Stoic work on ambiguity represents one of the most innovative, sophisticated, and rigorous contributions to philosophy and the study of language in western antiquity. This book is both the first comprehensive survey of the often difficult and scattered sources, and the first attempt to locate Stoic material in the rich array of contexts, ancient and modern, which alone can guarantee full appreciation of its subtlety, scope, and complexity.

The Stoics' primary motivation for interest in ambiguity was ethical and moral – a now surprising approach crying out for philosophical analysis and explanation. But, beyond this, identifying the nature and effects of ambiguity, and defining and classifying it, demanded application of concepts, categories, and techniques from grammar, semantics, stylistics, formal and philosophical logic, psychology, and epistemology – areas of philosophy in which the achievements of the Stoa are only now reaching a wider audience. The comparisons and contrasts which this book constructs will thus intrigue not just classical scholars, and philosophers, but also logicians, theoretical linguists, communication theorists, and historians of grammar and of literary theory. *The Stoics on ambiguity* is designed to be intelligible to readers with no Greek or Latin.

CAMBRIDGE CLASSICAL STUDIES

General Editors
M. F. BURNYEAT, M. K. HOPKINS, M. D. REEVE,
A. M. SNODGRASS

THE STOICS ON AMBIGUITY

THE STOICS ON AMBIGUITY

CATHERINE ATHERTON
Research Fellow, Girton College, Cambridge

CAMBRIDGE
UNIVERSITY PRESS

Published by the Press Syndicate of the University of Cambridge
The Pitt Building, Trumpington Street, Cambridge CB2 1RP
40 West 20th Street, New York, NY 10011–4211, USA
10 Stamford Road, Oakleigh, Victoria 3166, Australia

First published 1993

Printed in Great Britain at the University Press, Cambridge

A catalogue record for this book is available from the British Library

Library of Congress cataloguing in publication data

Atherton, Catherine.
   The Stoics on ambiguity / Catherine Atherton
      p.   cm. – (Cambridge classical studies)
   Includes bibliographical references and indexes.
   ISBN 0 521 44139 0
   1. Stoics.   2. Ambiguity.   I. Series.
B528.A84   1993
188–dc20   92–2469   CIP

ISBN 0 521 44139 0 hardback

For Robert

... der menschliche Wille erhält seine Stärke nie durch logische Spitzfindigkeiten

Carl von Clausewitz, *Vom Kriege*

CONTENTS

PREFACE AND ACKNOWLEDGEMENTS

This book began life as one chapter – admittedly a very long one – of my Cambridge doctoral dissertation. My first debt, therefore, is to David Sedley, who with consistent generosity and insight continued to point out new sources and new lines of attack, not to mention new weaknesses in my arguments and interpretations, long after his duties as my supervisor had been more than amply fulfilled. It was he who first made me realise the fundamental importance of puzzles and paradoxes to the development of Stoic logic; I am in his debt for an ever-growing appreciation of the dialectical subtleties of Hellenistic philosophy; and any skills I have managed to acquire in analysing ancient texts and reading papyri I owe largely to him.

Myles Burnyeat, one of the editors of this series, read drafts of both thesis and book, and without him neither would, I think, ever have been finished. Whatever is to be found in this book of the chief Stoic linguistic excellences, clarity and conciseness, is there almost entirely as a result of his meticulous attention to matters of style and presentation. It was he who first set me searching for the modern philosophical and linguistic contexts within which the Stoic achievement could best be understood and evaluated, and the rigour and thoroughness of the dissections he performed on my work often left me gasping for breath. Eventually I learned how to disagree with him (sometimes), but only because I had begun to learn how to argue – from him.

My Ph.D. examiners, Jonathan Barnes and Malcolm Schofield, provided invaluable comments, both on particular points of interpretation, and on the general scope of my thesis. Malcolm Schofield read an earlier draft of this book as well, and his expert, always gentle, and supremely clear, criticisms led me to a number of major revisions, especially of Chapter Three. Michael Reeve, also an editor of this series, made innumerable helpful suggestions. I am happy too to have the opportunity to make public my debt to Geoffrey Lloyd, Nicholas Denyer, John Vallance, and the late G. E. L. Owen, whose welcome improvements to the dissertation can still be seen in the book. But I alone take responsibility, of course, for its final contents and appearance, warts and all (above all, rather).

The delicate matter of money cannot be ignored. While writing this book I was privileged to be Junior Research Fellow – later Woodhouse Fellow in Classics – at St John's College, Oxford, and then Eugénie Strong Research Fellow at Girton College, Cambridge. But I do not know what to thank these two great Colleges for most: financial generosity, intellectual stimulation, or sheer good company. The British Academy receives my warmest thanks for appointing me to the Post-Doctoral Research Fellowship in the Humanities which I am now holding at Girton.

Pauline Hire, my editor at Cambridge University Press, has been far more helpful, efficient, and tactful than any first-time author deserves. The patient and meticulous attention to detail of my copy-editor, Peter Singer, saved me from many infelicities and inclarities.

Finally, my gratitude goes to my husband, Robert Wardy, who has helped me unstintingly and resourcefully at every stage, from typing the thesis to criticising the final draft of the book, as only a loving spouse who is also a professional philosopher can do. This book is dedicated to him, by way of a very small return for what I owe him: but that is a debt I shall never clear, or want to.

TYPOGRAPHICAL CONVENTIONS

I have tried to be both clear and flexible: this has meant a loss in absolute precision, which could easily lead to confusion and distortion in dealing with ancient texts. Some of the categories and distinctions applied here are deliberately vague or ambiguous, in order to meet a number of different demands in different contexts. In particular, it would be inappropriate to adopt conventions that would force on ancient authors a distinction between lexemes and forms, or between types and tokens; or any one specific interpretation of what moderns typically refer to as the "use/mention" distinction; or some view on the relation between written and spoken language. Readers must be allowed to approach the texts without having theories forced on them in the guise of italics or quotation marks. Where a convention serves a variety of functions, context will easily disambiguate. Some of the distinctions and conventions described here may seem obscure or unnecessary; they will be explained and justified as we proceed.

1 *Italics* indicate that a word, or a sequence of words, is being mentioned (quoted, talked about, being used to refer to itself, *etc.*). Words, unless otherwise specified, may be either word-forms, word-types, or lexemes, in standard modern jargon.

2 Where it is necessary to distinguish a lexeme from its forms, *italics* will indicate the lexeme, referred to by its citation-form (*viz.*, the form by which it is standardly referred to, in dictionaries, *etc.*); forms will be enclosed in single quotation marks, '. . .'.

3 Single quotation marks also indicate quotations of passages from other authors, ancient and modern, except where these are set out separately from the main text; here quotation marks are not used. They are employed too for the titles of articles in the bibliography.

4 Double quotation marks, ". . .", indicate either (putative) reference to "meanings", which are introduced merely for ease of analysis and exegesis, or the first use of a perhaps unfamiliar

piece of jargon (often a translation of a Greek or Latin expression). They are also used as "scare quotes".

5 Angle brackets, ⟨...⟩, following standard practice, indicate editorial additions to texts. Outside quoted text, however, and item 4 notwithstanding, they also mark (putative) reference to *lekta*, in order to signal their special technical status in Stoic semantics.

6 Braces, {...}, indicate the use of tokens, *i.e.*, of particular, unique inscriptions, or of such inscriptions as a means of reference to particular, unique spoken utterances.

7 Italics are used for titles of books (except those in Greek) mentioned in the text, footnotes, and bibliography; for emphasis, in the main text and in quotations; and for transliteration of Greek or Latin words or their abbreviations (for instance: *i.e.*, *lekton*, *ambiguitas*).

ABBREVIATIONS

A.D. = Apollonius Dyscolus; *adv.*, *coni.*, *pron.* = *de adverbiis, de coniunctionibus, de pronominibus* (*On Adverbs, On Conjunctions, On Pronouns*), in *G.G.* [*q.v.*] 2.1 (Leipzig, 1878), *ed.* R. Schneider; *synt.* = *de syntaxi* (*On Syntax*), in *G.G.* 2.2 (Leipzig, 1910), *ed.* G. Uhlig; *rhem.* = *de verbo* (*On the Verb*), in *Librorum Apollonii deperditorum fragmenta*, in *G.G.* 2.3 (Leipzig, 1910), *ed.* R. Schneider.

C.A.G. = *Commentaria in Aristotelem Graeca* (Berlin, 1882–1909); cited by vol., page and line.

Döring (*e.g.* 'fr. 112 Döring') = K. Döring, *Die Megariker. Kommentierte Sammlung der Testimonien* (Amsterdam, 1972).

DK (*e.g.* 'B42 DK') = *Die Fragmente der Vorsokratiker, ed.* H. Diels (Berlin, 1934/7, 5th edn.; repr. with *Nachträge* by W. Kranz, 1951/2 (6th edn.), 1954 (7th edn.); latest (18th) edn. 1989).

D.L. = Diogenes Laertius, *Lives and Opinions of the Eminent Philosophers.*

D.T. or D.T. *ars gr.* = *Dionysii Thracis ars grammatica*, in *G.G.* 1.1, *ed.* G. Uhlig (Leipzig, 1883).

D.T. Sch. = *Scholia in Dionysii Thracis artem grammaticam* (*Scholia on the 'Art of Grammar' of Dionysius Thrax*), in *G.G.* 1.3, *ed.* A. Hilgard (Leipzig, 1901).

EK = L. Edelstein and I.G. Kidd, *edd.*, *Posidonius. Volume 1:*

The fragments (Cambridge, 1972); I.G. Kidd *ed.*, *Posidonius. Volume 2: Commentary* (Cambridge, 1988).

Galen *P.H.P.* = Galen *de placitis Hippocratis et Platonis* (*On Hippocrates' and Plato's Doctrines*), *ed.* P. De Lacy (with translation and commentary), *Corpus medicorum Graecorum* V.4.1.2 (2 vols., Berlin, 1978–80).

G.G. = *Grammatici Graeci*, *edd.* G. Uhlig, R. Schneider, A. Hilgard and A. Lentz (Leipzig, 1867–1910; 6 vols.; repr. Hildesheim 1965).

G.L. = *Grammatici Latini*, *ex. rec.* H. Keilii (Leipzig, 1857–80; 7 vols. + supplement; repr. Hildesheim, 1961, 1981).

Halm = *Rhetores Latini Minores*, *ed.* K. Halm (Leipzig, 1863; repr. Frankfurt-am-Main, 1964).

K = *Galeni Opera Omnia*, *ed.* C.G. Kühn, Leipzig, 1821–33; cited by vol., page and line.

Loeb = The Loeb Classical Library, Harvard University Press (Cambridge, Mass.) and W. Heinemann (London).

LS = A.A. Long and D.N. Sedley, *edd.*, *The Hellenistic Philosophers* (Cambridge, 1987; 2 vols); all references enclosed in brackets thus: '(30A3)', following references to ancient works, are to texts in this collection.

L.S. = C.T. Lewis and C. Short, *A Latin Dictionary* (Oxford, 1880).

LSJ = H.G. Liddell and R. Scott, *A Greek-English Lexicon*; new edition, revised and enlarged by H.S. Jones, *et al.* (9th. edn., Oxford, 1940; repr. 1961; Supplement, *ed.* E.A. Barber, 1968).

O.C.T. = Oxford Classical Texts.

OLD = *Oxford Latin Dictionary* (Oxford, 1968).

P.L. = *Patrologia Latina* (*Patrologiae cursus completus* ...), *ed.* J.P. Migne (Series 1, vols. 1–79, Series 2, vols. 80–217, Paris 1844; Series 2a, Paris, 1845; Indices, vols. 218–21, Paris 1862–4).

R.E. = *Paulys Realencyclopädie der classischen Altertumswissenschaft, Neue Bearbeitung begonnen von G. Wissowa, fortgeführt von W. Kroll und K. Kittelhaus, hg. von K. Ziegler und W. John* (Stuttgart; Series 1, 1893–; Series 2, 1A, 1914; Suppl., 1903–).

R.G. = *Rhetores Graeci, ed.* C. Walz (Stuttgart, 1832–6; 9 vols. in 10).

Sp. – *Rhetores Graeci ex. rec.* L. Spengel (Leipzig, 1853–6, 3 vols.; repr. Frankfurt-am-Main, 1966).

Sextus *M.* = Sextus Empiricus *Adversus mathematicos* (*Against the professors*).

Sextus *P.H.* = Sextus Empiricus Πυρρώνειοι ὑποτυπώσεις (*Outlines of Pyrrhonism*).

Suda = *Suidae Lexicon, ed.* A. Adler (*Lexicographi Graeci* 1) (Leipzig, 1928–38; repr. Stuttgart, 1971).

S.V.F. = I. von Arnim, *ed., Stoicorum Veterum Fragmenta* (Leipzig, 1903–5; 3 vols.; vol. 4, Indices, M. Adler, Leipzig, 1924).

Teubner = edns. B.G. Teubner, Leipzig.

TLG = H. Stephanus, *Thesaurus Linguae Graecae, edd.* C.B. Hase, W. Dindorf, L. Dindorf (3rd edn., Paris, 1831–65; 8 vols. in 9).

TLL = *Thesaurus Linguae Latinae* (Leipzig, 1900 (vol. 1), 1904 (Index), 1913 (vol. 2)).

1
INTRODUCTION: THE SCOPE OF THIS BOOK

The subject of this book is some of the most impressive and original work on ambiguity to survive the wreck of western antiquity: that of the Stoa.

At some point in the long history of their school Stoics constructed at least one definition of ambiguity, the earliest to survive in the western philosophical tradition, and remarkable in any case for its complexity, subtlety, and precision. It shows that its authors saw themselves as defining a linguistic phenomenon, ἀμφιβολία, which can easily be recognised today as familiar to users of most, if not all, natural languages: that one and the same linguistic item can mean or signify two or more different things. (This rough-and-ready characterisation will serve for the moment.) Two Stoic classifications of types of ambiguity, neither explicitly associated with the definition, are also extant; as these seem to differ from each other in small but important ways, they make it probable that at least one other definition was also arrived at, and this too may have survived, albeit in a mutilated form, and not explicitly attributed to the Stoa.

Three chapters of this book will be devoted to close analysis of these three main pieces of evidence. They will reveal that Stoic philosophers had identified a range of linguistic and semantic concepts and categories with which ambiguity is intimately connected, and which serve to delimit or define it. Brief as they are, the texts to be examined will repay detailed study not only by students of ancient philosophy, at whom this book is primarily aimed, but also by workers in a variety of modern disciplines, above all by philosophers of language, theoretical and comparative linguists, and philosophical logicians: although they may all need to be convinced of the fact.

What these texts do not reveal, in a general, explicit way,

is what originally prompted Stoic interest in ambiguity. No ancient authority says in so many words why Stoics, as self-professed philosophers, found it worth while to define and classify ambiguity. If their motivations and anxieties are to be comprehensible, their conceptions of the purpose, structure, and contents of philosophy, of its internal and external boundaries, of the goal of human existence, and of the right way to achieve that goal, must all be determined. Stoic interest in ambiguity was the inevitable consequence of the basic doctrines about human nature, language, and rationality on which the whole Stoic system was based. Once ambiguity's place in the Stoic scheme of things is clear, it will be possible to trace the ways in which the form and content of Stoic work on ambiguity were shaped and constrained by its origins; and judgement by the school's own lights can be passed on its success in the projects it set itself.

This interpretative and evaluative task is one of the two chief purposes of this book. It prepares the way for its companion, which is to assess, as far as possible, the merits and defects of Stoic work from other appropriate perspectives, including those of relevant modern concerns and interests, both inside and outside philosophy. To do so it will be necessary to abandon the special viewpoints of both the Stoics' own philosophical teachings and their philosophical and intellectual milieu. One result of this shift will be a questioning of the lines of division which moderns (philosophers, logicians, linguists, and others) and ancients (Stoics and rival philosophers, as well as non-philosophical professionals such as grammarians and rhetoricians) alike draw between what they conceive of as different disciplines or sciences, including philosophy itself.

Given that part of the purpose of this book will be to try to analyse and explain some of the differences, in conception and method, between a range of modern and ancient perspectives on ambiguity, then restricting our inquiry to the particular contributions, however rich, which Stoics made to what are now called grammar, semantics, and epistemology, and to the other ancient disciplines or theories comparable with modern endeavours, would be a false economy even were the details of

2

the Stoic enterprise not hopelessly distorted or understanding of them severely curtailed in the process. For the exegetical need for these larger contexts also reflects the fact that Stoic ideas of what philosophy was like, and what it was for, are vastly different from those which dominate the field today. The Stoic motivation for studying ambiguity might be called pragmatic, but not in the sense that it contributed to some narrowly practical goal, whether writing good Greek or understanding the classics, arguing in court or doing grammar – or even doing logic, if that is conceived of as just another intellectual discipline, or as a tool of philosophy or of the sciences. The point was that seeing or missing an ambiguity could make a difference to one's general success as a human being.

To grasp the reasoning behind and the impact of that approach to ambiguity, a good deal of ancient testimony by and about Stoic philosophy will have to be considered and assimilated. Chapter Two begins with a brief summary of the available evidence, which is dealt with more thoroughly as required at various points throughout the book. Information has to be extracted, and with difficulty, from a lamentably small array of texts, few of them attributed or attributable to particular thinkers within the school. Virtually all primary Stoic writings had disappeared by the end of antiquity, Stoicism having finally lost the battle against Neoplatonism, neo-Aristotelianism, and Christianity; and what survives tends to do so, unfortunately, only by courtesy of more successful rivals. Three of the most important texts have already been mentioned: the definition, discussed in Chapter Four, and the two classifications of ambiguity kinds, subjects of Chapters Five and Six. Use will be made throughout, where appropriate, of the ideas, materials, or theories which may have been borrowed from, or shared with, the Stoa's predecessors and contemporaries in other schools of philosophy, and of critical exchanges and disagreements between schools and individual thinkers. A faithful portrait of the Stoic study of ambiguity will require the sketching in of much non-Stoic background,

3

not merely in order to eliminate, so far as possible, the distortions introduced by indifferent, prejudiced or ignorant sources, but also in order to reconstitute the assumptions and concepts common to all ancient writers in the field. Neither of the projects proposed – reconstructing the authentically Stoic contribution, and making comparative assessments – would otherwise be possible. Those familiar bug-bears, what is to count as a formative "influence" on Stoicism, and how one can be recognised – familiar because of the dearth of first-hand, early sources – raise their heads here too. Where explicit evidence of positive or negative reactions to others' work is unavailable, talk of "influence" must be decently muted. I have tried to indicate and assess whatever comparisons with earlier or contemporary ancient work on ambiguity seem relevant to understanding the Stoic contribution, whether because the latter fits into a known tradition, or because it significantly does not.

Chapter Three offers an introduction to Stoic philosophical doctrine, in so far as it shaped the Stoics' interest in ambiguity, and suggests some of the ways in which the distinction and classification of ambiguities were set to work, and justified in theory as integral to certain philosophically vital tasks: the precise formulation of argument and doctrine, and the construction of universal canons of correct discourse. The Stoics' reputation in antiquity for terminological and semantic innovation is examined here too, and an assessment offered of its place in the Stoic conception of philosophy, especially with reference to ambiguity's potential heuristic or creative value. Detailed comparisons are offered with relevant work of Aristotle, Epicurus, and modern theoretical linguists and philosophical logicians.

The obscurity and difficulty of the definition must be at least partly the fault of the almost complete absence from the sources, which here fall below even the wretched standard usual for Stoic philosophy, of anything which might serve as direct commentary. The closest approach to ancient exegetical material is made by the two Stoic classifications of ambiguity types, which are themselves recalcitrant, sometimes ungovernably so: with the result that explaining the definition is often a matter of indicating probable connections and contexts, and of exploring what might have been the point of the apparently precise and subtle distinctions in play. The definition has to be understood in a variety of theoretical contexts, both ancient and modern, which include Stoic semantics itself, ancient debates about the functions and origins of language(s), the distinctions between ambiguity, vagueness, non-specificity, and metaphor, the relation between spoken and written language, and the nature and extent of contextual and selectional restrictions on semantic interpretation.

Chapters Five and Six turn to the Stoic classifications. Each is preserved by a later, non-Stoic author; and for very different reasons each must be treated with minute care if the information it contains is not to be distorted, or missed altogether. Both lists, and especially that preserved by Galen, comprise strikingly original contributions to the study and taxonomy of ambiguity. They do so, however, within a form of typology that was standard in antiquity for the classification of ambiguities, but which bears little relation to the two most popular and influential modern modes of classification: the application of precise and exhaustive grammatical categorisations by linguists, within a given model or description of a single language;[1] and the application of non-language-specific linguistic categories by linguistic philosophers, philosophers of language or philosophical logicians seeking for a variety of reasons to identify and explain general features of (all) natural language(s).[2] The similarity of the Stoic lists to later

---

[1] *E.g.* for modern English: Hirst 1987: 149; from a simplified, pedagogic perspective, Taha 1983; for modern Chinese: Chao 1959/60: 3ff.

[2] Thus Robinson 1941: 141ff. lists ambiguity in singular terms, including proper names, and general terms ("Lockean" ambiguities, "sliding" terms, and relational univocals); the classification is clearly intended as an investigation into the properties of ordinary language in so far as they affect or determine the nature and limits of thought. Black 1952: 187 contends that familiarity with 'the types of shifts of meaning' associated with ambiguity is useful for detecting and correcting errors of reasoning; he picks out four (or five, with metaphor): sign/referent, dictionary *vs.* contextual meaning, connotation/denotation, and process/product, in single terms (188ff.). Likewise Waismann 1953: 11–18 concentrates exclusively on ambiguity in single terms, by way of a preliminary to constructing a model of natural language(s) as comprising different "strata". Quine 1960: 129ff. identifies a variety of ambiguities, both lexical and syntactic, as part of a study of 'the indeterminacies and irregularities of reference that pervade [language]' (125).

5

classifications may in part simply reflect Stoic influence in the field (the use made of Stoic material by rhetorical and grammatical writers will be explored in Chapter Eight), but is rather, I think, one facet of a radical difference in approach to the study of linguistic phenomena between modern and ancient theorists.

At the same time, the classification preserved by Galen seems not to favour either of the two major rôles assigned to ambiguity by Stoic philosophy, the formation of deceptively persuasive arguments (dealt with in Chapter Seven) and the origin of undesirable stylistic obscurities (discussed in 3.4).[3] Neither rôle seems to have exclusively determined this classification's arrangement, content, or choice of examples; and it can thus be called "neutral", as lacking reference to any privileged discourse or to any particular purpose, philosophical or otherwise, of discourse. The classification reported by the other source, the rhetorician Theon of Alexandria, looks to have a more stylistic bias; but, given Theon's own interests, it would be surprising if it did not.

Against the Stoics' achievements in classification must be set a range of weaknesses even within the terms which (as far as can be judged today) they themselves set, the narrowness of their grammatical concepts and categories being but the most obvious of these. This criticism holds even for the Stoics' own (native or adopted) tongue, Greek, and the fact that they probably credited their grammatical apparatus with universal validity only makes its limitations the more crippling. Of course, the Stoics were not linguists in the modern mould, with the goal of classifying types of ambiguity by way of the grammatical and lexical categories prescribed by some model of a language. But the grammatical categories applied in the classifications seem to be inadequate or inappropriate for the purpose in hand, and, anyway, are awkwardly combined with principles of classification which are only loosely "grammatical", and apparently redundant into the bargain.

It would be both unfair and unilluminating to blame the

---

[3] All references of the form 'o.o' are to sections of chapters in this book.

Stoa for neglecting approaches and methods alien to their enterprise. If comparisons are none the less both necessary and proper, it is because only by means of them can the uniquely Stoic motivation behind the classifications be grasped, and the lists themselves judged against the Stoics' own standards of success. A single example will suffice. A feature of the classifications and of Stoic work generally which would strike a modern philosopher of language or logician as a great defect is the failure to construct theoretical accounts of possible systematic relations amongst significations of a polysemous expression. But to take the absence of Stoic accounts of this sort as a defect would (as we shall see in 3.5) represent a misunderstanding of the whole Stoic philosophical project.

Chapter Seven concentrates on the rôle which was almost certainly the source of most anxiety for Stoic dialecticians, and which was standardly assigned to ambiguity by ancient philosophers: the creation of fallacies, of deceptive likenesses of sound arguments. This chapter is intended as a study in the logic and epistemology of the Stoa, in the form of an account of probable Stoic responses to a number of related problems: how arguments can go wrong by the presence or exploitation of ambiguities; why such arguments can still be persuasive; and how they can be detected and disarmed. The relation between ambiguity and the psychological states whose articulation in language is central to the Stoic understanding of human reason will be explored and possible weaknesses in the Stoic account sounded. The examples of ambiguities listed in 3.3 which are of crucial importance for Stoic doctrine and its correct exposition will be a useful adjunct to this chapter.

Chapter Eight turns to the broader context of Stoic work, to ancient rhetorical and grammatical theory, and tries to identify the ways in which Stoic material and methods were adapted to non-philosophical contexts – "non-philosophical", it should be emphasised, for non-Stoics, for the Stoa itself counted rhetoric as a subdivision of philosophical discourse, and what ancient theoreticians came to call Stoic "grammar" found its place originally within another subdivision, dialectic. Professional rhetoricians and grammarians, meanwhile, understandably tended to regard their disciplines as more or less autonomous. In them ambiguity was standardly assigned three fairly rigidly defined functions. As a stylistic defect it was discussed by literary critics and by teachers of composition; as a cause of legal dispute, over ambiguously-framed statutes, laws, and other documents, it found a minor but secure niche in rhetorical theory; less commonly, it was invoked as an explanatory mechanism by one sort of grammatical theory. Little survives of Stoic work in either of the first two areas, but Stoic definitions and classifications certainly had some influence. The mere fact that one of the two to survive is recorded in a rhetorical primer suggests as much, and there is evidence from other sources too.

The final chapter presents a very brief summary of results: of doctrines which can be more or less securely attributed to the Stoics, and of the most important points of agreement and contrast between their contribution, on the one hand, and the contributions of their ancient rivals or models and their modern counterparts, on the other. It will come as no surprise to learn that Stoic concerns and motivations, as well as their methods, conceptual apparatus, tools of analysis, and so on, are as a rule radically different from those of their modern counterparts in philosophy, and still more so from those of the other theorists – linguists, psycholinguists, or literary critics – whose work I shall call on from time to time to illustrate comparisons and contrasts in methods, theories, and motivations. The same holds, in fact, for all ancient writers on ambiguity. But identifying significant differences (and not only those peculiar to the Stoa) is as profitable an exercise as detecting what correspondences and parallels there may be.

On occasion throughout this book I have brought into the discussion whatever modern theoretical uses of or approaches to ambiguity seem to promise the most instructive parallels with ancient and Stoic work, or, more usually, still more instructive dissimilarities and asymmetries. If this comparative project is to be informative about both Stoicism and modern versions of philosophy, logic, or grammar, then the comparisons must be relevant, sharp, informed, and specific. Sometimes – too often – the state of the ancient evidence makes it impossible to meet all these criteria; I have always tried to indicate where interpretation ends and speculation begins. As for the skeletal remarks made so far on the subject of ancient-and-modern comparisons, and the assumption of their value and appropriateness, these will be, respectively, fleshed out, and defended, in the course of this book by what is surely the only acceptable method: demonstrating their worth in particular cases. Here I shall make only a short, general plea for their usefulness and validity.

The classicist, classical philosopher, historian of ideas or of linguistics, and philologist, may already feel justified in passing on to Chapter Two, in the hope of finding something to interest and even enlighten in this tribute to the Stoic intellectual achievement. The modern philosopher, or theoretical linguist, in contrast, may well not have found what has been said so far anything like a winning *captatio benevolentiae*, and may object that the game is not worth the candle: that, even if old theories, arguments, definitions, or classifications can only be understood as wholes and in their original settings, any sufficient reason for going to all the trouble of resurrecting them at all has not been given. What do Stoics have to teach today's students of philosophy, or of linguistics, about ambiguity (or anything else)? Why ever do today's students of ancient philosophy go to such extraordinary lengths?

What this study of Stoic thought aims to provide for such a critical reader is a set of alternatives: some common to all the ancient world, others unique to the Stoic school. At their most generous, the Stoics promise a comprehensive alternative vision of philosophy itself, one which includes natural science, psychology, stylistics, and grammar, as well as epistemology, ethics, and semantics; of unfamiliar motivations for doing philosophy and for studying ambiguity as a philosophical enterprise; and of unfamiliar philosophical methods. The ancient texts also reveal alien conceptions of what logicians and grammarians do, and why, and of how what we call natural and "artificial" or "formal" languages should be studied.

9

Stoics – perhaps surprisingly – did not try to eliminate ambiguity, but not because they thought that this would distort the essential nature of "natural" language, or because they saw themselves as constructing an ideal non-ambiguous language, the language of logic or of science, to replace it; and they saw ambiguity as a problem when they did not see, say, vagueness at all. To try to share these fundamentally different points of view is at the very least a prophylactic against parochialism.

But there is far more than warnings, however useful, to be won from close scrutiny of Stoic work on ambiguity. Ancient philosophical and linguistic ideas are worth reviving, not just because they are profoundly different, but because the reasons for those differences, and the arguments for the alternatives, can be cogent and pressing enough to make us notice, appreciate, strengthen, or reconsider, familiar categories, distinctions, and problems, and because, properly understood, the ancients can make illuminating and valuable contributions to our rethinkings or revisions. When supported by careful argumentation, and nested in a comprehensive theoretical framework, the potential of the ancient alternatives is great indeed. What is more, despite their very different ultimate concerns and motives, the Stoics who composed the definition and the classifications we shall study were confronted by many of the very same questions that face modern philosophers, logicians, and linguists who try to analyse ambiguity or types of ambiguity. They must ask what sorts of thing are ambiguous, what it is to have two or more meanings (or senses, or significations, or ...) in the relevant way, how to classify ambiguities, and what types of ambiguity there are according to the favoured mode of classification; what linguistic meaning itself is, where it comes from, what things have it, and how many types of it there are; what effects ambiguity can have on the psychological processes of ratiocination and cognition; and how the presence of ambiguity in natural languages is to be coped with in the context of formal languages, if it is not simply to be ignored. The Stoics saw the need to be precise and explicit about such problematic items as the bearers of meaning and ambiguity, contexts, literalness, negation, singular definite terms, reference, autonymy or linguistic reflexivity, and the autonomy of language; and they had very different and definite ideas about where ambiguity enters into logical theory. In some cases not only can their theses and the solutions they offered to the problems they perceived be reconstructed, they can also be compared usefully and even favourably with their modern counterparts. The point is to use a past philosophy, not to confirm the superiority of one or other of its descendants, or to put today's preoccupations and limitations "into perspective" (whatever that would mean), but to add something to the understanding of the problems and issues still found perplexing today, and to offer alternative approaches to different, but equally pressing, difficulties.

These are the positive lessons to be learned from the Stoa's ingenuity and enterprise. There are negative ones too, the significant omissions and inconsistencies. There are many gaps and flaws in present-day knowledge of Stoic philosophy, and it is good sometimes to be able to put forward at least persuasive reasons for believing that some of the gaps and flaws were in the school's own teachings, and not in what our authorities have chosen to record. But the reasons for the authentic, non-accidental silences, are of more lasting concern. It would be impossible here even to touch on all the ways in which modern theorists have analysed, deployed, or deplored linguistic ambiguity, and from the point of view of the Stoa's interests in the subject – or even those of the ancient world at large – largely irrelevant to boot. The modern reader would not be astonished to learn that antiquity lacked anything resembling psycholinguistics, machine translation, or communication theory, and so never had to worry about coping with the effects of ambiguity in these fields. Yet concentrating on what have been explicitly characterised by their authors as philosophical interpretations or uses of ambiguity – a policy apparently justifiable by appeal to the simple fact that a Stoic would approach ambiguity in his capacity as a *soi-disant* philosopher – would be disastrous. The breadth and depth of the Stoic concept of philosophical activity mean that orthodox assumptions about the boundaries and proper methods of philosophy cannot be allowed to stand unchallenged. Hence work in linguistics above all, for which parallels are to be found comfortably inside Stoic philosophy, cannot be overlooked.

On one side, then, is the creative task of putting together from scattered materials the network of ideas and values in which ambiguities could reasonably be taken as threats to be isolated and disarmed, which was manifestly the line taken by the Stoa and by most ancient thinkers. The Stoic position, as already suggested, is unique both in its conception of what is constituted by specifically philosophical activity ('the practice of expertise in utility', according to one definition[4]) and for the detailed programme it actually carried out, that of identifying individual problem ambiguities and of defining and classifying ambiguity in general. On the other side is the task of discovering what Stoics did not see in or do with ambiguity: what uses they did not make of it, and what misuses or abuses it did not occur to them it could serve, and why: for it is no mere trivial accident that the ancients did not invent, say, pragmatics, psycholinguistics, or the concept of the formal language. The Stoics, like all ancient thinkers who interested themselves in ambiguity, seem to have assumed intuitive recognition and resolution of ambiguities by speakers as the pretheoretical basis on which theoretical procedures, such as definition and classification, can be tacitly grounded. But ancient thinkers do not appear to have regarded such intuitive behaviour, or the knowledge underlying it, as phenomena requiring analysis and explanation, within (probably) some broader account of language knowledge. Ancient writers do observe that ambiguities in discourse (often, because of the writers' interests and purposes, written discourse) can be and are resolved by appeal to context and situation; but they nei-

---

[4] Aetius I, *pr.* 2 (= *S.V.F.* 2.35 (26A)): 'ἄσκησιν ἐπιτηδείου τέχνης'; the Greek text goes on to explain that 'virtue singly and at its highest is utility', 'ἐπιτήδειον δὲ εἶναι μίαν καὶ ἀνωτάτω τὴν ἀρετήν.' Philosophy was also defined as 'the pursuit' or 'practice' of wisdom: Seneca *ep.* 89.5; Philo *cong. erud. gratia* 79; Sextus *M.* 9.13; or of 'correctness in the mind' or '...in rationality': Seneca *ibid.*; Clement *paed.* 1.13.101.2.

ther clearly discriminate between these two groups of relevant factors, nor see the difference between them as important, nor use or explain their observations within a theory of what it is to know a language, and of how and where such knowledge can be distinguished from the non-linguistic knowledge with which it interacts. In fact, surprisingly little attention appears to have been paid in antiquity, at least systematically, to the whole question of language knowledge.

The choice of philosophy of language, linguistic philosophy, theoretical linguistics, and philosophical logic as affording the most suitable comparisons can be defended on another ground than their actual or apparent similarity of subject-matter. These disciplines are (to be brief and perhaps tendentious) the safest bets for theoretical and methodological sophistication. They are most likely to set themselves the goals of, and even to achieve, explicitness, generality, and rigour in matters of definition, classification, and identification and sifting of relevant material; and least likely to be satisfied with *ad hoc* analyses of individual cases or texts, or with undefined and unexamined "common-sense" notions of linguistic properties.[5] Both despite and because of their vast differences in everything from terminology to institutional organisation, and in part because of their technicality and rigour, they offer the most appropriate and illuminating set of comparisons and contrasts.

Before turning to the sources and their interpretation, I shall present a tentative outline of the nature of ambiguity and the problems it raises, by way rather of an advance warning, than of any attempt at settling them.

---

[5] A similar point is made by Scheffler 1979: 2f., who, however, does not mention work in theoretical linguistics. At the other extreme, the opening words of one, once extremely influential, literary critical work, Empson 1953: 1, may be cited: 'An ambiguity, in ordinary speech, means something very pronounced, and as a rule witty and deceitful. I propose to use the word in an extended sense, and shall think relevant to my subject any verbal nuance, however slight, which gives room for alternative reactions to the same piece of language'; in a footnote Empson adds that 'naturally the question of what would be the best definition of "ambiguity" ... crops up all through the book'.

Modern theoretical linguists tell us that native speakers of many – perhaps all[6] – natural languages seem to have intuitions of, and about, the presence of what modern Anglophones usually call "ambiguity". That is, speakers (or, more properly, users) are said to have learned to recognise, with a large degree of agreement and regularity, and simply and precisely in virtue of being native speakers, something in stretches of talk or writing in their own language which Anglophones may explicitly describe as being "ambiguous" or "open to two (or more) interpretations" or as "saying two (or more) things" or "having two (or more) meanings (uses, senses)" or the like. Further, perceived cases of it may lead to a request from listener to utterer for a decision between two or more paraphrases or interpretations of a given utterance or inscription; and, although some unnoticed cases may lead to confusion and worse, others (probably the majority) go unremarked, causing no disturbance in the smooth flow of discourse and associated interactions (*cf.* Lyons 1977: 396–8, 400). The claim, therefore, is that "ambiguities" observably shape linguistic behaviour, that they can be perceived and explicated by users, and that speakers regularly distinguish between cases requiring explication and cases where none is needed. Chomsky 1985b: 100, to give but a single example, asserts that in appropriate contexts speakers will not only fail to detect ambiguities, but will even reject alternative meanings, when they are pointed out, as 'forced or unnatural'.

In modern English the word *ambiguous* is also frequently applied to "doubtful" or "uncertain" persons, utterances, states-of-affairs, and so on, wherever there is (felt to be) insuf-

---

[6] It is, of course, impossible to determine empirically whether all natural languages contain ambiguities. The question is whether ambiguity is an essential feature of natural languages, to be explained at a theoretical level by, say, the necessarily limited number of phonemes and morphemes which any one language(-system) can possess. The point is argued by *e.g.* Jesperson 1964: 319f. Whether ambiguity could qualify as a "design feature", as something essential to something's functioning as a language (on this concept, see *e.g.* Hockett and Altmann 1968), would be determined by a theorist's evaluation of the purpose(s) ambiguity might serve, and hence by underlying assumptions about the nature and function of language – as Harris 1980: 21f. has pointed out with regard to design-feature accounts in general. Ancient views on the "naturalness" of ambiguity differed widely: see 3.1, 4.6.

ficient relevant information for choice between alternatives, where feelings or intentions are undecided, and the like; and the narrower use of the term favoured by linguists, lexicographers, and philosophers to denote only one very specific property of linguistic items is plainly an artificial restriction on the looser usage of the speakers whose productions are being studied and analysed.[7] Many linguists today maintain that such intuitive responses and behaviour express some sort of formally untaught, "tacit", linguistic knowledge, to which direct access is denied. Just what that knowledge is, if it exists, whether it is a realisation of an innate endowment or "universal grammar", and whether it is licit, or indeed practicable, to use native-speaker intuitions as guides to its content and scope, are some of the most closely-fought issues in and about

---

[7] To classify the experience of narrow linguistic ambiguity by speakers merely as a special case of that familiar mental state, uncertainty between two or more options perceived as more or less distinct and mutually exclusive, whether taking a decision, settling one's feelings, interpreting an utterance, *etc.*, would be to neglect the fact that speakers regularly cope with what they would recognise as ambiguities in other contexts, or in isolation, without any conscious experience of uncertainty and with little or no overt hesitation or deliberation. Latin and Greek speakers, to judge by available evidence (which of course is primarily for literary usage) employed *ambiguus* and ἀμφίβολος in much the same way as modern English speakers employ *ambiguous*: see LSJ *s.v.* ἀμφίβολος esp. III, IV (ἀμφιβολία is apparently first in Herodotus 5.74, of the condition of (being attacked on) both sides; *cf.* 7.9, n. 67). The *TLG* gives "qui undique feritur" as the basic meaning of ἀμφίβολος, and "ambiguus, anceps, dubius", as metaphorical extensions, while ἀμφιβολία is both linguistic ambiguity and "incertitudo consilii de re quapiam, haesitatio hominis ambigentis quid sit agendum, vel utrum ex duobus sit agendum". *Cf.* L.S. *s.vv.*, esp. *ambiguus* II ABC, and *OLD s.v. ambiguus* (the meaning "linguistic ambiguity" is only item 8 out of a total of 10, although the abstract noun *ambiguitas* is used solely of it or its possessors). The *TLL* gives *dubitatio* and *controversia* as synonyms of *ambiguitas s.v.*, and has "quod in ambas partes agi potest" as the core meaning, which extends to doubtful persons, objects, language, *etc.* After reporting what is in effect the one extant Stoic definition of ambiguity (see ch. 2), the Suda defines ἀμφίβολοι as persons "considering from every direction", 'πανταχόθεν βαλλόμενοι' (which might also mean, significantly, "being struck from every direction"); or "being at a loss, being in the grip of different arguments, out of ignorance of what is to be selected and whether they will do this or that" (*ed.* Adler, vol. 1, p. 152).

Aristotle seems to be the earliest extant author to use ἀμφιβολία in the narrow linguistic sense "semantically multiple", *rhet.* 1.15.1375b11, 3.5.1407a37f., *top.* 8.7.160a29, *poet.* 25.1461a25 (where it is used of a single word); in the *Sophistical refutations* (the "*s. el.*") the meaning is narrower still, one species of ambiguity: 4.166a6ff., and see Appendix. Plato's use of ἀμφίβολον at *Crat.* 437a3 is linguistic (of the word ἐπιστήμη, *knowledge*), but it means "inconsistent" (*i.e.*, in context, that ἐπιστήμη is open to an "Eleatic" as well as a "Heraclitean" etymology) rather than "ambiguous".

modern linguistics.[8] I shall simply note the current theoretical importance of native-speaker intuitions; while my preliminary, working characterisation of ambiguity will not appeal to them explicitly, it will subsequently prove impossible to ignore them: ambiguity is a property of linguistic items such that these items have more than one definite and specific use, meaning, interpretation, *etc.*[9]

This not especially illuminating characterisation is, of course, meant as a rough guide, and not a definition. It is deliberately imprecise as to bearers, and as to uses, significations, meanings, *etc.*, and it is intended to embrace lexical and grammatical ambiguity, that is, ambiguity of single terms and of syntactic complexes, and any other types too, if they exist (the Stoics thought they did). It also leaves unspecified what criterion or criteria will be used to test for the presence of ambiguity, and/or *who* is to say when ambiguity occurs: that is, whether all, or just some speakers of a language, members

[8] For a brief introduction to Chomsky's linguistic theory: Horrocks 1987: chs. 1–3. Chomsky 1967, 1981, 1985 are all useful, compendious statements of principles and methods. I have throughout avoided a too detailed account of any one or more of the varieties of Transformational and other Generative Grammars devised over the last three decades; of Chomsky's own changing conceptions of what a grammar is, what the relation is between grammar and semantics, which criteria grammars must meet, and so on; or of the numerous, and admittedly important, differences between Chomsky and his various groups of followers down the years. This is partly for reasons of space, but largely because such detail would be otiose: it is the most central and basic principles and methods of (Transformational) Generative Grammar, including and especially "innatist" or "realist" grammars, which afford the most revealing comparisons with Stoic and ancient grammatical theory and practice (see further, 3.5, 6.2.3). I have also made no specific reference to Chomsky's most recent theoretical developments, concerning the "ruleless" core grammar. His commitment to innatism and to its consequences for the status of languages and of linguistics remains, however: *e.g.* 1986: 15ff., 145ff. I trust that this silence on details will not prove too distortive.

[9] Edlow's definition of ambiguous discourse as 'discourse which admits of (at least) two paraphrases, x and y, such that x and y are not paraphrases of one another' (1975: 423) is, I think, unsatisfactory as it stands, for the reason stated by Lyons 1977: 404: like the translation technique it is not 'of itself sufficient to distinguish ambiguity from generality of sense' (*cf.* 4.5, n. 6). Wiggins 1971: 33 also argues that although 'completely different paraphrases' are possible of certain words, such as *good*, in different contexts, these can none the less make 'exactly the same input to the sense' (his examples are *good food* and *good knife*). The attempt of Kress and Odell 1982: 191, Odell 1984: 118 to give criteria for multivocality and ambiguity in terms of "metaphrases" is marred by reliance on the unexamined concept of "meaning" which enters into a central concept in their scheme, that of the "metaphrase*".

of a linguistic community, must acknowledge the semantic multiplicity, and in the same way or ways, and, if so, which group or groups are privileged. Here the place of ordinary speakers and their intuitive judgements must become problematic, whatever their epistemic status or their methodological or theoretical rôle. Also left unspecified is whether speakers must acknowledge that all occurrences (utterances, inscriptions, tokens, *etc.*) of designated bearers are ambiguous; whether any expression must in fact have a determinable number of meanings or interpretations; and many other matters too. The rough definition thus relates ambiguity implicitly to users of a language, and explicitly to the "language" itself; but it does not fix precisely what a "language" is (a set of behaviours? a system of rules or conventions? of normative regularities? of physical or of abstract objects of a certain kind (*viz.*, sentences)? of internalised rules?). The nature and status of the objects which grammarians study, or ought to study, are today perceived as crucial to preserving the status of their subject as a science, and to identifying it as a science of this or that sort. Ancient grammarians, and their critics, disagreed about much the same matters, in radically different theoretical and metatheoretical contexts.[10] The definition leaves open too the relevant and distinctive uses, aspects, situations, or contexts of language(s), and what connection there is between the ambiguity recognised by native speakers of a language and the ambiguity yielded by theoretical descriptions of that language.[11] Also left undecided is whether ambiguity is

[10] Sextus *M*. 1.57ff. sketches the main lines of disagreement; and the debate can be followed in the numerous critical comments on Dionysius Thrax's definition of grammar: 5.2f., with D.T. Sch. 6.31ff., 118.19ff., 165.16ff., 167.5ff., *etc.*

[11] Lyons 1977: 400–4 argues for the theoretical status of ambiguity as defined and described by grammarians; *cf.* Scheffler 1979: 2f. for a similar point about lexicographical principles. Robins 1980: 35ff. briefly lists the general options for the ontological and epistemological status of linguists' "abstractions". The model assumed, not to say enthusiastically endorsed, by most modern linguists is, of course, the modern one of an empirical science constructing and testing a theory from and against data. Some have challenged the idea that linguistics, albeit empirical, can be empirical in the way that physics or biology are: *e.g.* Itkonen 1978; others envisage a non-empirical linguistics, studying abstract objects: *e.g.* Katz 1981, 1985b; Montague 1974 (linguistics as a branch of mathematics). Katz 1985a: 14 argues that '[w]hat kind of science one takes linguistics to be ... depends

language-specific, and what relation holds between ambiguity as language-specific, within some grammar of a given natural language, and ambiguity as a feature of natural language *tout court*.

My definition can thus be seen as setting the stage for comparisons to be drawn later. The questions it raises are some of the most important faced by today's linguists and philosophers: yet only some of them would have been interesting or even intelligible to the Stoics or the ancients – the theoretical status standardly given to native speakers' intuitive judgements, even when these are not used to model competence directly, would have been found particularly baffling. It is widely accepted today that linguistic descriptions must be able to accommodate and explain the fact that some (utterances of some) sentences (and perhaps other linguistic items too) are recognised by speakers as open to more than one interpretation: models of the language(-system) must, minimally, assign two (or more) structural descriptions to sentences utterances of which are treated as ambiguous by users: examples, from a huge range, are Katz and Fodor 1963: 174ff.; Chomsky 1971: 75f., 1985: 109, n. 18; Gleason 1965: 462; Bierwisch 1970: 167; Katz 1985b: 194ff.; Stitch 1985: 132; Horrocks 1987: 12ff. Conversely, intuitive judgements are to be the arbiters of the correctness of theoretical predictions: thus Odell 1984: 123 assumes that '[t]he effectiveness of any criterion for ambiguity should be judged in terms of how well its results fit our linguistic intuitions'. At the same time, it is taken as obvious that intuitions on this, as on all key linguistic properties, being incomplete, changeable, even contradictory, and liable to be shaped unawares by theory (especially through schooling, so that the influence tends to be prescriptive), need not, perhaps even cannot, give rise to a single, coherent, "natural", account of what constitutes ambiguity. Theorists may try to explain such divergences by pointing to the indefinitely wide range of

on how one resolves the ontological issue', that is, the ontological status of grammatical objects. Stoic views on this issue are discussed in 4.3, 6.2.3. The *locus classicus* for the theoretical status of the "linguistic object" in general is Saussure 1916/1983: 23/8.

learning conditions to which individual speakers are exposed. But native-speaker perception of ambiguities is also observably affected by the quantity and quality of contextual (and situational) information available; so that identification and description of ambiguities by linguists who use the evidence supplied by intuitions are themselves guided by what linguists judge to be contextual (and situational) factors, on the one hand, and what they judge to be the contextualised item, on the other. In their turn, again, these judgements will be determined by (metatheoretical) considerations of what belongs in a description of "the language(-system)" and what does not. In the professional literature, therefore, "descriptions" of ambiguity will describe, not intuition's unpredictable Proteus, but whatever creature is constructed by theoreticians operating within a framework of broader assumptions about language and, accordingly, about the purpose and characteristic methods and subject-matter of their disciplines.

So, while linguists today frequently use ambiguities as tests of their own and their rivals' theories, ambiguity as classified and described is as much a product of theory, in fact of particular theories, as are the other cardinal linguistic properties – grammaticality, meaningfulness, synonymy, and so on. (Stitch 1971 is, in part, a rare attempt to reconcile the theoretical status of these properties with the assumption that native-speaker judgements of ambiguity, grammaticality, *etc.* are 'the grammarian's principal data' (477).)

The formulation, comparison or refinement of linguistic, above all syntactic, descriptions through the analysis of ambiguities is especially characteristic of Transformational Generative Grammar, figuring both in attacks on the perceived inadequacies of other theoretical models (of "phrase structure" grammars, for example), and in arguments for the existence of "deep structure" and for users' construction of theories of their languages out of the random and patchy "data" of experience: *e.g.* Chomsky 1959: 57, 1967: 430, Allen and van Buren 1971: 103. Ambiguity, as we have seen, is one of the properties of language which grammars must explain. But use of ambiguity by linguists is not confined to exponents of some version of TGG. In 1933 Sapir argued that the 'psychological reality of phonemes' is in part shown by the way phonological differences between homonymous words are experienced by users as phonetic differences – which do not in fact exist (1933/1985). Dik 1968: 227ff. has used cases of structural ambiguity in co-ordinate constructions to demonstrate the superiority of his own "functional" grammar over both constituent and TF grammars. Bach and Harnish 1979: 138ff. have rejected the notion that the speaker's 'system of (semantic) representation for specifying meaning' is the 'language itself' on the basis of 'the ambiguity (lexical or syntactic) of most sentences', and they advance considerations governing the correct theoretical description of different sorts of ambiguities to support their "inferential semantics" (144ff.). Hockett 1987: 19 takes hearers' awareness of ambiguities as evidence for "hearer construal". Indeed Chomsky himself has credited Hockett with 'the first general discussion of how ambiguity can be used to illustrate the inadequacy of certain conceptions of syntactic structure' (1967: 430, n. 32 (441)). Hockett's own argument, using Rulon Wells's famous example *old men and women* (1947: 93), was that "hierarchical structure" is a grammatical primitive (1954: 217ff.). In a passage already referred to (1985b: 100), Chomsky uses an ambiguity to show both how multiple meanings may not be obvious and how hitherto "obscured" linguistic intuitions can be brought to conscious knowledge. Perception of ambiguities has been deployed as evidence for a "modular" structure in real grammatical knowledge (an idea which helped renew interest in Transformational Generative Grammar): *e.g.* Frazier 1988. Other examples – from an enormous number – can be found in Chomsky 1965: 16ff. and Lakoff 1971: 238–45.

Modern linguists' theoretical deployment of native-speaker intuitions, including ones about ambiguities, has been frequently explained and defended (*e.g.* Robins 1980: 149, 269f.; Horrocks 1987: 11ff.), and related problems and restrictions often discussed (Lyons 1977: 27f., Palmer 1981: 27f., and (polemically) Baker and Hacker 1984: 247f., 292f., 320). A useful summary of the justifications for using ambiguities as "controls" and as sources for grammatical generalisations can be found in Kooij: 'It is no exaggeration to state, that in general the degree to which a grammatical description is capable of recognizing that otherwise identical sequences of linguistic elements are homonymous and should be assigned to more than one grammatical structure, has become one of the major tests for the adequacy of such a description, and also, that this is largely due to the impact of Transformational grammar' (1971: 62). He goes on to discuss why this should be so, with particular reference to Hockett's (1954) argument, already mentioned, for the primitiveness of "hierarchical structure", the fundamental point being that descriptions which do not recognise structural ambiguity are debarred from making some of the significant generalisations about structural similarities and differences vital to the whole enterprise of descriptive grammar (1971: 62ff.).

Such heuristic and diagnostic uses of ambiguity tend to assume a database of decontextualised sentences "open to more than one interpretation", whose structures must be described within a theory of the language (however "language" is understood, and whatever metatheoretical constraints there may be on the theory). Not only would the Stoics find this conception of grammar, and its associated theoretical and metatheoretical disputes, impenetrable (including the whole model of a theory explaining data), they would have challenged the authority it accords to ordinary speakers, awarding it instead for the appropriate expert, the fully experienced and elaborately trained dialectician – an ideal language user, but not the one Chomsky meant.

The characterisation I have given of ambiguity is further meant to suggest (not to fix, of course) dividing lines between ambiguity and what linguists, philosophers of language, philosophical logicians, and perhaps native speakers too, will regard as different but related phenomena. These will include, *imprimis*, cases of obscurity, in which no single, determinate meaning (use, sense, *etc.*) will or can be assigned to a bearer; cases of vagueness, where the criteria for correct application of an expression are imprecise, perhaps irremediably so; cases of generality or non-specificity; cases of multiple applicability (to any of a set of particular objects); and perhaps metaphorical usages too. It simply leaves room for such distinctions, whether or not exactly formulable. Again, some of these related linguistic properties would look familiar to a Stoic; others he would find quite alien, and the accounts of them in the modern literature inappropriate or even incomprehensible.

Mapping this part of linguistic territory constitutes a problematic by itself, and firming up my trial description may turn out to produce unwarranted or unprofitable restrictions. The study of ambiguity tends always to have a blurring effect – not always acknowledged, still less exploited – on the over-rigidly compartmentalised disciplines which seek to define and understand it: for example, those between the different "levels" of linguistic description, or between linguistics as narrowly conceived and pragmatics. It creates or gives new directions to disagreements which can go to the heart of a theory, its methodology, or metatheory. There will be debates amongst linguists, for instance, as to whether this or that utterance, inscription, or sentence of a language is ambiguous, and, if so, whether this or that description of that language adequately explains why, what precisely is being explained, what counts as an adequate explanation, and why such explanations are called for at all. There will be debates amongst philosophers of language as to why ambiguity exists, whether it is an intrinsic feature of natural languages, or can be eliminated from them, or from the artificial languages of logic or science, as to how, and how far, semantic models of fragments of natural languages can or should "explain" ambiguities, and as to what grounds justify postulation of an ambiguity as an explanatory mechanism for some logico-linguistic phenomenon. And there will be protests from literary critics, theoreticians of culture, and some philosophers and linguists, that these disputes dangerously neglect crucially important aspects not only of ambiguity, but of language itself, that is, their "creative", "aesthetic", or "social" functions.

The sheer breadth and intricacy of the difficulties associated with ambiguity can cause confusion and obstruct constructive communication between disciplines. A linguist may appeal in elucidating the notion of ambiguity to such things as "meanings" or "semantic representations" in a way that would make a philosopher of language blench. A philosopher may assume the possibility of morphological analysis or token replicability in a way that would make a linguist blench right back. Both may merely gesture at ambiguity's rôles in nondeclarative discourse, if they do not ignore them altogether. In part, such neglect is clearly the result of professional interests deliberately narrowed to a single field of study in order to achieve both greater precision and greater ease of inquiry and exposition. Logicians, for instance, will be primarily concerned with the properties of forms of artificial calculi, perhaps viewed as idealised fragments of natural discourse. Psycholinguists will want to understand how language-users' understanding is interferred with or otherwise affected by the presence of ambiguities, and will use ambiguities to provide information about language "processing". Lexicographers will need to decide how to classify entries, so that they, like all other theoreticians with an interest, direct or indirect, in ambiguity, will make assumptions, if only for the purposes of simplification and clarity, which may restrict or even reduce the theoretical value of their own work (that information content must be unique; that ambiguities are either "surface" or "deep" grammatical phenomena; that there are such things as "words" which all belong in dictionaries and have neatly specifiable definitions; and so forth).

It is probably true to say, as a broad criticism, that workers in these various disciplines do not always or consistently keep in view the fact (and the implications of the fact) that understanding of ambiguity is, in a variety of ways, theoretically grounded, or fully appreciate the range and seriousness of the problems they must solve (or at least acknowledge as problems) if they are to pursue their own, narrower interests; and they may also fail to reflect on or expound in detail the reasons they have for undertaking their own studies, or even to offer a precise and satisfactory definition of ambiguity.

Reluctance to engage with and accommodate the demands of linguistic theory can be a defect, too, in ancient writings on ambiguity, although the range of disciplines with interests in the subject is, in large part, startlingly different, and, where parallels can be found, the disagreements in conceptual frameworks, methods, and motivations more than serve to puncture any complacency we may feel, whether on account of the illustriousness of our predecessors, or of our glittering improvements on their work.

The principal disciplines which take an interest in linguistic ambiguity today are, indeed, some of the late twentieth century's shiniest intellectual products. Research into and analysis of natural language might be said (and have been said, many times) to dominate at least the Anglo-American branch of philosophy. The rise of descriptive, comparative, and historical linguistics as empirical sciences has marked similar radical, qualitative changes in the interpretation and understanding of linguistic phenomena: indeed in the range of such phenomena considered appropriate to scientific investigation and explanation. Literary theory has undergone a series of remarkable transformations which have brought about, *inter alia*, a drastic re-evaluation of ambiguity's rôles in texts – a revision which brings to the surface a vital distinction, unseen until now, between (most) ancient and (most) modern approaches to ambiguity.

Ambiguity was standardly in antiquity and to some extent still is today regarded by theoreticians in different disciplines as a difficulty or defect, something to be coped with, not courted, and eliminated if possible. Ancient theorists, critics, and teachers of style and composition tended to see ambiguities as stylistic infelicities (3.4), making an author's meaning obscure or indeterminate; and they were commonly identified by logicians and philosophers as sources of innocent or fraudulently induced intellectual error (7.1, 7.9), and by rhetoricians as potential sources of legal debate (8.2). What these very different groups had in common was a basic conception of language as a conduit for or means of transferral between minds of a single, detachable, preselected message or meaning,[12] encouraging on the one hand rigid and unsubtle literary critical methods,[13] and on the other an almost total philosophical neglect of "non-descriptive" or "non-cognitive" uses of language.[14] The availability of the modern jargon, that of language's "descriptive" function (*e.g.* Lyons 1977: 50ff.), is itself indicative of the survival of this immensely powerful conception of linguistic meaning and activity.[15] The Stoics shared it, and arguably their version of it brings their stylistics, semantics, and psychology at least very nearly to grief (3.4, 4.4, 4.5, 6.2.3, 7.7, 7.9).

The negative attitude to ambiguity has, however, lost ground. Literary critics, above all, would tend to regard linguistic ambiguity as a source of great richness in texts, and to question the assumption of a single authorial voice, especially one in control of a single authored message. Conversely, linguists standardly ignore ambiguity's potentially deleterious effects on (certain kinds of) communication, in order to treat it as a "narrowly" or "strictly" linguistic phenomenon to be

---

[12] This is what is claimed as the "telemental fallacy" by Harris 1981: 9, according to which 'linguistic knowledge is essentially a matter of knowing which words stand for which ideas', words being man-made symbols for 'transferring thoughts from one mind to another'. It is one half of "the language myth", its companion piece being the "deterministic fallacy". Fallacy or not, it was certainly the predominant preconception of ancient theories of language: see further, 3.1, 3.4, 3.5, 6.2.3.

[13] This fundamental defect in ancient literary criticism is associated by Russell 1981: 4 with the immense influence of rhetorical training, whose explicit aim is to teach ways of clothing a predetermined meaning in the, or the most, appropriate words.

[14] The neglect was not total: Peripatetics, for example, constructed classifications of non-declarative sentences (*e.g.* Ammonius *int.* 2.9ff.), Stoics of non-assertoric *lekta* (*e.g.* D.L. 7.66-8; Ammonius *int.* 2.26ff., and see 3.1, 6.2.4, 6.5.2). Different types of sentence are treated by Ammonius as productions of different psychic powers, the declarative sentence alone "expressing", ἑρμηνεῦον, the soul's cognitive faculty. Such classifications of sentence types appear to go back at least to Protagoras: D.L. 9.53f.

[15] *Cf.* Quine 1960: 129: 'either [the ambiguity] is resolved by broader circumstances of utterance ... or else communication fails and a paraphrase is in order'. His model for a scientific language eliminates ambiguities along with indexicals, 1976: 235ff., and he recommends considering larger discourse segments, rather than short forms, in order 'to overcome the difficulty of ambiguity or homonymy', 1961: 58. Black 1952: 184 asserts that in some cases 'the process of communication has then broken down and the offending words are ambiguous', ambiguity occurring 'whenever signs function defectively'; positive uses of ambiguity are permitted, but only as exceptional (185, 186f., 198), much as metaphor is 'no substitute for clear ideas' (197). Robinson 1941: 146ff. argues that ambiguity is 'an ever present defect' (154) (but see n. 18, below).

accounted for in theory as much as are grammaticality, mean-ingfulness, synonymy, and so on. For psycholinguists the fact that ambiguity constitutes a potential interference with com-munication is no reason to relegate it to a position of theoreti-cal or methodological inferiority – in fact, the opposite is true, for ambiguity's heuristic value is immense.[16] Some linguists, philosophers and philosophical logicians have begun to advo-cate a keener and more sympathetic awareness of ambiguity's importance both for natural languages and for understanding them theoretically,[17] and of its creative value for ordinary users or even for scientists.[18] There were no such revolutions in antiquity. What set the Stoic philosophical system apart is that it combined conventional assumptions about language, sometimes ones which were never even articulated, with origi-nality and conscious heterodoxy on other matters, supremely so about motives and reasons. The Stoa too considered ambi-guity a bad thing: but they would not have agreed with their contemporaries, or with us, as to why.

But as, in any case, I shall be concerning myself not so

---

[16] A "modular" approach to language may be a mere methodological convenience, in which case its potential dangers of distortion and incompleteness are fairly obvious (*e.g.* Kooij 1971: 5); at the other extreme it may instead be a result of commitment to a theory of mind (*e.g.* Fodor 1983, Chomsky 1980: 4off.). Whether psycholinguistic experimental projects, including those concerning the "process-ing" of ambiguities, can be treated as evidence for how users' linguistic knowledge (competence) is structured itself depends on what data the associated grammar is supposed to explain, and of course, more fundamental still, on whether it is claimed as "realist" or not (in the psychological sense).

[17] Scheffler 1979: 1f., for instance, 'attempts a direct study of lapses or deviations from the prevalent semantic ideal, its aim being to further theoretical comprehen-sion of such "deviational" phenomena as ambiguity, vagueness, metaphor, and related aspects of language. The characterisation of such features as "deviational" is, however, relative to an ideal conception that can itself not be taken for granted. This characterisation must emphatically not be taken to imply that these features are isolated, fragmentary or merely privative. On the contrary, they are pervasive, important, and deserving of systematic study in their own right. Beyond the ideal code, the bare letter of language, they contribute to its typical shape and force, its normal appearance and flow. Any advance in our understanding of these features will, moreover, not only enrich our appreciation of language, but also help to clarify the status of attempted idealisations.' The ideal of idealisation is still alive, but not dominant.

[18] The creative aspects of language use, even by ordinary speakers, are emphasised by Harris 1981: 151ff. Robinson 1941: 148 has argued that ambiguity is often an advantage in philosophy and science as in poetry, specifically through "relational univocity" (149).

much with ambiguity, as with some small portion of what has been said and written about ambiguity, a certain fuzziness is a necessary precaution at the outset. The characterisation I have offered is, as I said, only a rough demarcation of the territory we shall be exploring in company with the Stoics. Ambiguity, as we shall see, is very much what you make of it.

2

SOURCES AND MATERIALS

The obvious starting-point for this investigation should by rights be surviving Stoic literature on ambiguity, especially works from the school's early, formative years. But such first-hand material as has come down to us is so minuscule in quantity, and so resistant to secure interpretation, that we must look elsewhere for information.

The first decades of the school, under Zeno (334–262 B.C.E.), the founder, and his successor Cleanthes (331–232), seem to have produced few treatises explicitly or exclusively about ambiguity. Only Sphaerus (mid/late 3rd cent. B.C.E.) is credited with a work *On Ambiguities* (D.L. 7.178 (*S.V.F* 1.620, p. 140, l. 17)), and nothing of it survives. Of course, any of the works known to have been written on logical matters, or on poetry, may have contained scattered references to or treatments of ambiguity or particular ambiguities: but nothing of these survives either.[1]

The authoritative texts on ambiguity were, presumably, like so much else in Stoic logic, the work of the school's third leader. Chrysippus (*c.* 280–*c.* 206; head from 232), whose dominant position in the school is beyond question, wrote at least seven, and almost certainly eight, treatises on ambiguity

---

[1] The most that can be said is that discussions of ambiguity would not have been out of place in Zeno's *On Utterances, Handbook* (of dialectic?), *Solutions, Refutations, On Listening to Poetry*, and the five books of *Homeric Problems* (D.L. 7.4 = *S.V.F.* 1.41, p. 15, ll. 1–6); in Aristo's *Reply to the Orators, Reply to Alexinus' Objections* (almost certainly a response to Alexinus' polemical "parallels" to Zenonian arguments: 3.2), and *Reply to the Dialecticians* (D.L. 7.163 = *S.V.F.* 1.333, p. 75, ll. 22–4; on the Dialectical School of Diodorus Cronus, see 7.6, nn. 27, 28); in Cleanthes' *On Insolubles* (presumably "insoluble arguments", *i.e.* paradoxes and puzzles: 7.6, n. 43), *On Dialectic, On Modes* (possibly a rhetorical work *On Tropes*: 3.5, n. 75), and *On Predicates* (D.L. 7.175 = *S.V.F.* 1.481, p. 108, ll. 3–6); or in Sphaerus' *Dialectical Handbook* and *On Predicates* (D.L. 7.178 = *S.V.F.* 1.620, p. 140, ll. 15–16). On the chronology of these central figures in Stoic (and Hellenistic) philosophy: Sedley 1980.

(D.L. 7.193 = *S.V.F.* 2.14, p. 6, ll. 23–30 (37B2)).[2] His follower Diogenes of Babylon (*ob. c.* 152) may also have written
on the topic; his interests in language and logic are well documented, and his reworking of a famous argument of Zeno's
about the *locus* of the soul's ruling part, which will be discussed in 7.7, is typical of his formalising and clarificatory
contribution.

Beyond this point we cannot go. All these texts have been
lost, and all that is known for certain even of Chrysippus'
work is his famous dictum that 'every word is by nature ambiguous', the meaning and importance of which will be explored in 6.3.5.2, together with some very brief passages in
the extant fragments of a book of his *Logical Questions*, to
which I shall return shortly; the possible contents of some of
the lost works are discussed later too.[3] Two of them were
expressly introductory in character, and one a *resumé*, which
gives some slight support to the idea, one I shall be exploring
in connection with the classifications in particular, that the
study of ambiguity was exploited pedagogically by Stoic dialecticians. The books' position in the bibliography preserved
by Diogenes Laertius (7.189ff. = *S.V.F.* 2.13–18 (part, 37B,
321)) suggests that they concerned language and the constituents of discourse; and this admittedly superficial assessment is
at least in complete agreement with what can be learned from
other sources about ambiguity's place in dialectical theory.

The single extant Chrysippean text in which ambiguity
is discussed is a book of his *Logical Questions*, Λογικὰ
ζητήματα, probably listed by Diogenes in the logical portion
of his Chrysippean bibliography under the title of miscel-
laneous *Questions*, in no fewer than thirty-nine books: 7.198
(= *S.V.F.* 2.16, p. 8, ll. 24–27). The surviving book is preserved, incomplete, and sadly mutilated by the impact of

---

[2] Chrysippus' dominance is demonstrated forcefully by *e.g.* Frede 1974a: 26ff. Pachet
1978: 364 claims that Chrysippus seems to have worked more on syntactic than on
lexical ambiguities, but that would be a dangerous conclusion to draw from so little
evidence; see also 6.2.3.

[3] On the lost *Reply to Those Who Do Not Distinguish*, see 7.4; *Reply to Panthoides'
'On Ambiguities'*, 4.6, n. 22, and 7.5, n. 30; *On the Mode Ambiguities* and *On
Conditional Mode Ambiguities*, 3.2 and 7.6, n. 42.

volcanic material, burial, and the passage of time, as *PHerc.* 307 in the Biblioteca Nazionale in Naples. Despite its immense interest and importance, the very grave textual and exegetical difficulties it presents have persuaded me to postpone the separate treatment which the entire work demands, and I shall have only a very little more to say about it here. First edited and given a brief papyrological and philosophical commentary by Crönert (1901: 550ff.), the text was printed in 1903 by von Arnim as *S.V.F.* 2.298a (pp. 96–110), together with a few readings (from nineteenth-century copies of the papyrus) and suggested integrations of his own, but without a full papyrological commentary or *apparatus criticus*. The work is now badly in need of a new edition and thorough philosophical analysis. Some new readings are available, but a complete edition is urgently needed.[4] One influential current interpretation (*e.g.* Baldassari 1985: 103ff.), that much of *PHerc.* 307 is principally an investigation into ambiguity can, however, already be safely rejected, not only because of counter-evidence from the text itself – which shows that, while a number of ambiguities are indeed examined, nothing determinate at all emerges as *the* theme of the text – but also because it appears to rest on an insufficiently precise understanding of the Stoic concept of ambiguity.[5]

Later Stoics confirm the school's interest in and anxiety about ambiguity, but little appears to have been done by way of original contributions to the field. An exception might be found in the rhetorical work of Posidonius (*c.* 135–*c.* 50) (see 8.2).

---

[4] See Marrone 1982, for a selection of new readings of the whole papyrus, and her 1984a, 1984b, and 1988a for new texts of fragments 1-3 and columns 1, 2, part of 5, 6, 7, and 10. Also relevant are Bréhier 1951: 24ff.; Pachet 1978; Sedley 1982a: 251, 1984; Hülser 1982: 4: 442ff. (§698); Barnes 1984/5; Inwood 1985a: 94, 1985b: 82f.; Marrone 1987, 1988b.

[5] I must immodestly refer the reader to my criticisms of almost all previous interpretations in my edition and philosophical commentary forthcoming in the Clarendon *Later Ancient Philosophers* series, and, meanwhile, to my Ph.D. dissertation *The Stoics on Ambiguity*, at pp. 203ff., which also presents full texts of two of the columns, 4 and 5, that do deal with ambiguities (pp. 226ff., esp. 247–69). Cols. 8, 11–13 also concern ambiguities, and portions of provisional texts of cols. 3 and 8–15 are provided too (pp. 284–8).

This lack of irreproachable first-hand evidence is fairly typical, especially on the more technical issues in Stoic philosophy. It should not worry us unduly. Of Chrysippus' 311 books on logical topics (D.L. 7.198 = *S.V.F.* 2.16, p. 8, l. 27)), the Herculaneum text, after all, may be the only survivor. Scholars of Stoicism resign themselves to dealing with second-hand reports from hostile, ignorant, or at best indifferent writers who quote or paraphrase Stoic authorities incompletely and out of context. The variety of exegetical problems posed by the authors who preserve Stoic material on ambiguity – most prominently, Diogenes Laertius, Galen, Theon of Alexandria, Sextus Empiricus, Alexander of Aphrodisias, Simplicius, and St Augustine – is wide and challenging. Each source is tackled on an individual basis, as required, in the course of this book; but a general introductory survey may be found helpful.

Diogenes Laertius, who lived probably in the third century C.E., is the single most important source for the school's dialectical teachings; and it is Diogenes who preserves the one extant Stoic definition of ambiguity. Yet, while he presumably had enough interest in the subject to make him want to write about philosophers, Diogenes seems not to have been a professional philosopher himself. Significantly, his work is properly given the title *Lives and Opinions of the Eminent Philosophers*, and in it information of varying quantity and quality about philosophical doctrines rubs shoulders with chat about his subjects' origins, way of life, friends, wives, money troubles, and so on, with their pithy witticisms to each other and to students, and similar anecdotal material. The section dealing with Zeno of Citium is unusual because the "philosophical" section contains both a general survey of key Stoic logical doctrines (7.42ff.), and a much longer, more detailed, and apparently well-informed report covering much the same ground (7.49ff.), including our definition (7.62). The first account is much the briefer, but it does contain an assessment of the role of dialectic in a wider psychological and ethical framework (45, 48), as well as an analysis of the range of intellectual accomplishments it comprises (46f.), and it differs from the second, longer exposition (48–82) in its taxonomy of the topics embraced by logic. As for the second account, what distinguishes it is its unusually high number of *laudationes*. Disagreement has been rife among scholars as to just how much of Diogenes' second account of Stoic logic is taken directly from an earlier doxographer, Diocles Magnes, how much is Diogenes' paraphrase of it or reports or paraphrases of other authorities, and what relation it bears to the first, shorter account.[6]

This particular question need not be felt as too troublesome. It is clear that the definition of ambiguity comes from some exceptionally knowledgeable authority, whoever it may have been and however Diogenes got hold of it. On the other hand, because it is possible that some sort of selection or re-ordering of whatever authentically Stoic material was available might have been carried out by Diogenes and/or his source(s), the definition may not now be in exactly the place it occupied in the Stoics' own exposition of their dialectical doctrines. Diogenes' account provides excellent evidence for the existence of disputes within the school as to what the subdivisions of "logic" are, what they should contain, and how they and their contents are to be ordered.[7] Ambiguity appears to have been one, albeit minor, subject of disagreement, since in the longer description of dialectic it is listed almost at the very end

---

[6] The problem has been most recently treated by Mansfeld 1986: 351ff. Crucial is the interpretation of 7.48, which promises an excerpt from Diocles, but does not indicate its extent: a summary of scholarly views in Mansfeld 1986: 329, 353ff. Mansfeld himself argues that it includes only 7.49–53, the whole preserving 'a plurality of traditions' (371).

[7] Some Stoics wanted to establish a third, epistemological, subdivision of the "logical" section of Stoic philosophical teaching, in addition to the two more usual subdivisions, dialectic and rhetoric: D.L. 7.41f. (31A1–5). In D.L.'s first, briefer, account, psychology and epistemology are indeed listed and described as a part of dialectic, 43, 45f., rather than as a preface to dialectic proper, which is what they are in the second account, 49–54. In contrast, division and definition are part of dialectic at both 44 and 60–2, although, again, some Stoics wanted these to constitute a separate subdivision: 7.41f. (31A1–5)). More significantly, perhaps, neither of D.L.'s accounts corresponds in its arrangement to the order of the Chrysippean bibliography also reported by D.L. 7.189ff. (= *S.V.F.* 2.13–18 (part, 37B, 321); *cf.* Mansfeld 1986: 357–8, 371–3); and, for what it is worth, the three principal divisions of the bibliography were all (presumably: none of the titles of the physical works have survived) referred to as τόποι, literally "places". As the longer of the two accounts relies a good deal on authorities later than Chrysippus, especially Diogenes of Babylon, such correspondence in its case at least is not to be expected.

of the section dealing with linguistic matters, after definitions of definition and division at 60–2, and thus a good way removed from stylistics at 59–60: whereas, in the summary of this same range of subjects at 7.44, it is located after grammatical, stylistic, and literary topics, but before euphony, music, definitions, and divisions. It is thus unclear not only why ambiguity occupies the position it does in Diogenes' longer report, but also, given that it was intended to stand there, that this was the standard location assigned it.[8] This is no small uncertainty, for there is evidence that ambiguity was of interest in a number of ways to Stoic philosophers – as a source of fallacious reasoning, as a stylistic defect, as a vehicle for easy exposition of several key linguistico-logical doctrines – and it would be gratifying to know where in the handbooks it was defined and its species classified, and, if in several places for different purposes and audiences, what and who they were.

When we come to study the definition and the classifications in detail, and what Diogenes and other authors have to tell us about Stoic interest in ambiguity, these points will be brought up again, and their implications considered.

The two Stoic classifications of ambiguity types are recorded by two very different authors. The great medical and philosophical writer Galen devoted an entire, if small, treatise to the defence of the Aristotelian system for classifying ambiguities expounded in the *Sophistical Refutations* and to the

---

[8] Mansfeld 1986: 367 takes the definition to be no more than a 'Nachtrag' to Stoic grammar: 'one would have expected it either before or after the section on *poiesis* and *poiema*', an assessment of ambiguity's position in dialectic that I shall, I hope, prove quite wrong. Further, he suspects that 'the jumble of definitions' (366) at the end of this part of D.L.'s account 'derives from a collection of *horoi*, or rather from the *horikon eidos*' of 7.42 (31A1, 3) (see previous note) (367). The topic of ambiguity, of course, does not belong primarily in books about definitions, and there is no reason to believe that the material on definition comes from such a separate subdivision of logic – even if some Stoics thought that that was where it properly belonged (see n. 7). Definitions are central to epistemology, but, while they are linguistic items, what they define – *viz.*, concepts – are not: disagreement about their exact location in expositions of dialectic or logic is quite understandable. Hülser simply prints D.L. 7.60–2 (30C, 32C, 37P) as the 'Übergreifender Text' for a section on 'sprachliche Zeichen im Verhältnis zu ihrer Bedeutung' (1982: 3: 388f., §621). Elsewhere, he curiously, and without explanation, lists ambiguity and divisions as items moderns would want to transfer to the portion of dialectic dealing with significations (1979: 287).

criticism of a Stoic rival system. His attitude, as so often to Stoic ideas and arguments, is hostile and dismissive; but there is no good reason to believe that he has deliberately misreported the classification itself, or that he has otherwise distorted the material available to him, an offence of which he is beyond reasonable doubt guilty on other occasions. His failure to understand either Aristotle or the Stoics, and the fact that his criticisms of the Stoic classification and the taxonomic principles behind it are mostly misdirected or simply wrong, are rather the result of a misreading of the *Sophistical Refutations*, of too cursory an examination of the Stoic system, and of too rigid an adherence to (apparently) general principles of analysis.

The merits and defects of the other source, the rhetorical writer Theon of Alexandria, are of another kind entirely. Into the little handbook he wrote for primary teachers of rhetoric he inserted a report of a classification of ambiguity types, which he attributes to "dialecticians", and whose close resemblance to the list recorded by Galen establishes its Stoic origin. Unlike Galen, Theon was no philosopher, and certainly not hostile to the Stoa; but, unlike Galen again, he wanted the list to serve a strictly limited, practical purpose: to familiarise his readers with material which their small charges would in turn find useful when they came to compose speeches or parts of speeches; and he seems to have felt no compunction about rearranging or changing it as he thought fit. Despite these drawbacks, Theon's report is invaluable. The dialecticians whose work he records and adapts can be seen to be working in a slightly different field from the Stoics known to Galen – their ambiguity is more the ambiguity which troubles educated users of a language – and probably with a slightly different conception of ambiguity as well.

The author whose interpretation demands the most painstaking attention to his own philosophical aims and allegiances is probably Sextus Empiricus. He poses many complex exegetical problems, and I shall mention only two of them.

First, his hostility to the Stoics is explicit, general, and pervasive. They share the weight of his opprobrium, however, with other doctrinaire schools of philosophy (Platonists, Peripatetics, Epicureans, and others) and with professionals in other disciplines too, such as doctors, mathematicians, rhetoricians, and grammarians, and often it serves Sextus' purpose not to distinguish too sharply among the recipients of his criticisms either in his reports of their theories or in the criticisms themselves. In brief, it is not always clear exactly whose doctrines he is retailing and attacking. This is precisely the case with his account in Book 2 of his *Outlines of Pyrrhonism* ('*P.H.*') (229ff.) of what some doctrinaire philosophers had to say about fallacious arguments and ambiguity. A large part of Chapter Seven will be devoted simply to extracting authentically Stoic tenets and arguments from this text.

Second, Sextus' reports of dogmatic theories and arguments must be handled with considerable caution. His purpose, briefly, is to induce in the reader a reluctance to give philosophical allegiance to any one school or any one of its theories, by presenting propositions and arguments opposed to every and any given doctrinaire tenet, whether in physics, ethics, or logic, including refutations, valid, apparently, by the dogmatists' own lights, of the dogmatists' positive arguments for their theses. Sextus' immense battery of arguments will be seen to counterbalance the ostensible probativeness or persuasiveness of his opponents', and so will lead to skeptical "suspension of assent" (until such time as genuine proof is discovered) to any "dogmatic assertion", and thus, inevitably and effortlessly, to tranquillity and happiness.[9]

The problem is not that Sextus is not immensely learned, philosophically sophisticated, or deeply serious in his (non-dogmatic) commitment to the goal of serenity, for he is all these things. It is rather that his project is essentially and comprehensively negative and critical. The dogmatist philosophers, like the other professionals, were in the business of advocating their own theories, and presenting what they saw as the best arguments in their favour, as well as of refuting

---

[9] On the goal of freedom from disquiet in Pyrrhonist skepticism and its relation to open-minded and open-ended inquiry: Burnyeat 1980: 49ff.; Sedley 1983, esp. 22f.

objections raised by members of rival dogmatic schools, and raising objections in their turn to their rivals' theories. Sextus' brief is to find telling criticisms, not to present fully and in detail what his opponents argued in their own favour, even if a recognised skeptical strategy was to set one school's or philosopher's theories against another's, to illustrate their radical lack of agreement, and thus foster a reluctance to trust any of them.[10] It is impossible to be sure that Sextus has always reported faithfully everything relevant to the doctrinaire thesis he is attacking; that is, everything its authors said or would have said, and in the way they said or would have said it. He can sometimes be discovered in a piece of sloppy reporting, by comparing his account with that of an independent source,[11] or convicted out of his own mouth, on the basis of his own reports elsewhere, of invalid, weak, or irrelevant argumentation;[12] and readers must be on their guard constantly, when they use his reports as an authority for other philosophies, against the effects of the inherent selectivity and negativity of his project. The key text in *P.H.* 2 is, again, just such a case. Sextus does not say explicitly what systematic connection the dogmatist dialecticians saw between ambiguity and fallacy, or even that there is a systematic connection at all, beyond what he himself represents as the practical uselessness of doctrinaire teachings about both; and his account of those teachings can be seen to be arbitrary and distortive. None the less, the uniquely Stoic link between ambiguity and fallacy can be identified, in fact from Sextus' own use of the Stoic logical apparatus. What is more, a defence against Sextus' attacks on Stoic teachings about both topics can be (re-)constructed, in part again from information Sextus himself supplies.

Further evidence about the Stoic treatment of fallacious

---

[10] The skeptical method of ἰσοσθένεια – the counterbalancing force of opposed propositions, whether to do with the senses or with theory – is described by Sextus himself at *e.g. P.H.* 1.8, 26, 196. Its use by the two main Skeptical tendencies (Academic and Pyrrhonist) is explored by *e.g.* Striker 1980.

[11] This seems to be true of Sextus' report of Chrysippus' response to the Sorites or "Heaping" argument: 7.4, n. 19.

[12] As with his attack on dogmatist teaching about sophisms: 7.6.

arguments which exploit ambiguities – or, more strictly, which exploit equivocations, for such fallacies depend on a shift – an illicit shift – in the meaning of ambiguous expressions – comes from the sixth-century Neoplatonist commentator on Aristotle, Simplicius. When combined with evidence from Sextus and Cicero about the response devised by Chrysippus to another type of "puzzle" argument, the "Sorites", Simplicius' report of what the "dialecticians" recommend as response to "syllogisms due to homonymy", brief though it is, and patently out of its original setting, allows a reconstruction of a complete Stoic strategy for coping with such fallacious arguments, as well as fruitful speculation about Stoic views on context and disambiguation.

Another Aristotelian commentator, Alexander of Aphrodisias, increases the small store of information by describing, in all the full and precise technical detail that might be expected of so gifted a logician, a Stoic thesis concerning the ambiguity of the standard or ordinary negative sentence in Greek. This remarkable report is better known for its sequel, in which another Stoic thesis – that singular definite terms have (inherently tensed) existential import – is recounted and refuted. Both are invaluable for increasing modern understanding of Stoic "philosophical logic", and of the characteristic Stoic approach to ordinary linguistic properties.

The most unexpected source is perhaps St Augustine of Hippo, who provides evidence, of immense value despite its indirectness, about one of the most important strands in Stoic work on ambiguity, that relating to autonymy or linguistic reflexivity; and he does so in two different books. His *On Dialectic* is an incomplete survey of largely Stoic and Peripatetic logical material, including accounts of ambiguity and homonymy, with some additions of Augustine's own. In parts incoherent and unsophisticated, it is still useful just because it is relatively unadventurous and faithful to its sources. The slightly later *On the Teacher*, a contribution to epistemology, is more subtle and searching. It deals with the whole topic of signs, but especially linguistic ones, and it is in this context that Augustine advances his own version of what today would usually be termed the "use/mention" distinction. His thesis still bears marks of Stoic influence, but is no longer a borrowing from any source or sources. It is chiefly these two texts which together suggest the probable explanation of Chrysippus' thesis that 'every word is by nature ambiguous': every word is also its own name. Other relevant material is drawn from Aulus Gellius, who explicitly attributes the thesis to Chrysippus, from the classification reported by Galen, and from the numerous minor, scattered reports of bits and pieces of Stoic semantic theory.

There are many other sources for Stoic dialectic in particular and Stoic philosophy in general, and it would be impossible to describe or assess them all here. Instead I have discussed each as required in the course of my inquiries, just as I have explored the limitations imposed by their own perspectives and purposes on the testimony of our major authorities, those who make the largest contributions to our knowledge of Stoic work on ambiguity. In identifying the place of that work in the Stoic conception of philosophical activity, a very large number of sources, of widely varying reliability and informativeness, must be used, as the next chapter will show.

MORALITY TALKS: THE ORIGINS AND LIMITS OF STOIC INTEREST IN AMBIGUITY

3.1 Philosophical ideals

This book is intended to explore all the subjects dealt with by Stoic philosophical doctrines in which ambiguity was either given some rôle or function, or on which it had some bearing: epistemology, grammar, semantics, logic, stylistics and rhetoric, philosophical method, and the principles of definition and classification. My project would be incomplete, and inadequate in its coverage of these particular areas, were it to treat them in isolation from each other and from the principal tenets of Stoicism. Even the smallest detail, in semantics or taxonomy, has a place and a value in this larger context, and that is as it should be, since the Stoa prided itself on the coherence, the organic systematicity, of its teachings, which must be accepted in their entirety or not at all: hence the comparisons of its philosophy to a walled garden, a city, an egg, and – most appropriately – a living creature (D.L. 7.40 (26B3), Sextus *M*. 7.17ff. (part, 26D)).

What follows is an outline account of some of the chief teachings, primarily in logic and ethics, which are of most immediate relevance to the Stoic theory of ambiguity. It is not comprehensive, and it is neither a hostile critique nor an apologia. Whatever critical objections are raised are, for the most part, themselves intended and exploited as convenient explanatory devices, pointing the way to what Stoics said or (tentatively) might have said in defence of the way they approached ambiguity and of the importance they attached to it. Many points, especially in grammar, logic, semantics, and epistemology, are discussed at greater length, and usually with less sympathy, at various points throughout the rest of the book. The immediate task is to show that by examining Stoic philosophical doctrines, in particular those relating to ethics, language, and epistemology, it can be understood both how ambiguities could be thought of as presenting problems to moral agents, and why these problems were thought to be serious. I do not propose to present a critique of the moral teachings which in the last analysis justify and explain the Stoa's anxiety about ambiguity, for that would not further my purpose in this book, and I shall take the relevant moral and ethical principles as given. On the other hand, the Stoics' account of how ambiguities can be troublesome at all does raise important epistemological issues relevant to my project. Some of the obscurities and difficulties in the Stoic descriptions of language and cognitive processes have already been touched on, and I shall be returning to them at a number of points later on.

The Stoics standardly divided their philosophical doctrine into three: ethical, physical, and logical.[1] "Logic" was itself divided into the sciences of rhetoric and dialectic, and sometimes into epistemology as well, with, in one variant, a fourth subsection for the theory of definitions (D.L. 7.41–2 (31A1–3)).[2] Stoic "logic", in this broad sense, is something of a curiosity to modern eyes. Its precise subdivisions and their order tended to fluctuate – as shown by, for instance, the lack of unanimity about the place of epistemology and the study of definitions – but its general contents and structure can be determined. They were probably to a large extent the work of Chrysippus, third head of the school and its greatest dialectician (D.L. 7.180 (31Q): 'most people thought that if the gods did dialectic, it would be the Chrysippean kind'), and of his immediate successors, although the order of exposition fol-

---

[1] *E.g.* D.L. 7.39 (26B1–2). The trichotomy is standard in the doxographies: *e.g.* D.L. 3.56; Sextus *M.* 7.16 finds it implicit already in Plato, but 'most explicitly' in Xenocrates and the Peripatetics. The Peripatos and the Stoa disagreed as to whether logic was a part of philosophy, or its "instrument", ὄργανον: *e.g.* Alexander *an. pr.* 1.7ff.; Ammonius *an. pr.* 8.15ff. (part, 26E). Variations in the doctrinal and pedagogic ordering of the subdivisions were common: D.L. 7.40f. (26B4); Plutarch *st. rep.* 1035A (26C). I ignore Aristo's unorthodox formulation: D.L. 7.16of. (part, 31N).

[2] See Ch. 2, n. 7.

lowed by our main source for this part of Stoic philosophy, Diogenes Laertius, may well be later (*cf.* Mansfeld 1986: 371ff.). In current jargon, it would take in (optionally) epistemology and part of psychology, phonology, grammar, semantics, stylistics and poetics, definition and division (which may be separate), philosophical and formal logic, and the theory of the fallacy.

What unites these diverse disciplines and their various subject-matters can best be summed up by defining Stoic dialectic as the science of "rational discourse" (λόγος). Rhetoric, traditionally of immense social, political, and artistic importance, was given independent status; dialectic seems to absorb all other types of linguistic production, including poetry (D.L. 7.60). Chrysippus described dialectic's subject-matter as 'signifiers and significates' (D.L. 7.62; compare Seneca's division between *verba* and *significationes*, *ep.* 89.17), but his aim was not to confine dialectic to the study of meaning, and it neither began as nor developed into what today would be called semantics. Further, dialectic clearly never enjoyed any neat, straightforward dichotomy between "what signifies" and "what is signified". The subject-matters of the two subdivisions of their very nature inevitably intertwined, and it is no more use looking for a single, sharp principle of division than for a single modern paradigm – whether a conceptual scheme or a discipline – against which Stoic dialectic as a whole can be measured. From its early, quasi-Socratic origins as the 'science of rational discourse by question and answer' (D.L. 7.42 (31A5)), when Zeno, the school's founder, recommended its study to his pupils as necessary for the solution of fallacies (Plutarch *st. rep.* 1034E (31L5)),[3] it became a complex and

---

[3] Zeno's conception of dialectic seems not to have been entirely defensive, however: Epictetus *diss.* 4.8.12 (31J) suggests he wanted a broad, positive, if vaguely conceived, study of 'the elements of reason'. Stobaeus 2.22.12ff. (=*S.V.F.*1.49 (31K)) may perhaps be a contemptuous allusion to the contemporary Dialectical school (on which see 4.6 and 7.6, nn. 27, 28); certainly it does not accord with Aristo's rejection of dialectic as useless and irrelevant to human concerns (D.L. 7.160f. (part, 31N)), since the dialecticians' techniques could, in principle, be applied to 'good things' rather than 'chaff and rubbish'. On pre-Chrysippean dialectic: Frede 1974a: 12ff.; Long 1978: 102ff.; Hülser 1979a; Schofield 1983; and further, 3.2.

comprehensive theory of cognition, language, argument, and proof, indispensable for both philosophical exposition and a life in accordance with Stoic doctrines.

Mature Stoic dialectic was by no means restricted to the conduct of formal or public philosophical debate. The true dialectician is the master of all forms of rational interchange and inquiry (D.L. 7.46–8 (31B)). The ability to use and understand language, both publicly, and privately as "the language of thought", is distinctively human, a salient and inalienable characteristic of the rational mortal animal, whose λόγος enables it both to grasp logical connections (Sextus *M*. 8.275f. (53T)), and to make mere vocal noises into significant talk: D.L. 7.55f. (part, 33H); Galen *P.H.P.* 2.5.9ff., p. 130, ll. 7ff. (53U).[4] Only in rational discourse is it possible to articulate the internal, psychic entities called φαντασίαι, "presentations" or "impressions", which are altered states of the "mind", διάνοια, that is, of the soul's directive component, the ἡγεμονικόν.[5] Impressions can be excited by objects of thought or of perception: D.L. 7.51, 52 (39A4, 40P); Sextus *M*. 7.234ff. (part, 53F). For an impression to be "rational", λογική, is precisely for its content to be presentable to the receiver of the impression, or to the outside world, in language (Sextus *M*. 8.70 (33C)), language itself being 'significant vocal sound sent out from the mind': D.L. 7.56 (33H); Galen *P.H.P.* 2.5.12,

---

[4] It is not clear who invented the distinction between προφορικός, "pronunciative", *logos* (*i.e.* speech), and ἐνδιάθετος, "internal", *logos* (*i.e.* reason); on the two, see Pohlenz 1939: 191ff., 1970–2: 21; Mühl 1962; Nuchelmans 1973: 127f.; Ebbesen 1981a: 1: 128ff. In some form or other it was certainly used by the Stoa: *e.g.* Sextus *P.H.* 1. 65), and the school plainly regarded significant discourse as unique to rational creatures and as an expression of – as sound made significant by – internal psychic states correlated with *lekta* (on which see main text). The basic idea that language and thought are forms of *logos*, one internal, one external, of course goes back to Plato *Sophist* 263d6ff. The Stoic contribution to what Nuchelmans calls the philosophical tradition of 'the lingualisation of mental phenomena' (1973: 19), which is manifest, for example, in the equivalence Chrysippus assumes between thought and internal speech (see Galen *P.H.P.* 3.7.42, p. 220, ll. 16–18), will prove important later: see esp. 3.4, 3.5, 6.2, 6.3, 7.7, 7.9.

[5] Chrysippus and Cleanthes famously disagreed about the nature of impressions: Sextus *M*. 7.228–31, with D.L. 7.50 (39A3); *cf. e.g.* Rist 1969: 136. Their disagreement took the characteristic form of a dispute over how to interpret Zeno: 3.2. I adopt Chrysippus' view, that the impression is an ἀλλοίωσις, "alteration", of the soul's ruling part.

p. 130, l. 14 (53U6). Rational impressions, thoughts, νοήσεις, are a human (and divine) prerogative. The process is succinctly described at D.L. 7.49 (33D): 'first comes the impression; then the mind, which is capable of expressing itself, enunciates in language the experience it has because of the impression'.

The relevant portion of psychology, which is primarily a part of physics (D.L. 7.157ff.), is thus needed to explain the structure of the soul, and the genesis, structure, and typology of impressions. Epistemology, wherever precisely it is located in the exposition of Stoic philosophy, provides a theoretical account of their relative cognitive value, the highest in the scale being the "cognitive" or "apprehensive", καταληπτική, impression, whose truth, accuracy, and clarity are guaranteed.[6] Thoughts can be stored, combined, organised, compared, and analysed: hence arise concepts, memory, imagination, ratiocination and inference, definition, expertise, science – and virtue: e.g. Cicero acad. 2.21, 22, 30f. (39C, 40M, N). To undergo such mental operations and processes, and to be communicated from mind to mind, primarily by means of talk and writing, impressions must possess some sort of non-physical structure or representation, for, by the principles of Stoic materialism, both thoughts, and the soul of which they are altered states, are bodies. The soul must be corporeal, since it affects and is affected by the body it animates, and only bodies act or are acted on (e.g. D.L. 7.56 (33H); S.V.F. 1.518, 2. 790 (45C, D)); as for thoughts, they are nothing more than the soul in such-and-such a condition (e.g. S.V.F. 2.826 (part, 53K)), and, in consequence, cannot be directly passed from mind to mind, or shared by two or more minds.

Now at least some of the structures familar from ordinary language – principally that of nominal-subject-plus-verb – are reflections or analogues of the possible structures of the contents of impressions (the correspondence is not accidental, as

---

[6] The most important texts on this part of Stoic epistemology are collected as LS 40; and cf. esp. Sandbach 1971a; Frede 1983; Arthur 1983. There is a long-running dispute as to whether there can be non-perceptual cognitive impressions: see e.g. Striker 1974: 107ff.; Bonhöffer 1890: 228ff., for the two sides of the case, and Frede 1983: 72ff. for a persuasive settlement.

I shall argue). But structured complexes of this latter sort cannot be simply linguistic, for impressions are not bits of talk. Nor can they be what impressions convey from mind to mind, since, again by the Stoic metaphysical principles just described, linguistic items are corporeal too: they are manifestly produced by speakers, and have effects on hearers. They are in fact bits of battered air, shaped by the tongue and other organs of articulation, and their properties will be corporeal likewise (D.L. 7.55, 56 (33H)). What is new and important is that this air is special: it has content or meaning: it is *logos* in one of its many guises. The suitability of air to vocal communication could even be counted as evidence of divine providence (*cf.* Seneca *quaest. nat.* 2.29)

Some types of linguistic item, nouns and pronouns, standardly stand for or signify things in the world. Other words, although significant, do not signify in this way; and this group includes verbs (ῥήματα) which signify members of one group or species of what were called by the Stoics λεκτά (D.L. 7.58, 63–4 (33M, F, G)). The *lekton* was the invention of Stoic dialecticians. In mature Stoicism it is "what is said" or "sayable", in the special sense that this is what is or can be communicated[7] between speakers of a common language by the production of a significant utterance. It is also the content of a rational impression (not, of course, the impression itself) considered as something articulated or articulable in language-

---

[7] On the 'systematic ambiguity' of participles ending in -τόν, 'between being an object of φ-ing and being φ-able': Geach 1969: 31. That *lekta* "subsist in accordance with [κατὰ] a rational impression" (D.L. 7.63 (33F2)) suggests that they automatically accompany, or supervene on, any impression in a suitable soul, but this leads to difficulties: 7.7, 7.9. To indicate its status as a term of art and to preserve this ambiguity, I prefer simply to transliterate λεκτόν, with Long 1986: 135 (although I do not agree with him that *fact*, *statement* or *state-of-affairs* are ever appropriate equivalents). On *lekta* in causation theory: 6.2.3, 6.3.4. On the incorporeals in general in Stoic metaphysics: esp. Pasquino 1978: 383. I disagree with Long and Sedley 1987: 1: 200f. that *lekta* are 'parasitic on' language, as being largely analysable into words: it is true that some linguistic items are parts of *lekta* (see 6.3.4, 6.3.5.2), but it is predicates and complete *lekta*, not sentences, which make possible the articulation of extra-linguistic reality. Further, not only do *lekta* have the crucial rôle of structuring impressions, they are also immune to the ravages of anomaly and ambiguity, always retaining the structures which can be lost or obscured in linguistic complexes. Since they can serve as correctives on language, they must, to that extent, be independent of it.

like structures, and is thus defined as 'that which subsists in accordance with a rational impression' (D.L. 7.63 (33F2); Sextus *M.* 8.70 (33C)). *Lekta* also have a part to play in Stoic causal theory, as the incorporeal effects of corporeal causes, although they can also themselves somehow give rise to impressions in the minds of hearers (Sextus *M.* 8.409 (27E)). They constitute the crucial link between minds and linguistic behaviour, and the Stoics' account of them connects the part of dialectic dealing with impressions and linguistic items to the part dealing with propositions and logic. Understandably, *lekta* were frequent bones of contention between Stoics and their philosophical rivals, with the Stoics maintaining that without such "meanings" all learning, teaching, philosophical doctrine, science and expertise – in fact, all normal life – would be impossible.[8]

Some *lekta* are complex: some are questions, commands, oaths, and the like; and some of them, the sort to be true or false,[9] are the *lekta* from which arguments are constructed. These are ἀξιώματα, today more or less standardly, and more or less correctly, treated as "propositions" (*e.g.* D.L. 7.65ff.; and generally LS 34).[10] The basic structure of the proposition

---

[8] See Sextus *M.* 1.20–5, presumably borrowed from a Stoic source; Plutarch *adv. Col.* 1119C-1120B (part, 19K). The general Stoic strategy of arguing that skepticism destroys normal human existence is well illustrated by Cicero *acad.* 2.19ff.

[9] There is a propositional component in oaths (*cf.* n. 83), and other items besides *axiōmata* can be true or false (arguments, impressions), but they are the primary bearers of truth-values, by reference to which these secondary items are defined: see esp. Sextus *M.* 7.244 (39G7–8), 8.10 on the relation between *lekta* and impressions. On the senses of *true*: 3.5.

[10] To the extent that *axiōmata* are the primary bearers of truth-values, the contents of certain types of thoughts, and the significations of declarative sentences, they perform some of the functions that are or have been assigned to propositions by modern logicians. But *axiōmata* form part of a unique metaphysical system, in which only *lekta*, time, space, and place are incorporeals: *e.g.* Sextus *M.* 10.218 (27D). Though always and by definition either true or false (*e.g.* Cicero *fat.* 20f., 38 (38G, 34C)), they can change their truth-value, and are inherently tensed (*e.g.* the "reasonable", εὔλογον, proposition, ⟨I shall be alive tomorrow⟩, at D.L. 7.76, with Lloyd 1978: 293f.). They are also (unlike states-of-affairs, to which they are sometimes compared: *e.g.* Hülser 1979a: 296) inherently structured in quasi-linguistic fashion, with a basic "logical form" of predicate+subject (see main text). Further, there are distinct varieties of complete *lekta* which are questions, commands, *etc.* (*e.g.* D.L. 7.66–8) – even, it seems, different *axiōmata* corresponding to active and passive synonymous sentences (D.L. 7.64) – so that *axiōmata* cannot

is that of nominal-plus-predicate, the former being a "case" (πτῶσις), or nominal in a grammatical case, and the predicate, at its simplest, one sort of incomplete *lekton*, signified by a verb. (On this interpretation of Stoic "cases", see further, 6.3.) What are now called intransitive, transitive, passive, and impersonal constructions were all recognised. Our principal source is, besides D.L. 7.63f., with 58, a happily far more detailed quotation from Porphyry in Ammonius (*int.* 44.19ff. (33q)); the latter ostensibly concerns verbs, ῥήματα, but this must be one more instance of a confusion typical in non-Stoic authorities.[11] This subject/predicate structure is fixed, not by linguistic considerations *per se*, but by the metaphysical scheme which informs the Stoic world, since propositions articulate possible states-of-affairs in basically the correct fashion: it is not that all are true, but that by means of them true and false claims about the world can be made. Their structure makes possible the distinction in thought, impossible in the universe of concrete spatio-temporal particulars, between objects, denoted by cases, and their activities, passivities, and states. For the new Stoic twist to the old problem of explaining true or false talk is that, according to Stoic metaphysics, out there in the world there *are* only spatio-temporal particu-

be regarded as the "sense" or "propositional/descriptive content" common to sentences or utterances with different "forces", as required by modern truth theoretic semantics. If there is a Stoic pragmatics, it is 'fused', as Hülser 1979a: 287 puts it, into the semantic portion of dialectic, and it can be allowed (with Denyer 1988: 377, n. 1) that the Stoics did not identify indicative mood with assertoric force (assertable contents also occurring unasserted, *e.g.* as antecedents of conditionals) only provided no commitment is made thereby to a general Stoic sense/ force theory. Nor are they distinguished from some Stoic counterpart to the "statement", "saying the same thing of the same thing", which is postulated by some modern logicians. Again, they are not "Russellian" linguistic propositions, being in some respects more like Fregean "thoughts"; they can contain deictics, which take their reference from context (*e.g.* D.L. 7.70 (34κ6)); and they can be generated (D.L. 7.64 (33G); *cf.* perhaps Suda *s.v.* ἀξίωμα, a proposition 'ἔχει τὴν γένεσιν' from a predicate and a case), as well as being "perishable" (Alexander *an. pr.* 177.25ff. (38F)). Finally, the Stoics cannot have conceived of them in the mathematical terms of "functions", "arguments", or "variables", an analysis often applied in the literature: *e.g.* Inwood 1985a: 93f.; Egli 1987: 119f., 125.

[11] Ammonius *an. pr.* 68.4ff. (=*S.V.F.* 2.236), for example, makes *lekta* the Stoic equivalents of vocal sounds, while Apollonius *synt.* 43.15ff. reports that the Stoics called infinitives "verbs", and finite verbs "predicates" (*cf.* 429.10ff.), although he has probably fumbled a real distinction here, between predicates and verb-forms.

lars, all activities, passivities, and states being just (conditions of) the objects which they go to constitute. Without predicates, the only linguistic activity would be naming this or that object, or this or that condition of an object; with them, saying something about the object, truly or falsely, becomes possible.

Thus Seneca reports (*ep.* 117.13 (33E); *cf.* Long 1986: 136f.) that there is in the world just the single and indivisible wise Cato, the body which is Cato qualified in such a way (as regards his soul) that he has (and is in part constituted by) the quality walking, or wisdom; for a man's wisdom or walking, on the Stoic view, are also bodies, being but the man in this or that condition. In thought, on the other hand, a thing and its being so qualified can be contemplated separately, as in ⟨Cato is wise⟩. Here, presumably, the formal differentiation of the linguistic expression *is wise*, corresponding to the predicate ⟨... is wise⟩, reflects the fact that wisdom is not being named, as it would be by the noun *wisdom*, but predicated of something. (I am ignoring a possible distinction between predicates in general, and συμβεβηκότα, predicates actually belonging to subjects: see Stobaeus 1.106.5ff. (= *S.V.F.* 2.509 (51B)), Sextus *M.* 8.100, with Lloyd 1970: 232f.). Such *lekta* can be produced, understood, and assessed, even if there is no wise Cato (when the quality wisdom is predicated of him falsely, there being no such thing as Cato's wisdom), or even no longer such a thing as Cato at all (*cf.* Alexander *an. pr.* 403.14ff.).

I focus here on propositions in part simply because the only secure information available about the structures of *lekta* concerns propositions. More importantly, propositions are strictly the objects of assent, and thus play a rôle central to Stoic epistemology and moral philosophy: Stobaeus 2.88.2ff. (= *S.V.F.* 3.171 (33I)); Sextus *M.* 7.154 (41C8).[12] Two broad

---

[12] Frede 1983: 69 (*cf.* 1986: 105ff.) has argued that 'there is more to a rational impression than just the propositional content ... To have a rational impression is to think a certain proposition in a certain way', so that the manner of representation of the objects represented therein may differ enormously. As the propositional content of the impression remains constant, however, this distinction, important as it is for the Stoics' ethics and psychology, does not seem relevant to their semantics.

divisions, in fact, can be discerned within Stoic dialectic which cross Chrysippus' division of its subject matter into "signifiers and signified". One deals with impressions and the criteria of truth; the other treats of language and logic. They are bound together by *lekta*, which both structure impressions and give meaning to utterances, including definitions of the conceptions by which 'things are understood': D.L. 7.42 (31A3). Propositional *lekta* are at once the prime objects of assent, and the constituents of arguments and proofs. Thus the principal propositional syntax of subject-case + predicate makes possible a mental operation of articulation, and with it the human capacity for all the rational activities premissed on judgement and assent. In its turn, the principal linguistic syntax of nominal + verb, by reproducing this structure, means that speakers can express impressions in speech and, in a sense, share them with others, make them as public as private, internal states can be. Again, god's guiding hand is doubtless responsible for the happy situation that natural languages – some, like Greek, more than others? *Cf.* Galen *P.H.P.* 2.2.22, p. 108, ll. 14f. – tend to reproduce key logical structures, on to which ontological divisions in turn are mapped.

Lekta naturally had immense importance for the Stoic theory of meaning. The part of Stoic dialectic which superficially resembles what are now called phonetics and phonology, the study of speech-sounds and their patternings in natural languages, classified (some of) the articulate sounds of a language (Greek, in this instance) and their permissible groupings into syllables and larger complexes. What might be called Stoic "grammar" identified (some of) the lexical and syntactic elements of that language as a subset of the possible sound sequences already identified. What might be called Stoic "semantics" described the ways in which these elements are grouped as signifiers, perhaps with a broad dichotomy into lexical and formal or grammatical semantic classes, and crucially invoking *lekta* to explain semantic relations.[13] Some

---

[13] Rules of syllable-formation and -combination, a standard feature of ancient grammars, will have been required if the distinction between inarticulate and articulate vocal sound (as at D.L. 7.55–7 (part, 33A, H)) was to be precise and comprehensive. The question whether there was such a thing as specifically Stoic grammar has

lekta are (constituents of) the structures of interest to logicians, above all the propositional-like items which go to form arguments.

For the Stoa, of course, dialectic is a single, unified science, within a philosophical system whose own unity was famous: *e.g.* Cicero *fin.* 3.74, 4.53. The contents of what I have described as distinct subjects, some with the approximate labels of modern sciences and disciplines, turn out to be only rough equivalents of their modern counterparts. Besides fundamental differences in scope, methods, and conceptual frameworks, they are also different precisely because they do belong to one section of one division of a whole philosophical system. Stoics argued forcefully too on one side of an important ancient debate that logic is an integral part of philosophical doctrine, and is not simply taken over, as an independent body of theory, to be put to use *ad hoc* in constructing, analysing, and assessing arguments. The debate centred on what are today called formal and philosophical logic, but correct understanding of Stoic teaching in these fields would have required a thorough acquaintance with the rest of dialectic.[14] What is needed now is precisely an account of the content and aims of Stoic philosophy which will explain at once dialectic's privileged position, in all its richness, complexity, and technical sophistication, as an integral part of that philosophy, and the Stoa's interest in ambiguity. Hitherto dialectic has been referred to as a "science", ἐπιστήμη, a concept whose scope must now be explored if a distinction crucial to the correct understanding of the purpose of Stoic dialectical teaching is to be drawn.

Sciences are the province of the Stoic sage, the paragon of

been brilliantly explored by Frede 1977, 1978. I apply the label cautiously to this portion of Stoic doctrine because Stoic grammatical studies were subsumed under the broader discipline of dialectic, and because ancient "grammar" is anyway not directly comparable with its modern counterpart – and that is so even leaving to one side Stoic unorthodoxy in the field (*e.g.* the secondary status of linguistic syntax (see 6.2.4, 6.5.2), and the considerations brought to bear on the construction of grammatical categories (see 6.3.5.2)). The semantic status of two of the Stoic parts of speech (*viz.*, article and conjunction) is unclear; but, more generally, caution must be exercised in attributing to the Stoics a "semantics" in the same sense as it is to modern philosophers of language: 6.2.3, 6.3.5.2.

[14] The key text, Ammonius *an. pr.* 8.2off. (part, 26E), is further discussed in 7.6.

human success, who, within the natural bounds of human capacity,[15] is infallible, and who possesses all the virtues (*e.g.* Plutarch *st. rep.* 1046EF (61F)), one of which is actually dialectic itself: D.L. 7.46 (31BI). The "apprehensive" or "cognitive", καταληπτική, impression, whose truth, accuracy, and clarity are guaranteed, is what makes "science" in the Stoic sense possible. Sciences are systems of "cognitions", καταλήψεις, which are assents to impressions of this kind: *e.g.* Sextus *M.* 7.151–7 (41C). (The topic of assent will be taken up a little later.) Bodies of knowledge are tightly-knit systems of these cognitions, immune by reason of their comprehensiveness and truth to change through rational argument; and they are the privilege of the wise, who can put them to work as entirely reliable criteria for the assessment of the truth or falsity – more precisely, of the apprehensiveness – of all incoming impressions: *e.g.* Stobaeus 2.68.18ff. (= *S.V.F.* 3.112 (part, 41H)). Scientific knowledge so conceived is internal to the agent/knower, since – again in accordance with Stoic metaphysical laws[16] – cognition is corporeal, and knowledge a firm and unchangeable state of the wise man's soul, directing his responses to the impressions his soul receives.[17] Besides dialectic (and rhetoric), the principal Stoic virtues – courage, practical wisdom, justice, and temperance – are all "bodies" of knowledge in the twin sense that they are both states of the wise man's soul (*e.g.* Seneca *ep.* 113.24 (61E)) and organically unitary cognitive systems formed from prescriptive "theorems", θεωρήματα: *e.g.* Stobaeus 2.58.5ff., 63.6ff. (= *S.V.F.* 3.95 (part, 60K), 280 (part, 61D)).

---

[15] The sage is not literally infallible; rather, he 'does all things well, that is, what he does', Stobaeus 2.66.14ff. (= *S.V.F.* 3.560 (61G)); D.L. 7.125. His infallibility lies in his never mistaking truth for falsehood or for plausibilities whose truth is unclear – he never assents to a non-cognitive impression (*e.g.* Stobaeus 2.111.18ff. (= *S.V.F.* 3.548 (part, 41G)), *PHerc.* 1020, col. 4, col. 1 (= *S.V.F.* 2.131, part (part, 41D)), Sextus *M.* 7.156f. (41CI0)) – and in his grasp of the universal truths and their relations, which grounds his whole conduct of life (*cf.* Kerferd 1978).

[16] *E.g.* Alexander *mant.* 161.26ff. (= *S.V.F.* 3.63): virtues make use of the sense-organs in the process of choice; also 115.32ff. (= *S.V.F.* 2.797). Texts illustrating Stoic materialism are collected as LS 45.

[17] *E.g.* Stobaeus 2.73.16ff. (= *S.V.F.* 3.112, part (41H)); Plutarch *st. rep.* 1042E–F (60R); in fact the virtues, being states of the wise man's soul, are themselves living creatures: Seneca *ep.* 113.24 (61E).

Unsurprisingly, suspicions were often entertained in antiquity about the possibility of such human perfection, and the Stoics had to defend their claim that men could come to be wise in this lofty sense (see further, 3.2). An effective defence was of the last importance because the Stoic sage is not only cognitively perfect, he is the only happy man, and is so precisely because of his virtue: he has the wisdom which allows him to adjust his individual wants and needs to the ineluctable sequence of causes and events, fate, which orders the whole cosmos. One of the central tenets of Stoic philosophy is that the universe is a divine, rational, and coherent ordering. The Stoic god, who is also providence and fate, is the immanent active element in this ordering: *e.g.* D.L. 7.147 (54A); Cicero *nat. deor.* 1.39 (54B). The Stoic defence of their ideal rests on the thesis that the sage, although like a god on earth (D.L. 7.119; Plutarch *comm. not.* 1076A (61J)), has merely brought to perfection the rationality common to all which sets our species apart. All human beings have the spark of divine reason in their souls: Stobaeus 2.65.8 (= *S.V.F.* 1.566 (part, 61L)); hence they have within themselves the makings of happiness: for to be happy is to live in accordance with nature, and that, for humans, is just to live rationally, rationality being our unique, distinguishing property, and the gift of divine, rational nature: Seneca *ep.* 124.13f. (60H); D.L. 7.86 (57A5). Although people may be unable to exercise the dialectic which is a science and a virtue, a system of cognitions impregnable to argument or persuasion (Stobaeus 2.73.16ff. = *S.V.F.* 3.112 (part, 41H)) – and the Stoics went so far as to admit that not even the great men of their school had been sages (Sextus *M.* 7.432f.) – they can still, in virtue of this natural ability to use reason and language, acquire the rudiments of Stoic dialectical doctrine, which sketches the theoretical content of the wise man's knowledge, and emphasises the necessity of conducting one's life in accordance with its principles (D.L. 7.46–8 (31B)).

This is not a matter either of being clever logicians, or of making good prudential choices. Happiness, deliberately defined in commonplace and popular terms as 'an easy flow of life' (*e.g.* Stobaeus 2.77.16ff. = *S.V.F.* 3.16 (63A)), consists in living virtuously, for the natural goal of every living thing is to achieve its own unique perfection, and virtue is the perfection of our unique gift, reason: Seneca *ep.* 76.9f. (63D). Everything else, strictly, is irrelevant to this end. All the other, so-called "good" things of life, which are relegated to the status of "preferred", προηγμένα, objects, are to be chosen only in so far as they do not conflict with virtue, but rather provide material about which virtuous choices can be made (Cicero *fin.* 3.50 (58I); Plutarch *st. rep.* 1048A (58H)). The Stoa followed philosophical convention and ordinary non-philosophical beliefs in equating the good with the beneficial (*e.g.* Sextus *M.* 11.22 (60GI)), but earned harsh criticism for their claim that, although other things too, the preferred objects and activities, are 'in accordance with nature' (*e.g.* D.L. 7.107 (58m)), virtue and virtuous activity alone constitute "benefit", ὠφέλεια (*ibid.*). 'Virtue is a harmonious disposition, choiceworthy for its own sake, and not out of some fear or hope of anything external; and happiness consists in virtue, since virtue is a soul made with a view to harmony in the whole of life' (D.L. 7.89 (61A); and *e.g.* Cicero *fin.* 4.26ff. (part, 64K) for one hostile commentary on this doctrine). In contrast, what is preferred is no more than "serviceable", χρήσιμον; it is not "indifferent", ἀδιάφορον, in that our natural impulse is to get and keep it, yet is so in that it can make no contribution to happiness or misery, that is, it is morally neutral (*e.g.* D.L. 7.104f. (58B); and further, 3.2).

The arguments devised to construct and defend this Socratic, radically rationalistic philosophy, which are ultimately drawn from Stoic theology, need not be examined here.[18] Let us

---

[18] The equation of rationality with moral virtue seems to have been achieved by way of a matrix of arguments. Since god is good, he must be beneficial, and only moral goodness is consistently and innately beneficial (*e.g.* D.L. 7.101ff. (part, 58A)): so, god must be morally good: Clement *paed.* 1.8.63.1f. (= *S.V.F.* 2.1116 (part), 60I)). Second, since the universe is perfect, it must actually contain moral virtue: Cicero *nat. deor.* 2.37ff. (54H). Next, god is also perfect reason, as is shown by a variety of considerations, principally the order and beauty of the universe, and the (imperfect but perfectible) rationality of his creation, humankind (*e.g.* Sextus *M.* 9.104ff. (part, 54F)); his necessary moral goodness must be perfected rationality, which is realisable in the man who lives according to the will of the divine ruler, and whose reason is a part of the universal, divine reason: D.L. 7.88 (63C3–4).

suppose that the crucial connection has been established: to be happy is to be virtuous, and to be virtuous is to be perfectly rational, in a universe which reason pervades and rules, even down to its humblest inhabitants. The Stoic sage is born to virtue only in the sense that all humans have the innate potential for perfecting the gift of reason, and thus of living fully in accordance with their own nature (*e.g.* D.L. 7.87–9 (part, 63C)). The path to virtue[19] is difficult, none the less, and exhaustive philosophical training seems to be necessary. Dialectic, in particular, as will be seen, equips the agent with indispensable cognitive capacities. Another crucial ingredient was the observation, imitation, and performance of actions which, if performed by a sage, would be wholly rational and consistent – that is, virtuous – and which for any agent are dictated by relevant moral principles. These are "appropriate acts" or "duties", καθήκοντα, such as honouring one's parents, repaying debts, even caring for one's health and doing dialectic (*e.g.* D.L. 7.108f. (59E); Seneca *ep.* 120.3ff. (part, 60E); Cicero *fin.* 3.58f. (59F); Plutarch *st. rep.* 12.1038A). What differentiates the wise man's activities is not any particular action, or type of action, but the cognitive apparatus he can bring to bear in any situation calling for action: his theoretically coherent, pragmatically tested, comprehensive knowledge of the principles which govern action, argument, and, ultimately, the whole rational ordering of the cosmos: *e.g.* Sextus *M.* 11.200f. (59G); D.L. 7.88 (63C3–5). Above all, the sage can completely control the capacity that enables any human agent to decide and act on a decision: that of assent to (propositional) impressions.

It is here that dialectic demonstrates its practical value. As a body of theoretical knowledge, dialectic furnishes relevant technical information about the sorts of item that constitute, structure, and characterise minds, language, and the arguments by which men seek to reason and convince. As a

[19] Strictly, there is no "progress" toward virtue, in that the transition from vice to virtue is instantaneous: Plutarch *quomodo ... profectus* 75C (61S). But some notion of "advance" to this goal was clearly accepted, as is shown by *e.g.* Plutarch *st. rep.* 1043D, despite such texts as Plutarch *comm. not.* 1063AB (61T).

rigorous discipline, it trains perceptions, strengthens and organises the powers of reasoning, and confers the power of granting and withholding assent exclusively according to the objective properties of impressions. It has the dual nature, at once practical and theoretical, which characterises the whole of Stoic philosophy, of equipping a person to act correctly in any situation, providing both general doctrines and precepts for action: Seneca *ep.* 95, esp. 10ff. (part, 66J). Dialectic is neither a purely intellectual discipline, nor a mere cluster of skills, but, in Posidonius' words, 'the science of true and false and neither': D.L. 7.42, 62. His definition is not a radical departure from the past; he is merely emphasising dialectic's already central heuristic and diagnostic rôle.[20]

Dialectic's significance is ultimately explained by the fact that it is assent which governs a human being's life for good and ill, for happiness or misery. The paramount importance of assent is itself explained by its being within our power (*e.g.* Epictetus *diss.* 1.1.7ff. (62K), 1.17.21ff.) and by its intimate relation to action.[21] Assent to certain impressions constitutes an "impulse", ὁρμή, in the human soul to perform some action: *e.g.* Stobaeus 2.86.17ff., 88.2ff. (=*S.V.F.* 3.169 (part, 53Q), 3.171 (33II)). Many of the actions performable by human agents have moral value; these are the "duties" already described, which, as observed, can lay the groundwork for eventual translation to a wholly virtuous and blessed existence. Agents must learn to withhold assent from impressions where such assent will be an unstable, extravagant impulse to action, uncontrolled by right reason – from those, in fact, which are one of the "passions", πάθη, mistaken value-judgements[22]

---

[20] The definition means that dialectic provides theoretical descriptions of and practical guidance in distinguishing actual occurrences of both the bearers of truth and falsity (primarily, propositions, but also impressions and arguments, including proofs: see n. 9), and the items from which these are specifically distinct (primarily, non-assertoric, truth-valueless *lekta*, not just from questions, *pace* Nuchelmans 1973: 62). Posidonius' own particular interest in proof is well attested: *e.g.* Galen *P.H.P.* 4.4.38, p. 258, ll. 19–25 (=T83EK, pp. 26f.).

[21] Hence Epictetus' emphasis on the importance, and the divine origin, of the "control of impressions" (*diss.* 1.1.7ff. (62K)), and the quarrel between Stoa and Academy about whether assent must precede action (Plutarch *st. rep.* 1057A (53S)).

[22] I am assuming a Chrysippean monistic psychology, according to which virtue and vice alike are states of a single, wholly rational soul: *e.g.* Plutarch *virt. moral.* 440Eff. (61B).

about what is good and bad, beneficial and harmful, which encourage the descent into vice and misery: *e.g.* Stobaeus 2.88.8ff. (= *S.V.F.* 3.378, 3.389 (part, 65A)). Further, if agents are to regulate their actions with full understanding, they will need intelligent and informed assent to Stoic philosophical doctrines, as these articulate and explain the rational principles governing both the macrocosm of divine reason and the microcosm of human morality. Because agents have the power of assent they can learn to live uncomplainingly and intelligently in accordance with fate, grasping both its general, benevolent, despotism, and also, to a certain extent, the particular contributions people are ordained to make as individuals.[23]

Hence dialectic was conceived of as a system of subordinate virtues, or interrelated bodies of knowledge which control and direct assent and impulse: D.L. 7.46f. (31B1–6); *PHerc.* 1020, coll. 4, 1 (= *S.V.F.* 2.131 (part, 41D)). If assent is properly governed, the goal of human existence can be achieved, consistent rational selection of preferred items, 'the primary things in accordance with nature': see Stobaeus 2.79.18ff., 82.20f. (58C), and generally LS 58. Now the Stoics did not altogether disprize non-moral "goods". The wise man will still, if he can, make a judicious selection of all the other objects and activities which it is his (and human) nature to prefer – health, wealth, riches, a good reputation, and so forth – and is in fact able to exercise his virtue only in this way. But he will not actually "desire" such things, and under some circumstances, he may select what he would otherwise reject, and would certainly do so had he the knowledge that this is what is fated for him: *cf.* Epictetus *diss.* 2.6.9 (= *S.V.F.* 3.191 (58J)).

The interest in ambiguity shown by Stoic dialecticians now begins to explain itself. If the information on which assent

---

[23] Note esp. Cicero *div.* 1.127 (55O): only god can grasp completely the causes of what is to come, and men must make shift as best they can with signs and portents; also Sextus *M.* 11.64ff. (58F), with Epictetus *diss.* 2.6.9 (58J), Alex. *fat.* 191.30ff. (55N): any man naturally selects the preferred things, but the wise man will adapt his choices to circumstances, knowing they are not arbitrary, or the result of a malicious plot, but the design of a benevolent fate.

must be grounded is insufficient, unclear, irrelevant, or otherwise unsatisfactory, the danger arises that a poor decision may be made. The sage is characterised by his unfailing ability to treat impressions according to their merits – he will always take the quality of the impression into account when judging it, and his own mental and physical condition at the time[24] – and while the rest of humanity does too, it does not do so always and consistently. Frequently people assent to impressions which are false or unclear, taking the plausibility of an impression, that is, its attractiveness, or power to induce assent (cf. D.L. 7.75 (38D)), as grounds for accepting its truth, or even its apprehensiveness. Diogenes Laertius quotes this instructive example of a plausible proposition: 'If something gives birth to a thing, it is that thing's mother'. The generalisation looks true – but a hen is not the mother of the egg she lays (ibid.).

Diogenes preserves another crucial piece of information about the place of the study of ambiguity in dialectical education. The Stoic dialectician must be able to discern 'what is true and what false, what plausible [πιθανόν] and what said ambiguously' (7.47 (31B7)). The coupling of ambiguity with the "plausible" is not casual. The Stoic taxonomy of impressions gets under way precisely with a four-fold division by appeal to the concepts of plausibility and its opposite: the doctrinally significant point is that not all plausible impressions, those to which ordinary agents are inclined to assent, are true (e.g. Sextus M. 7.242–3 (39G2–3)). A fallacious argument is a prominent instance of plausibility's threatening to get the better of truth, and ambiguities were particularly associated with fallacies (as I shall show in Chapter Seven).

It it easy to understand how unnoticed ambiguities could be thought to give rise to this unfortunate situation. An agent may either fail on occasion to observe a normally obvious ambiguity, or be subject to the sort of gross conceptual confusion which underpins blank ignorance of such linguistic dis-

---

[24] This probably explains the late qualification to the Stoic definition of the cognitive impression, that it must have no "impediment": Sextus M. 7.253ff. (40K); also the dispute over whether the sage could lose his moral virtue when drunk or insane: D.L. 7.127 (61I2–3)).

tinctions. Of the many impressions which arise through the medium of language, the greatest importance will attach to those which convey philosophical truths and their supporting arguments, and those which must be correctly related to some appropriate piece of doctrine if assent is to be properly regulated. If agents do not realise that an ambiguity in the linguistic expression of a proposition or argument conceals its falsity or unsoundness, or if it leads them to gross misinterpretation, their moral welfare may, in extreme cases, be directly at stake, at least by reinforcing vicious tendencies. At best, people may be induced to accept a falsehood – any falsehood – which could subsequently involve them in self-contradiction, and hence in doubt, confusion, and vacillation. It is, after all, the mark of the fool that his assents are weak and shifting: he is always in danger of having to retract, to change his beliefs (Sextus *M.* 7.151 (41C3); *cf.* Frede 1983: 85f.) – and may be, uncomfortably, all too aware of his own repeatedly proven fallibility. The danger is more direct where the ambiguity which escapes an agent is that of a key moral or philosophical term, since here the ambiguity's potential for interference with decision-making would be both grave and manifest, and Stoic doctrine in fact seems to have presented several such cardinal distinctions at the linguistic level (3.2). But the Stoic tenet (D.L. 7.110) that any falsehood produces a disturbance in the soul, which can give rise in turn to the gross psychic instability or excessive impulse which is a bad emotion, widens even this generous basis for concern about ambiguities: the doctrine must apply to false propositions or false arguments accepted as a result of some undetected ambiguity in their expression. Such errors will be a constant potential source of psychological disturbance, in the simple sense that coming to realise an error, through further experience, or through formal education, typically means a more or less painful process of psychic adjustment to the new information; only the sage, secure in his all-embracing knowledge of the world, is immune from these periodic corrections.[25]

---

[25] Of course, it may be doubted that smoothness of life and tranquillity do form a plausible conception of happiness: I merely acknowledge this Stoic view, and exploit its explanatory power.

It may seem unlikely that such apparently trivial errors could be so dangerous. Certain errors of judgement are indeed more easily extirpated than others (*e.g.* Stobaeus 2.88.8ff. (= *S.V.F.* 3.389 (65A, esp. §8))), and they may include some of those due to the misapprehension or ignorance of ambiguities. The real threat lies in consistent mistaken evaluations of objects, actions, states, and persons, since these judgements, in the Chrysippean Stoa, are precisely the bad emotions, πάθη, which are wild impulses to wrong action; an agent in the grip of such a passion is not easily convinced of his error.[26] Now it would be absurd to suppose that ingrained vices can be corrected by learning a few new definitions or other rote lessons – the whole corrupt *logos* of a person's soul must be changed – or that ambiguities alone could produce such corruption. The persuasive, general case against ambiguities is that such superficial linguistic similarities can insidiously assist in the production and concealment of potentially dangerous confusions and distortions in an individual's conceptual scheme: authentic distinctions lose out to spurious identities hidden even from agents themselves in their own internal descriptions of and reasoning about the nature, content, and purpose of their beliefs and actions. The specific, and compelling, case is that conceptions, especially those of moral and ethical values, inform and structure moral character, and that moral character chiefly determines an individual's choice of courses of action and thus his or her entire welfare. Mistaken value-judgements could obviously be encouraged or further ingrained by failure to perceive conceptual distinctions not visible on the surface of language. As virtue – and hence happiness – are all-or-nothing matters (*e.g.* D.L. 7.127 (611)), even what appears to be the slightest moral failing will take on monumental proportions. A mistake about concepts induced by a mistake about language may make one's whole life wretched and pointless.

---

[26] For Posidonius such judgements cannot be bad impulses of a single, rational, soul; but the power of ambiguous language to mislead the rational part of the soul would remain. I concentrate on Chrysippean monistic psychology because that was school orthodoxy.

An example may be helpful; it will also serve to introduce an important qualification into this account of Stoic interest in ambiguity.

According to Stoic moral theory, there are two major types of thing – action, state, object – which are "indifferent", ἀδιάφορον, but in crucially different ways: *e.g.* D.L. 7.104 (58B). There are those which can contribute nothing to happiness or unhappiness, that is, which are morally neutral, neither good nor bad, neither beneficial nor harmful; these are called indifferent "simply", ἅπαξ. And there are those which excite neither impulse not rejection, that is, are preferentially neutral, such as having an even or an odd number of hairs on one's head: by nature we neither choose nor avoid such things. The distinction between these two categories, the Stoic story runs, can go unappreciated by the morally uneducated. This does not mean, of course, that a type or instance of the preferentially indifferent, say, straightening a finger, might be confused with a type or case of the morally indifferent condition, such as health or riches. The error lies rather in the moral categorisation of these items.

Suppose an agent believes that whatever is preferentially indifferent to her is indifferent to her happiness, and that she also believes that whatever is preferentially non-indifferent to her, *is* so relevant. She will have two conceptual categories, of two types of indifference, and will believe they coincide exactly. Another agent might not have two such clearly distinguished conceptions, one of preferential indifference, the other of indifference-to-happiness. He might operate with catch-all categories of "preferred" and "rejected", no sharp distinction being drawn in his scheme of things between what he likes to have, do, or be, and what he believes contributes to his happiness.

A Stoic would presumably say that both agents are morally defective, in that they associate what they prefer/reject with what is relevant to happiness, and do so because they have a faulty understanding of what being happy is (*viz.*, leading a virtuous, rational life). Stoic indoctrination would correct their conceptual scheme, and help them apply it correctly and consistently, so that wealth, health, and so on, will be identified as indifferent to happiness/morally indifferent ("mindifferent"), but not as preferentially indifferent ("prindifferent").

It cannot be argued that what these agents are insensitive to is the existence of two types of actions, states, *etc.*, answering to the same term, *indifferent*, yet falling under two different conceptions and definitions, as these are prescribed by Stoic doctrine. The second agent has not arrived at any sort of dual categorisation at all, while what both crucially lack is a true conception of the happy life. Nor is their fault one of simple linguistic ignorance about the meaning(s) of *indifferent*: for the "mindifferent" meaning of *indifferent* (understood as *simply indifferent*), "what is neither good nor bad, and makes no contribution to happiness or unhappiness", is reported to have been a Stoic innovation, ἀδιάφορον thus doing the work of the Aristotelian jargon 'οὔτε ἀγαθὸν οὔτε κακόν' (Simplicius *cats.* 386.24–6, 410.29–30, 412.1–3). (In consequence, *indifferent* clearly passes one at least of the Stoic tests for ambiguity: that its multiple meanings belong to the same "usage" (ἔθος): see 4.8.)

The Stoics are making moral claims about what sorts of thing there really are; they are not interested, at any rate primarily, in analysing ordinary people's actual linguistic usage. They are in the business of sorting and correcting concepts; and it turns out that ordinary people just do have defective concepts of, amongst other things, happiness, which may at best link general welfare with moral activity, yet are far more likely to associate it, crudely, with getting what one wants and not getting what one does not. Certainly, on a Stoic view, what ordinary people have failed to realise is that ἀδιάφορον is ambiguous; but this does not represent a gap in their ordinary linguistic knowledge. Speakers of Greek may well be blankly ignorant of the fact (let us take it as a fact) that ἀδιάφορον is ambiguous, according to Stoic technical usage, while their usage of the word yet remains correct by ordinary standards. (Whether it is so by Stoic criteria of linguistic correctness is unclear: see 3.4.) And, even if Greek is in this and similar cases counted as defective, such defects do not seem to have been much remedied by, or to have established a case for, disambiguating neologisms (see further, 3.5). Clearing up errors and confusions associated with ambiguities is, after all, not going to be a simple matter either of learning what nowadays would be called dictionary definitions, or of a minor readjustment of linguistic habits. Some definitions will only appear in Stoic texts, and, where the confusion is an important one, removing it will necessitate education in and adherence to the principles of Stoic philosophy. Given this peculiar combination of Stoic readiness to assume linguistic authority, and the Stoics' overriding concern with moral goals, the sorts of linguistic and conceptual confusion and error of most concern will thus be of a very particular sort.

Further, conceptual difficulties may arise for agents in a variety of ways. Agents may, of course, lack some key concept altogether. They may possess it in what Stoics would call an incomplete or distorted form, as with normal, pre-philosophical conceptions of happiness. They may be operating unawares with concepts which Stoics would claim as "fused", the "fusion" being of two or more concepts which correspond to genuinely distinct categories of object and which the ideal agent, the sage, would keep separate – as with the agent who, lacking a (sharp) distinction between a thing's relevance to general welfare and its capacity to stimulate desire or repulsion, fails to see that things can be "indifferent" in two crucially distinct ways. (Contrast the condition of someone who, never having heard of anaerobic respiration, thinks breathing simply is breathing *air*: such a person would still have it clear that breathing is breathing *something*, and that it consists in the intake and expulsion of a gas.) Again, agents may have failed to form the normal concept which users of a language tend naturally to form, their conceptual scheme thus failing in this respect to accommodate nicely some single, clear-cut standard meaning or set of meanings. (Stoics did not have to worry about the Lockean possibility of users' all forming undetectably different concepts on the basis of their experiences; conceptual variations between individuals will be small and isolated.) Or they may combine two or more of these defects, since the conceptions in question may be the naturally acquired ideas ("preconceptions", προλήψεις) formed without benefit of a specialised artistic, technical, scientific, or philosophical education, or else "technical" conceptions of this kind.

Given this matrix of possibilities, the danger which Stoics detect in ambiguities requires a subtle and delicate formulation. If analysis of ordinary usage neither as a topic in its own right, nor as a stimulus or contribution to philosophical advance, can be expected, it is justifiable none the less to look for meticulous attention to the intersections of whichever Stoic doctrines in psychology, epistemology, and semantics bear on the issues of the formation and individuation of concepts; and it is far from clear that the Stoics gave these the care they demand. In particular, it will prove hard to analyse satisfactorily, in the terms fixed by Stoic teaching, either the impressions, φαντασίαι, which agents have, or their errors of reasoning – crucial aspects of the failure to conceptualise properly – where ambiguities are involved. I shall return to this problem in 7.7 and 7.9.

The rest of Stoic theorising about ambiguity, about which rather more direct information is to be had, now begins to fall into place. The secure identification of even central technical cases in philosophy as genuine ambiguities, immune to the objection that the concept of ambiguity being invoked is itself vague, imprecise, or downright incorrect, will be smoother with the help of, preferably, an authoritative definition of ambiguity, or at least of one which is defensible, workable, and open to improvement. The Stoics did not present themselves as the consummate dialecticians of theory, and they need not have claimed ultimate reliability for this or that definition; but they did maintain that out of definitions 'grows and is constructed the whole rational system of learning and instruction', as Augustine reports (*civ. dei* 8.7 (32F)). Sextus *P.H.* 2.205ff. informs us that 'the doctrinaire philosophers' claim definitions as necessary 'for cognition and for instruction'; the presence here of the term κατάληψις suggests a Stoic origin for this view, and it is fairly clear how it would be applied in practice. On the one hand, the definitions of both ambiguity itself and particular ambiguities would play a central pedagogical and methodological rôle, not merely by simply communicating information, but also by fostering clarity, precision, and carefulness in all forms of discourse – qualities which would help prevent the sort of disturbance caused by error. On the other, definitions, linguistic articulations of conceptions, ἔννοιαι, were central to Stoic teaching and methodology (cf. D.L. 8.48 (32A)), their importance being cardinal where the concepts articulated were the naturally-formed preconceptions, προλήψεις, which were one of Chrysippus' criteria of truth (D.L. 7.54 (40A3)). The elevation of the study of definitions to the status of a separate subsection of logic was justified on the grounds that 'things are grasped through conceptions' (D.L. 7.42 (31A3)). Exactly what Chrysippus was claiming, and how conceptions produce cognition, have been disputed. The point of interest here is that it seems to have been conceded at some stage that such conceptions require the sort of exact formulation which only the philosopher or scientist can provide, if their correct application to particulars is to be possible (cf. Epict. diss. 2.17.5ff.; on the use and status of "preconceptions", see 3.5).

It thus becomes appropriate to ask whether the Stoics believed the concept of ambiguity to be in some sense "natural" – acquired, presumably, on the basis of cognitive impressions in the normal course of learning a language – and to what extent ordinary speakers had any authority over what counts as an ambiguity (both in general and in particular). The definition recorded by Diogenes Laertius, to be studied in the next chapter, hardly looks like an articulation of a naturally acquired conception; it calls on categories and distinctions which only a dialectician could be expected to grasp, ones only to be acquired by instruction and practice (διδασκαλία and ἐπιμέλεια, Aetius plac. 4.11.1ff. = S.V.F. 2.83 (39E, esp. §3)) in this expertise or science, as the next chapter will show. Yet at its core there could still be an account of a non-technical notion: a simple notion of simultaneous semantic multiplicity, shared by all language users, produced in them by linguistic practice, and informing their impressions of their own and others' linguistic behaviour.

The question then would be how the dialectician goes about reliably testing his elaboration or correction of the preconception. His formal definition, even if imperfect, will make the content and boundaries of the conception analysed clearer and sharper; but explicitness and precision are not enough if what is sought is a formulation of the single genuine concept of ambiguity. Rather, the dialectician must be deriving authority for his definition from his expert investigation into the general properties of language, formal and semantic, in so far as these bear on the property of ambiguity. The following chapter, and Chapter Six as well, will show how analysis of the concept of ambiguity must have been inextricably tied to analysis of other linguistic properties, categories, and concepts. In 3.3, 3.5, and in Chapters Six and Seven, the sorts of challenges the Stoics had to face to their claims to linguistic authority will be examined. The questions of the whole basis of the Stoic definition – why *this* concept is the correct one, and how ordinary users and the experts have access to it – and of how it can be safely emended if required, which find such striking parallels in modern linguistics and philosophy of language, will form one of the main themes of the next four chapters.

Since other forms of ambiguity could be dangerous, or at least unwelcome, taxonomies too have to be constructed: hence the material found in Diogenes, Galen, and Theon. By offering particular instances, such lists make application of the concept articulated in the definition easier to teach and to learn; the Stoics stressed the need for practical experience for the dialectician, as well as the mastery of abstract principles (*cf.* e.g. D.L. 7.48 (31B8); Augustine *civ. dei* 8.7 refers to the Stoic passion for the *sollertia disputandi*, the "skill of reasoning"). (Some ancient lists of ambiguity types seem to have been constructed with a view to easy identification of the appropriate disambiguating procedure, but this was apparently not the approach taken by the Stoa.) The classifications might also have served as vehicles for instruction in other areas of logic, as will emerge in Chapter Six.

The close relationship perceived by the Stoa between rationality and the ability to use and understand language – as shown, for example, in Chrysippus' denial that children learning to talk can strictly be said to "speak", *loqui*/λέγειν, at all, any more than parrots and crows can (Varro *ling. lat.* 6.56 (= *S.V.F.* 2.143) – makes dialectic's claims to enhance people's understanding of ambiguities, and their ability to cope with them in discourse, more intelligible, at least in broad outline. Linguistic knowledge is not conceived of as a distinct, let alone unique, form of knowledge. It is but one aspect of a general, pervasive, rationality; and, just like people's natural but imperfect rational abilities to understand cause-and-effect sequences or arguments, their ability to use and understand language is open to correction and improvement, even at the most basic levels of purity of speech (eliminating solecism and barbarism: see 3.4) or of identifying, distinguishing, and avoiding ambiguities. This is not merely because Stoicism alerts us to the most prominent and dangerous cases. It also gives a thorough theoretical grounding in relevant portions of grammar and syntax, in relevant linguistic properties such as autonomy, reference, and autonymy, and in the notions of context and usage, whose importance for the Stoic treatment of ambiguity will be explored later. It teaches people, not that there are ambiguities, but how to diagnose possible cases with the help of a firm conception articulated in a clear and precise definition; it helps them stay on the alert for ambiguities with the assistance of classifications; it makes them aware of the dangers ambiguities can pose; and, quite simply, tells them whether a given utterance is indeed a case of ambiguity. Similarly, Stoic philosophy cannot provide the first samples of cognitive impressions: but it can tell people what such an impression is, and allow them to recognise such an impression for what it is when they have one, rather than responding to it unreflectingly (*cf.* Frede 1983: 84).

Later sources confirm the importance attached by Stoic dialecticians to the identification and distinction of ambiguities. Seneca, for example, criticises the Epicureans for omitting logic from their philosophy: 'then, when they were forced by reality to distinguish ambiguities, and to expose falsehoods lurking under the appearance of truth' ('deinde cum ipsis rebus cogerentur ambigua secernere, falsa sub specie veri latentia coarguere'), they had to introduce "Canonic" (*i.e.* epistemology) anyway (*ep.* 89.9ff., esp. 11). Seneca also provides one of the most striking testimonies to the importance of ambiguity when he describes the function of wisdom: after showing us the *ratio* of the whole, and the creative powers of bodies, including the soul's, it moves on to what is incorporeal – that is, to the περὶ σημαινομένων part of dialectic – and teaches 'how what is ambiguous in life or language may be distinguished: for falsehoods are mixed with truths in both' ('quemadmodum discernerentur vitae aut vocis ambigua, in utraque enim falsa veris inmixta sint', *ep.* 90.29). Here Seneca is criticising Posidonius' extremely ambitious claims for philosophy's field of action, but he none the less concedes that difficult practical choices (the 'vitae ambigua') and linguistic ambiguities ('vocis ambigua') are alike soluble with the aid of practical wisdom.[27] Also memorable is the sarcasm of the author of the *ad Herennium*, who complains (2.16) that the dialecticians are so obsessed with finding ambiguities that they dare not open their mouths even to say their own names.[28] Philo portrays logic's dissolution of ambiguities and sophistries as a necessary preliminary to education in the doc-

---

[27] 'Vitae ambigua' are distinguished by natural philosophy, which also eliminates our mistakes: *quaest. nat.* I *praef.* 2. On the other hand, Seneca urges us elsewhere that it is best to proceed 'leaving behind ambiguities and syllogisms and hair-splittings and the other trivial pursuits of uncommitted cleverness', 'relictis ambiguitatibus et syllogismis et cavillationibus et ceteris acuminis inviti ludicris', when on the path of moral persuasion: *ep.* 108.12; *cf.* also 45.5, 9, 83.8ff., and 89.9, with its accounts of the contents of the three parts of philosophy. Seneca's attitude to dialectic is not to be extracted from a single, definitive text.

[28] This text is also important for explaining Chrysippus' claim that 'every word is ambiguous': 6.3.4.

trines of natural and moral philosophy (*agri.* 16 (=*S.V.F.* 2.39)).[29]

Ambiguity itself may have been explained by the Stoa as one of the signs of humanity's degeneration from a state of purest rationality, in which the contents and structures of the world found perfect matches in the constituents and structures of language.[30] (It is easy to see how a historical story might be told, for instance, about the moral corruption of humanity which has spawned the now standard meanings of the ethical terms "correctly" defined by Stoic philosophy, to be listed in 3.2.) Views about the naturalness or inevitability of ambiguity differed widely in antiquity, and were closely linked with disputes about the origins of language, as to whether languages are natural or conventional, and in what sense. The existence of homonymy might indeed be used as proof of the conventionality of language, in the sense that names are wholly arbitrary impositions on objects, on the grounds that natural connections of resemblance between words and what they name ought to have ensured a different name for each different type of thing. This argument is actually attributed to Democritus by Proclus (*in Crat.* p. 5.25ff. Pasquali (=B26 DK); but note Olympiodorus *Phil.* p. 242 St. (=B142 DK), where Democritus is said to have referred to the gods' names as 'ἀγάλματα φωνήεντα'; on the whole point, see Stephanus *int.* 9.34ff.). Proclus' response (p. 7.6–9) is that there is nothing remarkable if a name 'resembles', 'ἐνεικονίζεται', several things. Epicurus, in contrast, allowed for ambiguities in the very first stage of linguistic development, when words are emerging from the vocal cries naturally and unreflectingly evoked by internal states and perceptions

---

[29] This passage comes after what is known to be a Stoic comparison – *e.g.* D.L. 7.40 (26B3) – of the three divisions of philosophy to the plants (physics), fruit (ethics), and surrounding wall (logic) of a field, which suggests Philo is retailing Stoic views here too.

[30] Language's power to reveal the "true nature" of signified objects, now lost, is described by *e.g.* Philo *de opif. mundi* 150. An attempt by Ammonius *int.* 34.10ff. (*cf.* Stephanus *int.* 9.7ff.) to reconcile Plato's and Aristotle's opinions on the naturalness of language involves a careful, if unconvincing, distinction between two senses of φύσει, *naturally* and two of θέσει, *conventionally*. See further, 4.6.

of external objects. The next stage is one of clarification and elimination of redundancy (*ep. Hdt.* 76 (19A3)).[31] Aristotle explained homonymy as due to the finite number of names available for an unlimited number of things (as if all that were in question were extensional multiplicities) (*s. el.* 1.165a10–12). The Stoa itself took language to be "natural" in the sense that words are, so to say, coded descriptions, decipherable by etymological research, of the things they name, and linguistic structures to represent deeper semantic and ontological structures. Lexical and syntactic ambiguities have helped distort and even wholly conceal these pristine correspondences.

Ambiguity's current grip on language need not, of course, demonstrate decline from some original linguistic "state of grace": the primitive names from which all other words have been derived might themselves have been ambiguous.[32] Such a position is unlikely, however, to have appealed to the Stoa, because it could easily be understood as introducing at least one form of intrinsic defect, homonymy, into language, which would have then to be refined and corrected, rather than being a perfect, possibly god-given, instrument of communication. The twin attritions of constant use and moral degeneration have thrown up accidental ambiguities all the same, and language has thus been subject to the sorts of degenerative changes that allow the discipline of etymology to make a useful, if humble, contribution to the system of human knowledge (see further, 3.5). On the other hand, some important connections may arguably have been preserved for us, albeit imperfectly, by the presence of systematically ambiguous terms (see 3.2 and 3.5). The question of the "naturalness" of language will come up again for us in 4.6.

A final comparison may be illuminating. The detection of ambiguity was crucial for the Stoa, as it was for the medieval schoolmen, who took logic's task to be 'to provide the tools for discovering the truth', by giving a theory (and a method)

---

[31] A broader comparison between the very different Democritean and Epicurean views about the nature of language, on the one hand, and about knowledge, on the other, is drawn by Vlastos 1946: 52.

[32] *Cf.* Blank 1982: 23, n.17.

of verification, a semantics, and an account of proof: Ebbesen 1977: 103. Stoic dialectic too is the science of distinguishing true from false, and it offers firm definitions of truth and its bearers, of meaning and its bearers, of the nature of demonstration, and of the connections between all these. The thought that distinguishing ambiguities helps us along the path to truth becomes a commonplace (*e.g.* Simplicius *cats.* 237.7ff.). Where the Stoics differ is in the goal to which dialectic and the discovery of truth are directed. Dialectic is no intellectual exercise, and no mere tool of philosophy; it is an intrinsic part of the technique of living a happy and successful life as a rational animal. Ambiguities are obstacles because they can stand in the way of the achievement of a firm, internally coherent, and correct conceptual scheme by reference to which all judgements of propositions and arguments are to be made (including, and especially, those which lead to action), securely, consistently, and without doubt or confusion. Language alone cannot be relied on, credulously, as a sure guide to the types of things there are, and to their properties and relations. If the truth does set us free, finding the truth still begins with the apparently lowly task of noting the mismatches between the world and how we talk about it.

3.2 Exposition and argument

Exposition and explanation of Stoic doctrines frequently involve, even if indirectly, reference to πολλαχῶς λεγόμενα, that is, to semantically multiple expressions or to the range of objects they denote. What follows is a list of the most important examples; some of them are exclusively the creations of Stoic philosophical doctrine; others combine technical Stoicism with ordinary usage or standard philosophical conceptual schemes.

Logic:[33]
    γράμμα, *letter*, D.L. 7.56: basic speech sounds, their written symbols, and the names of the sounds are all (called) letters

---

[33] Other possible πολλαχῶς λεγόμενα from logic which are not explicit in extant Stoic texts include ὀνόματα (used of proper names or of words generally: 6.3.5.2), and perhaps ἐπιστήμη, *knowledge*, of which Stoic theory identifies four varieties,

69

('τριχῶς δὲ λέγεται τὸ γράμμα ...'). Sextus *M.* 1.99 begins his account of technical grammar '*Element* having three meanings ...', 'τριχῶς λεγομένου τοῦ στοιχείου ...', and remarks that the "power", δύναμις, of the element, *i.e.* the actual speech-sound, 'is called an element in the strict sense by the grammarians', 'αὕτη γὰρ καὶ κυρίως στοιχεῖον παρ' αὐτοῖς προσηγόρευται'. (It is presumably on the basis of this or a similar grammatical text that the defective text at D.L. 7.56 has been corrected to read 'ὅ τε χαρακτὴρ τοῦ στοιχείου ⟨ἥ τε δύναμις τοῦ στοιχείου⟩ καὶ τὸ ὄνομα', 'the (written) symbol of the element, ⟨and the power of the element⟩ [*i.e.* its sound], and its name', as well as '⟨τὸ στοιχεῖον⟩ ὅ τε χαρακτὴρ τοῦ στοιχείου καὶ τὸ ὄνομα', ⟨the element [*i.e.* the sound]⟩ and the symbol of the element and its name'.)

αἴσθησις, *sense(-perception)*, D.L. 7.52: the portion of breath extending from mind to sense-organs, cognition through senses, the apparatus of the sense-organs, and their activity, are all (called) perception ('αἴσθησις δὲ λέγεται τό ... καὶ ἡ ... καὶ ἡ ... καὶ ἡ ...').

Physics:

ποιόν, (*what is*) qualified, Simplicius *cats.* 212.12–213.1 (28N).[34]

κόσμος, *cosmos, world(-order)*, D.L. 7.137 (44F): god, the current world-order, and the complex of these, are all (called) world ('λέγουσι δὲ κόσμον τριχῶς ...').

στοιχεῖον, *element*, Stobaeus 1.129.1ff. (= *S.V.F.* 2.413 (47A, esp. 6–9)): fire, any element, and any primary constituent are all (called) an element ('τριχῶς δὲ λεγομένου κατὰ Χρύσιππον τοῦ στοιχείου, καθ' ἕνα μὲν τρόπον ... καθ' ἕτερον ... κατὰ τὸν τρίτον λόγον λέγεται στοιχεῖον ...', 'element being said in three ways according to Chrysippus, in one way ... in another ... in the third way element is said ...'). These meanings are of course in addition to that listed under logic, "element of speech".

Ethics:

ἀξία, *value*, e.g. Stobaeus 2.83.10ff. (= *S.V.F.* 3.124 (58D, esp. 2–3)): things may (be said to) have ἀξία in possessing intrinsic worth, in meeting the expert's appraisal, or in pos-

---

although our source does not expressly present this as a case of ambiguity: Stobaeus 2.73.16ff. (= *S.V.F.* 3.112 (part, 41H)), with Brunschwig 1978b: 69f.

[34] The differences between the various types of *qualia* are too complex to be usefully summarised here: please refer to the Simplicius passage cited in the main text, and to the schematic précis in Reesor 1989: 5.

sessing relative or selective worth ('... τὴν δὲ ἀξίαν λέγεσθαι τριχῶς ...', '... value is said in three ways ...'). Its opposite, ἀπαξία, also 'λέγεται τριχῶς', 'is said in three ways', 'ἀντιτιθεμένων τῶν σημαινομένων τοῖς ἐπὶ τῆς τρίττης ἀξίας εἰρημένοις', 'with the significations being opposed to those described in the case of threefold value' ('τρίττης', 'threefold', is Wachsmuth's emendation of the MSS 'πρώτης'). D.L. 7.105 (58B) has a similar report, and yet another account of value and disvalue can be found in Sextus *M.* 11.62ff.; and *cf.* Görler 1984.

ἀδιάφορον, *indifferent*, D.L. 7.104f. (58B): things can be (called) indifferent "simply", ἅπαξ, in making no contribution to happiness or its opposite, or they may be (called) indifferent in exciting neither impulse nor repulsion ('διχῶς δὲ λέγεσθαι ἀδιάφορα ...'). Stobaeus 2.79.1ff. (=*S.V.F.* 3.118), in contrast, describes the second group as indifferent "absolutely", καθάπαξ, since the first does at least awaken desire or its opposite. Sextus *M.* 11.59f. reports a tripartition, the additional grouping being of items which are objects of impulse or repulsion, but are otherwise undifferentiated, *e.g.* coins of the same value and appearance. According to Simplicius *cats.* 410.29f., as noted in 3.1, the use of *indifferent* as meaning something neither (morally) good nor bad was a Stoic innovation.

ἀγαθόν, *good*: see 3.5.

Note also:

ἄλογος, *irrational*: Galen *P.H.P.* 4.4.9ff., pp. 252, ll. 20ff.; on which see further, 3.5.

ἀπαθής, *unemotional*, D.L. 7.117: an ordinary person is ἀπαθής in lacking proper feeling, in being callous, the sage in not being prone to passions ('φασὶ δὲ καὶ ἀπαθῆ εἶναι τὸν σοφόν ... εἶναι δὲ καὶ ἄλλον ἀπαθῆ τὸν φαῦλον ...').

ἄτυφος, *without pride*, ibid.: an ordinary person is ἄτυφος in being rash, the sage in being rightly unconcerned about reputation ('ἄτυφον τ' εἶναι τὸν σοφόν ... εἶναι δὲ καὶ ἄλλον ἄτυφον ...')).

αὐστηρός, *harsh, austere, ibid.*: wine taken as a medicine may be αὐστηρός, harsh, and the ordinary αὐστηρός person is harsh too; but the sage is αὐστηρός in not being given to pleasure ('... καὶ αὐστηροὺς δέ φασιν εἶναι πάντας τοὺς σπουδαίους ... καὶ ἄλλον δὲ εἶναι αὐστηρόν ...').

ἄθεος, *godless*, D.L. 7.119: there are two types of ungodly person: everyone who is not a sage is ungodly; but in addition some ordinary persons are without any religious feeling at all ('διττὸν δὲ εἶναι τὸν ἄθεον ...').

In my descriptions of these items I have tried to capture the emphasis of many of the original Greek texts on there being different types of thing sharing a name but being different in kind and so in definition; and also the lack of any obvious distinction between singular definite terms (*e.g. world, element*) and descriptive or predicative terms (*e.g. indifferent, qualified*). The second feature can be straightforwardly accounted for by the principles of Stoic metaphysics and semantics, according to which all such expressions will count as "general terms" or "appellatives", προσηγορίαι, and will designate or refer to or signify (objects characterised by) common qualities.[35] The first calls for more comment. It may be asked, as a first stab at the problem, whether these πολλαχῶς λεγόμενα give rise to genuine cases of ambiguity: but that, of course, depends on what one counts as an ambiguity. It must rather be asked whether *the Stoics* would have counted them as producing genuine cases of ambiguity, and whether their grounds for doing so were good ones. The evidence of Diogenes' definition, and of the classification preserved by Galen, strongly suggests that the shared names will indeed qualify as linguistic ambiguities, and more precisely as cases of homonymy in single terms. Whether Stoic semantics gives an adequate account of such ambiguities is another matter. It would take us too far out of our way to explore the evidence here, and the question of the ambiguity of "nominals", both appellatives and proper names, is postponed until 6.3.4 and 6.3.5.2.

These technical ambiguities would also, of course, not be simple puns, whose shared orthography and pronunciation could reasonably be attributed to mere historical accident. Their meanings will be conceptually related, in that the definitions which are linguistic articulations of the relevant concepts would overlap to some significant extent. This conceptual relatedness may perhaps explain the preference for talk of πολλαχῶς λεγόμενα, "(things/expressions) said in many

---

[35] The case of *world* is different in that one of its referents, god, is a peculiarly qualified individual; but that need not detain us here. That ancient grammar as a whole treated adjectives and common nouns as one word-class may be due to Stoic influence: Robins 1979: 28.

ways", the flavour of which might best be captured by referring to the relevant terms as *systematic* ambiguities. A modern comparison, in point both of systematicity and (typically) dependence on linguistic *fiat*, may be helpful, and I offer Chomsky's use of *grammar* and of *theory of language* (1985: 103: the former is systematically ambiguous between the native speaker's internalised theory of his language and the linguist's reconstruction of it, the latter between 'the child's innate predisposition to learn a language of a certain type' and 'the linguist's account of this'). The systematic character of these key Stoic ambiguities will be taken up again in 3.5.

That only two of the accounts – those of disvalue, and of the good, which will be discussed later – mention significations explicitly, and that the explanations function (broadly speaking) by distinguishing the relevant characteristics of (types of) named objects, and not the senses or meanings of words, suggest that what was felt to be important was getting across the various Stoic ontological and conceptual schemes which reveal the properties and organisation of the contents of the world. The associated ambiguities, multiply significant linguistic items, do not in themselves play a prominent part in the exposition or explanation of these schemes. This, I think, substantiates the earlier claim (3.1) that what makes technical ambiguities important for the Stoa is their capacity to conceal conceptual distinctions, some subtle, some gross, and thus to hide crucial dissimilarities between (types of) object. Description of these differences must be all the more explicit precisely because the objects share a name.

I will return later to the most important feature of these technical ambiguities, their capacity for engendering error and confusion. I turn now to other uses of ambiguity in the exposition and defence of Stoic doctrines.

A typical rôle of ambiguities for Stoics was in the clarification, or tactful correction, or whatever it is called, of a formulation of a doctrine by a respected member of the school, whose authority could not be openly flouted. The usual beneficiary was Zeno, who occupied an awkward position in Stoic ideology, at once supremely authoritative and obscure, in frequent need of respectful exegesis. For example, a famous argument of Zeno's for the existence of god (or the gods) was subject to a polemical and disturbing "parallel", παραβολή, by his contemporary Alexinus: 'a man may reasonably honour the gods; those who are non-existent one may not reasonably honour; therefore, there are gods' became 'a man may reasonably honour the wise; those who are non-existent one may not reasonably honour; therefore, there are wise men' – an unwelcome conclusion, given that the Stoics had not a living instance to produce (or none at all, as Sextus comments; and *cf.* Plutarch *st. rep.* 31.1048E, *comm. not.* 33.1076B). Zeno was rescued by the discovery (if that is what it is) of an ambiguity in the verb τιμάω, *honour*, meaning either "worship" (in Zeno's syllogism) or "hold in respect" (in Alexinus') (Sextus *M.* 9.136 (54D4)).[36] Another argument, proving that the wise man will not get drunk, was saved by a similar move.[37] The strategy was not explicitly sanctioned by the Stoa, it seems, but it could sometimes serve the purpose of preserving doctrinal continuity, or at least its appearance – even if appeals to Zeno's authority were at least as likely to be inspired by rivalries within the school.[38]

[36] This must be a Stoic manoeuvre, since no other school is likely to have come to Zeno's rescue, while a second damage-limiting operation on Zeno's syllogism is unquestionably Stoic, attributed expressly to Diogenes of Babylon: *M.* 9.134–5.

[37] *Cf.* Schofield 1983, esp. 34–44, who observes, 42–4, that detection of an ambiguity was almost certainly employed as a defence of Zeno in at least two cases (he does not consider the first of those described in the main text), one of which was in connection with the issue, whether the wise man will get drunk. Seneca criticises Posidonius' detection of an ambiguity in *ebrius, drunk*, as clever but philosophically useless; what is needed is a frontal attack on the immorality of drunkenness: *ep.* 83.11.

[38] Conflicts in the school were frequently generated by disagreement over how to interpret something Zeno had said. His reputation within the school is discussed by Schofield 1983: 49ff., 1991, esp. 81, n. 29 (with useful references), 94ff. Sedley 1989: 98 contends that Zeno's position was unassailable: but just what did Zeno's exegetes think they were about? Athenodorus excised awkward passages from Zeno's *corpus*: D.L. 7.34. Cleanthes, remarkably, was prepared to attribute to Zeno distinctions and concepts never explicitly formulated in years of personal instruction. In this context, Chrysippus' assertion that he need only to be told the doctrines, he would find out the proofs thereof for himself (D.L. 7.179), looks curiously double-edged, even if unintentionally so (and that, I suppose, is the crux of the matter).

On occasion Chrysippus too could be the beneficiary of this strategy. His own improved definition of the impression (over Zeno's) was itself emended or defended by a *distinguo* in the meaning of ψυχή, *soul* (Sextus *M.* 7.234ff. (part, 53F) (= the whole animate principle of a creature, or its ruling part, the mind, which is called the soul "specifically", ἰδίως)). An alternative way of correcting Chrysippus' definition was to appeal to "implicitness", συνέμφασις (Sextus *M.* 7.233, 239), but Sextus considers the appeal to ambiguity 'more subtle', 'γλαφυρώτερον'. Sextus' account of the corrective or explanatory process is unfortunately not general enough for us to reconstruct whatever criteria there may have been for applying these concepts in appropriate ways in other cases.[39]

Less common in Stoic circles, it would seem, was a use of ambiguity familiar to all philosophers, ancient and modern; it is perhaps the commonest of all, and an obvious feature too of non-philosophical discourse. This is to criticise a theory (thesis, argument, *etc.*) on the grounds that it exploits, probably unwittingly, a crucial ambiguity whose recognition wholly disarms one's rival.[40] If it really was absent from the Stoic armoury, the omission is a surprising one. Perhaps the true explanation is that the sources far more often, and far more fully, report anti-Stoic polemics than Stoic replies to objections.[41]

There are some possibilities. One of the unattributed criti-

---

[39] As there is a Stoic ambiguity kind "Elleipsis" or "deficiency", it would be gratifying to know where expressions are ambiguous owing to some sort of omission, and where they each have one, albeit partly implicit, signification; but the Stoic criteria for the distinction, if any, are unknown: 6.4.4.

[40] Richmann 1959: 87 emphasises the importance of such manoeuvres, and thus of identifying ambiguities, in the conduct of philosophical argument. The tactic is also mentioned by *e.g.* Scheffler 1979: 4f., and more generally by Kooij 1971: 1, quoting Kaplan 1950. A few examples: Kripke 1980: 59 criticises Frege for using *sense* in two senses; Hockett 1968: 62f., Itkonen 1978: 82, and Hall 1987: 71 all criticise Chomsky for using *know* in two senses. A related defect is the extension of a word to a new, and typically improper, meaning with little or no warning or justification: so *e.g.* Ong 1982: 87 on Derrida's use of *écriture*.

[41] In fact considerable ingenuity may be required to reveal some seemingly eccentric and redundant piece of argument as a sophisticated and thought-provoking riposte. An outstanding example is Chrysippus' argument concerning Dion and one-footed Theon: Philo *aet. mundi* 48 (= *S.V.F.* 2.397 (28P)), as reconstructed by Sedley 1982b (briefly at LS 1987: 1: 175f.).

75

cisms reported by Sextus, *M.* 10.85ff., of Diodorus Cronus' arguments against motion, or, more precisely, of Diodorus' reply to an initial objection, is that it overlooks an ambiguity (10.99), and this criticism may well be Stoic.[42] It is even possible that a central thesis of Platonism, the existence of forms, was analysed by Stoics as a case, on a grand scale, of failing to appreciate an ambiguity; but I think the possibility a remote one. Syrianus (*metaph.* 105.17ff. = (part) *S.V.F.* 2.364 (30H)) contends that 'the forms were introduced by these god-like men [*i.e.* the Platonists] neither on the basis of the usage of names in ordinary speech [πρὸς τὴν χρῆσιν τῆς συνηθείας τῶν ὀνομάτων παρήγετο] as Chrysippus and Archedemus and most of the Stoics later thought (for there are many differences between forms in themselves and those mentioned in ordinary speech) ...'. The most obvious Platonic source for this interpretation of the forms is *Rep.* 10.596a6–8: 'for we are, I think, accustomed to posit some one form in the case of each group of the many things, to which we apply the same name'. Chrysippus' point, I take it, would be that the meaningfulness of such sentences as *Man is a rational, mortal animal* was incorrectly explained by Platonists by the postulation of the forms as objects of reference for general names such as *man*, much as an object of reference is posited for *Socrates* in *Socrates is a rational, mortal animal.*[43] In the usual Stoic scheme of things, here attributed by Syrianus to Cleanthes (105.28f.), Platonic forms are no more than a sort of erroneous hypostatisation of "concepts", ἐννοήματα, that is, mere mental constructs, the internal or intentional objects of our conceptions, ἔννοιαι (*cf.* D.L. 7.60f. (30C); *S.V.F.* 1.65 (30A)).

---

[42] The complaint is based on a general claim about past-tense sentences. 'These men married' has two different meanings according as it signifies an "inflection" (a "past-tense transformation", in a modern, misleading, jargon) of one proposition (⟨These men are marrying⟩) or of several (each of the form ⟨This man is marrying⟩). The appeal to the operation of "inflection" certainly suggests a Stoic origin: Alexander *an. pr.* 403.14 ff., with Lloyd 1978: 291; and see 6.2.3. Another objection to Diodorus points to the ambiguity of (*being contained in a*) *place, M.* 9.95, but I have not traced this to a Stoic source.

[43] Stoics actually used the "No-man" puzzle to show that forms could not be individuals (Simplicius *cats.* 105.8ff. (30E)), and they did assume that singular subject terms have existential import: see main text, below.

Hence it might be thought that "general terms" or "appellatives", προσηγορίαι, signify not only the qualified corporeal
things which are their true *significata* (assigned them at e.g.
D.L. 7.58 (33M)), but also these concepts, including Platonic
forms. But Chrysippus' identification of them as mere
language-generated illusions suggests a reluctance to grant the
Platonic usage any semantic authority: Platonic forms, at
least as Platonists imagine them to be, simply are not there at
all.[44]

One other notable absence from the Stoic repertoire is
a familiar tactic which precisely counterpoints the last: the
claim that an opponent's thesis, argument, *etc.*, involves unwarrantably postulating a non-existent ambiguity. The with-
drawal of licence for the ambiguity may, but need not, be
based on an appeal to ordinary intuitions about language.[45]
Strictly, of course, the correct criteria for rejection or introduction of an ambiguity should be the same; but they may not
be, and they frequently diverge according to the writer's preoccupations and intentions.[46] The whole topic is of immense

[44] If concepts *are* significations of common nouns, they might be so only derivatively
or catachrestically. The Stoic definition of ambiguity distinguishes "strict" from
"non-strict" meanings (see 4.7), and this may be one application of that distinction. The definition also provides for different "usages" (see 4.8); so that Platonic
and Stoic philosophical "usages", say, might share terms but not ambiguities.
Syrianus reports two other views of forms: that they are *lekta*-like in being subsistent on the mind; and that they combine features of *lekta* and concepts.
Chrysippus' dismissal of universals as language-generated might seem to recall the
positivist claim that '*the whole controversy about universals* rests on the misleading
use of universal words' (Carnap 1937: 311; author's emphasis). But Chrysippus
does not seem to have urged a solution by way of resorting to talk about words
('the formal rather than the material mode of speech', *ibid.*). Rather, Platonic
forms and Aristotelian universals are diagnosed as mental constructs.

[45] *E.g.* Baker and Hacker 1984: 181: if the ordinary speaker's use of *true* does not
conform to the philosopher's, that does not make it e.g. ambiguous; it would be
absurd to regard all context-dependent sentences as ambiguous (203). I assume
that this absurdity is premissed on ordinary usage and on native-speaker judgements, to which Baker and Hacker 1984 frequently defer, if not always with
explicit acknowledgement of their importance. The entry for "ambiguity" in the
index to this volume lists only references to linguists' uses of it, not to the authors',
in the course of their criticisms of others' arguments and doctrines – a not uncom-
mon lacuna: see next note.

[46] *E.g.* Kripke's criticism of Donnellan's postulation of an ambiguity in the use of
definite descriptions (between the referential and the attributive) assumes a distinction between semantic ambiguity and pragmatic multiplicity of use, and, although
he does ask what ordinary speakers would say or think in the relevant cases, he

interest for the questions it raises about the proper source(s) of authority for pronouncements, especially by philosophers or logicians, on matters pertaining to ordinary language use. It also brings to the fore the – for us intractable – problem of when a difference in meaning was put down to ambiguity, and when to a difference in "usage", ἔθος, or to one between terms' signifying "strictly", κυρίως, and non-strictly. While the Stoic definition of ambiguity explicitly excludes both non-strict significations and semantic variations between usages, and, as has been seen, the meanings of at least some of the systematic ambiguities were internally distinguished, as, say, "simple", ἅπαξ, or "absolute", καθάπαξ, information about the general meaning and scope of all these conditions is, sadly, negligible (see 4.7, 4.8). On the other hand, the Stoa's apparent failure to identify, as a matter of wider linguistic theory, the ways in which the meanings of a term may be related, could well be significant (see 3.5).

The school seems to have had no doubts about its linguistic authoritativeness, however, as the following case, I think, clearly demonstrates. According to Alexander (*an. pr.* 402.3ff.), some persons claimed that in ordinary usage negative sentences having singular terms, demonstrative pronouns, or definite descriptions as subjects, are ambiguous. The contradictory of ⟨Καλλίας περιπατεῖ⟩, they urged, cannot be (the proposition signified by) the Greek sentence Καλλίας οὐ περιπατεῖ, which has two possible meanings, the ordinary conjunction ⟨There is a certain Callias, and this man [referring to the Callias in question] is not walking⟩ – in which

also allows for theoretical considerations: Kripke 1979, esp. 13, 18f., referring to Donnellan 1966: 297; also Donnellan 1979: 41f. Kripke cautions that '[i]t is very much the lazy man's approach in philosophy to posit ambiguities when in trouble ... Do not posit an ambiguity unless you are really forced to, unless there are really compelling *theoretical or intuitive grounds* to suppose that an ambiguity really is present' (1979: 19; my emphasis). Baker and Hacker 1984 also deploy ordinary-speaker judgements, *e.g.* at pp. 212f.; the compositional principle of truth theoretic semantics entails postulating 'a host of ambiguities among apparently unambiguous expressions' (p. 213), *i.e.* among expressions which appear to "Everyman" (the ordinary speaker) to be unambiguous. Baker and Hacker, of course, have highly unorthodox views on the use made of linguistic intuitions by modern theorists; see esp. their chs. 7–9.

the predicate alone is negated – and the negated conjunction ⟨Not (there is a certain Callias, and this man is walking)⟩, which is the contradictory proper, and whose status should be signalled by prefixing the whole sentence/proposition with the negative particle (external negation) (402.8ff., 16ff.). The argument turns on the claim that ⟨Καλλίας περιπατεῖ⟩ and ⟨Καλλίας οὐ περιπατεῖ⟩ might be false simultaneously, which for genuine contradictories cannot be the case – as long, that is, as these propositions are interpreted as equivalent to ⟨There is a certain Callias, and he is walking/not walking⟩, the negation being internal, and provided too that Callias does not exist, the existential conjunct being false in both cases (402.12ff., 20ff.).

This section repeats much of what was said earlier, (*an. pr.* 177ff.) in connection with the problem sentences *Dion is dead*, *this man is dead*, and, as Lloyd 1978: 289, n. 25, points out, the earlier discussion confirms that Alexander's opponents are Stoics here too; so his report is an invaluable supplement to the doctrine of negation of simple and of complex propositions recorded by D.L. 7.69ff. (34K) and Sextus *M.* 8.88ff. (34G) respectively.[47] The passage shows that the second technique I have described – refusing to admit an ambiguity claimed by an opponent – was certainly known to the ancients; and it has such a familiar ring not just because of its similarity to modern debates about the scope of operators and failures of reference, but also because it concerns the purported logical properties and behaviour of ordinary sentences in a natural language. It has been both claimed – by Geach 1972: 75 – and denied – by Mates 1961: 31 – that in treating negation as propositional the Stoics were deliberately violating ordinary Greek usage. Yet some of the evidence suggests Stoic sensitivity to the range of possible negative propositions in Greek (Diogenes lists three, all simple), while, whatever the

---

[47] I am unconvinced by Cavini's claim, 1985: 84, that the sources also point to a Stoic 'polemica antiaristotelica' on the connected questions of the scope of negations and of the existential import of singular definite sentences or propositions. That the Stoics differed from Aristotle, as they seem to have done, and that his commentators realised this fact, is no proof of influence or contact between them.

facts of the Greek language, there is no hint that the Stoics' contemporaries, or later philosophers, thought that the Stoa had gone against ordinary language or – and this is important – that appealing to ordinary use or understanding of the negative was appropriate in this case. Alexander does contend that the Stoic analysis will not apply to process-sentences such as *A house is being built* (*an. pr.* 403.2ff.), but this is surely a point about the logic of processes, not an appeal to usage, any more than is his rival claim that *Socrates* changes its meaning between *Socrates is dying* and *Socrates is dead* (403.24ff.).

The Stoics' apparent neglect of non-language-specific, "systematic" ambiguities – those (species of) ambiguous expressions which (are taken to) perform a set of identical or closely related semantic functions in all natural languages – seems to set the school apart from modern philosophers of language and philosophical logicians as well. Identification or postulation of such ambiguities may be the task of any philosopher in the course of developing or in defence of a favoured doctrine, or of the linguist, philosopher of language, or philosophical logician trying to trace and classify universal features of natural languages. Of the former type is the conventionalist, logical positivist thesis that one and the same sentence (or different tokens of the same type-sentence) may make an analytic or a synthetic statement (*e.g.* Pears 1953, Brotman 1956); of the latter, the claims that definite descriptions are ambiguous – semantically or pragmatically – between their "referring" and their "attributive" uses, and between rigid and non-rigid designation, and that sentences which can be used to perform non-standard speech-acts have additional meanings (see Kripke's (1979) criticisms of Donnellan 1966; and *cf.* also Donnellan 1979)). Kaplan 1979 proposes a "Dthat" operator which would turn ordinary descriptions into rigid designators, such descriptions thus being ambiguous, without the operator, between rigid and non-rigid designation. Quine 1960: 134ff. lists types of syntactic ambiguity which are clearly intended as perfectly general in their application to natural languages. Roberts 1984 uses a difference in the scope of disjunctions to distinguish ambiguity from generality. And so on.

The tactic is so common that further examples would be tedious.

I suspect that Stoic neglect of such methods or areas of inquiry may to some unknown extent be only an illusion produced by the scarcity and poor quality of our sources, especially by the dearth of first-hand material of a more advanced or technical nature. No doubt general logical doctrines played some part in Chrysippus' *On the mode ambiguities* and *On conditional mode ambiguity* (D.L. 7.193 = *S.V.F.* 2.14, p. 6, ll. 25–6), for example, but nothing of their contents is known. Again, the fragments of Chrysippus' *Logical Questions*, mentioned in Chapter Two, preserve a complex and apparently aporetic discussion of the possible ambiguity of one sort of imperative sentence. The text of this discussion being as uncertain as its interpretation is difficult, I have decided not to attempt to establish either the one or the other here. (The arguments of *Logical Questions* cols. 12–13 can be pursued in Barnes 1984/5 and Inwood 1985a: 94, 1985b: 82f.) I mention this particular passage all the same because it seems to show that questions very much like ones pursued by modern philosophers of language or philosophical logicians were of interest to Stoics, although, surely, for ultimately different reasons. The fact that there is little evidence for such work outside the rarefied atmosphere of the *Questions*, and, in particular, none in the doxographical summaries of Stoic dialectical doctrines, suggests, however, that it was not thought a central or important enough topic to be condensed for consumption by the beginner (or by the amateur of philosophy), who would be introduced instead to some sort of definition, perhaps with an associated classification, and to examples of ambiguous philosophical terminology.

3.3 Technical vocabulary and everyday language

In the second book of his *Outlines of Pyrrhonism*, Sextus Empiricus criticises as useless and redundant, even by their own standards, the technical apparatus constructed by doctrinaire dialecticians to deal with fallacious arguments (*P.H.* 2.229ff.).

He goes on to make similar complaints about the "dogma-tists'" treatment of ambiguities (256–9). In Chapter Seven I will examine this whole crucial and fascinating text in the detail it deserves. Here I will simply begin to explore Sextus' chief criticism of dialectic's redundancy in the face of ambigu-ities, that it can add nothing to the abilities of ordinary speak-ers or of technical experts, so that all that is left to the doctri-naire dialecticians is endless and useless squabbling about the meanings of their own technical terms (258) – like those which concerned us in 3.2.

The charge as presented apparently assumes that it will in-variably be clear which words are ambiguous, and that only their meanings, in particular uses or contexts, will be uncer-tain. (For the present I am observing Sextus' tactical restric-tion of the area of debate to lexical ambiguity.) Nothing is said about borderline cases, when it is unclear whether a term is ambiguous at all, and when more basic disagreements may arise, one party stoutly maintaining the presence of an ambi-guity, the other just as stoutly denying it. Stoic dialectic's rôle, I surmise, is to provide a precise, formal definition of ambigu-ity and related concepts by which such problem cases can be decided, its privileged position being guaranteed by its access to the spectrum of linguistic expertise which is needed to con-struct the definition and to deal with the troublesome features of discourse that give rise to uncertainties and disagreements.

Sextus would not have found this reply convincing. As a Pyrrhonist Skeptic, he is unconvinced of the doctrinaire dia-lecticians' ability to pronounce definitive judgement on any-thing at all. But, without endorsing his sort of skepticism, some modern readers too may feel uneasy with the response I have made on the Stoa's behalf. It is the Stoics' assumption of authoritativeness in ordinary, non-technical usages that seems questionable to us: why should this, or any, definition of am-biguity be final and decisive? If ordinary speakers disagree about which terms are ambiguous, and do so not by reference to some agreed criterion, but because a conceptual dispute exists, then that may be all there is to say on the matter: no alternative adjudication is possible because the only standard of correctness surely just is what ordinary speakers have to say. If there is lack of agreement, no higher authority exists to be appealed to. Moderns might decide to abide by the decision of the lexicographer; but they would still have to face the problem of deciding where dictionaries get their authority from: *cf.* Scheffler 1979: 3f., and also Harris 1980, esp. 130ff., for criticisms of lexicographers' allegedly pernicious influence on linguistic concepts.

An ancient critic of the Stoa, also unpersuaded by Sextus' arguments, would all the same be still less likely to share, or even understand, these modern qualms. Sextus' examples of non-technical ambiguities are carefully chosen as much to highlight some of the weaknesses of ancient treatments of ambiguity and of the ancient theories about language within which they were framed, as to illustrate the ordinary ability to cope with ambiguities. Ancient readers familiar with this feature of their intellectual milieu would appreciate Sextus' slyness. Of the broad assumptions behind his polemic one in particular must be uncovered if the rôle which Stoic dialectic could have been assigned in the life of ordinary agents is to be grasped. Direct evidence for the details of Stoic policy in this area is unavailable, and indirect evidence incomplete and circumstantial; and it should be noted that in what follows I shall be constructing a possible Stoic defence, not reconstructing it from accidentally scattered materials.

One of the earliest, deepest and and most abiding concerns for ancient theorising about language was the setting up of canons for correctness or purity in speech, that is, for "Hellenism" (and later for "Latinity" as well). It has frequently been remarked, but perhaps not always sufficiently appreciated, that ancient grammar – including the "technical" grammar that is the forerunner, of sorts, of modern linguistics – was profoundly and explicitly prescriptive, and typically unashamedly élitist too. Its main task was to provide criteria for lexical and grammatical purity, to apply these to problem cases in the standard authors, and to supply the rules to persons who wanted to be able to speak and write correctly (see further, 8.4). Stoic grammar is known to have shared this viewpoint; and the work of Stoic grammarians was clearly influential on the whole tradition.[48]

The list of appropriate criteria was fiercely debated in antiquity, with Sextus himself predictably entering the fray on the side of those who took as the sole standard the actual usage of Greeks, disregarding etymology, antiquity, use by revered authors, and all the other options defended by grammarians and rhetoricians. Technical grammar is thus deprived of its *raison d'être*: if everything to be learned about how to speak properly can be had from one's linguistic community, with a little help from the lowly grammar-teacher in the local primary school, the *soi-disant* Professor of Grammar will be out of work in a trice.

Sextus' tactic at *P.H.* 2.256ff. is, I think, largely similar, only here the Professors of Dialectic are being handed their notice. In Stoic circles they would also be theoreticians of grammatical principles, and almost certainly they saw their work, at any rate in the early days of the school, as in part at least a contribution to a theory of style, particularly that portion of it which dealt with Hellenism.[49] Sextus assumes that ordinary speakers of a language will be able to recognise and

---

[48] The Stoic definition of Hellenism at D.L. 7.59 refers to "technical usage", that is, as Frede 1978: 41 points out, to one governed by the prescriptions of an "expertise", τέχνη; *cf.* the definition of "solecism" in Cyrillus' *Lexicon* as 'when someone speaks inexpertly', 'ἀτέχνως' (*Anec. Gr. Par.*, ed. Cramer, vol. I, p. 190). This definition is not obviously incompatible with barbarism's being there defined as 'language contrary to the usage of reputable Greeks', since reports of Stoic adherence to a doctrine of "technical" analogy must be exaggerated (*cf.* Frede 1978: 72f.) – just as, perhaps, are those of the whole "great debate" between analogists and anomalists: *cf.* Blank 1982: 1–5 (Frede 1978: 73 may be underestimating Varro's self-interest in exaggerating the scale and scope of earlier disagreements). It is conceivable that Crates wrongly thought of Chrysippus and Aristarchus (the Alexandrian grammarian) as champions of anomaly and analogy respectively (as Varro claims, *ling. lat.* 9.1) without sparking off any controversy – certainly Aristophanes' and Aristarchus' supposedly technical, analogistic criteria do look to be limited to nominals and/or directed to resolving textual cruxes (see Charisius (*G.L.* I) 117.1ff., with Taylor 1987a: 11ff.) – until Varro and exponents of the new technical grammar began to take an interest in formal analogy.

[49] *Cf.* Frede 1978, esp. 44ff. Philo *cong. erud. gratia* 146 (= *S.V.F.* 2.99) may be recycling a Stoic view of the relation between philosophy and grammar (philosophy defines everything to do with vocal sound, the parts of speech, *etc.*), although the sharp division between philosophy and a separate grammatical discipline is obviously not an early Stoic product. Simplicius *cats.* 9.19ff. presents the opposite view.

cope with ambiguities, if necessary by explicit requests for clarification. But the educated ancient reader would find this as contentious as Sextus' preference for ordinary usage as the sole standard of linguistic correctness. In an ancient context it would be perfectly normal to argue that ordinary speakers can go wrong in their use of language, and that they then need guidance from grammarians, who in their turn ultimately follow the professional researchers' abstract criteria of correctness. The same attitude to speakers' behaviour and to grammatical rules will hold, I contend, in the case of ambiguities: speakers may need to be told the right and the wrong way to interpret a word in this or that context, or how to go about settling its meaning, just as they may need to be told the right and the wrong way to use it.

The point of this refinement to my formulation of the Stoic response is not that the Stoics did not assume authority in linguistic matters (they did, obviously), but that their doing so is a standard and permissible move in the ancient game. It is objectionable only in so far as they do not provide a justification for the authoritativeness to which they lay claim (just as they must be able to defend their chosen standards of Hellenism). The Stoa was quite willing to meet this requirement, by producing its elaborate and highly original account of grammatical and semantic concepts and categories, crowned by their splendidly precise and sophisticated definition of ambiguity. The school was quite unhampered by broad theoretical or methodological anxieties about the authoritativeness or otherwise of ordinary speakers' intuitions; and Sextus would take issue with the alleged grounds of Stoic authority, and, in the end, with the assumption of the possibility of authoritativeness for any grammatical expertise – not with the conception of grammatical activity, which informed the whole ancient debate, as the provision of norms for speaking, writing and understanding good Greek or Latin. Sextus himself defends the ancient basic formal grammatical education, γραμματιστική, which taught reading and writing, on the grounds that it is "useful" for living an ordinary life, since it allows us to record in writing what would otherwise be forgotten (*M.*

1.52), frees us from the risk of ridicule for speaking incorrectly (1.206), and equips us to express ourselves clearly, and appropriately to our subject-matter and our company (1.191f., 1.194, 1.234f.).[50] A wholly different, descriptive grammar is beyond Sextus' ken, and he rejects only existing theories' pretensions to authoritativeness, for they are redundant as well as internally incoherent.[51]

Sextus' neglect of syntactic ambiguities, and so of native-speaker understanding of these, is explicable given this same context. Sextus' strategy, I believe, is to bring to the fore cases where the dividing line between linguistic and non-linguistic knowledge is unclear. Highlighting syntactic ambiguities would have drawn attention more sharply to what it is more plausible, or at least intuitively more obvious, to interpret as a special linguistic ability, and would thus have directed the ancient reader to the familiar debate about standards of linguistic correctness – which in turn would have made Stoic claims about ambiguity, based as they were on a broad, complex, and sophisticated grammatical and semantic theory, far more attractive. Of course, knowledge of lexical ambiguities also, and necessarily, involves linguistic knowledge, however that is conceived: one could not be said fully to know a word, ambiguous or not, if one did not know how it is pronounced

---

[50] The defence of Hellenism rests, I think, in part on an older notion of it as "good Greek" in a broad sense, including but going beyond purity, as analysed by Aristotle (*rhet.* 3.5.1407a19ff.); and it is not entirely clear that Sextus has not fudged the issue, although his criticisms of the internal incoherence of prescriptive grammar are certainly weighty.

[51] Hence, what are to modern eyes the truly interesting difficulties lie just below the surface of the polemic: If each man can have a συνήθεια, a "customary usage" (*M.* 1.187), how is this a *common* usage? What is the relation between it and the shared normative regularities of languages? Why should one accept the judgement of other speakers on one's utterances (*M.* 1.191–2)? How are different συνήθειαι (232ff.) related? Where does linguistic knowledge end, and non-linguistic begin, and what should go into a description of a language? These questions are of no interest to Sextus, who wants to fill in some of the details of the Skeptic life-plan – *cf.* esp. *M.* 1.193 – and to avoid handing dogmatist dialecticians an obvious objection to his argument at *P.H.* 2.257; his goal is not to construct an alternative technical grammar. συνήθεια is a test for the purity of utterances rather than a form of knowledge deserving of exploration in its own right, and Sextus admits – indeed his case rests on – the non-technical status of an ordinary speaker's knowledge: *e.g. M.* 1.87, 179; such knowledge is not distinguished by any special name (it is just εἴδησις, *M.* 1.87) or status.

(and, perhaps, spelled, in some cultures) and what its syntactic and formal properties are – precisely the sort of knowledge about lexical items to which ancient grammarians laid claim. But by focussing narrowly on the meanings of single terms, and avoiding all mention of syntactic ambiguity, Sextus manages to avoid obvious trespassing on the grammarians' territory; for, after all, what really distinguishes the layperson from the expert is that the expert knows what a given technical term means, even if the layperson knows, in some sense, everything else about it (how to pronounce it, how to spell it, what part of speech it is, and so on).

The suggestion Sextus needs to avoid is that native speakers may well not be competent to detect ambiguities and decide on interpretations for themselves in such matters, on the grounds that an expression's having this or that syntactic structure would be a matter for judgement by grammarians. If there is a failure here to distinguish understanding that an expression is (structurally) ambiguous from having access to some theoretical description of its possible structures, then, for the purposes of understanding Sextus and his Stoic opponents, this is to be accepted as a common feature of the ancient grammatical landscape, as shaped by the enormous practical power and theoretical hegemony of prescriptive grammar.

3.4 Stylistics

Stoic philosophy, as we saw (3.1), uniquely restricts what is good or beneficial to moral virtue and virtuous action, including the justice which binds human societies. Coupled with humanity's natural sociability and fellow-feeling – the desire both to associate with and to benefit others – virtue's pre-eminence ensures that the canons of correct style will ultimately be determined by moral and ethical precepts. In the Stoic system this means that as a speaker, just as in other social and political rôles, one's natural desire, when this is properly understood, is for others to be swayed chiefly by morally correct principles, with a view to development toward a perfectly happy virtuous existence, and for them to choose the "preferred objects" (those "in accordance with nature", health, money, and the like) only when morality permits. This feature of Stoicism seemed, if anything, odder to ancient than to modern readers, who are both less familiar with, and less impressed by, the importance and usefulness of a conventional rhetorical education. Its implications for ambiguity, which is presumably to be understood as a potential offence against the stylistic virtue of clarity (defined at D.L. 7.59) are fairly obvious, although no direct evidence shows they were recognised by the Stoa: standardly, ambiguities are to be avoided lest they present others with the opportunity for false assents (or unwarranted withholdings of assent).[52]

The outcome is plain enough in the case of philosophical terminology. Potentially misleading syntactic ambiguities will also be undesirable, whether in argument, exposition, or narrative. Ambiguities which might confuse or mislead hearers properly engaged or intending to engage in the pursuit of "preferred" objects are to be avoided too, I assume, since the ordinary human desire is that one's fellows possess these items, wherever moral considerations do not forbid it. There is a ban on ambiguity in orthodox stylistics too (see 8.2, 8.3):[53] what set Stoic concern for clarity and correct discourse apart was the school's ethical motivation.

---

[52] I refer to Atherton 1988 for a fuller defence of this view of Stoic rhetorical theory and practice. It has been claimed, by Baratin and Desbordes 1987: 44f., that Hellenism subsumes all the other qualities of style, which 'participent de cette norme neutre, génériquement définie par la notion d'ἑλληνισμός'. But there is no indication of such a broad, quasi-Aristotelian, conception of Hellenism or "good Greek" at D.L. 7.59. The Stoic ideal of discourse is indeed best interpreted as forming a unity, each virtue entailing the other (as in the moral sphere), but, significantly, that is not the way it is presented in the Diogenes doxography. A direct Stoic association of ambiguity with inclarity is suggested by the definitions in one of the classifications of the ambiguity kinds "Significant" and "Non-significant Part": see 6.5.1. It is consistent too with ambiguity's usual place in orthodox stylistics: see 8.3.

[53] Modern literary theorists or rhetoricians may here raise doubts whether ambiguity, even if precisely definable and identifiable, is under authorial control, or whether such control would be desirable, or whether it is always an advantage, by some scale of values and purposes, to have it excluded from a text; and they will find ambiguity's relegation (Stoic or traditional) to the stylistic blacklist theoretically crude, naive, incoherent, and so on. But such objections will not help us

This bare outline of the Stoic plan may seem straightforward. On closer inspection it proves unsatisfactory and incoherent. The Stoic stylistic canons must be understood as practical guides for composition, and some ancient speakers are known to have accepted them in this rôle.[54] The canons will be redundant if they remain mere abstract desiderata. Now no evidence exists of practical guidance as to when and which (types of) ambiguities may be dangerous. But the problem is not just that all injunctions to be "clear" are useless without the aid of practical experience, examples, models, etc. (as ancient teachers of composition, like their modern counterparts, knew very well). Lost Stoic lectures and manuals on stylistics might have dealt with such things. Chrysippus' comments on the allowances to be made for stylistically crude speakers suggest that a more detailed treatment of stylistic topics lies in the background (Plutarch st. rep. 1047AB (31H)). The Stoic notion of clarity – 'language presenting what is thought in a way that is easily understood' ('λέξις γνωρίμως παριστῶσα τὸ νοούμενον', D.L. 7.59) – can be grasped in an untechnical way, even accepted, without much difficulty. If it remains the case that language can be said to be "clear" relative only to some subject-matter, to some audience, in some context, and if, in consequence, some sort of categorisation of contexts and audiences is still required from the Stoa, then that, again, may be the fault of the sources. Alternatively, Stoics might not have thought this expectation reasonable: Stoic stylistic criteria are, after all, presented as canons of excellence for undifferentiated "discourse", λόγος (D.L. 7.59), and language must be "appropriate", πρέπον, to its "content" or "subject-matter", πρᾶγμα, with no parallel allowances being made, explicitly

reconstruct either standard ancient prescriptions for compositional excellence or the unorthodox but equally prescriptive canons of Stoic stylistics, and so are not pursued here. This is not to deny that their methods may help detect revealing inconsistencies, assumptions, etc., in our sources, or that, on a broader scale, they help to identify one of the principal weaknesses of ancient literary theory, its presumption of an easy distinction between medium and message. The Stoic understanding of that distinction is criticised in the main text.

[54] Cf. Atherton 1988: 401f. Most revealing is Cicero's description of Stoic orators and oratory at Brutus 118.

at any rate – for situation of utterance, audience, or the emotional or other state of the speaker.

The real difficulties with the Stoic definition of clarity are, I think, far less tractable than these. Even given the Stoic story about what is and what is not basically valuable and important to human beings, and the stylistic evaluations and prescriptions founded on it, the Stoic conceptions of clarity in particular, and stylistics in general, still remain unacceptable, because they appear to rest on an inadequate and incoherent model of the relation between the mind and language. I shall leave to one side the (to us) enormously implausible presumption that, given the requirement on language to be appropriate to subject-matter, the world must already be neatly and exhaustively divided up into things whose nature, properties, moral importance, and interconnections can be apprehended (as they are by the sage) and clearly, appropriately, and concisely "put into words". Here the Stoic model of discourse – which allowed the school to criticise Homer for using articles when he should have used pronouns because 'not using the natural words is a vice' (A.D. *pron.* 7.21–3) – differs from the standard rhetorical one only in that there is but one "right" form of words for each message, not several candidates amongst which a speaker must choose the best suited to his objectives. Exception will also be taken to the implicit assumption that language's function is solely or primarily one of describing things, whether well or badly. But this sort of picture of what the world and language's relation to it are like is not uniquely Stoic, and if one wants to challenge its Stoic version, it is the exclusive distinction it constructs between moral and other sorts of goodness which must be tackled too, and this I have determined to pass by. It might also be objected that the excellences do not constitute a set of qualities any one or any combination of which might be present in a text apart from the others: as Baratin and Desbordes point out, 1987: 45, it is hard to see how discourse could be correct, concise, appropriate, and elegant, say, but not clear. The Stoic excellences may, in practice or theory, have far more closely resembled a composite, Aristotelianising notion of "good

Greek" (*rhet.* 3.5.1407a19ff.) than a set of discrete items as
defined and inculcated by later stylistic tracts; this may reflect
the influence of Theophrastus (*cf.* Innes 1985: 255ff.), just as
does the content of the Stoic theory – four of the five excellences, at least in name or form, were taken over from him.
But it is the second stage of the process of communication –
what Stoic stylistics assumes about the relation of thought
to language – which creaks so badly as to suggest imminent
collapse.

Clear discourse 'presents what is thought in a familiar,
easily accessible way' (D.L. 7.59). It is uncertain whether
'what is thought' is the articulated content of an impression (= (roughly) a *lekton* or set of *lekta*), or some external
object of thought. The Stoic definition of λέγειν, speaking,
does not help, since it employs the obscure quasi-technical
term *pragma* ('τὸ τὴν τοῦ νοουμένου πράγματος σημαντικὴν
προφέρεσθαι φωνήν', "producing the vocal sound significant
of the *pragma* being thought", Sextus *M.* 8.80), which, in
this context, is probably co-extensive with *lekton* (see further,
6.2.3). Now, if "what is thought" is "a/the object of thought",
then there may be room, given that generous and confident
assumption of a set of objective values and a neatly divisible
world, for discourse that is appropriate and clear. Language
achieves presentation of an object or situation to the mind *via*
the senses of hearing or vision. For the Stoics language was a
prime instrument of expression of subjective experiences, that
is, of rational impressions or thoughts (D.L. 7.49 (39A2)), and
as such it does not *directly* convey information about "things
out there". Yet the question why sloppy, vague, and muddled
thoughts are not, on this account, "clearly" and "appropriately" expressed in sloppy talk, was never even raised. A fairly
straightforward passage is supposed to link impression with
logos (D.L. 7.49 (39A2)); so, if thoughts are confused, incoherent, and imprecise, a higgledy-piggledy jumble of words,
dotted with hesitations, retractions, contradictions, barbarisms, solecisms, and so on, seems to be just what they need by
way of "clear" and "appropriate" linguistic expression. Similarly, if I am unaware that there is a crucial ambiguity present

in the verbal formulation of an argument which I am constructing, proposing, or considering, then that ambiguity – at
first blush a prime instance of inclarity – must figure in the
only possible "appropriate" and "clear" linguistic expression
of the argument which is the content of my thought.

This anxiety is not isolated. Chapter Seven will confront
other difficulties in the Stoic account of how ambiguity affects
the proper functioning of reason.

3.5 Stoic philosophical method and the Stoic concept of language

The Stoics' belief in the providential arrangement of the cosmos, which accounts for god's gift of reason and language to
humans, committed them to the basic reliability of the natural
human capacity for apprehension of the world, including the
fundamental correctness of language, in both structure and
vocabulary. Reason and language are inextricably entwined.
Our ability to talk about the world is an intrinsic part of and
vehicle for our rationality, not a casual adjunct to it.[55] We
could not be moral agents, or occupy a unique position in
the order of the universe as divinely-appointed seekers after
knowledge, without the capacity to control our assents to the
impressions produced in our souls, or the power of reason to
understand, assess, and collate those impressions. It is impressions' internal structuring, by means of *lekta*, which explains
how impressions can be the objects of rational assessment or
judgement, and how they can be communicated or explained
to others. Communication itself is necessary if people are to
come together in families, tribes, cities, and all the social
groupings which are the natural result of their need for com-

---

[55] This may explain Plutarch's report that the Stoics prized human form over wisdom
in the body of a beast; note especially the words put into the mouth of practical
wisdom, '… let me go and have no thought for me, for I am being destroyed and
corrupted into the face of an ass' (*comm. not.* 11.1064B). Because of their different
physiology, some non-human animals will crucially lack even the power of articulate speech.

panionship, security, and procreation, and which are also a prerequisite for moral activity.[56]

Unfortunately, language does not enjoy, or no longer enjoys, a thorough-going isomorphism with *lekta*.[57] Ambiguity itself may be the result of language's decline and man's corruption, like his weakness for unnecessary and misleading euphemisms (Cicero *ad fam.* 9.22.1, *off.* 1.35, 128).[58] Anomalies too were of interest to Chrysippus.[59] Yet language's imperfect reproduction of the structures of *lekta* was not seen as a serious obstacle to apprehending the world and communicating our findings. The very fact that Stoics feel able to pronounce on both the existence and – in principle, at least – the limits of language's corrupt state and of its potential for misleading its

---

[56] Cicero *fin.* 3.62ff. is a Stoic account of the origins of society (part, 57F). Man is naturally sociable and gregarious: Stobaeus 2.109.10ff. (– *S.V.F.* 3.686 (67W)).

[57] The basis of the supposed world/*lekton*/language isomorphism can itself be challenged. Harris 1981: 27 complains that even if, say, Socrates and anger are two bits of reality, '... it is puzzling to know what counts as evidence for answering the question whether these bits of reality would, if in fact Socrates were angry, be structurally related in exactly the way reflected in anything that might count as the structure of the sentence "Socrates is angry"'. In brief, he wants an explanation of how language can be 'systematically unmisleading' (24). The Stoic account is vulnerable to just this objection. The structure of the proposition ⟨Socrates is angry⟩ is supposed to capture a distinction between Socrates as a whole and a (possible) state of his soul. The "evidence" for this is that Socrates' anger must itself be corporeal – for it affects/effects other things – so any distinction between him and his soul-so-disposed must take place outside the corporeal realm, *viz.*, at the level of the *lekton*. The "fact" that in the world there are just Socrates and his anger is marked by the predicate ⟨... is angry⟩ being true of him. But the *precise* dependence/correspondence relation of this quasi-linguistic structure with the "angry Socrates" complex goes unaccounted for. For further criticisms of Stoic semantics, see esp. 6.2.3.

[58] See 3.1. It is this gradual but still limited deterioration of language which solves the puzzle (noted by Blank 1982: 2, n. 17), how it is that the Stoics can claim both that there is such a thing as correct language and also that language is infected with anomaly.

[59] See esp. Varro *ling. lat.* 9.1: Chrysippus 'proposes to demonstrate that similars are signified by dissimilar words, and dissimilars by similar expressions'. Varro comments that Crates apparently misconstrued Chrysippus' real position regarding analogy and anomaly; perhaps the point is that Chrysippus was interested primarily in semantic anomaly (*cf.* Simplicius *cats.* 396.3ff., on ἀθάνατος, immortal), although *ling. lat.* 10.59 confirms an interest in the formal aspects as well. Blank 1982: 2 rightly points out the difficulty inherent in making anomalists out of rationalist Stoics; on the whole anomaly/analogy "debate", see Blank 1982: 1ff., 11ff.

93

users, speaks of confidence in the availability and satisfactoriness of other means of achieving philosophical enlightenment. The Stoic definitions and classifications of ambiguity and its types are not only sharp, precise, and authoritative; what they capture are objective, isolable phenomena. That Stoics apparently felt no need to urge or practise the actual elimination of ambiguities by introducing additional terminology, even in the case of crucial philosophical terms, and were content with distinguishing meanings, would have been mere folly if language's defects could not be picked out and allowed for, so that they need no longer obstruct the discovery, consolidation, or communication of the very truths about the nature of things which force language's defects on our attention.

Introducing two or more new terms to take up the semantic slack is not by itself, in any event, going to solve such problems; their meanings will still have to be defined, and this cannot be done in isolation from the relevant portions of Stoic philosophical doctrine. The preservation of ambiguities may actually help to make underlying conceptual associations more obvious. Stoic terminological innovations, even if they do capture some underlying difference, will, of course, seem vulnerable to the charge of pointlessness until and unless they acquire independence, which is unlikely in any number of cases; perhaps they were always meant to play a pedagogic rôle, as *aides-mémoire* for the student, rather than initiating a programme of linguistic revisionism.[60] In antiquity the complaint was rather that such verbal distinctions, like the Stoics' numerous semantic innovations, were arbitrary, lacking any foundation in reality. But what Galen in particular seems to have found immensely irritating was the Stoic failure to stick to standard Greek usage – a point to which I shall return.[61]

---

[60] Chrysippus even sanctions using *good* of objects other than virtue and virtuous action so long as it is clear to the user what he is doing: Plutarch *st. rep.* 30.1048A (58H). But this must be an instance, not of ambiguity, but of non-strict usage: see 4.6. Cicero *fin.* 5.89 (*cf.* 4.22) makes the criticism that Chrysippus uses *good* the way everyone does outside school hours.

[61] Brunschwig 1978b: 61 observes Galen's frequent 'note xénophobe assez déplaisante'. *Cf. e.g. diff. puls.* 2.10, 8.631K, (= *S.V.F.* 2.24): Chrysippus is the first to break his own new linguistic laws, and is not even a native Greek speaker; 3.1,

It is worth noting, however, that language retains some, limited, cognitive value. Where standard scientific resources fail to provide cut-and-dried confirmation of Stoic theses, recourse can yet be had to information provided by linguistic and paralinguistic phenomena: the idioms and gestures used by philosophically uneducated speakers, the mechanisms of speech production, and elaborate and ingenious etymologies (which won the school as much derision as praise: *e.g.* Cicero *nat. deor.* 3.62). Etymology may also have been used to construct rules for linguistic correctness, and even to show up the limits of rationality in language (*cf.* Frede 1978: 72f.). The justification once again must be that humans and their languages are, or at least were, basically rational, and in harmony with the objects of perception and judgement, and are so as a dispensation of the benevolent divine force which granted the extraordinary gifts of reason, speech, and assent. Individual words can preserve traces of pristine resemblances to the objects they name, and everyday idioms and gestures, even the mechanics of vocal articulation, may point to truths, recoverable by the expert, which are unprovable, and untestable by sensory evidence. Yet this means of access to hidden facts is restricted. Chrysippus himself – and his pronouncements and practice would have carried considerable weight – does not treat ordinary language as scientifically heuristic, on a par with syllogisms or sense-experience. Idiomatic expressions, like gestures and etymologies, are not signs in the appropriate sense; they lack the power to reveal; they can only suggest and confirm.

8.642K (=*S.V.F.* 1.33): the same goes for Zeno; *inst. log.* 4.6, 11.11, *al.*, and esp. 17.7, where the injunction in cases of disagreement about meanings to 'understand the word according to Greek usage' may well be directed against the Stoa. Verbal inventions typically help make important Stoic conceptual distinctions explicit. Thus, Chrysippus' distinction between δεῖσθαι, *being in need*, and ἐνδεῖσθαι, *being in want*, ridiculed by Plutarch *comm. not.* 20.1068C–E (*cf.* 23.1070AB) as a case of useless καινολογία, rests on a special interpretation of χρεία, *use*, and would be unintelligible and pointless without this doctrinal underpinning. Long 1978: 108 points out that the names for the dialectical sub-virtues at D.L. 7.46f. (31B1–5) (see 3.1) are all neologisms. The Stoic reputation for καινολογία seems to have spread far and wide: note *Sch. in Lucianum* (*ed.* Rabe) 128.18–129.16: 'but the Stoics, being people who make a display of precision and who like to use strange words . . .'.

The passages on which I base this interpretation of Chrysippean etymology (*contra e.g.* Dahlmann 1932/1964: 6) are from Galen (*P.H.P.* 2.2.4ff. and 3.1.9ff., pp. 104, ll. 3ff., 170, ll. 6ff.). The context is Galen's criticism of Chrysippus' procedure when arguing that the *locus* of the ruling part of the soul is the heart. The crucial methodological announcement comes from Chrysippus' *de anima* I, which Galen quotes:

... thus the place [*sc.* of the ruling part of the soul] seems to elude us, since there is neither clear sense-perception of it, as there is in the case of the other parts [*sc.* of the soul: *cf.* 3.1.11, p. 170, ll. 10–15], nor proofs ['τεκμηρίων'] through which one might construct a syllogistic argument for this [*sc.* that the soul's ruling part is located in the heart]: for otherwise the disagreement amongst both doctors and philosophers would not have grown so great. (3.1.15, p. 170, 11. 23–7)

Even if Chrysippus' application of his method is sometimes suspect (see esp. 2.5.19, p. 130, l. 32; 3.3.4ff., p. 192, ll. 18ff.; 3.7.38ff., p. 220, ll. 2ff.), his theoretical understanding of the material he then presents – the etymology of καρδία, *heart* (3.5.27, p. 206, ll. 12ff.), the analysis of the articulation of the pronoun ἐγώ, *I* (2.2.9ff., p. 104, ll. 27ff.; *cf.* 3.5.24–6, p. 206, ll. 3ff.), the long lists of quotations from the poets, and of ordinary speakers' usages and gestures – is clear. None of it can count as evidence or proof: at best, it is "plausible", πιθανόν, "reasonable", εὔλογον, or "consistent with", ἀκόλουθον, the material, that Chrysippus' favoured thesis is true (*e.g.* pp. 200, l. 22, 206, l. 15, 208, l. 5, 218, l. 29). Similarly, the gesture which accompanies the utterance of ἐγώ is said to be performed 'naturally and appropriately' (p. 104, l. 31; when Nigidius Figulus called attention to the fittingness of the mode of articulation of personal pronouns in Latin – reported by Gellius *noct. att.* 10.4.1–4 – he must have been adapting Chrysippus' claims for Greek). Elsewhere, Chrysippus is said to have asserted that 'doctrines about divine matters [*i.e.*, presumably, those revealed at initiation ceremonies] are reasonably [εἰκότως] called "completions" [τελετάς]', because of the word's similiarity to τέλος (*end, completion, perfection*) (*Etym. Mag. s.v.* τελετή, p. 751.16–22, ed. Gaisford, col. 2108). As Chrysippus raises no doubts about the reliability of the particular linguistic, articulatory, and paralinguistic items he cites, his refusal to grant them genuine heuristic power must be due to some other reason, and I take this to be a widespread failure of language genuinely to reveal the properties of objects.

It is true, of course, that Stoic etymological theory developed into a complex and comprehensive discipline, as is shown by such texts as Chapter Six of Augustine's *de dialectica*; and Cleanthes had already warned against 'trusting just anyone', 'πιστεῦσαι τῷ τύχοντι', when tracing the origin of words, in his treatise, Περὶ μεταλήψεως, *On [Semantic] Change* (Athenaeus *Deipnosoph.* 11, 471b (*ed.* Kaibel vol. 3, p. 35, ll. 9ff.)), as if expert guidance were already available. But the theory of its very nature had to remain merely confirmatory, providing only a systematic account of the types of correspondences between known properties of objects and known properties of their names,[62] while unable to meet the needs of any genuinely heuristic, explanatory, or probative Stoic project. Varro associates the third, philosophical, level of etymological inquiry, at which ordinary usages begin to be explained, with Cleanthes (*ling. lat.* 5.8), while disclaiming certain knowledge for himself: such knowledge is reserved – perhaps recalling Socrates in the *Cratylus* (*e.g.* 396d2ff.)? – for initiates of the divinely-inspired fourth and highest level (hence his own, modest assertion 'opinionem aucupabor'). Stoic rationalising accounts of divine names and titles, as "in line with the powers" (κατὰ τὰς δυνάμεις) of god, combine etymological and non-etymological elements (as at Cicero *nat. deor.* 2.45–72), suggesting that the former could not stand alone.[63]

---

[62] Lloyd 1971: 62ff. and Amsler 1989: 22 take the doctrine of *lekta* – what Amsler calls the Stoic 'intensional theory of meaning' – to be central (however problematically) to the school's etymology; but this theory must relate physical objects in the world and their properties to the properties of other physical objects, *viz.*, the bits of battered air which are their names: *cf.* Long 1986: 137, and see 4.4 on the materialism of Stoic language theory.

[63] It is true that Diogenes of Babylon is reported by Philodemus *music.* 1, fr. 23 Kemke (=*S.V.F.* 3.II.64, p. 224, ll. 29–31) to have supported his claim that 'well-regulated and serious music' is directed chiefly toward honouring τὸ θεῖον, "the divine", with the observation, not necessarily of his own devising, that 'καὶ αὐτὰ σημαίνειν τὰ ὀνόματα, τό τε θεωρεῖν ⟨καὶ τὸ⟩ν θεατὴν ⟨καὶ τ⟩ὸ θέατρον',

There is no evidence, however, that ambiguities were put systematically to work in philosophy even to the limited extent to which etymologies were made to prove their usefulness. At this point, now that the motivation behind Stoic interest in and concern about ambiguities has been sketched, and the ways in which this interest and concern manifested themselves in projects with practical applications – isolating key ambiguous terms, drawing up stylistic canons, and so on – have begun to emerge, it will, I think, be instructive to look beyond the Stoa, at some alternative approaches to ambiguity, and alternative assessments of its importance. These comparisons will of necessity be unsystematic: I offer them as especially instructive in part because they will not, and cannot, form a coherent set. It is not just that the state of the evidence does not permit sure-footed construction of an orderly account of the place of Stoic work on ambiguity in the history of philosophy or of the language sciences. Indeed, what evidence there is suggests the opposite, that there simply is no neat, comprehensive story to tell about influences on the Stoa, or of its influences on later thinkers; and it would be absurdly limiting to restrict our vision to what is historically possible (let alone probable, or certain). Of course, some theorists, in grammar especially, borrowed and adapted Stoic material; Chrysippus (almost) certainly reacted to Diodorus Cronus' teachings on the subject (as will be seen in 4.6); and he and other Stoics may have been reacting to Platonic, or earlier,

---

'the names themselves signify this, *observing* and *observer* and *theatre*' (*cf.* Bk. 4, ch. 2, V 1ff., =Neubecker 1986: 42f., with commentary 131f.). But σημαίνειν could mean no more than "indicate, point to the fact that" here. D.T. Sch. 454.21ff. asserts that etymology is 'σύντομος καὶ ἀληθὴς τοῦ ζητήματος ἀπόδοσις ... ἢ ἐπισημασία ἐπὶ τῶν πλείστων τὸ πιθανὸν ἔχουσα· οὐ γὰρ ἐπὶ πάντων ἐστιν αὐτὴν εὑρεῖν' 'a concise and the explanation of the problem item, or an indication which is plausible in most cases: for it is not possible to discover it in all': the point of the second definition, however, is that etymology is merely plausible because it cannot explain all words, either because their origin is now lost, or because explanation must come to a halt somewhere – both commonplaces in the literature. Reliance on idioms as guides to real state of affairs is not confined to ancient Stoics. A description of the basis of the Alexander technique observes: 'Common language expressions such as "things are getting me down" or "I'm feeling uptight" suggest a feeling for how our relationship with gravity is disturbed': John Nicholls, 'The Alexander Technique', leaflet for the Society of Teachers of the Alexander Technique, n.d.

treatment of ambiguities. But illuminating comparisons are to be found which have no rôle to play in such genetic accounts, however speculative, and the question of historical contact between the Stoa and other thinkers is irrelevant to their importance and interest – although the simple fact that contacts and responses cannot be traced with any certainty, and look unlikely in any case, must be significant for the history of Hellenistic philosophy.

I begin with the ancient philosopher whose work on ambiguity rivals the Stoics' in innovation and sophistication, but who made use of it in ways which their philosophy did not and, I believe, could not accommodate. It is as well to remember first the important similarities between their approaches to ambiguity. Aristotle, like the Stoa, took it to be a prime cause of fallacy, and his classifications of linguistic sophisms call out for comparison with the Stoic lists of ambiguity types, to be explored in Chapter Seven (where it will also prove useful to note the crucial differences between the Aristotelian and Stoic analyses of fallacious argument as a whole.) Aristotle's hostility to ambiguity as a defect of style was almost certainly shared by the Stoa, as observed in 3.4, and the Stoic taxonomy of stylistic excellences, including clarity, may well ultimately derive from his work in this field,[64] although the motivations behind his and the Stoa's concern with stylistics could hardly be more different. There is no evidence either that the Stoa, despite its intense interest in literary exegesis, set about solving textual or critical "problems" by positing ambiguities, a procedure explained in Chapter 25 of the *Poetics*;[65] but this

---

[64] The main texts are: *poet.* 22.1458a18ff., 'the excellence of language is to be clear and not mean', and *rhet.* 3.2.1404b1ff., 'the excellence of language is to be clear and appropriate', esp. 37–9, 'of words, homonymies are useful to the sophist ... synonymies to the poet', 3.5.1407a19ff., 'the principle of language is good Greek', esp. 32ff., on the need to avoid ambiguities. For a reconstruction of the relation between Stoic, Aristotelian, and Theophrastean stylistics, see Atherton 1988: 419f.

[65] Three types of Aristotle's literary "solutions", λύσεις, *poet.* 25.1460b6ff., can be interpreted as appeals to ambiguities in texts, although only one is explicitly called "ambiguity", ἀμφιβολία, 1461a25f.; the example is apparently ambiguity of a single word (in the example, πλεῖον or πλέων), not an "Amphiboly" as defined in the *s. el.*: see 6.3.3, 6.7.2, and Appendix. The others are "Accent", προσῳδία, *poet.* 1461a21–3, and "Division", διαίρεσις", 23–5, neither of which is treated consistently in the *s. el.* as a genuine ambiguity-kind: see 6.2.4 and Appendix. Aristotle

might be a false impression created by the patchiness of our sources. Even if the school did not formally draw up comparable, highly particularised, lists of appropriate exegetical procedures, Zeno certainly initiated a tradition of detailed commentary on the classics (*cf. e.g. S.V.F.* 1.274), primarily designed, of course, to tease (or force) out fortunate anticipations of or support for Stoic doctrines.[66]

Aristotle seems also, however, to have had reasons for interest in ambiguity which were unknown to, or had little or no attraction for, the Stoa. He anticipated later rhetorical tradition in identifying ambiguously-framed laws as one source of legal disputes (*rhet.* 1.15.1375b11–13), an approach which seems to have had no place in Stoic rhetorical theory before Posidonius (see further, 8.2). He also constructed a classification of apparent rhetorical syllogisms, "enthymemes", parallel to that of apparent dialectical, "sophistical", refutations, one group of which is 'due to language', 'παρὰ τὴν λέξιν'. Two of these have rough counterparts in the *s. el.* (*rhet.* 2.24.1401a1ff.).[67] Whatever the explanation – most likely, the non-existence of a special form of rhetorical reasoning in Stoic theory – there is no sign of a comparable Stoic doctrine of specifically rhetorical fallacies, linguistic or otherwise.

A more striking difference can be detected in the Stoics' apparent failure to draw up anything like the *Topics'* general guidelines for constructing and testing arguments on any topic and definitions of any subject, including ways of detecting, exploiting, or eliminating ambiguities.[68] Parallels to

certainly does not mark these three off as a group from other 'linguistic', 'πρὸς τὴν λέξιν' (1461a9f.) solutions. For detailed commentary: Gudeman 1934: 429–35; *cf.* Pfeiffer 1968: 69ff. on Aristotle's Homeric problems and solutions, and 70, 144f., 226, 263, on Peripatetic use of the ζήτημα or "question" format.

66 Zeno is credited with five books of *Homeric Problems*, D.L. 7.4, Aristotle with six of *Homeric Puzzles*, D.L. 5.26. On the "problems" *genre*, which was probably a Peripatetic speciality, albeit not exclusively, see, besides references in n. 65: Flashar 1975: 359ff.; Blank 1982: 9f.

67 The two are Homonymy, and Combination/Division: *rhet.* 24.1401a13–b3. Aristotle's treatment of them, and indeed his whole treatment of apparent syllogisms in the *Rhetoric*, are looser and less rigorous than those in the *s. el.*, however. See further, 6.2.4, n. 37, on Theon's version of the Combination/Division modes.

68 Key passages are: *top.* 1.13.105a23f., 1.15.106a1ff.: provision of premisses or arguments by distinguishing senses, 'ποσαχῶς ἕκαστον λέγεται'; 1.18.108a18ff.: such

Aristotle's guidelines for identifying and dealing with ambiguous definitions and *definienda* may have been set down in, say, Chrysippus' staggering collection of treatises, now lost, on the theory and practice of the art of definition (D.L. 7.199f. = *S.V.F.* 2.16, pp. 8, 1. 33–9, 1. 11 (321)). But, to be brief, and to simplify a little, there seems to have been little room in the logical part of Stoic philosophy for the sort of dialectic described and prescribed in the *Topics*: the public, formalised, highly rule-governed attack on and defence of some given, reputable belief or ἔνδοξον, to which the technique of developing a plausible case for just about any position was central. Far from taking bouts of semi-formalised, but free-ranging, debate between his students to be a valuable part of their philosophical education, Chrysippus seems to have wanted to restrict discussion, perhaps to those fairly far along the philosophical course (Plutarch *st. rep.* 10.1037B).[69] The (Arcesilean) technique of arguing for the opposite side (that is,

semantic distinctions as useful for clarity, *i.e.* for (a) making plain just what one is committed to in an argument; (b) making sure that arguments are relevant to the matter in hand; and (c) not getting deceived in argument – as well as for deceiving others: thus *s. el.* 16.175a5ff., a comparable defence of the usefulness of studying sophisms, claims *inter alia* that, as most fallacies are linguistic, they improve our ability to see 'ποσαχῶς ἕκαστον λέγεται'; 1.7.103a6ff., with two important concrete examples, *same* and *different*, at 1.18.108a38–b6; 2.3.110a23ff.: the *topos* of "many senses" and how it is to be used both *pro* and *contra* a given position; 6.1.139a24ff.: the ways in which a definition can fail, including the case where either *definiens* or *definiendum* is or contains a homonymy, 6.2.139b19ff., 10.148a23ff.; also *an. po.* 1.11.77a5ff., 24.85b9ff., 2.13.97b36f. The *Rhetoric* refers the reader to the *Topics* for the correct treatment of the commonplace (for constructing enthymemes) "in how many ways", 2.23.1398a28f.

69 Chrysippus is reported to have said that 'it will be possible even', 'ἔσται δὲ καὶ', for people with a cognitive impression of something to argue against it as best they can, and 'sometimes', 'ποτὲ', for those without such an impression to make out a case on either side. As the quotation is very short, and out of context (from the *Physical Theses*), misinterpretation is more than likely, but it looks as though Chrysippus is contemplating two non-standard sorts of case. Long and Sedley 1987: 1: 190 are thus correct in saying that Chrysippean dialectic 'provides its expert with the ability to practise dialectic in the Aristotelian sense', the vital point being that it was almost certainly intended only for the man whose allegiance to Stoicism was already settled. Chrysippus was, admittedly, deeply impressed by the seriousness of the concern for dialectic evinced by Plato, Aristotle, and above all Socrates, so much so that 'it is not plausible that they are so completely wrong, if they were on the whole the sort of men we suppose them to be', Plutarch *st. rep.* 24.1046A. Yet this could be read (again, the context is lost) as much as a preliminary to a revisionist reading of them, as a promise to follow their example.

from Chrysippus' perspective, against what is known to be true) is, in contrast, proper only 'to those who suspend judgement about everything, and it furthers their ends, whereas for those who are producing knowledge in accordance with which we will conduct our lives, the opposite holds' (1036A (31P2)). The genuine Stoic dialectician, it is true, the descendant of Plato's philosopher-kings (Schofield 1980a: 286), is able to defend himself in argument against all comers, since his system of cognition cannot be weakened or changed by reasoning, and he can always give an account of it (D.L. 7.47 (31B6); cf. Cicero acad. 2.144f.): but a Stoic education is not a training in or for free debate, or the testing of ordinary opinions as a preliminary to philosophical or scientific advance.[70]

This last point brings us to a feature still more conspicuous by its absence from the Stoic context, in comparison with the Platonic–Aristotelian: any systematic use of homonymy, ambiguity, or related concepts as general instruments for identifying and solving philosophical problems, or for analysing, constructing, and disarming philosophical arguments. Of course, just as key Stoic terms may be (systematically) ambiguous (3.2), so too are many Aristotelian ones, as, say, a glance at the "philosophical dictionary" (meta. 5) will confirm. It is not remarkable in itself that Stoic sources never speak of anything resembling Aristotle's supremely innovative use of the concept of an expression's having (in G.E.L. Owen's phrase) "focal meaning", 'being said in relation to one thing and some one nature', πρὸς ἕν καὶ μίαν τινὰ φύσιν λεγόμενον (famously at meta. 3.2.1003a33–b16, 6.4.1030a27ff.), with its ultimately

---

[70] This is not the place for a full-scale comparison of Stoic and Aristotelian dialectic. The contrasts indicated here and in the main text are no more than a sketch of potentially fruitful areas of difference. Mature Stoic dialectic, as seen in 3.1, was not a method, or a set of techniques, but an organic virtue, and a body of knowledge, extending to all forms of public and private discourse (barring rhetoric), of which question-and-answer was just one: cf. D.L. 7.42, 48 (31A5, B8). (Compare the way it enormously outgrew its early concern, inherited from the minor "Socratic" philosophers, with sophisms and their solution: see 7.1.) The mass of argumentation Chrysippus famously produced against the cognitive value of ordinary experience was interpreted as Skeptic/Academic in form and inspiration, not Aristotelian: see Plutarch st. rep. 10.1036C, 1037AB (31P4) with Cicero fin. 2.2 (68J) on Arcesilaus' method; Cicero acad. 2.75, 87; and cf. D.L. 7.184 (31O). See also Schofield 1980a: 287f., and my n. 72, infra.

cardinal importance for the evolution of his metaphysics and ethics.[71] Nor is it strange that they do not report the kind of sifting of the philosophical tradition, using ambiguity (or something like it) as one of the tools of analysis, which is a distinctively Aristotelian method.[72] It is rather the almost complete absence from what is known of Stoic theorising of any interest even in formulating rules as to how significations of ambiguous terms may be systematically interrelated (using "categories", genera and species, or some other taxonomy) which is so striking.

There are, it is true, a few exceptions to this lack of interest in the intricacies of semantic multivalence. There is a hint of one in Simplicius' reference to Chrysippus' name for "conventional", ἐθική, as opposed to "natural" privation, στέρησις (cats. 394.31ff., 395.8ff.). Such terms as ἀχίτων, undressed, ἀνυπόδητος, unshod, ἀνάριστος, unbreakfasted, 'signify both not having something pure and simple, and signify also a kind of implication, whenever it [sc. the "not having", ἀέχεια, apparently a coinage of Iamblichus', whom Simplicius seems to be reporting or paraphrasing here] also occurs by way of privation', 'σημαίνει μὲν καὶ ψιλὴν ἀναίρεσιν, σημαίνει δὲ καὶ

---

[71] See esp. Owen 1986b, 1986c. Relevant earlier studies are Robinson 1941: 143; Hintikka 1959/1973; Patzig 1961; and see also Hintikka 1971. The concept of focal meaning, its origin, and importance have of course been hotly disputed. I ignore most of this discussion on the grounds that focal meaning and and its applications were, to all appearances, equally unknown to the Stoa. Interest in homonymy and synonymy in the Academy is well documented, though also much debated, above all as to whether and how Aristotle and Speusippus disagreed about homonymy and synonymy: see Boethus ap. Simplicium, cats. 38.19f., 36.28 ff., with Hambruch 1904: 28f.; Cherniss 1944: 57f.; Anton 1968; Barnes 1971; Heitsch 1972; Tarán 1978; Ebbesen 1981a: 1: 3ff.; and also Anton 1969.

[72] The classic analysis of Aristotle's dialectical method is Owen 1986d; cf. e.g. Hintikka 1973: 4f. Mansfeld 1989, esp. 338ff., claims to have detected Chrysippus in something like an Aristotelian-style dialectical examination of opposed views, viz. those concerning the location of the ruling part of the soul, as reported by Galen P.H.P. 3.1.10ff., p. 170, ll. 9ff. But there is no sign that Chrysippus actually set out anyone's view except Plato's – hardly the mark of an Aristotle at work – while his conclusion (3.1.15, p. 170, ll. 23–7; quoted p. 96) shows that the disagreement has been outlined to provide evidence that standard cognitive methods (perception, proof) are obviously inapplicable in this case. What follows is a collection of merely plausible or reasonable considerations he believes can none the less support the Stoic orthodox view that the ruling part has its locus in the heart: it is not a sifting or assessment of rival reputable views, ἔνδοξα, in order to arrive at the truth or an approximation of it.

παρέμφασίν τινα, ὅτε καὶ κατὰ στέρησιν γίνεται' (395.11–12), so that 'we do not say that the ox is tunicless or that we ourselves are unshod when we are in the bath, or that the birds or ourselves are unbreakfasted at day-break: rather, there must be co-implication of what is customary and when it is customary' (395.12–15). (Note the explicit appeal here to 'what we (do not) say'.) The use of the Stoic term (*co-*)*implication*, (συμ)παρέμφασις, suggests that Simplicius, or Iamblichus, is reporting Chrysippus with some fidelity (*cf. e.g.* Chrysippus *Logical questions* = *S.V.F.* 2.298a, col. 10, p. 107, l. 9; col. 12, p. 108, l. 22; Alex. *pr. an.* 402.26). A little later, 396.19ff., Simplicius also reports Chrysippus' attention in his *On Privatives* (Περὶ τῶν στερητικῶν) to the many anomalies present in words for privations (such as ἀθάνατος, *deathless*, suggesting death is something the gods have been deprived of). So it is possible that Chrysippus, like Aristotle before him (*meta.* 4.22.1022b32ff., *an.* 2.10.422a20ff.; *cf. an. po.* 1.12.77b24ff., *phys.* 5.2.226b10ff., *E.E.* 3.2.1230a37ff.; also *an. pr.* 1.46.51b 5ff.), had called attention to some systematic semantic variation in privatives formed with ἀ-. He certainly did distinguish between meanings of ἄλογος, *irrational*, as will emerge later in this section (pp. 119–22), and he inquired whether people with cataracts should be called "blind" (Simplicius *cats.* 401.7ff.). But perhaps Simplicius would have fully reported any such close, and piquant, similarity between the two philosophers: he is already citing Iamblichus for the view that the Stoics had taken most of their teachings about opposites from Aristotle (*e.g.* 394.31ff.).

The second exception emerges from reports that the meaning of the technical term *indifferent*, ἀδιάφορον, "having no bearing on happiness or unhappiness", is what it means *simpliciter*, ἅπαξ (D.L. 7.104 (58B1)) or καθάπαξ (Stobaeus 2.79.1). Its other meaning, "exciting neither impulse nor repulsion", must, accordingly, and understandably, have been qualified or conditional in some way. The terms of the distinction recall the rescue of yet another argument of Zeno's (like those discussed in 3.2) by the following route: some properties are "absolutely", καθάπαξ, better than others, such as rationality and intelligence; others, such as poetic skill or musicality, are not (Sextus *M.* 9.108ff.). Nothing is known, however, of any universal criteria that may have been worked up to support and justify these distinctions.

The third case can be stated in a little more detail. Sextus reports (*M.* 11.22ff.) that the Stoics added to the standard definition of the good as "benefit or not other than benefit" that '*good* has three meanings, and they sketch each sense again under a separate account', 'τριχῶς ... ἀγαθὸν προσαγορεύεσθαι, ἕκαστον τῶν σημαινομένων κατ' ἰδίαν πάλιν ἐπιβολὴν ὑπογράφουσιν' (25). The second intension/extension includes the first, and the third the other two (30), thus: that by which or from which benefit arises, *i.e.* virtue, is included in that which happens to produce benefit, *i.e.* virtue and virtuous actions; which in its turn is included in that which is capable of producing benefit, *i.e.* the virtues, virtuous actions, friends, the wise, the gods, and other good supernatural beings. The Stoic position is not like that of Plato and Xenocrates, for, says Sextus, these two philosophers believed that the Form of the Good, and particular things which are good, *i.e.* which partake in it, are good in quite different and unrelated senses, just as are the significations of the Greek word κύων, *dog*, which can signify the Dog Star and the dogfish as well as the domestic pet (28f.).[73] That the Stoics whose views Sextus reports felt justified in taking *good* as being in some way ambiguous or multivalent strongly suggests that they belonged to some later phase of the school. A comparison can be made with the complex classifications of goods made by Stobaeus, who might seem to allow for good things that are not virtues (or virtuous actions or persons), but does not do so, since all goods are so called by way of their relation to virtue: 2.58.5ff., 70.21ff., 71.15ff., 73.1ff. (= *S.V.F.* 3.95 (part), 104 (part), 106 (part), 111 (60J–M)). Similarly, the senses of *good* all depend on the primary goodness of the virtues: no independent source of benefit is possible.

---

[73] This discrimination may be the Stoics' own, but this is, I think, ruled out by the opening words of *M.* 11.30.

It is easy enough, of course, to see conceptual connections even now, with the paltry evidence at our disposal, between the (meanings of the) technical πολλαχῶς λεγόμενα, "(things/ expressions) said in many ways", listed in 3.2. In Sextus' report about the Stoic good, the expression 'τριχῶς ... ἀγαθὸν προσαγορεύεσθαι' appears, and this may be genuinely Stoic too, although Sextus does not say he is quoting his source *verbatim*. So perhaps the ambiguity of such conceptually complex terms was indeed given special treatment, albeit indirectly, with their significations receiving the special description πολλαχῶς λεγόμενα, or the like, to show that at the linguistic level what are in question are not simply crude puns. (The nearest modern comparison is with "polysemy", as opposed to "homonymy".[74]) The problem for the Stoa would then be to determine what counts as an appropriate conceptual connection; for example, whether things which are ἀνδρεῖος will count as appropriately related. The word *ἀνδρεῖος* is the illustration of one of the ambiguity species ("Homonymy in Simples") in the classification preserved by Galen (discussed in 6.3.4). Yet the two sorts of thing which are ἀνδρεῖος – brave men, articles of male apparel – do share a conceptual association of a sort, as well as the name: the definitions of (the concepts associated with) both qualities or both types of *qualia* would overlap to some extent, if only minimally, because both stand in some relation to adult human males. So what is needed is a formal, firm and universal distinction between this sort of link, and whatever it is the significations of κόσμος, say, or στοιχεῖον, have in common; and no Stoic responses to this requirement are known.

The surviving Stoic definition does allow for the effects of context on ambiguities (as 4.9 will show), and this would at least be consistent with awareness of the extreme context-

---

[74] The distinction is common today: *e.g.* Lyons 1977: 550ff., who notes the problems it occasions for linguists who want to use relatedness of meaning as a test of the distinction between polysemy and homonymy; also Hirst 1987: 5, Quine 1960: 129f. To my knowledge it has no direct parallel in the ancient world, its other closest (collateral) ancestor being a distinction between homonymy and metaphor (on which see further, 4.7).

sensitivity of Aristotelian-type πρὸς ἓν λεγόμενα; but they, of course, are also systematically related to some basic meaning or concept, and it is precisely the more-or-less fixed set of different relations in which they stand to it which determine the range of possible contextualisations. The definition also marks off "strict" from "non-strict" meanings (4.7); but nothing is known of general Stoic rules for distinguishing them. There are cases too where a description is to be expected but is not to be found. The "true impression", for instance, is one of which a true assertion can be made (Sextus *M*. 2.244 (39G7)), and "true arguments" have true premisses besides being valid (*e.g.* D.L. 7.79 (36A8)), so that the basic concept of the "true" proposition – what is true or false by definition (*e.g.* D.L. 7.65 (34A)) – turns out to be what explains how these other items can be true. Yet the sources do not suggest they were connected explicitly in just this way. Given the Stoic belief in the basic rationality of language, and in the possibility of portraying at least some ambiguities as throwing useful light on important conceptual connections once their meanings are carefully distinguished, it is thus highly puzzling that more effort was apparently not spent on explicit theoretical identification and classification of internal relations between the significations of ambiguous terms. The conclusion which suggests itself most strongly is that the Stoics were not interested in such schemes: that they thought it sufficient to identify particular cases of ambiguity – ones considered important in virtue of their place in theory and teaching – and to clarify their meanings, and the relations between their meanings, on an individual basis. If broad-based investigation into the varieties of ways of meaning was indeed considered unnecessary, perhaps this neglect was unwarranted: for how much may have been lost in terms not only of clearer, more memorable instruction, but of theoretical rigour and precision?

The evidence also forcefully suggests a crucial lack of contact between the early Stoa and Aristotle's work, although ambiguity is not included in Sandbach's list, 1985: 53f., of significant silences – that is, of ideas, themes, arguments, *etc.*, absent from Stoicism, to which thinkers influenced by

Aristotle could reasonably be expected to react in some way. It points too to an important gap in the Platonic Academy's influence over the school. Leaving aside rhetoric and literary criticism, Aristotle's interests in ambiguity can be located in two traditions, to some extent at least centred on the Academy: of using homonymy and ambiguity as general philosophical tools, and of abusing them for their usefulness to sophists. Broadly conceived, the method of looking to ambiguities to solve philosophical puzzles is older than Aristotle; he himself mentions thinkers who solved Eleatic arguments by making *being* or *one* ambiguous (*s. el.* 33.182b13ff.). It is clear too that classification of fallacies as linguistic was already a recognised procedure, and the tradition of writing about sophisms seems to have continued.[75] The Stoa, however, seems to have bypassed systematisation of modes of signifying, in favour of the taxonomy of ambiguity types, while retaining, and taking very seriously indeed, the connection with fallacy. To modern scholars, the extent to which Plato

---

[75] On the first point: note, besides the general boast of originality at 34.183b34ff., the rejection of a dichotomy of fallacies into πρὸς τοὔνομα, "verbal", and πρὸς τὴν διάνοιαν, "semantic" (*s. el.* 10.170b12ff.), attributed to Speusippus by Cherniss 1944: 57, n. 47, although a similar distinction is associated with Protagoras at D.L. 9.52; the rejection also of a classification of "Secundum quid" (*i.e.* "(only) in some respect"), "Accident" and "Many Questions" sophisms as due to ambiguity (17.175b19ff., 24.179b38ff., 30.181b19ff.; the last may be Aristotle's own idea); and the dismissal of a claim, attributed by Poste 1866: 151 to those behind ch. 10's verbal/semantic dichotomy, and so by Cherniss to Speusippus, that all fallacies are due to ambiguity (or, more plausibly in the context, that all *linguistic* fallacies are due to ambiguity) (20.177b7ff.). On the second: Xenocrates is credited with ten books on *Solution of Matters Connected with Arguments* and two books of *Solutions* (D.L. 4.13); Heraclides Ponticus with two books of *Eristic Solutions* and one of *Solutions* (D.L. 5.88); and Theophrastus with a work *On Many ⟨Senses⟩* (and/or *On How Many ⟨Senses⟩*), in which he identified the reverse of Aristotelian amphiboly, that is, cases wøhere a word-compound is unambiguous although one or more of its elements is ambiguous (Alex. *top.* 378.24ff., and further, 6.3.6). He also wrote two books on *Sophisms*, one on *Solution of Syllogisms*, one on *Solutions*, three on the Liar Paradox, and a treatise on the theory of eristic arguments (D.L. 5.42, 45, 47, 49; *cf.* Replici 1977: 185ff., 221f.; Graeser 1973: 2f., 46f.), but very little is known of what he said, not even whether he furthered Aristotle's systematisation of fallacies. Prantl 1855: 39 speculated that Clearchus' *On Riddles* (Wehrli 1948, frr. 31–6) connected riddles with fallacies. Finally, Ebbesen 1981a: 1: 14ff. has argued convincingly that Galen's apparent allusion in his *On Linguistic Sophisms* (ch. 3, 10.6G, 18E, for mode of reference see 5.1.2) to a work or part of a work on fallacies by Eudemus is actually an allusion to the sophist's primer *par excellence*, the *Euthydemus*.

himself endorsed Socrates' low estimate in the *Euthydemus* of the philosophical value of the study of language – the dismissal of the sophists' play on ambiguities as just that ('παιδιά', 'προσπαίζειν', 278b3), and the relegation of 'the correctness of names' and the distinction of near-synonyms, Prodicus' favoured technique, to a lowly propaedeutic position (277e3ff.) – is just one puzzle amongst many posed by the dialogue: its evaluation of Socratic dialectic in relation to sophistic; the extent to which solutions to the eristic puzzles had been developed; the importance attached to their solution; and so on. But in antiquity not only did the usefulness of distinguishing meanings become something of a commonplace (*e.g.* Simplicius *cats.* 237.7ff.; Galen *inst. log.* 17.5ff.; Epictetus *diss.* 1.17.11f.), but the *Euthydemus* itself took on almost textbook status.[76] Given that ambiguity's principle rôle for the Stoics was to be as a source of fallacious reasoning, as will emerge in Chapter Seven, then to that extent they too can be seen as the heirs of the *Euthydemus*. What should be guarded against is any tendency to read Stoic work on ambiguity in the light of Aristotle's.

A glance sideways, at the Stoa's chief Hellenistic rival, the Epicureans, also fails to reveal any traces of contact: a comparison of the Stoic and Epicurean attitudes to ambiguity, and, more broadly, to the philosophical importance of ordinary discourse, will be informative just the same.

It might be objected that Epicurus' work on ambiguity cannot be a useful source of comparisons for the trivial

---

[76] According to Simplicius 'everyone agrees' with what Plato says in it, that 'verbal ambiguity has given dialectic an enormous impetus', since 'there is nothing against sophistic nuisances like the distinction of words', *cats.* 22.11–13 (*cf.* 237.7ff.). The author of the *Didascalicus* (on whom see Witt 1971: 104ff.; Whittaker 1990: VII–XIII) even claims that Plato had described the whole sophistic method in the dialogue, distinguished between linguistic and non-linguistic sophisms, and given their various solutions: 6, p. 159.38–42 Hermann, Whittaker 1990: 14. This view of Plato goes back at least to Eudemus, who is reported as saying that 'Plato, by introducing ambiguity, solved many puzzles about things', 'Πλάτων τε γὰρ εἰσάγων τὸ δισσὸν πολλὰς ἀπορίας ἔλυσεν ἐπὶ τῶν πραγμάτων': Simplicius *phys.* 98.1–3, 242.31–242.3. See also previous note, for a probable reference to the *Euthydemus* by Galen.

reason that none survives. There is certainly no use looking to Epicurus for definitions of ambiguity or of types of ambiguity or of modes of multiple signifying. But the non-existence of such material is no mere accident of transmission. Epicurus rejected definition and division *en masse* as uninformative and redundant (Cicero *fin.* 1.22 (19H); *cf.* anon. *in Theaet.* 22.39ff. (19F); Erotianus 34.10ff. (19G)) – including, presumably, the definition and classification of ambiguity. Probably he plumped instead, where necessary, for "outline descriptions", ὑπογραφαί (*cf.* Asmis 1984: 44), that is, sketches of the initial content of concepts, or of the distinguishing features of types of object, as opposed to the precise and exhaustive definitions which are the outcomes of investigations (*cf.* Asmis 1984: 43, n. 26). The notion of ambiguity may itself have been given this treatment, but there is no evidence as to its content, or for an accompanying classification of types.

Epicurus' famous hostility to dialectic (*e.g.* D.L. 10.31 (19I); Cicero *acad.* 2.97 (20I)) was blamed for his failure to teach 'how ambiguities are distinguished', 'qua via ... ambigua distinguantur', or to fix the meaning of such a key term as *pleasure* despite his frequent assertion 'that the force of words should be carefully expressed', 'diligentia oportere exprimi quae vis subiecta sit vocibus' (Cicero *fin.* 1.6, 22 (19H)). It is especially attractive to follow Sextus' lead (*M.* 7.15) and see Epicurus as rejecting dialectic as conceived of by the Stoics, with its heavy emphasis on the epistemological importance of definition, insistence on identifying the constituents and structures of language and its significations, commitment to linguistic precision in theory and practice, and an assumption of linguistic authority. All that is required in this department of philosophy, according to Epicurus, is a true Canonic (*cf.* Seneca *ep.* 89.11; D.L. 10.29f.) which is underpinned by physics (Cicero *fin.* 1.63). Unlike the Stoics too, Epicurus came to recommend the shunning of innovation and technicality in language as far as possible (*e.g. nat.* 28, 31.14.8–12 (19E, part); D.L. 10.31 (19I); *ep. Hdt.* 72 (7B6)); and this was no mere rhetorical appeal to simplicity. His call for brief, easily-memorable formulae (*ep. Hdt.* 36) is grounded in their practical utility: the rejection of neologism and jargon, in the epistemological priority of basic significations. Here Epicurus' attitude to Stoic-style dialectic, including the distinction of ambiguities, starts to make sense.

His thesis that the basic or ordinary significations of words must form the starting-point for philosophical and scientific investigation was travestied as recommending appeal to the usage of peasants (Cicero *fin.* 2.12, 50). What Epicurus really opposed was a philosopher's or scientist's attempting to to free himself from the legitimate and positive, because largely natural, constraints of ordinary language (D.L. 10.31, 34 (191, J). His own famous description of his methodology[77] lays down that part of what is needed if there is to be something to which puzzles and disputed matters can be referred for judgement is that 'τὰ ὑποτεταγμένα τοῖς φθόγγοις' should be grasped, and that 'the primary thought-content associated with each vocal sound be looked at, and have no further need of any proof' ('τὸ πρῶτον ἐννόημα καθ' ἕκαστον φθόγγον βλέπεσθαι καὶ μηθὲν ἀποδείξεως προσδεῖσθαι', *ep. Hdt.* 37f. (17C); *cf. rat. sent.* 37 (22B2)). This much-disputed passage raises the obvious problems of what these ultimate items of reference are, and why anything 'underlying vocal sounds', or any ἐννοήματα, should be useful and informative, let alone non-arbitrary and authoritative, reference-points.

These prescriptions have their basis in Epicurus' epistemology and theory of the origin of language. Some words still in use were formed and acquired their significations before a more sophisticated civilisation deliberately extended significations, overlaid them with erroneous beliefs, and invented new terms for new, unperceived items. But all naturally-formed words originated as cries in automatic, unreflective response to feelings, πάθη, and to impressions of the external

---

[77] I follow Asmis 1984: 24 in reading *ep. Hdt.* 37f. as a statement of Epicurus' methodology, rather than of his epistemology: but of course the former is premissed on the latter. Although preconceptions are not mentioned until 72f., and the term *idea*, ἐννόημα, is used here instead, this is probably due simply to Epicurus' reluctance to introduce a piece of jargon so early in his exposition: see Asmis 1984: 22; LS 1987: 1: 89; 2: 92.

world, φαντασίαι. These cries then came to be recognised as useful labels for internal states and external objects or states-of-affairs. After this "natural" stage came conscious, communally-based sharpening and clarification, to reduce the impact of redundancy and ambiguity[78] on communication, as well as the introduction of technical meanings or terminologies (*ep. Hdt.* 75f. (19A)). But, as Sedley 1983: 20f. points out, Epicurus is unlikely to be urging either a return to the messy, ambiguous, long-winded sort of discourse men had before they set to work tidying it up, or deferral to the usages of poetry, science, or philosophy, which later invented new, abstract or metaphorical, meanings, and even new words. What one must check is how things really are in the world, using our internal and external perceptions, as we do with any problem (*cf.* Glidden 1983: 218). On the other hand, while particular homonymies were linked with particular bits of faulty reasoning or particular false beliefs (*e.g. nat.* 2, 20 I, pp. 215f. Arr., *nat.* 14, 16 II, pp. 276f. Arr.), there is no sign that Epicurus explicitly included ambiguity in a system for classifying or explaining either such unforced errors or deliberate sophistries. He does seem to have been familiar with the idea that all error may be due to language, but from the brief fragment in which it is mentioned it is impossible to say whether he ever accepted it as his own (*nat.* 28, 31.10.2–12 (19D)). And he appears to have rejected a logical or semantic solution to a version of the Veiled-Father sophism (on which see 7.1), in favour of a response based on the method of "practical reasoning" (ἐπιλογισμός) (Sedley 1973: 71ff.).

The crucial link seems always to be that between words and things in the world – which leaves the nature and rôle of preconceptions unclear. That mental preconceptions and exter-

---

[78] Sedley 1973: 18 suggests that Epicurus' own emphasis on the natural origin of language is partly lost in other Epicurean accounts of the origin of language, such as Usener 334–5, Demetrius Lacon *PHerc.* 1012, col. 45.9–12 (as read by Sedley 1973: 18, n. 89), Lucretius 5.1028–90 (19B), Diogenes of Oenoanda 10.2.11ff. (19C), where no mention is made of the subsequent, deliberate elimination of ambiguity and prolixitiy. The naturalness of language is itself a necessary consequence of the doctrine that there cannot be a preconception of a thing before it exists, so no-one could have invented language: Lucretius 5.181–6, 1046–9 (19B4).

nal objects alike are what 'underlie words' is strongly suggested by *ep. Hdt.* 37f. (17C), and, if so, this can be partly at least explained by the mechanics of Epicurean concept-formation (*cf.* Asmis 1984: 25ff.; but see Glidden 1985 for a quite different view, that "preconceptions", προλήψεις, are objective features of the world which the mind "notices" and which are the *denotata* of words). Certainly their reliability and self-evidence is best explained by adopting one part of Diogenes Laertius' confusing and probably confused account, that they are no more than stored memories of impressions (D.L. 10.33 (17E)), on which internal, unreflective processes of generalisation, abstraction, and assimilation have worked, and through which objects in the world and the types into which they naturally fall can be recognised. In which case it is easy to see why ignoring them, and imposing new significations of one's own on words, would amount to philosophical suicide; to endorse Diodorus Cronus' radical linguistic conventionalism – probably referred to in disparaging terms at *nat.* 28, 31.13.23ff. (19E, part; *cf.* Sedley 1973: 21ff., 41ff., 62ff.), and condemned in the lost *On ambiguity* (mentioned at *nat.* 28, 31.14.26f.) – is to give up science and philosophy altogether, since without such preconceptions no investigation can be begun. Any, even partial, arbitrary departure from 'the words belonging to things' (D.L. 10.31 (19I)) is a step down that dangerous path.[79]

Epicurus' theory of meaning and his account of the origin of language are without doubt crude and inadequate as such.[80] But what they were intended to show is how

---

[79] Epicurus himself, it seems, was willing to risk at least one step along it. At *ep. Men.* 123 (23B3) (*cf.* Cicero *fin.* 1.47) he asserts that the impious man 'is not he who denies the gods of ordinary people, but he who ascribes what the many believe to the gods'. Here Epicurus is distinguishing true preconceptions of the gods from false beliefs about them, a prime example of what can easily be seen as mere ideological arbitrariness in selecting some conceptions as "universal" and "genuine": *cf.* Schofield 1980a: 306f. Epicurus' semantic innovation points beyond itself to a very serious difficulty for his philosophy.

[80] It is here, I think, that Epicurus' contempt for dialectic (and for grammar: Sextus *M.* 1.49, 272) comes home to roost. In particular, he has no theory to explain linguistic or logical structures or their origin – how word-complexes function as linguistic wholes – or how words not related to preconceptions have meaning. All preconceptions appear to be similar in internal structure (*cf.* Asmis 1984: 25, 44f.), or at least little effort is expended on keeping differently-structured ones apart;

correct language use is a necessary condition of the success of scientific inquiry, provided the primary significations have been understood and inquirers are careful to check problems against them. Neologism and semantic innovation are not outlawed altogether – the term πρόληψις, *preconception*, was itself Epicurus' own invention (Cicero *nat. deor.* 1.44 (23E3)) – but a crucial part of the philosopher's duty is to identify and adhere to the basic meanings of the words he employs when initiating and conducting inquiries. The whole project rests on the assumption that these basic meanings are recoverable, that the gold can be sifted from the dross: for example, that the notion of a god's taking any interest in the world can be rejected as spurious on the grounds that it contradicts the genuine preconception of god as a blessed being, free from care (*ep. Men.* 123f., with Lucretius 6.68ff., Cicero *nat. deor.* 1.43ff. (23B, D, E)).

In brief, Epicurean methods of scientific inquiry assess empirical evidence on the basis of a prephilosophical, pretheoretical body of naturally-formed words and meanings deriving its authority from its causal proximity to the external world and to language users' own internal states – the result of what Goldschmidt 1978: 157 calls 'un véritable dédoublement

contrast the careful Stoic statement of the contents of such preconceptions as "man": Cicero *acad.* 2.21 (39C), with Sextus *M.* 11.8–13. Glidden 1985: 199 has claimed that experience – presumably along with the automatic processes of generalisation and abstraction – is what makes it possible for preconceptions to acquire a propositional character; but an explanation is still required of how the quasi-perceptual/perceived *Gestalt* which is a preconception gets to be the semantic content of a sentence. Elsewhere (204), he admits that as far as linguistic structure, syntax, *etc.* are concerned – everything but a simple bearer/name story – 'there really is no such thing as Epicurean semantics'. Plutarch's complaint that Epicurus' rejection of the *lekton* does away with all meaning and discourse (*adv. Col.* 1119F (19K)) is thus only partially answered by the substitution of preconceptions for *lekta* (as suggested by LS 1987: 1: 101). For all its defects, the Stoic theory at least tries to account for how language, and not just naming, is possible. On the other hand, Epicureans and Stoics alike seem to have regarded primary concept-formation as a simple, automatic process of selecting similarities amongst impressions (*e.g.* Cicero *acad.* 2.30 (40NI), *nat. deor.* 1.49 (23E7)), as if similarity were natural, objective and context-free and detecting it natural and involuntary – which is especially curious given the Stoics' criticism of Epicurean epistemology, that it neglects the power of convention (*nat. deor.* 1.81ff.), and given both Epicurean and Stoic claims for the reliability of people's concepts of the gods: see already n. 79.

du monde réel' represented by the *simulacra*, and thus by the preconceptions which, somehow, they go to form.[81] The Stoics also assigned great importance to preconceptions, and thus implicitly conceded ordinary usage some authority, while allowing for their clarification, correction, and expansion. Epicureans and Stoics alike claimed universality, and thus natural authoritativeness, for their favoured preconceptions – of god, for instance – the former distinguishing naturally acquired ideas from culturally-determined false beliefs, the latter splitting natural preconceptions away from non-natural conceptions.[82] Here it is tempting to cry: a distinction without a difference. But there is a fundamental disagreement involved. Stoics did not see preconceptions as bed-rock reference-points to which all scientific inquiry must ultimately be referred. Of course, ordinary preconceptions had to be conceded some measure of truth, since to do otherwise would be to contradict Stoic confidence in the ultimate reliability of the natural human cognitive apparatus. Such untrained, untested conceptions will, however, be incomplete, and inadequate for the purpose of achieving comprehensive and systematic understanding. They must be supplemented by the technical conceptions defined by the doctrines of Stoic philosophy, and

---

[81] It seems that preconceptions were also criterial in the sense of being employed in settling everyday, nonscientific inquiries: at D.L. 10.33 (17E4) the matter to be settled is 'Is that thing standing over there a horse or a cow?', a simple case of identifying a macroscopic object. Schofield 1980a: 295 has argued that this is not so for Chrysippus (esp. D.L. 7.54 (40A3)), who, he claims, restricted preconceptions' criterial (and mainly negative) rôle to philosophical investigation. But Schofield's case rests on what is surely an implausible distinction between the informational content of an impression and its being reported in language. The impressions of a mature rational adult will be informed by the conceptions she has, including, most fundamentally, her naturally-acquired preconceptions; despite a common origin, they will be qualitatively different from the impressions of a child precisely because the latter lacks the conceptions that constitute rationality: Aetius 4.11.1ff. (= S.V.F. 2.83 (39E, esp. §4)). This "informing", I take it, operates at two levels. At a physical level, conceptions – ἐννοήσεις, ἔννοιαι – are physical objects, that is, stored impressions (Plutarch *comm. not.* 47.1084F–1085A (39F)), which will variously "match" parts of those complex alterations of the mind which are impressions. At a semantic level, impressions are given quasi-linguistic, transmissible content by *lekta*, which themselves correspond (indirectly) to concepts, as well as to things in the world; concepts, ἐννοήματα, are themselves articulated in meaningful discourse or *logos*.

[82] See n. 79.

organised into a coherent whole – processes which may well involve the distinction of hitherto unrecognised ambiguities. Thus, the Stoics famously contended that the conception of the good is natural (D.L. 7.53 (60C)); but what this means is that 'nature has given us the seeds of knowledge' of such matters (Seneca *ep.* 120.3 (60E2)), and specifically that people already understand the connection of the good with what is natural (Cicero *fin.* 3.33f. (60D)) and beneficial (Sextus *M.* 11.22 (60G1)), not that they already possess the elaborate knowledge of the meanings of *good* described by Sextus (see p. 105, above). In other words, *good* will pass from non-technical to technical status in a speaker's usage as he acquires a Stoic education. Ordinary conceptions may also be encrusted with irrelevant and misleading accretions, or embedded in faultily constructed schemes: associating the good with bodily comforts or worldly success, for example. The Stoa's sophisticated conceptual constructs, supported by complex argumentation, in which distinction of ambiguities plays such an important rôle, make no concessions to, and have no use for, ordinary language, however purified. What has been seen of the Stoa's assumption of independent authority in ordinary as well as in philosophical usage is full evidence of that; and when Chrysippus exploited ordinary linguistic and paralinguistic behaviour as philosophical resources, it was as plausible supports, not as privileged foundations, for his favoured doctrines.

I turn now to modern comparisons.

It should already be clear that the Stoic attitude to ambiguities is also profoundly different from that of modern linguistic philosophers. Ordinary significations of terms are not unworthy of attention – as is shown by their being included in explanations of ambiguities – but superior status will be given to the pronouncements of Stoic philosophical doctrine, which confidently assign significations to terms drawn alike from ordinary language and from the terminology of philosophy. The Stoa is simply not in the business of making the explication of ordinary usages a central philosophical project, of taking such linguistic investigations as starting-points for the ultimate goal of regulating and organising concepts.

As for knowledge of the meanings of technical terms, including ambiguities, in philosophy, it is plain, but unsurprising, that they did not constitute a separate category of philosophical knowledge. Knowing the "real" significations of, say, κόσμος, world(-order), γράμμα, letter, or ἀδιάφορον, indifferent, is not a component of ordinary linguistic knowledge (although linguistic knowledge is necessary for their correct use), and is not to be had without understanding of the physical, ethical, and logical theories in which the associated concepts are nested. But knowing what the technical terms of any discipline or science mean is, in large part, simply a matter of absorbing definitions, theses, and arguments relating to the correct use of such terms in technical discourse. I take it that Stoics saw themselves as usefully bringing to light categories which might well been hidden by the surface forms of language; and that they subscribed, perhaps as a matter of explicit philosophical policy, to the psychological importance of correct and precise verbal distinctions.[83] They certainly thought such distinctions important enough to introduce a number of their own, and, along with a closely related

---

[83] Two Chrysippean terminological innovations – ἀληθορκεῖν, swear truly, εὐσυνθετεῖν keep faith (in a contract or agreement) – and one semantic innovation – for ψευδορκεῖν, swear falsely – deserve attention. Evans 1974: 45ff., nn. 2, 3 argues that they reflect an interest in Austinian performatives, with Chrysippus wanting to make (more) obvious at the linguistic level the distinction between whether what is promised (sworn, contracted) actually comes to pass, and whether the promise (oath, contract) is kept (that is, whether one promises well or amiss). But they could have another explanation, one which does not ascribe to Chrysippus any such concern with pragmatics, and which rather calls on two doctrines independently known to be as important as they were controversial. He may want to show how the two Stoic principles of bivalence (every proposition's being true or false) and of individual moral responsibility, for the keeping of oaths as in other areas, can be reconciled. At the time of promising (swearing, contracting), the proposition about the future state-of-affairs which the promise contemplates is already true or false (what Evans calls the 'purely predictive element in swearing', 45). But this does not absolve promisors from responsibility for fulfilling or not fulfilling their promises, since they still have or lack the intention of fulfilling them, and since it is up to them whether the state-of-affairs comes about (or fails to come about) as a result of their actions rather than of some other cause.

formalistic tendency in logic,[84] this laying down of the linguistic law met with a great deal of exasperation, and open mockery, from the school's rivals and commentators. Alexander, for example, (*top.* 301.19ff. (part, 27B)) sees the Stoic insistence that the verb *be* apply only to bodies as a case of mere lexical legislation ('νομοθετήσαντες αὐτοῖς'). Inwood 1985a: 145 mildly chastises the school for failing to introduce a new word for the sorts of pleasure and pain which are not bodily sensations, but voluntary mental states; the criticism seems appropriate, whether or not justified, precisely because of the Stoics' reputation for neologism.

Complaints about this tendency would be soundest where the distinctions might be understood as arbitrarily distorted interpretations of actual usages. It is not always clear, however, that this was truly a Stoic flaw. Plutarch *comm. not.* 21.1068D–1070B wants to show that 'in their enthusiasm for neologism', 'ἐπιθυμίᾳ καινολογίας', the Stoics will go to any lengths, even self-contradiction, to overturn the "common notions" whose champions they none the less claim to be. If Chrysippus really had been playing fast and loose with ordinary conceptions – for example, claiming that these distinctions are what ordinary speakers would themselves introduce to explain their usages – then Plutarch's criticism would be justified. In fact, more subtly if no more convincingly, Chrysippus' self-confessed aim was to back up distinctions

---

[84] For criticisms of Stoic logical formalism, see Porphyry *ap.* Amm. *int.* 73.19ff.; Boethius *hyp. syll.* 1, III. 4; Alex. *an. pr.* 264.14f.; Galen *inst. log.* 1.4, 5 (Galen's indifference to the different names for premisses), 4.4, 4.6 (the importance of using good, pure, clear, Greek); *cf. diff. puls.* 2.10, 8.631K, (=*S.V.F.* 2.24); and see n. 61 above. Presumably Stoic too are Ptolemy's targets at *crit.* 4.5–6, p. 8, ll. 5ff. Lammert (with Blank 1982: 35 and n. 57). Despite Galen's objections to Chrysippean formalism in his use of the logical connectives at *inst. log.* 4.6, Brunschwig's analysis of Sextus *M.* 8.128 suggests that extra-logical considerations may have been relevant to the Stoic conception of the conjunction: one whose conjuncts are all true is a "better" conjunction than one not of this kind, 1978: 65f. Aulus Gellius *noct. att.* 16.3.12f. (probably a passage of Stoic origin) imposes a comparable constraint on the disjunction: 'omnia autem quae disiunguntur pugnantia esse inter sese oportet ... Ex omnibus quae disiunguntur unum esse verum debet, falsa cetera', 'but all disjuncts ought to conflict amongst themselves ... Of all disjuncts, one alone should be true, the others false'. On the Sextus passage, see also p. 124 below. The Stoa was much criticised for introducing purely verbal distinctions; thus, Cicero *fin.* 5.89 attacks the Stoic use of *good* (above, n. 60).

already and independently sanctioned by the principles of Stoic philosophy; and the difficulty was that he could not consistently claim to find genuine evidence of – only plausible support for – such distinctions in current usage.

Galen complains several times (*e.g. inst. log.* 3.2, 3.5; also *meth. med.* 10.55 K) of what he regards as empty "verbalism", of redundant coinages and baseless semantic distinctions – although, at least in the context of a primer, his impatience is directed rather at useless finessing of the fine old Greek tongue, and he seems not to have been altogether successful in separating disdain for Chrysippus' foreign origins from indignation at unwarranted and philosophically perilous linguistic invention.[85] His interpretation of one of Chrysippus' descriptions of the emotions is detailed enough to be instructive (*P.H.P.* 4.2.8ff, p. 240, ll. 11ff.). Chrysippus wants "passions" or "bad emotions", πάθη, to be "irrational", ἄλογα, movements of the soul in the sense that they are 'not obedient to reason' (*e.g.* 4.2.12, p. 240, ll. 23f.); the other sense of *irrational* is something like "reasoning badly" (ll. 26f.). Galen, while praising Chrysippus for his careful avoidance of ambiguity here at least (4.2.20, p. 242, ll. 14ff.; but *cf.* 4.3.9f., p. 248, ll. 28ff., 4.4.8, p. 252, ll. 16ff.), and accepting a distinction between emotion and error (esp. 4.2.28, p. 244, ll. 10ff.), rejects Chrysippean moral psychology, and argues that passions are irrational in that they occur in, or are states of, some irrational part or power of the soul (*e.g.* 4.4.5, p. 250, ll. 29ff.). Chryippus' language, he claims, is ambiguous and contrary to normal usage, because there are only two possible meanings of ἄλογος: "lacking reason altogether" (of non-human animals, and certain putative non-rational states or powers of the human soul); and "having one's reason in a bad and blameworthy condition" (of humans who possess the faculty of reason, but misapply it); this is one case of a systematic ambiguity of words formed with the privative prefix ἀ- (4.4.9ff., p. 252, ll. 20ff.).

What is more, Galen asserts that Chrysippus is aware of

---

[85] See previous note, and also n. 61.

this fact about *irrational*, and that he and the Stoics 'profess to be explaining the language' of the Greeks (4.4.15f., p. 254, ll.10f.). The first claim he supports with a passage from Chrysippus' *Cure of the Passions* (4.4.16f., p. 254, ll. 13ff.; *cf.* 4.4.23, p. 256, ll. 2ff.) where the way in which people – ordinary people, it seems – say that the emotions are movements of the soul "contrary to nature", παρὰ φύσιν, is called 'not inappropriate', 'οὐκ ἀπὸ τρόπου', 'since all such movements and states are disobedient to reason and reject it; accordingly we say too that such individuals [*i.e.* ones in the grip of a passion] are moved irrationally, not as reasoning badly, as someone might use the word with respect to being the opposite of [reasoning] well, but with respect to the rejection of reason' (*cf.* 4.2.12, p. 240, ll. 26f., 4.4.23, p. 256, ll. 1f.). So the appropriateness of Galen's critical intervention depends, in part, on Chrysippus' purpose. Chrysippus may indeed have wanted to explicate the normal meaning(s) of *irrational*, in which case Galen's refusal to admit a third (or fourth), specifically Stoic, signification would be correct (assuming always that his report of Greek idiom is reliable). But if, instead, Chrysippus were appealing to some non-standard use of the term, one in accordance with Stoic doctrine only, or were making an implicit distinction between what speakers mean and what they say or think they mean, then it would be inappropriate to convict him of getting ordinary usage wrong, whether wilfully or out of ignorance.

In the passage in which Galen explicitly considers the standard use of *irrational*, what Chrysippus is doing, quite clearly, is offering an explanation of why 'some people', 'τινων' (4.4.16, p. 254, l. 14), say that the passions are 'contrary to nature', 'παρὰ φύσιν' (l. 15): they are 'disobedient to reason' (l. 16). Chrysippus cannot seriously have believed that, when ordinary speakers of Greek called an emotion, such as fear or desire, "contrary to nature", what they would have said if asked what they meant was that it was "disobedient to reason". The precise correlation of human nature with rationality is Stoic, and technical, not a feature of ordinary concepts or of everyday discourse. (If it were, Stoic philosophy would never have needed inventing.) Chrysippus' explanation of this use of the phrase may fail to convince, but it constitutes a philosophical thesis, couched in terms of a Stoic metaphysical and psychological scheme: it is not a description of what a native Greek speaker would have said about standard use of the phrase. Chrysippus adds that 'we say such persons [*sc.* those in the grip of a passion] are irrationally moved', 'ἀλόγως φαμὲν φέρεσθαι τοὺς τοιούτους' (1. 17); here, 'we say' might be 'we Stoics say', not 'we Greeks say', and there may be no need to take the contrast with the sense "reasoning badly" as calling to mind some other item in a list of standard Greek significations of the term.

Elsewhere Chrysippus certainly does offer an explanation of 'ordinary usage too' (*cf.* 'καὶ ἐν τῷ ἔθει', 4.2.12, p. 240, l. 25):

... it is with respect to this [*sc.* irrational, disobedient to reason] movement [*sc.* in the soul] that in ordinary usage too we say that certain persons are pushed and moved irrationally without reason ⟨and⟩ judgement; for we do not use these words as if ⟨a person in such a condition⟩ is moved erroneously, disregarding something which is in accordance with reason, but most of all with reference to the movement he describes, it not being natural for the rational creature to be moved thus in his soul, but in accordance with reason. (4.2.12, p. 240, ll. 24–9).

Here the claim that 'we use these words' [*sc. irrational, irrationally*]', 'ταῦτ' ἐπισημαινόμεθα' (l. 27), is obviously a claim as to how "we ordinary speakers" use words. But again there is no good reason to convict Chrysippus of reading Stoic theses into what people say they mean, the intuitive judgements about usages which they would themselves offer to justify and explain their linguistic behaviour. I have already described Chrysippus' use of ordinary linguistic and paralinguistic behaviour, the method sketched earlier as part of a sort of Stoic "ordinary language philosophy", premissed on the Stoic belief that scattered fragments of truths about the world lie hidden in ordinary persons' frequently messy, unreflective habits of speech and thought. Here Chrysippus is offering to explain the intuition that *irrational* does not always mean, and cannot always be explained as meaning, "reasoning badly", by bringing in a Stoic idea, namely that the passions are move-ments of the soul which are "disobedient to reason". The link between this and the intuition is that ordinary people would agree that such movements are "unnatural" for rational beings. What Chrysippus does not claim (wisely) is that what people mean – that is, what they would say they meant – is that such movements are unnatural in so far as they are disobedient to reason. The passions' being irrational movements in *that* sense is what explains the intuition: it does not itself constitute the intuition. This way of speaking could indeed reflect a prethe-oretical conviction that for human beings to behave "irratio-nally" is for them to behave "contrary to nature" precisely in that they are suffering some unnatural disturbance of their entire, wholly rational, souls (the φορά which is at the core of Chrysippus' explanation: see ll. 21f., 27f.). But the Greek idiom is just as consistent with the idea that such "irrational" persons have lost control of the non-rational – child-like or bestial – parts of their souls, and the "irrationality" in ques-tion might as well lie in these psychic parts' lack of reason as in their or the entire soul's disobedience to it. So it is surely significant that Chrysippus is careful never to locate this "movement" any more precisely than as being 'in' or 'of the soul', 'κατὰ τὴν ψυχήν' (4.2.12, p. 240, ll. 28f.), 'ψυχῆς' (4.2.18, p. 242, l. 11). In brief, Chrysippus is using ordinary language to justify his psychological monism only in that he illustrates the consistency between his psychological theory and the intuitive behaviour and judgements it can explain.

A comparable accusation – that of introducing private mean-ings and thus creating unacknowledged ambiguities – is made against the Stoa by Alexander in his *de fato*. Alexander no-where names his opponents, but the consensus is that they are Stoics (*cf.* Sharples 1983: 19), and in the particular cases which interest us they are Stoics almost beyond doubt. Alexander's complaint is that his opponents have assigned their own meaning to the terms τύχη, *luck*, and τὸ αὐτόματον, *chance*, viz., "a cause obscure to human reasoning", and similarly to the phrase τὸ ἐφ’ ἡμῖν, *that which is up to us/depends on us/in our power*, viz., "that which comes about through us" (173.13ff., esp. 174.1–3; 181.7ff. (part, 62G), 211.30ff.). The former definition, although not a Stoic invention, was adopted by the school (*e.g.* Simplicius *phys.* 333.1ff. (= *S.V.F.* 2.965)); the latter is clearly Stoic doctrine: *e.g.* Cicero *fat.* 41–3 (62C5–10), Aulus Gellius *noct. att.* 7.2.6ff. (62D). The Stoics thus fail, Alexander charges, to preserve anything of ordinary usage but the words themselves (173.26f., 182.23f.). How fair are these criticisms? As Alexander is attacking determinism in general, and not even Stoic determinism in particular, it would be optimistic, perhaps, to expect a full and balanced exposition of the Stoic theory. It is certainly possible to mount a defence on the Stoa's behalf.

If the Stoics had argued that they were preserving the standard intensions or concepts associated with *chance*, *luck*, and *up to us* then they would indeed be open to attack. Yet they may well have sought to preserve only the extension of those concepts: that is, they may have re-allocated the range of events which would fall under the term *luck* as standardly used to a new concept, "cause obscure to human reason", and have argued that they are commonly attributed, out of ignorance, to luck or chance as vulgarly understood; and likewise in the case of τὸ ἐφ’ ἡμῖν, it turns out that where people believe they have the power of 'choosing the opposite' of what they do (181.5f., 211.32f.), they in fact do not – rather fate is acting through choices and actions determined by character. Alexander offers his own explanation of what luck is (172.17ff.), couched in a philosophical jargon no ordinary person, presumably, would or could employ in explaining what he or she meant by *luck*, together with several clear cases to which the word would ordinarily be applied (172.15ff., esp. 23–5), and a comparable account of τὸ ἐφ’ ἡμῖν, based on how 'everyone' understands human nature (178.8ff., esp. 17–20). But that people use the words in question to mean something else, that they have different concepts determining their correct application in ordinary language (whatever weight is attached to their own explanations of their meanings, and whatever relation these have to what philosophers say about what they mean), would not affect the Stoic position.

Of course, if the Stoics are indeed flouting 'the common and natural conceptions' (172.17, cf. 4–6; 182.20–2) of all men, then this breach must be explained and isolated (how can people be so wrong? if wrong in this case, why not in others too, where the Stoics accept the relevant concepts as correct and reliable? how do such wrong concepts come into being?). They will not, however, be guilty of sophistry, of deliberately misleading their hearers with ambiguities, as Alexander asserts (173.22f., 182.29–31). If they are doing away with lucky events and with freedom of choice or responsibility as ordinarily understood (173.27–174.1), then the mere fact that people commonly believe in such things is no defence – unless all ordinary concepts constitute wholly reliable, accurate pieces of knowledge about the world. If other philosophers share these beliefs in their capacity as ordinary perceivers and knowers, their profession can confer no privileges; if as philosophers, their views are open to philosophical challenge; and if as philosophers they defend the reliability of the views of the many or the wise, the ἔνδοξα, then their position is equally vulnerable, in the general as in the particular.

Chrysippus could never have contemplated the possibility of being stymied by ordinary usage. The existence of workaday meanings of a word or phrase could, at most, produce an ambiguity: they cannot themselves be appealed to against a Stoic innovation, for this is guaranteed by other, far loftier and securer, sources of knowledge. Stoics could appeal to homely idioms to support sophisticated logical ideas – Sextus reports (*M.* 8.128) their defence of the idea that a conjunction which contains even a single false conjunct is not "sound", ὑγιές, by a comparison with the ordinary practice of calling "unsound" a garment with the smallest tear in its fabric[86] – without compromising their philosophy's power to reveal semantic distinc-

---

[86] *Cf.* Brunschwig 1978: 65f.

tions, or questioning the propriety and usefulness of capturing these by neologism. Similarly, Stoics never dreamed that philosophy's principal task was to study, analyse, or describe so imperfect and so limited an instrument as language. Assumption of linguistic authority is not unique to the Stoa, of course,[87] and introduction of new terms or of new significations is proper if precise, informative, backed by cogent argument, and employed expressly and solely to provide technical terms or meanings. The sheer breadth and quantity of Stoic innovation on both fronts are unusual none the less.

A final comparison with another modern discipline in which ambiguity has a key rôle to play will round off this attempt to supply Stoic theorising about it with a richer, more intelligible context. It can be briefly stated. Ambiguities were not interpreted by Stoics as important features of natural languages to be described and explained by grammarians or linguists: today, they are widely used as devices for formulating and testing theoretical descriptions of natural languages or fragments of natural languages, and one of the explicit purposes of most such descriptions is to account for native speakers' intuitions of and about ambiguous utterances and inscriptions, by assigning different lexical or syntactic structures to ambiguous sentences. Ambiguity is, in fact, to be reckoned a cardinal linguistic property, alongside grammaticality, meaningfulness, and synonymy.[88] Of course, it would be as much a waste of time to look in Stoic – or any ancient – theorising about language for analysis or reconstruction of the native speaker's intuitive capacity to detect and understand ambiguities or other linguistic features, as to expect accounts of the connections and distinctions between semantic and pragmatic ambiguities or of the complexities of discourse disambiguation.[89] But also

---

[87] Thus, Simplicius defends Aristotle against Nicostratus' charge that it is absurd to disapprove of the idiom ἔχεσθαι γυναῖκα, *having a wife*, on the grounds that in mentioning and judging ordinary usage, 'τὸ ἐν τῷ ἔθει', he is simply fulfilling the function of the dialectician: *cats.* 371.23ff.

[88] On ambiguity's rôles in modern linguistics: ch. 1, pp. 18–21.

[89] As explored by *e.g.* Bach and Harnish 1979: 4f., 20ff., 80, 101f., 244f.; *cf.* Sperber and Wilson 1986: 13, 34, 188.

lacking from Stoic linguistic theory is a descriptive account of the full range of the grammatical and syntactic properties and structures, of ancient Greek, or Latin, or "language" as a whole.

It is surely no coincidence that the only extensive information available about Stoic syntactic theory (from Porphyry, as reported by Ammonius *int.* 44.19ff. = *S.V.F.* 2.184 (33q)) is restricted to the proposition and to the subject–predicate relation, both of fundamental importance to Stoic metaphysics and logic. Stoic syntactic theory, which primarily governs relations within and between *lekta* (see 6.5.2), looks hopelessly inadequate for determining the "regularity" or "concinnity", καταλληλότης, of any given *logos*, the task implicitly assigned it by the definition of solecisms at D.L. 7.59; and this is so even though any concept of ambiguity, including the Stoic one, must presuppose adequate independent criteria for grammaticality or acceptability – that is, for what are to count as genuine utterances of the language in which the ambiguity occurs (see 4.3). The incompleteness and crudeness of Stoic syntactic theory surely reflect the school's overriding concern with structures relevant to the operations of logic, and its very alien concept of the relation between the objects of logical and of linguistic theorising. *Lekta* are of fundamental importance not because they form part of the – now central – philosophical-cum-linguistic project of constructing a systematic, comprehensive, detailed theory of meaning for natural languages, but because they are supposed to explain the publicness of linguistic meaning, and hence the possibilities of communication, instruction, and the acquisition of knowledge through language, and, in the last analysis, the possibility too of a systematic ascent to a state of moral perfection and perfect happiness. I shall return to these crucial, basic differences between modern and Stoic conceptions of syntax and semantics in 6.2.3 and 6.3.5.2.

It is not even clear, in fact, that Stoics would have conceded such abilities to ordinary speakers, at least in a full or strict sense, precisely because they lacked the theoretical knowledge (of definitions, classifications, *etc.*), as well as the guided and organised experience of discourse, which are only to be had by dialectical training. Stoic dialectic is able to distinguish what is said ambiguously (D.L. 7.47 (31B7)), as if nothing else could, and no person but the man with dialectical knowledge – an extraordinary claim, whose remarkableness lies rather in its ambition than its uniqueness. Behind it lie Stoicism's pretentions to authoritativeness in philosophy, in the principles of science, and in all linguistic matters. The Stoa prescribes the constituents of speech and writing, correct grammatical categories and the properties of their members, the true nature and varieties of syntax, the rules for grammatical correctness, and the proper definition and classification of ambiguity. Ordinary people have only a sorry approximation to the true dialectician's faultless knowledge of his language, and their meagre abilities have no intrinsic interest, except in proving god's beneficence even to us lowly, but still rational, creatures, and in providing plausible support for Stoic theories. Like all ancient workers in the field of language, the Stoics were not concerned either to construct a grammar for explaining native-speaker intuitions about their own language, or to accommodate ambiguity within a formal model of a language-system or a semantic theory for natural languages.

The Stoics' assumption of authoritativeness on linguistic matters such as purity and ambiguity is to be ultimately explained by their confidence in their philosophical system as a whole. So, in a different way, is the belief that their philosophy is also empowered to prescribe meanings for terms employed by the individual sciences, some of them directly shared with philosophy – meanings (both scope and intension) which would presumably have been fixed exclusively by the doctrines of Stoicism. The early years of the school seem not to have been marked by a deep or formative interest in mathematics or the other sciences, but later texts assert their subordination to philosophy, and this presumably extended to terminology as well.[90] Stoics could also claim

---

[90] This is strongly implied by D.L.'s (7.132f.) and especially Seneca's (*ep.* 88.25ff. (26F), =(part) fr. 90EK; probably Posidonian: *cf.* Kidd 1978: 8–10) account of the

authoritativeness for their definition of ambiguity as a criterion to be used by all scientists, as well as by philosophers (see 7.6). A training in dialectic, partly precisely in virtue of the firm definition of ambiguity which it provides and explains, would also ensure that control of assent which is as important to investigative scientists as to philosophers.

Whether the Stoics would have been justified in their faith in the usefulness of their definition depends in part on what emerges from the examination of it in the next chapter. Account must also be taken the fact that it seems to have been called on to function as a criterion of ambiguity in all types of discourse – which in turn is to assume that such a universal definition is possible; and so it must also be asked whether, in principle, any definition of ambiguity can be formulated that is not directed to some specific purpose, but is comprehensive in scope, embracing all forms and subjects of discourse. This is another of the questions which the following chapter will address.

3.6 Conclusions

One modern linguist has characterised most premodern interest in ambiguity as typically "practical": ambiguities were seen as important because they threatened some "practical" project, such as arguing well, or composing good, clear prose, which is how Aristotle and Quintilian, for example, approached them (Kooij 1971: 1ff.). For this to be true of the Stoa, we must specify carefully how *practical* is to be understood. Like other Hellenistic philosophies, Stoicism was above all a theory for expounding and recommending a way

relation between philosophy and the special sciences, which are not part of philosophy, as logic is, but its necessary instruments. It is suggested too by the Stoic explanation of the relation between philosophy and logic, as contrasted with that between medicine and logic: Ammonius *an. pr.* 8.20ff., 9.1ff. (part, 26E). Philo *cong. erud. gratia* 146 (= *S.V.F.* 2.99) makes similar claims for philosophy's importance, by its providing definitions of the basic theoretical items deployed by geometry, logic, and grammar (*cf.* n. 49). As for Chrysippus, he seems to assume that philosophers and doctors will employ the same general methods of inquiry and argument, sense-perception (including self-perception) and syllogism from τεκμήρια, "proofs" or "pieces of evidence": see Galen *P.H.P.* 3.1.10ff., p. 170, ll. 9ff.

of life; it was a systematic assault on what was perceived as the principal problem of human existence, that of achieving and sustaining a happy life. At this level of generality, the Stoa can be said to have distinguished itself from its predecessors and rivals alike by its motives for taking ambiguity as philosophically important. Since happiness consists in moral goodness, and human good is perfected rationality, any failure to recognise ambiguities in philosophical argument, disquisition, or exposition, can result, not in some minor intellectual error – a botched definition or a shaky conclusion – but, by way of deep conceptual confusions, in blocking access to the truths and supporting proofs which systematically define and explain the governing principles of the universe, and the comprehension of which guarantees correct, successful conduct of an individual life.

That goal is, in one sense, "practical"; its location within a profoundly rationalist and moralistic "philosophy of life", however, and its promise of achievement through complex and subtle theoretical analysis of the properties of language, makes wholly inappropriate a comparison with Quintilian's professional interest, or even with Aristotle's classification of linguistic fallacies in the *s. el.* – although not with the monumental discovery and application of the notion of πρὸς ἕν λεγόμενα. It might be objected that other Hellenistic schools, above all the Epicureans, also offered a "philosophy of life", and thus could have shared the Stoa's motivation. I have tried to show that the Epicurean assessment of the importance of all dialectical matters, including the treatment of ambiguity and of ordinary language, was very different, and for reasons which go to the heart of the epistemological, methodological, and philosophical disagreements between the two schools.

Besides its "practical" motivation for studying the topic at all, what may seem most alien and implausible about the Stoa's attitude to ambiguities is its confidence, its authority, or authoritarianism, according to one's taste. The Stoa is sure that it has identified all major ambiguities, not by analysing usages, questioning users, comparing Greek with other languages, or by other essentially linguistic or pragmatic

129

techniques, but by application of substantive doctrines independently arrived at. The school's assurance that its identifications were correct had to be secured by mastery of relevant background material in grammar, semantics, and associated disciplines; and in one field, certainly, where comparisons are proper only with Aristotle himself, the Stoa towered above all its Hellenistic rivals: in the power and precision of its technical work in definition and classification. It is to the first part of this programme to which I now turn.

4

THE STOIC DEFINITION OF AMBIGUITY

4.1 Sources

The only securely Stoic definition of ambiguity to survive is preserved by Diogenes Laertius 7.62 (37P). Its author is not identified. Crinis, who dates from the late second century B.C.E., is credited with the definition of "partition", μερισμός, which immediately precedes it; but since Chrysippus, Diogenes of Babylon, Antipater, and Posidonius are all cited as authorities in this same section of Diogenes' account of Stoic philosophical doctrine, they too must be reckoned amongst the candidates for authorship. At all events, as observed in Chapter Two, Diogenes' debt is obviously to some unusual, and unusually well-informed, source; and so it is obvious too that the definition he records must be granted special status, of the same high order, despite its humble and rather obscure doxographical origins, as the rest of the second account. The Suda reports the same definition *s.v. ἀμφιβολία* (*ed.* Adler, vol. I, p. 152), with one important omission (of the condition that significations belong to the same usage), and a couple of lesser changes (in the explanation of the example).

The definition itself, at least at first blush, appears to boast the qualities of precision and formality for which Stoic dialectic was honoured – or reviled – in antiquity. It is also dense and, at least today, obscure; it is not even clear why it has the position it does in Diogenes' account(s) of dialectic. It has been put in the part of dialectic whose subject-matter is "vocal sound", φωνή, and its subdivisions, primarily human vocalisations, the rational utterances which articulate in language the contents of the world and of speakers' minds. What is puzzling is that it should apparently find itself out on a limb, at the very close of Diogenes' exposition, after definitions of definition, 7.60 (32C1–3), and of various modes of logical division, 7.61f. (32C5–8, 30C); the juxtaposition of the definition with these is so striking that an easy first response is to see our definition as "state-of-the-art", paraded as a paradigm of what the Stoic technique of ὁρισμός can achieve.[1] Allowances must anyway be made for distortion of the original Stoic ordering of their material, as well as for Diogenes' adaptations and abbreviations of his immediate source(s). Part of the earlier account's list of dialectical topics runs: '... poems, and ambiguities, and euphonic vocal sound, and music, and definitions, according to some, and divisions, and expressions' (7.44), as if ambiguity really belonged with stylistics. Ambiguity's being listed in two different places in the two accounts might be explained either by Diogenes' having relied on different sources, or by his having carelessly selected from one comprehensive survey two different and incompatible, but equally authentic, organisations of the contents of dialectic and logic.

There is certainly no reason to believe that ambiguity's rôle in an account of the virtues and vices of style (which is the rôle apparently assigned it at 7.44) exhausted its interest for the Stoa.[2] The definition's isolation in 7.62 can be interpreted rather as a sign that ambiguity was taken to have bearings on a number of issues and problems within dialectic. Its potential impact on an agent's moral welfare, and its complex interconnections (described in the previous chapter) with epistemology, formal logic, and stylistics, make it impossible to subordinate it to any single topic or discipline within dialectic's broad sweep. That it falls within this part of dialectic, rather than in the part which deals with the σημαινόμενα of linguistic items, is pretty well self-explanatory (ambiguity is by

---

[1] The definition seems to be yet another illustration of the Stoics' rejection of a Platonic model of definition, that by way of division; it is striking that in Diogenes' account definition and division are nowhere explicitly linked. Known Stoic definitions rarely conform to Platonic precepts; those of sign and of proof at Sextus *P.H.* 2.104 (35C1), 135 (36B1) are two important examples.

[2] Mansfeld 1986: 367 claims the section on ambiguity as no more than a *Nachtrag* to Stoic grammatical doctrine, probably displaced from that on poetry. Given ambiguity's importance elsewhere, this is implausible, as this book is intended to show.

definition a linguistic phenomenon (4.3)); but to grasp the meaning and scope of some of its elements, the account of *lekta* and of their complexes must be put to use, just as it must be to understand the classifications. This interconnectedness is no accident. It is a foreseen and desired outcome of the unity and unified purpose of the logical portion of Stoic doctrine, from epistemology, through phonetics and grammar, to philosophical and formal logic.

4.2 The use of definitions

According to Galen, the Stoics whose classification of ambiguity types he records also produced a definition of ambiguity, but he neither reports it nor attributes the list to any Stoic or Stoics by name. Galen's only comment is that scrutinising the numerous conflicts between his and the Stoic views 'belongs to another discipline', a curious observation which perhaps suggests a certain methodological naiveté.[3] Although, as noted in Chapter One, native speakers of natural languages do seem to have a pretheoretical notion of ambiguity (in that they will intuitively recognise and even label certain utterances as ambiguous), at the theoretical level it cannot be treated outside a semantic and syntactic model, whether with universal application or tied to a particular language; and the strengths and weaknesses of any definition, and of any associated taxonomy, will be determined in part by the qualities of the model to which it is bound. Even an apparently straightforward decision to accept as the extension of *ambiguous* only such utterances or inscriptions or other items as are acknowledged as ambiguous by native speakers is a theoretical decision (*cf.* Scheffler 1979: 2f.). In the context of modern linguistic theory, for example, different theoretical descriptions of a language (-system) will produce different definitions of ambiguity and different lists of ambiguities (*cf.* Lyons 1977: 400).

---

[3] *De sophismatis* ch. 4, 12.15–17G, 21E (for text and mode of reference: 5.1.2, 5.1.3). Galen proposes to pass by the Stoic definition 'even if it seems to conflict with many of our [views? ambiguity modes?],' 'πρὸς πολλὰ τῶν ἡμετέρων', as if this would have no impact on the scope of the Stoic classification.

Of course, criteria of adequacy for any definition must be formulated independently of attempts to construct particular definitions, and the Stoa is known to have offered just such criteria.

Another necessary condition for classification is to have some prior, theoretically-grounded – even if not explicit, comprehensive, or even coherent – conception of what counts as, say, an ambiguity. In the case of ambiguity this will be shaped by what are considered the relevant linguistic pieces of evidence, and by whatever theoretical framework is set up to describe the components and structures of (the) language – in its turn again partly determined by whatever assumptions are made about what can and cannot be adequately or legitimately described within a linguistic or semantic theory. A definition will be "successful" to the extent that it captures, precisely and without redundancy, all the items which this broader framework fixes as ambiguous; it can be marred equally by its own inherent defects and by any faults in the framework. That is not to say that a definition and a taxonomy cannot be mutual modifiers. But it is pointless for classifiers to fix or for critics to assess a classification if the classifiers' account of what ambiguity *is* is passed over.

Galen, oddly, seems to have missed this point: and, to some extent as a result of this error, his criticisms of the Stoic classification turn out to be misplaced, and his own version of Aristotle's classification of linguistic fallacies gravely flawed, as Chapters Five and Six will confirm. His assumption appears to have been that all that need be done is to scrutinise the definition by the criteria of a science of definition, and he does not raise the possibility that the substantive content of the definition, whatever its formal merits or defects, may have a direct bearing on what goes into the classification and what it leaves out. In contrast, the modern reader will readily concede that without this other Stoic definition there could be no hope of a final adjudication on the scope and quality of the classification even were the rest of Galen's report both clear and well preserved (which is hardly the case).

Nor – and this is crucial – can it be presumed that the

definition reported by Diogenes is or resembles the definition not reported by Galen. It might well turn out that the definition admits species or instances of ambiguities excluded by the classification and/or excludes others which the classification accommodates. As a matter of fact the definition and the two classifications do turn out to be mutually illuminating: as signposts both to territory subject to continuing dispute, and to areas already peacefully settled. Galen characterises his Stoics as "more sophisticated", and their work might have been widely influential, even authoritative. But, if there is nothing improper in using it as a guide to the highest achievements of Stoic dialectic in the field, the fit between definition and classifications must still be discovered, not assumed. Each word and phrase in the definition will be analysed in turn, and related where possible to known Stoic doctrines. Sometimes discussion is postponed until Chapter Six, so that Stoic material from the classifications can be reviewed at the same time. Comparative material from ancient and modern treatments of ambiguity will also be examined wherever this seems appropriate.

4.3 Diogenes Laertius 7.62: the text

The text given here is that of the *O.C.T.*, ed. H. S. Long (1964), to which I refer for information on the manuscript tradition; the most important variants are discussed where relevant in the commentary.

1 ἀμφιβολία δέ ἐστι λέξις δύο ἢ καὶ πλείονα πράγματα σημαίνουσα
2 λεκτικῶς καὶ κυρίως καὶ κατὰ τὸ αὐτὸ ἔθος, ὥσθ᾿ ἅμα τὰ πλείονα
3 ἐκδέξασθαι κατὰ ταύτην τὴν λέξιν· οἷον Αὐλητρὶς πέπτωκε· δηλοῦνται γὰρ
4 δι᾿ αὐτῆς τὸ μὲν τοιοῦτον, Οἰκία τρὶς πέπτωκε, τὸ δὲ τοιοῦτον, Αὐλήτρια
5 πέπτωκε.

2 λεκτικῶς FP ἐκτικῶς B   καὶ κυρίως *om*. F   τὰ *libri: om.* Suda; τινὰ Arnim   καὶ κατὰ τὸ αὐτὸ ἔθος *om*. Suda   3 ἐκδέξασθαι B ἐκλέξασθαι P δέξασθαι F   ταύτην τὴν BP: τὴν αὐτὴν Suda, Arnim

Ambiguity is an utterance signifying two or even more *pragmata*, linguistically, strictly, and in the same usage, so that the several *pragmata* are understood simultaneously in relation to this utterance; for example, Αὐλητρὶς πέπτωκε: for by it are indicated both something like this, "a house has fallen three times" ["Οἰκία τρὶς πέπτωκε" = "Αὐλὴ τρὶς πέπτωκε"], and something like this, "a flute-girl has fallen" ["Αὐλήτρια πέπτωκε" = "Αὐλητρὶς πέπτωκε"].

4.4 'λέξις', 'utterance'

What is ambiguous is *lexis*, defined elsewhere (7.56, 57 (33H, A)) as "articulate vocal sound". The Greek term is of course closely linked etymologically with λέγειν, λόγος and thus with λεκτόν, while the things these terms name are bound together in Stoic semantic and linguistic theory. My preferred translation *utterance* is less misleading than most, but the following provisos should be noted.

First, what is in question is the product of an act of uttering, not the act or process of uttering. Second, this use of the term λέξις is a technicality peculiar to the Stoa, and λέξις itself has properties fundamental to the school's conceptions of language and ambiguity, as I shall show. Third, λέξις is speech only primarily, not exclusively, and utterance must be made to bear this extra semantic burden; the Stoa had no jargon term comparable with the modern linguist's *inscription*. (Thus the Inwood and Gerson 1988: 84 translation *speech*, for example, is unacceptable.) This dual rôle is what explains the fact that individual articulate sounds, their written symbols, and their names (D.L. 7.56) can all be called στοιχεῖα, "elements", or "basic constituents", of *lexis*. Similarly, λόγος, in these linguistic/semantic contexts, is any significant utterance (chiefly, it seems, such *lexis* as constitutes a syntactically complex utterance: D.L. 7.56, 57), but the "parts of *logos*" – nouns, verbs, and so on – are obviously not just parts of significant talk, but of significant written discourse too. Finally, ambiguous utterance is significant (hence 'σημαίνουσα', 'signifying', in the next clause of the definition), but what differentiates *lexis* from the "vocal sound", φωνή, made by animals, and is its principal characteristic, is simply its being articulate. By the same token, *expression*, the usual translation of λέξις – *e.g.* LS 37P, 1987: 1: 228; Pachet 1978: 364 – must be inappropriate. A λέξις may "express" nothing at all, at least not in the crucial sense that what it expresses is the content of a rational mind, for that is the differentiating property of significant discourse, *logos*. The Stoic hierarchy of vocal sound/*lexis*/*logos* can in fact be seen as implicitly excluding animal communication from consideration as in any important way comparable with human linguistic interaction, the dialectical object of attack probably being Epicurean accounts of the origin of human language in spontaneous cries like those of animals (*cf.* esp. Lucretius 5.1028ff. (19B); and see already 3.5), rather than Aristotle's concession that even the inarticulate noises of the beasts 'mean something', 'δηλοῦσί γέ τι' (*int.* 2.16a28f.), for Stoics too would no doubt grant so much, with suitable qualifications. Later on, more complex distinctions of types of sounds and producers were to be devised, using the categories meaningful/meaningless, inarticulate/articulate, articulate/literate (*i.e.* writable), inanimate/non-human/personal: *e.g.* Diomedes (*G.L.* 1) 420.9ff.; Priscian *inst.* 1 (*G.L.* 2), 5.5ff.; D.T. Sch. 130.12ff., 181.18ff.

An utterance is a (permitted) sequence of elements.[4] The elements of speech are not terminologically distinguished from the elements of written language; indeed, the tacit assumptions are made that components of articulate (Greek) speech stand in a direct one-to-one correspondence with the letters of the (Greek) alphabet, and that vocal elements are simply strung together in a line to form utterances as letters are put together to form inscriptions. (Thus the translation of Egli 1967: 16, 26f. and Hülser 1979b: 48f., 107 (n. 31a), 113f. (n. 37), 1982: 3: 300, *Phonemreihe*, is even less appropriate than *utterance*.) These assumptions, when conjoined, will have grave and unfortunate consequences for this portion of Stoic dialectic, and in fact for all ancient theorising about language.

An utterance is characterised as any articulate vocal sound

---

[4] It is not known whether the Stoics made a study of the rules governing permitted sequences, a common and methodologically important feature of technical grammar: *e.g.* D.T. *ars gr.* §§ 7ff. with Scholia; and *cf.* Blank 1982: 8ff., 24ff. The Stoic classification of the elements (D.L. 7.57) did differ from the orthodoxy slightly, in making θ, φ, and χ semivowels: Sextus *M.* 1.102; Priscian *inst.* 1 (*G.L.* 2), 11.22ff.

sequence, regardless, not only of semantic content, but also of duration and syntactic status. It is not a word (although it may be a word) (*cf.* Hülser 1979b: 113). The illustration of ambiguity reported by Diogenes – which is the same in all important respects as the example of the first ambiguity species in both classifications – explains why the authors of the definition chose utterances as bearers of ambiguity. The illustration will be more closely examined in 6.2.2 and 6.2.3, and it needs only a brief description here. The core of the ambiguity is the sequence of elements α, υ, λ, η, τ, ρ, ι, ς, which is "common to" – that is, is shared by – both the single term αὐλητρίς, which means "flutegirl", and the phrase αὐλή τρίς, which means "a house three times". (Inwood and Gerson 1988: 84 n. 40 capture this point when they describe the illustrations as stemming from 'alternate [*sic*] divisions into words of the same syllables'.) Neither the common noun nor the complex can be ambiguous: the bearer must be the articulate string, or *lexis*.

So here is one clear instance in which the taxonomies and the definition prove mutually supportive and explanatory. Utterances can be ambiguous by Stoic criteria which are classifiable neither as words (parts of speech) nor as complexes of these, that is, as *logoi*, which is the dichotomy adopted as a division of ambiguity bearers by Aristotle in his *Sophistical Refutations*, by Galen in the treatise in which he records the Stoic classification, and by almost all later rhetorical and grammatical writers in antiquity (see 6.2.2, 6.2.3, 6.5.3, 8.2, 8.3). Thus the Stoic definition and Galen's classification prove themselves innovatory from the start.

At the same time they raise many important issues: not least, whether the admission of significant *lexeis* which are not also words or word-complexes as bearers is legitimate, and, next, which considerations can legitimately be appealed to to decide that question. Unclear too is whether the definition extends to what are now called "homographs", that is, symbol-sequences which are ambiguous as written, but automatically disambiguated in speech (such as 'read', which may be the present tense or the past participle of the verb *read*); and whether it embraces cases of the converse phenomenon, "homophony", that is, apparently identical phonological structures with different morphological structures and different graphic representations (*e.g. abroad/a broad, an ocean/a notion*).

Attention is drawn to this second set of difficulties from another direction: there is evidence, albeit not conclusive, suggesting that the *lexis* used as an illustration would not have been ambiguous in speech. Further, Galen, when comparing the Stoic classification with Aristotle's, criticises the former for failing to include a type of ambiguity Aristotle and Galen claim is due to "accent". The two Stoic classifications certainly do not include a class of such ambiguities, ones which – roughly – result from the fact that in ancient Greek certain letter-sequences, although phonetically identical, were prosodically differentiated in speech (and, later, differentiated in writing too, by prosodic signs, as they are in modern typographical practice); for example, the sequence of letters ο, ρ, ο, ς might be ὄρος, meaning "mountain"; or ὀρός, which means "whey"; or even ὅρος, which means "term" or "definition". Hence the general question how Stoics regarded the relation between written and spoken discourse must be tackled, including one variation of it that has not yet been mentioned, whether sentential intonations might have been held to produce or remove ambiguities.

I have postponed discussion of these issues until 6.2 and 6.5, when they can be studied in light of the classifications. This temporary respite will also allow me to continue more or less without interruption our analysis of a very dense and obscure text. The definition has already been seen to depart significantly from ancient orthodoxy, in the matter of the bearers of ambiguity.

4.5 'δύο ἢ καὶ πλείονα πράγματα σημαίνουσα', 'signifying two or or more *pragmata*'

I have translated the participle as '... signifying ...', which is both conventional and convenient (because lacking any specific theoretical connotations). The noun has simply been transliterated, for reasons to be made clear shortly. The remaining words, '... two or even more ...', probably suggest that ambiguities typically have just two significations, more being rarer, but not unknown.[5]

What, then, is the relation between the utterance which signifies, and what is signified or indicated? In particular, does the word πράγματα represent a genuine addition to the definition? There may be other things besides *pragmata* which can be signified, but ones irrelevant in this field; equally, *pragmata* may be everything signified or signifiable, yet have properties beyond, and identifiable independently of, merely constituting one set of semiotic *relata*. In both cases, πράγματα could not be a bland and uninformative placeholder, as, say, *things* would be in modern English. The sources do in fact frequently link *lekta* and *pragmata* in such a way that the multiple significations of ambiguous *lexeis* might seem to be identical with *lekta*. But there are problems with such a view, whatever we think about the larger relation of *pragmata* and *lekta*, and there is good reason to believe that ambiguities in particular and *lexeis* in general can also mean things which are not incorporeal significations: primarily, things in the world, material particulars or their shared common qualities (*cf.* Nuchelmans 1973: 70).

These problems are complex in the abstract and are best discussed in the context of what are known to be authentically Stoic illustrations of species of ambiguity, including the example reported here by Diogenes. I have accordingly again postponed discussion of the scope of the term πράγματα until 6.2.3. Here I shall simply assume, trivially, that Stoic ambiguities have meanings and significations of some sort, and that there are distinctly two or more of these, and, non-trivially but also, I think, uncontroversially, that these significations at least include *lekta*, in order to deal here only with the further,

---

[5] The Greek may also mean *e.g.* "two or, if you like, more" or "two, or more as well", without the suggestion that having more than two meanings is unusual. But ἀμφιβολία still, I think, carries with it a connotation of twoness or doubleness, and it would be more likely for the Greek to convey the thought that, despite their name, ambiguities may signify more than two *pragmata*.

distinctly non-trivial, difficulties which this broad characterisation throws in our path. I shall also make the assumption,
to be justified in 6.3.4 and 6.3.5, that complete *lekta* contain
"cases", πτώσεις, as (what are today called) subjects, and, for
some types of predicate, (what are today called) objects too,
which are not themselves *lekta*, but nominals – common
nouns, adjectives, proper names, pronouns, infinitive phrases
– in one or other of the standard grammatical cases. Such
words typically signify particular individuals or commonly
qualified objects.

One problem to be faced, fairly obviously, is that there is no
specification of the conditions an utterance must meet to signify two or more *pragmata*, as opposed to a single *pragma*
applicable to numerically distinct, but qualitatively identical,
situations or objects (what Dik 1968: 254f. calls "interpre-
tational" or "referential", as opposed to "syntactic" and
"semantic", ambiguity). This problem can be framed quite
generally, as just shown, or more precisely, with reference to
different types of signified object: the Stoics will then need
to distinguish utterances signifying a number of appropriately
different *lekta*, common qualities, *qualia, etc.*, from those
signifying a number of appropriately identical *lekta, qualia*,
qualities, *etc.* The key, of course, is to determine what is
meant by a signification's being appropriately the same as, or
different from, another, by marking off sentences with two
or more syntactic or lexical structures, from those sometimes
superficially similar sentences which none the less each express
or represent one "state of affairs"; *I am now writing* is not
ambiguous, although the reference of *I* changes with every
speaker (*cf.* Denyer 1988: 378).[6] From a Stoic perspective,

---

[6] Note the ambiguity (semantic multiplicity) of *He's a friend in need* (compare *A
friend in need is a friend indeed* with *A friend in need is a real nuisance*) as against the
generality (multiple applicability) of *He is my friend*. The distinction is not always
obvious: arguably, the verb *like* could be vague, general, or ambiguous in *I like my
friends more than I do ice-cream*. (The oddity of this sentence can be better appreciated by comparing it with *I like my friends more than I do my enemies* and with *I
like ice-cream more than I do cake*). Suitability for co-ordination, which is (roughly)
the conjoining of forms within a single construction, is one now widely recognised
test for ambiguity: see Lyons 1977: 404ff., and esp. Dik 1968 on co-ordination
generally. On tests for ambiguity in linguistic theory: *e.g.* Zwicky and Sadock
1975.

what is required is an explanation of how, for example, ⟨someone is walking⟩, ⟨a man is walking⟩, or ⟨this man is walking⟩ (the examples are from D.L. 7.70 (34κ6–7) and Sextus *M.* 8.96ff.) can each be a (token of a) single proposition or single semantic content, despite their being applicable to any number of different individuals and states-of affairs.[7]

There is even good reason to believe that it cannot be a sufficient condition for identity of *lekta* that they share the same constituents and structure. Different tokens of the same proposition-type, for example, may have different truth-values, as Denyer 1988: 378ff. and Frede 1983: 90 have observed with reference to propositions containing deictics. The same presumably holds for proposition-types and -tokens made ambiguous by the presence of an ambiguous appellative, προσηγορία, signifying two or more common qualities (or the individuals they qualify), and may well hold too for ones containing proper names. It is not clear whether Stoics considered all these ambiguous rather than multiply applicable (see further, 6.3.5.2), but the need to account for such cases as the following might have prompted them to this belief. As regards constituents and structure, *Ajax duelled with Hector* (a standard example: *e.g.* Quintilian 7.9.2; and *cf.* Ebbesen 1981a: 1: 163ff.) signifies just one proposition-type. The reference of (each occurrence of) *Ajax* can, however, be different on different occasions of utterance, and hence "one and the same" proposition apparently be at once true and false, true of Ajax son of Telamon, false of Ajax son of Oileus. This is impossible unless either the difference in reference produces

---

[7] Could there be "ambiguous *lekta*" in this sense? Chrysippus might even have mentioned them in his *On the syntax of the parts of speech* (Περὶ τῆς συντάξεως τῶν τοῦ λόγου μερῶν): for Dionysius of Halicarnassus reports (*comp. verb.* 31 = *S.V.F.* 2.206a) that there he discussed '... the syntax of the proposition, of true ones and false and possible and impossible, contingent and truth-value changing and ambiguous and other suchlike ones'. Even were this report entirely reliable, the problem of distinguishing ambiguous propositions from general ones would remain. But Dionysius, no philosopher, might well have misunderstood and misreported what he read, there is no supporting evidence, and I am reluctant to give his report much credence. At best, *ambiguous* might have some non-standard meaning.

different proposition(-type)s, or there are numerically different occurrences or tokens of "the same" proposition(-type)
just as there are tokens of word-types, proposition-tokens
and other *lekta*-tokens thus being countable items; and D.L.
7.68f., for instance, does report that the conditional proposition ⟨if it is day, it is day⟩ consists of the same proposition
repeated.[8]

The Stoics nowhere draw an explicit distinction between
type and token, and their failure to do so has important consequences for their classification of ambiguities (see 6.3.6). Almost nothing is known of their criteria either for identity of
type, or individuation, at the level of *lekta*; and nothing in the
definition explicitly addresses the problem. Its last clause –
that '... several *pragmata* are understood simultaneously in
relation to this utterance' – shows either that the problem of
individuation had not been faced, or, more charitably, that a
solution, now lost, had been found. Not only does this final
proviso appear to make free use of the Stoic semantic theory
(assuming that *pragmata* are or include *lekta*), it also takes for
granted that, at the point of understanding, distinctions of the
sort I have been seeking, so far without success, are straightforwardly available. For it must be clear that two or more
appropriately different *pragmata* have or have not been understood in connection with a given *lexis*: how else can there be a
case of *ambiguity*?

A further assumption implicit in our definition is that it will
be clear when indicating two or more *pragmata* is a case of
ambiguity, and when, although two or more *pragmata* are
indeed indicated, they are rather (members of) different species in a genus, or (members of) different subclasses in a larger
class, rather than (members of) quite different classes of thing.

---

[8] Nuchelmans 1973: 83 argues that it is the fact that the proposition is a 'definite
thought-content', the 'particular meaning or thing meant', which makes its identity
in general dependent neither on tokens nor on types of *logoi*, although precise
wording can be relevant; and he claims that different references for different subjects (proper names, demonstratives) would result in different propositions. The
Stoa seems never, however, to have produced anything like the "statement", *i.e.*
"saying the same thing of the same thing", which would most naturally complement
such a view.

It might be claimed, for instance, that there is a very general term, *hard*, which applies to chairs and questions alike, rather than an ambiguous term, *hard*, which can be simultaneously true and false of a chair and a question, or even two words, *hard₁* and *hard₂*, applying to chairs, *etc.*, and questions, *etc.*, respectively (Quine 1960: 129ff.); or, to use a philosophical example, that there are not different senses of *mean*, but only different kinds of meaning (Alston 1971: 46). The same point is made by Wiggins 1971: 28 – even if we can devise two separate, and apparently correct, lexical entries for a word, 'this cannot prove that one general account could not have been given to cover both simultaneously' – and by McCawley 1980: 7: 'our failure to come up with a single definition that covers both "illegitimate person" and "nasty person" may be merely the result of insufficient ingenuity on our parts, and we have no justification for calling *bastard* ambiguous just on the basis of an argument from ignorance'.

In 3.5 I observed a failure on the part of the Stoics to construct a conceptual framework for just such distinctions as these. They can be found, in a variety of guises, in other ancient authors. Boethius, for instance, draws an appropriate dividing-line between ambiguities, which have many meanings, and cases 'secundum modum', 'according to the mode [of signifying]': 'these do not signify several things, but in many ways' ('haec enim plura non significant, sed multis modis', *P.L.* 64, *div.* 888D); an example is *infinitum*, which means one thing, "what has no limit", but does so in more than one way, since the limitlessness in question may be in measure, number, or species. The Stoics, for their part, might have appealed here to an independently constructed system of genera and species – these being the conceptions, ἐννοήματα, which are the internal objects of the concepts, ἔννοιαι, explicated in definitions – in order to settle the question of the relation of extensions, that is, whether or not all members of some given group of *qualia* fall under the same genus or species. It can only be assumed on a principle of charity that concepts and hierarchically arranged definitions do indeed supply the requisite semantic resources, for their availability and applicability are not explicitly signalled here.[9]

Another problematic group of utterances or sentences for modern linguists are those which are grammatically well formed but absurd or nonsensical; they include utterances or sentences which can be interpreted grammatically or lexically in two or more ways but which we are unwilling to call ambiguous because only one meaning "makes sense", that is, is also semantically acceptable. (Hockett 1987: 23f. cites *I left the car to get cleaned up* as ambiguous – was the speaker dirty, or the car? – but not *I left the car to get a lube job*, because people do not get lube jobs.) If the Stoa developed something resembling theoretically-grounded selectional criteria, no trace of them survives; but the Stoa is not alone in antiquity in its neglect of the issue to what extent ambiguity can or has to be systematically linked with semantic or pragmatic acceptability. Discussion by almost all ancient authors is scattered and unsatisfactory. It may be that because the ancients did not distinguish, as modern linguists and philosophers tend to do, the sentence as utterance-token in actual or potential contexts of discourse, from the sentence-type or from the sentence as a "linguistic object", they operated with an almost entirely intuitive notion of context.

A close association of knowing the correct meanings of technical terms with understanding technical doctrines may lead to the false impression that the former is entirely separate from, and owes nothing to, any kind of specifically linguistic knowledge. I have already argued (3.3) that this tendency may help account for the way Sextus chooses to argue for the

---

[9] Richman 1959 argues that it may well be impossible always to discern a true case of ambiguity because it seems both that this can only be done by 'direct understanding of the meaning of the term in question', and also that 'appeal to such understanding is unsatisfactory in adjudicating disputes as to the presence or absence of ambiguity' (92). It might be easier just to admit that there are no hard and fast divisions between ambiguities and non-ambiguities, even within descriptions of particular languages. But that may be unwelcome to theoreticians who want to construct logical models for natural languages, as well as for the Stoics, who will be unable to admit such radical undecidability into their model of the world.

uselessness of doctrinaire dialectic as a means of distinguishing lexical ambiguities. More tentatively, his manner of argument may perhaps reflect and exploit a general failure on the part of ancient writers about language to categorise knowledge into linguistic and non-linguistic, or at least to set up such categories systematically. Obviously, it was recognised in antiquity that people learn and know how to speak languages, and obviously too efforts were made not only to identify and codify what were taken to be the important features of particular languages (leading to the practical projects of constructing grammars, glossaries, *etc.*), but also, at a higher level of abstraction and of theoretical explicitness and complexity, to analyse language in general – to identify its origins and functions, the relations between words and word-complexes, on one side, and minds and bits of the world, on the other, and so on. Whatever their exact theoretical context, such speculations typically involved attempts to determine those properties of language which make it capable of performing the functions it does perform: for example, the natural appropriateness of names to their objects; the distinction between noun and verb (first at Plato *Sophist* 261dff.); or the way inflection makes learning a language possible (Varro *ling. lat.* 8.3, 5). General cognitive categories, of correlative knowers and objects of knowledge – in a broad sense – were also formulated. But knowing a language[10] does not seem to have

---

[10] Although Harris 1981: 171 is no doubt justified in claiming that what he calls the "orthological dogma" – the thesis that some usages are (more) correct, others less so or not at all (*cf.* his 1980: 7, n. 3) – is dominant in the western grammatical tradition, it is far from clear that knowing a language – as opposed to grammar, the study of language, whose status as a discipline was of course repeatedly questioned – was itself commonly thought of as a τέχνη. Thus solecism can be defined as "inexpert speech" (it occurs ' ὅτε τις ἀτέχνως διαλέγεται', *An. Gr. Par.*, ed. Cramer, vol. I, p. 190) because speaking correctly is speaking according to the rules laid down by a prescriptive grammar. On the other hand, I remain unconvinced of Lyons' 'interesting hypothesis', 1963: 185, that for Plato speaking Greek, ἑλληνίζειν, as opposed to speaking foreign languages, at least for a Greek, 'would not fall within the field of τέχνη', and likewise for all native speakers' knowledge of their mother-tongue (*cf.* 221). For it is not altogether clear to me what Lyons intends when he claims that 'since indeed you know how to speak Greek', 'ἐπειδήπερ ἑλληνίζειν ἐπίστασαι', at *Charmides* 159a6f. (184), 'may well, in the context, be ironical' (185), or how this would prevent its being normal Greek, and thus liable to the analysis Lyons favours for other constructions of

been regarded as a unique kind of knowledge, radically different from knowing other sorts of thing – still less, as deserving
of study in its own right: and this despite the fact that language (true language, not mere parroting of the human power
of articulate speech) was frequently claimed, by the Stoics
amongst others, as a uniquely human possession; thus Cicero
off. 1.50, for instance, contrasts the human bond of 'ratio et
oratio' with the tighter connection of belonging 'to the same
people, tribe, and language', 'eiusdem gentis, nationis, linguae'
(57) (*cf.* Quintilian 2.20.9; Diomedes (*G.L.* 1) 300.12ff.).

This is a large claim, and it would take a lengthy mono-
graph to argue it fully. It would require, in particular, detailed
consideration of the ways in which rationality (itself often
made a human prerogative, of course) and the faculty of language were linked in theory. The broad outline of the Stoic
view at least is quite plain. To speak is to give voice to psychic
states wholly unavailable to animals; their impressions can
never give rise to such complex ideas as 'If something is a
man, he is a rational, mortal animal' (Cicero *acad.* 2.21 (39C)),
embodying both generality and logical connectedness. Language just is rationality in one of its guises, and, as understanding what many words mean requires a grasp of such
complex concepts, there must be constant, simultaneous, if
largely unreflecting, resort to reason's other key manifestation, the ability to grasp logical connections: Sextus *M.* 8.275f.
(53T).[11] As for the the general question, all I shall try to do

---

ἐπίστασθαι with a personal subject and governed infinitive, as 'one of the principal
sources' for expressions of the form τέχνη τοῦ *so-and-so* (183; *cf.* §7.17, 159–63).
He merely suggests, parenthetically, of "Ἕλλην μέν ἐστι καὶ ἑλληνίζει' at *Meno*
82b4, that it may be 'more normal?' (*ibid.*). At *Theaetetus* 163b1–c3, the only
languages mentioned are foreign, and so this passage cannot be used as evidence
for Plato's, or his character Socrates', views about native-speaker knowledge, as
Lyons would like (221). An awkward question *is* suggested – how any language
can be learned if perceiving is knowing – but curiously is not pursued: *cf.* Bostock
1988: 85. The 'διδάσκαλος τοῦ ἑλληνίζειν' at *Protagoras* 327e2–328a1 (184) is compared with those able to teach virtue, Greek, and a handicraft, in such a way that
the parallel would collapse were knowing Greek not a τέχνη: but here the comparisons are drawn by Protagoras, not (even) by Socrates.

[11] This internal relation between syntax (of the *lekta* which articulate impressions)
and rationality (which manifests itself in meaningful discourse and in logical
association of *lekta*) was not always appreciated, at least by non-Stoics. At *de*

here is survey relevant evidence from ancient accounts of how ambiguous sentences are to be used and dealt with by hearers and readers of texts. The relevance of such sentences lies in their showing, quite trivially and unmistakably, that what it is appropriate or correct to understand by an utterance in a given situation will in part be determined by the circumstances (very broadly construed) in which it is produced. Further, certain interpretations of isolated ambiguous sentences which seem grammatically possible will none the less be consistently rejected or at least differentially treated by speakers.

Such "performance phenomena" are naturally of great importance for theorists who want to construct a comprehensive account of linguistic understanding; and they are taken into consideration too even when the questions of the nature, structure, and mechanisms of speaker understanding are, for whatever theoretical or methodological reason, shelved in favour of the question, what is to go into a description of a language, that is, what is strictly "linguistic" and what is not. The principal area of disagreement, briefly, is the extent to which selectional restrictions on lexical items should and can

---

abstinenta 3.3ff. Porphyry argues that neither pronunciative, προφορικός, λόγος – that is, speech – nor internal, ἐνδιάθετος, λόγος – the power of ratiocination – belong only to humans. (On the distinction, see 3.1, n. 4.) The first point would presumably have been conceded by the Stoics. It is supported by the consideration that, merely because the sounds animals make are just so much noise to humans, they need not be so to other animals (3.3.4f.; *cf.* Sextus *P.H.* 1.74). Porphyry never explains, however, why articulateness should be a necessary condition for linguistic status; perhaps his view was extracted or adapted from Aristotle; *cf.* Kretzmann 1974: 17 on *int.* 2.16a26ff.: inarticulate animal noises, besides being natural, do not function as names because they are not determinate enough to be sharply describable or predictably repeatable. Porphyry also claims that animal languages, while not conventional as human tongues are, none the less conform to νόμοι – those of nature and the gods: 3.3.3. Even more striking is the way his argument passes to proof of animals' ability to reason, to "do dialectic", 3.7.1, without so much as a glance at the question of any special grasp of broadly structural or syntactic features of language; the latter seem to be included implicitly in the definition of προφορικὸς λόγος as 'vocal sound emitted by means of the tongue which is significant of internal, psychic states', 3.3.2. Sextus *P.H.* 1.65ff. similarly exploits the distinction between the two types of *logos*, in order to call into doubt the sharp Stoic demarcation between humans and animals, without explicitly considering where understanding of linguistic structure lies. This suggests, perhaps, that such understanding was not regarded as the product of a special language faculty, as opposed to that of a general faculty of reason (on which see already n. 10).

be built into any model of a language, realist or not (*cf.* Lyons 1977: 418ff.). Ancient authors tend to display a mighty in-difference to such problems: contextual factors are discussed only piecemeal, without a theoretical account of context, and for other purposes than understanding language knowledge or constructing grammars. Thus the "dialecticians" who drew up the classification of types of sophism reported by Sextus *P.H.* 2.229ff. do seem to have distinguished at least implicitly between the well-formedness and the acceptability of proposi-tions, but in order to explain the plausibility of certain types of sophism (see further, 7.5, 7.6). I shall return to the topic of the effect of context on ambiguities in 4.9, 6.3.6, and 7.3.

Another lacuna in the definition is that it does not, at least explicitly, raise the possibility that users of language may not be able to say in all cases whether or not they meant or under-stood one, two, or more *pragmata*, with reference to any given utterance, when this failure is due not to ignorance of the language, or of the situation of utterance, or of the world at large, but to a radical, irremediable uncertainty as to what is or is not included in the range of meaning of any utterance of that type. In other words, if the Stoics saw the need to distin-guish ambiguity from vagueness, only the end result of their ponderings on the problem is available (that there are indeed cases in which meanings are distinct), and not the consider-ations that led them to it or the *differentiae* they discovered and applied.

The second proviso in the definition, that the ambiguous utterance signify "strictly", might have been directed partly to filling that need. Such a condition would by itself reveal noth-ing about the conditions for its application to particular cases (see further, 4.7), and, in any case, explicit evidence for it is not to be found. Far more plausible is the supposition that the Stoics, and the ancients in general, simply did not see vague-ness as the problem – one of immense theoretical importance and complexity – which occupies modern philosophers of lan-guage, formal and philosophical logicians, and theoretical lin-guists. The questions what vagueness is, of just what it is a

property, and how it is related to (other) cardinal linguistic
features such as generality and ambiguity; whether it is intrinsic to natural languages, and, if so, why; what are its implications for the understanding of the nature and structure of the
mind, for the notion of the correctness of descriptions of objects, and even for the identity criteria of objects themselves;
whether it makes the acquisition and use of natural languages
possible; how it affects the construction of theories of meaning and of comprehension for natural languages, the interpretation of natural languages as or by means of formal systems,
and their relation to scientific discourse and to formal calculi:
these and similar difficulties have such significance today precisely because of the intimate relation in which vagueness
stands to the projects ordained by certain highly influential
modern ideas of what sorts of things philosophers should do
(*e.g.* construct semantic theories for natural languages; inves-
tigate their key properties, or those appropriate and necessary
for scientific discourse; use linguistic phenomena as means of
access to conceptual structures) and of what logics are (languages of a sort).[12] Again, vagueness has been used to argue
the untenability of all orthodox theories of meaning in which
linguistic rules are fixed independently of particular commu-
nicational situations: *cf.* Harris 1981: 181ff.

In general, it seems reasonable that ancient language theorists failed to single out vagueness as moderns do in large part
just because they did not see the relation between natural and
formal languages, or the very concept of (a) language, or the

[12] The classic works on vagueness are Peirce 1902; Russell 1923; Black 1949;
Waismann 1953 ("vagueness" *vs.* "open texture"; *cf.* Harrison 1972: 137ff.,
Scheffler 1979: 49ff.); Quine 1960: 125ff. Scheffler 1979: 37 briefly outlines some of
the philosophical and logical problems to which vagueness gives rise. Lakoff 1970
offers a test for distinguishing vague from ambiguous sentences using Verb-Phrase
deletion (the ... *and so did* ... move). On specific issues: Black 1970; Haack 1978:
162ff.; Scheffler 1979: 65ff.; Quine 1981: 31ff. ('What price bivalence?', on "the
logic of vagueness" and challenges to traditional two-valued logics and to standard validity); Wright 1987: 4, 343 n. 1, 349 (the problems for realism posed by
vague or "tolerant" predicates); Dummett 1975 (strict finitism not a possible
philosophy of mathematics because it uses vague predicates such as *intelligible*);
Unger 1979 (identity criteria for physical objects); Quine 1960: 84ff., 125f.; Wright
1975, 1976 (vagueness and mastery of observational predicates); Lyons 1977:
407–9 (vagueness and generality).

way languages are learned, as of central philosophical importance or as deeply problematic for some other science or discipline. A case could be made out that, in fact, they hardly
noticed vagueness at all. One outstanding illustration of the
gulf between ancient and modern appreciation of vagueness
may be mentioned. Recent scholarship has shown that the
Sorites or Heaping paradox ('One grain of wheat does not
make a heap; neither do two grains; or three; *etc.*'), which for
modern philosophers is a potential threat to the coherence of
a wide variety of ostensibly vague predicates and concepts,
was in antiquity exploited and understood as an epistemological puzzle, not as an ontological, conceptual, or linguistic
one; it was certainly so understood by the Stoa.[13] Strictly
speaking, the Stoa cannot be said to have "eliminated" vagueness, for the upshot of the school's (that is, Chrysippus') response to the Sorites was that any "vagueness" people might
experience is the result of their own sloppiness, lack of powers
of observation, and careless, untrained habits of thinking and
talking: vagueness itself has no basis in reality, in theory, or in
the languages people use. In an important sense, it is just not
there to be eliminated.

This response to the Sorites might reasonably be thrown
out of court as hopelessly feeble. I merely observe that the
Stoic failure to recognise the enormous non-epistemological
difficulties associated with vagueness seems to have been general in antiquity. Burnyeat 1982: 318ff. also notes the restriction of ancient soritic arguments to implicitly quantitative
terms; the point I want to emphasise here is their restriction to

---

[13] Two different interpretations of Chrysippus' solution to the Sorites (briefly summarised at LS 1987: I: 229f.) are to be found in: Barnes 1982, who argues for the
philosophical importance of soritic predicates, 34f.; Burnyeat 1982, esp. 335, 336,
n. 50, on the epistemological nature of the puzzle, and 318ff. on the medical
context. On the dialectical tactics recommended by Chrysippus: see 7.4, 7.6.
Burnyeat 1982: 324 suggests that Chrysippus' *On Soritic Arguments Against Vocal
Sounds*, φωναί (D.L. 7.192 = *S.V.F.* 2.14, p. 6, l. 11 (37в1)) concerns arguments
which (in modern terms) 'purport to show that certain predicates are incoherent'.
But φωναί are not even words, as Burnyeat's translation would have it, let alone
predicate(-expression)s; and the work is listed in a subsection of books which
almost all deal with utterances, *lexeis*, anomaly, and solecism (as Burnyeat himself
observes, 1982: 324, n. 24).

the problem of knowledge (not, of course, the problem of knowing *a language*). The authors of the Stoic ambiguity definition probably never even noticed that they could not assume that it would always be clear, even if only to a sage, that, and when, an utterance had definitely more, or not more, than one signification.

4.6 'λεκτικῶς', 'linguistically'

How can an utterance signify, but only λεκτικῶς? And why this first qualification on the mode of signification of ambiguous utterances? Direct evidence is sparse.[14] Any connection with *lekta* is implausible, for, given the mention of *pragmata* in the definition, a further proviso that an ambiguous utterance signify only *lekta* would appear to be either redundant or contradictory. A more profitable line of inquiry is to consider what the Stoics might be trying to exclude as candidates for ambiguity. The next two conditions in the definition rule that signification must also be strict, and within the same usage: λεκτικῶς must have at least a core of meaning different from both.

One sort of use of linguistic items both theorists and ordinary speakers might want to exclude is the code or password. Substitution cyphers could yield non-articulate sequences,

---

[14] Apollonius Dyscolus uses it, *adv.* 195.16, with *synt.* 2.8f., apparently as meaning "functioning as a word, *lexis*" or perhaps "signifying a *lekton*" (since for Apollonius all *lexeis* signify *lekta* or νοητά (*synt.* 2.10ff.)). Neither meaning is appropriate to the definition, where *lexeis* are not words, and *lekta* have probably already been implicitly mentioned (see 6.2.3). λεκτικῶς is also used to mean simply "linguistic", as at Olympiodorus *cats.* 30.6f., 'τὴν λεκτικὴν ἐνεργείαν', Ammonius *int.* 39.23ff., 'τῆς λεκτικῆς καλουμένης φαντασίας'. The word is also used, again at a much later date and not (or not obviously) in a Stoic context, in opposition to συμβολικῶς, the contrast being between the way words have meaning and the way marks of punctuation used in association with texts do. The context is an argument that conjunctions are to be associated semantically with the latter and not the former: Simplicius *cats.* 64.18ff, with Dexippus *cats.* 32.18ff. Private significations of code-words could be contrasted with their ordinary meanings as "symbolic", but the parallel with textual signs is hardly convincing. It is possible, but highly unlikely, that the authors of the definition also distinguished between different modes of signifying of different classes of words or parts of speech: 6.3.5.2. (Pachet 1978: 364 translates 'à la lettre', Inwood and Gerson 1988: 84 as 'literally', but this would be 'αὐτοῖς τοῖς ὀνόμασιν/αὐταῖς ταῖς λέξεσιν' or similar.)

which would fall outside the scope of our definition. But whole-word codes employ only the phonological (and graphic) structures permitted by the rules of a language. Suppose two spies are given a code-word in order to recognise each other and so initiate a clandestine conversation. Now the code-word – *Glasnost*, say – does not mean what it means for them ("I am a friend") by the rules or conventions of the Russian language, according to which it means "openness" or the like. The word has been arbitrarily assigned the signification "I am a friend" purely by an agreement to use the word in that way. Its linguistic meaning remains unchanged: in fact, if it did not, the word could no longer be used as a codeword to mean "I am a friend". Spies would soon go out of business were it always possible, at least in principle, simply to consult a dictionary (perhaps supplemented by a grammar) in order to discover the meanings of their coded messages.

There is no evidence that the Stoics were actually troubled by codes (or cyphers). Yet the case of codewords and passwords gives a useful insight into what has been argued to be one of language's distinctive features: its autonomy. Harrison 1979: 6 urges that the 'autonomy of language is pretty clearly closely connected with the utility of language as a system of communication'. It 'excludes the assignment of private and personal meanings or grammatical interpretations to utterances in a natural language. The utterance itself dictates its linguistic meaning, not the speaker or the hearer. This should not surprise us. A system of communication is necessarily "public" in the sense that it excludes private and personal interpretations of the symbols used in it'. A language could not function as a semiotic system were its rules, including those determining the semantic content of its constituents and their complexes, not independent of any given speaker's usage. What matters, very roughly, is how the users of a language in general speak; any person with the appropriate physiological equipment and intellectual faculties can have access to those rules, however they are described at a theoretical level, simply by being a member of a language community. Modern linguists agree that language is arbitrary: but this sort

153

of arbitrariness has little to do with the *ad hoc* and deliberate arbitrariness of the password.[15]

The Stoics may well have wanted to dispute the claim that language is (or is intrinsically) arbitrary; their etymological researches especially are premissed on the opposite view of the relation between words and what they name (see 3.1, 3.5). My contention is rather that they did grasp and acknowledge its autonomy, and that they are indicating as much here, for the very good reason that ambiguity had already become the focus of a Hellenistic dispute about the autonomy of language. Diodorus Cronus seems to have exploited this difficult issue with his customary originality and *éclat* in order to challenge claims to linguistic expertise. The reports have Diodorus arguing that no word is naturally ambiguous, on the grounds that it will have only whatever meaning may be accorded it by a speaker on any occasion of utterance, and actually calling several of his unfortunate slaves after various particles and conjunctions (frr. 112, 113, 114 Döring) '... in order to mock the grammarians' definitions and those who say language is natural'. Diodorus' claim is reported by Gellius, *noct. att.* 11.12.1ff. (= fr. 111D (37N)), along with Chrysippus' counterclaim that every word is ambiguous (on which see 6.3.5). On Diodorus' view, obscurity is still possible (*i.e.* if I say one thing and you understand another), and so is deliberate ambiguity (a form of equivocation), on the grounds that 'nemo ... duo vel plura dicit, qui se sensit unum dicere'. What is eliminated is the intrinsic ambiguity attaching to a word as part of a language system. He was himself committed, reportedly, to the absolute arbitrariness of names: fr. 114 Döring.

Modern semanticists will perhaps find it diverting to offer interpretations of the weaknesses in Diodorus' position. A typical response would run like this. If speaker's meaning is the only meaning, a language cannot be a public semiotic system of any sort. Linguistic communication is not achieved by arbitrary and private assignment of meanings. Diodorus'

---

[15] Arbitrariness, as opposed to iconicity, as a design feature of languages: *e.g.* Hockett 1958: 577 (a narrow definition), 1987: 9ff. (broader); Lyons 1977: 70f., 102ff. (also broad); and seminally Saussure 1916/1983: 67ff.

undoubted success in naming or renaming his slaves as he pleases is irrelevant. The "autonomous idiolect" (to borrow Norman Kretzmann's happy phrase)[16] only appears possible because audiences will continue to translate his usage into theirs.

Modern philosophers disagree about the semantic status of proper names (see further, 6.3.5.2). I shall follow their disputes only to highlight their profound differences from ancient views in general and Stoic views in particular. Diodorus' purpose, according to the sources, was explicitly polemical, and his challenges have to be assessed in the context of ancient controversies. The sample response outlined above is not what Diodorus would have expected. Very different assumptions about the origin and nature of language are under attack.

The Stoics counted themselves amongst those who believe that words are natural: in a variety of ways, of which simple onomatopoeia is merely the most basic, phonology regularly and systematically mimics, or in some other way captures and reproduces, semantic content. Derived usages are also systematically related to origin. At the same time, the Stoics could easily have recognised language's publicness and autonomy, whatever their position on the old νόμος/φύσις (nature vs. convention) debate about the origin of language; for the dispute which Diodorus made fun of did not concern language's alleged origin in some sort of public, social convention, or (significantly) in a series of acts of naming by a legendary or mythical name-giver, but rather whether or not words, whoever imposed them, or even if they were not imposed at all, as Epicurus argued,[17] are somehow naturally suited to signify whatever it is they do signify (cf. Allen 1947: 36f.; Fehling 1965: 218ff.). The very naturalness of the (correct) names for things confers an authority on them which the individual cannot hope to match.

---

[16] Kretzmann 1971: 127: "autonomous idiolects" vs. "autonomous languages".

[17] In the case of the first, "natural", stage of language formation (*ep. Hdt.* 75f. (19A)), that is; later generations extended meanings and invented new words as required: see already 3.5.

But the Stoics would have been highly unlikely to sanction the phenomenon of ambiguity as entirely natural.[18] They would have had to square the naturalness of homonymy with the thesis that names are reproductions in sound of things (thus laying themselves open to the obvious objections, that it is arbitrary to claim that the one-to-one correspondence fails in just some cases, and that there will anyway be no way of telling for certain which these are). Grammatical ambiguity will be just as awkward an intruder if (the Stoic view) the world was at one time consistently and straightforwardly articulable in language. Now the value of explanations which appeal to changes in words whose pristine form is unknown can reasonably be questioned; but at least the Stoa was able to offer an account of the origins of ambiguity which did not threaten to invalidate their entire etymological project. Hence, although in other contexts (now unknown) λεκτικῶς may have had connotations of naturalness or appropriateness, I assume it cannot have done so here.

The thrust of the report of Diodorus' attack on "naturalists" and grammarians is that all words (*i.e.* all members of all word-classes) can legitimately be assigned any semantic function, including that of proper names, whose naming and vocative functions can also be lumped together. This is surely an authentic feature of Diodorus' arguments. His targets would not have seen how his peculiar taste in proper names presents no threat to the autonomy of language precisely because the whole issue was dominated by the wide-spread assumption, mightily influential for all that it is rarely expressed, that naming is the basic function of words. Diodorus is said to have given his slaves conjunctions for names to prove that every word or vocal sound, φωνή, is significant (fr. 112 Döring), as

---

[18] This does not, incidentally, undermine Chrysippus' contention, reported by Aulus Gellius, that all words are 'naturally ambiguous'. In 6.3.5 I shall argue that Chrysippus' apparently bizarre claim amounts to the thesis that all words (can be used to) signify themselves as well as whatever they signify extra-linguistically. "Autonymy" will thus be a property of words *qua* words, regardless of origin, whether natural or conventional. It has already been noted (in 3.1) that homonymy was paraded as a proof of the conventionality of language; *cf.* Ebbesen 1981a: 1: 177ff.

if only one sort of signifying were in play; and one response to him was that *however, ἀλλά μήν*, for example, has a corresponding 'σημαινόμενον', 'signification', but lacks the form or character of a name (fr. 113 Döring).[19] (The dialogue which may have inspired Diodorus to this gimmick, Plato's *Cratylus*, opens with Hermagoras' outline of Cratylus' extreme naturalism, including its application to Hermagoras' own name (383b).)[20] In Stoic dialectic too a one-to-one, word(-form)/object correspondence, a picking out of a thing and attaching a linguistic tag to it, informs or is mimicked by all other signifying by all types of nominal, by verbs (which signify predicates), and perhaps by other words too. If the Stoics would have accepted talk of linguistic "rules" or "norms", as seems reasonable, they would have thought of the semantic subgroup of these as, in part, rules for linking atomistic meanings with more or less invariant words. Stoic semantic theory, although it identifies several sets of semantic *relata*, does not fix their relations with technical labels, and the function of "signifying" is not minutely or consistently analysed (see further, 6.2.3, 6.3.5.2). So, although it is possible that the condition that ambiguities signify λεκτικῶς was intended to exclude the way proper names attach to their bearers (the way they do in Diodorus' challenge), just as modern linguistics may exclude proper names from the scope of linguistic ambiguity (*cf. e.g.*

---

[19] Contrast fr. 115D: in justifying the extended use of ὄνομα of all words, a distinction is invoked between the *onoma* proper, which is 'ὀνοματικὸν καὶ σημαντικόν' and all parts of speech, which must be either 'σημαντικόν' or 'συστατικόν'.

[20] The autonomy of language is of course implicit in the thesis of its naturalness: if each thing has its own natural name, irrespective of what people actually call it, then the name/thing relation must be independent of users. The problem (as Socrates points out) is that people manage to communicate perfectly well with non-natural, supposedly non-existent, names, 434b9ff. When Cratylus counters that this is merely courtesy of usage, ἔθος, Socrates returns that "usage" is just convention, συνθήκη, under another name, 434e4–8 – which implies, but does not make explicit, that language, being a matter of agreement, must be something fixed between individuals, if only temporarily, and not alterable entirely at the whim of one or other of them. It is remarkable that in outlining his own conventionalist position Hermagoras is to all appearances blithely unaware of any distinction between individual and collective convention: *cf.* 383a4–b2, 384d2, 7f., 385a2ff., 385d7–e3. His unconscious switching between the two now seems painfully, suggestively, obvious, but we are left to draw the appropriate conclusions for ourselves.

Lyons 1977: 398; Kooij 1971: 5), it is surely highly implausible. It may just be the case that for the Stoa proper names are fully ambiguous. How, then, to deal with Diodorus' use of connectives and the like as proper names?

Perhaps this was simply not Diodorus' point. His play with proper names is reported to be a criticism of the belief that language is natural, and of all "natural" grammatical distinctions, not as a continuation of his denial that there is such a thing as ambiguity at all. Yet if the way proper names are taken to signify is not pertinently different from other modes of signifying, and if, say, *however*, ἀλλὰ μήν, is also significant in whatever way is accepted by the Stoic definition, it does look very much as though Diodorus has, simply on the strength of his own, private decision, created a new ambiguity, and that any (significant) word could be made ambiguous by the easy trick of imposing it on some hapless slave. If the word is given public recognition as a name (and is not immediately shifted by Diodorus to some other, equally eccentric function), it seems merely arbitrary to deny it the status of a name as well as a conjunction. Diodorus might well have been influenced in his choice not only by the contemporary debate as to whether all words signify, but also by the (to us chilling) comparison which the archetypical conventionalist, Hermogenes, chose for his thesis of complete arbitrariness: the meaning of words can be changed at will just as the names of slaves can be (*Cratylus* 384d3–5; *cf.* Isidore *orig.* 1.29.2).[21] But the problem of "arbitrary ambiguity" does not go away if the usurped term is not, or not fully, already significant.

[21] Varro also makes use of slaves' names as evidence for various contentions. The way in which slaves easily use their fellows' names in all the grammatical cases after hearing only the nominative shows the usefulness of inflection, *ling. lat.* 8.6. Simple objects are given simple names, just as in a household with a single slave only one name is needed, 8.10; Sextus *P.H.* 2.257, in contrast, imagines a household with several slaves all with the same name, when even the slaves recognise the need for clarification of the ambiguity (see further, 7.5, 7.6, on this passage). The arbitrariness of *derivatio voluntaria* (= derivation) is contrasted with the determinism of *derivatio naturalis* (= inflection) by supposing a case in which three men might each purchase a slave in the same market and each give their new possession a different name (8.21). Neologism by appeal to analogy should not be rejected out of hand: who, after all, has slaves 'with the old names', 'priscis nominibus'?, 9.22.

Diodorus need simply substitute a term which his opponents agree to be significant independently of his use of it.

The Stoics' answer might be that there are indeed natural correspondences between phonological and/or morphological properties, on the one hand, and, on the other, semantic and/or grammatical ones. *However*, for instance, cannot be rightly used as a proper name because it does not have the right structure *qua* utterance (*e.g.* it has no gender, is uninflected, *etc.*). This is presumably the sort of response for which Diodorus was amply prepared: he could reply that he was, as an obvious and uncontestable matter of fact, using *however* as a proper name, and using it successfully, and anyone else who liked could do so too. He could also point out that hard-and-fast rules governing the phonology or morphology of names, or of any other so-called "part of speech", had yet to be drawn up, and that no-one had so much as sketched how they might even be possible.

Now it would not have been open to the Stoa to call on an account of how proper names signify which, if it does not assign them a unique rôle (and this may anyway be impossible), at least distinguishes them from other signifiers in such a way that Diodorean "performative nomination" fails to create ambiguity. Yet there is an alternative. The distinction in play does not arise from the fact that Diodorus' performative nomination is the conscious act of an individual. Such nomination may also be the act or series of acts of a group or a whole community; it may be sacred, ritualistic, or merely playful; and it may be as much the outcome of speakers' adopting a name more or less unconsciously, as of a deliberate "speech-act" of naming. But to inform the rest of the linguistic community that such-and-such a name or nickname has been assigned, the resources of the continuing and unchanged language(-system) must be utilised. Diodorus can only use *however* as he does by telling people he is so doing, or, perhaps less securely, by having others observe and record his appropriate and consistent linguistic behaviour, *viz.*, his use of *however* to refer to one of his slaves. And in so doing he reveals the crucial fact: what matters is not how he alone uses the name, but how he and at least one other person use it. Diodorus and the slave form a minimal linguistic community. (Compare pet names used by lovers, or in families.) If the slave does not know or get to know (by being told, or by learning that he has to respond appropriately to the utterance of *however*, in certain contexts, by Diodorus) that he is (now) called *however*, Diodorus' ostensible nomination is empty, and the new "name" so much battered air. *However*, on this account, may turn out ambiguous, but not because of what Diodorus alone decides to do. It is ambiguous because a linguistic community has agreed to assign it more than one signification. Of course, if the slave does not realise he has been renamed, Diodorus might perhaps be able to continue thinking of him as the one called *however*, and referring to him as such in his private ponderings (if he could follow such a "private rule": I shall not pursue the matter). In such circumstances, *however* cannot, though, be said to refer to the slave by the public rules of a language. Diodorean "private ambiguity" is either not ambiguity, or not private.

The proviso that ambiguities signify λεκτικῶς is certainly not signalled as an attempt to meet Diodorus' challenge by insisting on the publicness and autonomy of ambiguous utterances. It is still curious that the only recorded Stoic response[22] to the serious threat which Diodorus' arguments represented to the whole elaborate structure of Stoic philosophy is Chrysippus' assertion that 'every word is naturally ambiguous, since from the same word two or more things can be understood'. Chrysippus' point might be the simple one that, as a matter of fact, people just do understand two or more things by the same word: so there must be such a thing as ambiguity.

---

[22] Chrysippus' *Reply to Panthoides' 'On ambiguities'* (D.L. 7.193 = *S.V.F.* 2.14, p. 6, l. 27 (37B2)) could conceivably be Gellius' ultimate source, but this interpretation of its contents is as speculative as Ebert's: see 7.5, n. 30. (Chrysippus also composed Πρὸς τὸ περὶ σημασιῶν Φίλωνος (D.L. 7.191 = *S.V.F.* 2.13, p. 5, l. 23), which might concern either semantics or sign-inferences.) Döring *ad* frr. 111–15D = 1972: 128, claims that Diodorus' denial of ambiguity is a 'rigorose Weiterführung' of Eucleides' rejection of the form of reasoning by παραβολή, "analogy" or "parallelism" (D.L. 2.107), but he does not make clear precisely wherein the connection lies. On this mode of argument, see 3.2.

The problem then is that appeals to people's understanding of words on actual occasions of use are not going to disconcert Diodorus. There can be no guarantee that a particular hearer's understanding of this or that utterance as meaning two or more things is not the result of the hearer's own incompetence: he might just happen to believe, incorrectly, that it has two meanings, either in general, or in this context. But Chrysippus would hardly want to deploy such casual misunderstandings as a counterattack on Diodorus, thus readmitting ambiguity only on condition that what chance hearers understand by utterances on chance occasions can constitute what utterances mean.

Chrysippus' claim that 'every word is naturally ambiguous' has almost certainly to be interpreted as assigning to all words the functions both of being their own names – "autonymy" – and of non-reflexively signifying something else as well (as will be argued in 6.3.4, 6.3.5). His return of fire will thus hit the target only if he can demonstrate that words do not derive their meanings from individual and arbitrary decisions by speakers on occasions of utterance. If Chrysippus' doctrine of "universal ambiguity" really constituted a rejection of Diodorus' autonomous idiolect (and their juxtaposition in Gellius' report suggests that it did), it must rest on the premiss of linguistic autonomy. His response makes sense only if words are autonomous signifiers, both reflexively and non-reflexively. Their being linguistically significant is independent of what any given user makes of them.

This reconstruction of Chrysippus' response to Diodorus is speculative. I have presented the case against him none the less because the threat he poses is so grave: it is the undermining of the fundamental Stoic doctrine that a publicly-accessible language is necessary for human cognitive and moral activity. Diodorus does not deny that utterances may be communicative; as speakers can still be meaningfully described as expressing themselves obscurely, there must be an implicit assumption at work that some communication is non-obscure and successful. What is worrying is the invention of a new domain of private usage. If words mean just what a speaker wants them to mean, there can be no place for the description and prescription of meanings which is central to the Stoic philosophical project. Private semantic legislation has to be eliminated, for otherwise it will not be just the Stoic theory of ambiguity that collapses: so will all the Stoa's claims to possess and promulgate the authoritative discourse about the world. Of course, it will still be perfectly possible for linguistic communities to invent and adopt new usages (as the Stoics themselves did: 3.3, 3.5). The definition even makes allowance explicitly for different usages in different linguistic communities (4.8). If my understanding of λεκτικῶς is correct, what would be done away with would be private innovation. This still leaves the task of defining precisely what it is that fixes meanings as "linguistic", what sanctions them and not Diodorus' idiolect. But the distinction is crucial all the same, and its presence in our definition would be a great credit to its authors.

The definition will also proscribe another version of Diodorean idiolect, according to which the meaning of an utterance is indeed that given it by the speaker, but has to be selected from the meanings assigned to utterances of that type by the rules of the language in question. That is, the assigned meaning would not be chosen entirely at random, but taken from some publicly accessible and fixed range of meanings. Where the speaker assigns one meaning only, ambiguity would be impossible. But the Stoic definition gives no rôle at all to speakers' intentions: signifying is something utterances do, not speakers. What matters is whether some audience understands several *pragmata* by an utterance (see 4.9), provided that these are the utterance's "linguistic" meanings, *i.e.* not ones arbitrarily assigned by speakers or hearers.

4.7 'κυρίως', 'strictly'

Two of the verbal and semantic oppositions standard in ancient grammarians and other writers on language are those between "proper", κύρια, and "common", κοινά, names and between "strict", κύρια, and "loose/metaphorical/catachrestic" terms and phrases.[23] The first pair cannot be relevant here. A first guess, then, must be that the Stoics were trying to draw some sort of distinction between "narrow" and "extended" uses of expressions. This is hardly surprising. Modern studies of ambiguity frequently attempt similar distinctions, although disagreement is rife about particular cases or particular rules, even as to whether the whole project is well founded and likely to be fruitful and informative. At stake are very important issues: whether some significations are more basic or central than others, which are somehow derived from the central core of meaning, and may not be significations of the same order or type as these others; in what ways whatever distinctions are made are relevant to a description of a language or to an associated theory of ambiguity; and how metaphorical meanings are formed and understood.[24]

The modern controversy usually acknowledges that the notion of "neutral" or "natural" signification is incoherent, uninformative, and ideologically fraught. Ancient theoreticians of language had normativeness in their blood, and insisted on such distinctions as those between "prose" and "poetic", or "low" and "refined" vocabularies, or "strict" and "loose" usages, all ultimately resting on an impossibly rigid dichotomy

---

[23] "Proper" vs. "common" nouns: e.g. D.T. 24.5f., 33.6f, Sch. e.g. 214.17ff., 356.16–18; A.D. e.g. pron. 10.11, 25.14, synt. 142.6; an example at Simplicius cats. 25.25. "Proper" vs. rare, unusual, etc.: note Aristotle's contrasts between "proper" names and rare, coined, metaphorical, altered, foreign, and obsolete words: poet. 21.1457b1ff., 22.1459a4ff., and cf. 25.1461a9ff.; also rhet. 3.2.1404b26ff, and Plato Cratylus 401b10ff., 408e8ff., 434c7f. Aristotle distinguishes homonymous from metaphorical expressions at e.g. top. 6.2.140a6–8. On "strict" vs. loose, metaphorical, etc., usage, see also Simplicius cats. 10.27f. (Theophrastus' distinction between strict and metaphorical language), 18.29ff. (strict vs. troped expressions), 41.4ff. ("strictly" vs. "catachrestically"), 81.7ff. (strict vs. metaphorical usage); Themistius an. po. 5.5 ("strictly" and "simply" vs. "commonly"); an example at Simplicius cats. 32.25f. Galen has a distinction between signifying ἰδίως and non-ἰδίως: inst. log. 17.6.

[24] There is a very useful summary and nominalistic critique of the major modern theories of metaphor in Scheffler 1979: 2ff., adopted by Kittay 1987: 178; both authors present their own theories. Kittay's is notable for its general analysis of the rôle of metaphor in cognition and conceptualisation, Scheffler's for its basis in an inscriptionalism with which Stoic semantics is in some ways comparable (see further, 6.2.3).

between "the world" and "the word".[25] In many ways the Stoa stood well outside the mainstream rhetorical and grammatical traditions, as noted in 3.4, and any Stoic distinction between "strict" and "loose" usage will presumably have to pay heed to (amongst other things) the unconventional significations of technical terms emphasised or assigned by Stoic philosophy. The school may even have regarded metaphors and other tropes, sometimes explained as compensations for the poverty of ordinary discourse (*e.g.* Cicero *de or.* 3.155), as symptoms of language's debased condition. But it remains quite obscure which criteria are to be appealed to when judging whether a term in ordinary use (as opposed to one which had undergone some semantic shift or refinement at Stoic hands) had both a "strict" and a loose signification, and which meaning was in play in which contexts. It would be interesting to know, in particular, where idioms were located in this classification of types of meaning. There is certainly no discussion in Stoic circles of what distinguishes metaphors from homonyms, as there is in Aristotle[26] and his commentators.

Simplicius, for example, in the context of a discussion about the criteria for the correct division of types of homonyms (*cats.* 31.24ff.), reports that Porphyry had drawn up a set of criteria based on what terms are available, whether ordinary or more arcane, for things, coupled with an unexamined (at least in this context) notion of "rightful" usage, that is, of a name's belonging "properly" to a thing (32.12ff.). The nub of the distinction is that homonymy occurs when a name is transferred to a thing lacking its own, proper name; if the thing receiving the name has its own name as well, the new name will be used metaphorically: 'for troped expressions will not be homonymous with what is said strictly', 'οὐ γὰρ τὰ

---

[25] Theon, for example, divides the sources of inclarity in narrative (the heading under which he locates the Stoic classification of ambiguity types) into "things" and "words": 5.2.1; *cf.* Quintilian 3.5.1, 8. *pr.* 6: 'orationem porro omnem constare rebus et verbis'.

[26] See esp. Hintikka 1971: 143f.; and *cf.* Kittay 1987: 2–4 (Aristotle on metaphor and the use of analogical reasoning).

τροπικῶς ῥηθέντα ὁμώνυμα ἂν εἴη τοῖς κυρίως λεγομένοις', 32.25f.[27] Simplicius goes on to observe that Porphyry's classification is not entirely consistent (some words are sometimes homonyms, sometimes metaphors: 33.4–16), but the grounds for the distinction are clear; and it is clear too that no appeal will be made to the intuitions speakers may have about the senses of terms, or how they are actually used, or to etymology, the modern linguist's standard methods.[28]

The qualification "strictly" in the Stoic definition, if it is to be substantive and informative, must bring with it explicit and precise distinctions like those formulated by Porphyry. Yet the Stoa seems to have neglected almost entirely the tasks of identifying and classifying the possible relations between the significations of ambiguous expressions, and there is no evidence either that they systematically set about marking off strict multiple significations from cases where the term is "multivalent", but not strictly ambiguous (see 3.5). The same seems to hold for "strict" and non-strict meanings, despite a small amount of evidence that these categories were applied to their terminology by the Stoics themselves. Chrysippus wrote a work *On Zeno's having used words strictly* (D.L. 7.122) and is reported to have understood the concept of the impression 'not strictly', 'οὐ κυρίως' but rather as 'simple alteration', 'ψιλὴ δὲ ἑτεροίωσις' (Sextus *M*. 7.376). (The comparable opposition at *M*. 8.400, 'καταχρηστικώτερον' (Chrysippus) *vs.* 'κυρίως' (Cleanthes), might be Sextus' own.) Alexander *an*. 72.5ff. makes this same contrast one of understanding the term τύπος 'more generally', 'κοινότερον', not 'strictly',

---

[27] Aristotle *rhet*. 3.2.1405a34ff. already has the basic idea. For the notion of transfer from proper or natural usage, see Cicero *orator* 92; Quintilian 9.1.4

[28] In modern linguistic theory the distinction between homonymy and metaphor is commonly discussed under the rubric of the principles which determine how items are to be listed in the lexicon which complements the grammatical component of any description of a language. Homonymy – when two or more distinct lexemes share a set of forms – and polysemy – when a single lexeme has two or more meanings – are standard categories: *e.g.* Lyons 1977: 550, Palmer 1981: 202. The difficulties lie in deciding between one polysemous lexeme and a set of homonymous lexemes, and in drawing up criteria for the distinction. (A further problem may therefore be posed for theoreticians who assume that the number of lexemes, and of their senses, is fixed for a language: Lyons 1977: 550.) The whole enterprise is criticised by Quine 1960: 129f.

'κυρίως'. Simplicius reports what might be an original Stoic description of the distinction between opposites 'most strictly', 'κυριώτατα', and 'secondarily' 'δεύτερον' (*cats.* 388.30, 32). A very important general question is thus left hanging: exactly why its authors might have thought their definition should pick out metaphor, or catachrestic usage, say, as linguistic phenomena close enough to ambiguity to need distinguishing formally and explicitly from it. Examination of the first two requirements in the definition – that ambiguities signify *pragmata*, and that they do so "linguistically" – has suggested that it was compiled partly from the internal resources of Stoic semantic theory, and partly in response to an attack on that theory, and on all similar theories, by an outsider. It has not, at least primarily, been the result of an investigation into ordinary speakers' unreflecting use of the term ἀμφίβολος, or into their intuitions about its meaning or scope. Recognition of the need for the requirement that significations be "strict" may also have been borrowed from outside, the likeliest source being rhetorical and grammatical/literary critical texts, where explicit distinctions between acceptable metaphors and unacceptable ambiguities would have been found useful for teaching composition or for defending canonical authors from charges of stylistic infelicity.

Several qualifications should be made to this account. First, the motivations even for Stoic stylistic experts would not have been so narrowly pragmatic (as noted in 3.4). Second, it is possible that the drawing of the line between strict and non-strict signifying was forced on the Stoa by philosophical rivals, who detected a weakness in the Stoa's use of ambiguity as a method of philosophical explanation and exposition: but the sources are silent on this point too. The problem certainly had a philosophical context outside the Stoa. Simplicius reports that it was Theophrastus and his followers who began the investigation of what Simplicius himself terms 'λέξις ἤ λέξις', including the distinction between strict and metaphorical *lexis* alongside general questions of grammar and stylistics (*cats.* 10.23ff.). This project can be seen as part of

Theophrastus' formalisation of Aristotle's stylistic teachings. It is probable that the Stoa had some knowledge of Theophrastus' own stylistics – at least, it adapted his doctrine of the excellences of discourse[29] – and ideas about the difference between strict, metaphorical, *etc.*, usages could have come from the same source. Finally, "transferred" usages were much appealed to in etymological accounts of word-formation, including that attributed by Augustine to the Stoa, and this, rather than ambiguity, may have been the chief locus for discussion in Stoic circles of what is/are to count as the strict signification/s of an utterance. Augustine himself makes ample use of it in his own classification of ambiguity types in Chapter 10 of his *de dialectica*.[30]

4.8 'κατὰ τὸ αὐτὸ ἔθος', 'in the same usage'

This condition is absent from the Suda version of our definition, its only important omission. In his *apparatus criticus ad loc.*, Bernhardy 1853: vol. I.I: 298 (followed by Schmidt 1839/1979: 51/73, n. 74 (1979: 140)) suggests emending the Diogenes text to 'κατ' αὐτὸ τὸ ἔθος', 'according to ordinary usage itself'; but our text is both intelligible as it stands, and more likely to be correct: why confine ambiguities to ordinary usage (which seems to be is what is intended)? Accordingly, it is adopted here, as it is by the editors of the *O.C.T.* and the Loeb.

The general thrust of this condition on ambiguities is still fairly clear, but its precise object of attention is now lost to sight. Ἔθος in rhetorical and grammatical texts can apply equally to the dialects ("common", "Doric", etc.) and literary

---

[29] See Atherton 1988: 419f. on the probable origins of this portion of Stoic stylistic theory.

[30] Here Augustine offers a complex taxonomy of different sorts of ambiguities (ch. 10, 18.25ff.C, 116ff.P; reference is by the page and line number of Crecelius' edition ("C", 1857) and the page number of Pinborg's edition ("P", 1975a); the chapter divisions are those of the Maurist edition). Here "transference", *translatio*, is prominent (19.4ff.C, 116–17P, and *cf.* Barwick 1957: 63). There is a strikingly similar account of the varieties of meaning change in Bloomfield 1935: 426–7.

idiolects (*e.g.* "Homeric usage") of Greek, and to non-Greek tongues.[31] It occurs in the Stoa's own definition of solecism, 'language contrary to the usage of reputable Greeks' (D.L. 7.59), and it was apparently employed by Chrysippus as equivalent to *ordinary usage* (Galen *P.H.P.* 4.2.12., p. 240, l. 25; already quoted in 3.5). The meaning "(linguistic) usage" is to be distinguished from the sense "custom" or "habit", as in the title of Dionysius the Apostate's Περὶ τῶν βαρβαρικῶν ἐθῶν, *On Barbarian Customs* (D.L. 7.167);[32] but, at the same time, ἔθος perhaps carries with it connotations of the public nature of language, just as social usages are public, and suggests that, although words are ultimately natural (see 3.5), and although syntax can reflect basic natural structurings (see 3.1), some elements of language may have a conventional basis – especially the jargon terms of expertises.[33] Given the standard use of ἔθος as *language*, Stoics might want to exclude too what Augustine was to call ambiguities of 'different origin' ('diversa origo'), a class of such oddities as *tu*, which is *you* (*tu*) in Latin but *of the* (τοῦ) in Greek.[34] In brief, ambiguity is a feature of many (of all?) languages, but can be a property of an utterance only within the rules of some one of them.

Yet it is not known what Stoic identity criteria were for

---

[31] Alone, ἔθος can mean "(ordinary) usage": *e.g.* Simplicius *cats.* 371.23–6; Pachet 1978: 364 is perhaps reading 'κατ᾽ αὐτὸ τὸ ἔθος' when he translates 'dans son sens ... ordinaire'. Τὸ κοινὸν ἔθος is "common usage", *i.e.* κοινή and not other dialects: *e.g.* A.D. *adv.* 132.27, 155.10, *synt.* 8.3f.; or poetic usage: *e.g.* A.D. *synt.* 223.13f., 251.8f. Dialects are frequently referred to as ἐθνικὰ ἔθη: *e.g.* A.D. *synt.* 62.10f., *cf.* 301.6f.

[32] Perhaps also at Plutarch *st. rep.* 20.1043D, where Chrysippus' *On Ways of Living* is quoted as mentioning those who 'have advanced to some degree and have been engaged in exercises and habits [reading 'ἔθεσι' for 'ἤθεσι'] of such a kind ...'; certainly at Simplicius *cats.* 395.8ff., a report of a Chrysippean theory of the "customary privation", ἐθικὴ or ἠθικὴ στέρησις, ἠθικὴ being the emendation of the *editio princeps*; here ἔθος clearly means "usage, custom" in a perfectly general sense.

[33] Kooij 1971: 5, n. 2, with reference to Quintilian's observation, 7.9.2, that *Ajax* will be ambiguous, comments that it will be so 'at least to literate people': whether or not proper names were ambiguous for the Stoa, could "literate persons" be said to possess a shared usage?

[34] *De dialectica* ch.11, 19.24–6C, 118P (mode of reference: n. 30). Augustine seems to be saying that such cases are only of interest to people who conduct discussions in several languages at once; this explains the example without justifying the assumption that it is an example of ambiguity.

languages: whether, say, κοινή, Attic, and Doric count as well as Greek, Latin, and Persian.[35] Usages within languages or dialects, such as the technical jargons of professionals, may also qualify, especially where the distinction between ordinary and philosophical usage is concerned, or even the shared idioms of even smaller groups, such as families or clubs.[36] As for the motivation behind the proviso, Stoic interests would perhaps have been determined, at least in part, by the need to meet or anticipate criticisms from rival philosophers, who could have constructed the following dilemma: If the Stoic definition makes no allowance for ambiguity's language-relativeness, then either an utterance ambiguous in one will be ambiguous in all or an utterance will not be ambiguous unless it is ambiguous in all. Diodorus Cronus' attack on ambiguity (4.5), which relies on the supremacy of speaker's meaning, could easily be adapted to a "proof" that distinctions between general usages are, like "natural" parts of speech, mere grammarians' constructs.

4.9 'ὥσθ' ἅμα τὰ πλείονα ἐκδέξασθαι κατὰ ταύτην τὴν λέξιν', 'so that several *pragmata* are understood simultaneously with respect to this utterance'

The bearer of ambiguity is an utterance or articulate sequence (4.4). The example, however, puts a core bearer of ambiguity (αὐλητρίς) into a minimal sentential context (... πέπτωκε), perhaps to ensure that what is signified is a *lekton*, perhaps simply to make its ambiguity more plausible, by presenting an

---

[35] The emphasis might go the other way: if the definition were composed at a relatively early date (3rd or 2nd cent. B.C.E.), then the distinction between different dialects of Greek might have been felt as more important than that between Greek and other languages. Greek interest in dialects began early, even before the rise and spread of κοινή: *e.g.* Herodotus 1.142; Plato *Prot.* 341c6ff., 346d, *Crat.* 401c2ff., 408e8ff., 434c7f.

[36] Also unknown, if less problematic, are individuation criteria for usages, in the sense that the Stoa would not want to treat them, any more than they would contexts, as abstract objects: they must be individuated by reference to users, their knowledge, or their linguistic behaviour: see 6.2.3 on this whole issue. Ebbesen 1981a: 1: 30 gives ἕξις as an example of a term which would perhaps fail this ambiguity test, given that it has different meanings only in the different usages of the Peripatos and the Stoa.

utterance which might actually figure in a conversation or in a text (see further, 6.2.3, on these problems). At all events, in determining whether a candidate ('... this utterance ...', or, if the Suda text is preferred, '... the same utterance', which comes to much the same thing) is or is not ambiguous it must have to be considered either in isolation, or in some particular context or situation of utterance. I take it that the minimally ambiguous utterance (that is, the shortest utterance the removal or alteration of which would remove or alter the semantic content(s) of the whole) is to be the bearer, because this guards against the "leakage" of ambiguity into the context – the unwelcome and absurd outcome that any arbitrarily large utterance in which the minimal utterance is embedded will be rendered ambiguous: say, the *Iliad* by a single homonym. The obstacles that the Stoa's materialism might have put in the path of constructing the obviously necessary generalisations, about contexts, about ambiguous utterances in particular, and about all linguistic items in general, will be set out in 6.2.3.

4.8 showed that the exact Stoic meaning of *usage* is lost, but the broad thrust of the condition that utterances signify 'within one and the same usage' is plain: to eliminate putative "ambiguities" taken from different dialects, languages, *etc.*, which just happen to share an orthography or a phonological shape. Here, the definition seems to be drawing distinctions within groups of hearers sharing a single usage, for this last condition leaves open the possibility that an utterance may be ambiguous for, say, Dion but not for his (less learned, sensitive, ingenious, experienced, *etc.*) compatriot Theon. At least, no reference is made to who is to do the "understanding" of the multiple significations. (Since no subject is indicated for the verb 'ἐκδέξασθαι', I have translated as if it were passive and not middle. The sense "understand, take (in a certain sense)" is common enough; there is a Hellenistic parallel at Polybius 10.18.2 (with 'τοὺς λόγους', 'the discourses').)

Further, it seems that an utterance may meet all other conditions, and yet fail to be ambiguous, because, as a matter of fact, no-one who hears or reads it understands multiple meanings by it.[37] This might be taken as restricting the Stoic conception of ambiguity to what has been called "psychological ambiguity", when a linguistically ambiguous utterance actually engenders confusion in an audience.[38] But there is no reason to think that the Stoics would have considered it improper to think of (occurrences of) utterances in isolation from any particular context, and to describe them as ambiguous or not, as much as their contextualised counterparts. This distinction is an intuitive one between (occurrences of) utterances in particular contexts or situations of utterance, and (occurrences of) utterances not so contextualised, or not yet contextualised, not a theoretical one between linguistic ambiguity attaching to the "maximally decontextualised" objects of linguistic or semantic theory, and psychological ambiguity attaching to utterances and inscriptions in actual discourse: for the Stoa lacked any such theoretical distinction. Von Arnim wished to read 'some', 'τινά', *pragmata*, instead of 'the several' *pragmata* here; the Suda text omits the definite article 'τά', 'the', so that just 'several' *pragmata* are understood. All these variants amount to a tacit, but entirely reasonable, condition that the number of meanings an utterance has on any one occasion of utterance need not exhaust its semantic multiplicity. But they do not help elucidate the conditions under which that semantic multiplicity is ascribed to *this lexis*.

What will still be needed is some account of the criteria of identity of utterances such that "the same" utterance can be coherently described in theory as ambiguous in this context but not that, or ambiguous in isolation but not in this or that context. If it is granted that such criteria can be established, as

---

[37] A more innocuous reading is that 'several *pragmata* are admissible with respect to this utterance': *cf.* Pachet 1978: 364, '. . . si bien que la même expression admet plusieurs sens'; the additional point might be that the significations must not be absurd, impossible, *etc.* This would at least acknowledge the difficulty noted earlier (4.5), that not all grammatically possible meanings are semantically acceptable. The meaning "accept, approve" seems rare with the compound ἐκδέχομαι, as opposed to the simple verb, however.

[38] On this distinction: *e.g.* Richman 1959: 87; Edlow 1975: 425 has suggested psychological ambiguity as an explanation of Chrysippus' thesis that 'every word is ambiguous', but this is unlikely in itself, and a far more plausible account can be found: see 6.3.4, 6.3.5.

well as individuation criteria for times and contexts (see 6.2.3 on these difficulties), "the same" utterance may be correctly described as ambiguous at t, and not at t_1: so that the way lies open to a distinction between ambiguity and equivocation (discussed in 7.2), and to an explanation of how it is intuitively obvious that "the same" *lexis* can be ambiguous in a context C but not in a broader, richer context C_1 which includes C.

Yet a weak point seems to be left in the Stoic defence of dialectic's usefulness for distinguishing ambiguities. If the Stoic definition does not provide a final, neutral arbiter of all disputes, in all usages, what is its use? Perhaps the authors of the definition were thinking too much of making their position secure against a charge of countenancing spurious ambiguities – utterances manifestly disambiguated by their contexts which would yet count as ambiguities because they meet the other conditions of the definition – at the expense of a certain open-endedness in the decision-procedure for ambiguities which dialectic promises to provide.

4.10   Example

Some of the problems associated with the example have been touched on already, in 4.4 and 4.9, and I refer to discussion there and in 6.2.3.

4.11   Conclusions

Where questions about the Stoic definition of ambiguity could be framed that were precise enough to be interesting the evidence has sometimes (it has to be admitted) simply given out. It has not proved possible to discover much of substance about the notion of usage, or about the difference between strict and non-strict signifying, while the provision that ambiguities signify λεκτικῶς has been interpreted only by recourse to speculation on the basis of a Hellenistic debate about language. But some features of it have, I think, been convincingly shown to be Stoic innovations: notably taking *lexeis* as bearers of ambiguity, and making explicit allowance for the effects of context and of different linguistic communities; probably, too, the stipulation that rules of meaning be public. These have raised crucial questions, above all about identity criteria for bearers and contexts, within and between media, and about the rôle of context in making and eliminating ambiguities, which still require exploration. In Chapter Seven I shall approach some of these difficulties afresh, with the help of new material from the two classifications. Examination of these lists may also help with clarification of the nature of the project Stoics were undertaking when they defined and classified ambiguity: that is, what sort of thing the definition and classifications were intended to explicate and organise, and which material, and which sorts of discourse, were thought relevant to them.

Applying the definition correctly must have required a broad philosophical and rhetorical education, as well as familiarity with technical concepts and categories, some of them exclusive to Stoic dialectic and metaphysics (*lexis*, linguistic signifying, *pragmata*) if the notions of usage, strict usage, and context or situation were to be applied with any precision and consistency. Assessing an utterance for ambiguity in Stoic circles might perhaps begin, in some cases, with the observation that an audience is uncertain in which of two ways to understand it; yet the process as a whole was surely never, and never intended as, an explication of that intuitive response.

It should be clear too that the definition is neutral as regards types of discourse, whether distinguished by purpose, literary genre, institutional or cultural context, or any other factor, despite ambiguity's particular importance for both the stylist and the logician. Whoever created it plainly wanted their definition to have its own location within the ample setting of dialectic, without subordinating it to some narrower discipline or topic or a range of these. If it has no positive rôle in Stoic contexts, ambiguity is at least not defined as a form of interference with, or failure of, communication or expression:

and that in itself represents an important conceptual link with modern understanding of the subject. It will be interesting to see how the two classifications compare with the Stoic definition on these two counts.

THE STOIC CLASSIFICATIONS 1:
THE SOURCES

5.1 Galen *On Linguistic Sophisms*

5.1.1 The contents of the work

Only one surviving classification of ambiguities is attributed to the Stoics by name. It is recorded by Galen in the fourth and final chapter of his little work *On Linguistic Sophisms* (variously *de captionibus* (or: *sophismatis*) *in dictione* (or: *penes dictionem*) in the manuscripts).[1] What that chapter preserves – the title of the treatise notwithstanding – is a list of types of ambiguity. Galen does treat it as a classification of linguistic fallacies; but this is explained by the nature and purpose of the work, not by anything in the Stoic system itself. Ostensibly, the Stoic classification is not even his central concern, which is rather to establish as correct and complete the classification of linguistic fallacies developed by Aristotle in his *Sophistical Refutations*. The Stoics appear merely to provide a form of inductive proof of Aristotle's success, and are attacked as, in comparison, unmethodical, unoriginal, and unobservant.

Thus, ironically, this Stoic system owes its survival to pro-Aristotelian bias, itself possibly only assumed for polemical purposes. The irony is double. With all its faults, the Stoic list is innovative, precise, and backed by a semantic and syntactic theory far more sophisticated than anything available in the *s. el.* Yet its very sophistication and complexity may have

---

[1] Galen's own bibliography mentions the treatise as Περὶ τῶν κατὰ τὴν λέξιν σοφισμάτων (19.47 K.), although the only independent manuscript gives the title as Περὶ τῶν σοφισμάτων παρὰ τὴν λέξιν, and this is how Galen himself describes linguistic fallacies here (*e.g.* 1.11, 3.4, 3.10G, 1, 5, 6E). As Müller observes, Galen must be deliberately recalling Aristotle's division of fallacies into two groups, παρὰ τὴν λέξιν, "due to language", and ἔξω τῆς λέξεως, "independent of language", at *s. el.* 4.165b23–4, and accordingly he takes κατὰ as a mistake (*Script. Min.* 2 (Teubner 1891), lxxix–lxxx; I owe this last reference to Gabler 1903: 17).

contributed to its eclipse. Aristotle's classification of linguistic and extra-linguistic fallacies enjoyed tremendous influence in the logical traditions of later antiquity and the Middle Ages – in fact its impact is still felt today – and, as a result, so did the division of ambiguity types on which his system of linguistic sophisms rests.[2] In contrast, the Stoic ambiguity classifications, along with the rest of Stoic logic, had effectively dropped out of sight by the end of antiquity. (Simplicius reports that by his day most Stoic books had disappeared: *cats.* 334.2–3.) All the same, Stoic survivals in rhetoricians' and grammarians' definitions and classifications of ambiguity are at least as common as material of Aristotelian origin, while logicians continued to preserve Stoic teaching in this field, albeit in a mutilated form, long after Stoicism itself as a distinct philosophy was a spent force.

The first requirement is a clear picture of the content and structure of the Stoic classification. The chief obstacles are Galen's own open hostility, his exegetical limitations (he apparently understood neither the system he purports to defend, nor the one he attacks), and, not least, the brevity of his exposition: for Galen limits himself to the name or general description of each Stoic "species", "division", or "kind" (διαφορά) of ambiguity, followed in each case by a single illustration and (with one exception) an explanation of the example. The nature and scope of each kind has therefore to be puzzled out from a tiny amount of material. Further, each illustration has been selected by Galen himself, from what might have been a lengthy list in his Stoic source; and deliberately or unconsciously he may have modified or misreported any or all of the authentic explanations. Inferences about the purpose of the original classification (by whom, and for whose use,

---

[2] On the survival of Aristotle's taxonomy of fallacies even in modern logic textbooks (admittedly in a very much modified form), see Hamblin 1970, esp. ch. 1; for a comprehensive survey of the ancient revival of interest in the *s. el.*, see Ebbesen 1981a: 1: 52ff.; and of scholastic writings on it, his chs. 4, 5. Ebbesen also has an interesting account of Stoic teaching on fallacies and ambiguity, 1981a, ch. 2.3 (21–51), to which I am much indebted. A description of Aristotle's classification of fallacies due to language is to be found in the Appendix.

it was compiled, and where precisely it belongs in Stoic dialectic) must be extremely cautious.

Yet Galen's hostility proves something of a blessing. The correct response to his criticisms of the Stoa is to check whether or not they are justified. He is (I am convinced) mistaken in all significant respects; but to reach that conclusion we must focus sharply on the Stoic principles of division and on the logical and semantic framework within which they were formulated, thereby both broadening our understanding of the Stoic classification and highlighting the differences between it and its Aristotelian counterpart.

5.1.2   Editions of the text

The text of the relevant portion (ch. 4) of the *de sophismatis*, although for the most part better preserved than the rest of the work, is a source of difficulties; Ebbesen's recent edition, 1981a: 2: 1ff. (ch. 4 is at 21–5), helpful elsewhere, sheds little light on the more troublesome obscurities. His critical introduction, viii–xii, is extremely thorough.[3] Previously the best edition had been Gabler's ('G'; 1903), which also contains Latin observationes. Earlier editions are: the Aldine ('A'; 1525); that of Basle ('B'; 1539); the Charterian ('Ch'; 1679); and Kühn's ('K'; 1827: *Opera Omnia*: 14:538–98). There is also a Latin translation (by Limanus, 'Li'; 16th cent.). Kalbfleisch ('Ka') read the chief manuscript, and Gabler includes many emendations of his in the text or apparatus criticus. Arnim's edition, *S.V.F.* 2.153, pp. 45–6, contains some helpful emendations, also recorded by Gabler. The text in the *TLG*, *s.v.* ἀμφιβολία, suggests several emendations later adopted, presumably independently, by other editors, including a correction of Galen's explanation of the first species, Common, on the basis of Theon's account of it. Edlow 1977: 88–112* 'substantially' (87) reproduces (but does not always

---

[3] Ebbesen 1981a: 2: ix–x observes that scholiasts on the *s. el.* had recorded extracts from the *de soph.*, but no new material has emerged for ch. 4, the scholiasts being interested primarily in Galen's comments on the *s. el.* itself.

translate) Gabler's text. Hülser 1982: 3: 396ff., fr. 633, reproduces Edlow's (that is, Gabler's) text of ch. 4; his translation
follows Edlow's. There is a partial translation into French in
Baratin and Desbordes 1981 at 133–40 (ch. 4 is at 138–40).
Long and Sedley print and translate a composite text, based
on Gabler's, Arnim's, and Ebbesen's versions, with two emendations by Sedley, as their 37Q.

The only independent manuscript (all the others are copies
of this) is in Milan (Ambrosianus Q 3 Sup., gr. 659, = 'M').
According to Ebbesen 1981a: 2: ix, it is fourteenth-century,
not sixteenth-, as claimed by Gabler 1903: v (or fifteenth-, as
claimed by Nutton 1978: 348). All references to the *de soph.*
will be by the page and line number of Gabler's 1903 edition
and the page number of Ebbesen's, 1981a: 2: 1ff., which conveniently incorporates the Gabler pagination and lineation. I
have indicated Gabler's and Ebbesen's numbers in the text
and translation which follow. They are based on Ebbesen's
text, but with a few differences; editorial changes are indicated
in the *apparatus criticus*. Additions in the translation enclosed
⟨thus⟩ correspond to editorial additions; those enclosed [thus]
are intended only to make the English a little smoother. Numerous problems in the text and translation are fully discussed in my commentary. Of course, it is sometimes impossible to capture a Greek ambiguity even less than adequately in
English, and my version ranks fidelity to the original over ease
of reading.

5.1.3   The text, ch. 4, 12.10–14.5G, 21–23E

(p. 12 Gabler)

⟨ Ἐπεὶ δ'⟩ εἴρηταί τινα καὶ τοῖς Στωικοῖς   10
περὶ τούτου ⟨τοῦ⟩ μέρους, δίκαιον ἐπελθόντα ἰδεῖν, εἴ τις ἔξω   11
πίπτει τρόπος τῶν εἰρημένων· εἴη γὰρ ⟨ἂν⟩ ἐπαγωγ⟨ικ⟩ή   12
τις αὕτη πίστις, καὶ δίκαιον ἄλλως μηδεμίαν δόξαν ἀνδρῶν   13
εὐδοκίμων πάρεργον τίθεσθαι. τὸν μὲν οὖν τῆς ἀμφιβολίας   14
ὅρον, εἰ καὶ πρὸς πολλὰ τῶν ἡμετέρων μάχεσθαι δοκεῖ, τό   15
γε νῦν ἐατέον, ἑτέρας γὰρ καὶ ὑπὲρ τούτων [νοσεῖν] σκοπεῖν   16
πραγματείας· τὰς δὲ διαφορὰς τῶν λεγομένων ἀμφιβολιῶν   17
αὐτὰς ληπτέον· εἰσί γε πρὸς τῶν χαριεστέρων λεγόμεναι τὸν   18

(p. 13 Gabler)

ἀριθμὸν η΄. μία μέν, ἣν κοινὴν ὀνομάζουσι τοῦ τε ⟨δι⟩ ηρημένου   1
καὶ τοῦ ⟨ἀ⟩διαιρέτου, οἷα ἐστὶν ἡ αὐλητρὶς πεσοῦσα· κοινὴ   2
γὰρ αὕτη τοῦ τε αὐλητρὶς ὀνόματος καὶ τοῦ διῃρημένου.   3
δευτέρα δὲ παρὰ τὴν ἐν τοῖς ἁπλοῖς ⟨ὁμωνυμίαν⟩, οἷον   4
ἀνδρεῖος, ἢ γὰρ χιτὼν ἢ ἄνθρωπος. τρίτη δὲ παρὰ τὴν ἐν   5
τοῖς συνθέτοις ὁμωνυμίαν, οἷον ἄνθρωπός ἐστιν. ἀμφίβολος   6
γὰρ ὁ λόγος, εἴτε τὴν οὐσίαν εἴτε τὴν πτῶσιν εἶναι σημαίνει.   7
τέταρτον δέ ἐστι παρὰ τὴν ἔλλειψιν, ⟨ὡς τίνος   8
σὺ εἶ;⟩ καὶ γὰρ ἐλλείπει τὸ διὰ μέσου, οἷον δεσπότου ἢ   9
πατρός. πέμπτη δὲ παρὰ τὸν πλεονασμόν, ὥσπερ ἡ τοιαύτη   10
ἀπηγόρευσεν αὐτῷ μὴ πλεῖν. τὸ γὰρ μὴ προσκείμενον ἀμφί-   11

10 Ἐπεὶ δ' add. Ka: δὲ post εἴρηται add. Ch K   11 τούτου τοῦ G: τὸν τοῦ
M A B: περὶ τῶν τοῦ μέρους δικαίων ἐπελθοῦσιν ἰδεῖν K: περὶ τούτων, ⟨ἃ
κατὰ⟩ μέρος δίκαιον ἐπελθοῦσιν ἰδεῖν Arnim   12 ⟨ἂν⟩ ἐπαγωγ⟨ικ⟩ή add.
Arnim   13 μηδεμίαν G: μὴ δὲ μι M μὴ δὲ μὴ A B   14 τίθεται M A B:
corr. Li (ponere)   16 ἐατέον Ch K: θετέον M   νοσεῖν om. Li Ch K
σκοπεῖν σκ- e corr. M   17 πραγμα᾽ M πράγματα A B πραγματείας ἐστι
Ch K   18 εἰσίν M A B   γε leg. δὲ vel γὰρ TLG   λεγομένων M:
λεγόμενοι TLG: corr. Arnim
1 μίαν M A B: corr. Li (una)   ⟨δι⟩ηρημένου TLG Ebbesen: εἰρημένου
M: om. A B: εἰρομένου propos. Ka Arnim   2 ⟨ἀ⟩διαιρέτου TLG Ebbesen:
διαιρετοῦ M edd.   παῖς οὖσα M Ch K: om. A B: corr. Ka Arnim   κοινὴ
... αὐλητρις om. A B   3 ⟨δι⟩ηρημένου Ka, propos. TLG Arnim: εἰρημένου
M edd.   4 δευτέρον M A B: corr. Li (altera)   ἁπλῶς M: corr. Li
(simplicibus)   5 τρίτον M A B: corr. Li (tertia)   τὴν e corr. M
8–9 τέταρτον M A B: corr. Li (quarta)   ὡς τίνος συ εἶ; Sedley: ὃ ἔστιν ὡς
συὶ καὶ ὡς M A B: ὃ ἐστι σου· καὶ γὰρ Ch K: σός ἐστιν [ὡς] υἱός· καὶ γὰρ G οἷον
οὗτος τούτου – vel σὸς vel σου παῖς· ἐλλείπει ⟨γὰρ⟩ vel sim. propos. Ebbesen
10 πέμπτον γὰρ (non δὲ) M A B: corr. Ch (quinta Li)

180

(p. 12 Gabler)

⟨Since⟩ the Stoics too have had something to say 10
on this topic, it is right to go on and see if any [Stoic] mode [of 11
ambiguity] falls outside the ones mentioned
[*sc.* the Aristotelian modes]: for this will be an inductive 12
proof of a sort [*sc.*, of the correctness of the Aristotelian 13
classification of linguistic fallacies], and, in any case, it is not right
for any opinion of gentlemen
of good reputation to be set down as trivial. The [Stoic] definition of 14
ambiguity,
even though it seems to conflict with many of our ⟨beliefs ?⟩ [*or*: 15
with many of our modes of ambiguity?]
must now be passed over, for examining these belongs to another 16
field of inquiry. But the species [*or*: divisions, kinds] themselves of 17
what they call "amphibolies"
must be grasped. By the more sophisticated [Stoics] they are said 18

(p. 13 Gabler)

to be eight in number: (1) The first [species], which they call 1
"common to what is divided
and undivided [*or*: indivisible]",⁴ is this sort of thing, αὐλητρίς 2
πεσοῦσα; for this is common
to the word αὐλητρίς [=*flutegirl*] and to the divided [*sc.* to αὐλή 3
τρίς, = *a house three times*].
(2) The second [species is] due to ⟨homonymy⟩ in simples, *e.g.* 4
ἀνδρεῖος; for [it can be said of] either a shirt [=*pour homme*] or a 5
man [=*manly*]. (3) The third [species is] due to
homonymy in compounds, *e.g.* (*a*) *man is*; for the sentence is 6
ambiguous, whether it signifies that the being [*or*: substance] is,
or that the case is. 7
(4) The fourth [species is] due to elleipsis, ⟨as *whose* 8
are you ?⟩; for it omits the mediate term, *e.g.* [*or*: *i.e.*] *master's* 9
or *father's*. (5) The fifth [species is] due to pleonasm, such as this 10
sort [of ambiguity],
he forbade him (*not*) *to sail*; for the (*not*) by its addition makes the 11
whole ambi-

---

⁴ '⟨ἀ⟩διαιρέτου' could also standardly be translated *indivisible*, and this is appropriate to the unitary word *flutegirl*; but 'διηρημένου', 'divided', in the following line (l. 3) suggests *undivided* may be the translation required here.

δοξον ποιεῖ τὸ πᾶν, εἴτε τὸ πλεῖν ἀπηγόρευσεν ἢ τὸ μὴ πλεῖν. 12
ἕκτην φασὶν εἶναι τὴν μὴ διασαφοῦσαν τί μετὰ τίνος ἄσημον 13
μόριον τέτακται, ὡς ἐν τῷ καινυκενηπαρελασσεν. τὸ 14
γὰρ ⟨η⟩ στοιχεῖον ⟨ἢ πρῶτον ἢ τελευταῖον⟩ ἂν γένοιτο 15
⟨ἢ⟩ διαζευκτικόν. ἑβδόμη δέ ἐστιν ἡ μὴ διασαφοῦσα τί μετὰ 16
τίνος τέτακται σημαντικὸν μόριον, ὡς ἐν τῷ 17
(p. 14 Gabler)
πεντήκοντ᾿ ἀνδρῶν ἑκατὸν λίπε δῖος Ἀχιλλεύς. 1
ὀγδόη ⟨... δ᾿ ἡ⟩ μὴ δηλοῦσα τί ἐπὶ τί ἀναφέρεται, 2
ὡς ἐν τῷ Δίων ⟨ἐστὶ καὶ⟩ Θέων ⟨εὕροις ἄν⟩· ἄδηλον γάρ ἐστιν, εἴτε 3
ἐπὶ τὴν ἀμφοτέρων ὕπαρξιν ἀναφέρεται εἴτε ἐπὶ τοιοῦτον 4
οἷον Δίων Θέων ἐστὶ ἢ πάλιν. 5

12 εἴγε (post πᾶν) M A B Ch: corr. K 13 μὴ διασαφοῦσαν TLG Arnim:
μηδὲν σαφοῦσαν M 14 rest. Arnim ex Il. 23.382: καὶ νῦν καὶ μὴ παρέλασε
M A B 15–16 suppl. G: ἂν μὴ γένοιτο M: μὴ γένοιτο ἂν leg. TLG
1 sec. Ar. s. el. 4.166a37f. rest. Ch: πεντήκοντ᾿ ἀνδρῶν ρ᾿ λείπεται M A B
2 ⟨.... δ᾿ ἡ⟩ supplevi pro quo spatium XIII f. (G), XX–XXIII (Ebbesen) litt.
relictum in M A B δέ ἐστιν ἡ suppl. G δηλοῦσα τί Ch K: δηλονότι M A B
3 Δίων ... ἂν Sedley: Δίων Θέων εὕρω M: Δίων Θέων εὕρων A B: Dion Theon
est Li edd. ἄδηλος M A B: corr. Li (incertum) 4 τοιούτων M A B:
corr. Ch

valent, whether he forbade him to sail or not to sail.   12

(6) The sixth they say is [the species] which fails to make clear which   13
non-significant

part is ranged with which [non-significant] part, as in   14
καινυκενηπαρελασσεν;

for the element ⟨η⟩ might be ⟨the first letter [*sc.* of the word ἧπαρ,   15
liver, or the last letter [*sc.* of the word κενή, *empty*]

or⟩ the disjunction [*i.e.* 'or' in 'καί νυ κὲν ἢ παρέλασσεν ...', '... and   16
now he would have driven past, or ...' (*Il.* 23.382)]. (7) The seventh
[species] is that which fails to make clear with

which [significant part] is ranged which significant part, as in: 17
(p. 14 Gabler)

> *Noble Achilles left 50 [out] of 100 men [or: ... 100 [out] of 50 men or*:   1
> *... 150 [of] men].*

(8) The eighth [species] ⟨... is that⟩ failing to make clear what is   2
being referred to what,

⟨as you might find in⟩ *Dion* ⟨*is also*⟩ *Theon*; for it is unclear   3
whether

it is being referred to the existence of both [*sc.* of both Dion and   4
Theon], or to something

like "Dion is Theon" or *vice versa* [*sc.* "Theon is Dion"].   5

Abbreviated titles of the Stoic species in Galen's list:

1. Common   5. Pleonasm
2. Homonymy in Simples   6. Non-significant Part
3. Homonymy in Compounds   7. Significant Part
4. Elleipsis   8. Reference

At one juncture, in the description of the very first species, the *TLG* and Ebbesen emend on the basis of a parallel passage in the rhetorician Theon of Alexandria, who records the only other recognisably Stoic ambiguity classification to survive today.

5.2 Theon *progymnasmata*

5.2.1 The contents of the work

Very little is known about Aelius Theon himself. Even his *floruit* is uncertain, and he is dated variously to the late first century B.C.E, to the first century C.E. as a contemporary of Quintilian, to the second century C.E., and even later; the most plausible date is probably the mid-first century C.E., and it is possible Theon exercised some influence on Quintilian (Lana 1951: 150, with Butts 1986: 6). Of the seven works with which the Suda credits him, whose titles strongly suggest he was a professional rhetorician, only his *progymnasmata* or *Preliminary Rhetorical Exercises* (henceforward the "*prog.*") has survived, but incomplete.[5] The *prog.* belongs to an old and familiar genre (Reichel 1909; Clark 1957: 177ff.; Bonner 1977: 250ff.): it is a teacher's handbook (Butts 1986: 23) of the earliest stages in education in rhetorical practice and theory for pupils who had attended a grammar school.

The classification itself is employed as a list of some of the sources of obscurity in narrative, traditionally one of the divisions of the rhetorical speech to be practised and mastered before embarking on rhetorical training proper.[6] What sets Theon's treatment apart is precisely his explicit inclusion of the Stoic list, for in all other respects it is wholly conventional:

---

[5] Or rather, the Greek manuscripts end in the middle of the chapter on "Law"; four further chapters are preserved in the Armenian tradition. On the manuscript traditions in Greek: Lana 1959; in Greek and Armenian: Butts 1986: 17ff., 23ff. On the later rearrangement of material "On narrative" in the *prog.* (into which the Stoic classification is inserted): Butts 1986: 8ff.; on the original order of the chapters: Butts 1976: 11ff.

[6] Accounts of the rhetorical theory behind the *prog.* also in *R.E. s.v. Theon* (5), vol. 5a, pp. 2041–54; of the contents and structure of the *prog.*: Butts 1986: 7ff.

in tackling ambiguity as a stylistic defect; in approaching narrative by way of the stylistic excellences – clarity, conciseness, and plausibility – and their opposites; in the further division of these into the fields of "subject matter", πράγματα, and "style", λέξις; in its dichotomy of the stylistic component into single terms and complexes; even in its list of the sorts of obscure single terms defined.[7]

The classification is not ascribed to any Stoic(s) by name, but to "the dialecticians", which was not, of course, exclusively a designation of logicians from the Stoa.[8] Theon may not even have known his authorities' true identity, although he does voice conventional pieties regarding the traditional philosophical training for orators (*prog.* 59.1–4), and has at least a smattering of Stoic and other philosophical views on rhetoric, epistemology, ethics, and politics (*cf.* Reichel 1909: 23ff.; Butts 1986: 6f.). The principal exegetical difficulty is not, however, whether the list is essentially Stoic – even the most cursory comparison with the authentic *de soph.* classification shows that it must be of Stoic origin – but how far it has been altered – expanded, cut, or reorganised – by Theon himself. On a first or casual first reading, *prog.* 81.30–2, for instance, might seem to imply that every ambiguity belongs in the Common species. I strongly suspect that here Theon has opted for an informality and simplicity of presentation in keeping with both the elementary nature of his treatise and the broad-based education he favours. His descriptions of two of the species, Elleipsis and Reference, seem to have been infelicitously abbreviated and simplified; the same deliberate brevity may well account for this slight confusion at the beginning of his report.

---

[7] The three narrative excellences are standard: *e.g. ad Her.* 1.14; Cicero *inv.* 1.28; D.H. *Lys.* 18; Quintilian 4.2.31ff.; as is the division into "things" and "words": *e.g. rhet. Alex.* 30.1438a27f.; *ad Her.* 1.15; Cicero *inv.* 1.29; Quintilian 4.2.36ff. Theon displays some knowledge of Aristotle *rhet.* 3.2.1404b1ff.: see also n. 12.

[8] On the other hand, not even the staunchest admirer of Diodorus and Philo will want to attribute it to the Dialectical school (on which see further, 7.6). Butts 1986: 305, n. 35 (p. 376) misinterprets *prog.* 81.31: first, he takes the words 'πρὸς τῶν διαλεκτικῶν' to relate to the first type of ambiguity only; second, he renders them 'in oral presentations', apparently as if the text read 'πρὸς τῶν διαλέκτων'.

5.2.2   Editions of the text

References will be by the volume, page and line number of the edition of Spengel ('Sp.') in his *Rhetores Graeci Minores*, (Leipzig, 1853–6; 3 vols.); the classification is at vol. 2 (1854), 81.30–83.13. Spengel has no notes on the text of this passage in his *praefatio* (2: v–vii); his text is basically that of Ch. E. Finckh ('F') (Stuttgart, 1834), who did not have direct access to any of the manuscripts (Butts 1986: 60). The *TLG*, *s.v.* ἀμφιβολία, immediately following the text of the *de soph.* classification already mentioned in 5.1.2, reports an obviously correct emendation of the account of the first species, but does not present a complete text. Butts's new text of the classification,[9] where it does differ from Spengel's, seems inferior; but no serious textual problems are apparent either.

Additions in the translation enclosed thus: [...] are again my own, and are again intended only to make the translation smoother and more idiomatic. I have myself numbered the different types for ease of reference. Again, it is often impossible to capture a Greek ambiguity in a translation.

---

[9] Butts 1986: 304.107–310.153: his text and translation unfortunately do not run parallel, and, while the introduction is very useful, with a detailed account of the various conjectures concerning Theon's dates (1–6), the rendering and exegesis of the relevant portions of text are not wholly reliable; see n. 8. On the manuscripts: n. 5.

5.2.3　The text, p. 80.30–p. 81.13 Spengel

(p. 80 Spengel)

Ἀσαφῆ δὲ τὴν ἑρμηνείαν ποιεῖ ἡ λεγομένη ἀμφι-　30
βολία πρὸς τῶς διαλεκτικῶν, παρὰ τὴν κοινὴν τοῦ ἀδιαι-　31
ρέτου τε καὶ διῃρημένου, ὡς ἐν τῷ αὐλητρις πεσοῦ-　32

(p. 82 Spengel)

σα δημοσία ἔστω· ἕν μὲν γὰρ τί ἐστι τὸ ὑφ' ἕν καὶ ἀδιαί-　1
ρετον, αὐλητρὶς ἔστω πεσοῦσα δημοσία, ἕτερον δὲ τὸ　2
διῃρημένον, αὐλὴ τρὶς πεσοῦσα ἔστω δημοσία. ἔτι δὲ καὶ　3
ὅταν τι μόριον ἄδηλον ᾖ, μετὰ τίνος συντέτακται, οἷον　4
ουκενταυροις ὁ Ἡρακλῆς μάχεται· σημαίνει γὰρ　5
δύο, οὐχὶ κενταύροις ὁ Ἡρακλῆς μάχεται, καὶ οὐχὶ ἐν　6
ταύροις ὁ Ἡρακλῆς μάχεται. ὁμοίως δὲ ἀσαφὴς γίνεται　7
φράσις καὶ ὅταν τι σημαῖνον μόριον ἄδηλον ᾖ, μετὰ τί-　8
νος συντέτακται, οἷον　9

　　　οἱ δὲ καὶ ἀχνύμενοί περ ἐπ' αὐτῷ ἡδὺ γέλασσαν.　10

ἀμφίβολον γὰρ πότερον ἐπὶ τῷ Θερσίτῃ ἀχνύμενοι, ὅπερ　11
ἐστὶ ψεῦδος, ἢ ἐπὶ τῇ καθολκῇ τῶν νεῶν· καὶ πάλιν,　12

　　　δῆμον Ἐρεχθῆος μεγαλήτορος, ὃν ποτ' Ἀθήνη　13
　　　θρέψε Διὸς θυγάτηρ, ⟨τέκε δὲ ζείδωρος ἄρουρα⟩.　14

πότερον τὸν δῆμον ἢ τὸν Ἐρεχθέα φησὶν ὑπὸ τῆς Ἀθη-　15
νᾶς τραφῆναι καὶ τεκεῖν τὴν γῆν. παρὰ ταύτην δὲ τὴν　16
ἀμφιβολίαν τὰ Ἡρακλείτου τοῦ φιλοσόφου βιβλία σκο-　17
τεινὰ γέγονε κατακόρως αὐτῇ χρησαμένου ἤτοι ἐξεπίτη-　18
δες, ἢ καὶ δι' ἄγνοιαν. παρατηρητέον δὲ καὶ τὸ μὴ ὑπερ-　19
βατοῖς χρῆσθαι, οἷά ἐστι τὰ πολλὰ τῶν Θουκυδίδου· οὐ　20
γὰρ καθόλου τὸ τῶν ὑπερβατῶν γένος ἀποδοκιμάζομεν·　21
ποικίλη γὰρ διὰ τούτου καὶ οὐκ ἰδιωτικὴ γίνεται ἡ φρά-　22

32 ΑΥΛΗΤΡΙΣ Sp. αὐλητρὶς Butts
3 αὐλὴ τρὶς πεσοῦσα *TLG* (Lederlinus *rest. e* Quint. 7.9.4, D.L. 7.62) F Sp.:
αὐλητρὶς παῖς οὖσα *codd.*, *edd.* ante F (*cf.* Galen *de soph.* 4, 13.2G 21E
αὐλητρὶς παῖς οὖσα M)　　5 ΟΥΚΕΝΤΑΥΡΟΙΣ Sp. οὐ Κενταύροις Butts
14 *add.* Heinsius Walz Sp. *ex.* Hom.: *in app. crit.* Butts　　15 φασὶν Butts

(p. 81 Spengel)

Expression is also made obscure by what is called "ambi-	30
guity" by the dialecticians, (1) [first] owing to the [ambiguity which	31
is] "common to what is undivi-	
ded [*or*: indivisible]¹⁰ and divided", as in *let an αὐλητρις having fall-*	32

(p. 82 Spengel)

en become state property: for one thing is what is single and undivi-	1
ded [*or*: indivisible], *let an αὐλητρίς* [*=flutegirl*] *having fallen become*	2
state property, and another thing is what	
is divided, *let an αὐλή τρίς* [*= a house three times*] *having fallen*	3
become state property. (2) And again, [there is obscurity/ambiguity]	
whenever some part is unclear, with which [part] it is arranged, *e.g.*	4
Heracles fights ουκενταυροις: for it signifies	5
two things, "not with centaurs (οὐ κενταύροις) Heracles fights", and	6
"not amongst	
bulls [*or*: in Tauri] (οὐκ ἐν ταύροις) Heracles fights". (3) Likewise,	7
there is obscure	
language too whenever some significant part is unclear, with	8
which [significant] part it is arranged, *e.g.*:	9

'They [*sc.*, the Greeks] despite their anger at him [*or*: it] laughed gaily' [*Il.* 2.270]:	10

for it is ambiguous whether they are angry at Thersites (which	11
is false), or at the drawing down of the ships; and again,	12

'The people of great-hearted Erechtheus whom Athena, Zeus' daughter,	13
once nourished and the fruitful earth brought forth' [*Il.* 2.547–8]:	14

[it is ambiguous] whether it says that it was the people or	15
Erechtheus who were nourished by Ath-	
ena and whom the earth brought forth. It is because of this	16
ambiguity that the books of Heraclitus the philosopher are obscure	17
to such a degree, whether he employed it intention-	18
ally, or else out of ignorance. (4) One must also take care not to	19
employ hyper-	
bata [*sc.* transpositions], such as are very frequent in Thucydides;	20
for it is not that	
we entirely disapprove of the genus of hyperbaton;	21
for by means of it language becomes varied and unusual.	22

---

¹⁰ This ambiguity of ἀδιαίρετον has already been mentioned, n. 4. Again, the Stoics may well be emphasising the unity – semantic as well as graphic or phonological – of the noun αὐλητρίς.

σις· μηδὲ μεταξυλογίαις, καὶ ταύταις διὰ μακροῦ· τὰ   23
γὰρ ἐγγὺς λαμβάνοντα τὴν ἀπόδοσιν οὐ λυπεῖ τοὺς   24
ἀκροατάς. καὶ μέντοι καὶ τὸ ἐλλείπειν τινὰ ὀνόματα πρὸς   25
τὴν σαφήνειαν ἐναντίον ἐστί. παραφυλακτέον δὲ καὶ τὸ   26
παραλλήλους τιθέναι τὰς πτώσεις ἐπὶ διαφόρων προ-   27
σώπων· ἀμφίβολον γὰρ γίνεται τὸ ἐπὶ τίνα φέρεσθαι,   28
οἷον ἐπὶ μὲν τῆς αἰτιατικῆς, ἐφ' ἧσπερ καὶ μόνης τῶν   29
πτώσεων πολλοὶ γίνεσθαι τὴν ἀμφιβολίαν νομίζουσιν,   30
ὡς παρὰ Δημοσθένει κατὰ Μειδίου, ἴσασιν Εὐαίωνα   31
πολλοὶ τὸν Λεωδάμαντος ἀδελφὸν ἀποκτεί-   32
(p. 83 Spengel)
ναντα Βοιωτὸν ἐν δείπνῳ· ἄδηλον γὰρ πότερον   1
Εὐαίων ἀπέκτεινε Βοιωτὸν ἢ Βοιωτὸς Εὐαίωνα, ὅπερ ἐστὶ   2
ψεῦδος· ἀλλὰ καὶ ὁ Λεωδάμαντος ἀδελφὸς πότερον Εὐαί-   3
ων ἐστὶν ἢ Βοιωτός; ἐπὶ δὲ τῆς εὐθείας, ὡς παρ' Ἡρο-   4
δότῳ ἐν τῇ πρώτῃ, εἰσὶ δὲ καὶ Αἰγύπτιοι Κολχοί·   5
ἄδηλον γὰρ πότερον οἱ Αἰγύπτιοι Κολχοί εἰσιν ἢ τού-   6
ναντίον οἱ Κολχοὶ Αἰγύπτιοι. τὸ δ' αὐτὸ καὶ ἐπὶ τῆς γε-   7
νικῆς καὶ δοτικῆς, Κολχῶν δὲ ὄντων Αἰγυπτίων· καί,   8
Κολχοῖς δὲ οὖσιν Αἰγυπτίοις· ἐπὶ μὲν οὖν τῆς αἰτιατι-   9
κῆς ἀναμφισβήτητόν ἐστιν, ἐπὶ δὲ τῶν ἄλλων πτώσεων   10
φανερόν, ὅτι προσθέσει ἄρθρων οὐκέτι ἀμφίβολος γίνεται   11
ἡ λέξις· εἰσὶ δὲ Αἰγύπτιοι οἱ Κολχοί· δῆλον γὰρ γέγονεν,   12
ὅτι περὶ Κολχῶν λέγει, ὡς εἰσὶν Αἰγύπτιοι.   13

(5) [One must take care] not [to employ] interpolations either, that   23
is, lengthy ones;
for early resumption of one's account does not trouble   24
one's audience. (6) Moreover, omitting certain words is   25
contrary to clarity. (7) One must also guard against   26
applying parallel cases to different per-   27
sons; for it becomes ambiguous to whom [*or*: to which things?]   28
[each of the cases] is being referred;
e.g. in the accusative, in which alone of the   29
cases many people think this [sort of] ambiguity occurs,   30
as in Demosthenes' *Against Meidias* [§71, p. 44.10f. *ed.* Goodwin]:   31
'Many people know that Euaion [or Boiotos] (Leodamas' brother)   32
kill-
(p. 83 Spengel)
ed Boiotos [or Euaion] (Leodamas' brother) at a dinner-party'; for   1
it is unclear whether
Euaion killed Boiotos, or Boiotos Euaion, which is   2
false; but also, is Leodamas' brother Euai-   3
on, or Boiotos? But [this sort of ambiguity also occurs] in the   4
nominative [case], as in Hero-
dotus Book I [*sic*; but = 2.104.1], 'Egyptians too are Colchians':   5
for it is unclear whether the Egyptians are Colchians or the oppo-   6
site, that Colchians are Egyptians; and the same in the ge-   7
nitive and the dative too, *of Colchians being Egyptians/of Egyptians*   8
being Colchians, and,
to Colchians being Egyptians/to Egyptians being Colchians; so with   9
the accusa-
tive [case] it is undisputed, and with the other cases   10
obvious, that by addition of [definite] articles the expression is no   11
longer ambiguous:
The Colchians are Egyptians; for it is now clear   12
that it says about Colchians that they are Egyptians.   13

Abbreviated titles of the types of ambiguity in Theon's list:
1. Common   5. Interpolation
2. Part   6. Elleipsis
3. Significant Part   7. Reference
4. Hyperbaton

5.3 Comparisons

Galen and Theon are very different authors to use and interpret. While Galen's true purpose in composing the *de sophismatis* is not altogether obvious, his declared motive in including the Stoic list is clear: to lend indirect support to his proof of the superiority of the Aristotelian system. It is thus in his best interests at least to seem to be making an accurate report of what the reader is surely meant to take as that system's most serious competitor in the field. Of course, it is no longer possible to judge the faithfulness of his account or to verify whether the Stoic classification he reports really is the best – or even the best Stoic – rival he knew. It would be an understandable, if improper, ploy to imply that the Stoic classification is the best rival to Aristotle's, when in fact it is not. Edlow 1975: 426f. observes that Galen must 'expound the Stoic system fully' if he is going to use it as he does 'in all conscience': the question is just how tender Galen's conscience was on such points. Further, Galen distorts the Aristotelian theory, as will emerge in 5.4. Still, the evidence strongly suggests that he has nowhere deliberately twisted the facts to fit his proof: where he goes wrong he is almost certainly guilty of no more than misinterpretation of a highly complex and not always consistent text.

With the Stoic classification the situation is interestingly different. Every one of Galen's criticisms of it fails to hit the mark; yet in every instance much or even all of the evidence by which his verdict is overturned comes from his own report of the system. If Galen has done injustice to his Stoic authorities, deliberately or in blind incomprehension, he cannot have done so very thoroughly; whereas, were all available material on the system of linguistic fallacies presented in the *s. el.* derived from the Galen text alone, the modern picture of it would be seriously distorted.

Even within the narrow confines of the *de soph.*, then, Galen's trustworthiness as a reporter of other people's doctrines seems to vary widely; and to show why, his own biases, interests, and areas of competence and ignorance must be examined. To explore this intricate topic would take me far out-side the scope of this chapter, and I shall note only that Galen's untrustworthiness is an exegetical hazard made still more dangerous by its unpredictability. The specific form and effects it will have must always be puzzled out from whatever his acknowledged or tacit bias is in relation to each topic or question. This is true of the *de soph.* It is also true, for exam-ple, of Galen's invariably unfriendly attitude to atomistic the-ories, which are lumped together more or less indiscriminately in, for instance, the *de elementis sec. Hipp.* (1.415ff.K) and the *de const. med.* (1.245ff.K). It is no use looking in either work even for careful doxographical reports of the various theories, for Galen's sole purpose is to undermine them (partly because of their alleged anti-teleology: *e.g. de usu partium* 11.8, vol. 2, p. 135, ll. 14ff. Helmreich), and all he requires is something common to them all which he can then attack (*de elementis* 417). The argument in the *de const. med.* is more complex, since Galen's sights are trained there on Anaxagoras, Emped-ocles, and Asclepiades, as well as on Democritus and Epi-curus, but is basically an extension of that deployed in the *de elementis*. At least in the *de soph.* something approaching the Stoics' own words, not merely the crudest of hostile summa-ries, is on offer.[11]

Galen's hostility to the Stoics in the *de soph.* is not hard to detect; the remaining puzzles are only indirectly connected with it, but will help with understanding the Stoic list, and are therefore given a section to themselves (5.4). None of these considerations applies to Theon's report. The *prog.* is what it seems: a handbook for elementary teachers of rhetoric. Theon has no partisan axe to grind (at least in philosophy), no duty to reproduce his authorities fully and precisely, and no self interest to serve by appearing to do so. In so fully reporting a

---

[11] I am indebted to John Vallance for signposts in the, to me, trackless and inhospita-ble terrain to be crossed in assessing Galen as a source; and for a case-history I refer to his account of Galen's staggering unreliability in reporting Asclepiades' physical theory, largely explained by his eagerness to find sticks with which to beat Methodics: 1990, esp. 32–43, 53–8. Galen's quotations in the *P.H.P.* from Chrysippus' *de anima* have a similar value to his report of the *de soph.* classification: on the former, see already 3.5.

classification from apparently quite outside his own discipline he seems to be unique amongst rhetoricians, and grammarians as well, although some of these authors were plainly aware of what they may acknowledge to be dialectical (which usually means Stoic) teaching on the subject. There is also the question, arising quite naturally from recognition of Theon's unique position, where he found his Stoic list: that is, not only whether his immediate source was some earlier rhetorical treatise or a Stoic text, but also under which broader rubric the classification was located. The importance of this second query will become clearer as we proceed.

Theon's unconcernedly eclectic use of sources, a characteristic amply illustrated by his two lists of causes of linguistic obscurity at *prog.* 81.8–83.13, 129.11–130.36, is the chief difficulty in dealing with his evidence. The second list falls under the heading of the exercise which commonly figures last in primers of this sort, one closely linked with a topic familiar enough from more advanced rhetorical textbooks: legal controversy arising from laws, wills, and other written documents, which is one of ambiguity's two "homes" in ancient rhetoric (see further, 8.2). The associated theory of *stasis* (literally "position, stance", also called, *inter alia*, *status*, literally "state, condition", *controversia*, "dispute, point of dispute") is complex and ramified; roughly, it constructs a set of criteria for identifying all possible types of issue on which legal cases may turn. Here, it is the interpretation of an ambiguously-framed document. The system itself was adopted in one form or another in virtually every subsequent rhetorical handbook. The exercise "law" looks forward to the more advanced, practical training centred on *stasis* theory. Theon follows tradition here, just as he does in treating ambiguity as a defect of style. The list of the causes of obscurity is itself an ill-organised and idiosyncratic hodge-podge that can function as a reliable guide neither to the Stoic nor to the Aristotelian elements (much altered and interpreted by Theon) which figure among its constituents. It remains, never the less, deeply interesting for the historian of Stoic influence outside the philosophical schools, and I shall discuss it in more detail in 8.2. I shall also refer to it while investigating the individual Stoic ambiguity species in the following chapter.

Its companion list at *prog.* 81.8–83.13 is more sharply divided into what look to be "Aristotelian" and "Stoic" portions. It comprises, besides the dialecticians' classification, a list of types of single term liable to create obscurity which may be dependent, at some remove, on similar lists in the *Rhetoric*, and probably in the *Poetics* as well (81.8–29). It contains word-categories – "poetic", "tropic", "archaic" – not mentioned by Aristotle, however; and it is presented in a rigid, summary format appropriate to its function and context but alien to the more wide-ranging and discursive treatment accorded to stylistic matters by Aristotle, especially in the *Rhetoric*.[12] Learned comparisons of authorities are not to be expected in a teacher's handbook.

There is, accordingly, no guarantee that the differences between the *de soph.* and *prog.* classifications are not wholly or in part the result of Theon's, or his source's, silent tinkering with the Stoic model.[13] These differences apply to the examples provided, but also extend to the species themselves and their order of appearance. What follows is a schematic summary, using the shorthand titles listed earlier:

De sophismatis		*Progymnasmata*	
1. Common	(1)	1. Common	(1)
2. Homonymy in Simples		(*)	
3. Homonymy in Compounds		(*)	
		2. Part	(6)
		3. Significant Part	(7)

---

[12] Compare with *prog.* 81.8–29 (poetic, invented, tropic (or figured), archaic, foreign, homonymous), the "blacklist" at *rhet.* 3.2.1404b28–30 (unusual, compound, coined). Note that Theon also knows both the Stoic and Aristotelian definitions of synonyms, but not as such: *prog.* 129.13f., 130.1f.

[13] Ebbesen 1981a: 1: 37 is noncommittal on the extent of Stoic influence on Theon's classification. Barwick 1957: 17, by contrast, seems to assume without further comment that it is Stoic through and through. Edlow 1975, 1977 appears not to know it at all. LS 1987: 2: 231 feel that Theon's list 'seems to derive ultimately from the same classification' as does Galen's.

4. Elleipsis	(6)		
5. Pleonasm		(*)	
(*)		4. Hyperbaton	
(*)		5. Interpolation	
		6. Elleipsis	(4)
6. Non-significant Part	(2)		
7. Significant Part	(3)		
8. Reference	(7)	7. Reference	(8)

The number to the left of each column indicates its position in that list; in the case of the *de soph.* classification, the numbering is an explicit part of Galen's report, and presumably authentic. The number to the right, in brackets, indicates its position, if any, in the other list. An asterisk * against a species in a list shows that it is present in the other list but absent in this one.

The most obvious questions concern the species themselves: which (if any) of the two species present in the *prog.* list alone – Hyperbaton and Interpolation – are Stoic; why three species – the two Homonymies and Pleonasm – are found in the *de soph.* classification alone; why two more species – Part, Non-significant Part – should look very much alike, and yet be differently described; and, finally, what differences, if any, exist between the species present in both lists, Common, Elleipsis, and Reference. Furthermore, variations in the order of presentation have to be accounted for. The *de soph.* sequence, although problematic, is not arbitrary: it promises an orderly progression from less to more complex linguistic ambiguity-bearers, from undifferentiated articulate sequences, through single terms, and non-syntactically ambiguous sentences, to bearers whose constituents can be grouped in various ways to produce different sets of words or different grammatical constructions of one and the same set. At the same time, the choice of ambiguity bearers made by the "more sophisticated Stoics" is not entirely happy, and it is hard to see the rationale behind some of the distinctions they have made. I shall attempt both to justify these doubts and to reconstruct the arguments they may have used to form and consolidate their principles of division.

It should already be obvious that the authenticity of the *prog.* classification would be more or less secure were it to display a structure at least close to that of the *de soph.* system. But to dismiss as Theonic intrusions all dissimilarities between them would be too crude a procedure. I shall argue that Hyperbaton and Interpolation could indeed have been inserted by Theon: but from the same, broader-based Stoic classification (of sources of obscurity) which provided the material on ambiguity. On the other hand, the new location of Elleipsis and the absence of Pleonasm may well be due to genuine disagreement between the authors of the lists as to whether they are true ambiguity species, and I shall try to trace out the arguments that might have been deployed in support.

One further question can no longer be postponed: can either classification be judged the "better" of the two, by some appropriate scale of values? External evidence cuts both ways. Galen describes his Stoics as "more sophisticated": but it is always possible that Galen did not honestly select the best Stoic classification he knew. Theon, for his part, is unlikely to have included the dialecticians' list unless it seemed to him relatively straightforward, and consequently likely to be of use to teachers in the classroom, because easily comprehensible to and memorable by mere schoolboys (with a few judicious alterations by Theon himself); yet that need not mean that it was "less sophisticated", or less successful. Where direct, internal comparison is possible the *de soph.* list does, I think, emerge as a little more flexible in its handling of the bearers of ambiguity. The modern reader will always be at something of a disadvantage because the definitions of ambiguity on which the classifications were based are not known (for certain, at least). In any case a firmer idea will be required of the criteria for the success of ambiguity classifications, and I shall return to this issue in 6.1.

This tricky internal comparison between the classifications can be supplemented with another type of external information, that drawn from the *prog.* as a whole. What are most clearly Theon's additions and alterations can be picked out by forming a picture of his own interests, requirements, and areas of expertise. In this connection, illustrations as well as species must be scrutinised and, if necessary, jettisoned. The most outstanding example is the insertion of Hyperbaton and Interpolation, best accounted for as one manifestation of Theon's concern with the topics of linguistic clarity and obscurity, the concern which motivates his use of the dialecticians' classification. Authentically Stoic differences are most plausibly explained by the hypothesis that the *prog.* Stoics produced their classification as part of a general theory of style, more precisely as part of an account of the linguistic "virtue" clarity and its corresponding "vice", obscurity. In contrast, the *de soph.* classification seems not to have been inspired by an interest in ambiguity's rôle within any one discipline or field of discourse. Here, naturally, caution is necessary. A classification adapted to the needs of the theorist or teacher of style is precisely what Theon requires in the context of the *prog.* There must be independent grounds for believing features of the list to be genuinely Stoic before they can be employed as evidence for Stoic concentration on ambiguity as, or as causing, a stylistic defect; and I shall argue that good grounds do in fact exist for such a belief.

So long as it remains obscure what a Stoic dialectician would count as an accurate and correct definition of ambiguity, neither system can be judged by their authors' own lights. All that can be done is to work from within the classifications, eking out our meagre supply of information by comparisons of the lists with each other, and again of them with the Aristotelian, grammatical and rhetorical systems. Thus whatever flaws I have tentatively identified in either Stoic system may have been wrongly described, or may be the result of a misreading of the text. Apparent inconsistencies or omissions may have been defended in commentaries and monographs now lost, while, on the other hand, the supporting arguments I have supplied may have had no corresponding Stoic originals. Similarly, the responses I have made to Galen's attacks on what he detects as faults in the *de soph.* list are merely speculative reconstructions based on very limited evidence. What Theon and Galen record are, after all, mere taxonomic skeletons, stripped of the flesh of research, debate, retraction, and reformulation. Only in the authentic divergences between the classifications is there any hint of the thoughtful and fruitful investigations and disagreements in which they must have had their origin.

5.4 Galen's use of the Stoic classification

It may be tempting, at first sight, to take the appearance of a Stoic classification of ambiguity in a work entitled *On Linguistic Sophisms* as (at the very least) yet more evidence for a connection of some sort between ambiguity and fallacious argument in Stoic dialectic. Indeed, the opening sentence of Galen's fourth chapter might appear to support the stronger assertion that what he goes on to expound is a list not of ambiguities, but of linguistic fallacies, parallel to the Aristotelian system with which Galen later compares it. Galen writes:

⟨Since⟩ the Stoics too have had something to say about this topic, it is right to go on and see if any [Stoic] mode falls outside the ones mentioned [*sc.* the Aristotelian ones]; for this would be an inductive proof of a sort [*sc.* of the correctness of the Aristotelian classification of linguistic fallacies], and in any case it is not right for any opinion of gentlemen of good reputation to be set down as trivial. (12.10–14G, 21E)

An argument for the stronger claim would go something like this. Galen's avowed purpose is to prove the correctness and exhaustiveness of Aristotle's classification of linguistic fallacies. The outline of his proposed proof runs as follows:

Since the task before us is to demonstrate that sophisms due to language occur in just so many ways as Aristotle said those due to ambiguity ⟨occur⟩ ... (4.7–9G, 7E)

In his first chapter Galen quotes[14] and puzzles over the sentence in the *s. el.*, 4.165b27–30, which prescribes the forms such a proof will take, both inductive and syllogistic:

---

[14] Galen's text (or his memory of it) differed slightly from ours. He has 'ἕτερος' instead of the MS 'ἄλλος', 4.165b28, and 'ταὐτὸν' for 'ταὐτό', b30, both here and at 11.5G, 19E. Elsewhere he has 'ταὐτά' for 'ταὐτό' (3.16, 19G, 6E).

Having listed these modes, he at once demonstrates that he has not omitted a single one, and that it is impossible for any one of the fallacies due to language to fall outside the [modes] mentioned. The argument through which he demonstrates these points is this: 'Proof of this is by means of induction, and also a syllogism, if some other is taken, and that in so many ways by the same words and word-compounds [λόγοις] we may fail to signify the same thing. (3.2–9G, 5f.E)

The merits and demerits of Galen's interpretation of this admittedly terse and obscure remark of Aristotle's need not be explored here.[15] I want to observe only that, whereas Galen's second and third chapters are devoted to finding the premisses which he believes should constitute Aristotle's syllogistic proof, the fourth is explicitly presented as 'an inductive proof of a sort' of the *s. el.* system. If the Stoics turn out to have identified an ambiguity mode unknown to Aristotle, Galen's boast that his favoured classification is the true one will be a hollow one.

It is irrelevant in this context that the Stoic list actually contains as many as six modes which cannot be accommodated within its Aristotelian rival (which escapes Galen entirely). But for Galen's induction to be in his eyes appropriate and effective he must believe himself to be comparing classifications of items of the same type: that is, of linguistic fallacies, not of ambiguities. Galen never says in so many words that the Stoics had constructed anything but a list of species of ambiguity. And yet his assumption that the two systems can be profitably compared is surely some evidence that they really are parallel, and that consequently what he records is a Stoic classification of species of sophism due to ambiguity.[16] That bodes ill for the argument of my Chapter Seven. There I

---

[15] On Galen's reading of this passage: esp. Ebbesen 1981a: 1: 78f.; also Edlow 1977: 71. On Galen's arguments in *de soph.* chs. 2 and 3: Ebbesen 1981a: 1: 78–82; also Edlow 1977 chs. 5, 6, 8. The *de soph.* is excellent evidence that the long tradition of commentary on the *s. el.* had already got underway in Galen's time: see ch. 1, 3.22–4.2G, 6–7E, where Galen criticises two groups of commentators for their failures, respectively, to try to explain *s. el.* 4.165b27–30, and to explain it if they did try.

[16] This seems to be the interpretation of Long and Sedley, to judge by their description of the context of the Stoic classification in the *de soph.*: 'Galen's defence of his classification of linguistic fallacies against the Stoic one' (1987: 2: 231). But at 1987: 1: 230 the classification is explicitly a classification of ambiguities, which 'provides plentiful material for the resolution of fallacies'.

shall contend that the peculiar relation between ambiguity and the sophism in Stoic logical theory is always indirect: ambiguity produces either a formal defect, incoherence, or at least one false premiss, and hence a false argument. There are no Stoic species of argument made defective by the presence in them of an ambiguity. Stoic arguments are systems of *lekta*, and simply not the sorts of thing in which ambiguities can figure.

The objection can be overcome. By reading the important first sentence (already quoted) of *de soph*. ch. 4 in the light of the syllogistic proof conducted earlier in the treatise, the stronger claim I have sketched can be safely rejected, while leaving Galen with, by his own lights, a sound basis for induction (even if his conclusions must be rejected). There will be no need to posit a quasi-Aristotelian theory of the Stoic "linguistic fallacy".

At the end of *de soph*. ch. 3, Galen believes he has already demonstrated deductively that Aristotle's classification is the only correct one. Galen's proof has two premises, each buttressed by a prosyllogism: (a) ambiguity is the sole cause of linguistic sophisms (ch. 2); (b) there are six and only six (*i.e.* only the Aristotelian) modes of ambiguity, *viz*., Homonymy, Amphiboly, Combination, Division, Accent, Form of Expression (ch. 3; see Appendix A for a full description). In his second chapter, ambiguity is identified as the only essential "vice", κακία, of language, λέξις, or the sole cause of its only defect, obscurity, ἀσάφεια, which is the same as "not signifying well", τὸ μὴ εὖ σημαίνειν (6.10–13G, 9E). Correspondingly, there is only one genuine linguistic "virtue", ἀρετή, which is "signifying well", or "clarity", σαφήνεια. (Not signifying at all is not a defect of language, but its destruction, for language which does not signify cannot be performing its specific function, and ceases to be language: 5.10–6.10G, 9–11E, esp. 5.19–20G, 9E.[17]) This theory represents a radical

---

[17] That homonyms do not signify at all – since they fail to make clear what the speaker wishes to argue – was argued by the school of Nicostratus: Simplicius *cats*. 26.21ff. The idea that each thing has its own κακόν and ἀγαθόν of course appears in Plato *Rep*. 10.608e6ff.; but Galen distinguishes, as Plato's Socrates does not, between that which impairs and that which destroys.

departure from traditional teaching on style that identifies a plurality of excellences and defects, amongst which ambiguity, under the rubric of obscurity, is assigned a regular, if not exalted, position (see 3.4, 6.6.2, 8.3).

It is Galen's concentration on a very narrow range of linguistic exchanges – those between the sophistic questioner and his interlocutor/victim – which probably explains his unorthodox approach to language. Galen sees ambiguity only as it is exploited by sophists in order to produce fallacies and so secure victory in argument. This approach dominates even *de soph.* 3, which sets out to prove the correctness of the Aristotelian division of ambiguity species: note especially 9.18–10.4G, 17E, on sophistic procedure, while Galen's motive for proposing an analysis of λόγος" (a "compound of words") is that 'premisses too are λόγοι' (7.14f.G, 12E).[18] At the start of his second chapter, Galen asserts:

That point at any rate is clear to all, that all linguistic fallacies must come about by some defect of language; for sophists, holding fast to this ⟨defect⟩ as to a governing principle [ἀρχή] ⟨....⟩[19] and deceive those who have less experience in these matters, and do not perceive the deception. (4.11–15G, 7E)

This conception of the sophist's deliberate and illicit use of ambiguity is of course reminiscent of the *s. el.* (*e.g.* 1.165a13–17), and it is possible that Galen's own views on what he saw as the very close links between fallacy and ambiguity were at least confirmed by a reading of the Aristotelian treatise. Yet Galen can hardly be said to be following faithfully in Aristotle's footsteps. The *s. el.* is not just about the ways relatively inexperienced youths can be taken in by silly puzzles. Some ambiguities elude even the experts; and for some people the

---

[18] The text states that we must first grasp what is 'λόγος τε καὶ ἐκ λόγων λόγοι γὰρ καὶ αἱ προτάσεις'. The first five-word sequence is obelised by Gabler and Ebbesen, each proposing a different reconstruction. The sense of the last five words is plain, however.

[19] Unless '... καὶ ...' is simply omitted, as by Kühn and the Charterian edition, there must be a lacuna between '... holding fast ...' and '... and they deceive ...'. In his *app. crit. ad loc.* Ebbesen proposes 'παρακρούονται' or 'σοφίζονται'; either is appropriate, but neither will add anything substantial to the sense.

detection of ambiguities is a valuable tool in the solution of philosophical problems (33.182b22–7). The awkward inconsistencies between the *s. el.* and Galen's reading of it come into sharp focus at the end of *de soph.* 4, where the "fact" that sophists exploit the possibility of a word's being variously accented seems to be taken as unimpeachable evidence that there is such a thing as the ambiguity mode Accent, one unrecognised by the Stoa (15.15f.G, 25E). Aristotle, in contrast, is not sure there are any Accent fallacies, or even that Accent is a form of ambiguity, as we shall see a little further on.

Someone convinced by Galen's argument about the special status of ambiguity might try to construct on its basis a general account of linguistic excellence, applicable to the writing and criticism of both prose and poetry. But this is not Galen's programme. Other alleged "defects" of language, apart from ambiguity (such as verbosity, or excessive brevity) qualify as such only if they produce ambiguity or obscurity, which Galen seems to regard as co-extensive, if not as identical (7.7G, 12E): the disjunctive 'ambiguity or obscurity', 'τὴν ἀσάφειαν ἢ τὸ διττόν', here may suggest that Galen was not altogether happy with his manoeuvre, but the final sentence of his ch. 2 makes it obvious he had no qualms: 'If this [*sc.* obscurity] alone is the vice of language ['εἰ δὲ μόνη κακία λέξεως αὕτη'], and our earlier claims [*sc.* those made in ch. 2] are correct, and if all linguistic fallacies occur as a result of its vice, then all linguistic fallacies will be due to ambiguity' (7.8–10G, 12E). A literary critic, in particular, would no doubt find much to quarrel with in Galen's identification of ambiguity as the sole cause of obscurity, and obscurity as the sole defect of language.[20] But Galen is looking at its effect only on argument, and on a special form of argument: the terse, constrained question-and-answer discourse between sophists and their victims. Hence he can, by his own criteria, afford to

[20] On Stoic and ancient theories of the excellences of language, see 3.4, 8.3. One fairly typical later stylistic treatise, Ps.-Herodian *de soloecismo et barbarismo*, p. 308.14ff. Nauck, lists six stylistic excellences, purity, clarity, conciseness (a hint of Stoic influence), use of the proper names for things, good composition of words, and appropriateness.

ignore such problems as are posed by the arrangement of subject matter, choice of vocabulary, and sentence-construction, and such as are dealt with by Theon in his account of the excellences and defects in the language of narrative, as also, in a variety of contexts and formats, by other, traditional writers on style.[21]

It may perhaps be unfair to accuse Galen of offering a crude and inadequate general stylistic theory. Yet his analysis would fail to convince even were its object exclusively the correctness or otherwise of strictly philosophical or scientific discourse, of whose intelligibility such faults, distinct from ambiguity, as verbosity, over-conciseness, poor organisation, and the use of irrelevant illustrations (or no or too many or too few illustrations) may all prove destructive.

At all events, the implications of Galen's theory for classifiers of ambiguity are plain. Given that ambiguity has but one rôle to play – the creation of fallacies – then to approach it as, say, Aristotle had done outside the *s. el.* would be quite useless. Galen would have no interest in it as a source of literary critical problems, as an offence against good Greek, or even as exploited by unscrupulous orators to form apparent enthymemes (see 3.5). There is certainly no room for ambiguity as a topic of independent importance, requiring observation and analysis outside the boundaries of any one context or application: precisely the approach I believe was taken by the Stoics whose work Galen reports.

So intent is Galen on showing up ambiguity's dangers that he not only overlooks a step in his argument, but he also seriously misinterprets three of the Aristotelian system's fallacy modes, Accent, and Combination and Division. A brief description of these may be helpful.

Considered as a single type of ambiguity, Combination-

---

[21] The Stoa too seems not to have isolated distinct stylistic virtues and vices for various types of discourse, but any similarity with Galen's equally unorthodox approach is superficial, for, while he focusses on a single form of discourse purely for the purposes of this proof, the Stoics refused to countenance varieties of discourse for broader, philosophical reasons: see 3.4.

Division will produce ambiguities where a set of words can be differently combined or divided syntactically into one or other of a selection of syntactic groupings, e.g. 'ἐγώ σ' ἔθηκα δοῦλον ὄντ' ἐλεύθερον', I made you, free, a slave/a slave, free' (4.166a36f.). As two modes of fallacy, each exploits this syntactic fluidity contrariwise, Combination when the sophist combines a group of words which his victim had assumed were syntactically divided, Division when he divides a group which the victim had assumed to be syntactically combined. Aristotle signals the distinction between Combination and Division in these two different rôles, as fallacy modes and as ambiguity types, at 4.166a35f. He does not consistently treat Combination and Division as fallacy modes due to ambiguity; he is uncertain whether what is in question is exploitation of the multiple meaning of a single *logos*, or of the set of single meanings of several *logoi* which happen to be composed of the same words in the same order.

Much the same holds for Accent sophisms: Aristotle apparently hovers between treating words formed from identical letters, but differently pronounced, as ambiguous, and treating them as several distinct words distinguished by prosody. Aristotle is not even sure there are really any Accent fallacies at all, 21.177b35–7, and only a single, feeble, example is offered, at 177b37–178a3, where the word (or words) in question is (or are) οὐ, *not*, and οὖ, *where*.

The argument of *de soph.* ch. 2 is supposed to allow the conclusion (not explicitly drawn) that all modes of fallacy due to language are modes of fallacy due to ambiguity, since all linguistic fallacies are caused by ambiguity. It is nowhere argued, however, that all Aristotle's ambiguity modes are as a matter of fact exploited to cause sophisms, and this despite Aristotle's own cautious comments on the Accent mode:

It is not easy to devise an argument [*or*: statement, λόγος] dependent on accent in unwritten dialectical exchanges, but rather in written ones and in poems (4.166b1–5)

There are no arguments dependent on accent, whether written or spoken, except perhaps a few [πλὴν εἴ τινες ὀλίγοι γένοιντ'ἄν]. (21.177b35–7)

Aristotle, as noted, gives only one example of the Accent fallacy mode; yet of only two sample fallacies provided by Galen, one turns on accent (10.2f.G, 17E).[22]

Galen's tacit assumption that all modes of ambiguity are actually modes of linguistic fallacy does not in itself vitiate his demonstration: none the less, it should have been stated and argued for. This omission, I think, is to be explained by his single-minded hostility toward ambiguity as the tool of tricksters and charlatans preying on the unwary tyro. Galen does not ask whether every last one of the Aristotelian ambiguity modes really does produce fallacies because in the *de soph.* that is the only rôle ambiguity has.

In the *s. el.* Combination and Division are without question genuine fallacy modes. What is doubtful, as already observed, is whether the sophisms which fall under these modes are due to ambiguity. On occasion Aristotle asserts they are not, but the issue is never satisfactorily settled. The problem will repay a little further exploration. There are passages in the *s. el.* (6.168a26–8, 20.177b1–9) which show Aristotle behaving as if three of his modes – Combination, Division, Accent – were due not to ambiguity at all, but rather to what Edlow 1977: 19, 21, 24ff. calls "linguistic confusion": he sometimes argues as if they occur where quite different words or *logoi* are mistaken one for the other (I would add: or are illicitly substituted one for the other), not where the same word or *logos* signifies two or more things. Aristotle's difficulty is that he has not yet pinned down identity criteria either for words or for their combinations, and as a result is uncertain whether or not a change of accent or of syntax respectively will produce a new word or sentence.

Galen shares this uncertainty. At 15.10–15G, 25E, he asserts that 'the division [διαλήψει] of the whole' and 'the empty time', 'ὁ κενὸς χρόνος' – *i.e.* the pauses between words in a *logos* or the punctuation which indicates them – are 'extrinsic', 'ἔξωθεν', to the *logos*, and that it is these which make it

---

[22] The text is unclear, but the sophism must in some way exploit the (assumed) ambiguity of ορος (= ὅρος, *boundary*, *landmark*; or = ὄρος, *range of hills*). The other, interestingly, exploits autonymy: see 6.3.5.2.

ambiguous in the Combination/Division mode(s), where the syntactic relations between words are unclear. If by this he means that marks of syntactic grouping are extrinsic to an intrinsically-structured *logos*, the *logos* cannot be ambiguous: Combination/Division will change it into a different *logos*, with its own syntax. If a *logos* is not so structured, on the other hand, the ambiguity-bearer will be a mere collocation of single terms (as the definition "composite of words", σύνθεσις ὀνομάτων, would suggest (7.16f.G, 13E)). Treating a sentence no differently from a shopping list is hardly a satisfactory state of affairs, but it appears not to have caused Galen any anxiety. He seems to have compared words to stones, and the *logos* to the wall or building formed from them, as if there existed only the stones and what is put together from them (8.1–3G, 13–14E), and the structure of the whole were irrelevant. The Stoics, as we shall see, avoid the whole mess by assigning (primary) syntax to the complex λεκτόν (6.2.4, 6.5.2, 6.5.4).

Similar problems beset Galen's treatment of Accent: by classing it too as a form of "potential" ambiguity (8.10G, 15E), that is, one where it is merely possible for the bearer to signify more than one thing, he is able to overlook or sidestep the need to determine exactly whether words (and *logoi*, if they are held to form a separate group of accent ambiguities) whose prosodic features are deliberately ignored are genuine ambiguities, or not. His comments on such cases certainly suggest that he has not made up his mind on this issue (see esp. ch. 3, 9.4f.G, 9.10G, 16E). His failure to decide is not unreasonable – the issue is indeed a difficult one – but his failure to acknowledge the difficulty is culpable.

Galen also fails to grasp the facts that Combination and Division, which he treats as a single fallacy mode (*e.g.* 2.5–9G, 4f.E), cannot be two distinct species of ambiguity, and thus that his proof that there are just six, the six Aristotelian, ambiguity modes, cannot hope to succeed. There are indeed six Aristotelian fallacy modes due to language: there are not six Aristotelian species of ambiguity. In one key passage, quoted by Galen himself, Aristotle can be interpreted as saying that there are six ambiguity types;[23] but Galen should not have accepted this one passage as authoritative if his intention was to reconstruct Aristotle's own system. Combination and Division are so-called in the *s. el.* because the sophist who uses them illicitly "combines" or "divides" a pair or group of words which his interlocutor has assumed are (respectively) divided or combined syntactically, assent having been given to a premiss on the basis of that assumption. The underlying linguistic phenomenon, whether it is a form of ambiguity or not, is single: it is the sophist's exploitation of it which can take either of two forms, division of what should be combined, combination of what should be divided. It is important to remember, when comparing the Aristotelian and Stoic systems, that the latter is not (primarily) a classification of ways in which people can be deceived by language. Rooted in this difference in intent are revealing terminological distinctions which will emerge later.

Finally, Galen overlooks Aristotle's observation, *s. el.* 6.168a17ff., that all the fallacy modes can be grouped under the general heading of *ignoratio elenchi*, specifically a non-linguistic mode: *s. el.* 5.167a21ff. Aristotle's treatment of the whole topic has far more flexibility and investigative verve than can be accommodated by Galen's rigid formatting of the problem.

In the light of this analysis of Galen's motives and arguments it is easy to see why a Stoic classification of ambiguity species can be employed as an inductive check on an Aristotelian classification of linguistic fallacies. As far as Galen is concerned a classification of one will simply be a classification

---

[23] This is the quotation, from 4.165b28–30, which Galen muses over near the start of the *de soph.*: 'καὶ ὅτι τοσαυταχῶς ἂν τοῖς αὐτοῖς ὀνόμασι καὶ λόγοις οὐ ταὐτὰ δηλώσαιμεν'. It is far from clear how this sentence should be read (in particular, 'ὅτι' might mean "that" or "because", and the function of the first 'καὶ' is obscure). Aristotle does, however, appear to be talking about the possibility or the fact that 'we may not indicate the same things with the same words and *logoi*' (*i.e.* that we may say something ambiguous) in 'as many ways' as he has just listed at 165b25–7: and that list comprises six items. I have to admit to a suspicion that Galen simply did not read beyond, say, ch. 4 of the *s. el.*, and so never encountered any of the passages which conflict with the programmatic passage he cites and uses.

of the other. He can override the original aims, whatever they were, of the Stoic authors since, in his eyes, ambiguity is merely the cause of linguistic fallacy, and all modes of ambiguity are modes of linguistic sophism. He will be effectively blind to the possibility that the Stoic or any other classification could have been compiled for different purposes. In short, Galen has chosen not to examine the phenomenon of ambiguity independent of its abuse in eristic combat.

This assimilation of ambiguity to deliberate and fraudulent equivocation – changing the meaning of an ambiguous expression between several occurrences of it as an illicit strategy of argument – is understandable, given the thesis Galen explicitly sets out to prove. The puzzle is rather that Galen should have thought this particular theory of Aristotle's worth proving. He is neither an Aristotelian scholar, nor a partisan Peripatetic, except in logical matters. He does invoke the favoured Aristotelian philosophical method, dialectic, in the shape of discovery of premises (ch.1, 4.4–6G, 7E), and seems to allude to it again, at the beginning of his fourth chapter, where the introduction of the Stoic classification is justified (quoted earlier, p. 199), a passage which cannot fail to recall, for example, *top.* 1.13.105a21ff.: 'As for the tools by which we shall have a good supply of arguments, they are four in number: one, the getting of premises; two, being able to distinguish in how many ways each thing is said; three: the discovery of differences; four: the investigation of similarity'. Yet its promise of balance and fairness is soon reneged on by the ill-founded, irrelevant, and rather testy criticisms which occupy most of the rest of the chapter.

Barnes 1991: 55 has dismissed the work as 'a juvenile essay on ambiguity'. More charitably, and I think more accurately, Ebbesen 1981a: 1: 79 feels that the 'treatise is a sophist's ἐπίδειξις, a display of the proof-procedure that he [Galen] persistently claimed was the feature of his own philosophy that made it superior to everyone else's'; and it is true, and remarkable, that the main *de soph.* proof does seem to consist of an example of each of the aspects of logic – demonstration from axioms, division into genera and species, proof-discovery by identifying appropriate axioms – which Galen considered vital. (Elsewhere, 1987: 109, Ebbesen describes the work as 'an oversize note' on *s. el.* 4.165b24–30, the passage which inspired Galen's proof-discovery.) Nutton 1978: 348 suggests instead that Galen's aim, wholly consistent with his usual concern with clarity, was 'didactic, not exploratory' – that is, to make difficult Aristotelian and Stoic (and other) material easy of access and intelligible to students – and sees the *de soph.* as 'a pendant to the logical investigations' of the first two books of the *On Demonstration*. Galen's procedure bears out both these interpretations; yet his simplification of his material, whether as a concession to his audience's youth and inexperience, or as a deliberately provocative and unorthodox polemical gesture, vitiates his use of it. In both form and content, the *de sophismatis* does indeed look to be a hymn of praise to Galen's favourite virtue, clarity (which even Aristotle may lack on occasion: ch. 1, 3.20ff.G, 6E). It comprises a display of dialectical prowess in the discovery of premisses and proofs, in their lucid exposition, and in the demolition of objections, while the argument itself hinges on clarity's crucial importance for language's proper functioning. All the while, however, Galen's position is fatally weakened by his failure to take into account all the factors inimical to clarity and intelligibility in philosophical and scientific reasoning.

Galen's ostensible position is that by reconstructing the proof alluded to by Aristotle himself at *s. el.* 4.165b27–30 we shall improve our own understanding of it: but he nowhere argues that or why it is important to grasp the Aristotelian system in the first place, or that knowledge of the correct division of ambiguity species is useful or necessary for the logician or the scientist, despite the importance he attaches elsewhere to the ability to recognise and solve sophisms (*e.g. an. pecc. dign.* 2.3, pp. 55.4ff. Marquardt (*script. min.* 1), 5.72K (=(part) *S.V.F.* 2.272)), and to ambiguity as a producer of sophisms (*e.g. P.H.P.* 2.4.4, p. 116, ll. 28ff., 2.5.48, p. 136, ll. 34ff.), and despite too the scorn he lavishes on the charlatans, the sophists, who masquerade as doctors (*e.g. nat. fac.* 2.44, 2.56–7K). I do not think the possibility can be wholly discounted that the Stoic classification, despite its officially lowly position, of affording indirect proof of its rival's excellence, in fact furnishes the *de soph.* with its real *raison d'être* – yet another swipe at the Stoa: in which case, of course, the classification's official position is merely an implicit part of his offensive.[24]

On the other hand, the general link between fallacy and ambiguity may simply have won considerable support in Galen's eyes from its Aristotelian authority. In the *P.H.P.* Galen distinguishes four types of premiss (or ἀξίωμα or λόγος) – not types of argument – and identifies each in turn as the subject-matter of a different work of Aristotle's, as follows: *Sophistical Refutations*: sophistical; *Rhetoric*: rhetorical or persuasive; *Topics*: dialectical or "gymnastic"; *Posterior Analytics*: scientific (2.3.12, p. 112, ll. 3–8). The sophistic sort is associated particularly with 'certain homonymies and forms of expression' (2.4.4, p. 116, ll. 30–1). In this context Galen must be anxious to highlight the connection between ambiguity and fallacious argument because (as 7.7 will show) he is about to diagnose a Stoic argument, about the seat of the ruling part of the soul, as unsound because of its exploitation of an ambiguity.

Galen's assumption that the Stoic and Aristotelian systems are parallel must be dispensed with if *de soph.* ch. 4 is to yield up reliable evidence about the location and significance of the theory of ambiguity in Stoic dialectic. But the absence of any systematic, one-to-one connection between types of ambiguity and types of linguistic fallacy does not mean that links between particular sophisms or sophistic patterns of reasoning and particular ambiguities or patterns of ambiguity were not forged by Stoic dialecticians. Indeed, with the help of external testimony, examples of some of the Stoic modes, and fallacies known to Stoic logicians, can be connected. One source of material for the Stoic classifiers was definitely ambiguity as deployed to produce fallacious argument, and one of their

---

[24] Galen's conception of logic and its importance to medicine is discussed by Barnes 1991, esp. 52f.

motivations the felt need to systematise those ambiguities. Yet this part of the process of classification could have been conducted independently of any logical analysis of the general relation between ambiguity and the sophism, while remaining open to the investigation of ambiguities having no connection at all with sophistic argument. The classification suggests a Stoic interest in ambiguity in part in its own right, and one certainly not restricted to any single area of dialectic. In the next two chapters I aim to prove both these points in detail.

5.5 Authorship of the Stoic classifications

Theon's mode of reference to his ultimate authority as "the dialecticians" suggests that the system was not compiled by, or primarily for the use of, teachers or students of rhetoric; but neither is it proof that it was designed for the formal logic class. Ambiguity has its own distinct niche in Stoic dialectic, which in its mature form embraced far more than formal logic: stylistic theory and literary criticism, for example. There is no reason to believe Theon had a dialectical education, although his inclusion of the Stoic list argues a commitment to his contention that the rhetorician can benefit from philosophy (59.1ff.). It is accordingly most plausible that Theon (or his secondary, rhetorical source, if he had one) came across the list in a Stoic treatise on style: an interpretation supported, as we shall see, by certain features of the classification itself.

As for the *de soph.* list, Galen states that it is the work of the 'more sophisticated [χαριεστέρων]' Stoics (12.18G, 21E, 14.5f.G, 23E). Edlow 1977: 132 thinks it 'reasonable to suppose that the more subtle men of the Stoa ... are Chrysippus and his followers, especially Diogenes of Babylon'. Given Chrysippus' enormous influence in all areas of Stoic logic, it would indeed be reasonable to suppose that one or other of his classifications survived and became authoritative and well known (he may have produced more than one, of course; his ancient reputation – if it was deserved – was for 'arguing repeatedly about the same philosophical tenet' (D.L. 7.180)).

It is fairly clear that Galen must have regarded Chrysippus as one of the "more subtle" or "sophisticated" Stoics.[25] Chrysippus 'sometimes says what is false . . . but not what is simply stupid' (*P.H.P.* 2.5.61, p. 140, ll. 1–3). He is criticised elsewhere in this same work (3.1.21, p. 172, ll. 10 ff.; *cf. inst. log.* 4.6) for lack of method, ignorance of the proper canons of scientific inquiry, and terminological laxity. These are precisely Galen's grounds for dissatisfaction with the authors of the *de soph.* classification, but they are hardly criticisms Galen limits to Chrysippus in particular or the Stoa in general.[26] The relevant *de soph.* passage is anyway worth quoting in full (I translate Ebbesen's text):

It [will be] clear [to] anyone who paid attention to what was said earlier [*i.e.* in *de soph.* chs. 2 and 3] that all [the Stoic species] fall under the modes listed [*sc.* the Aristotelian ones]: but its lack of method and expertise [will be] perfectly clear; for from what has been said no-one could formulate a proof that in one mode some other ambiguity could not be located;[27] and saying that homonymy occurs in complexes too [*sc.* as well as in single words] is the work of men who do not even listen to words at all. And how is it not simple-minded for specific divisions to be counted in ⟨addition

---

[25] Chrysippus did, of course, acquire a reputation for subtlety and obscurity, to which in their different fashions Epictetus' allusion to Chrysippus' books on the Liar, *diss.* 2.17.34, and Lucian's mockery of his clever way with fallacies, *vit. auct.* 22 (part, 37L), both testify.

[26] Galen attacks both the Rationalist and (especially) the Methodist doctors for their ignorance of logic and their inability to use, compose, or recognise proper demonstrations: *meth. med.* 10.32K, 10.109K (Rationalists), 10.37K (Methodists). But the Stoics more than anyone else seem to have irritated Galen with their mixture of terminological "fussiness" (*i.e.* when Galen does not think the distinction at stake is real or important) and "laxity" (when he does): see *e.g. inst. log.* 4.6–7.

[27] Gabler's text has 'οὔτε γὰρ . . . ἀποδείξιν ⟨ἂν⟩ τις λάβοι τοῦ μηδὲ καθ' ἕνα τρόπον ἕτερον ἀμφίβολόν τι δύνασθαι συστῆναι'. One might be tempted to translate 'a proof that no ambiguity could be located in some other mode', the charge being that the classification cannot be proved complete, rather than that its modes or species cannot be proved mutually exclusive. But the opposition between '. . . ἕνα . . .' and '. . . ἕτερον . . .' makes this extremely unlikely – what has not been proved is that an *alien* ambiguity cannot find its way into *a* mode – and in any event the alternative translation would make Galen awkwardly repeat himself, for the charge of incompleteness is made at 15.7ff.G, and in very specific terms, the precise failure being to omit Form of Expression and Accent ambiguities. The general complaint will be that the Stoic list actually and obviously omits certain particular modes from a classification already known to be authoritative.

to⟩²⁸ generic kinds, as they do in the case of those [fallacies? ambiguities?]
due to Division, by their separating Non-significant ⟨and⟩ Significant Part?
For ⟨one⟩ could of course get even more of the specific divisions in this
fashion; and moreover one could in this way make yet more specific so-
called divisions of homonymy too²⁹ ... besides, there are yet more modes
of what they call "homonymy in a sentence" [ἐν λόγῳ], for some arise by
juxtaposition of like grammatical cases, as in *May Meletus Socrates overcome*, while the other modes ...³⁰ ⟨but⟩ these are fewer; yet that is worth
puzzling over, how they came to omit Apparent ambiguities,³¹ and still
more so, those in the Accent mode³² ... (14.6–15.10G, 23–25E)

Galen thus complains that the Stoic list is inadequate because: materials for a proof of the mutual exclusivity of its
species are not forthcoming; the species "homonymy in word-
compounds" is a contradiction; it includes specific alongside
generic types, but only in one instance (*viz.* Significant/Non-
significant Part), failing to do so with the two Homonymies;
and it omits Apparent and Accent ambiguities entirely.

These criticisms fall under the general description of the
list as obviously 'ἀμέθοδόν τε καὶ ἄτεχνον': that is, as lacking
method, and as failing to exhibit application of the rules and
principles of technical expertise. Its authors have failed by the
lights of the conception of "expertise", τέχνη, to which Galen
subscribes and which he ascribes to Chrysippus and the other
philosophical giants: expertises consist in the knowledge of
the differences, διαφοραί, of each thing (*adv. Lyc.* 3, 18A.209K
= *S.V.F.* 2.230).³³ Further, the classification is unoriginal,
containing no new modes or types in addition to Aristotle's.
The charges are grave: we must try to answer them.

---

²⁸ Gabler has '⟨προσ⟩καταριθμεῖσθαι' at 14.14G, 23E, the point being that the
generic *differentia* "Part" has been replaced by two specific *differentiae*, which are
now counted in addition to the other, generic, types.

²⁹ Such homonymy types are listed by *e.g.* Simplicius *cats.* 31.22ff.

³⁰ Some words have been lost after 'the other modes ...'; presumably Galen went on
to describe other forms of Amphiboly, on which see 6.7.2.

³¹ "Apparent" ambiguity covers "Form of Expression" in the *s. el.* list (10.12G,
18E).

³² On Accent ambiguities: 6.2.3, 6.2.4.

³³ Note that διαφορά is the term apparently used by the *de soph.* Stoics themselves
for the "kinds" or "species" of ambiguity: see 6.1.

THE STOIC CLASSIFICATIONS 2:
STOIC TYPES OF AMBIGUITY

6.1   Taxonomic principles

Except in dealing with Reference before the two species not found in the *de soph.*, *viz.* Hyperbaton and Interpolation, my investigation will adopt the order of presentation used by Galen, which seems to be authentic. At 12.17G, 21E Galen refers to 'the species [or 'kinds', or 'divisions', 'διαφοράς'] of what are called "amphibolies"'. Ἀμφιβολία is a mode of linguistic fallacy in Aristotle's *s. el.* list, ambiguity in general elsewhere (*rh.* 1. 15.1375b11, 3.5.1407a37f.; *top.* 8.7.160a29; *cf. poet.* 25.1461a25); for the Stoics it is always ambiguity in general, as the definition preserved by Diogenes confirms (7.62); and Galen here signals the difference in terminology (*cf.* Ebbesen 1981a: 1: 36). The term διαφορά, *differentia* or *species*, may be authentically Stoic (it is used at D.L. 7.42 (31A2), 'τὰς τῶν φαντασιῶν διαφοράς', for example; and *cf.* Sextus *M.* 7.241; Alexander *mixt.* 217.2ff., 7f.), but even this is not beyond doubt. Certainly the Stoics did not mention τρόποι, "modes", of ambiguity, as Aristotle spoke of "modes" of sophism. For his part, Theon, unlike Galen, does not number his ambiguity kinds, nor, indeed, has he any general name or description for them.

One of the main tasks will be to identify and assess the principles of classification adopted by Galen's and Theon's Stoics. Both groups used a basic form of differentiation by bearer – utterance; single word; word-complex – on the last of which have been imposed, not altogether with success, three other criteria: whether the ambiguity is due to the presence of some single (homonymous) term(s); or is one of grouping, which includes syntactic association; or is one of reference. A fourth criterion is quite foreign: utterances due to Elleipsis and

Pleonasm are due to the bearer's being deficient or excessive. Other, ample, evidence of inconsistencies, overlaps, and omissions in the Stoic lists will come to light. But without so much as a glance at the lists one problem will be glaringly obvious. Nothing definite is known about the definition(s) of ambiguity constructed by these Stoics, and without them it cannot be absolutely certain what the classifications were intended to capture.

It cannot even be assumed that the lists are meant to cover all ambiguities in all languages.[1] The Stoic definition of *lexis* reported by Diogenes Laertius makes a distinction between Greek and other tongues in that being articulable is defined as being divisible into the letters of the Greek alphabet (7.56). Yet the definition of ambiguity itself makes explicit provision for rejecting utterances drawn from different usages (as we saw in 4.8). Given the ethnocentricity of ancient theorising about language, such inconsistency is not surprising. The Stoics presumably did not make a conscious decision to concentrate exclusively on the properties (including ambiguity) of Greek. When the classification was compiled there was simply no other language of interest, even to grammarians, let alone philosophers, in the West; then, when Latin came on the scene, Greek still retained much of its status as the language of philosophy and the model for grammatical concepts and categories.[2] It would, however, be more accurate to say that the Stoics saw their doctrines about the constituents and struc-

---

[1] Edlow 1975: 424, *cf.* 435 (followed by Baldassarri 1984: 48) claims that the Stoics' 'overriding concern is to distinguish and describe those forms of ambiguity they find most interesting, especially those by appeal to which fallacies or sophisms due to language may be identified. Unlike Galen, the Stoics carry out their enterprise without systematic reference to a strict set of taxonomic principles that govern such ambiguity'; their achievement is 'perceptively observing this phenomenon, case by case', although some 'subtle kinds of ambiguity' are captured (435). Edlow does little to counter Galen's criticisms of the Stoic list as 'unsystematic but also nearly incoherent' with the species being 'neither jointly exhaustive nor mutually exclusive' (426, a reference to the passage quoted at the end of 5.5). In what follows I hope to do the Stoics more justice on all points, and to correct the view that the classification was compiled largely with an eye on sophistic material and with no view to exhaustiveness.

[2] Edlow 1975: 424 explicitly limits the Stoic classification to 'eight kinds of ambiguity that occur in Greek'. On Greek linguistic ethnocentricity: 8.4, n. 31.

tures of *lexis* and *logos* as broadly applicable to every language, or to language in general. Neither classification is to be understood as a strictly grammatical construction, that is, as a systematic listing of the possible forms of ambiguity in some one language, by reference to a comprehensive range of word-classes, grammatical functions, syntactic structures and relations, *etc.*, such as is common in modern linguistic textbooks (*e.g.* Hirst 1987: 149). It was just not the Stoics' intention (whatever may have been achieved by the professional grammarians who extended Stoic work) to describe Greek, nor to construct a comprehensive prescriptive grammar for it.

Both lists, however, also reflect the limitations imposed by familiarity with a single language. In particular, both external evidence, and the understanding of syntactic relations manifested in the classifications, show that it was the syntax of grouping which dominated the Stoic conception, and that even this was narrowly and crudely conceived. No explicit mention is made, for example, of syntactic ambiguity through syncretism, when (roughly speaking) a single word-form can be one or other of two or more words associated with the same lexeme (*e.g.* 'loved' could be the past tense or the past participle of the lexeme *love*).[3] One of the commoner sources of ambiguity in modern English (*e.g.* the sentence *they all put on their hats*), this is far less frequent, but still to be found, in highly inflected Greek.[4] Such a heavily restricted grammatical theory is itself, in large part, the product of a dialectic whose primary concern was with logic, and thus with those properties and structures of sentences which are important for the operations of logic. The theory can rightly be called flawed, because it lacks distinctions which the ambiguity classification requires and whose absence it highlights; but it should not

---

[3] More precisely, two or more morphosyntactic words may share or realise the same word-form: *cf.* Lyons 1977: 73f.

[4] Syncretism did, of course, occur in ancient Greek, and was noticed even by non-grammarians: Origen *selecta in psalmos* 4.5 (*P.L.* 12.1141D), for example, observes that ὀργίζεσθε signifies both the 'προστακτικὸν κατηγόρημα' and the 'ὁριστικὸν/διαβεβαιωτικὸν κατηγόρημα', *i.e.* it means both "be angry" and "you are angry" (*cf.* Nuchelmans 1973: 64). For a single grammatical example (one of many) of such ὁμόφωνα, see Apollonius *synt.* 318.5ff. (nominative and accusative cases).

217

be treated as a failed attempt at comprehensive grammatical description or prescription. The Stoic classifications depend rather on general principles and categories culled from semantics and philosophical logic, even if they do contain observations specific to constructions in Greek, and they apply general grammatical categories and concepts. They offer very little by way of a grammatical explanation of what causes the ambiguities; and, more seriously, their broader semantic and logical framework is thin and sketchy.

The lists should, minimally, capture all, and only all, utterances which will fall within the scope of the associated definition (and *vice versa*). The comprehensiveness of a classification is a function of the concept (*e.g.* of ambiguity) with which it is associated; and this will prove a useful exegetical principle. There is no reason to think, on the basis of anything Galen says, or, as will emerge, of the evidence of the classification itself, that the list was meant to be or to be understood as limited in any way, except in that it will automatically be restricted to what its associated definition admits as cases of ambiguity. Classifications and definitions ought also to be coherent – an utterance which finds an entry into one must not be excluded by the other, and *vice versa* – although all this means today, given the disappearance of the Stoic definition(s), is that anything inferred from the content of the two lists about the associated concept(s) of ambiguity must be consistent (which is trivial). It does not mean that an utterance must be assigned to one and only one kind, as Galen believes (that is the clear implication of 14.9–11G, 23E; quoted in 5.5). There is, in fact, nothing in the descriptions of the kinds or in their illustrations to suggest that mutual exclusivity was thought necessary by the classifications' authors, and Galen neglects to explain why mutual exclusivity should be a prerequisite. Galen himself believes the Aristotelian system (as interpreted by Galen) can boast this virtue; the fact that he is wrong is irrelevant here, since what is at issue is whether the *de soph.* (or *prog.*) Stoics would have agreed that mutual exclusivity of kinds is a prerequisite.

The general issue of exclusivity will bear further scrutiny, both in the abstract, as presenting a problem for all classifiers of ambiguity, and also because it promises to furnish a useful tool for the analysis of individual Stoic kinds and the distinctions between them. A classifier may (i) accept some degree of overlap between kinds (*i.e.* will admit cases which could equally well fall into two or more kinds, and others which can only be explained as combining elements from two or more kinds) provided that for each kind there is at least one ambiguity(-pattern) not otherwise classifiable. At opposite extremes are the viewpoints (ii) that no ambiguity can be multiply classifiable; and (iii) that some ambiguities are properly classifiable in two or even more ways, there being nothing to choose between the taxonomic modes or criteria, and any ambiguity which falls under one heading will automatically fall under the other(s) (making one or other kind redundant would, however, be simply arbitrary). It remains to be seen which policy found favour with these groups of Stoics.

Another problem to be faced is that of determinacy, that is, whether undecided, or undecidable, cases of ambiguity are permitted. This difficulty has briefly raised its head before, in connection with the final condition attached to the Stoic definition preserved by Diogenes Laertius (see 4.9). It shows itself here again not only because it is to be expected that Stoics would, if possible, prefer a determinate classification, blaming mere human fallibility in constructing or applying it in uncertain cases, but also because two of the kinds, the two Homonymies, seem to be intended to distinguish between homonyms in isolation and in context. In some sense "the same" utterance must turn out to be ambiguous (in isolation, and in some contexts) and not ambiguous (in other contexts), and, in particular, will be ambiguous (in a narrow context) and not ambiguous (in some second, richer context embracing the first). The question is whether the Stoic classification copes successfully with this commonplace experience of ordinary language users.

Given Stoic interest in the Platonic analytical scheme of division and definition, it is obvious and reasonable to ask what sort of division these examples represent, judged by the

Stoa's own principles. Two chief types are known (D.L. 7.61f. (32C5–8)): διαίρεσις, "division" (by species), and μερισμός, "partition" (by topic). All the evidence indicates that the former must be in play. Partition is distribution into subject areas or headings: for example, dialectic into the topics of significations and vocal sound, with all their sub-partitions (D.L. 7.43f. (31A7–8)). Division is of a genus into species and sub-species. It is easy to apply this model to the present texts: the genus, ambiguity, is divided by way of *differentiae*, διαφοραί, into types or species whose definitions determine the concept to which utterances of that kind conform.

Although complete texts and translations of the classifications have already been provided (5.1.3, 5.2.3), the texts in which each species is described are repeated here for ease of reference.

6.2   The species of ambiguity 1: Common

6.2.1   *Common: texts and translations*

de soph. 13.1–3G, 21–2E

μία μέν, ἥν κοινὴν ὀνομάζουσι τοῦ τε ⟨δι⟩ῃρημένου	1
καὶ τοῦ ⟨ἀ⟩διαιρέτου, οἷα ἐστὶν ἡ αὐλητρις πεσοῦσα· κοινὴ	2
γὰρ αὕτη τοῦ τε αὐλητρὶς ὀνόματος καὶ τοῦ διῃρημένου.	3

(1) The first [species], which they call "common to what is divided   1
and undivided [*or*: indivisible]", is this sort of thing, αὐλητρις   2
πεσοῦσα; for this is common
to the word αὐλητρίς [=*flutegirl*] and to the divided [*sc.* to αὐλὴ   3
τρίς =*a house three times*].

prog. 81.31–82.3

παρὰ τὴν κοινὴν τοῦ ἀδιαι-	31
ρέτου τε καὶ διῃρημένου, ὡς ἐν τῷ αὐλητρις πεσοῦ-	32
(p. 82 Spengel)	
σα δημοσία ἔστω· ἓν μὲν γὰρ τί ἐστι τὸ ὑφ' ἓν καὶ ἀδιαί-	1
ρετον, αὐλητρὶς ἔστω πεσοῦσα δημοσία, ἕτερον δὲ τὸ	2
διῃρημένον, αὐλὴ τρὶς πεσοῦσα ἔστω δημοσία.	3

... owing to the [ambiguity which is] "common to what is undivi-   31
ded and divided", as in *let an* αὐλητρις *having fall-*   32

(p. 82 Spengel)

en become state property: for one thing is what is single and undivi-   1
ded, *let an* αὐλητρίς [=*flutegirl*] *having fallen become state property*,   2
and another thing is what
is divided, *let an* αὐλὴ τρίς [= *a house three times*] *having fallen*   3
become state property.

6.2.2   Common: title and examples

Both classifications begin with the same species. Its full description, on Theon's authority, is 'common to what is undivided [*or*: indivisible] and divided', 'ἡ κοινὴ τοῦ ἀδιαρέτου
καὶ διῃρημένου', 81.31f.; *cf.* 130.14f. Ebbesen emends the obviously corrupt parallel text in the *de soph.* to bring it into line
with Theon's description (as was also suggested by the editor
of the *TLG*), and in this he is no doubt correct: 1981a: 2: 21,
ad loc. (*cf.* 1981a: 1: 36, n. 30 (p. 41)). The *prog.* version displays an opposition both sharper and more immediately comprehensible than that afforded by earlier attempts to correct
the *de soph.* passage.

Had Galen's and Theon's examples been lost the modern
reader would be hard pressed to see the real point of this
characterisation. It might have been urged that Common is
identical with the Aristotelian modes Combination and Division, "what is undivided and divided" on this view being a
logos, a word-complex, which can be variously construed (as
observed in 5.4). This is Theon's own interpretation, *prog.*
130.13–15; Galen too takes Common ambiguities to be a
sub-set of Combination and Division, as will emerge later; it
is found in the grammarian Fortunatianus (see 8.3); and it has
ensnared at least one modern scholar: Butts 1986: 305, n. 35
(*cf.* Ebbesen 1981b: 335). But they can all, I think, be proved
wrong.

I argued, briefly, in 4.4, that what is "common", strictly, can
only be the sequence αὐλητρις, for what is ambiguous, strictly,
is neither a word nor a syntactic complex of words.[5] It is a

[5] Edlow 1975: 434, 1977: 67 suggests that this species gets it name because it is
"common" to the next two species, Homonymy in Simples and Homonymy in

lexis or sequence of articulate sounds or their written symbols, shared by both the noun or single word (= "the undivided") αὐλητρίς, *flute-girl*, and the phrase (= "the divided") αὐλή τρίς, *a house three times*. The Stoic definition names the bearers of ambiguity as *lexeis* precisely to accommodate such ambiguities; and identifying the bearer here as a *lexis* makes good sense of the characterisation of the species. The genitive phrase in the description usefully limits and delineates this "common" nature (all ambiguities might loosely be called "common", to several significations). It has the further advantage of generality, making unnecessary any enumeration of the species of compound linguistic items which constitute the "undivided" category. The absence of a qualified noun (if one should be understood)[6] perhaps argues a terminological deficiency, and would certainly cause obscurity were the illustrations no longer available. A similar problem is raised by the title of the second and third *de soph.* species (see 6.3.3).

If this is the right way to take the ambiguity bearer in cases of Common, and if it is from the "common" quality of its members that the ambiguity type or species gets its name, it might suggest that the descriptions of the kind originally began something like this: 'παρὰ τὴν κοινὴν ⟨λέξιν⟩ ...', 'due to the ⟨utterance⟩ common to ...'. Depending on what the ante-

---

Compounds, and hence is both lexically and syntactically ambiguous, while he acknowledges (albeit in parentheses) that 'the ambiguity really is common to the articulate sound' (1977: 67). What Edlow calls the 'phonological unit (describable as one word) αὐλητρίς' plainly cannot mean both "flutegirl" and "court three times", any more than it does when 'describable as two words' (1975: 434). It will have one or other signification according as it is regarded as one or two units. As a single *lexis*, it has both. Nor is what makes the utterance "common" that, in a complete phrase such as αὐλητρις πεσοῦσα/πέπτωκε, one word (the participle or verb) combines syntactically with the remainder of the phrase, whether this is read as one word or two. For not only would Galen's and Theon's explanations then have to be disregarded altogether, which would be unacceptable, but in other cases of Common the division into two words may in fact not result in a broader syntactic re-arrangement, one word of the phrase combining syntactically with some third word (that is, there will be no one word in the ambiguous phrase with which the core *lexis* combines, however it is read). Baldassarri 1984: 48 makes the odd and obviously incorrect claim that Galen describes the Common example as one of 'omonimia comune'.

[6] Ebbesen 1981a: 1: 36, n. 30 (p. 41) is uncertain on this point too, and makes no suggestion.

cedent of 'One ...', 'μία[v]', is in 13.1G, 21E, however, Galen's words suggest rather that what is common is the first ambiguity (ἀμφιβολία) or the species (διαφορά) (this is not a list of particular ambiguous utterances). Theon is content to leave the adjective hanging, there being no suitable substantive in sight.[7] As for the example, Galen first appears to take what is common to be αὐλητρὶς πεσοῦσα as a whole (13.2G, 21E), which cannot be the case; but then he analyses αὐλητρὶς alone (13.3G, 22E), and I take this to be correct.

Diogenes Laertius' report of the Stoic definition of ambiguity provides another vital piece of information. His single example, αὐλητρὶς πέπτωκε, is almost identical to the illustration of Common in the *de soph*. It can hardly be doubted, then, that Galen's order of presentation of the kinds is authentically Stoic. Diogenes, or his source, would most likely have chosen as an illustration the very first he met with, that is, the first example of the first kind. His report may also be evidence that Theon's version is not Stoic as it stands, but an expansion of it culled from rhetorical treatments of ambiguity (see 6.2.5).

6.2.3 Common: species

Common ambiguities could not, then, be captured by a definition which confines the range of ambiguity bearers to words and their complexes. A theoretical *onoma/logos* distinction is, of course, as old as Plato (*Sophist* 262a1ff.). It is first explicitly used as an exhaustive dichotomy of linguistic items for the classification of ambiguities by Aristotle (*e.g. s. el.* 4.165b29); it is crucial too in Galen's defence of the *s. el.* system (ch. 3, 7.18–8.6G, 13–14E), and in Alexander of Aphrodisias' discussion of Aristotle's treatment of ambiguity in the *Topics* (*e.g. top.* 152.12ff., 378.2ff.). Boethius divides ambiguities exclusively into *aequivoca* or ambiguous *partes*, single terms, and ambiguous *orationes* (*P.L.* 64, *div.* 888D, 890A–C). Ancient

---

[7] The only nouns available are 'ἑρμηνείαν', 80.30, not an obviously Stoic term; and 'ἀμφιβολία', 80.30–1, which would produce a very awkward text ('What the dialecticians call "ambiguity" also makes language unclear, by the ⟨ambiguity⟩ which is common to ...').

school grammarians also tended to operate with a dichotomy between the "word", *lexis* (typically equivalent to "part of speech"), and the "sentence", *logos*, a *lexis*-complex, the definitions of which standardly combine phonological, semantic, and syntactic criteria (see 8.1). Whatever definition the *de soph.* Stoics adopted, it must have identified bearers as *lexeis*, as articulate sequences which can be treated as one word or as several. Another Stoic kind, Non-significant Part ("Part" in the *prog.*), will be seen to point firmly to this same conclusion (6.5.3). The Stoic definition and the two classifications are therefore innovative; but is the introduction of *lexis* as an ambiguity bearer justified? And what, precisely, is the *lexis* in question: a sequence of articulate sounds, of written symbols, or both?

I shall tackle the second question first. It is not a great deal more tractable, but the relevant evidence is a little easier to identify, and it will lead naturally back to the problem of the legitimacy of Common ambiguities. So: would the example of Common have been ambiguous both written and spoken, according to contemporary conventions governing pronunciation and scribal practice? And, whatever the answer to this particular query, will utterances be admitted by these Stoics as ambiguous which are ambiguous in one or other medium only?

There are good grounds for believing that some written utterances, such as αὐλητρίς, could, as a matter of fact, in some contexts, have been interpreted as one or as several lexical components (and not just because this example is paraded in other classifications of ambiguity). Many of the typographical conventions familiar today for ancient Greek were largely and for a long period unknown in antiquity: for example, spaces between words (so standard a rule that it can be used in a working definition of a word(-form) for some languages); capital letters to mark the beginning of sentences, proper names, nominals, *etc.*; punctuation marks; and so on. (Partly, no doubt, this was a result of the absence of pressures from publishing institutions employing mechanical methods of reproduction.) Ancient textual marks, by contrast, seem only to have developed relatively late, in the Alexandrian period, and then for paedagogic purposes (Allen 1987: 125). The earliest surviving reference to what may be a prosodic symbol is in Aristotle (*s. el.* 20.177b6), but the identity of the "additional signs", (παράσημα) he mentions there is much disputed (contrast Blass 1890: 92 with Laum 1928: 105f., Sandys 1921: 97; and see also Allen 1973: 3, n. 2). Signs fall into two main categories, those indicating pitch, vowel length, and breathing, and those marking transitional (junctural) features, that is, those which indicate that a letter sequence is to be read as a single word or as more than one (apostrophe, comma, hyphen: *e.g.* D.T. Sch. 312.34f, 305.32f.).[8] Junctural signs were not regarded as accentual signs (*e.g.* Sch. 135.12ff., 30ff.), and accentual signs were themselves not regarded as elements or letters (*e.g.* Sch. 496.11ff; *cf.* Allen 1973: 3ff., 244f.). A small illustration from Sextus *M.* 1.59: grammarians are expected to explain the correct pronunciation of the Attic idiom, common in Plato, ἦ δ' ὅς, *he said*; Sextus makes the sole issue the positioning of breathings on syllables, nothing being said about word-divisions or pitch. (Pauses and other transitional features are today very commonly accorded phonemic status, as "suprasegmental" phonemes realised alongside letter phonemes.)

---

[8] Pfeiffer 1968: 178ff. carefully distinguishes between them, the latter, he claims, being 'indispensable for the Greek *scriptura continua* from the beginning'; there is a very small amount of papyrus evidence to support this claim. Junctural signs certainly only become relatively common after the first century B.C.E., and they were not standard until the end of antiquity: for an ancient witness, see Galen *de soph.* 4, 15.19–16.3G, 25E. Aristophanes of Byzantium is traditionally credited with the invention (*c.* 200 B.C.E.) of symbols for punctuation, quantity and pitch; but against this, see Pfeiffer 1968: 179 (Sandys 1921: 126–7 claims Aristophanes systematised earlier efforts). Allen 1973: 10f. claims that prosodic features tend to have a grammatical rather than a lexical function; but this does not diminish their importance in the present context, since 'the delimitation or characterisation of the grammatical unit "word"' (*ibid.*) by juncture/disjuncture and accent must feature amongst the identity criteria of (some) bearers of ambiguity. (I cannot agree with Ong 1944 that punctuation marks were not regarded as indicators of semantic, as opposed to rhythmic, units until the seventh century C.E.: the evidence from the later Latin grammarians at least – especially from Diomedes (*G.L.* 1) 437.10ff., whose account is the fullest – shows clearly that all three marks had semantic or pragmatic rôles. Diomedes' rules for use of the full stop (*distinctio*) shows this particularly clearly: 437.24ff.)

It was recognised, then, that prosodic features not represented in the letter script – pitch, vowel length, aspiration, and juncture – required additional symbols, and also that a number of different speech sounds may have identical representations in the alphabetic script (and *vice versa*). The grammarians acknowledged that their native tongues display no straightforward correspondence between speech sounds and their sequences, on the one hand, and conventional written symbols, on the other.[9] Yet the alphabetic symbol system was never replaced for the purposes of linguistic analysis, merely standardised by the application of orthographic rules, and supplemented by prosodic marks of varying complexity; and transcription as a purely descriptive goal was never envisaged. It is a commonplace of modern criticism of ancient occidental grammar that it lacked the concept of the phoneme.[10] (On the

[9] The grammarians sometimes refer to vocal elements as στοιχεῖα and to the written characters as χαρακτῆρες: *e.g.* D.T. Sch. 183.16f., 484.12ff.; or to the former as ἐκφωνήσεις and to the latter as χαρακτῆρες: *e.g.* Sch. 32.14ff. Dionysius himself seems to fail to distinguish the two (9.1ff.): hence the elaborate explanations from his many commentators: *e.g.* 197.15ff., where letters are made out just to be elements lacking phonological patterning. Priscian observes that strictly *litterae* are signs, *elementa* the sounds, *pronuntiationes*, but that this strict usage is often ignored: *inst.* 1 (*G.L.* 2) 6.22–7.7. The sense of *element* "speech sound" is attributed to 'the philosophers': *e.g.* 36.8ff., 356.1ff., and its triple use – of the speech sound, its written shape, and its name – which is also Stoic (see 3.3, 4.4), and which passed into Latin grammar (*e.g.* Priscian *inst.* 1 (*G.L.* 2), 7.26 and ff.), is attested by Sextus *M.* 1.99.

[10] Ebbesen's claim that '[p]honemic analysis of language is ancient. Alphabetic script presupposes it', 1981b: 333, like Allen's that 'the post-Eucleidean spelling of Greek ... comes reasonably near to being phonemic', 1987: 10, must be hedged about with suitable qualifications. Adoption of an alphabetic script presupposes only some degree, not necessarily conscious, of phonemic analysis; and it seems no alphabet is completely phonemic (*cf.* Robins 1979: 13, 1980: 98ff.). Harris 1980: 15 (*cf.* Allen 1981: 115, 1987: 8ff.) argues that the invention of the alphabet required, not precisely the right number of symbols to differentiate every phonetically different pair of words, but only sufficient 'symbols having fixed segmental values to ensure the elimination of most practical ambiguities of word identification', and urges that the practice of representing speech in this way leads to 'the conceptualisation of the spoken word as a "chain" of fixed articulatory positions' (16); on the second point, *cf.* Fudge 1990: 31. DeFrancis 1989: 83f., 100ff. provides examples of ways in which writing systems compensate for the ambiguity of their symbols.

Care must also be taken to define what "phonemic" analysis could be in the context of such a claim. What are sometimes called ancient "phonetics and phonology" (including that portion of Stoic dialectic devoted to language sounds) were limited to the identification and some sort of description of the elements and

other hand, modern linguistics too has been found guilty of the crime of "scriptism", the delusion that standard orthography faithfully captures the features of spoken language, while yet paying lip-service to the priority of spoken language.[11]) Moreover, what transcriptional devices there were were devised to meet needs which were at once practical and normative, characteristic of an age in which recitation was still the preferred method of reading but pronunciation was rapidly changing and contact with other cultures increasing, so that Greek and Latin were beginning to be taught as foreign languages. Scholars were motivated by urgent requirements to (re-)construct what was presented as the "correct" pronunciation of the literary texts whose canonical status merited preservation, as well as to direct readers to what was presented as the "correct" phrasing, and thus the interpretation, of otherwise largely unbroken lines of writing (*cf.* Robins 1979: 17f.), especially where non-native speakers were concerned (*cf.* Allen

patterns of human vocalisations conventionally corresponding to the characters of the Greek and Latin alphabets and to their combinations: what was studied was the δύναμις or *potestas* of the στοιχεῖον or *littera*. Ancient language specialists did not set about identifying (let alone constructing a theory of the principles behind) all the phonemes of Greek or Latin, with their positionally determined variants (allophones) and their combinations, on the basis of "parallel" *vs.* "complementary" distribution. On ancient speech analysis: Robins 1979: 12f., 16f., 23f., 32f.; Allen 1981.

11 "Scriptism", 'the assumption that writing is a more ideal form of linguistic representation than speech', is the coinage of Harris 1980: 6, who roundly condemns its influence on modern linguistics; one of his examples (8) is precisely an "ambiguous" sentence which when spoken, in context, need not be ambiguous at all. Some examples: Frazier and Rayner 1982 (*cf.* Frazier 1988: 16) use a study of the eye-movements of readers of 'temporarily ambiguous' sentences as empirical evidence for the immediate use of syntactic information during language comprehension, regardless of whether the spoken representations of the sentences are or are not ambiguous. Chomsky describes and uses the notion (what might be called the "occidental scriptist variant") of "left" and "right-branching" structures (*e.g.* 1985a: 89f.). Hall 1987: 4 calls attention to the infelicity of the Transformational Grammar jargon *rewrite rules*. Lyons 1981: 217f., who speaks of words (*viz.* the components of the abstract language system) being 'inscribed' in a physical medium, phonic or graphic), claims that he is using the term in a 'technical sense', but the choice of *inscribe* in such a context, rather than, say, *represent*, is striking. For a modern statement of the grounds for the (ostensible) priority of speech: Lyons 1972; for a compendious statement of Lyons' own views, 1981: 218ff. (I have ignored altogether the question of whatever influence writing may have had on the actual phonetic, phonological, and morphological properties of ancient Greek and Latin.)

1987: 125).[12] The limitations of standard ancient orthography (amply described by Ebbesen 1981b: 333–7) meant that skill and experience were needed to assign to any given graphic sequence its correct (or optimal) phonological and morphological structures, including the resolution of ambiguities; and "reading" with due reference to accent and punctuation was a normal and important part of grammatical instruction (the *locus classicus* is D.T. *ars.gr.* §2).

One particular case of the general failure to adopt prosodic signs early and systematically is the late appearance and even later wide acceptance of a now universal convention for written ancient Greek, that of indicating the (suprasegmental) feature of low (or falling) pitch with a grave accent marker (`), where determined by phonological context, on a syllable which carries the high (or rising) pitch in the isolated forms of a lexeme (*i.e.* on the final syllable of oxytones). Other, rival, ancient conventions for the use of accentual signs appeared late as well (Allen 1973: 244f.), and none of these could plausibly have influenced what is known of of Stoic theorising in the field. Both readings of the Common example would almost certainly have been represented by the same undifferentiated graphic sequence in the majority of ancient texts, especially at the comparatively early period in which the Stoic definition and the two extant classifications would probably have been composed, in the hey-day of Stoicism.

The real problem is that it is not absolutely certain that they

[12] Pfeiffer 1968: 181 confines his account explicitly to accentual signs as ways of eliminating ambiguities (*cf.* Allen 1987: 125); but interest in dialect forms, primarily the chief literary dialects, which was stimulated in Alexandria by the rise of textual and literary criticism, just at the time when what was to become the "common" dialect began to spread through the Hellenistic world, must also have contributed to the importance of the discipline of orthography, and to the development of its symbols (*cf.* Robins 1979: 17). The new literary interest in orthography is briefly described by Ebbesen 1981b: 336. On the history of orthography and transcription: Robins 1980: 95ff.; on the various ancient and Byzantine prosodic symbol systems, Blass 1890: 132ff., Schwyzer 1938/53/59: 373ff.; and Bonner 1977: 209ff. on scholarly disputes about the need for changes in Latin orthography. Given the great importance attached to instruction in correct "reading" of texts in Hellenistic and Roman times, or to the services of a skilled reciter, as noted by Roberts 1910: 328, Hockett 1987: 54 is surely being too optimistic when he writes that the 'Greeks and Romans managed just fine with no spaces between words'.

would instead be distinguishable in speech, by pitch or junctural features or both.[13] The scholarly consensus is that there would very probably have been some difference in pronunciation, at least regarding the contextualised final (intrinsically acute) syllable of αὐλή and the middle syllable of αὐλητρίς. The possibility remains, however, that the final acute may have been wholly neutralised by its position (as argued by Wackernagel 1893, Vendryes 1929: 37ff., Sommerstein 1973: 160f.); if so, it will have been indistinguishable from the grave accent of the middle syllable of αὐλητρίς. This view is supported, for example, by a passage in Apollonius Dyscolos discussing the ambiguity, ἀμφιβολία, of such items as καταγραφω, καταφεροντος, and ἀποικου, whose pitch, τάσις, does not reveal whether they are two words or one (*synt.* 435.4ff.). The various rival theories have been summarised by Allen, whose own view (1973: 247; and *cf.* 1966b, 1974: 115f.) is that in such phonological contexts, given the relatively strong word demarcation in Greek, there may 'have been a general requirement (except after pause) that the high pitch should contrast with a preceding low', without, however, its being possible to specify how marked the contrast should be. Final acutes are retained before pauses (and enclitics), but it is unclear too which junctural features, if any, would have been in play. Of course, αὐλητρίς could be deliberately made distinct from αὐλή τρίς, by means of a pause, or something like a pause, in speech (as *abroad* and *a broad*, can be in modern spoken English). The question is whether the two readings were *automatically* distinguished.[14]

Several anecdotal versions survive of an example which would surely have to be classed as Common, one which raises the same problem as does the αὐλητρίς case, that of the pitch of contextualised acutes, and which takes the form of a spoken

---

[13] There is the further complication of possible differences in word-stress and/or intonation; I have decided to pass over this immensely difficult area altogether because the evidence is even less firm here than it is for other features of pronunciation. On stress in Greek: Sturtevant 1940: §108; Allen 1966a, 1987: 130ff.

[14] Edlow 1977: 67, n. 55 asserts that 'presumably neither expression was pronounced without pause' and that the 'spoken accents were identical' in each. The first claim may well be true; the second is far more doubtful than he appears to realise.

riposte. Stilpo, on seeing a freezing-cold Crates, remarks 'ὦ Κράτης, δοκεῖς μοι χρείαν ἔχειν ἱματίου καινοῦ', 'Crates, I think you have need of a new cloak/of a cloak and a mind too'; his witticism plays on the sequence (= the *lexis*) καινου (= καινοῦ, *new*; καὶ νοῦ, *and a mind too*) (D.L. 2.118; *cf.* 2.36, 6.3, and Theon *prog.* 100.13–18, where the story is told of Antisthenes and Isocrates respectively). Yet this does not prove pronunciation was *precisely* the same.[15]

The case of αὐλητρίς must remain ultimately unsettled, with the proviso that a pitch differentiation of some sort would be counted more probable by the majority of scholars in the field than a total neutralisation.

The possibility is now open, therefore, that ambiguities in the written medium only ("homographs") were admissible. Perhaps the obvious defects of contemporary orthography were attributed by the Stoics to faulty and misleading convention, as distinct from the less grossly corrupt "natural" spoken language, whose primacy went unchallenged. Another of the Stoic ambiguity kinds, "Non-significant Part", is illustrated by an utterance which seems to be open to two readings only if written (6.5.3), while another example, that of "Significant Part", could be disambiguated in speech (6.5.2). Edlow's conclusion that 'the evidence points to the fact that the Stoics are concerned with ambiguity in *speech* (rather than in written language)' (1977: 68; his emphasis) is therefore unacceptable.

His evidence for this claim seems to be two-fold. There is the presence of the provision that ambiguities signify λεκτικῶς in the Stoic definition of ambiguity (D.L. 7.62), which he takes to mean "verbally, in speech", but which is open to another,

---

[15] Note how the syntax of the whole sentence changes with the way καινου is understood; it would be gratifying to know how Stoic dialecticians described the various syntactic rôles and relations assumed by αὐλητρίς (as subject case), and again by αὐλή (subject case), and τρίς (adverb). Curiosity is fuelled by the fact that what looks to be a deficiency in the Stoic system could be remedied by use of a more precise and wide-ranging vocabulary for description of syntax than the Stoic classifiers seem to have had or thought appropriate; further, 6.5.2, 6.7.2. Stilpo's witticism perhaps points to an interest in ambiguity which may have been inherited by Zeno; see 7.1, and also 6.4.3, in connection with Elleipsis.

and I think far more persuasive, interpretation (4.6);[16] and, in any case, the example cited by Diogenes at 7.62, and by Galen and Theon, might not be ambiguous in speech. Edlow also makes much of the absence of an Accent kind from the *de soph.* list, which is one of the Stoics' failings in Galen's eyes (15.8ff.G, 24f.E; quoted in part in 5.5).

This alleged "missing" Accent species does deserve investigation. Some Greek words (*i.e.* "lexemes" in standard modern jargon) have citation- and other forms differentiated in speech by accent (pitch), vowel length, or breathing, or some combination of two or more of these: a common example, which perhaps owes its later popularity to Aristotelian authority (*s. el.* 20.177b3), is: ὅρος, *mountain*; ὅρος, *term* or *definition*; ὀρός, *whey*. This phenomenon came to be acknowledged by classifiers of ambiguity, as demonstrated by a report in Olympiodorus (*cats.* 33.8ff., *ad* 1a1) that the Aristotelian commentators offered 'additional specifications' ('προσδιορισμοί') of homonyms, additional, that is, to Aristotle's stipulation that they share a name (and not a definition). Homonyms must also share a written form (γραφή), pitch (τόνος), grammatical case (πτῶσις), and breathing (πνεῦμα). Olympiodorus himself adds that the homonyms must belong to the same part of speech and have the same gender. (For example, the form, (φωνή) 'ἔχεις' (a plural form of the noun ἔχις, *viper*, or a form of the verb ἔχω, *have*) is not homonymous; neither are ἄργος

---

[16] Edlow 1975: 427, 1977: 59, followed apparently by Baldassarri 1984: 48, and definitely by Hülser 1982: 3: 396, §63, as well as by Ruef 1981: 151, n. 287 (p. 197), who then draws the further conclusion (shared by Barwick 1957: 18) that Augustine's classification of ambiguities in *de dialectica* chs. 9–10, prefaced as it is by an explicit distinction between written and spoken ambiguities (16.7–8C, 108P), cannot display any Stoic influence. λεκτικός is indeed listed in LSJ as meaning "good at speaking" (Xenophon *mem.* 4.3.1, *Cyr.* 5.5.46) and "suitable for speaking, colloquial" ([Demosthenes]? 61.2, Aristotle *poet.* 4.1449a24, *rhet.* 3.8.1408b33). Ammonius uses the phrase 'ἡ λεκτικὴ φαντασία' to refer to the mind's speech-producing faculty (*int.* 22.34–23.2). Such a restriction would be intolerable, however: it is arbitrary as a matter of theory, as well as counter-intuitive, and a gross limitation on the dialectician's field of competence, to admit only spoken word(-form)s as ambiguous, and never their graphic equivalents. Silence on the topic of identity criteria might constitute a serious weakness in the whole semantic project, but, no more than the assumed priority of spoken discourse, need it imply that one (or other) medium alone was excluded altogether.

(*Argos*, the name of a city) and ἀργός, *shining* or *lazy*, being differently accented, the same word; nor are κενός, *empty*, and καινός, *new*, being differently spelled – not, by this date, differently pronounced.) This last-named condition, like the provision that homonyms have the same gramatical case, implicitly restricts homonymy to nominals,[17] whereas the proviso that they belong to the same part of speech implicitly eliminates any such limitation. Olympiodorus may thus be combining, not altogether consistently, several rival lists of 'additional specifications'. That pitch, length of syllables, and breathing came generally to be considered as much part of words as their constituent letters or letter sounds is also shown by later lists of the types of barbarism, which tend to appeal to precisely these four features (*e.g.* anon. *de barb. et sol.* 290.1–8 Nauck; ps.-Herodian *de barb. et sol.* 309.7 Nauck). Similar phenomena were observed in Latin: Boethius, for example, lists as one mode of distinguishing equivocals that by pronunciation and spelling (*e.g.* pōnē, *place* (2nd person singular imperative of the verb *ponere*) *vs.* pŏnĕ, *behind* (adverb and preposition); *queror, I complain, vs. quaeror, I am asked*) (*P.L.* 64, *div.* 890BC).

Aristotle's uncertainty in his *Sophistical Refutations* as to whether fallacies which are constructed by deliberately overlooking the fact that phonemic (vowel and consonant) sequences may be prosodically differentiated, are or are not due to ambiguity, is perhaps the earliest surviving theoretical tribute to the puzzlement these identity criteria can cause (*cf.* Ebbesen 1981b: 335f.; and see 5.4). Apparently he could not decide, or had not yet decided, whether words formed from the same letters in the same order, but differently pronounced (with different pitches, breathing, or vowel length), are ambig-

---

[17] The commentators are quick to claim that Aristotle's use of ὄνομα in his famous definition of homonyms is not so restricted: *e.g.* Simplicius *cats.* 25.10ff.; Ammonius *cats.* 17.16ff., 18.18ff.; Philoponus *cats.* 15.15f. It is interesting that Olympiodorus seems to have known lists which did confine homonymy to nominals. Ebbesen 1981a: 1: 184 points out that much more weight was attached in such lists to nouns than to other parts of speech, and to orthography than to sameness in pronunciation. Modern linguists wrestle with comparable criteria, in different theoretical dress and contexts: *cf. e.g.* Lyons 1977: 550ff.

uous, or are distinct words that are changed one into the other by the change in prosody. Galen, as observed already in 5.4, is confused too, but not to the point of excluding Accent from the Aristotelian modes, or of forgiving the Stoics for omitting it.

Now even were Edlow correct in supposing that the Stoics focussed on spoken ambiguities, an Accent kind for written *lexeis* whose prosodic differences go unrecorded in the standard orthography might still be expected. As it is, the best, most charitable explanation to suggest itself is that authentic words – roughly, parts of speech – unlike mere utterances, were considered phonetic and phonological, as well as semantic and grammatical units. There would have been a Stoic assumption that prosody is integral to a word(-form). (In modern jargon: homonymous lexemes will by definition be associated with forms (all or some of) which have a constant phonemic and prosodic shape (in isolation); non-contextual changes in suprasegmental features will produce different words (*i.e.* forms of different lexemes, or different forms of the same lexeme).) But this comfortable explanation cannot boast direct evidence in its support. The sole extant definition of ambiguity fails to address the issue explicitly. Theon knows of Accent ambiguities (*prog.* 129.12, 17–22, where they are restricted to written expressions), but there is no Accent kind in his Stoic list either. There is certainly no evidence that separate classifications of written and spoken ambiguities were devised or contemplated.

As for indirect evidence, what little there is is hard to interpret. The Homeric scholiasts report a number of readings suggested by Cleanthes and Chrysippus which show that they took accentual changes to produce semantic changes: 'αὐΐαχοι' for 'αὐϊαχοι' ('shouting hoarsely' for 'shouting together') in *Iliad* 13.41 (Chrysippus; Scholia Vol. III, p. 407 Erbse)'; 'ἕ', which Chrysippus claims is superfluous, for 'ἕ' ('himself') at *Il.* 15.241 (IV, p. 65 Erbse); 'ὀλοόφρονος' for 'ὀλοόφρονος' ('thinking of all' for 'crafty, baleful') at *Od.* 1.52 (of Atlas; Cleanthes; Sch. *ad. loc.*, p. 33, l. 26–p. 34, l. 1 Ludwich). It is possible that these changes in pronunciation were thought to give rise to new words. More damaging, perhaps, is the report that Chrysippus criticised Homer for using a plural verb, 'δῶσι', with a singular subject at *Iliad* 1.129. The scholiast replies that this word is in fact an expanded form of 'δῷ' (the 3rd person singular of the 2nd aorist subjunctive, not the 3rd plural); and it is possible that Chrysippus may have been misled by the absence from his text of the *iota mutum*, which would not have normally been marked at that time (and was not until after the end of antiquity), into reading 'δῶσι' (= 'they will give').

If this speculative diagnosis is correct, Chrysippus will have overlooked the failure of conventional orthography to capture distinctions in morphology and meaning. And if so, it makes a little more sense, although it is still an embarrassing lacuna in their theory of language, if the Stoa never developed an account of identity criteria for utterances, both written and spoken, and so never came to grips with the whole question of how and when changes in prosodic features constitute lexical changes. In fact, there does not seem to be a Stoic definition of "word" at all. Any conception and associated definition of ambiguity will necessarily be shaped by the criteria adopted for the identity of bearers within and between media. Even the purely pragmatic tasks of prescribing or maintaining the appropriate pronunciation and punctuation of a text will make reference, implicit or explicit, to some conception of ambiguity, although such identity criteria will not by themselves ensure correct recitation and interpretation. In whatever specific discipline, however, theorists of language cannot properly neglect the task of articulating a conception of ambiguity, or of constructing one, and thus of facing head on the problem of the relation between written and spoken discourse.

Yet no evidence survives of explicit conditions being formulated by the Stoa which would determine when a non-ambiguous phonic sequence could correspond to an ambiguous graphic sequence – that is, when an utterance ambiguous according to the Stoic definition is not "articulate vocal sound" after all – or *vice versa*. No anxiety appears to have

234

been felt that what a speaker might intuitively regard as "the same" utterance may by Stoic standards be both ambiguous (when written) and non-ambiguous (when spoken). The original Stoic conception of the elements of spoken and written *lexis* as standing in a straightforward one-to-one correspondence seems never to have been revised. The Stoics never, apparently, explored the difficulties which Aristotle succinctly raised when he argued that 'in writing, the word is the same provided it is written from the same letters in the same order ... but the sounds are not the same: so that the [fallacy] due to division is not [due to] ambiguity' (*s. el.* 20.177b4–7).

The root cause may perhaps lie in the Stoic doctrines that all utterances must be bodies in order to be causal agents: D.L. 7.56 (33H, part). The elements of *lexis* will, I take it, be particular bits of sound, of battered air, primarily, and secondarily marks on a surface representing these.[18] The lexemes constructed by many modern linguists and semanticists are abstract items associated with word-forms having representations in different media: hence, the problem of what counts as identity between media is still a pressing one, despite the pretty well universal assumption that speech is the primary medium. Equally, the relation between actual bits of talk (or writing), which are unique, physical objects or events, and what it is that the linguist puts into a description of a language, must be specified. The Stoics, in contrast, had a theoretical basis from which, at least in the context of the study of ambiguity, it could apparently confine its interest to individuals. *Lexeis* are physical objects, and, although the relevant individuating criteria are admittedly unclear, utterances will presumably be individuals in some sense, each being this bit of air shaped in such a way, or these marks having such-and-such a shape and

---

[18] The theoretical primacy of speech is a commonplace in antiquity; thus in the definition of the elements of *lexis* at D.L. 7.57, the speech-sounds are listed first, and utterances are defined as a certain sort of vocal sound. Written language will have been granted some measure of independence, however, if homographs were permitted to count as cases of ambiguity, and written (representations of spoken) *lexeis* will count as *lexeis* too, being themselves composed of "elements", in a different sense of *element* (see 3.3, 4.4).

arrangement.[19] Arguably, it would be appropriate to focus on the behaviour and properties of such individuals because they can form part of a real stretch of discourse (other bits of air, other marks) which someone might encounter (get impressions of) and misinterpret.

The definition reported by Diogenes Laertius offers a small confirmation of this interpretation, in the provision that the two or more significations be 'understood simultaneously in relation to this utterance' (see 4.9). In determining whether a given utterance is or is not ambiguous, the possible or actual behaviour of "the same" utterance ("same" by criteria yet to be described) in a different context, if any, and on a different occasion, is irrelevant: all that matters is whether this unique individual meets these conditions for being ambiguous.[20] (If this interpretation is right, then the correct convention for mentioning the example of Common will be {αὐλητρίς}, to indicate that we are dealing with a series of tokens on each

[19] The uniqueness of individuals was a necessary premiss of Stoic epistemology: *e.g.* Cicero *acad.* 2.56ff., 83ff. (401, part, J, part); Sedley 1982b: 263ff. It is not clear how utterances are individuated. *Bona fide* individuals are or have particular qualities: *e.g.* D.L. 7.58; and they may perhaps be collections of common qualities: Porphyry *cats.* 129.8ff.; Dexippus *cats.* 30.20ff. (28J). It is not enough for utterances to be individuals that they are different bits of matter (air, in this case) (*cf.* Sedley 1982b: 255–9), so that merely numerically distinct utterances (both acts and products) of "the same" word, or other linguistic item, must be differentiated in some other way if they are to be full individuals. Also required is some account of how utterances can be alike, *i.e.* be commonly qualified, whether they are "tokens of the same type" or "forms of the same lexeme" – see main text. It may be that utterances were not in fact given "qualified" status on the grounds that they, like armies or ships (*cf.* Simplicius *cats.* 214.24ff., esp. 27–30 (28M3)), are not proper unities. Chrysippus' *On soritic arguments against vocal sounds* (D.L. 7.192 = *S.V.F.* 2.14, p. 6, l. 10 (37B1)) was perhaps a contribution to this topic. But utterances must still be concrete particulars after a fashion; they are certainly not types or abstractions of any kind.

[20] Edlow 1975: 424f. (followed by Baldassarri 1984: 48) claims there 'is evidence that in the discussions of Aristotle, the Stoics, and Galen, it is words (or word-types) and sentences (or sentence-types) that are ambiguous rather than particular utterances (or word-tokens, sentence-tokens) ... that is, the datable *uses* of words and sentences.... Although the Greeks do not seem to distinguish the ambiguity of a word or sentence (the token) in a datable context from that of a word or sentence in abstraction (that is, free of any context, the corresponding type), their discussions presuppose that ambiguity of discourse is left unresolved by the contexts in which it occurs' (italics in original). But the evidence points rather the other way as far as the Stoics are concerned (whatever Aristotle and Galen did), and suggests that they even used contextual disambiguation as grounds for a taxonomic principle: see 6.3.4.

occasion of use, albeit tokens of an as yet theoretically unde-termined type.) This does seem to let the Stoics temporarily off the hook of providing identity criteria, whether within or be-tween media, and whether tokens of the same type, or forms of the same lexeme, are in question. But at a deeper level it not only raises the tricky problem of distinguishing a bearer from its context: it calls into question the possibility of any such discipline as Stoic semantics at all.

Most modern linguists and semanticists are happy to con-struct criteria of identity by appeal to such abstractions as lexemes or types. Others may not want to admit these into their ontology, and will therefore try to restrict their objects of study to utterances or inscriptions, which they may charac-terise as "replicas".[21] Of course, the motivations behind these modern and Stoic approaches are very different: the former is a response to the recent drastic overhaul of the traditional semantic apparatus, the latter to a materialist system which only accommodates non-physical meanings (*lekta*) at the edge, so to say, of its ontology. But the two afford some interesting comparisons. The modern theoretician is at least taking into consideration the need for generalisation in linguistics and semantics, if only by characterising the objects of study as "replicas", apparently implying the existence both of some original of which other utterances or inscriptions are copies, and of firm criteria for replication.[22] The Stoics, in contrast, seem not to have written the need for generalisation in cases

---

[21] Quine's hostility to lexicographers' and grammarians' postulation of "words" which are not forms (*e.g.* 1960: 129) is perhaps the most famous, and influential, example of the tendency away from abstraction. I am indebted to Scheffler's stimulating study, 1979: 8f., 11ff., as my model for the modern theory used in the main text.

[22] These conditions may be problematic: why is one item privileged as the original? On the original/replica relation: Lyons 1977: 18. Scheffler 1979: 12ff. seems to make theoretical use of tokens without any qualms. Criteria of "identity" for replicas or tokens are also needed, especially in speech: *cf.* Lyons 1977: 15ff., 28ff.; Hockett 1987: 52ff. Harris 1980: 134f. argues that it is actually impossible to specify type/token identity criteria, and that linguists' compulsion to do so is one result of the power of the dictionary. And this is not even to touch on the issue of how to treat different "words" as "forms" of the same "word". The criticisms of Scheffler's system by Eikmeyer and Rieser 1983: 396ff., Maloney 1984: 195, n. 4, are too lenient on these points.

of ambiguity explicitly into their definition, or to have applied it in their classifications. The problem the Stoics face is to find a way in which the particular utterances which are *lexeis* can be legitimately regarded as tokens of a type, or forms of the same word, about which appropriate generalisations – such as assigning ambiguity to them in isolation or in context – can be made.

For linguists and semanticists, the study of ambiguity allows both the construction and the testing of generalisations about what are assumed to be the important features of a language, especially syntactic ones. Individual ambiguities must also be explained within favoured descriptions of particular languages, and typologies assembled and compared; both procedures require generalisations about relevant objects and properties. For more logically-inclined semanticists, ambiguity must be understood in general terms, as a widespread phenomenon in natural languages, if only to make its elimination from artificial languages possible, or easier. There are profound and wide-ranging debates about the proper content, theoretical status, and even the possibility, of linguistic descriptions, and of the semantic apparatus required to give explanations of what utterances mean or of how users understand them; about the nature and ontological status of the object(s) of study, "language(s)"; and about the relation between natural and artificial languages. Yet there is general agreement on the need for linguistic and semantic generalisations, including ones about ambiguities. It is standardly taken to be impossible to construct theoretical descriptions of any sort, whether of a whole language(-system), or of a class of ambiguous sentences, if all one's ontology admits are unique individual utterances. (*Cf.* Baker and Hacker 1984: 221: 'There is no such thing as an explanation of the meaning of an expression which in principle is applicable only to a single token: it is type-expressions that are explained and defined'; and Appiah 1986: 4: 'But we cannot suppose that the rules that give the grammar of a sentence are attached to tokens: for competent speakers have a capacity they can exercise with any

238

token of the type. So what we need is to give the declarative meaning of sentence-types ...'. Only such extreme inscriptionalist semantics as Scheffler's (1979) attempt to make do with only individual *significata* and token signifiers, without even covert reference to sets or types.) Trivially, such generalisations can be made only if a theoretical account is also available of the linguistic items which are ambiguity-bearers. Any useful, precise definition of ambiguity must be securely located within a framework of linguistic categories and concepts, beginning with the basic account of what it is that signifies multiply: and linguistic signification, and *a fortiori* ambiguous signification, cannot be attributed to a single *lexis*.

Now Stoic dialecticians will also want to make general statements about the constituents and features of language. For example, and in particular, they offer definitions of the parts of speech, which have grammatical and semantic as well as phonological properties, and they have an account, albeit restricted and indirect, of possible syntactic relations (see 6.5.2). Further, although the constituents of *lexis* are defined as the letters of the Greek alphabet (D.L. 7.56), and although the Stoic account of linguistic purity is restricted to the rules for correct Greek (7.59), the Stoics seem to have assumed that their accounts of the parts of speech, and of syntax, would apply to any human language. (A Skeptic argument was indeed launched against the possibility of any discourse (Sextus *M*. 1.127ff.), on the tacit assumption that its constituents – syllables and words – are material particulars. The Stoics may not have been its particular targets,[23] but the need to have a reply to it available would still have been pressing.) Provided that appropriate identity criteria for "words" could be assembled – all words seem to be Stoic parts of speech of one variety

---

[23] No target is specified. The notion of "co-remembering", συμμνημονεύειν, in Sextus' argument, *M*. 1.129, by which people are able to grasp long syllables, is put to work at *P.H.* 3.108 to explain how people get an idea of movement – which looks very much like something Diodorus Cronus might have argued ('we get a concept of motion and having moved [τοῦ κεκινῆσθαι]'; *cf.* Sextus *M*. 10.85ff.) – and is mentioned at *M*. 10.353 as a dogmatist ploy for explicating the notions of part and whole.

or another, so there would be no danger of suitable bearers being neglected (see 6.3.5.2) – they could, in theory, have also appealed to such functional features, and designated members of the classes which they called "parts of speech", together with sequences of these, as bearers, without immediately abandoning the requirement that individuals be the focus of concern. Provision would still have to be made for identifying as ambiguous only some inflected forms of some words (*e.g.* 'αὐτοῦ' is ambiguous between "his/its" and "there", but 'αὐτός' has no parallel double meaning), and the working assumption will have to be that this can be done by reference to formal categories. Certainly there seems to be no simple Stoic definition of "word" which might be appealed to here. (The Stoic definitions of barbarism and solecism (D.L. 7.59), for instance, are framed as if an exhaustive division could be drawn between phonological, prosodic, and orthographical errors (those in *lexis*), and errors in combinative syntax (where the *logos* is 'incongruously combined', 'ἀκαταλλήλως συντεταγμένος'); the possibility of single-word solecisms, ignored here, was to exercise later grammarians.) But the Stoics did not pursue this strategy; and the obvious reason for their failure to do so is that not all Stoic ambiguities are words or sequences of these.

So the criticism still holds that they did not then proceed to revise appropriately their patently inadequate account of the constituents of the Greek language; and it holds not because the Stoics "really ought" to be describing (a) language, or explaining native speakers' intuitions of identity of utterances (which would be absurd), but because their own theoretical motivations demand the collection and collation of utterances. Only thus can definitions and classifications be constructed, and students instructed in the dangers of a corrupt and slippery language. Meeting it might not even involve what Stoic ontology would regard as unacceptably irreducible abstractions (appeal to items and structures at a non-linguistic level, that of the *lekton*, would not be disallowed, of course). For example, if utterances are authentic *qualia*, and if an account can be given of how they are commonly qualified, then all their

240

phonological and grammatical properties should be specifiable exhaustively in terms of their states and relations.[24]

Another item in the definition reported by Diogenes confirms the need for phonological, orthographic, and morphological identity criteria. I argued in 4.6 for interpreting the provision that ambiguities signify λεκτικῶς as the requirement that ambiguities have multiple significations according to the public rules or conventions of language. But a public set of rules for meanings is only possible if different *lexeis* (different tokens of the same type, different forms of the same word) can be securely identified appropriately as "the same". The need for relevant generalisation is intensified by the fact that the difference between two of the ambiguity species – the two Homonymies – in the list recorded by Galen seems to rest on a set of such "identity" criteria, as will emerge in 6.3; and, further, because the problem also arises in the case of those utterances which are (also) *logoi*, word-complexes.

Logoi cannot be neglected because yet another of the Stoic kinds, Significant Part, classifies what might be called "grouping" ambiguities, where two or more syntactic construals are possible of the constituents of a syntactic complex, and where the ambiguity is resolvable in speech by suitable pauses (or what can conveniently be treated as pauses).[25] A classic example in Greek is *I made you being free a slave/being a slave free*, ἐγώ σ' ἔθηκα δοῦλον ὄντ' ἐλεύθερον (most famously at Aristotle *s. el.* 4.166a36f.). Written utterances of such sentences are

---

[24] Kirwan 1979: 44 advocates abandoning the whole project of defining identity criteria for equivocal items on the grounds that such criteria are 'far less straightforward' than Aristotle's treatment of them would suggest, and treating ambiguity instead as the signifying of two or more things by occurrences of a single morpheme or phoneme, without bothering ourselves with the problem what are to count as occurrences of the same word. It may well be that identity criteria for words are less than straightforward. Ambiguous signifying cannot, however, be isolated from other sorts of meaning, and cannot be located at one or other of two very different levels of analysis, of which one is non-semantic (how can phonemes be significant?) and the other illicitly assumed as a "given" for the description of ambiguities. So Kirwan's recommendation means not only underestimating Aristotle's appreciation of the difficulties involved (see 5.4, 6.2.4), but also ignoring the whole question of when it is theoretically appropriate for talk of ambiguity, and so of meaning, to enter into a linguistic description.

[25] Ebbesen 1981b: 332 notes that medieval schoolmen working on similar cases of ambiguity took such features to be pauses.

readily taken as ambiguous; spoken ones are more problematic. The real issues at stake (to put them in a form recognisable to ancient theoreticians) are, what counts as a *logos*, and, accordingly, whether word sequences of this type are syntactically ambiguous, or rather sets of two or more syntactically different *logoi* which (as a rough characterisation) happen to share the same word(-form)s in the same order. As with utterances of the αὐλητρίς sort, claims that these sentences are not ambiguous when spoken could be supported by accounts of ordinary pronunciation, with appeals to prosodic or junctural features in the case of αὐλητρίς and the like, to intonation and emphasis in the case of syntactic complexes. The major differences in the analysis of complexes lie in an assumption that constituent forms are morphologically distinct, and in the fact that syntactic groupings are in play. I shall return to the question of the identity of *logoi* when I come to consider the species Significant Part (6.5.2).

Today's typographical conventions tend to eliminate Common "ambiguities" automatically, in modern English as in ancient Greek, although in speech they still seem possible (*e.g. my wife is abroad/a broad*). Whether they are mere puns, or partial ambiguities, or ambiguities *tout court*, can only be determined by reference to some conception of ambiguity and of its bearers. Ancient grammarians confirm that one reason diacritical signs were developed was precisely in response to the felt need to clear up certain forms of ambiguity from literary texts. A Dionysian scholiast describes one species of diacritical sign as 'the distinction of something written which has an ambiguous construction' (312.34f.; *cf.* 305.32f.). Augustine comments on the usefulness of prosodic signs for distinguishing ambiguities (*quaest. in Heptat.* 1.162 (*P.L.* 34, 592); *ep. ad Paulinum Nolanum* 149.4 (*P.L.* 33, 362)). Gradually, application of the signs became general, even where ambiguity was not a potential danger. But without gaps between words or prosodic signs, and with spaces or punctuation, where they were employed, typically marking only the end of a clause or sentence, certain letter sequences in written texts can be interpreted as one word or several, as in the αὐλητρίς example, and as any papyrologist or palaeographer will confirm; and where the corresponding phonological string is also constant, there seem good *prima facie* grounds for taking the utterance, written or spoken, to be ambiguous.

Yet a very strong case (and this is the second of the two problems outlined earlier (p. 224)) can be constructed for the opposite view, for not treating such cases as cases of ambiguity. The point is that ambiguity should be a property of authentic linguistic items, these being theoretically defined as either forms constituting utterances, for homonymy or lexical ambiguity, or as strings of forms, for grammatical ambiguity. This approach to utterances seems to have very general support in modern linguistic and semantic texts (*e.g.* Lyons 1977: 18ff.), although a distinction may well be drawn between, say, free forms (words proper) and bound ones (which never occur in isolation), a distinction which goes back to Bloomfield 1926: 155f.; here the relevant forms are word-forms. In Stoic or standard ancient jargon, it would mean that ambiguity could belong only to (some) parts of speech (roughly, members of word-classes, although parts of speech are indeterminate between classes of lexemes and classes of forms), or to complexes of these. (The common modern distinction between system-sentences and utterances (*i.e.* signals) of (parts of) sentences, although relevant to the question of the bearers of ambiguity, can be put to one side for the present.) I am not pretending that rhetoricians and grammarians employing the usual dichotomy of bearers – words or word-complexes – consciously rejected, and on just these grounds, the Stoic assignment of ambiguity to varieties of utterance, including the undifferentiated sort. The argument against the Stoic position I wish to rehearse here would all the same, I think, have been comprehensible to all the ancient protagonists, and attractive to most.

It starts with the presumption that meanings and ambiguities cannot be made or eliminated by private usage. This is not to deny either that ancient conventionalists – those who believed that all words signify by virtue of arbitrary assignment of meanings to words, there being no "natural" (*i.e.* mimetic) link between them and their *significata* (see 4.6) – made the entirely reasonable point that meanings could be changed by communities; nor that sometimes the extreme case was advanced that an individual could use any word in any sense he chose (Sextus *P.H.* 2.214 is perhaps deliberately ambiguous between the two positions, Plato's Hermogenes unwittingly so, *Cratylus* 384d2–8, 385a4ff., 385d7–e3). But this latter view was commonly regarded as absurd, and as inevitably destructive of language (*e.g.* Ammonius *int.* 132.17ff.), while the former makes no compromise over the non-subjectivity of linguistic rules. Its adherents will have granted that only the utterances regulated by public usage can be linguistically significant, even if that usage is a product of human invention. (In other words, meaning is not speaker's meaning: it is precisely because language does not derive its semantic content from private *fiat* that it is a public semiotic system.) It is only such utterances too which can be ambiguous, not because they could be intended by a speaker on some one occasion to have two or more significations, but because a speaker could in perfect accordance with the rules of language produce an utterance with either of the significations assigned to it by public usage. So the question is: of what do properly constructed human utterances consist?

People typically do not say (mere) phonological sequences, but rather, words (forms) or sequences of these, usually in combinations permitted by the syntactic rules of the language (-system). This principle, which can be traced back to Bloomfield (1926: 155f., 1935: 138, 158), is common in generative grammar (Lyons 1977: 387). Utterances are defined as acts of speakers or the resulting signals (Lyons 1977: 26), but the assumption is that any utterance will always be analysable into forms of words (26f.). As Kooij remarks: 'many discussions of ambiguity only start *after* one possible source of ambiguity has been eliminated, *viz.* after sentences have been unambiguously transcribed morphemically ... In the vast majority of cases, this means an orthographically unambiguous transcription as well; and orthographic conventions may serve to solve various kinds of potential ambiguities' (1971: 9; Kooij's emphasis). Given the post-Bloomfieldian concern to produce parallel but independent analyses of utterances at the different levels of representation (phonological, grammatical, and lexical), '[i]t can be disputed ... whether sentences that *are* unambiguous morphemically ... but ambiguous syntactically ... are also "homophonous", or whether they are different on the level of phonological representation as well, by the introduction of prosodic features' (1971: 10; Kooij's emphasis). Kooij goes on to consider just this question (1971: 11–55).

The ancient grammatical tradition had no metatheoretical anxieties about the interdependence of linguistic levels, and it did not set out to map the actual sounds of Greek or Latin onto phonological abstractions. But it did produce a comparable distinction between the constituents of sound-sequences and of syntactic structures. The latter are *lexeis*, "words" (a different usage, of course, from the Stoic), which, morphological analysis being unknown (*cf.* Robins 1979: 25f.), are the minimum syntactic and semantic units, and are distinguished from the phonological units, letters, and syllables, which lack meaning as well as syntactic status. The assumption is that all discourse (*logos*) is analysable without remainder into "words", even though there may well be disagreement about what sorts of word there are and about what is to count as a *bona fide* word (see 6.3.5.2 on this dispute). Mention of Common ambiguities is rare, perhaps significantly, in rhetorical and grammatical ambiguity classifications, and they are frequently classed as just another species of ambiguity in single terms (see 6.2.5, 8.1). This can hardly be explained by the still relatively infrequent and sporadic use of diacritical signs. More plausibly, it is a reflection of this standard theoretical dichotomy, already noted, of grammatical and semantic entities into words and sentences. (Whether it also had intuitive support is unclear; the theoretical frameworks in which the distinction was embedded were certainly vastly different from their modern counterparts.) Significantly, perhaps, what would be classed as Common *lexeis* are far more frequently met with in, for example, the Homeric scholia, where different interpretations hinge on a particular decision to read a given sequence as one word or several. Chrysippus and Cleanthes are themselves reported to have made suggestions in just such cases (Chrysippus: 'περὶ κῆλα' for 'περίκηλα' at *Od.* 5.240 (Scholia vol. I, p. 265, l. 26 Dindorf), 'ἀμβωμοῖσι' for 'ἀμ [=ἀνὰ] βωμοῖσι' ('on its stand', of a chariot) at *Il.* 8.441 (Scholia vol. II, p. 375 Erbse); Cleanthes: 'ἀναδωδωναῖε' for 'ἄνα δωδωναῖε' ('the (air) given up (from the earth)' for 'Lord of Dodona') at *Il.* 16.233 (vol. IV, p. 219 Erbse; *cf.* Plutarch *quomodo poet. aud.* 11.31 DE)). In the nature of such evidence, theoretical questions of word and *lexis* identity are never touched on.

It may be objected that as a matter of fact speakers do not (as a rule) utter words, but bits of talk which can be analysed into or described as words (*i.e.* forms of lexemes). It is true that single-term utterances (*Yes, Tomorrow, etc.*) constitute only one species of utterance; that boundaries between forms in speech are not always marked; and that linguists deal, strictly, with "norm-shapes" of words, not actual bits of talk (Hockett 1987: 44–5). Moreover, the relation between the intuitive notion of the word and the theoretician's construct is unclear; it has been queried whether it is even theoretically possible to give stringent type/token identity criteria for words, or to distinguish forms within the spoken medium; and objections have been raised to the whole idea of a fixed lexicon for a language (*cf. e.g.* Harris 1980: 132ff., 156, 1981: 150ff.). None the less, it is words (forms) which, in the sense relevant here, constitute meaningful utterances. No competent speaker of ancient Greek could have learned, or taught, or selected from his or her stock of words and phrases in the course of a conversation, an item such as αὐλητρις: it simply is not the sort of thing to function as a lexical or grammatical item. αὐλή τρίς, *or* αὐλητρίς, *or* both, could appear in or be selected from stock, but neither is ambiguous. It makes no sense, the argument runs, to give room in a conception or codification of ambiguity, which is a mode of linguistic meaning, to mere articulate sound sequences, or to the corresponding graphic symbols. (It is this which may underlie the everyday, intuitive, distinction between puns and ambiguities.) The Stoics actually

246

had a terminological distinction between the "pronunciation", προφορά, of vocal sounds and the "saying", λέγειν, or "enunciation", ἐκφορά, of signified items, a sound/content dichotomy which is fundamental to Stoic philosophy of language. Yet, despite the already familiar *lexis/logos* opposition, no comparable terminological distinction was developed between this sort of "saying", where what is "said" is the significations of linguistic items, and the quite different "saying" which is uttering or articulating significant bits of authentic talk: λέγειν does for both.[26]

It might be urged too that a "Common" utterance could be claimed quite strictly and straightforwardly to have two or more significations provided it is identical with both a word and a phrase. Yet Galen's Stoics, to judge by his report of their explanation of the example of Common, described the utterance as only "common to", that is, as "shared by" – not as identical with – both noun and phrase (13.2f.G, 21f.E), which have different and differentiating grammatical and semantic properties. What Common ambiguities have in "common" is a graphic sequence (and, perhaps, in some instances, a phonological structure as well); and this "sharing", where a sequence comprises the same written elements, in the same order, whether it is treated as a single term or as two terms, is not obviously identity, precisely because it does not meet what seem to be minimal criteria for an adequate description of the ambiguity bearer as a fully linguistic item. A Common ambiguity such as αὐλητρίς seems in danger of turning out to be an ambiguity only because of the accidental deficiencies of a conventional orthography.

---

[26] When Chrysippus wanted to draw attention to the pronouncing/signifying division, he appears to have applied the term λαλεῖν to the former: 6.3.4. On ἐκφορά: see D.L. 7.57, 63, and esp. 192 (= *S.V.F.* 2.14, p. 6, ll. 3, 8, where are listed Chrysippus' *On Enunciations Definite as regards the Subject* and *On Singular and Plural Enunciations*), with cols. 1 and 2 of *PHerc.* 307, a book of his *Logical Questions* (already mentioned in Ch. 2) (text in Marrone 1984a). Chrysippus does not always use προφέρω in contradistinction to ἐκφέρω: note Galen *P.H.P.* 2.2.10–11, p. 106, ll. 1f., '... καὶ τῆς ἐγὼ φωνῆς τοιαύτης οὔσης κατὰ τὴν ἑξῆς ὑπογεγραμμένην δεῖξιν συνεκφερομένης. τὸ γὰρ ἐγὼ προφερόμεθα ...'. The λέγειν/ προφέρεσθαι dichotomy seems to have been used by Alexander: Simplicius *cats.* 41.23f.

247

Further, bearers of ambiguity surely have to be the sorts of thing that are significant, with reference to whatever "signifying" is taken to be in the wider linguistic or semantic theory within which the account of ambiguity is nested; broadly functional criteria can then be overlaid on the phonological or graphic descriptions of bearers. But it is quite unclear that αὐλητρις does signify, and, if it does, how. It is not only very hard to find a way of describing what it might signify or indicate that is not intolerably vague,[27] but "αὐλητρίς" and "αὐλή" are surely not signified by it at all: rather, the word αὐλητρίς and the words αὐλή τρίς are formed or formable from it, and it is they which signify. Galen's account of the example (13.2f.G, 21f.E), after all, says that αὐλητρις is common to, or shared by, the noun and the word-complex, not that it *means* both. The difficulty will then be that αὐλητρις turns out not ambiguous after all: for it does not itself signify anything. It seems that the *de soph.* Stoics must admit that Common ambiguities are not ambiguous, or that they are not bits of the language; instead, such utterances can be formed into a word or a word-complex each of which will be univocal. All that can be said about Stoic "utterances" on the basis of such descriptions of Stoic semantics as D.L. 7.55–7 (33A, H) is that they get to be significant by being *logoi* or parts of *logos*. If, however, a grammatical description of αὐλητρις is attempted, one which will give it definite grammatical and semantic status, the ostensible bearer disappears. Another "common" utterance might be indisputably open to two or more interpretations when spoken as well as when written, as the present example is not. Yet it would then still be a matter

---

[27] It would seem very odd to say, for instance, that τρίς refers to or denotes three times as αὐλητρίς refers to or denotes (the class of) female flute-players or as αὐλή refers to or denotes (the class of) domiciles. Compare the English *abroad*, which in speech can be one word or two, and say that what this signifies is "on foreign soil" or (in American/English slang) "a woman". *A broad* might be said to refer to women, but *abroad* does not refer to or denote on foreign soil, although it does mean "on foreign soil". I have been unable to find another, more precise but still consistent description of the significations (if there are any) of αὐλητρις taken alone.

for argument whether "ambiguous" status should be granted before or after formal (morphological) analysis has been completed.

Nor, I think, can it be the wider complex of which the core Common ambiguity is a part which is strictly and properly ambiguous. This seems to be the assumption behind the example supplied by Diogenes: at least, he observes that there are two things, which look like complete *lekta* – propositions, in fact – signified by αὐλητρις πέπτωκε, *viz.* ⟨a female flute-player fell⟩ and ⟨a house three times fell⟩. Theon's explanation of his example is also of the larger complex, and although his illustration may be his own expanded version of the Stoic original (see 6.2.5), there is no reason to think he has departed from the substance of the Stoic account. It seems arbitrary, of course, to deny that αὐλητρις signifies in isolation, while claiming that it somehow manages to signify as part of a larger *lexis*. As for αὐλητρις πέπτωκε itself, it does not look like a proper *logos*, for only one of its components is clearly and consistently a (and the same) part of speech. It looks rather like something from which one or more *logoi* might be made: in each, a subject nominal signifying a commonly-qualified material object (a κοινῶς ποιόν), will be syntactically joined with a predicate. The second "indicated" *pragma* also includes τρίς, an adverb or its "indication". In brief, these examples as wholes, too, have to be counted as *lexeis*. This is consistent with the definition Diogenes is illustrating, but it leaves the original problem untouched: there has simply been a substitution of a longer for a shorter *lexis* of which, again, one component is not a part of speech or a complex of these, yet from which two univocal *logoi* can be formed. As Theon says (82.1–3), there is one thing which is one and undivided, and another which is what is divided. Yet it remains obscure how else the whole example, any more than the core ambiguity αὐλητρις, is going to be significant according to the principles of Stoic semantics, except by going to form those *logoi*.

To supplement these objections the observation might be made that an audience's or reader's reaction to the utterance of a "Common" ambiguity could well be, not: what does it mean? but rather: which (univocal) utterance (which word or word-complex) is it? Such appeals to particular intuitive linguistic responses cannot by themselves undermine any theoretical account of ambiguity or its bearers, and intuitions are, of course, notoriously shaped by hidden theoretical assumptions; but if theory and intuitions do part company, some theoreticians might agree that explanations must be had. Unsurprisingly, neither Stoics nor their ancient critics seem to have taken this line. It is obviously not an adequate response to the argument that as a matter of fact such sequences, written or spoken, might be interpreted in more than one way. The Stoic definition does carry the proviso that an ambiguity has the result that the ambiguous item's two (or more) significations will be simultaneously understood (4.9); but this is plainly not a *sufficient* condition of ambiguity.

For the purposes of my interpretation of the Stoic theory of ambiguity I have accepted and set to work the semantic apparatus of Stoic dialectic, including the *lekton*. The sharing of *lekta* by minds might itself be interpreted as an early version of the "telementational" view, standard in the West since antiquity, of how language works: language is a medium of communication of thoughts between minds (*cf.* Harris 1981: 9). Although Stoics would naturally deny that thoughts can strictly be conceived of as being "put into" words, *lekta* appear to function as intelligible contents of both impressions and *logoi*, allowing the *logoi* to function as causes of the impressions. The critical importance of *lekta* for Stoic claims to explain human linguistic knowledge and communication has already been stressed (3.1). Given the examples of ambiguities supplied by Galen and Theon – especially those of Homonymy in Compounds, Elleipsis, Pleonasm, Significant Part, and Reference – it would be perverse to deny that the authors of the classifications at least included *lekta* amongst the possible *significata* of ambiguous signifiers. The Common examples too, as observed, are optimally interpreted as signifying complete *lekta*. The presence of a finite verb, signifying a predicate, or of a participle, which some Stoics classed with verbs (see 6.3.5.2), should bring it about that the significations of the whole example turn out to be complex *lekta*.

Yet Theon's original example, if it was the same as Galen's, will have included, not a finite verb, as Diogenes' does, but a participle; and the Stoics are known to have disagreed as to whether participles are to be grouped with verbs or with nouns (see 6.3.5.2). Certainly they did not form a separate part of speech, and may not have signified incomplete predicates of such a sort that connecting them with suitable subjects will produce a complete *lekton*. Hence, although Diogenes' Stoics might have specified, albeit arbitrarily, that any ambiguous *lexis* must contain a finite verb, Galen's and Theon's seem not to have done so. There are thus grounds for beginning to suspect that the semantic categories and distinctions available to all these Stoics may have been imprecise or incomplete.

The definition in Diogenes specifies explicitly that ambiguous *lexeis* signify two or more *pragmata*, and the example is most readily seen as signifying two or more *lekta*; it is not yet clear if *pragmata* and *lekta* are co-extensive, but, if they are, the definition will gain in precision, since *pragmata/lekta* will form a single class of significations, whose properties might be further and independently investigated and classified. One very grave objection to this interpretation exists, however: it is virtually certain that nominals do not signify *lekta*. I shall argue this point later, in 6.3.4, and for the present shall simply assume its correctness. On that assumption it has to be concluded either that the definition in Diogenes excludes ambiguous nominals (homonymies) altogether, or that *pragmata* there are not *lekta*.

The first of these alternatives is surely unacceptable. Galen's classification includes a species of homonymy in single terms (and another in term-complexes, 6.3.3), as does just about every ancient classification of ambiguities which aims even feebly at comprehensiveness (see 6.3.2), and it would have been an eccentricity well worthy of comment had even a minority of Stoics gone against so popular, and so reasonable, a practice. In Galen's list the illustration of the second Stoic kind, "homonymy in single terms", is ἀνδρεῖος, meaning both "manly, courageous" and "*pour homme*" (see further, 6.3.4). It would have been classed by the Stoa as an appellative, προσηγορία, signifying two different common qualities or two different sorts of *qualia*.[28] So presumably ambiguities classified in Galen's list can indeed signify items which are not *lekta*, whatever else they may be.

Unfortunately this portion of Stoic semantics cannot be clarified by unpacking the concept of the πρᾶγμα. Some sources tend to suggest that πρᾶγμα has the same extension as λεκτόν, but that in semantic contexts it connotes something like the content of a thought, in contradistinction to that content as what can be said or signified in discourse (whether silent, to oneself, or aloud, to others). Diogenes reports a distinction between "pronouncing" a vocal sound and "saying" a *pragma* (7.57 (33A)); it is *pragmata* 'which also happen to be *lekta*', '... ἃ δὴ καὶ λεκτὰ τυγχάνει', when they are "said". The distinctions are nice: it is precisely the contents of rational thought which can be articulated into the *lekta* communicable by speakers of a language using the appropriate bits of sound, whose structures typically borrow those of the *lekta*. "Speaking", λέγειν, is defined as 'pronouncing vocal sound significant of the *pragma* being thought', Sextus *M*. 8.80 (*cf.* Mignucci 1967a: 94; Cortassa 1978: 391, n. 1). The terms λεκτόν and πρᾶγμα are even used interchangeably in some contexts. Diogenes Laertius (7.65 (34A)) and Aulus Gellius (*noct. att.* 16.8.1), for instance, reproduce the same definition of the proposition, except that one uses πρᾶγμα and the other λεκτόν in the *definiens*. The Chrysippean bibliography in Diogenes Laertius has a section devoted to *pragmata*, which almost without exception is a list of books clearly concerning varieties of *lekta* (D.L. 7.190ff. = *S.V.F.* 2.13, p. 5, l. 4ff.). The predicate and the *lekton* clearly had their beginnings partly in the Stoic theory of causation, and there is some evidence that

---

[28] This is clear from a comparison of D.L. 7.58 (33M) with Simplicius *cats*. 212.12ff. (28N), where the Stoic uses of the term *qualified* are described. Presumably a brave person would count as "qualified" in the strictest of the three senses listed there; an article of masculine apparel, as "qualified" in at least the first and possibly the second sense also.

the *pragma* too originally had a rôle in this context.²⁹ The most striking difference between the two terms is that no explicit mention is ever made of "incomplete" *pragmata*, although the phrase 'πρᾶγμα αὐτοτελές' at D.L. 7.65 (33A), 66, does imply that there are such things.³⁰

In other texts *lekta* seem to be just one sort of *pragma*, with πρᾶγμα and σημαινόμενον being more or less synonymous. Diogenes describes the content of the second subsection of dialectic as 'περὶ τῶν πραγμάτων καὶ σημαινομένων' (7.63), and immediately expands on that as '... the doctrine concerning *lekta*, both complete – both propositions and syllogisms – and incomplete, *i.e.* predicates, both direct and reversed'. (Diogenes' list is something of a jumble, and my translation tries to make some sense of the seven occurrences of καί in it.) The heading looks like a restriction of the section of dialectic dealing with significations to incorporeal significations, that is, to *lekta* only; but this is surely incorrect. Other things besides *lekta* must fall within the compass of this part of dialectic, above all the significations of nouns. The report that predicates are defined both as a type of *pragma* and as a species of *lekton* (7.64) will actually be a double classification, first within a genus, then within a species of that genus.³¹

The safest course seems to be to take the meaning of

---

²⁹ On the Stoic causal triad: 6.3.4. The origins of the *lekton* as predicate lie in Stoic aetiology and metaphysics rather than in semantics, and it is as plausible that the term *pragma* was extended from its original use to mean "effect (of)" ("what is done by") a cause to all *lekta*, including those which are the effects of discourse on the mind, as that it had an independent use inside dialectic proper: see Nuchelmans 1973: 47ff.

³⁰ *Pragmata* cannot, therefore, be "states of affairs" (*pace* Long 1971a: 107, n. 10; LS 1987: 1: 196 = 33F1). The incomplete predicate ⟨... writes⟩ (D.L. 7.63 (33F3)) is not a state-of-affairs. Complete non-assertoric *pragmata* such as questions, imperatives, oaths, and the like (D.L. 7.66ff.) in no way resemble states-of-affairs, and there is no Stoic equivalent of "propositional content". It cannot, in any case, be illuminating to compare *axiōmata* to facts (as at LS 1987: 1: 201), since there are false as well as true statements ('putative facts' (*ibid.* 202) are not facts at all, but, if anything, "factoids"). Finally, arguments and syllogisms, which cannot be compared to complexes of facts or states-of-affairs, are complexes of *lekta*, which are redescribable as *pragmata* in such contexts.

³¹ Each of the three definitions of predicates outdoes its predecessor in technicality, but the last is flawed by its narrowness (not all predicates form propositions with nominative cases: see Porphyry *ap.* Amm. *int.* 44.19ff. (33q)); the others are all very vague. The substitution of 'incomplete *lekton*' for '*pragma*' in the third looks like a gesture at precision.

πράγματα, in the context of the Diogenes definition at least, as "(signified) things",[32] so that any possible type of signification will qualify, including, but not only, *lekta*. The unwelcome result for the definition as a whole will be a blurring of precision, and this deficiency may well not have been made up by the main body of Stoic semantics. Its authors cannot be assumed to have had the same purposes as modern linguists or philosophers in defining meaning in general or ambiguity in particular. Yet there are distinctions amongst types of signifying, and types of multiple signifying, which any definition of ambiguity should capture, and I think it is vain to look for them, at least in an explicit formulation, here or elsewhere in Stoic semantic theory. In fact, explicit descriptions of types of signifying, or even rigid implicit distinctions conveyed by choice of terminology, are largely missing from Stoic sources (see further, 6.3.5.2).

At the same time, the mere appearance of *lekta* in a materialist philosophy, which confines activity and passivity to bodies, is at the very least disconcerting.[33] Their elusiveness in the sources – we have no direct definitions of *lekta*, only definitions of them *qua relata* to users, impressions, *logoi*, and causes – and the fact that there are no good grounds to postulate such odd entities independent of the constraints of Stoic metaphysics, help explain this discomfort. But there is more to it than this. *Lekta* are what "subsist on rational presentations", which might be understood as their "supervening on" such things (and on sentences expressing rational presentations). Some problems with that view are brought to light by ambiguity itself, and I shall explore these in 7.7 and 7.9. What

[32] *Πρᾶγμα* itself is variously translated: *cogitatum* (Schmidt 1839/1979: 20/49f. and n. 35 (1979: 112f.); *cf.* Hülser's n. 24a, p. 112); *entity* (Mates 1961: 11, n. 3); *thing* (Rist 1969: 153, and nn. 1, 5); *state-of-affairs* (besides the references in n. 30, see Blank 1982: 33, n. 48; LS 1987: 1: 202 (34A); Reesor 1989: viii, 33, 45, *al.*, although she prefers *meaning* at 158; see also her discussion of the antecedents of the Stoic *pragma*, 148ff.); *unité de sens* (Hadot 1980: 315); *sens* (Pachet 1978: 364 (implicitly)); *chose* (Pachet 1978: 364 (explicitly); Delamarre 1980: 339).

[33] Nuchelmans 1973: 52ff. traces the *lekton*'s development from 'an event that occurs at the periphery of the domain in which bodies act and are acted on' to 'the thought expressed or that which is signified by words, without any qualification' (52, 56).

seems doubtful in general is that *lekta* can be inserted into an account of how linguistic communication works without giving them the causal rôles their incorporeality denies them. I think great precision is needed in describing what is being effected, and what is effecting it, in such cases.

First, the Stoa seems to have had difficulty describing in exact terms the semantic "loading" of speech (or inscriptions) by utterers. The Stoic definition of *logos* stipulates that it comes "from the mind", ἀπὸ διάνοιας, of the speaker. This is clear from D.L. 7.55 (33H) and from Galen's accounts of Diogenes of Babylon's and Chrysippus' versions of an argument originally formulated by Zeno, to the effect that the ruling part of the soul is located in the heart (*cf.* 3.5). Galen reports Diogenes' version *verbatim*, and the crucial passage reads as follows:

But certainly that at least is true – that rational discourse is sent out from the mind. At any rate, people say even when defining it that it is "significant sound sent out from the mind". And besides, it is plausible that the rational discourse is imprinted, and so to say stamped, by the conceptions in the mind ... [καὶ ἄλλως δὲ πιθανὸν ὑπὸ τῶν ἐννοιῶν ἐνσεσημασμένον τῶν ἐν τῇ διανοίᾳ καὶ οἷον ἐκτετυπωμένον ἐκπέμπεσθαι τὸν λόγον ...] (*P.H.P.* 2.5.11f., p. 130, ll. 12–16 (53U6–7))

The comparison is thus with the straightforwardly physical, directly causal relation of "stamping" or "imprinting" by one object on another; Galen himself refers to such a process when he applies the words 'τυπουμένου' (2.4.40, p. 124, l. 34) and 'συντυποῦντος' (p. 126, l. 2) to the *pneuma* which constitutes vocal sound, as being 'shaped' or 'impressed' by the *pneuma* in the heart.[34] Now the corporeality of conceptions, ἔννοιαι, is not in doubt: *e.g.* Plutarch *st. rep.* 47.1084F–1085A (39F); and

[34] Diogenes' choice of vocabulary here recalls, surely intentionally, descriptions of the relation of a (cognitive) impression to its impressor (*cf.* D.L. 7.50): the point is to emphasise the physicality and immediacy of the relation between concepts and *logos*. Sedley (forthcoming) argues that 'ἐνσεσημασμένον' at *P.H.P.* 2.5.12, p. 130, l. 15, may also mean "made significant"; but the question is how exactly this semantic loading occurs. David Sedley very kindly made this unpublished manuscript available to me, and I am grateful to have had the benefit of his illuminating discussions both of this passage in Galen and of the Stoic conception of the mind; I remain stubbornly convinced that the Stoics' semantics is deeply unsatisfactory, in the way argued in the main text.

they are to be distinguished from concepts, ἐννοήματα, which are their internal objects, and which do not even achieve the level of objectivity and independence accorded to *lekta*, being mere mental constructs: *e.g.* Stobaeus 1.136.21ff. (= *S.V.F.* 1.65 (30A)). But this cannot get Diogenes all the way to his goal, which is an explanation of how the pattern imposed on air, φωνή, transforming it into discourse, λόγος, is specifically *semantic*. *Lekta* are not, and are not reducible to, physical stuffs in such-and-such a state or arrangement. Any relevantly informative description of the patternings – one which reveals and reproduces their semantic content – must, however, make reference to these non-corporeal items. The effect of conceptions on *pneuma*, or of rational discourse on a hearer's mind, is not *just* that of a stamp on wax or metal; and a description of physiological changes in tension, *etc.*, simply is not an account of semantic loading. The problem is not a trivial one. If it "just so happens" that the contents of thoughts and of sentences uttered to convey them are identical – the same *lekta* – no genuine explaining of linguistic meaning has been done *at all*. All that has been performed is a gesture toward the providential arrangement of the universe.

The same gap between *explanans* and *explanandum* opens up in Chrysippus' version of the argument. 'It is reasonable', he is reported to have written, 'that the thing with reference to which the meanings in this [*sc.* rational discourse?] are generated [εἰς ὃ γίγνονται] and from which discourse ⟨is generated⟩, should be the chief part of the soul' (*P.H.P.* 2.5.15, p. 130, ll. 24f.). (De Lacy translates 'εἰς ὃ γίγνονται', p. 130, l. 24, as 'to which ⟨the meanings⟩ go', but I strongly suspect that the phrase is rather an example of Chrysippean stylistic inelegance, since the ensuing argument concerns the *source* of vocal sound and of discourse, not their recipients (ll. 25–8), above all the region where ratiocination, thought, and silent rehearsal of speech, all take place (ll. 29–31).) Of course, "meanings", σημασίαι, may, in some sense, be the conceptions to which Diogenes refers, and thus *bona fide* physical objects. But the only meanings which could be said to be "in rational dis-

256

course" (if that is what the text means) are surely *lekta*, given that they, and not concepts, are explicitly associated with both linguistic and psychical processes (*i.e.* with communication through speech, and with impressions). Yet the only known Stoic explanation of the causal or quasi-causal properties of *lekta* is notoriously thin. Since direct mental apprehension of *lekta* and other incorporeals is possible (D.L. 7.53 (39D7)), the Stoics had to argue that rational impressions are somehow produced in the hearer's mind "in relation to", ἐπί, *lekta*, rather than "by", ὑπό, them, in the same way as the recruit copies his drill-sergeant's movements without physical contact between them (Sextus *M.* 8.409 (27E)). The comparison cannot even get off the ground, at least in this form, because the sergeant and the recruit, unlike the *lekton* and the impression, are both physical objects capable of activity and passivity. Furthermore, they are autonomous, conscious agents, capable of deliberate action and reaction.

Consider what happens when someone hears or reads a bit of discourse and gets a rational impression as a result. What, exactly, is the impression a result *of*? The Stoics will not want to say it is the effect of a *lekton*. They will admit that when the effects of *logos* on the portion of *pneuma* which constitutes the soul, including its ruling part, the mind (διάνοια), are not being described simply in terms of the physical changes in its internal state of tension or relaxation (and thus describable by a formula in which only physical changes (in tension, *etc.*) are mentioned), such effects must be described in terms of the *lekta* which articulate the content of the impression whose content is shared. (Of course, the physical conditions of the soul can only be described by using *lekta*, as the significations of *logoi*; but that is not the point at issue here. It is true too that the Stoic universe is "rational all the way down": even inanimate objects are given shape and form by the active cosmic principle. That thesis, however, is irrelevant to consideration of *particular* semantic contents.) What the Stoics will not permit is a move from description in terms of *lekta*, to description in terms of *lekta* as causal agents: they will say rather that there is a change in the soul, and that on the soul in this condition, the *lekton* which is the articulation of the semantic content of the impression somehow supervenes.

Yet to try to use *lekta* to explain a person's understanding what is said to them in their own language – which is what *lekta* are supposed to account for (Sextus *M*. 8.12 (33B2)) – while not allowing *lekta* to effect understanding, is not just a case of having one's metaphysical cake and eating it too. A sequence of sounds or of marks on a surface is not rational discourse. Its being rational discourse, for the Stoa, is its standing in a certain relation to a *lekton*, which is not and can never be described as "such a body in such a condition". Speech-sound or letter sequences cannot be understood as parts of a process of linguistic communication merely by describing their physical configurations or the physical impact they have or may have on a soul. If such descriptions of particulars and their alterations are all that is permitted, then no real explaining of linguistic or semantic processes as such seems possible. That is, if descriptions in terms of semantic contents are allowed, but as merely supervening on physical objects, without, so to say, doing any work, no genuine explaining gets done of what is supposed to be being explained, of how people communicate when they are barred by the laws of Stoic metaphysics from actually sharing thoughts. For what precisely is *not* being explained is how it comes about that the semantic content of *this* sentence is the same as the semantic content of *this* impression. The ostensible explanation boils down to saying that, as a convenient matter of fact, such-and-such a *lekton* always supervenes on such-and-such an impression or stretch of discourse. If the *lekton* had some sort of causal rôle, it might begin to explain the identity in question: it might be responsible for its own reduplication. That story might well be equally unconvincing (and if *lekta were* effective in this way, denying them corporeality would seem inconsistent (*cf.* Hülser 1979a: 289)): it would at least be an attempt at explanation at the appropriate level. Again, were the *lekton* a physical object, it could cause a similar "patterning" in a set of semantically similar objects, as the seal-ring moulds the wax. But it is not a physical object. Only *pneuma* in the heart could *literally* shape *pneuma* in the lungs.

This vital weakness in Stoic semantics – its failure to convince us that the *lekton* is anything more than a providential *deus ex machina* – poses a general objection to any Stoic theorising about ambiguity which makes use of it, as the one studied in Chapter Four seems to have done. Other specific difficulties can be constructed from the school's own teaching about meaning: above all, that of fixing the way that *lekta*, impressions, and conceptions are related, in such a way that confusion over ambiguities can arise; this will come up for discussion again in 7.7 and 7.9. The apparent Stoic failure to be precise and specific about the contribution to semantic contents of words other than nouns and verbs has already been noted; this too will be taken up again, in 6.3.5.2. On a more general level, the Stoic theory must come in for the standard criticisms levelled against both "atomistic" and "surrogationalist" theories of meaning, as well as against the metaphorical conception of language as a medium or conduit for the transmission of thoughts or ideas, such meanings being associated with bearers (*i.e.* words) of fixed form, by agreement within a linguistic community (Harris's "telementational" and "deterministic" fallacies, 1981: 9ff.; and, for the "conduit metaphor", Reddy 1979).

On the other hand, it would be unwise to construe the Stoic "theory of meaning" as a semantic theory as those are understood today by philosophers of language or theoretical linguists, and either criticise it for failing to live up to expectations created and imposed by alien disciplines and methodologies, or praise it for anticipating them. In so far as the Stoa aimed to explain linguistic comprehension and communication, primarily by way of the theory of the *lekton*, then – however far short this intention fell of a genuine explication of these phenomena – comparison with modern semantics is appropriate. But it would be as absurd to suppose that the Stoics could be described as setting about this task by attempting to construct an exhaustive catalogue of all the enormous variety of possible sentence structures, whether in rational discourse *per se* or in this or that natural language, as that what they were aiming for was a complete formalisation of a natural language as a necessary preliminary to the construction of a theory of meaning for all the well-formed expressions in it (or a set-theoretic semantics for a formal logical language, or a formal model of native-speaker competence).

The attractions of the first of these mistaken approaches can be resisted by bearing in mind that the Stoic conception of syntax apparently did not extend much beyond a naive and inadequate notion of "grouping" – a limitation implicit, as already noted, in the definition of solecism as 'a *logos* incongruously constructed' ('ἀκαταλήλλως συντεταγμένος') (D.L. 7.59) – and that little care seems to have been lavished on distinguishing types and modes of linguistic signifier (see 6.3.5.2, 6.5.2). Further, what information there is on the constituents of complex *lekta* is overwhelmingly concerned with the structures of truth-value-bearing *lekta* of a more or less simple predicate + subject form (D.L. 7.64 (33G); Porphyry *ap.* Amm. *int.* 44.19ff. (33q)). It is surely significant that certain non-declarative types of complete *lekta* – such as oaths or expressions of wonder or disgust – were defined as systematic, non-truth-valued, variations on ἀξιώματα (D.L. 7.67f.; and esp. Simplicius *cats.* 406.20ff.). Other sorts of complete *lekta* were studied: Chrysippus, the key figure here, wrote on imperatives, questions, and interrogatives (D.L. 7.191 = *S.V.F.* 2.13, p. 5, ll. 26ff.), the fragments of his *Logical Questions* show him at work on imperatives (cols. 11–13), and so on; and allowances must be made for lost evidence. But the heart of Stoic semantics was an account of the constituents of certain types of truth-bearer – the objects of assent fundamental to the school's logic, epistemology, and ethics.

The second sort of misreading misfires because missing altogether from Stoicism is the basic, structural feature of much influential modern linguistics and semantics: the notion that what is needed is a theoretical calculus or language in which the constituents and structures of a natural language can be exhaustively and perspicuously rendered. This does not mean that the Stoa (and it hardly stands alone in the histories of grammar and semantics) did not imagine that the constituents and structures it described were universal features of natural languages: there is every reason to think that that is precisely what it did believe. But it did not arrive at this position by detailed empirical analysis of the "data" of a language or languages, on the basis of which models ("grammars") of them could be constructed, from which in turn could be selected those properties which are linguistic "universals" (it hardly needs saying that such "universals" – *e.g.* Chomsky 1985b: 113; Soames 1985: 231ff. – could not have been understood until very recently as constraints on possible grammars constructable by language learners). It is relatively easy to reconstruct the Stoic alternative to such essentially linguistic researches. The predicate + subject or verb + noun structure of *lekta* or *logoi* would have been arrived at by a process of philosophical argument – a matrix of metaphysical and theological considerations yielding the insight that this natural distinction between objects and their activities, passivities, or states, was and had to be reflected in human discourse by virtue of a divine dispensation. As for the doctrines that there are such-and-such types of words, that some of them inflect and others do not (witness the definitions at D.L. 7.58), and so forth, the best explanation of them may well be a simple, crude, linguistic ethnocentrism, buttressed by much the same reasoning as before – that such useful formal distinctions are providentially decreed and maintained, directly or indirectly.

What must be resisted is the temptation to reconstruct Stoic semantics as if it were or could be translated into a modern semantic theory, even a theory of an idealised fragment of (a) natural language, using *lekta* as 'idealised semantic constructs' whose designators form 'an artificial language', so that 'analysing expressions of spoken or written Greek in terms of [*lekta*], *i.e.* practically in terms of an artificial language, is the task of semantics (*peri sēmainomenōn topos*)', as Egli claims in his pioneering study of Stoic syntax and semantics (1987: 110, *cf.* 113). Interpreting the Stoic semantic project in this way distorts it almost out of recognition, and even seems to induce neglect for or misinterpretation of particular pieces of evidence. It seems that Egli implausibly takes subjects of propositions (*i.e.* πτώσεις, cases) to be qualities themselves (116, 121; and see further, 6.3.4); and at first he effectively ignores the rôle assigned to objects in the world as designations of certain types of word (parts of speech) (112), although later (125) a 'variant of the theory of multiple denotation' is claimed for the Stoa. The relation between other word-classes, such as adverbs and σύνδεσμοι (which latter comprise conjunctions and prepositions), and the class of *lekta*, is obscure (see 6.3.5.2), yet Egli asserts that Stoic word classes 'are partly defined in terms of the category to which loquia [= *lekta*] signified by elements of the class belong' (112) – a claim which can actually hold good only for verbs (D.L. 7.58).

Also unacceptable are the results of misapplications of modern theories of reference and of the proposition. Thus Egli asserts that the account in Sextus *M*. 8.100 (part, 341) of the truth-conditions for various types of propositions distinguished by their subject-case can be reformulated in Fregean terms as using 'assignment of individuals to variables': but, Egli's assertion (120) that '[t]he terminology used [in his account] actually occurs in Greek terms' notwithstanding, this interpretation rests on a number of non-translations, such as *assignment* for δεῖξις, *is true according to* for ἐκφερόμενον κατά, and *refers to* for πίπτειν ὑπό and τυγχάνειν with the genitive (119). (For a more accurate modern interpretation of these conditions, see Lloyd 1978; and *cf.* Imbert 1975: 365, n. 9 (p. 381), on the question of variables.[35]) Modern logic differs, Egli's story goes, only in that the existential quantifier is explicitly preposed and the bound variable explicitly exhibited thereafter, anaphora being used instead of a bound variable in the Stoic system (119, 125); the Stoics are said to have used 'predicate functors' instead of connectives (125), sentences are now 'zero-place predicates' (116, 125), and subjects are 'analogues to predicate functors' (127). Confidence is not restored

---

[35] As for Egli's assertion that a thing's μεταλαμβανόμενον is its truth condition, 1987: 125, the term's only use in the relevant passage – Alexander *an. pr.* 404.18 – is as an equivalent to ἐγκλινόμενον, on which see main text, pp. 264f., below.

by talk elsewhere of Stoic sentences or statements (no distinction, significantly, seems to be drawn between these) as consisting of a subject and a predicate (*e.g.* 110, 125), or by the
claim that the Stoics anticipated 'a Russellian [*sic*] theory of
presuppositions' (125). The Stoics were once thought to have
misunderstood and distorted Aristotelian syllogistic: now they
have most of mathematical logic under their belts, two thousand years before Frege.

The whole project of reconstructing Stoic semantics as if
it were an anticipation of the work of Montague, Chomsky,
or any other modern linguist, is equally misguided. Montague
is cited by Egli as an authority for 'the construction of a
theory of truth ... as the basic goal of serious syntax and
semantics' (113, quoting from Montague 1974: 188), Montague and Chomsky as offering *schemata* ("trees") for sentence analysis (111, 113). The mere fact that the vast metatheoretical differences between these two authorities are overlooked itself gives grounds for suspicion (does it really make
no difference what one's sentence *schemata* or grammatical
descriptions are schemata or descriptions *of*?). In any case,
lekta are not 'idealised semantic constructs', equivalent to
the "semantic structures" or "semantic representations" of
modern semantics and linguistics, as Egli asserts (126). They
were not introduced as theoretical or methodological conve-
niences, to permit the construction of a linguistic description
of a language, or the identification of the metatheoretical constraints on such descriptions: they are (subsistent) things in the
world, which are genuinely supposed to explain both causation and linguistic communication. Nor does the "predicate +
subject = proposition" syntax represent, as far as can be
judged today, a deliberate, idealising, simplification of natural
languages' structural multiplicity: it is rather a joint product
of Stoic metaphysics and theology. Further, what the Stoic
theory describes are *lekta*, their arrangements and structures.
But *lekta* are not linguistic objects; and comparing them with
the "sentences" – strictly, sentence representations – generated
by TG base- and transformation-rules cannot be genuinely

263

helpful, given that *lekta* could not have been conceived of as abstract representations of linguistic objects (symbols) of any sort – and given too that both the ontological coherence and explanatory adequacy of such underlying "sentences" have themselves been challenged (*cf. e.g.* Baker and Hacker 1984: 73ff.).

Even talk of Stoic "rules", whether of formation or transformation, is somewhat misleading. The definitions of the predicate as '*pragma* combinable with a thing or things' or 'incomplete *lekton* combinable with a nominative case to form a proposition' (D.L. 7.64 (33G)) can be interpreted as containing rules for forming propositions. None the less they are framed *as definitions*, not explicitly as formation-rules or -procedures (contrast the imaginary procedural rule: 'to form a proposition, combine a predicate and a (nominative or oblique) case'). Egli, understandably, prefers to frame the basic composition principle as 'A sequence consisting of subject and predicate is a statement' (1987: 110): but this fails to capture the essence of Diogenes' or Porphyry's reports, which unmistakeably make predicates the heart of any complex *lekton*. After temporarily accepting the correct Stoic model, 'The predicate is that which might be combined with a subject to form a statement' ((11) on 112), Egli asserts that another version of the combinative principle, 'a predicate may be composed with a subject to form a statement' ((2) on 110), can be inferred from this (112) – as if the distinction between rule and definition were irrelevant – and then proceeds to cite the relevant formation-rule as 'R1: A subject and a predicate form a statement' (114).

As for what Egli calls "transformations" of propositions (113f.; *cf.* Lloyd 1978: 291), these are more properly "inflections", ἐγκλίσεις, the same word being used of formal lexical patternings indicating case, tense, *etc.*; and they are of course inflections of ἀξιώματα, not of sentences, let alone of "strings" as proxy for sentences. Calling such items "transformed" (as Alexander does: *an. pr.* 404.18, 'μεταλαμβανόμενα') is harmless enough: presenting them as a product of an *Ur-*

Transformational Grammar is not.[36] Further, such "inflections" have their home as much in a debate in the philosophy of science (can a thing ever be said to be moving, as distinct from having moved?: Sextus *M.* 10.99f.) as in one in the philosophy of language (about the meaning of non-denoting singular terms: Alexander *an. pr.* 403.14ff.). And the only evidence that the Stoics regarded as parallel procedures both the (non-truth-functional) formation of propositions from predicates and subjects, and the (truth-functional) formation of propositions from propositions, is that the same phrase, συνεστὸς ἐκ, was applied to both (D.L. 7.68, 70 (34κ2–7)). The question whether or not such lax terminological habits produced no more than confusing coincidences is a thorny one: for similar cases, see further, 6.3.5.2 and 6.5.2. Yet Egli is sure that '[c]omplex expressions are valuated in function of their syntactic composition and the values of their parts' (127), as if the "values" in question were the same and the Stoics were well on the way to a compositional, truth-theoretic semantics.

Finally, a passage from cols. 1 and 2 of the *Logical Questions* (translated by Egli 1987: 118 from his text at Hülser 1982: 4: 445ff., §698) shows that Chrysippus may have been familiar with the general notion of recursivity, *viz.* the reapplication of a procedure to an item previously generated thereby. But it is not shown that recursive rules were actually used anywhere in Stoic dialectic (as Egli seems to imply at 117: the passage is too aporetic and fragmentary for that), or that he thought they had (systematic) application to *linguistic* items in particular.

---

[36] For a survival of the Stoic theory (in Nicostratus' criticisms of Aristotle), see Simplicius *cats.* 406.13f. (future-tense inflections of propositions). Egli 1987: 117 also allows, unusually, for "transformations" of sub-sentential items, that is, of predicates into subjects, by the "participle" and "nominative" transformations. One source, D.T. Sch. 518.17f., reports that the Stoic participle was sometimes called an ἔγκλισις of the verb, but there cannot have been an analogous "inflection" of the predicate into an appellative, since the former is a *lekton* and the latter a word (see 6.3.4). Priscian *inst.* 11 (*G. L.* 2), 549.1 also gives a Stoic definition of the participle as 'modum verbi casualem', 'mode of the verb inflected for case', where *modus* may conceivably render ἔγκλισις. On this portion of Stoic grammatical/semantic theory, see 6.3.5.2. What Clement *strom.* 8.9.26.3f. (55C) describes and illustrates, however, are the "cases", πτώσεις, of – that is, the nominals used to refer to – predicates and propositions: see further, 6.3.4.

Of course, it can be illuminating to construct parallels of this sort. It could be both useful and interesting to argue that the *lekton* played the rôle for the Stoa of the "deep" or "logical" structure of sentences of natural language which modern grammars are sometimes claimed to be on the path of identifying, for the edification of logicians and philosophers of language (*e.g.* Katz 1985a: 5, 12). It may be of equal interest to conjecture that the simplistic nature of Stoic syntax as we know it – always the "verb + noun = sentence" or "predicate + case = proposition" structure – may be matched by the standard modern assumption that the basic or nuclear sentence structure is that of (Noun Phrase + Verb Phrase) and its variants (the Stoics at least having a metaphysics to back up their "grammar"). I doubt, however, that Stoic dialecticians can be found guilty of linguistic Procrusteanism: one has surely to see, then ignore, the teeming variety of ordinary-language structures, for that charge to stick. In any case, the comparisons game – whether of grammars or logics – is worth the candle only so long as the rule-book is explicit that what are in play are analogies and disanalogies, not straightforward similarities and dissimilarities, between widely different systems, disciplines, theories, and methodologies. These principles have perhaps begun to be more widely respected in the case of Stoic formal logic (*cf.* Celluprica 1980: 123–7), and they should be just as closely adhered to when reconstructing the Stoic theory of meaning.

To recapitulate: the findings so far about Common ambiguities suggest grave inadequacies both in semantics and in the broader theory of language. Conventional mismatches between spoken and written utterances may have shaped the content and scope of the Stoic conception of ambiguity more than they ought; later writers on homonyms at least were apparently more sensitive to the need to supply criteria of word-identity within and between media (as Olympiodorus testifies), although the theoretical basis of their "additional specifications" for homonymy remains obscure. It proved hard to describe Common expressions in such a way that they

THE SPECIES I: COMMON

could count as genuine linguistic items – briefly, as words or their complexes, *logoi* – which might reasonably figure in a theory of ambiguous signifying. And if Common ambiguities cannot be described as signifying *lekta*, then even this degree of precision and clarity in defining just how they are ambiguous is lost. Finally, calling in *lekta* to explicate linguistic signifying and communication in general seemed to threaten either Stoic dialectic or Stoic ontology with destruction, according as *lekta* are conceded or denied the status of genuinely explanatory items. But direct evidence bearing on the *lekton* is too slight to bear the weight of such grave conclusions.

6.2.4   Common, Combination, and Division

In his second list of the causes of obscurity, at *prog.* 129.11ff., Theon implicitly identifies Common ambiguities with ambiguities in the modes Combination and Division, which are known to be Aristotelian (see 5.4).[37] This is wrong, as I shall argue; it is instructive none the less, as a signpost to the falsity of Galen's claim (14.6–8G, 23E; quoted in 5.5) that the Stoa had failed to identify any new – any non-Aristotelian – ambiguities. In his critical commentary on the Stoic system, Galen does not mention Common at all; earlier in his treatise he refers to it indirectly:

In compound words[38] too this [*sc.*, Combination and Division, which Galen treats as one mode] is possible, because of their resemblance to a

---

[37] Combination and Division are correctly treated by Theon as a single type of ambiguity, although he gives no sign that he knows they derive ultimately from Aristotle, and it is unclear whether he found these modes in the *Rhetoric* itself, or in a handbook drawing on it as source. I have no doubt that he did not extract them from the *s. el*, for the examples he uses are consonant only with the *Rhetoric*'s very loose interpretation of Combination and Division: contrast *rhet.* 2.24.1401a25ff., with *s. el.* 4.166a33–8, 20.177a33ff. It is odd, to say the least, that Theon should have confused the Stoic kind with the Aristotelian mode(s) after having correctly reported the former in our text; his attention to his Stoic source probably flags on at least one other occasion, however: see 6.6.2, in connection with Hyperbaton and Interpolation.

[38] Galen's use here of *simple*, ἁπλοῦν, and *compound*, σύνθετον, differs from the Stoics': for Galen, these terms indicate whether a word is simple or formed from simple words (*e.g.* Νεάπολις); for the Stoa, they distinguish isolated words from

267

word-compound [λόγῳ], as in Νεάπολις [= Naples/new city] and καλοσκάγαθος [= noble/fair and good]; and it might transform a simple word too – but not into another word, only ⟨the ambiguity mode⟩ Accent does that – but into a logos, as, plainly, αὐλητρις; and it might combine the compound into a word, like the preceding one. (9.7–12G, 16E)

I shall overlook the fact that Aristotle does not consistently treat Combination and Division (or Accent, for that matter) as modes of fallacy due to ambiguity, and that consequently Galen cannot be justified in blandly assuming that Combination and Division are a mode or modes of ambiguity. Such "ambiguities", I shall say, occur when a complex can be syntactically grouped in more than one way. What Galen is trying to do is to extend the Aristotelian classification in order to accommodate such ambiguities as αὐλητρις which are absent from the s. el. (as are those such as Νεάπολις and καλοσκάγαθος, comprising a similar though distinct group).[39]

To explain his manoeuvre I must turn once more to the conceptual scheme of de soph. ch. 3, discussed in 5.4, which restricts ambiguity either to single terms or to compounds (συνθέσεις) of these (7.13–8.3G, 12–14E.). Strictly, Aristotelian Combination and Division in the s. el. operate on word-complexes, transforming one into another by changing the syntactic relations between their constituent words, or, alternatively, changing the syntax of one and the same complex. But, says Galen, in the case of αὐλητρις, for instance, the transformation will be, not compound to compound, but compound to single term (by σύνθεσις) or single term to compound (by διαίρεσις), αὐλή τρίς becoming αὐλητρις (or vice versa).

Yet "combination" and "division" of this sort have nothing to do with the syntactic conjoinings and separations which Aristotle had in mind in the s. el. αὐλητρις is not a logos which

combinations of these: see 6.3.3. Galen approaches the Stoic usage when he defines a logos as a 'σύνθεσις ὀνομάτων' (7.16f.G, 13E).

[39] The difference lies in the fact that in the case of Newtown or fair-and-good one or both of the linguistic items forming the logos also contribute(s) to the (original) meaning of the single term. Quintilian's classification, unusually, preserves this distinction (7.9.4–6). In the Aristotelian commentators, an (unsatisfactory) explanation was offered for treating such words as νεάπολις as single λέξεις (i.e. as said ἄνευ συμπλοκῆς) on the grounds that 'what is signified is one': e.g. Simplicius cats. 43.20ff.

can be variously construed (for in that case it would be the unambiguous word-complex αὐλὴ τρίς). Neither, though, is it a single term which can be split up, syntactically or otherwise (for then it would be the unambiguous noun αὐλητρίς). The putting together and taking apart Galen mentions are not only obviously not construals – they are not syntactic operations on words whose morphology is clear but whose syntactic functions and/or relations are not – they also cannot be legitimately described as operations on words at all, unless "words" here are mere graphic or phonological sequences and not lexical or syntactic units. There is not one word, αὐλητρίς, which becomes two words, αὐλὴ τρίς, or *vice versa:* there is a sequence, of sounds or symbols, α, ὐ, λ, η, τ, ρ, ι, ς, which can form one genuine word, αὐλητρίς, or two genuine words, αὐλὴ τρίς.

Galen's dichotomy of linguistic items simply cannot accommodate bearers appropriate to this form of ambiguity even if *logoi* are no more than strings of words lacking syntactic ordering (a move which would allow Galen to depart altogether from Aristotle's conception of Combination and Division). There can be no genuine change from a word to a group of words (or *vice versa*) so long as the operative conception of "word" is what it should be: a semantic and syntactic unit. (Later it will emerge that for this same reason Galen is, strictly speaking, and although he does not realise it, unable to classify as ambiguities members of his sixth Stoic kind, Nonsignificant Part.) In contrast, the one Stoic definition of ambiguity which does survive would capture both Common and Non-significant Part ambiguities. (I am not, of course, suggesting that the Stoa was responding to the inadequacies of the *s. el.*) The real problem, as argued in 6.2.3, is that there are strong objections to recognising Common utterances as genuine instances of ambiguity; and these Galen does not see.

I have observed how Galen fails to distinguish between Combination and Division considered as two separate modes of fallacy, and as one species of ambiguity (5.4). Also unappreciated by Galen, and by Theon too, are the implications of Aristotle's names for his fallacy modes, names entirely appropriate to an analysis of sophistical tactics for winning arguments. In the one case, the sophist syntactically combines words in a premiss to which assent has been given on the basis that those words are syntactically divided (and combined with other words); in the other, the relation is reversed. The Stoic characterisations of both Common and the Part kinds are, in contrast, entirely neutral. Neither interpretation is "correct" by rules external to the understanding of the utterance or sentence *qua* utterance or sentence, perhaps in a given context, rather than, say, *qua* premiss or part of a premiss.

6.2.5   The later history of Common

There is anecdotal evidence that Common ambiguities were exploited before the founding of the Stoa (such as the example, καινου, described in 6.2.3), but Stoic dialecticians seem to have been the first to label and classify them. Their presence in any later, non-Stoic classification can thus be reckoned a sign of Stoic influence, even if indirect and unacknowledged. Both Quintilian 7.9.6 and Hermogenes 2, 141.26–30 Sp., for instance, have the illustration πανταλεων, which could be a proper name (Πανταλέων) or a phrase containing one (πάντα Λέων). Capella 5.229.21–230.6 and Fortunatianus 99.26–8 Halm both have *milesi* (=*mi Lesi* or *Milesi*; likewise, both *Milesus* and *Lesus* are proper names. The classic Stoic illustration, αὐλητρις, itself survived – flourished, if Quintilian's contemptuous allusion to it as 'illa vulgata', 7.9.4, is anything to go by. Here *vulgata* presumably means both "overfamiliar (as an illustration) in the rhetorical manuals", as well as "crude, implausible", for the context is Quintilian's classification of ambiguities as sources of legal dispute, and he refers to ambiguities of this type as 'ineptae sane cavillationes' (*ibid.*), silly quibblings of no importance for the rhetorician.[40] Quintilian's own version, like Theon's, takes the form of an imagi-

---

[40] Quintilian's attitude to the subtleties of classification is equally robust: see 6.3.6, 8.2.

nary law. Comparable examples can be found elsewhere in Quintilian, as well as in Hermogenes, Capella, and Fortunatianus; all these are framed as testatory clauses.

Thus Common finds its way into rhetorical *stasis* theory. It plays a small but regular part in treatments of ambiguity as a cause of legal dispute, occasioned by ambiguously-framed laws, wills, and other documents. It is puzzling, none the less, that it was an expanded, forensic, version of the example preserved by Galen and Diogenes Laertius which was chosen for the *prog.* Theon himself was familiar with the theory; the advanced *progymnasma* "Law" at 128.23ff. is a propaedeutic to higher level instruction in *stasis* theory (see 5.2.1), and according to the Suda (*s. n.*), Theon wrote, *inter alia*, *Rhetorical Hypotheses*, and possibly a *Handbook*, τέχνη, although this may be the *prog.* under another name. Perhaps he substituted for the illustration he found in his source a variant already known to him from his rhetorical studies, and more in conformity with his readers' special interests.

And yet the example does seem out of place in its narrower context within the *prog.*, a classification of the sources of linguistic obscurity in narrative, even if the dialecticians' ἀμφιβολία has been introduced in quite general terms at 81.30 as something that 'makes language unclear', 'ἀσαφῆ δὲ τὴν ἑρμηνείαν ποιεῖ'. A Stoic dialectician would be unlikely to tailor the illustration to rhetorical theory. Of the other examples Theon provides, just one (one of two instances of the species Reference) can boast a rhetorical pedigree (it is a quotation, from Demosthenes), and it may very well be Theon's own contribution. The most plausible conclusion is that Theon is inconsistently, if harmlessly, combining two paedagogical topics: *stasis* theory, to which the illustration of Common belongs, and the excellences and defects of narrative style, of which the ambiguity classification as a whole forms part.

This is the first indication that the *prog.* text may not be a (more or less) *verbatim* report of a Stoic list. The forensic version of the example might be a genuine Stoic variant; it might even be a deliberate borrowing-back from the rhetoricians,

271

intended to signal the array of types of discourse in which ambiguities occur and have to be recognised and dealt with. But the rest of the *prog.* report provides indisputable evidence that Theon has silently altered his Stoic original elsewhere. The absence from Theon's classification of the following two *de soph.* kinds, the two Homonymies, is the next striking piece of silent testimony to his free handling of his Stoic source.

6.2.6   *Common: conclusions*

Given the definition of *lexis* formulated by Diogenes of Babylon, as 'φωνὴ ἐγγράμματός' (D.L. 7.56), and given that this account is extendable to appropriate written representations of vocal utterances, the examples of Common presented by Diogenes, Theon, and Galen confirm that bearers of ambiguity for the Stoics will be varieties of articulate spoken and written *lexeis*; but this will hold only if certain scribal (or typographical) conventions are observed. There must be no marking of word-divisions, or of lowered final acutes, as there is today. In speech, continuous utterance, without a pause, may similarly fail to disambiguate, and the example αὐλητρις may thus also be a homophone, although this point remains unresolved. It became clear, however, that what counts as a single *lexis*, in speech or in writing, will determine what can count as a Common ambiguity. Perhaps utterances ambiguous in writing only may have been disqualified by the *de soph.* Stoics, but the issue proved a complex one, and a strong possibility remains that identity criteria for spoken and written items had not been developed.

Whether Common is hailed as a successful and important innovation, or as a misguided and unneeded excrescence, depends fundamentally on what conception of ambiguity is adopted, and, in particular, on whether the study of ambiguity should begin before or after morphological analysis (as it is now called it), and on whether scribal conventions should be relevant to deciding the scope and meaning of the term *ambiguity*.

6.3 The species of ambiguity 2: Homonymy in Simples, Homonymy in Compounds

6.3.1 Homonymies: text and translation

de soph. 13.4–7G, 22E

δευτέρα δὲ παρὰ τὴν ἐν τοῖς ἁπλοῖς ⟨ὁμωνυμίαν⟩, οἷον	4
ἀνδρεῖος· ἢ γὰρ χιτὼν ἢ ἄνθρωπος. τρίτη δὲ παρὰ τὴν ἐν	5
τοῖς συνθέτοις ὁμωνυμίαν, οἷον ἄνθρωπός ἐστιν. ἀμφίβολος	6
γὰρ ὁ λόγος, εἴτε τὴν οὐσίαν εἴτε τὴν πτῶσιν εἶναι σημαίνει.	7

(2) The second [species is] due to ⟨homonymy⟩ in simples, *e.g.*   4
ἀνδρεῖος, for [it can be said of] either a shirt [= *pour homme*] or a
man
[= *manly*]. (3) The third [species is] due to   5
homonymy in compounds, *e.g.* (*a*) *man is;* for the sentence is   6
ambiguous, whether it signifies that the being [*or:* substance] is,
or that the case is.   7

6.3.2 Homonymies: species

These two kinds, as their titles suggest, belong and must be
studied together. The distinction between them – almost unrecognised by modern scholars,[41] and missed altogether by the
single ancient author known to have commented on them –
represents a provocative innovation in the classification of
ambiguity types. It rests on the assumption that only some
(occurrences of) single terms characterised by homonymy in
isolation ('in simples') are so characterised in particular contexts. Certain linguistic environments are taken to disambiguate terms which out of context are homonymous, and which
are all classed as isolated homonyms under Homonymy in
Simples; under Homonymy in Compounds, by contrast, are
ranged only single terms not thus disambiguated.

Explicit and positive evidence for this interpretation does
not exist. Indeed, later writers on ambiguity seem to have
ignored this original offering of Stoic taxonomy (if it ever

---

[41] It is correctly identified only by Pépin 1976: 96f., Baldassarri 1984: 49 (who both
fail to see that it offers an explanation of Chrysippus' thesis that 'every word is by
nature ambiguous': *cf.* Pépin 1976: 95, n. 4, and Baldassarri 1984: 50 respectively)
and LS 1987: 2: 231; and suggested by Hülser 1982: 3: 401. See also n. 63.

came to their attention). But indirect evidence is available, and I shall present two different and complementary sorts of testimony.

First, there is the *de soph.* itself, with its examples and Galen's observations on them, as well as the titles of the kinds. The necessarily very close scrutiny of the Homonymy in Compounds example proves fruitful in another, unexpected, direction, since it reveals that this illustration must be understood as a case of autonymy, whereby a single term signifies both some extra linguistic object, and also, surprisingly, itself, that is, it is also its own name. A Stoic doctrine of autonymy can hardly fail to arouse interest today, as it seems to be the first known attempt at a precise and systematic explanation of how talk about language is possible, a phenomenon commonly accounted for nowadays by appeal to the distinctions between use and mention or between language and metalanguage. To all appearances, however, it went almost completely unnoticed in antiquity, and today only Augustine can be seen to have appreciated and deliberately exploited its usefulness.

Another, equally strong, argument in favour of understanding the example in this way is the explanatory power of a Stoic, and specifically a Chrysippean, theory of autonymy. When coupled with evidence that in Stoic semantics every word is (non-autonymously) significant, it allows a highly plausible reconstruction of the reasoning behind Chrysippus' notorious dictum that 'every word is by nature ambiguous'.

The second sort of testimony I shall present combines both of these striking innovations; and therein lies its real value. Augustine, I shall argue, developed his own versions of both these original Stoic contributions, and, crucially, developed them in tandem, as the cruder prototypes of his *de dialectica* (*On Dialectic*) gave way to the rather more sophisticated models of the *de magistro* (*On the Teacher*). The most obvious source for both is a Stoic ambiguity classification like the one Galen records.

One subject Augustine glances at in the *de dialectica*, and expands on in the *de magistro*, is the nature of the conditions under which disambiguation takes place. Regrettably, he restricts his later, maturer discussion to his version of the disambiguation of autonyms. The last part of my inquiry into the kinds follows up what very slight clues there are to Stoic teaching or speculation on this topic.

Not every Stoic classification necessarily included both these kinds. They represent a new and controversial approach to taxonomy in the field, and, besides earlier lists from which they were absent, there may well have been later systems whose authors deliberately rejected the pairing of the two Homonymies as inappropriate, inadequate, or ill-founded. I shall sound out a number of objections which could have exercised such an influence. It is extremely doubtful, however, that homonymy would have had no place at all in a Stoic classification. Homonymy is perhaps the single most common feature of grammatical, rhetorical, and philosophical lists of ambiguity species. Even if the list to which Theon had access did not include Homonymy in Compounds, and only some mode of homonymy in a more familiar guise, he cannot have reported it with complete accuracy.

An explanation for Theon's omission of Homonymy (or of the two Homonymies) is easily found. The first half of Theon's first classification of sources of linguistic obscurity – whose second half is the Stoic system itself – comprises a list of types of single term (81.8–29) (see also 5.2.1, 8.2 on this text). Its last entry begins (25–7) 'ὁμώνυμα δέ ἐστιν, ὧν φωνὴ μὲν καὶ ὄνομα τὸ αὐτό, ἕτερον δὲ τὸ σημαινόμενον ὑπὸ τῆς φωνῆς' ('homonyms are those things of which the vocal sound and name are the same, but what is signified by the vocal sound different')[42] and the accompanying illustration is παῖς, which signifies "child", "son" and "slave" (27–9). Theon would have felt fully justified in omitting the dialecticians' version of homonymy whether or not it comprised the two de soph. Homonymies. If he failed to appreciate the difference between them and any more

---

[42] Ebbesen 1981a: 1: 37 lists homonyms as one of the causes of obscurity identified by Theon's dialecticians. But ἀμφιβολία appears only after homonyms have been mentioned in the first half of Theon's classification. Schmidt 1839/1979: 51/73 and n. 74 (1979: 140f.) wrongly takes Stoic ἀμφιβολία to be 'Mehrdeutigkeit der Rede'.

standard and familiar version, as he may well have done, then, in his eyes, not to excise homonymy from the dialecticians' ambiguity classification would cause needless repetition.

If this was Theon's reasoning, then he was mistaken. He would have been misled primarily (and understandably so) by the titles of the *de soph.* kinds.

6.3.3 Homonymies: titles

These contain two important pieces of information.

In each case what is being classified is homonymy; and, unless the *de soph.* Stoics were quite hopelessly negligent, each kind will classify single terms characterised by homonymy. The Stoic definitions of homonymy and homonyms are unknown.

The phrases 'ἐν τοῖς ἁπλοῖς'/'... συνθέτοις' ('in simples'/'... in compounds') must preserve the distinction between the two species of homonymy. Galen's examples very strongly suggest that this involves a distinction between isolated and combined terms. It remains unclear what noun, if any, is to be supplied with each phrase (presumably the same with both), a problem which has already raised its head in the course of the discussion of the first Stoic kind, Common (6.2.2).[43] As for the distinction itself, there is evidence for a Stoic dichotomy between φωναὶ ἁπλαῖ (simple vocal sounds) and φωναὶ σύνθετοι (compound vocal sounds), although this cannot be precisely the division in play here. At *M.* 8.135f. Sextus classifies items like *Dion* as ἁπλαῖ φωναί and ones like *Dion walks* as σύνθετοι, and this dichotomy, and the argument in which it is used, appear to have been taken from a Stoic source (adapted and

---

[43] The missing term cannot be μόρια, *parts*, despite Galen's descriptions of Non-significant and Significant Part. The "parts" in question there are parts of articulate utterance, as I shall argue; so it would have to be assumed tacitly here that the simple and compound parts are all *significant* parts of *lexis*. Further, σύνθετα μόρια, following standard Greek usage (see LSJ *s.v.* σύνθετος), ought to be "parts which are compounds", not "parts combined (with other parts)". At D.L. 7.58 (33M), however, ἀσύνθετον applies to a type of predicate, and must mean "non-compound", *i.e.* "consisting of a verbal predicate only (without an oblique case)"; and Simplicius *cats.* 60.14f. (*cf.* 10.29) distinguishes between simple and compound *lexeis*.

compressed by Sextus), since the position under attack is that linguistic items are the bearers of truth and falsehood. Simplicius too may offer evidence for a Chrysippean, and hence presumably an influential, distinction between what is ἁπλοῦν in language and what is not; unfortunately, it is unclear how much of the report is a *verbatim* record of Chrysippus' views: 'Chrysippus too is puzzled as to whether perhaps the simple appellatives [τὰ προσηγορικὰ καὶ ἁπλᾶ] alone are contraries, but the others [*sc.* definitions] are not. For we include many other things in the latter, and ⟨utter them⟩ along with articles and conjunctions and other exegetical parts [μορίων] . . .' (*cats.* 389.22ff. = *S.V.F.* 2.174, p. 50, ll. 19–23).

Galen himself is convinced that the opposition between the two Homonymies involves a distinction between single and combined words: 'and saying that homonymy occurs in complexes [ἐν τοῖς συμπεπλεγμένοις] too [*sc.* as well as in single terms] is the work of men who do not even listen to words at all' (14.11–13G, 23E). A little later he refers to 'what is called by them [*i.e.* the Stoics] "homonymy in a word-complex [ἐν λόγῳ]"' (15.3f.G, 24E). In Galen's opinion, Homonymy in Compounds constitutes one-half of the Stoic version of Aristotelian Amphiboly, a species of ambiguity in which each of a combination of non-homonymous terms can perform more than one grammatical function in relation to its fellows.[44] In this he is undoubtedly wrong, and his own explanation of the illustrations proves him so.

6.3.4 Homonymies: examples

The first difference between the two illustrations to strike the eye is that one, ἀνδρεῖος, is a single term, while the other, ἄνθρωπός ἐστιν, is a grammatically complete two-word

---

[44] 15.3–6G, 24E, where Galen lists as one 'mode' of 'homonymy in a word-complex' the 'juxtaposition of like grammatical cases', as in εἴη Μέλητον Σωκράτην νικῆσαι (= *May Meletus defeat Socrates; May Socrates defeat Meletus*). His own example of Amphiboly at 1.12–2.1G, 2f.E is of just this type. The other kind Galen almost certainly has in mind as the second half of the Stoic counterpart to Amphiboly is Reference, and there too he is wrong: see 6.7.2.

sentence. The former Galen explains by listing, not its direct significations, but a choice of two objects or classes of object of each of which it can be said in one or other of its two possible meanings: a shirt or tunic (when it will mean "men's wear") and a man (when it will mean "brave") (13.5G, 22E). In the explanation of the significations of the other example (13.6f.G, 22E), the infinitive εἶναι corresponding to the finite verb ἐστιν in the illustration itself is used with τὴν οὐσίαν and with τὴν πτῶσιν alike; so I shall assume, for the time being, that the meaning of the finite verb must be constant, and that ἄνθρωπος alone is homonymous.

Galen's criticism of Stoic terminology can therefore be dismissed: Homonymy *in* Compounds is just that, not homonymy *of* compounds; and, being a form of homonymy, it cannot correspond to Aristotelian Amphiboly, which characterises *logoi*. But it would be absurd to classify under this kind any and every instance of a term, homonymous in isolation, when conjoined with other terms. In that case the two Homonymies would be a mere travesty of a classification of ambiguity species. The true distinction between them can be found with the help of a passage in Simplicius (*cats.* 24.13–20), where he reports the response of persons he calls 'dialecticians' to 'syllogisms [that is, fallacious syllogisms, sophisms] due to homonymy'. I shall analyse this passage more closely in Chapter Seven, in connection with the Stoic theory of the linguistic fallacy. The point to observe here is that the dialecticians recommend keeping mum – raising no objection – so long as the sophist posing the questions continues to transfer his selected homonym to 'another signification', 'ἄλλο σημαινόμενον': an objection should only be raised when he stops doing so. The considerations advanced in support of this policy by the dialecticians, who are almost certainly Stoics, are unknown, and Simplicius neglects to say that in each case the signification has to be that appropriate to its context; but this must be their key assumption, what makes their advice reasonable.

One of the features of the passage which strongly suggest that these dialecticians are Stoics is that the homonymy exploited in the sample sophism is ἀνδρεῖος.[45] What they could plausibly have claimed is only that context can disambiguate, not that it does always, and of necessity. The Homonymy in Compounds kind, I suggest, classifies just such terms, words that are characterised by homonymy in particular contexts. The first condition which must be met if this interpretation is to be correct is that the significations of (a) *man* in the example should be such that neither is eliminated by the context constituted by *is*.

Clearly, (a) *man* can be said to signify an *ousia*, a being or substance. Among material objects, according to Stoic metaphysics, are qualities which are either particular, and constitute individuals, or common, and qualify each member of a group of similarly – characterised items, such as natural kinds (a man, a horse: D.L. 7.58 (33M)).[46] The προσηγορία or "appellative" *man* will signify the common quality man, or anything possessing it, each κοινῶς ποιός which is a human being;[47] and the quality and the *qualia*, being corporeal, will alike be, and can be called, *ousiai* in this Stoic sense. On the other hand, it is usually the substrate underlying the object's qualities that in Stoic contexts is called a substance (*e.g.* 28q); and the possibility cannot be discounted that Galen has intruded a piece of Aristotelian terminology.

Some modern scholars have identified common qualities with cases as the incorporeal significates of appellatives

---

[45] Another feature is the appeal to the dialectical tactic of "falling silent": see 7.4.

[46] See Sedley 1982a: 260f. for a clarification of the difference between particular and common qualities. Pachet 1978: 365 claims a parallel case in Chrysippus' *Logical Questions* (= *PHerc.* 307, on which see ch. 2, p. 30): ῥυπαρός is used equally of a man and a tunic (col. 14 = *S.V.F.* 2.298a, p. 110, ll. 16–18). But, unlike ἀνδρεῖος, ῥυπαρός could have the same sense ("filthy, dirty") in both uses; and the more plausible explanation of Chrysippus' "question" in col. 14 is how such words, which look and behave like appellatives, προσηγορίαι, can be so when they signify purely superficial, temporary properties (such as being dirty).

[47] I make what seems the reasonable assumption that *man* can signify each of the generic *qualia* as well as the quality which, in a sense, they have in common. Qualities of the sort in question here, like man, are simply portions of breath characterising bits of matter (*substrata*): so a particular man, just in so far as he is a man, can be viewed either as qualified substance, or as a quality (*cf.* Simplicius *cats.* 212.12ff. (28N, esp. 7)).

(Mates 1961: 11; J. Christensen 1962: 50; Hadot 1966: 111; Pinborg 1975b: 81; Graeser 1978: 205; Hülser 1979a: 289), but evidence in support is unconvincing. Frede's claim, 1978: 31f., that cases are common qualities and must therefore be corporeal, and Egli's, 1987: 116, 121, that appellatives signify qualities which are appellative subjects, are unpersuasive too; and the notion must be rejected altogether that corporeal qualities are 'what corresponds to the different forms of a noun on the level of what is signified or meant' (Frede 1978: 31).[48] A case, not being a common quality, might be such a thing, but the evidence is against even this. Even if nouns do have correlatives at the level of the *lekton* – which itself seems highly unlikely – no source reports that Stoic cases are types of *lekta*; as Nuchelmans 1973: 57 points out, 'there is not a single passage where ... the subject is called a defective *lekton*'.[49]

---

[48] Also unacceptable is Rist's contention, 1969: 164–7, that common qualities are not (just) incorporeal, but are mental constructs, ἐννοήματα: see further main text, below.

[49] Sextus reports that *Dion* has an incorporeal signified *pragma*, but not that this is a case: *M.* 8.11 (33B2). Long 1971a: 76f., and n. 11, argues that Sextus is actually referring to a proposition, utterance of the name being equivalent to saying *e.g.* ⟨this is Dion⟩, which is perhaps supported by Alexander *an. pr.* 402.16ff.; the need to account for successful uses of names when their owners cannot be demonstrated makes it unlikely, however. From *M.* 11.28f. (a passage already discussed, from a different point of view, in 3.5), it is clear that someone certainly thought nouns signify cases, but not that such cases are incorporeal, or that the thesis is Stoic. Long 1971a: 105f. believes this text is 'probably based on Stoic doctrine'; but, even if it is Stoic, to interpret cases as the "grammatical functions" signified by nouns and classifying items of the same kind is both unsupported by the evidence and, I think, inconsistent with what is known of Stoic materialism. A Dionysian scholiast, 523.9–27, argues that a case is a noun's signification, σημαινόμενον, rather than its final syllable's "inflectional change", μεταπλασμός, without, however, expanding on what he means by *signification*, or attributing either position to the Stoa. Much has been made of the inclusion of a work *On the five cases* in the *pragmata* section of Diogenes Laertius' Chrysippean bibliography (7.192 = *S.V.F.* 2. 14, p. 6, l. 2; *cf. e.g.* Frede 1978: 31). Yet the last title in the subsection to which this work is assigned is περὶ τῶν προσηγορικῶν (p. 6, l. 5). In professional grammar προσηγορικὰ ὀνόματα are "appellative names" (as opposed to κύρια ὀνόματα, "proper names": *e.g.* D.T. 33.6–34.2), and it seems a reasonable assumption that here προσηγορικά are προσηγορίαι (defined at D.L. 7.58 (33M)), under a slightly different title; Simplicius may perhaps preserve an authentic Chrysippean use of the term (*cats.* 389.22 = *S.V.F.* 2.174, p. 50, l. 20, quoted p. 277 above). Furthermore, another title in the subsection (p. 6, l. 3) contains a form of the term ἐκφορά, *enunciation*, which was almost certainly a piece of Stoic semantic jargon for the "issuing", so to say, of incorporeal σημαινόμενα in speech (see 6.2.3, n. 26): at p. 6, l. 8, however, the same word figures in the first title of the *lexis* division of the

It is not clear, in any case, that taking cases to be the significations of nominals can explain the Stoic illustration. Suppose nouns have immaterial significations as verbs do. Unlike verbs, they will typically also refer directly to particulars in the world. Now, when I say (*a*) *man is*, I am not saying one or other of two things, that (i) a human being exists, or (ii) an incorporeal signification ⟨man⟩ exists. I am saying (i) only, and I say (i) by using language to express the *lekton* of which one component is, *ex hypothesi*, the incorporeal meaning ⟨man⟩; for the *lekton* just is the articulate content of the mental impression I am putting into words. What is required here, however, is an explanation of how (*a*) *man is* is ambiguous, not of how *man* manages to be significant.

It might still be contended that cases must be incorporeal, and stand to nouns as non-compound predicates do to verbs, on the grounds that case and predicate together form complete *lekta*, according to Diogenes Laertius' account of this portion of Stoic semantics (7.64 (33G)). That a combination of a material object – a piece of language – and an incorporeal *lekton* should be possible, and should itself be incorporeal, does seem somewhat bizarre, and is the principal objection to this interpretation of the nature of cases.[50] Against this must be set the positive evidence for cases being words.

First, the case can be said to "be", and this status, in Stoic metaphysics, is, strictly speaking, limited to corporeal objects: *e.g.* Seneca *ep.* 58.13ff. (27A), Alexander *top.* 301.19ff. (27B), Galen *meth. med.* 10.155.1ff.K (27G). The Stoic definition in Diogenes Laertius stipulates that an ambiguous utterance's

bibliography. A rigid line could not reasonably have been drawn between treatises concerned with linguistic items and those concerned with their significations (*cf.* Mansfeld 1986: 368f.). Accordingly, the appearance of *On the five cases* in this subsection is no sure guide to the ontological status of cases.

50 A passage in Chrysippus' *Logical Questions* (text and commentary in Marrone 1984b) shows that Chrysippus was at least aware of an argument to the effect that certain properties of verbs, *e.g.* tense, number, voice, do not attach to predicates or propositions. If the possibility of *lekta* sharing properties with linguistic items was indeed rejected, their being combinable with words seems still less likely. At the same time, accounts of types of predicate preserved by D.L. 7.64 and Porphyry *ap.* Amm. *int.* 44.19ff. (33q), and the Stoic notion of inflection of a whole proposition (Alexander *an. pr.* 403.14ff.), appear to show that formal distinctions of *lekta* as well as of cases are possible.

significations be strict, and the *de soph.* Stoics may have adopted the same policy.

Second, although in ancient grammar a case is an inflected form of a word, not the word itself,[51] the Stoics seem to have thought of cases in quite a different way, as words themselves. More precisely, they comprise at least some, and perhaps all, "declinable", πτωτικά, linguistic items. Thus, appellatives (*i.e.* common nouns, adjectives, and (on one view) participles), articular infinitives (or the articles employed in these), and demonstrative pronouns are definitely "cases"; proper names probably are; and other sorts of pronoun may be too, although no evidence is available directly for these.[52] The relation of the Stoic "case" to the standard grammatical case remains obscure; one explanation is that a Stoic case, referred to without any explicit grammatical qualification, is an inflected noun (or pronoun, *etc.*) in some, unspecified, case or other. Ebbesen 1981a: 1: 206 suggests that it probably has modern parallels in the word-type, lexeme, or citation-form of a lexeme, but, as the Stoic case is a corporeal object and a particular, the closest parallel must be the citation-form, at least for cases *simpliciter*.[53] So unorthodox was this concept of the case that

[51] *E.g.* D.T. Sch. 382.36ff., 523.9f.: a case is the τύπος, "shape, form", or μετασχηματισμός, "reformation", of a declinable word; precisely, of its final syllable; and *cf.* 230.34ff.: the cases belong to φωναί, not to meanings. There was a long-running dispute as to whether the nominative is a case (*e.g.* 230.24ff., 546.5ff., and see n. 60 *infra*). A related dispute concerned a distinction between something called "the generic noun", an abstract entity which gets determined by the forms (the nominative or naming case, the three oblique cases) it takes on in actual discourse (*cf.* Frede 1978: 67), the noun "in the mind" being sometimes inserted between the generic noun and the nominative, as it is human beings who perform acts of naming: *e.g.* D.T. Sch. 547.18ff.; Choeroboscus *in Theod.* (*G.G.* 4.2), 109.24ff. The generic noun was used to explain how nominatives can themselves be cases (*i.e.* derived forms). The Stoics are said to have subscribed to a similar idea, with the concept (usually an ἐννόημα; νόημα in the report) playing the part of the generic noun: Ammonius *int.* 43.9ff. (33κ)). But *lekta* seem not to have played any part in this curious explanation.

[52] Proper names, appellatives, articular infinitives, and demonstrative pronouns are dealt with in the main text. As for other species of pronoun, it is known that the Stoics argued that definite and demonstrative pronouns were all articles (indefinite and definite respectively) because the former were substitutable for the latter (see 6.3.5.2); and this is at least consistent with their all also being cases.

[53] Ebbesen 1981a: 1: 206 also argues that in 'metalinguistic statements [*e.g.* in the "Wagon" sophism to be discussed in the main text, pp. 285f., below] ... you are speaking about the "case" instantiated by the word you utter or about that word

it left no mark on conventional grammar, and the only information about it comes from Diogenes Laertius, Stobaeus, Clement, and Simplicius.

Diogenes reports that the proposition ⟨Dion is walking⟩ is constructed from a nominative case and a predicate: 7.70 (34K) (*cf.* 64 (33G)). Nothing in the context suggests that the subject-case is a *lekton* and not a word.

Stobaeus, in the course of an account of the Stoic interpretation of Platonic metaphysics, according to which forms are mere "concepts" or "mental constructs", ἐννοήματα, reports that

> They say that concepts are neither somethings nor *qualia*, but quasi-somethings and quasi-*qualia*, mental imaginings [φαντάσματα ψυχῆς]; and that these are called "ideas" by the ancients. For they [*sc.* the Stoics] say that the ideas are of the things falling under [ὑποπιπτόντων] the concepts, *e.g.* of men, horses, and, in more general terms, of all the animals and all the other things of which they [*sc.* the ancients] say there are ideas. The Stoic philosophers say these [*i.e.* the Forms] are non-subsistent [ἀνυπάρκτους], and that we share in the concepts, but get the cases which they call appellatives [τῶν δὲ πτώσεων, ἃς δὴ προσηγορίας καλοῦσι, τυγχάνειν]. 1.136.21ff. (= *S.V.F.* 1.65 (30A))

At least some cases, then, were appellatives for the Stoa.[54]

Simplicius reports as follows:

> Chrysippus, moreover, is uncertain whether the Form will be a particular something [τόδε τι]. We must take into account too the Stoics' usage with regard to the generic *qualia* – how, according to them, cases are pronounced [προφέρονται], and how τὰ κοινά are called by them 'no-things' [οὔ τινα], and how, as a result of their ignorance that not every substance signifies a particular, the "No-man" fallacy comes about, by [the fallacy mode] Form

itself'. I shall argue that Ebbesen's second alternative is the correct one, except that not all words are cases.

[54] Frede 1978: 32 contends on the basis of this passage that cases are so called because 'they fall (*cadere*, πίπτειν) under a concept'; but clearly what "fall" here are the external objects, not the cases. Sedley 1985: 89 (*cf.* LS 1987: 1: 182) sees in the claim that 'we share in universals' a report of an authentic Stoic but Platonising tenet regarding the proper way to express species membership. But surely Stobaeus' report makes clear that *fall under* is the correct term for this relation; and I suggest that it is 'we *humans*' who (alone amongst the animals, which otherwise only bear names) both "partake in" the concepts and "bear" the names, "partaking in" thus being equivalent to "sharing in a conceptual framework".

of Expression:[55] for instance, 'If someone is in Athens, he is not in Megara.'[56] (*cats.* 105.8–13 = *S.V.F.* 2. 278 (30E))

The observation that according to the Stoa 'cases are pronounced' can be connected with a terminological distinction recorded by Diogenes (7.57) and already noted in 6.2.3: 'speaking [λέγειν] differs from pronouncing [προφέρεσθαι]; for while sounds are pronounced, meanings are spoken [λέγεται τὰ πράγματα], which are also then *lekta*'. The relation between *pragmata* and *lekta* is not altogether clear (see 6.2.3), but by combining these two pieces of information it can be concluded that the sounds which are merely "pronounced" must include cases; and where cases signify common qualities, they will be appellatives.

Clement's account, *strom.* 8.9.26 (part, 330), of the Stoic analysis of effects might be read as evidence for the incorporeality of Stoic cases, yet in fact tells against it. Clement asserts that, according to the Stoa, effects are incorporeal, being either predicates, such as ⟨...is cut⟩, or propositions, such as ⟨a ship comes to be⟩; and further that the case of the former is *to be cut* (or *being cut*) (τὸ τέμνεσθαι), and of the latter *a ship's coming to be* (τὸ ναῦν γίνεσθαι) (what a modern grammarian might be tempted to call a "desentential transform").

---

[55] "Form of Expression", σχῆμα τῆς λέξεως, is one of the linguistic fallacy modes identified in the *s. el.* (see Appendix). It occurs when the superficial grammatical "form" of an "expression" is taken as a faithful guide to the nature of the thing signified by the word, *i.e.* to its proper category. Thus *man*, when it signifies "the common man", will signify a "such", τοιόνδε τι, not a "this", τόδε τι, formal appearances notwithstanding: *s. el.* 22.178b36–9. On the "No-man" fallacy: D.L. 7.82, 187; Elias *cats.* 178.1–12; Philoponus *cats.* 72.4, scholium (*cod. Marc.* 217).

[56] Edlow's attempt, 1975: 429f., 1977: 65f. (followed by Baratin and Desbordes 1981: 138; *cf.* Hülser 1982: 3: 397, §633), to forge a link between the Homonymy in Compounds illustration and the "No-man" argument fails because he completely misidentifies both the *ptōsis* and the *ousia* of Galen's report, the former as "particular case, instance" – on which see further, n. 60 – the latter as the "essence" man, which seems to have no place in Stoic metaphysics (unless Edlow means the common quality man; at 1975: 430, n. 31, he suggests *ousia* is an interpolation of Galen's). There is a connection with a fallacy-type, but not the one Edlow names: see further, main text. It is possible that the example *man*, one of the standard illustrations of the Platonic form or Aristotelian universal, was deliberately chosen to demonstrate how the word is "really" ambiguous: not between the form and the particular which partakes in it, as explained at Sextus *M.* 11.28f., but between the particular and its name. But the Sextus passage seems not to be Stoic: see 3.5.

284

He also claims that '... cases are generally agreed to be incorporeal; which is why that well-known fallacy is solved in the following way: "what you say [λέγεις] comes out of your mouth", which is true; "you say house; so, a house comes out of your mouth" – which is false: for we do not say the house, which is corporeal, but the case, which is incorporeal, and which the house gets [ἧς ἡ οἰκία τυγχάνει]'.

Now nothing incorporeal could reasonably be said by a Stoic to come up from the lungs and emerge from the mouth. What is required is a distinction between the word (*qua* the corporeal sounds uttered as a particular sequence by a speaker) *house*, and the thing in the world which it signifies (*cf.* Nuchelmans 1973: 73). In its pristine state, the reported solution must have distinguished the corporeal external object from the case, which will also be corporeal. For some reason Clement has misunderstood or misreported it, mistaking the incorporeal effect for its corporeal name or "case";[57] but there is good reason all the same to believe that the solution he knew was Stoic. The case *house* is referred to as 'what the house gets', a characteristically Stoic description, as the Stobaeus passage just quoted confirms.[58] What is more, a version of Clement's "house" argument is associated explicitly with the Stoa, and with Chrysippus in particular:

εἴ τι λαλεῖς, τοῦτο διὰ τοῦ στόματός σου διέρχεται.
ἄμαξαν δὲ λαλεῖς.
ἄμαξα ἄρα διὰ τοῦ στόματός σου διέρχεται. (D.L. 7.187 (37R))

[57] Frede 1980: 229f. believes that Stobaeus' allusion to appellatives as cases shows he is using appellative in an unorthodox way, *i.e.* of what appellatives signify; but this interpretation is based only on Frede's assumption that cases are the significations of nouns.

[58] The point of the description is elusive. Pinborg 1975b: 83, n. 26 suggests that objects in the world are τυγχάνοντα in the context of the Stoic semantic triangle (as described by e.g. Sextus *M.* 8.11f. (33B), 13, 75; Plutarch *adv. Col.* 1119F (19K)) because they "get" or "bear", τυγχάνειν, cases, the view adopted by LS 1987: 2: 182, *ad* 30A, ll. 6–7, 197, *ad* 33B, l. 5. (Frede 1978: 32 holds the same view, but his opinion of what cases are is very different, as noted in the main text.) The Stoic usage may have its origin in the ordinary Greek idiom *to get/bear a name*, προσηγορίας/ὀνόματος τυγχάνειν; examples of this usage at Sextus *M.* 8.80; Simplicius *cats.* 2.9f.; D.T. Sch. 125.4. Two other sources, Ammonius *an. pr.* 68.4ff.; Themistius *an. po.* 2.3, each preserve an alternative explanation of τυγχάνον, neither of which is convincing or even intelligible.

It differs from Clement's most importantly in that λέγεις has been substituted for λαλεῖς in the protasis of the major and in the minor. λαλεῖν can be used in much the same way as λέγειν, to mean "speak, talk of"; but unlike λέγειν it is often applied to the emission of any kind of vocal sound, even inarticulate, such as a baby's prattling or a bird's chirping (LSJ, *s.v.*). The choice of λαλεῖς in Chrysippus' version of the sophism may well have been intended to point the way to its correct solution, by emphasising the uttered term's phonetic – and thus corporeal – aspect. (Chrysippus is reported to have derived λαός, *people* from λαλεῖν, λαλός, on the grounds that human beings alone are capable of articulate speech (Herodian *pros. cath.* (*G.G.* 3.1) 5, 108.9ff).) It can thus safely be assumed that the versions of this puzzle and its solution known to Seneca (*ep.* 48.6f.) and Augustine (*de magistro* 8.23f.; *de quant. anim.* 32.65ff., *P.L.* 32, pp. 1071–2)[59] were Stoic, and I shall argue shortly that here in the *de magistro*, as well as in the *de dialectica*, Augustine is working from and reshaping Stoic material.

It is now plain that Stoic cases are linguistic items, that they are declinable parts of speech – in this instance, the article τό or the articular infinitive considered as one unit – just as *man* is in the Homonymy in Compounds illustration, and that some of them are used to refer to *lekta* (as with Clement's *being cut*). The Stoic usage also allowed the nominative to be correctly called a case, something imperfectly understood by ancient authors.[60]

---

[59] I owe this last reference to Nuchelmans 1973: 74.

[60] For a useful summary of theories about the origin of the word πτῶσις itself, see esp. Hiersche *et al.* 1955; and *cf.* Hahn 1951: 32, n. 9. I have deliberately avoided discussion of this intricate topic as it has no bearing on how the Stoic dialectician used the word. Stoic theories of its origin would perhaps be more informative, but nothing certain is known of them. It is clear that the Stoics used the term in a far more restricted way than did Aristotle, who applied it to all sorts of derived forms, not just inflections of nouns: *e.g.* verb-forms, *int.* 3.16b17, *poet.* 20.1457a18ff. (if this chapter is genuine); adverbs, *top.* 1.15.106b29ff., 5.7.136b15ff.; and *cf.* Alex. *top.* pp. 103f., Simplicius *cats.* 37.10ff. *Contra e.g.* Ammonius *int.* 42.30ff. (part, 33K). Aristotle does, however, seem to have accepted the nominative as a case as the Stoics did (*an. pr.* 1.36.48b37ff.), albeit with a distinction between the use of nouns in premisses and their use as simple terms which might conceivably be a parallel to the Stoic distinction between cases and the nominals of which they are

Although it does not mention cases, Philoponus' solution to this fallacy is in other ways strikingly similar to Galen's account of the Homonymy in Compounds example: 'Man is a creature; creature [ζῷον] is disyllabic; so, man is disyllabic' (*an. po.* 154.26f.). Philoponus explains: 'for the word *man* is double [*i.e.* ambiguous], [being said] of both the substance and the name. For both the thing and the name is called "man"' ('διττὸν γὰρ τὸ ἄνθρωπος, ἐπί τε τῆς οὐσίας καὶ ἐπὶ τοῦ ὀνόματος. καὶ γὰρ τὸ πρᾶγμα λέγεται ἄνθρωπος καὶ τὸ ὄνομα') (154.27–9). As Ebbesen, to whom I owe this reference, points out (1981a: 1: 221), Philoponus should strictly be talking about the word ζῷον, but the slip is unimportant; it may even be that Philoponus' ultimate source was Stoic, and that he failed to adapt to its context the example originally used, *man*. (The external object, a man, is here termed a πρᾶγμα, not a τυγχάνον, but this is not a serious objection either.) Could Stoic autonymy have found its way into non-Stoic philosophical circles, by way of ambiguity classifications, or of textbooks on sophisms? There are surprisingly few allusions to it in ancient authors. Philoponus' solution seems to have no parallel in the other Aristotelian commentators, and he may have been thinking rather of such passages as *s. el.* 14.174a 5–9, where Aristotle compares apparent solecisms to Form of Expression fallacies, on the grounds that 'man is both white and a thing and a name'. Aristotle's point is that such sophisms are, so to say, solecisms of things, category mistakes prompted by formal linguistic considerations, while true solecisms are confusions of the linguistic forms themselves (*cf.* Evans 1975: 51). "Alexander", in his commentary on this passage of the *s. el.* (137.20ff.), although he seems to have

cases. Edlow's explanation (1975: 429, 1977: 65–6) of what a case is here is still more implausible than his interpretation of οὐσία (*cf.* n. 56), for he relies on two Dionysian scholia (231.21f.; 383.5f.) (previously cited by Müller 1943: 98), in both of which cases are quite obviously not individuals in the world – as Edlow believes – but words standing for those individuals; and it is these cases, not their referents, which somehow "fall from" what the scholiasts call the "incorporeal and generic" word to form the particular cases (see n. 51). No scholiast, to my knowledge, explicitly makes cases external objects, despite the disagreements as to whether cases are forms of words or their significations. And, even were it a scholastic position, it need not also be Stoic.

understood it aright, notably fails to use the distinction else-where (167.30ff.) to solve a specially invented problem which seems to cry out for its application, treating it instead as an instance of a type of non-linguistic fallacy, Accident.[61] Barnes 1971: 77, n. 1 notes that Aristotle 'has the means of distin-guishing between the "use" and the "mention" of an expres-sion'. But Aristotle's failure to apply the distinction systemati-cally, or to explain it explicitly in terms of autonymy, as I assume Chrysippus to have done, makes it unlikely that the *s. el.* passage is the origin, or at least the unique origin, of the medieval formal/material supposition distinction (as Barnes also claims); and Stoic dialectic is the obvious complementary source.

This interpretation of the Homonymy in Compounds illus-tration could only be firmly accepted were a text to come to light in which Stoics were at least credited with something like the idea of autonymy. It is not even known what term, if any, might have been used of this sort of "self-signifying".[62] So far it has merely been proved consistent with the example's being ambiguous (between (*a*) *man is* and "*man*" *is*) as, say, ἄνθρωπος περιπατεῖ, 'a man is walking', or ἄνθρωπος φωνή ἐστιν, 'a man is a vocal sound', would presumably not be. A minor positive contribution comes from the author of the *ad Herennium*, who, in the course of a scathing attack on what he sees as the utter uselessness to orators of dialectical teaching on ambiguity, remarks that the dialecticians 'are so afraid of saying something ambiguous when they speak that they can-not say their own name' ('ita dum metuunt in dicendo ne quid ambiguum dicant, nomen suum pronuntiare non possunt', 2.16). The context is a summary treatment of ambiguity as a

---

[61] On Form of Expression, n. 55 and Appendix; on Accident fallacies: 6.4.3. For more on the Ps.-Alexander passage, 6.3.6.

[62] Terms meaning "reflexive" are known, but not in this context: certain pronouns are ἀντανακλώμεναι ἀντωνυμίαι, *e.g. myself* (A.D. *pron.* 67.27f., metaphorically from bodies "bent back on themselves"); some Stoics spoke of the participle as the ἀντανάκλαστος προσηγορία, "reflexive appellative", on the basis of its seman-tic relation (almost tautological) to the noun: *e.g. currens est cursor, A runner is running*, and *currens cursor, A running runner*: Priscian *inst.* 11, 548.15ff. Apollonius has the expression *what is understood externally*, τὸ ὑπακουόμενον ἔξωθεν, for mentioning words: see *synt.* 34.5ff., and further, 6.3.7.

cause of legal dispute, and the author is decrying the use of dialectical manuals on ambiguities by orators in training. Had these dialecticians subscribed to a doctrine of reflexive signification, then to pronounce one's own name would indeed have been, for them, to utter an ambiguity, under certain circumstances. An alternative explanation is that a proper name shared by several person(s) will be ambiguous, provided proper names are taken as genuine instances of ambiguity, as they tended to be in antiquity – understandably so, given the original meaning of ὁμώνυμος, "namesake" (*e.g. Il.* 17.720; Plato *Tht.* 147d1; A.D. *pron.* 4.2, 10.12; Porphyry *cats.* 65.12ff.; Olympiodorus *cats.* 27.10ff., 34.7ff.; Philoponus *cats.* 16.22, 17.26ff.; Simplicius *cats.* 21.1ff.; Elias *in Porph. isag.* 138.19ff.). Whether the Stoics did so too, is unclear: see 6.2.3, 6.3.5.2.

A more important source of information is Augustine's very suggestive combined account of his versions of reflexive homonymy and contextual disambiguation; these will be discussed in the next section.

6.3.5   Homonymies: Autonymy

6.3.5.1   Augustine's evidence

The *de dialectica* (chs. 8–10)[63] is unique amongst surviving ancient texts in offering arguments for the Chrysippean thesis,

---

[63] References are by the page and line number of the 1857 Crecelius edition and where necessary by the page number of Pinborg 1975a, who usefully indicates the Crecelius lineation and pagination, with English translation on facing pages. Chapter divisions are from the famous Maurist edition of Augustine's complete works. There is a French translation in Baratin and Desbordes 1981: 211–31, with chs. 8, 9 and 10 on pp. 223–31, and a German translation, with Pinborg's text, of part of chs. 8 and 9, in Hülser 1982: 3: 402f., §637. Amsler's recent discussion of the *de dialectica*, 1989: 44ff., is as unreliable as it is unintelligibly fashionable, and I have made no use of it in what follows. Ruef 1981: 148ff., curiously, correctly interprets Augustine's evidence for a Stoic theory of autonymy, yet claims, first, that the theory itself is probably older than Chrysippus because the whole controversy over ambiguity must be (150), and, second, that every isolated word 'gar keine Bedeutung hat, da es nicht imstande ist, als eindeutiges Zeichen zu fungieren' (149). In contrast, while Baratin and Desbordes 1982: 79 correctly identify the *verbum* of the *de dialectica* as a self-signifier, and have an interesting discussion of the 'analyse metalinguistique' (84) of the *de magistro* (examined later in this section), Baratin 1982: 14f. misinterprets the universal ambiguity of the *de dialectica* as universal *lexical* ambiguity of isolated parts of speech: see further, n. 71.

ascribed here by Augustine to the "dialecticians", that 'every word is ambiguous', 'rectissime a dialecticis dictum est ambiguum esse omne verbum' (ch. 9, 15.14C, 106P). In this and the following sections I shall try to reconstruct the true reasoning behind it. Augustine does not say explicitly that either of the two arguments he presents for the thesis is Stoic or "dialectical", but the first definitely emerges as his own, peculiar distortion of a genuine Stoic analysis of autonymy. The second could also be Stoic; and it assumes, and does not argue for, contextual disambiguation.

Augustine presents what leads up to his report of the thesis as some sort of proof of it: 'Itaque rectissime ...'. In the previous chapter (ch. 8), Augustine has been describing what happens when an ambiguous word (his example is *magnus*) is uttered. He characterises it as a sort of crossroads ('multivium', 15.11C), by which is meant that, unlike an obscure word, it offers a clear choice between different uses or senses, to be determined by context, as with: 'magnus, quae pars orationis? qui sit pes?' ('Great, what part of speech is it? which metrical foot?'), or 'magnus Pompeius quot bella gesserit?' ('Great Pompey, how many wars did he wage?'), 'magnus et paene solus poeta Vergilius' ('A great and almost unique poet was Virgil'), and 'magnus vos erga studia torpor invaserit' ('Great sluggishness toward your studies has taken possession of you') (15.6–10C). Of the word in isolation, Augustine concludes:

For this one thing which is said, great, is a name and a choric foot and Pompey and the sluggishness of indolence; and innumerable other things, even if they are not mentioned here, can be understood through this utterance of the word. .

(Nam hoc unum quod dictum est magnus et nomen est et pes chorius est et Pompeius est et neglegentiae torpor et si qua alia vel innumerabilia non commemorata sunt, quae tamen per hanc enuntiationem verbi possunt intellegi.) (15.11–13C)

That he is already thinking here of the thesis to be reported at the start of ch. 9, which he attributes to the "dialecticians" and which we know is Chrysippus', is confirmed by the last clause of ch. 8: for Chrysippus' explanation of it is reported to have been 'quoniam ex eodem duo vel plura accipi possunt', 'since two or even more things can be understood from the same word' (see 6.3.5.2). Yet Augustine seems quite unaware of the peculiarity of introducing *great* as an instance of *ambiguitas* and explaining that 'this one thing which is said' is Pompey or Virgil – while the same thing is also a noun and a certain kind of metrical foot. The point could be treated as an application of an earlier (ch. 5, 8.3f., 5f.C, 88P) distinction between the *verbum*, a word being uttered 'for its own sake', which takes on the position of the object of discussion normally occupied by an extra-linguistic item, and the *dictio*, a word uttered 'in order to signify something else' (*cf.* Ruef 1981: 148f.). But curiously, perhaps, Augustine does not explicitly call on this scheme here in ch. 8; and at the beginning of ch. 9 he seems to have forgotten it altogether, for he happily reports that every *verbum* is ambiguous according to the dialecticians. What is today usually characterised as a word's being mentioned is treated as just one quite straightforward aspect of its being ambiguous.

The same approach is taken in his ch. 10, which also displays a similar kind and degree of semantic confusion. Augustine lists and describes the species of *aequivoca* (obviously Aristotelian ὁμώνυμα), which, like *univoca* (= Aristotelian συνώνυμα),[64] are by definition things which bear names (17.9,

---

[64] Barwick 1957: 18f. argues that this distinction is drawn from Augustine's Stoic source, and only indirectly from the *Categories*, the Stoa having already taken over Aristotle's distinction and given synonyms and homonyms different labels: in fact, 'Homonymy in Compounds' and 'Homonymy in Simples' respectively. The example (*a*) *man is* is to be understood as a predicate, while the adjective σύνθετα qualifies the (omitted) noun κατηγορήματα, *predicates*. Barwick cites D.L. 7.58 (33M) in support: 'a verb is a part of speech signifying an ἀσύνθετον κατηγόρημα', a "compound predicate" being one formed from a case and the copula, a "non-compound", in contrast, comprising a single word only. Barwick's failure to preserve the vital Stoic distinction between *lekta* and linguistic items is regrettable and confusing, but reformulating his account to accommodate it does not help matters. He makes no attempt to explain the two significations of (*a*) *man is*, or how they can be understood as Aristotelian synonyms; or how Stoic and Aristotelian metaphysics can be reconciled; or why Aristotelian synonyms have become Stoic homonyms; or why compound predicates should be formed with the copula, when the distinction required is obviously that between verbal predicates and predicates comprising a verbal predicate and at least one oblique case; or, finally, what is to happen to all other homonymous parts of speech which do not signify simple predicates.

16.19C, 110P; 18.28C, 116P). Augustine's examples, however, are all words (*e.g. Tullius*, 18.1–3C, 114P; *nepos*, 19.4f.C, 116P). This is understandable in the case of what Augustine calls "*ab arte* equivocals" – the *ars* in question being grammar (17.6C) – for these are words which are differently defined according to the various special interests and techniques of the grammarian, as parts of speech, metrical feet, and so on (17.16f.C). What is curious is that Augustine does not say that *Tullius*, for example, signifies a *Tullius* which is a noun, another which is a dactyl, another which is an equivocal – rather, he says that *Tullius is* all these (17.17f., *cf*. 18–25) – and yet he sums up thus:

> Since it was open to me to define this one thing which I uttered, *Tullius*, in so many different ways, in accordance with the terminologies of the expertises, why should we doubt that there exists a genus of ambiguities arising from equivocals, which can deservedly be said to come into being from expertise? For we said that equivocals were those things which cannot be included under one definition as they are ⟨included⟩ under one name.

> (Cum igitur hoc unum quod dixi Tullius secundum artium vocabula tam varie mihi definire licuerit, quid dubitamus esse ambiguorum genus ex aequivocis venientium, quod merito dici possit ex arte confingere? Diximus enim aequivoca esse, quae non ut uno nomine ita etiam una definitione possent teneri.) (17.25–8C)

How can this definition of *aequivoca* – which are different sorts of items sharing only a name, 18.27f.C, 116P – be squared with Augustine's particular account of *magnus*? What the reader expects, is a nice combination of Aristotelian metaphysics and Stoic semantics: what she gets, is just a jumbling of the two.

It would, I think, be unfair to criticise Augustine too harshly. The *de dialectica* was written in haste, and by his own admission left unfinished.[65] And it is still a valuable source. Somewhere in his dialectical studies[66] Augustine must have

---

[65] Convincing cases for the authenticity of the *de dialectica* are presented by Pépin 1976: 21–60, Jackson 1975: 1ff.; the latter argues that it must have been written, together with the other treatises on the liberal arts, most of which were not completed either, between early March and late April 387, in which period the *de quantitate animae* was also composed.

[66] Barwick 1957: ch. 1 argues that Augustine is heavily indebted to Varro's *disciplinae* 2 (and so indirectly to Antiochus); but, as Ebbesen 1981a: 1: 32, n. 8 (p. 40) points out, all that Barwick establishes is that Augustine has borrowed a lot of Stoic

come across the notion of autonymy, and seen it connected with Chrysippus' thesis; but he misinterpreted the latter as universal lexical ambiguity, and had gone on to try – unsuccessfully – to unite both with Aristotelian homonymy.

In contrast, Augustine's defence of the thesis could be an authentically Stoic reply to what might have been, say, an Academic offensive. Specifically, it is a response to an attack put into the mouth of Cicero's Hortensius (in the now lost dialogue named after him). Hortensius' complaint runs like this: 'They [sc. Augustine's "dialecticians"] claim they listen out for ambiguities, to explain them clearly; yet at the same time they say that every word is ambiguous. How, then, are they going to explain ambiguities with ambiguities? That is to carry an unlit lamp into darkness' (15.15–17C). Augustine points out that, although isolated words are indeed ambiguous (15.20 16.1C), all explanations of them are sentences, *sententiae, disputationes* (16.1f., cf. 5f.C), and he goes on to conclude that 'omne igitur verbum non ambigua disputatione explicabitur' (16.6C). He must be making a further, implicit, assumption, that at least some linguistic contexts automatically disambiguate. (The possibility of non-linguistic disambiguation is ruled out: note 'nisi verbis', 16.3C. Augustine's defence could be read as claiming that all contexts always disambiguate, but there is no need to accept this construction.) That he may have misunderstood the Chrysippean thesis as referring to, or as including, universal *lexical* ambiguity does not affect the argument in any way.[67] Hence, the argument's tacit assumption of contextual disambiguation, for certain linguistic environments, could be Stoic, even Chrysippean.

Augustine, unfortunately, did not think it appropriate or

---

material, as Pépin 1976: 72ff. confirms (although his confidence that the Stoics borrowed Aristotelian logic (*e.g.* p. 72) is misplaced). Courcelle 1969: 167ff., curiously, does not so much as mention Stoic influence on Augustine.

[67] Misunderstanding of Chrysippus' thesis may have combined with the sometimes unfriendly reactions to Stoic classifications of ambiguity (of undoubted subtlety and complexity) to produce the innocently or maliciously distorted charge that any linguistic item at all is ambiguous, *i.e.* falls into one or other of the Stoic classes: *cf. e.g.* Quintilian 7.9.1; Augustine *dial.* 17.13C. Most interesting is Cicero's possible allusion to universal ambiguity in the *de inventione*: see 8.5. Augustine, after all, may well have known of the thesis from the *Hortensius*; on Augustine's knowledge of this work, see Jackson 1975: 103, n. 3.

necessary to name his authorities, on the grounds, perhaps, that he was trying to create something fresh – presumably by linking Stoic and Aristotelian accounts of ambiguity. It is illuminating to compare with these passages his semantic definitions earlier in the *de dialectica*, which comprise roughly equal parts Stoic influence and Augustinian originality, and achieve a stimulating, if partial, success.[68] In the *de magistro*[69] his ideas have already taken on more coherence and independence, but their Stoic origin is unmistakable.

Here three of the major themes I have been pursuing – ambiguity itself; contextual disambiguation; autonymy – and a fourth which will occupy Chapter Seven – the solution of

---

[68] For example, Augustine's tetradic semantic theory, outlined in his ch. 5, employs a distinction between the *dicibile*, 'quod in verbo intellegitur et animo continetur' (8.10C, 90P), the *dictio*, which is a word used to signify something other than itself, and the *verbum*, which is the word considered simply as a word. The *dicibile* thus looks to be Augustine's version of the *lekton*, with the Latin term as a straightforward translation (Jackson 1969: 21ff. identifies it as the content of a bit of thinking, transferable from mind to mind); yet a little further on, Augustine says that *dicibilia* actually *become dictiones* when uttered (8.16f.C 90P), while the claim that the *dicibile* is contained in the mind gives it a different, psychological, status from that of the *lekton*, which supervenes on certain sorts of impression. Similarly, the *verbum/dictio* distinction seems to be new, at least in precisely this form (*cf.* Burnyeat 1987: 11, n. 12). In ch. 8, however, Augustine treats the same word both *qua* phonetic item, and *qua* lexical item, as a signifier. The most informative passage on Augustine's tetradic semantic schema in the *de dialectica* is 8.8–23C, 88–90P. Todorov 1982: 38, in his discussion of Augustinian semiotics, is, I think, wrong to see 'the metalinguistic use of language' in the *verbum*, for Augustine says of it rather that it 'both is a word and signifies a word' (8.9–10C, 90P), the object-language/metalanguage model being modern in any case. For a modern parallel to Augustine's *ab arte* equivocals, see Quine 1960: 142.

[69] I am grateful to Myles Burnyeat, whose 1987 discusses the place of the *de magistro* in the development of Augustine's epistemology, for alerting me to the importance of this text. I have used the text of K. D. Daur and W. M. Green in the *Corpus Christianorum, ser. Latina 29, Aurelii Augustini Opera Omnia, 2ii* (Turnholt, 1970). (Baratin and Desbordes 1981: 232–46 have a French translation of chs. 20–38 (with omissions); chs. 22–3 at 232–6.) It was composed in 389. Parallels between it and the *de dialectica* – similar or identical definitions and etymologies, discussions of written *vs.* spoken discourse, self-referential *vs.* non-self referential words, and obscurity *vs.* ambiguity – are noted by Jackson 1975: 4; *cf.* also Pépin 1976: 97, and generally his 'Arguments pour l'authenticité' (of the *de dialectica*) at 33ff. Markus 1957: 65ff., who analyses its theory of signs, including the "use/mention" distinction (67f.), does not always do justice to the work's subtlety or its dialectical nature (for example, he feels it contains many 'palpable sophistries', 65, n. 3), but he does make the useful observation that when Augustine refers to the work at *retractiones* 1.12, no mention is made of the theory of signs (including its version of the use/mention distinction) which supports its general conclusion, *viz.* that learning through signs is impossible. This suggests the theory may later have lost importance in Augustine's own eyes.

fallacies – all converge in Augustine's exploration of the subtle and difficult nature of signs. A division has been drawn (4.7) between signs which signify signs and signs which signify things, *res*, while subdivisions of the former group comprise, respectively, signs which can signify themselves and signs which cannot. The distinction in play is that, for example, the word *coniunctio* and the words which are conjunctions fall into different grammatical categories, whereas the word *nomen* and the words which are nouns do not. But *coniunctio* is autonymously significant, signifying itself, the word *coniunctio*, as well as signifying the (class of) linguistic items called conjunctions, just as *nomen* is in signifying itself as well as the parts of speech which are nouns. The sort of linguistic reflexivity which Augustine is describing may be called "self-reference", to distinguish it from autonymy. It is interesting that Augustine approaches it as just another type of signifying.

Next (7.22), Augustine proposes an investigation of *significabilia*, that is, of the *res* signified by signs; but 8.22–4 are actually devoted to expounding Augustine's version of what may be called, for convenience, the use/mention distinction (*cf.* Markus 1957: 67). He distinguishes what seem to be two facets of a verbal sign, which can be used or understood either 'secundum id quod sonat' (*i.e.* in its phonetic aspect) or 'secundum id quod significat' (*i.e.* in its aspect as a signifier), a characterisation which has led to comparisons with Saussure (*e.g.* Mandouze 1975: 790f.). Augustine draws a second, less helpful, distinction, applied in parallel with the first, between some single item's two *partes* or sides, from either of which it can be used or understood – 'ex ea parte, qua signum est', 'from the side on which it is a sign', and 'ex ea parte rei, quam significat', 'from the side of the thing which it signifies' – as if this one item were both sign and signified. (*Cf.* Ebbesen 1981a: 1: 217: Augustine solves his version of the "wagon" fallacy (described in 6.3.4) '... by declaring that being a noun is a property of man inasfar as it is a sign, whereas man qua signified is not a noun but, for instance, an animal'.[70]) An

---

[70] Ebbesen 1987: 120 also reports that the scholastics described fallacies *in dictione* as having their *causa apparentiae* – *i.e.* what makes them appear valid: see 7.2 – 'ex

alternative explanation is that the *partes* which Augustine invokes will be points of view, as it were, from which a sign can be "observed" and understood or employed: a verbal sign can be taken either as a piece of language, a distinct object of study in its own right, or as a verbal token of whatever it signifies (*cf.* Madec 1975: 68), so that the object on which attention is focussed is the signified thing, through the now-transparent medium of the sign.

Augustine does not expand on these approaches to signs, and I have attempted to make them explain themselves, by cashing out Augustine's difficult metaphors; the first interpretation of the *partes* does less violence to the text, but is intuitively, and I think theoretically as well, the less attractive of the two. The discussion in 8.22ff. is really directed toward clarifying normally unreflecting assumptions about the correct way to understand and respond to certain sorts of questions, those in which words can be understood 'secundum id quod significat' or 'secundum id quod sonat'. What is unclear is whether instances of the latter are presented as cases of ambiguity. Near the beginning of his inquiry, the query 'homo homo est?', 'is a man a man?', is characterised as 'ambigua', 'ambiguous' (8.22), and Augustine's interlocutor, his son Adeodatus, dismisses its *ambiguitas* as not really troublesome (*ibid.*). Nowhere, however, is it asserted that *man* signifies both itself and the rational mortal animal. He seems to have felt ill at ease with the notion of reflexive signification, and tried to replace it with his own, parallel, distinction; but its ghost still makes its presence felt, for it is put to the same use as the Stoic distinction, an explanation of how it is possible to talk about as well as with words. Furthermore, Augustine uses it to explain away the sophisms which exploit language's capacity for glossing over that distinction, and on which the Stoic linguistic case/external object dichotomy was very probably brought to bear.

---

parte vocis', whereas those *extra dictionem* have it 'ex parte rei'. But this distinction rests on a distinction between object (*res*) and sign (*vox*), which, Ebbesen goes on to argue, caused no small difficulty for the schoolmen, since, unlike the *in dictione/extra dictionem* distinction, it was not originally Aristotelian, but Stoic: see 7.2.

To get Adeodatus to grasp his own distinction, Augustine brings out two closely connected sophisms. At 8.22 he asks: 'homo homo est?' and 'Do the two syllables ho and mo form homo?' Adeodatus assents to both premisses, but will not allow that he is himself 'those two syllables combined'. At 8.24 he asks: 'homo nomen sit?', 'is a man a name?'; Adeodatus agrees; Augustine inquires: 'quid? cum te video, nomen video?', 'What? When I see you, do I see a name?' A third fallacy is mentioned at 8.23, a "lion" variant on the "wagon". Augustine goes on to offer some guidance on coping with such fallacies: his advice may or may not be of Stoic origin, but it deserves mention in any event, for it involves what appears to be the only surviving ancient treatment by a trained logician of (something approaching) disambiguation. If someone asks 'Is man a noun?', it is proper to agree, for the questioner makes it clear he is to be understood as talking about the sign, the noun, *man* ('Satis enim significat ex ea parte se velle audire, qua signum est'). But suppose the question is: 'What is (a) man?' Augustine counsels: 'placita illa loquendi regula ad id, quod duabus syllabis significatur, animus curreret, neque quidquam responderetur nisi animal' ('by that well-known and agreed rule of discourse the mind would run off to the thing signified by the two syllables, and the only reply would be "an animal"'). This *regula loquendi* is defined a few lines later; to make Augustine's distinctions more natural, I shall temporarily abandon typographical conventions for distinguishing use and mention. If man is understood as a word, it is legitimate to conclude that 'you are not a man'; nevertheless this 'animum offendit', 'shocks the mind', because of 'ea ... regula, quae naturaliter plurimum valet, ut auditis signis ad res significatas feritur intentio', 'that ... rule, which naturally has the greatest force, that when signs are heard one's attention is drawn to the signified objects'. If the interlocutor concludes 'you are not a man' it must be pointed out to him that his inference is not drawn 'ex ea parte ... qua interroganti assentiebamur', 'from the side from which we assented to him when he asked the question'; if he admits it is indeed drawn 'ex ea parte', 'from that side', why should we hesitate to assent?

All we concede is that we are not the word man. The "natural rule of discourse", to the effect that signs signify external objects, remains valid unless some implicit or explicit qualification is made; and a word's context can reveal that it does not hold good in a particular instance.

Augustine's treatment of *magnus* and of the *ab arte* equivocals in the *de dialectica* appears to be a record, however confused and incomplete, of the Stoic theory of autonymy or reflexive signifying which very probably underlies the Homonymy in Compounds illustration in the *de soph.* classification. His defence of the Chrysippean thesis, with its assumption of the possibility of contextual disambiguation, might be Stoic too. In the *de magistro* Augustine has moved further away from Stoic models, although he has not yet entirely dropped the notion of autonymy. It surely cannot be the case that only active autonyms fall under Homonymy in Compounds; but perhaps it is no coincidence that Augustine's *regula loquendi* has validity exclusively for distinguishing his version of the use/mention distinction from ordinary extra-linguistic signification. A Stoic ambiguity classification in which the Homonymy in Compounds example was an illustration of contextual ambiguity due to autonymy could have stimulated Augustine, given his own growing interest in signs, to develop in tandem versions both of autonymy and of the rules for recognising and distinguishing what the Stoa would have treated as autonymous and non-autonymous modes of signifying.

6.3.5.2 *'Every word is by nature ambiguous'*

Chrysippus says that every word is naturally ambiguous, since from the same ⟨word⟩ two or even more things can be understood.

(Chrysippus ait omne verbum ambiguum natura esse, quoniam ex eodem duo vel plura accipi possunt.) (Aulus Gellius *noct. att.* 11.12.1 = *S.V.F.* 2.152 (37N1))

Autonymy can explain Chrysippean universal ambiguity on two assumptions: that Chrysippus was talking about single terms, and that all single terms are non-autonymously significant in some appropriate way.[71]

Only Augustine and Gellius indicate the scope of Chrysippus' claim, the original Greek not having survived. The most plausible Greek equivalent for *verbum* must be ὄνομα, despite Chrysippus' application of it to the proper noun as well. [ὄνομα in the wider sense is standard usage, and Chrysippus is known to have written treatises Περὶ τῶν κατὰ τὴν διαλεκτικὴν ὀνομάτων (D.L. 7.189 = *S.V.F.* 2.13, p. 5, l. 1) and Περὶ τοῦ κυρίως κεχρῆσθαι Ζήνωνα τοῖς ὀνόμασιν (D.L. 7.122), which both presumably concerned terminology.

Gellius' report of Diodorus Cronus' opposed thesis,

---

[71] Pinborg's contention, 1962: 168, that Chrysippus' thesis is explained by what he regards as the anomalous nature of language, and by the 'begrenzten Anzahl der Wörten und Begriffe', is more appropriate as an analysis of *s. el.* 1.165a10–13 than of any Stoic source. Similar objections apply to the suggestions of Long 1986: 134f. ('language has changed in the course of time and ... there can be no one to one relation between a word and its meaning'), Pépin 1976: 95, n. 4 ('l'inadéquation entre les mots et les choses'; but see already my n. 41), and Reesor 1989: 158. Schmidt 1839/1979: 30/59, n. 30 (1979: 119–24) seems to have been the first to interpret Chrysippus' thesis in this way. Baratin 1982: 13f. suggests, without any argument in support, that all words will be (lexically) ambiguous in so far as they are decontextualised parts of speech. But he is then forced to argue, absurdly (14, n. 13) that 'un énoncé [=*logos*] n'est ambigu que lorsqu'il ne permet pas lui-même de désambiguïser l'un des mots qu'il comporte': that is, all the examples of ambiguous *logoi* in the *de soph.* list will be ambiguous only in virtue of containing a non-disambiguated part of speech. Yet more oddly, he adds that 'On comprend par là la place marginale que ce phénomène occupe' in D.L.'s account. Colish 1983: 23, under the impression that a special explanation is required of ambiguity (*universal* ambiguity goes unmentioned) on the grounds that all words for the Stoa have a natural meaning, accordingly explains that 'words signify the speaker's intention as well as having an objective natural reference', as if intentions and linguistic meanings (or references) were on a par. Denyer 1985: 9 apparently interprets universal ambiguity as embracing, but wider than, universal lexical ambiguity ('for, as Chrysippus pointed out, no communicative sign has any one meaning intrinsic to it'), but attempts no explanation of why Chrysippus' assertion should have been framed as if it were about verbal signs alone – and it seems about just one sort of verbal sign, the single term – if he were talking about all signs, or of how this fluid semantics is to be reconciled with the typically rigid and atomistic accounts of meaning found in the Stoic sources which do survive. Edlow 1975: 425 (*cf.* Baldassarri 1984: 50) takes the thesis to rest on the 'fact' of psychological, as opposed to semantic, ambiguity, or 'ambiguity by association': again, it would be most curious were such an obvious threat to Stoic confidence in the communicative success of discourse not leapt on by the school's enemies, especially one adopting so different a concept of ambiguity from that articulated in the D.L. definition.

'nullum verbum est ambiguum" is also framed using *verbum* (and Diodorus also had in mind words' natural properties, it seems: 'ambigui enim verbi natura illa esse debuit', *noct. att.* 11.12.2f. (37N2)). But the opposition between the two theses seems at first glance perhaps a little too neat to be entirely credible. If my reconstruction of Chrysippus' reasoning is correct, he is simply taking for granted both the lexical and the autonymous modes of signification. On the other hand, the arguments with which Chrysippus must have supported his thesis have not survived; there is nothing unreasonable in seeing it as a direct and polemical response to Diodorus' universal denial. Nor can there be any difficulty in assuming that Diodorus framed his thesis with reference to ὀνόματα (of the three extant examples of the Diodorean autonomous idiolect, three are of single terms, and one of a two-word phrase functioning as one term),[72] and that ὄνομα became *verbum* in Latin. Aulus Gellius himself uses *verba* perfectly normally (as *words* in general) in 11.11 and 11.13, and also, for example, in 10.4.2, where the question 'φύσει τὰ ὀνόματα sint ἢ θέσει' is raised. So what Chrysippus said was probably 'every ὄνομα is by nature ambiguous'.

The second premiss for which a case has to be made is that all *onomata* are non-autonymously significant. This problem cannot be reframed as: are all *onomata* parts of speech (or, as Chrysippus called them, "elements", στοιχεῖα),[73] for there is no direct evidence that all parts of speech signify. But I shall still start with these.

First, it is tolerably clear that just about everything that might be called an *onoma* in ordinary discourse (the category is admittedly fluid and ill defined) would qualify as one or other of the Stoic parts of speech. Later grammarians, such as Apollonius, Priscian, and the Dionysian scholiasts, who preserve most of what little information there is about the Stoic parts of speech, do not complain that Stoic or Stoicising gram-

[72] Two of Diodorus' slaves were named μέν and δέ (frr. 114.2–4D), another ἀλλὰ μήν (frr. 112, 113D); see 4.6.
[73] Galen *P.H.P.* 8.3.12f., p. 498, ll. 1–8, esp. 7f. (= *S.V.F.* 2.148, p. 45, ll. 10f.); *cf.* D.L. 7.192, 193 (= *S.V.F.* 2.14, p. 6, ll. 17, 19 (?), 20).

mar – which, even if its history is unclear and much disputed, must have formed a distinct and rival tradition for some time[74] – neglected altogether any of the separate parts of speech identified by mainstream grammarians, as for instance participles, adverbs, pronouns, and prepositions. Rather, the Stoa seems to have consistently assimilated each of these to one or other of the parts (recorded at D.L. 7.57) already identified by Chrysippus, grouping adverbs and participles with nouns or verbs, pronouns with articles, prepositions with conjunctions.[75] Chrysippus did not, it seems, overlook or actively discount any of the later, orthodox, word-classes: rather, most of his five parts of speech were just broader in scope (and perhaps vaguer). Accordingly, all Chrysippean *onomata* could have been one or other of the

---

[74] The relation of Stoic grammar to that of Alexandria, the difference between the two, and even the existence of the former as a separate discipline, have all been much disputed. But all that is needed for the present argument is that there were Stoics who were elaborating what they or later thinkers would recognise as grammatical concepts and categories, even if these (still) formed part of dialectic; and it is quite plain that a Stoic dialectician in Chrysippus' time or after would have found the question: are all *onomata* parts of speech? perfectly intelligible. On Stoic grammar: esp. Frede 1977, 1978; Blank 1982: 1ff.; sources in Schmidt 1839/1979.

[75] Participle: Priscian *inst.* 2, 54.9–11; 11, 548.14–549.1 (various semantic and formal criteria); D.T. Sch. 518.17–22; Plutarch *quaest. Plat.* 10.6.1011D. Adverb: Priscian *inst.* 2, 54.10–12; D.T. Sch. 520.16–18. Pronoun and article: A.D. *pron.* 5.13–6.19, *cf.* 7.3–7, *synt.* 94.12f. (articles are called "indefinite parts" on the basis of such constructions as ὁ δειπνήσας παῖς κοιμάσθω, Let the [i.e. any] child who has eaten take a nap), with *adv.* 122.2ff.; Priscian *inst.* 2, 54.12–16; 11, 548.7–14; *part.* (G.L. 3) 492.10–12, 501.11–13; D.T. Sch. 518.33–519.5; and, for a Stoic survival, Wouters 1979: 68, 77 (a papyrus of c. 300C.E.). Preposition: D.T. Sch. 519.26ff. (formal similarities between prepositions and conjunctions); A.D. *synt.* 436.14ff., 457.13ff. (distributional and semantic considerations), *cf.* 488.2ff. (the ⟨παρα⟩ συναπτικὸς σύνδεσμος, ἐπεί, *since*, is formed from the conjunction εἰ and the preposition ἐπί). Schneider *G.G.* 2.3, pp. 30f. argues that both the scholiasts' and Priscian's source for the Stoic doctrine of the parts of speech is Apollonius, not Trypho, as the Marcianus scholiast claims (at *G.G.* 1.3, 356.21). The doctrine is set out and criticised at: D.T. Sch. 214.17–215.3, 356.27–358.9, 517.33–520.33; *cf.* also A.D. *pron.* 5.13–9.6, *coni.* 214.4ff. (probably), 218.20ff., 248.1ff.; Priscian *inst.* 2, 54.8–22; 11, 548.7–549.6, *part.* 492.10–15, 501.11–14.6. Chrysippus is invoked by D.L. 7.57 as one of the authorities for the five-fold division of the parts of speech; the only source actually mentioned at 7.58 (33M), however, where the definitions appear, is Diogenes of Babylon, and the other authorities referred to (by the phrase 'ὥς τινες') turn out, on comparison with 7.64 (33G), to be followers of Apollodorus – and Apollodorus is not one of the sources named at 7.57. Chrysippus' innovative division between proper and common nouns is set out, with supporting arguments (primarily formal in character), and criticised at *e.g.* D.T. Sch. 356.16–357.26, 517.35–518.16.

(Chrysippean) parts of speech. There were certainly no new post-Chrysippean Stoic parts, except for Antipater's μεσότης, and, whatever word-type this may have been (perhaps the adverb (*e.g.* Simplicius *cats.* 388.26, with Robins 1979: 28), but not the "middle" voice of the verb, the term's standard use (*e.g.* D.T. 48.1)), it did not make sufficient impact to find its way into the version of Stoic grammar which Apollonius and the scholiasts knew.

Were all Chrysippean parts of speech significant? One of the unresolved difficulties to emerge from the earlier discussions of Stoic semantics (4.5, 6.2.3) was that no firm conceptual apparatus and terminology seem to have been developed to distinguish and classify various modes of signifying or types of signified object. The remainder of Diogenes' two accounts of dialectic offers very little information. Chrysippus' description of the subject-matter of dialectic as "signifiers and significations" (D.L. 7.62, with 43f. (31A7–8)) was noted in 3.1. The subsections dealing with significations are largely to do with the varieties of *lekta*, above all with propositions and their combinations (43 (31A7)). But Chrysippus' own words reveal nothing more of what it is for a linguistic item to signify, and the term σημαίνειν itself appears to be used (quasi-)technically only twice in connection with single terms. (It is also, of course, used of *logoi*; see Nuchelmans 1973: 70.) It occurs in definitions of the "appellative", προσηγορία, which 'signifies a common quality', and of the "verb", ῥῆμα, which 'signifies a non-compound predicate, or, as some say, is an indeclinable element of speech, signifying something arrangeable with a thing or things [συντακτὸν περί τινος ἢ τινῶν]' (7.58 (33M)). The only other part of speech whose definition explicitly accords it semantic status does not "signify": the "(proper) name", ὄνομα, is the part 'indicating [δηλοῦν] a particular quality'. If Diogenes' report is reliable, then, as qualities are corporeal, and predicates a species of *lekton*, Stoic dialecticians must have been capable of great carelessness in their use of terminology; or else they thought it unnecessary or unimportant to employ jargon to capture different semantic relations, it being sufficient to identify the various *relata* (nouns and qualities; verbs and predicates).

Was the relation between proper names and individuals, at least, given a special label: *indicating*, δηλοῦν? The two significations of the example accompanying the definition of ambiguity in Diogenes Laertius are, however, said to be 'indicated [δηλοῦνται]' by it. Now, unless this definition belongs to Diogenes of Babylon – to whom the definition of the common noun, and the first definition of the verb, are attributed at D.L. 7.58 (33M) – the use of δηλοῦν in such different contexts may be unimportant: not all Stoics need have adhered to the same semantic terminology. Yet it would be unwise to repose too much confidence on jargon unsupported by other evidence, even where what seem to be quite faithful records of Stoic teaching have been preserved. It is far from clear, especially, that articles and conjunctions are significant in the way that nominals, verbs, and participles are. Chrysippus himself may have thought some parts of speech significant only in such a way that their capacity for autonymy would not make them ambiguous, by his own criteria of linguistic ambiguity. Frede 1978: 64ff., who gives a persuasive explanation of the Stoic decision, against the Peripatos, to include conjunctions and demonstrative pronouns amongst the parts of speech, sees great difficulties in fixing an exhaustive, kind-by-kind correspondence between parts of speech – particularly certain sorts of pronoun, articles, prepositions, and some types of conjunction – and elements of *lekta*. Some parts were perhaps distinguished only on formal (morphological), distributional, or functional grounds. I note that while Egli 1987: 116 freely assigns conjunctions counterparts at the level of the *lekta*, he observes that complex propositions are said to be formed "by means of", διά, ὑπό, and not "from", ἐκ, a conjunction, σύνδεσμος (D.L. 7.71f. (35A1–4)), a description suggesting that conjunctions at this level were not genuine parts of propositions, even if their counterparts at the level of sentences are definitely parts of the *logos*.

It will, I think, be worth while to rehearse the evidence that

303

Stoic parts of speech were all in some way at least significant. Chrysippus' influence within Stoic dialectic was immense; his opinions may well have shaped the Stoic material preserved in the grammatical doxography; and, his definition of ambiguity being unknown, the possibility cannot be discounted that whatever distinctions he drew amongst types of linguistic signifier were irrelevant to his thesis that every word is ambiguous.

Available testimony is either general, pertaining to the Stoic doctrine of parts of speech as a whole, or particular, pertaining to individual parts. Only two passages relate to Chrysippus by name, while two more refer to other individual Stoics (Posidonius (probably) and Charisius); but even these two may testify to later development or refinement of a basically Chrysippean approach to the elements of discourse.

General:

(i) The main thrust of Plutarch's attack on the Stoic doctrine of the parts of speech is an argument that only nouns and verbs signify (*quaest. Plat.* 10.1.1009D). He denies that conjunctions and articles signify at all, whether in isolation or combined with one another (*quaest. Plat.* 10.2.1010A), and the metaphors he uses to describe them suggest they have no semantic status at all (10.3.1010C–1011C, 7.1011E). Pronouns and participles, in contrast, are assimilated to other parts of speech, just as they are in Stoic theory (5–6.1011C–D), while prepositions are mere additions to sentences, just bits and pieces of words (since they also function as prefixes) (7.1011DE). This account seems to follow the Peripatetic, possibly Theophrastean (*cf.* Simplicius *cats.* 10.23–7, with Frede 1978: 63), distinction between parts of *logos*, *i.e.* the nouns and verbs which signify (or signify strictly or properly), and parts of *lexis* which do not, and are at best συσσημαίνοντα or *consignificantia* "co-signifiers" along with parts of speech proper (*e.g.* Priscian. *inst.* 2, 54.5–7). Thus Ammonius takes ἀλλὰ μήν to be a conjunction, and non-significant: *int.* 37.17–20 (= fr. 112D); and, besides offering a general defence of the distinction, he argues that Plato made it even before Aristotle (*int.* 12.12ff., 40.26ff., 48.30ff., 60.1ff.). Apollonius constructs a partial analogy between "independently spoken" (κατ᾽ ἰδίαν ῥηταί) vowels and verbs, nouns, pronouns, and adverbs, and between "dependent" consonants and prepositions, articles and conjunctions (*synt.* 13.1ff.)). Broadly comparable dichotomies have been advanced by modern linguists (*e.g.* "contentives" *vs.* "functors" or "function words", Hockett 1958, 1987: 27, 35, following Fries 1952).

(ii) One of the Dionysian scholiasts, who has a lengthy and very informative section on the Stoic and Peripatetic parts of speech, and who himself believes that all words (not just nouns and verbs) have their own σημασία, "meaning", roundly criticises the Peripatos (516.2ff., esp. 516.13–27) for restricting genuine semantic status to nouns and verbs, but, in contrast, is unhappy only with the Stoic divisions – or the absence of them – between parts of speech, and with their supporting arguments, which almost exclusively invoke phonetic and morphological considerations: he never complains that Stoic parts do not signify.[76] The scholiast's account is clearly neither sympathetic nor comprehensive (for instance, he fails to point out the semantic distinction between Stoic common and proper nouns); but the aspects of the Stoic doctrine he found objectionable are not the semantic ones.

Particular:

(iii) Apollonius Dyscolos records a criticism, attributed to a certain Posidonius, whom I take to be the Stoic Posidonius, of

---

[76] A typical Stoic argument is that participles are not genuine parts of speech because the latter have 'primitive forms', 'πρωτοτύπους φωνάς', whereas participles are derived from verbs: D.T. Sch. 518.19–21. Similarly, prepositions and conjunctions are grouped together as being morphologically invariable, ἄκλιτοι (519.29), and as sharing a phonological peculiarity in Aeolic (29–31), while proper names and appellatives have different declined forms, and only the former give rise to derivations (517.37–518.1). According to Apollonius, the Stoic grammarian Chaeremon argued that expletives, παραπληρωματικοί, count as conjunctions in virtue of their form, φωνή (*coni.* 248.1ff.): see main text, item viii. Semantic factors could be invoked, however: *e.g.* the near synonymy of common nouns and their corresponding participles was taken as evidence for their constituting a single part of speech: Priscian *inst.* 11, 548.15ff.

those who make conjunctions connect, but not signify (*coni.* 214.4–8).[77] But I cannot with complete confidence follow Kidd 1988: 200ff. in his contention that Posidonius was here arguing against his own school. The definition of the σύνδεσμος reported by Diogenes Laertius ('non-declinable part of speech binding the parts of speech together', 7.58), on which Kidd's interpretation is based, would doubtless not have met with Posidonius' approval; but Diogenes' whole account of the Stoic parts of speech is shown by independent evidence to be of limited scope and doubtful reliability. In particular, Posidonius' criticism assumes that prepositions, prefixes, and conjunctions form a single part of speech,[78] and he urges that prefixes must differ in meaning on the grounds that they produce differences in meaning in the words to which they are preposed. Now the Stoics are known to have called prepositions "prepositive conjunctions" (A.D. *synt.* 436.10ff.). No mention of these are made by Diogenes, however.

(iv) Diogenes Laertius' definition of the article is also flawed. His list of the μέρη τοῦ λόγου omits pronouns altogether, the article there defined being what the Stoics called the "indefinite article", and what moderns and the ancient professional grammarians call the "definite article". But (what we call) pronouns are Stoic articles too, what they called definite articles. The Stoics defended this unorthodoxy with a number of phonological considerations (A.D. *pron.* 6.7–14), while also observing that articles (*i.e.* standard definite articles) are substitutable for pronouns, and like them signify anaphora. (See also item (v).) Both Apollonius and the Dionysian scholiast are very critical of this portion of Stoic grammar. They pro-

---

[77] That this is the Stoic Posidonius (as assumed by *e.g.* Frede 1978: 64, and convincingly argued by Kidd 1988: 200ff.) is very strongly suggested by the context: Apollonius has just criticised the Stoa for introducing irrelevant dialectical considerations into grammar, and he goes on to use the protasis of a Stoic-style major premiss to illustrate the fact that conjunctions constitute a separate part of speech. The Stoic Posidonius' interest in conjunctions is shown also by fr. 192 EK.

[78] Apollonius has already pointed out the underlying assumption that prepositions and conjunctions form a single part of speech (*coni.* 214.7–8), which is the Stoic view reported by the Dionysian scholiast: 519.16–32.

vide strong evidence none the less that some Stoics at least believed that their articles, both definite and indefinite, were in some way significant.

(v) The same scholiast has the information that Stoic "definite articles" (*i.e.* pronouns) signify either δεῖξις, "demonstration", or ἀναφορά, "reference" (518.40–519.1). This is the orthodox description of pronouns' semantic rôle (*e.g.* 256.20–7, 516.14–16), and may not reflect an authentic Stoic analysis. At least it shows that Stoic pronouns were later assumed to signify in such a way that the doctrine concerning them could easily be assimilated to grammatical orthodoxy. Chrysippus must have held that deictic pronouns, such as οὗτος, *this (man)* (*here*), signify in some way; otherwise his claim that reference fails in such propositions as ⟨this (man) (here) is dead⟩ (Alexander *an. pr.* 177.25ff., esp. 28, 178.6) would be non-sensical. οὗτος as part of a proposition is described as a "deictic nominative case" (D.L. 7.70 (34κ6); *cf.* Sextus *M.* 8.96f.), and will thus, I take it, be the pronoun or a form of it, and it or the pronoun will be significant. In columns 4 and 5 of *PHerc.* 307,[79] the papyrus fragments of a book of his *Logical Questions*, Chrysippus raises a problem connected with the inability to use and understand deictic pronouns infallibly. The text is obscure and difficult, but Chrysippus' conundrum would simply be non-existent were these pronouns not assumed to signify (presumably, to refer to or denote objects in the world).

(vi) Both Theon's examples of the Stoic ambiguity kind Significant Part (*prog.* 82.10, 13f.) hinge on what would be described in traditional grammar as the ambiguity of reference of pronouns, one relative, one anaphoric. In the Stoic classification the examples are of the type of ambiguity which occurs when a set of significant linguistic items is open to a variety of syntactic groupings. Nothing in Theon's report at this point casts the shadow of suspicion on the illustrations' authenticity. At least one group of Stoic dialecticians must have thought

---

[79] Text, translation, and commentary for cols. 4–5 in Atherton 1986: 235–65.

that what Stoic grammarians labelled "anaphoric definite articles" were significant.[80] (On Theon's examples, see further, 6.5.2.)

(vii) The illustrations of the three Part kinds in the two classifications reveal that the "parts", μόρια, in question are parts of *lexis*, that is, bits of articulate utterance, not parts of logos (see 6.5.3). Significant Part ambiguities arise (as seen) when the syntactic arrangement of a number of significant parts of *lexis* is unclear, while "Non-significant Parts" are articulate sounds or sequences of such sounds, not fully-fledged words. Any genuine word must have been classed as significant, and *vice versa*, although the distinction actually drawn (however unsatisfactory for other reasons) was between significant and non-significant units of *lexis*.

(viii) The first-century B.C.E. Stoic Chaeremon claimed that expletives, παραπληρωματικοί, are conjunctions in virtue of their form, on the basis of both a distinction between conjunction-form, φωνή, χαρακτήρ, τύπος, and conjunction-meaning, δηλούμενον, and a more general form/meaning or form/function dichotomy (*coni.* 247.30ff.) (*cf.* Frede 1978: 66). This report is especially interesting because Chaeremon also argued that redundant conjunctions too are called conjunctions 'even though they conjoin nothing', implying that he took meaning and function as somehow equivalent. Plutarch claims that the fact that 'the dialecticians [presumably Stoics] need conjunctions above all for conditionalising and combining and disjoining propositions', 'τὸ δὲ τοὺς διαλεκτικοὺς μάλιστα συνδέσμων δεῖσθαι πρὸς τὰς τῶν ἀξιωμάτων συναφὰς καὶ συμπλοκὰς καὶ διαζεύξεις', does not show that the conjunction is a part of speech, rather than 'a kind of binding instrument', 'ὄργανόν τι συνδετικόν'; he himself regards it as such, words other than nouns and verbs signifying nothing either in isolation or combined with one other (*quaest. Plat.* 1011AB, 1010A). Similarly, Apollonius reports that the Stoics called the sequence δέ γε ('but at least') a "conjunction of addition",

---

[80] Relative and interrogative pronouns, according to Priscian *inst.* 11, 548.9, were grouped by the Stoa with their indefinite (standard definite) articles.

προσληπτικὸς σύνδεσμος, and the particles τοίνυν (*so then*), τοιγαροῦν (*therefore*), τοιγάρτοι (*accordingly*) "conclusive conjunctions", ἐπιφορικοὶ σύνδεσμοι, because of their use in arguments to introduce the minor premiss, πρόσληψις (*cf*. D.L 7.76 (36A1)) and the conclusion, ἐπιφορά (*cf*. D.L. *ibid*.) respectively (*coni*. 250.12ff., 251.27ff.). But it remains unclear whether Stoics regarded these as meaningful: their titles at least, formed to reflect their positions and/or logical functions, are against it. The latter group 'are called ἐπιφορικοί in that they are added on to the premisses', 'καθὸ ἐπιφέρονται τοῖς λελημματισμένοις' (*coni*. 252.3).

(ix) Alexander records a Stoic account of the semantics of sentences with singular definite subjects which confirms that proper names, demonstrative pronouns, and definite descriptions are all significant: *an. pr*. 402.3ff., esp. ll. 7, 9, 24, 29.[81] (The view that proper names signify in such a way as to be (referentially) ambiguous if they have two or more bearers – generally rejected by modern linguists and semanticists (*e.g.* Lyons 1977: 398; but note also Quine 1960: 130) – was common in antiquity; the theoretical tradition goes back at least to Aristotle, *s. el.* 17.175b15ff. There is no direct evidence for Stoic approval of it; but, equally, none against.)

There seems to be no ancient author who claims or suggests that Chrysippus denied either that any part of speech is significant, or that any word is a part of speech; and I have presented the evidence, such as it is, for thinking that he did not, and thus that autonymy, coupled with the notion that all words signify non-reflexively too, will account for his thesis that every word is naturally ambiguous. The problem is that the Stoics do not seem ever to have embarked on the project

---

[81] It was noted in 3.3 that the Stoics whose views Alexander reports took proper names to have tensed existential import. Definite descriptions – Alexander's example is *Callias the grammarian* (*an. pr*. 402.23f.) – pose the problem that what are standardly called definite articles are for the Stoa indefinite articles, which suggests that they may be on a par, oddly, with such expressions as *someone, a certain*: see D.L. 7.70 (34K7), with the analysis of *Callias is walking* as *there is a certain* (τις) *Callias, and he is walking* at Alex. *an. pr*. 402.17f. Still more curiously, given that relative pronouns are also indefinite (see n. 80), cashing out proper names, which are intermediate signifiers (*e.g.* D.L. 7.70), as descriptions, (*the person who ...*) must actually be self-contradictory (apparently not noticed by Lloyd 1978: 288).

of defining the semantic status and content of every part of speech; what has been found is support for the thesis that Stoic parts of speech signify, not concrete and precise evidence for the nature of their semantic rôle(s), just as it was observed that the definition of ambiguity preserved by Diogenes Laertius could perhaps have employed a distinction between signifying *lekta* and signifying other sorts of thing, but no more than that (6.2.3). Such a gap in Stoic theorising, combined with the difficulty and subtlety of the notion of autonymy, will go a good way toward explaining how the reasoning behind Chrysippus' *dictum* became obscured. It would, in any case, have found its natural habitat in the more technical Stoic handbooks on ambiguity: when they dropped out of circulation, it did too.

6.3.6 Homonymies: disambiguation and the principles of classification

If Homonymy in Compounds classifies homonyms not "deactivated" by context, then the *de soph.* Stoics must have had some criterion, now unknown, by which to judge when a term is so disambiguated. If they ever had a jargon term for contextual disambiguation, it has not survived. Even the name (if any) specifically for "context" is unknown, σύνθετον itself being ruled out because it is clearly just a word-complex in a fairly general sense, as the contrast with 'ἐν τοῖς ἁπλοῖς' shows. (A late source reports that the Stoic term for "syntax", that is, word-combination, is σύνθεσις: cf. Donnet 1967: 25, n. 7.) And there is no evidence for a theoretical and explicit notion of smaller σύνθετα being included in larger stretches of discourse.

Another plausible assumption is that a distinction between types and tokens (the latter being particular occurrences in particular contexts of ambiguous single terms) was drawn. But the distinction, if present at all, is so only implicitly; any description of it has been lost; and any consequences for the classification which its authors may have recognised are lost too. I suspect (*contra* Edlow 1975: 424f.) that the distinction, in explicit and systematic form, may be a modern importation (originally from Peirce 1966: 4: §537), the Stoics themselves regarding their example of Homonymy in Compounds simply as a *lexis*, and ambiguous in isolation, regardless of whatever we call tokens of it might signify in this or that wider context.

The bare fact that the two Homonymies are distinct kinds surely calls for some explanation. On the current interpretation, they do not classify different primary ambiguity bearers. Since what makes bearers multiply significant is different in each case – for the context in a Homonymy in Compounds utterance makes at least a passive contribution, the ambiguity of the whole being activated by the presence of the ambiguous single term – the Stoics may have reasoned that they must be genuinely different kinds. If so, ambiguities may have been classed not only by bearer (varieties of *lexis*), but also, roughly, by the factor(s) responsible for an utterance's being ambiguous. But the relation between Stoic ambiguity taxonomy and Stoic aetiology is so obscure that I am reluctant to pursue this possibility further.[82] For consistency's sake too the specific causes of ambiguity for isolated utterances must be classified by the same aetiological model; but this proves itself extremely awkward to apply. Even if explanations for kinds are reformulable in such a way as to identify some particular(s) as causally responsible,[83] it is far from obvious what type of cause, according to the Stoic classification of such

---

[82] There are surely no ambiguous utterances whose presence in some wider context would also necessarily make that context ambiguous too; that is, there are no utterances ambiguous in isolation which could be counted as "sustaining", συνεκτικά, causes of ambiguity for all contexts. On the other hand, utterances are obviously ambiguous in isolation, and in some contexts, and in the latter case the two together (utterance and context) might be conceived of as "joint-causes", συναίτια, of the ambiguity of the whole. That still leaves unclear why context is not conceded to be, and included in the classification as, a "joint-cause" for all kinds. On Stoic causes: sources in LS 55; "sustaining" causes are objects or their properties whose presence disposes the affected item to behave in a certain manner under certain narrowly-defined circumstances, and which if removed will remove the effect, *e.g.* the round shape of a cylinder is the sustaining cause of its rolling when pushed, placed on a slope, *etc.* (Cicero *fat.* 43 (62c8–9)); "joint-causes" are severally incapable of producing the effect they can produce jointly, and here there is no sustaining cause: Clement *strom.* 8.9.33.1ff. (55I, esp. §4)).

[83] For example, its not being clear what the grouping of a *lexis* or *logos* is, or what the reference of some constituent term(s) in a *logos* is, might be redescribed as the fact that the parts do not stand in definite morphological or syntactic groupings, or that the term(s) do(es) not clearly and definitely refer to only one individual or to two individuals.

things, these items are. In any event, there are exceptions. Galen's description of Elleipsis makes it 'παρὰ τὴν ἔλλειψιν', 13.8G, 22E (compare 'παρὰ τὸν πλεονασμόν', 13.10G, 22E); yet this must mean that the taxonomic principle in play is rather the defect held to be responsible for the utterance's having several significations, a principle not apparent elsewhere (see further, 6.4.4). Moreover, what identifies an utterance as elliptically ambiguous is some term's (or terms') absence; with the offending term(s) added, the ambiguity would disappear. But Stoic sources do not say what sort of cause an *absent* item might be.

The issue of context has brought back into view the question of the Stoics' taxonomic principles, and indicates that more than one taxonomic principle, over and above that of the bearer, was applied. It also prompts the question why, if linguistic context has so important a rôle to play, it was restricted to cases of homonymy. The context of Galen's Common illustration, for instance (a participle, πεσοῦσα, 13.2G, 21E), does not disambiguate the bearer; the failure is perhaps meant as an inducement to accept it as genuinely ambiguous.[84] The Nonsignificant Part example may, in contrast, have been disambiguated by its original Homeric environment (see 6.5.3). It would be uncharitable to assume that *de soph.* Stoics were unaware of the conflicting rôles assumed by context in these cases.

Context may enable reader or audience to grasp an author's or speaker's intended sense. It can do so in more or less subtle and complicated ways, for example if an inference, observation or connection is made that is consistent with only one of the isolated expression's possible meanings. Sometimes a context must be consciously scanned, or questions put to one's interlocutor; more frequently, as everyday linguistic experience teaches, the work is done without realising it. The

---

[84] Given that the Stoic definition stipulates that the individual ambiguous *lexis* be considered in isolation, or in some particular context (see 4.9), it is interesting to observe that a minimal context,... πέπτωκε,... *has fallen*, has been provided by Diogenes' source too, although its presence is perhaps to be otherwise explained: see 6.2.3.

unspoken assumption is that the speaker has said nothing contradictory or otherwise absurd or inconsequential; yet of course this must be a possibility, and not only where he or she is not altogether competent in the language, or not completely sane (where would humour be without ambiguity?).[85] In an actual stretch of spoken or written discourse the same (occurrence of a) term, assignable to Homonymy in Simples in isolation, may be ambiguous in one context, but not in another, wider and fuller, context including the first. It seems redundant and arbitrary to assign the term in the first context to Homonymy in Compounds, if in practice no difficulty is experienced in understanding the intended meaning, given the second, broader context. Where the complex, expanding context of real written and spoken discourse is in play, with all its possibilities for revision and clarification, correct allocation to Homonymy in Compounds cannot be straightforward, there being no immediately apparent, natural, restriction on what counts as a term's linguistic environment. And what of the more general situation of utterance, the speaker, the audience, their environment, relationship, shared knowledge and beliefs, and so on?[86]

Other, connected, problems were raised in 6.2.3: the exact nature of the items classified, and the identity criteria for *lexeis*. The modern response to the two Homonymies must be that Homonymy in Simples classifies types, whereas Homonymy in Compounds classifies tokens; or that one belongs to the lexicon (the assumption, as for all Stoic semantics, being that meanings are intrinsic, rather than contextually

---

[85] That assumption poses a theoretical difficulty for the Stoa since, strictly speaking, all but the Wise are insane. But it would seem sheer perversity to claim that ordinary speakers can never be certain whether an expression is being used in an absurd sense. The Stoics themselves must have drawn a distinction between the madness shared by all ordinary humans, and lunacy ("melancholy") as normally understood, since, on one view, even the sage can fall victim to the latter (D.L. 7.127 (621)).

[86] The modern distinction between context and situation (*e.g.* Dik 1968: 229; Lyons 1977: 418ff.) would be unavailable, or at least unobvious, to authors who had never heard of competence and performance, and did not feel it vital to keep linguistics and pragmatics wholly separate. That context affects perception of ambiguity is today a commonplace of linguistic and semantic theory: Richman 1959: 87; Chomsky 1965: 21; Dik 1968: 229; Lyons 1977: 400; Scheffler 1979: 16.

"activated"), and the other to a description of the language system. But the Stoa seems not to have developed a type/token distinction, and might have found it hard to accommodate such abstractions as types within their metaphysics; and of course they have no text/system dichotomy either. Yet the question what criteria there are for (qualitative) identity of utterances must still be answered. The Stoics must also provide criteria of identity and individuation for contexts; and this might even be impossible without appeal to abstract objects again.[87]

There is the further difficulty of determining what exactly is to count as disambiguation. Is it enough to say that one interpretation must be "absurd" or "unreasonable", for example, calling on an intuitive, pre-theoretical notion of absurdity or unacceptability? The idea seems to have been familar to Quintilian (see further, below), and perhaps to the grammarian Charisius.[88] Boethius draws a distinction between possible and impossible meanings of ambiguous sentences, *orationes*, and comments that a dialectical situation requires all meanings to be distinguished, a scientific or philosophical one only those which are possible ('ergo quoties ad contentionem venitur, dividenda possibilia et impossibilia sunt, quoties ad veri-

---

[87] Eikmayer and Rieser 1983: 396ff., in their criticisms of Scheffler's (1979) attempts to construct inscriptionalist theories of ambiguity, vagueness, and metaphor, argue that necessary generalisations about "contexts" (as well as about "discourse") are impossible within a purely inscriptionalist model; Scheffler's inscriptionalism has already inspired other criticisms of Stoic semantics, in 6.2.3. The Stoics would also presumably be unwilling to make semantic or grammatical generalisations into descriptions of such apparently abstract objects as the school grammarians' "generic name" (*e.g.* D.T. Sch. 546.5ff., 547.18ff., and n. 51 above). Further, time and place, although incorporeal (*e.g.* Sextus *M.* 10.218 (27D)), also require individuation criteria: for places, perhaps, by reference to occupants, since these, being bodies (*e.g.* Sextus *M.* 10.3f. (49B)), will be particulars (except that *lexeis* may not be genuine individuals: 6.2.3, n. 19), and are what permit a definition of place at all (*e.g.* Stobaeus 1.161.8ff. (49A, esp. §1)); for times, either by their being bodies themselves, as is the case with days or seasons (Plutarch *comm. not.* 45.1084CD (51G)), or by some (unique) specification of what is true (of a body) (see esp. Stobaeus 1.106.5ff. (51B, esp. §4)).

[88] Charisius lists *amphibolia* as a defect of language, but his account is incomplete. After the observation that ambiguity 'fit aliquando in uno verbo', the text runs 'ut si quis se dicat hominem occidisse, cum appareat eum qui loquitur occisum non esse' (*inst. gr.* 4 (*G.L.* 1), 271.26–32, esp. 30–2). Charisius may be pointing out that "ambiguities" of this sort, of which one grammatically possible reading is patently absurd, are not genuinely ambiguous, but are to be avoided none the less, presumably as having an unintentionally comic effect.

tatem, impossibilia relinquenda sunt', *P.L.* 64, *div.* 890A).[89]
None of these authors suggests his material has a Stoic origin,
however. Further, Quintilian, Charisius, and Boethius apparently have in mind selectional, rather than contextual, disambiguation, that is, an expression's being disambiguated
because, of several grammatically possible significations, all
but one are absurd in themselves (Boethius' example is *dico
hominem comedere panem, I say there is a man eating bread/a
man-eating bread*). Single terms, of course, can only be contextually disambiguated; Quintilian, Charisius, and Boethius are
all discussing word-complexes. This same criterion, of simple
absurdity or semantic unacceptability (notoriously slippery, as
modern linguists observe[90]), might be applied to both forms
of disambiguation, despite the fact that the *de soph.* Stoics
seem not to have taken selectional disambiguation into consideration: at least, the illustration of Significant Part has one
patently absurd sense which was not thereby disqualified (see
6.5.2).

A comment of the author of the pseudo-Ciceronian *ad Herennium* may also be relevant. It has already been mentioned,
in connection with the Chrysippean thesis that every word is
ambiguous (6.3.4). He complains that the dialecticians 'watch
out for every ambiguity, even those which on one side [*sc.* of
the case] cannot express any meaning', 'omnes ... amphibolias
aucupantur, eas etiam quae ex altera parte sententiam nullam
possunt interpretari' (2.16). Assuming (reasonably, given the
date of the *ad Herennium*[91]) that the dialecticians under attack
are Stoic, this criticism may testify to a trend in the technical
Stoic treatment of ambiguity. On the other hand, as noted
briefly in 6.3.4, and as will be seen in more detail in 7.4, the
response recommended by the "dialecticians" to fallacies that
exploit homonymies, as described by Simplicius (*cats.* 24.13–
20), makes no sense unless the speaker – even a designing
sophist – is assumed not to use language in an absurd and

[89] Boethius refers to interpreting 'reasonably' and 'unreasonably' only in order to
distinguish ambiguous from obscurely elliptical utterances: *div.* 889BC (*P.L.* 64).
[90] *E.g.* Shopen 1973: 73; Baker and Hacker 1984: 334ff.; Horrocks 1987: 2f.
[91] On the date and authorship of the *ad Her.*: Kennedy 1972: 110–13, 120ff.

unreasonable way. And not a single one of the apparently genuine Stoic illustrations in the *prog.* list, whose authors, I shall argue, were most probably interested in ambiguity as a stylistic defect, is a candidate for either selectional or contextual disambiguation.[92] So it looks as though there may well have been serious internal dissension on this whole topic.

I can see three solutions to the puzzle of why contextual disambiguation has been restricted in the *de soph.*

The first, and most drastic, is to cut the knot, and simply abandon the interpretation I have presented here – that just (*a*) *man* is ambiguous – in favour of what is called "dual focus homonymy", that is, of taking both *man* ... and ... *is* to be homonymous simultaneously, neither word disambiguating the other, both providing a suitable context for each of the other's multiple meanings. This would still be a form of homonymy, because it involves homonymous words, but a homonymy "in a compound", because there are two of them, forming a word-complex. I fear this approach is misguided. It requires us to reject Galen's implicit testimony that ἐστι in the example does not change its meaning (13.7G, 22E). It seems to represent no more than an interesting variant of Homonymy in Simples, since, on this hypothesis, the reason the whole *lexis* (*a*) *man is* is ambiguous is that it contains two homonyms so to speak "co-operating": and that is all. (A syntactic difference between the two readings might be grounds for introducing a new kind, but the two readings of the sentence appear to be syntactically identical.[93]) Finally, it is hard to think of two different senses for ... *is* in this context, one applying to persons, the other to cases.[94]

---

[92] For my interpretation of the *prog.* classification's original rôle, see esp. 6.4.6, 6.6.2. On the Part example: 6.5.3. The Reference illustrations, I think, are both Theon's own (6.7.3); the remaining examples, of Significant Part, are Homeric quotations, which can therefore be checked against their original context (6.5.2).

[93] Edlow 1975: 429, 1977: 65 claims that the example is constructionally ambiguous, as required by his own, erroneous, interpretation of it (see nn. 56, 60), not as suggested by anything in the Greek. Of course, (*a*) *man* ... could be subject or complement of the verb: but it could be so whatever its meaning.

[94] Were cases incorporeal, it could be argued that the use of the verb εἶναι of them would be improper. Like *lekta*, they will merely "subsist", ὑφιστάναι: *cf.* Goldschmidt 1972.

An alternative explanation is that the limitation indicates the origin of Stoic interest in ambiguity: that is, the dialectician's need to deal successfully with equivocations deployed to produce fallacies, or unknowingly abused in argument. Such terse, sophistic question-and-answer exchanges would be especially vulnerable to the exploitation of single term ambiguities, but their restricted context would still be sufficient to disambiguate them, and/or make claims of disambiguation plausible. (Particular exchanges may also be subject to disambiguation by factors outside the linguistic environment, in the general situation of utterance; thus, the dialecticians' advised assent to the premiss *Is the tunic ἀνδρεῖος?* only if the tunic – *viz.* some actual tunic about which the question is being asked – is indeed male attire: see 7.4.) A distinction still has to be observed, of course, between allowing, on the one hand, that "the shirt is brave" is technically a possible meaning of (what would today be called the type-sentence) ὁ χιτών ἐστιν ἀνδρεῖος, while claiming that this cannot be its meaning (*i.e.* the meaning attaching to one of its tokens) in some particular linguistic exchange, and asserting, on the other, that it is not a possible signification at all – which I take it would have been the approach of the *de soph.* Stoics. They manifestly did not focus exclusively on ambiguity as exploited to produce fallacies: their separation of the two Homonymies may never the less testify to their interest in that rôle.

Finally, it could be argued that there was a Stoic, and general, failure to develop a theoretical concept of context (in marked contrast to the attention lavished on it by modern theoretical linguistics: *e.g.* Lyons 1977: 570ff.), and that it is simply more obvious to intuition that single terms can be disambiguated by their contexts than that complete sentences can be by their (necessarily longer and more complex) contexts, even if they may be selectionally disambiguated, or at least present one optimal or most reasonable interpretation. Yet the Stoics are obviously not operating simply with and on intuitive judgements about ambiguities; while it is surely just as obvious that phrases and sentences get disambiguated as that single words do. Ps.-Alexander (on his identity, see

317

Ebbesen 1981a: 1: 70ff., 268ff.) even argues in the other direction, to apparent "ambiguation" by context, broadly construed: commenting on *s. el.* 24.179b38ff., he points out that
one might have the impression, φαντασία, that the expression
ἀγαθόν τι τῶν κακῶν, *a good thing belongs among the bad/to
the bad*, is ambiguous, when in fact it is not (so Aristotle,
180a16ff.), because slaves tend to have bad characters, and it
would seem unlikely for someone to say, of a bad master, that
he has a good slave. (On the *s. el.* passage, see 6.4.3.) He also
has his own, distinctly odd, version of word-complexes which
are univocal combined, ambiguous divided (137.20 ff.), apparently based on an idiosyncratic reading of *int.* 11.21a25 ff., and
points out too that it is the whole *logos* or premiss which is
made ambiguous by the presence of an homonymy (138.1–8).
Here a bias toward sophistical contexts, and relatively isolated
premisses, is to be expected. But how to explain comparable
limitations elsewhere?

The answer may lie in a failure to acknowledge the pragmatic resources and requirements of actual stretches of discourse, in all their variety. Thus Aristotle construes the notion
of context (*cf.* 'ἐν τῷ εἰρημένῳ') far more generously in his
discussion of "problem" words or phrases in literary texts
(*poet.* 25.1461a30ff., *cf.* 4ff.), presumably because experience
of such works has made him aware that an expression's immediate surroundings may not be enough to explicate or disambiguate, and that non-linguistic information may be relevant
too. Broader still is Boethius' advice that 'not every meaning
of expressions is to be distinguished as if [they were the divi-
sions] of a genus, however. For in the case of a genus all its
species are enumerated. In the case of an ambiguity, as many
[meanings] suffice as can serve that stretch of discourse which
one or other locution [*sc.* one or other interpretation of the
ambiguity, but it is worth noting that Boethius does not distinguish bearer from meaning] binds together', 'non tamen ita
dividenda est omnis vocum significatio tamquam generis. in
genere enim omnes species enumerantur, in ambiguitate vero
tantae sufficiunt, quantae ad eum sermonem possunt esse

utiles quem alterutra nectit oratio' (*div.* 890D). The advice is given despite the allusion a little earlier (889D) to the usefulness of the art of division of meanings 'against sophistical irritations, as Aristotle himself says' ('oportet autem maxime exercere hanc artem, ut ipse Aristoteles ait, contra sophisticas importunitates'). His and Aristotle's breadth of vision, their theoretical imprecision notwithstanding, suggests that not only the Stoics', but also Theophrastus', concentration on homonyms contextualised by simple sentences perhaps suffered, ironically, from too much freedom from such practical constraints:

For many [words] when used by themselves do not belong among those that have several meanings, but when put together with one another they do signify several things: and, again, some said by themselves signify several things, but when put together they do not, as was shown in Theophrastus' *On ⟨how⟩[?] many ways.*[95] For in *knowing letters* the two together are amphibolous, although neither of the words is homonymous by itself; the same [holds for] *Plato Dion beats*; for the words are single [*i.e.* univocal], the sentence formed from them amphibolous; yet in *an eagle flies, a dog barks,* the words are homonymous, the sentences single. (Alexander *top.* 378.24–379.3)

The illustration *knowing letters* is one of Aristotle's own examples of his ambiguity-cum-fallacy mode Amphiboly, in which the constituents of a syntactic complex may play one or other of several grammatical rôles in relation to each other (*s. el.* 4.166a18f.; and see Appendix A). Theophrastus seems to have arrived at his class of sentences by reversing Aristotle's Amphiboly mode. Amphibolies are ambiguous although no constituent is ambiguous in isolation: Theophrastean sentences are not ambiguous although one constituent is homonymous, in isolation, and they are thus also the complements of Homonymy in Compounds ambiguities, which are ambiguous because one constituent is homonymous and remains so in its given context. The implicit connection between the two classes

---

[95] ποσαχῶς and πολλαχῶς are both possible readings at 378.27 – the former is the reading at *top.* 154.16 – and clearly the work, or works, concerned semantic multiplicity.

is easy to see now. Whether there was a Stoic debt to Theophrastus' work, as there seems to have been in stylistics (see 3.4), is impossible to say.

The last condition on ambiguity laid down by the definition preserved by Diogenes Laertius suggested, as noted in 4.9, that a bearer cannot be counted as ambiguous unless some audience, unspecified, actually understands two or more meanings by it. This might seem to undermine the Stoic position that ambiguity can represent a serious threat to one's moral and general welfare. It surely is a plain fact about almost all types of discourse that what linguists identify as lexical or grammatical ambiguities get resolved by contextual or situational factors: *e.g.* Chomsky 1965: 21, Kooij 1971: 4f., Baker and Hacker 1984: 310. Two possible responses, at least, might be made on the Stoics' behalf. On the one hand, they made a dialectical training with a large experiential component necessary for the detection of ambiguities in all forms of rational discourse. The taxonomic principles of the *de soph.* list acknowledge the power of context to eliminate ambiguities, while the illustrations in the *prog.* classification which are drawn from literary texts are not contextually disambiguated, testifying to its probable origin in a practical stylistic manual. On the other hand, that contexts and situations disambiguate is of such importance for modern linguists because it is one of the principal phenomena to be faced in defining the limits of narrow linguistic competence, or the language-system, as against performance, a broader language competence, or text. The ancients did not make these theoretical distinctions, and in consequence the projects they entail, like this one, had no such urgency for them.

That dichotomy may seem a little too neat. At the end of his first discussion of ambiguity (7.9.4), Quintilian points out that, if an ambiguous sentence can be definitely interpreted in the way a client needs to win his case, then it is no ambiguity at all, but that other factors – what would be more natural, more just, more in keeping with the wishes of the author of the disputed document – can then be appealed to. Quintilian is not, however, consciously limiting the scope of "the linguistic", or openly rejecting clear-cut theoretical distinctions between what is "in the language" and what is not. Like the author of the *ad Herennium*, who makes fun of the dialecticians for finding ambiguities everywhere (2.16), he is criticising the detachment of ambiguities from the constraints of particular contexts and situations, and is responsibly carrying out the rhetorician's practical task of teaching the composition of speeches and discussing the difficulties an orator must tackle. The question: is this "ambiguity" really ambiguous?, has no importance in this context. In the *de inventione*, similarly, Cicero sets out the correct procedures for dealing with an ambiguously-framed document whose meaning is at issue in law (2.116ff.). He is concerned with the procedures appropriate to advocates bent on demonstrating that their favoured reading is the one intended by an author; his advice shows both how loosely the notion of context can be interpreted, and how complicated and lengthy a business it could be in practice to establish whether an expression is or is not ambiguous; but no general account of the effects of context is needed or attempted.

Again, in his classification of causes of linguistic obscurity in Book 8, Quintilian mentions not merely standard ambiguity, as described in his Book 7, but also that which

even if it cannot disturb the meaning, falls prey to the same linguistic defect, *e.g.* if someone were to say "he saw a man a book writing". For even if it is obvious that the book is being written by the man, yet [the writer] will have composed amiss, and created an ambiguity, as far as was in in his power to do so.

etiamsi turbare non potest sensum, in idem tamen verborum vitium incidit, ut si quis dicat "visum a se hominem librum scribentem". nam etiamsi librum ab homine scribi patet [and not the man by the book!] male tamen composuerit feceritque ambiguum, quantum in ipso fuit. (8.2.16)

Quintilian's mentioning such cases at all perhaps shows that they had come up for discussion previously, at least in the context of the correct canons of literary composition, where unlikely absurdities will be as unwelcome as outright inclarities. Hermogenes the rhetorician seems to have taken this line too (Ebbesen 1981a: 1: 128), and a Dionysian scholiast (474.27) justifies the need for punctuation in a Homeric line to separate the words *Achilles* and *old man*, on the grounds that these might otherwise be construed together, 'which is absurd'.

The rule seems to be that it is irrelevant for rhetoricians, stylistic theorists, and literary critics, who are dealing with the interpretation and construction of particular texts, whether or not a sentence "really" is ambiguous. What matters is the acceptability of a given sentence or a given reading, where "acceptability" is plainly not (wholly) grammatical, but judged by a variety of factors, and determined by the particular pragmatic interests of the writer. In contrast, technical grammarians (Apollonius Dyscolos is especially sensitive to the rôle of context in disambiguation: see 8.4) may want to ignore just such factors, and so may philosophers, but never because they are trying to construct a theory about what should go into a description of a language, or to fix the boundaries of language-knowledge. Here too, of course, purpose is relevant. Aristotle observed that only so many meanings of an ambiguous sentence should be distinguished as are relevant to immediate dialectical needs (*top.* 2.3.110b28, with Alexander's commentary *ad loc.*, *in top.* 153.30ff.). His appeal in the *Poetics* to the broader context and even to extra-linguistic factors to determine 'in how many ways this ⟨word⟩ might signify in the context', ('ποσαχῶς ἂν σημαίνοι τοῦτο ἐν τῷ εἰρημένῳ'), has already been mentioned. Boethius quotes a very similar example to Quintilian's, of which only one reading is possible and need be mentioned when distinguishing meanings of ambiguities ('dico hominem panem comedere', 'I say there is a man eating bread/a man-eating bread', *P.L.* 64, *div.* 890A); the context is the distinction between and definition of various forms of "division", as a general contribution to logic. The Stoic separation of the two Homonymies may, as already noted, have been inspired by sophistic chicaneries.

If the Stoics seem never to have moved much beyond a loose, intuitive conception of context and situation, then this will be a serious defect in their definition (and classifications) only if they aimed to provide criteria for rigid and mutually exclusive division into ambiguous and non-ambiguous utterances. To launch such a project is to neglect ambiguity's pragmatic fluidity; and without some sort of distinction between maximally decontextualised utterances and those produced in actual discourse, then, even if it is always possible to determine when a given expression is a case of ambiguity, the project is bound to come to grief.

6.3.7 Homonymies: conclusions

These few lines dealing with the two Homonymies in Galen's classification will preserve, if the interpretation I have argued for is correct, not one, but two major Stoic contributions to the study and classification of ambiguity: the notions of contextual disambiguation, and of autonymy. Unfortunately, however, external evidence consisted only of scraps of information, unconnected hints and – most interesting and rewarding of the meagre sources – Augustine's reworking of what (I trust) has been shown to be Stoic material.

That it proved impossible to find support for this interpretation in the work of the rhetoricians and grammarians, who had a strong professional interest in ambiguity, and who provide invaluable evidence for the spread of Stoic influence outside strictly philosophical circles, is of little moment. These writers would have been little stimulated by the idea of autonymy, which would be of interest mainly to philosophers of language and logicians; the study of the contribution of context to the creation and neutralisation of ambiguity in actual contexts, not Stoic taxonomic subtleties, alone had high, practical, value.

At the same time, it must be admitted that the decision to restrict contextual disambiguation appears both arbitrary and pointless, when it should have been founded on broad, but precise and coherent, assumptions about the way language in general is or can or should be used, and about the relation of language to its narrow and broad environments, both linguistic and situational. It is is deeply regrettable that the mode of preservation of the classification has destroyed its original context, along with whatever Stoic commentary there may have been on problem topics such as this.

The Stoic concept of autonymy did not achieve general philosophical currency in later antiquity, although Chrysippus' "universal ambiguity" did find its way, out of context, into an erudite, if unscholarly, anthology (Gellius' *Attic Nights*), perhaps in part because it gave an opportunity to picture two philosophers, Chrysippus and Diodorus, at loggerheads with each other. Its association with the "wagon" and similar fallacies,[96] attention-grabbing and easily memorable, won it little genuine respect, and it seems to have taken an Augustine to appreciate what must be two of the most striking products of Stoic dialectical ingenuity. But perhaps this peculiarly Stoic approach to language's reflexive capacity did not disappear altogether. Besides Philoponus' solution of the fallacy quoted in 6.3.4, a passage in Simplicius, *cats.* 31.4ff, also testifies to Stoic influence, although nothing like autonymy is explicitly mentioned (for details, see Ebbesen 1981a: 1: 218f.). The Ps.-Alexandrian commentary on the *s. el.* invents an alleged ambiguity which looks to turn precisely on a use/mention distinction (ἀγαθός, *good*, could be mentioned, as a slave's name, or used, to denote the slave), yet which is classified as a case of a non-linguistic fallacy mode, Accident (167.30ff.; on Accident sophisms, see further, 6.4.3). The Western schoolmen certainly did recognise this reflexive function of language (Ebbesen 1977: 107), and some of their accounts may betray Stoic influence.[97]

What is to be said of the Stoic notion of autonymy as a contribution to the school's philosophy? N.E. Christensen

---

[96] Although the text is poor, and one does not expect such a case here, where Galen is discussing potential ambiguities (those due to Accent, Combination, and Division), one of the two fallacies he describes in the *de soph.* does seem to turn on a failure to observe the use/mention distinction (or however it is described): (9.22–10.2G, 17E).

[97] Ebbesen 1981a: 1: 222, and n. 15 (p. 223), reports a 13th-cent. Latin *quaestio* in an unpublished commentary on the *s. el.* which claims a distinction between a term's signifying itself and its signifying its external signification; the example is *man*. Another scholiast solves the "wagon" sophism by distinguishing senses of λέγειν and λεγόμενα. Ebbesen 1981a: 1: 207f.

1962: 359 objects to the notion of autonymous use of words that it will 'introduce a great number of homonyms into our language, one for each word', which then have to be systematically eliminated by the use of quotation marks; and he himself offers an original alternative to the use/mention distinction in the shape of the thesis that a variety of *uses* of words exists, one of which will be the use of a word precisely in order to produce or display that very word, so that it can be talked about. His real objection to autonymous use (360) is not so much its practical inconvenience (which contextual and situational disambiguation will greatly reduce, even without benefit of textual symbols), as that it seems redundant: why bother to name a word, when producing it does just as well? The word will always be there to be produced, if it can be named by uttering it.

But the Stoics were not operating with the notion of words being *used* autonymously. Rather, words signify themselves, which could be redescribed as their being used to signify themselves; but that would surely not constitute a real distinction for a Stoic dialectician. The notion of "use" of language, as a systematic, basic contribution to semantics, to refurbish or replace a tattered or empty notion of "meaning", is a modern innovation. Then there is the important consideration that, although the ancients had some devices for indicating "use" as opposed to "mention" – notably, the prefacing of τό or τὸ ὄνομα or something similar to a word[98] – these were not thought of as necessary adjuncts, in the way that quotation-marks tend to be today, the omission of which would be held to be at least misleading, and even solecistic or ambiguous.[99]

---

[98] *E.g.* Boethus *ap.* Simp. *cats.* 25.9ff.: any word, *lexis*, of which one wants to ask, *is it homonymous?*, can be prefaced with the neuter article, regardless of the gender or grammatical rôle of the word in question: *e.g.* τὸ κύων; Apollonius *synt.* 45.13ff.: the article is preposed to the infinitive both 'ὡς πρὸς τὸ πρᾶγμα', 'as looking to the thing (or action) signified by the infinitive', and where the infinitive can be 'κατὰ τῆς φωνῆς λέγεσθαι', 'said of the word', *i.e.* of the infinitive itself.

[99] Quine 1951: 23, for instance, calls the sentence *Boston is disyllabic* false, and regards it as one of the class of sentences liable to give rise to the sort of 'confusion and controversy which have resulted from failure to distinguish clearly between an object and its name'; *cf.* N. E. Christensen 1962: 359. Contrast the complexity of the late antique discussion of sentences of this sort: Ebbesen 1981a: 1: 217ff.

Ancient readers' expectations about the "use" or "meaning" of words would be different from those of their modern counterparts, and they would not necessarily be thrown off their stride by an unmarked autonymy, because contemporary conventions did not dictate that such cases had to be marked by symbols or some other mechanism. Apollonius does observe (*synt.* 34.3ff.) that articles are used with every part of speech 'which signifies only the name of the word, so that the article is applied to what is understood externally', 'σημαίνοντι αὐτὸ μόνον τὸ ὄνομα τῆς φωνῆς, ὥστε πρὸς τὸ ὑπακουόμενον ἔξωθεν τὸ ἄρθρον ἀνατείνεσθαι', as in 'ὁ μὲν προτακτικός ἐστι τοῦ δέ', 'the [particle] μὲν precedes the [particle] δέ', or 'τὸ λέγε προστακτικόν ἐστιν', 'the [verb] *speak* is imperative'; while 'ὁ᾽ Ἀρίσταρχος', where 'we add the article with reference to the gender [of the word] which is thought of [along with the word]', 'πρὸς τὸ νοούμενον γένος τὸ ἄρθρον παρατίθεμεν', is opposed to 'τὸ Ἀρίσταρχοι', '*Aristarchuses*', which 'we say with reference to the name of the form, the word being [what is] understood', 'πρὸς τὸ ὄνομα τῆς φωνῆς φαμέν, ὑπακουομένου τοῦ ὀνόματος'. The reference to parts of speech signifying the names of words may even be a Stoic survival; but the care with which Apollonius introduces this use of the article is explained by his own need for clear and precise ways of mentioning the items whose grammatical properties he is analysing. Nontechnical authors feel no such compunction.

To this extent Burnyeat's contention that '[i]n a world without inverted commas Chrysippus' claim [*sc.* that every word is ambiguous] is simply true' (1987: 11, n. 12) seems acceptable. It is easy to imagine a language in which there is a rule that autonymy must be indicated by a special particle, so that without that particle a word could never be correctly used to signify itself; in modern English the quotation mark is fast acquiring the status of that special particle (to the extent that "gestural" quotation marks are now acceptable in conversation, if mention of a word is intended). The upshot will be that the existence of autonymy as a distinct form of ambiguity in a language will be a matter of convention, of the use of special symbols (which may be paralinguistic). Further, even within a language, if conventions regarding use of such symbols are fluid, as in ancient Greek (and Latin), autonymous ambiguity may itself be a fluid, unstable phenomenon, appearing in some texts and contexts, eliminated from others, in still others flickering uncertainly as an author's use of the symbols fluctuates.

Chrysippus and the *de soph.* Stoics seem to have accepted one convention as fixed, and this might be questioned much as the acceptance of written Common utterances as ambiguous was questioned, on the grounds that their alleged ambiguity may be a mere by-product of ancient orthographic practice. But the cases are not parallel: the real objection to Common was that no language user would utter the undifferentiated *lexis* αὐλητρίς, only the *logos* αὐλὴ τρίς or the *onoma* αὐλητρίς, so that ostensible spoken Common ambiguities, at the appropriate, grammatical, level of analysis, showed themselves in danger of dissolving altogether. The introduction of *lexis* as ambiguity-bearer seemed both insufficiently motivated, and inconsistent with the requirement that bearers of meaning be actual or potential utterances of speakers, and what came into question was what is to count as an utterance of a language, and not, as in the case of autonymy, what a *bona fide* utterance can (be used to) mean. So it is arguable that Stoics should have been more alert to the fluidity of Greek, as of other natural languages, in which all conventions and rules are changeable diachronically and variable synchronically.

Yet that may be to misread the underlying reason for their interest in autonymy. Modern logicians are not concerned with the description of particular natural languages; speakers' and writers' actual practices may be of interest, but they will not be allowed to determine, or influence the rigidity and explicitness of, rules for marking mention, or autonymy, or some functionally equivalent category, in formal languages (or in formalised fragments of natural languages). The Stoic perspective is comparable, if also importantly different. The identification of universal ambiguity can be seen, alongside the invention or systematisation of grammatical, logical, rhetorical, and poetical terminologies, as part of a continuing, systematic project to establish what today would be called a

327

theoretical "metalanguage", in which the properties of discourse can be labelled and classified. Stoic dialecticians may well have wanted to establish a single rule operative in this area of usage too, for every natural language, not for the trivial reason of imposing a new standard of linguistic correctness (like not splitting infinitives), but in order to rationalise language, or to restore part of its pristine rationality, in which state such distinctions would, at a guess, have been automatically marked. And that is necessary because it is this "ordinary" language which has to be used for the conduct of actual argument and all rational discourse, not the fixed abstractions of formal logic – to which, in any case, access is gained primarily through linguistic items and operations carried out upon these items. A new rule for "Hellenism" may be the result, but that is not surprising in a system in which solecisms are ultimately explained in terms of improper composition at the level of the *lekton*.[100]

If this interpretation of the origin of the Stoic doctrine of autonymy is correct, then it confirms that the *de soph.* classification is not to be taken as a (complete or partial) typology of ambiguities in ordinary Greek usage. Rules for general linguistic usage are being implicitly laid down: in the case of Common, as regards the category of possible utterances; here, as regards the category of possible meanings. This lesson will be learned again and again as the classification unfolds.

6.4   The species of ambiguity 3: Elleipsis, Pleonasm

6.4.1   Elleipsis, Pleonasm: texts and translations

The state of the texts is a serious obstacle to interpretation. The Elleipsis example has effectively been lost from the *de soph.*, and no example at all survives (if there ever was one) in the *prog.*

---

[100] This is implied by the definition of solecisms at D.L. 7.59. Primary Stoic syntax governs relations within and between lekta (6.5.2); its inadequacy reflects both the overriding Stoic concern with structures relevant to the operations of logic, and a very unmodern concept of natural languages: see 3.1, 3.4.

de soph. 13.8–12G, 22E

τέταρτον δὲ ἐστι παρὰ τὴν ἔλλειψιν, ⟨ὡς τίνος   8
σὺ εἶ; ⟩ καὶ γὰρ ἐλλείπει τὸ διὰ μέσου, οἷον δεσπότου ἢ   9
πατρός. πέμπτη δὲ παρὰ τὸν πλεονασμόν, ὥσπερ ἡ τοιαύτη,   10
ἀπηγόρευσεν αὐτῷ μὴ πλεῖν. τὸ γὰρ μὴ προσκείμενον ἀμφί-   11
δοξον ποιεῖ τὸ πᾶν, εἴτε τὸ πλεῖν ἀπηγόρευσεν ἢ τὸ μὴ πλεῖν.   12

(4) The fourth [species is] due to elleipsis, ⟨as *whose*   8
are you?⟩; for it omits the mediate term, *e.g.* [*or: i.e.*] *master's*   9
or *father's.* (5) The fifth [species is] due to pleonasm, such as this   10
sort [of ambiguity],
he forbade him (not) to sail; for the (*not*) by its addition makes the   11
whole ambi-
valent, whether he forbade him to sail or not to sail.   12

prog. 82.25f.

καὶ μέντοι καὶ τὸ ἐλλείπειν τινὰ ὀνόματα πρὸς   25
τὴν σαφήνειαν ἐναντίον ἐστί.   26

(6) Moreover, omitting certain words is   25
contrary to clarity.   26

6.4.2   *Elleipsis, Pleonasm: the problem of taxonomy*

These species show that a new principle of classification is being applied. Classifying an ambiguity as "deficient" or "superfluous" is to follow a quite different standard from that taken in the rest of the *de soph.* list: by reference to appropriate methods of resolution. No other species is explicitly distinguished by reference to a defect.[101] But the discrepancies

---

101   That only two of the Stoic modes are so clearly classed according to some defect, or its remedy, is almost certainly evidence against Barwick's claim, 1922: 97f., 1957: 103–7, that the so-called *quadripertita ratio* (the name used of it by Quintilian, 1.5.38) – the four-way classificatory scheme of addition, subtraction, transposition, and transmutation which dominates Roman grammatical and rhetorical theory – is specifically Stoic in origin (perhaps the work of Diogenes of Babylon). In particular, Barwick 1922: 94–6 believes it found its way into Roman grammatical texts by way of a Stoic classification of the virtues and vices of discourse. But in that case it would be more than reasonable to expect to find it in classifications of ambiguities, which will fall under the heading of the stylistic defect of obscurity (see 3.4, 8.3); and this the two surviving lists show definitely not to have been the case. Of course, all the species could probably be squeezed into the *quadripertita ratio*: but that is unsurprising, since the four categories are broad and flexible. For further, weighty, objections to Barwick's contention: Ax 1987: 29ff. On the origins of the *ratio*, with a lengthy list of related Greek and Latin terminology: Householder 1981: 7ff., esp. 8, n. 3. But Stoics did use the *ratio*: see my n. 120, below.

between Galen's and Theon's reports must be accounted for: are they the results of authentic disagreements between different and rival groups of Stoic dialecticians, or of Theon's tampering with his source?

6.4.3   Elleipsis: Galen's illustration (de soph. 13.8f.G, 22E)

Galen's explanation suggests the basic shape any reconstruction must take. What the ambiguity "omits" is 'τὸ διὰ μέσον', literally 'the in-between', a description elucidated by the words that follow, 'οἶον δεσπότου ἢ πατρός'. So *master's* and *father's* are those terms, or examples of those terms, of which one has been omitted, and the addition of one of which will disambiguate the whole. Since both terms are in the genitive case, the example must contain some word in the same grammatical case to which they correspond.

The most plausible reconstruction offered to date of the MS 'ὅ ἐστιν ὡς σὺι καὶ ὡς' must be Sedley's: 'ὡς τίνος συ εἶ', 'as, *Whose/Of whom are you?*' (3Q5; 1987: 2: 230, l. 9). First, it agrees well with the MS. It also guarantees that there is no word in the example to reveal the identity of one or other party to the relation. Last, it contains both a suitable genitive, *whose/of whom*, to agree grammatically with the omitted term, and a pronoun referring to the other party.[102] The sentence can be resolved by addition of this "mediate" term: *Of which ⟨master/father⟩ are you? Master's* and *father's* are perhaps called "mediate" not (merely) because they would occupy a central position in the expanded sentences, but (also) because they signal, indirectly, the relation which holds between the parties. As Edlow 1975: 432, n. 43 observes, the phrase τὸ διὰ μέσου seems to be 'a rare Stoic technical term, occurring no-

---

[102] Gabler's emendation '⟨ὡς⟩ σός ἐστιν [ὡς] υἱός', accepted by Baratin and Desbordes 1981: 138 ('c'est ton garçon'), Hülser 1982: 3: 397, §633 ('Der Sohn ist dein'), neglects the requirement for grammatical agreement between the omitted term and the term designating the other party to the relation. Gabler is also anxious to detect a connection between this illustration and Aristotle *s. el.* 24.179b39ff., on which see pp. 333–6. Ebbesen 1981a: 1: 36 suggests παῖς as the missing term, but this would introduce a second and independent source of ambiguity, the homonymy of παῖς itself (*slave; child; boy(-child)*).

where else [that is, not in this sense] in the doxographical tradition'. The absence of *slave* or *child/son* (agreeing with *you*, and so in the nominative case) must, I assume, have precisely the same result. Galen may well have listed only a couple of instances of the omitted "mediate/mediating" term.

The insight behind this example might be that genitives or constructions with the genitive are or can be ambiguous between different species of belonging/owning relations, a kind of shorthand for more precise expressions of these diverse types, whose contradistinctions may be obscured by conventional usage. On this interpretation, these Stoics will have identified a double use or sense of the genitive, to express both property-ownership and kinship, which were the two common types of genitive identified by the later grammarians: *e.g.* D.T. 31.5ff.; Sch. 231.28ff., 384.2f., 575.4ff.[103] They may have explained this feature of language as one more area in which its original precision and clarity have been blurred.

But such "ambiguity of the genitive", or of constructions using it, cannot be ambiguity of *any* use of the genitive or a genitive construction: that would be absurd. Kooij 1971: 108f. has shown the limits to the usefulness and applicability of even so vague a grammatical distinction as that between the objective and subjective genitive, and it is possible to doubt, with Sperber and Wilson 1986: 188, that the genitive is ambiguous at all, 'with as many senses as there are types of relationship it may be used to denote, or that all these relationships fall under a single definition which is the only meaning expressed by use of the genitive on any given occasion'. In any event, appealing to genitive constructions as the source of the ambiguity misses the point of the Stoic analysis of what is wrong with this sentence. What makes Elleipsis utterances ambiguous is, explicitly and by definition, an omission. In this particular case, the omission happens to be that of a term which would appropriately identify the rôle, in a relation between two parties, of one of those parties, and that relation happens to be expressed

---

[103] Carneades seems to have identified an interesting double use of the genitive: a mental impression is "of something" (τινός) both in being of an external object and in occurring in a perceiving subject: Sextus *M.* 7.167 (69D2).

by a genitive construction. Edlow 1975: 433 claims that Elleipsis ambiguity 'results from an omitted term preserving the ambiguity *of possessives* or *of the genitive construction*' (his emphasis): but nothing in the example or its general explanation entails that such constructions or the genitive case itself (in Stoic terms, words in the genitive case) are inherently ambiguous, or that they are being identified as the source of the ambiguity even in this one instance.

It would almost certainly not have been possible for Stoics to describe genitives *per se* as ambiguous. Gabler's reconstruction of the illustration (*the son is yours* [σός]) must be incorrect, but Edlow's analysis of it is worth examining. He suggests, 1977: 63, n. 38, that Elleipsis 'corresponds to Galen's mode Amphiboly (actual, syntactic ambiguity)', and contends in support that 'the son is yours' is ambiguous 'because of the syntax, a term's being in the genitive case (or its equivalent) rather than of the word itself (*e.g.*, the pronoun "you" in the nominative case)' (63). Whatever the strength of this argument, it surely could not have figured in a Stoic account of Elleipsis. Even allowing that the forms 'σός' and 'σοῦ' were accepted as equivalent by the rules of Stoic grammar (and they were as a matter of fact commonly interchangeable in ancient Greek), the now familiar concept of syntax to which Edlow refers is surely not even close to its *de soph.* counterpart, as far as can be made out from the rest of the classification, especially from the descriptions of the Part species, as I shall argue later. "Syntax" explicitly so called at the linguistic level appears to be solely or primarily the association or ranging together of an utterance's constituents, whether these are words or bits and pieces of words, that is, grouping or combination: it has not been extended to the determination of "selectional restrictions" (*viz.* by concord and rection) with which a system of morphological (inflectional) variations would be associated. It is especially revealing that the same verbs ('τέτακται' in Galen (13.14, 17G, 22f.E), 'συντέτακται' in Theon (82.4, 9)) are applied alike to the properly syntactic combination of genuine words ("significant parts") and to the juxtaposition of letters and syllables ("non-significant parts"). This restriction of linguistic syntax may be a result of the restriction of primary syntax to the syntax of *lekta* (as argued by Frede 1978: 56–8).[104] But the syntactic grouping of the *lekta* signified by 'whose are you?' seems straightforward enough. (If the Stoic verbal predicate analysis is applicable, the structure will be: predicate [= copula + oblique case] + nominative case.)

The classification's authors may still have regarded inflectional variation as "syntactic" in the sense that it is typically linked with or effected by the association of words in "groupings" or "arrangements" in *logoi*. Yet the fact remains that the chosen category for the example is "Deficiency". The Stoics have not opted for a more rigorously grammatical description or diagnosis of why the utterance is ambiguous. The same objection would apply to any suggestion that genitive-case nominals are being treated as a subspecies of homonym. It is not just that there is no evidence that cases were thought somehow to be accompanied by one or other of a set of additional significations, or that a theory of this sort would surely prove unwieldy and tortuously complex. The point is that if that were the Stoic analysis of their example, then it is mysterious, to say the least, that it was not put in one or other of the Homonymy species. It would be just like pointing out that the reference of the genitive-case noun is not fixed (which it is), while not putting it in the Reference species.

I realise that it is not original to cite in this connection the following Aristotelian passage:

Some solve the syllogisms [*i.e.* apparent syllogisms, fallacies] by ambiguity [τῷ διττῷ] too, *e.g.* that 'the father (or son, or slave) is yours [*sc.* your father/son/slave]'. And yet it is plain that if there is an apparent refutation by being said in many ways [παρὰ τὸ πολλαχῶς λέγεσθαι] the word or *logos* must belong to several things strictly [κυρίως]. But no-one says strictly that this man is this man's child, if he is master of a child; rather, the combination is accidental [παρὰ τὸ συμβεβηκὸς ἡ σύνθεσίς ἐστιν]: 'Is this yours [σόν]?' 'Yes.' 'But this is a child; so this is your child.' But it is not your child because it has come about accidentally that it is both yours and a child. (*s. el.* 24.179b38–180a7)

---

[104] Morphological variation might then be confined to cases, if these are indeed words, as argued in 6.3.4 – but see n. 50 there.

What seems to have been missed in the past is that Aristotle and the Stoics are not discussing the same expressions of possession.[105] Aristotle's point is that *the child is yours*, the sophist's desired conclusion (*cf.* 'that the father/son/slave is yours', 179b39), is not strictly ambiguous, and he appeals to ordinary usage to defend his claim. *This ⟨person⟩ is the child of this ⟨person⟩* or *this child is yours* cannot strictly mean anything but what they say; and, in particular, they cannot strictly be used to say of a slave that he is his owner's child. If the sophist's conclusion cannot strictly have two meanings, the fallacy as a whole cannot be due to ambiguity, and is located instead in the non-linguistic fallacy mode "Accident".

Now Aristotle does go on to explore the possibility that expressions of the form τό τοῦτο τούτων εἶναι, *this thing's belonging to these*, such as ἄνθρωπος τῶν ζῴων, *man ⟨is⟩ of/belongs to the animals*, or ἀγαθόν τι τῶν κακῶν, *a good thing is of/belongs to the bad*, (which, we would say, could be partitive or possessive genitives) are πολλαχῶς λεγόμενα, "said in many ways", are "semantically multiple", rather than always and straightforwardly being expressions of a thing's being a possession, κτῆμα (180a9f.). But he decides against it (180a16ff.), assigning them instead to another non-linguistic fallacy mode, *Secundum quid* (13f.), which works by removing necessary qualifications from expression. He does so again on the basis of ordinary usage: *e.g.*, even if a good slave has a bad master, ἀγαθόν τι τῶν κακῶν is still not ambiguous – he is good, and this man's, but not this man's good (16–18). The mere fact that they can be uttered without appropriate qualifications does not make them πολλαχῶς λεγόμενα: 'for it is not the case that if we ever signify something incompletely, then this has several senses', 'οὐ γὰρ εἴ ποτέ τι σημαίνομεν ἀφελόντες, τοῦτο λέγεται πολλαχῶς' (19f.).[106] He does not consider

---

[105] Edlow 1977: 62 claims that what Aristotle denies is that the fallacy turns on the ambiguity of *yours* in the premiss sentence *A is yours*. Gabler states explicitly, 1903: 24f., that he tried to restore the wording of the example on the basis of *s. el.* 24.179b39; and he nowhere suggests that the Aristotelian and Stoic illustrations may not be directly comparable; *cf.* LS 1987: 2: 231 *ad* 37Q, l. 9.

[106] The same point about the strict meaning of expressions of belonging is made at 176a38ff. Ps.-Alexander *s. el.* 164.11ff. thinks both οὗτος τούτου τέκνον; *Is this*

whether sentences like *this is yours* – one of the fallacy's pre-misses (180a4f.) – are ambiguous; perhaps they would count as univocal but "incomplete" expressions. Yet, on the reasonable assumption that Sedley's reconstruction of the text, or one very like it, is correct, it is just this sort of expression which the *de soph.* Stoics did diagnose as ambiguous.

Other Stoics might have disagreed. A comparable distinction to Aristotle's was drawn by members of the school defending Chrysippus' revised version of Zeno's definition of the impression or presentation, φαντασία, to which objection had been made on the grounds that its *definiens* and *definiendum* were not co-extensive, since not every τύπωσις, "moulding, formation", in the soul is an impression. The response was that in Chrysippus' definition the additional phrase 'ἐν ψυχῇ ὡς ἂν ἐν ψυχῇ', 'in soul *qua* soul', is 'implied', 'συνεμφαίνεσθαι', so that the whole definition, when 'stated explicitly', 'ἐξαπλούμενον', comes out as "ἑτεροίωσις ἐν τῷ ἡγεμονικῷ", alteration in the ruling part (of the soul) (Sextus *M.* 7.232ff.). This passage is interesting not only for its allusion to 'implications', 'συνεμφάσεις' (239), which we have already met (3.5), but also for being followed by a report of an alternative defence appealing to ambiguity (also discussed in 3.5). The possibility must accordingly arise that a systematic account of modes of signifying – *e.g.* strict, as in the Stoic definition; by implication, as here; ambiguous; perhaps others too – was developed by the Stoa. On the other hand, *ad hoc* application of intuitively clear but theoretically untested categories would explain the little material available.

Now it is highly unlikely that the Stoic analysis was formulated in direct response to the *s. el.* and stimulated by dissatisfaction both with the solution Aristotle criticises and with his own. Nothing in this or the *prog.* classification so much as hints at Aristotelian influence, and no ancient author seems even to believe that the Stoics drew up these or any other

---

man this man's child? and οὗτος τούτου; *Is this man this man's?* are treated as ambiguous by Aristotle's opponents, the point being that one could hope to get an answer to the latter from someone who knows the circumstances of utterance. But the text does not bear out his interpretation.

ambiguity systems wholly or in part as a response to Aristotle. The very fact that Aristotle is in a position to criticise a rival approach to such problem expressions shows that they were well known, at least in the Academy, from which they and the various proposed solutions could have reached early Stoics. The ultimate literary source for them is most likely Plato's *Euthydemus* itself (especially the "dog-father" fallacy, 298d8–e5, and generally the whole passage from 297d6ff.). The example may, then, represent an authentic Stoic link between ambiguity and fallacious argument.

Inspiration may also, or alternatively, have come from the Megarians, of whose head, Zeno's teacher Stilpo, this story was told:

> They say he used an argument like this about Pheidias' [statue of] Athena: 'Is Athena, Zeus' daughter, a god?' When one said yes, he said: 'Yet she/this [αὕτη], at any rate, is not Zeus', but Pheidias'.' And when one assented he said: 'So she/it is not a god.' (D.L. 2.116)

The story is probably apocryphal (Stilpo is further reported to have defended himself on a charge of impiety by pointing out that Athena is in fact a god*dess*), but it suggests that puzzles of this sort and different solutions to them may have been circulating during Zeno's philosophically formative years. The diagnosis recorded in the *de soph.* may not be original. But it is the first known attempt to incorporate it into a systematic division of ambiguity-types.

6.4.4 Elleipsis: the species

All Theon has to say, 82.25f., is that 'omitting certain words is contrary to clarity'. This might be a half-hearted and unilluminating attempt to précis his source's subtle examples and explanations. At all events, its interest and complexity should not be allowed to overshadow the facts that a single illustration of Elleipsis survives, and that the species may well have extended far beyond ambiguities associated with the genitive case. The diagnosis of the utterance as ambiguous makes no explicit mention of genitives or genitive case constructions, and describing these as ambiguous, even if only in certain contexts, would require all relations of possession to be assigned to a determinate number of categories (otherwise the expressions would be not ambiguous, but indeterminate. Galen's introduction to his explanation, 'οἷον δεσπότου ἢ πατρός', is itself ambiguous between listing just two options, and listing all of them). The real puzzle, and the challenge for the Stoics, is to fix what counts, and alone counts, as a genuine case of Elleipsis. If it, and Pleonasm too, are to count as genuine species, their members must share some intrinsic ambiguating feature. In ancient Greek, but not in English, *Dion gave Theon's book to the father* [τῷ πατρί], for example, is a possible sentence;[107] and since it is unclear whose father is intended, and since failure to specify still leaves the utterance entirely idiomatic and acceptable, this can surely be classed as a case of Elleipsis.

Again, the Stoics believed that a third-person verb standing in isolation could not constitute a complete sentence, since the *lekton* it signifies is ἐλλιπές (D.L. 7.63 (33F3); and *cf.* Donnet 1967: 31f., for Stoic influence in this matter on the professional grammarians). Presumably, however, they believed not that such a decontextualised verb was (*ceteris paribus*) ambiguous, but rather that it was indefinite, ambiguity arising only where a context or situation of utterance did not supply the necessary information, and rather offered a definite choice between two or more subjects. Ordinary linguistic experience confirms that

---

[107] The comparable English sentence would run ... *gave the book to his father*, which, if it counted as ambiguous, would be so probably because of the unclear reference of *his*; but see also n. 109. Another sort of candidate is that described by Joos 1968: 72: 'In certain languages, notably Latin [he might have added Greek as well] a finite verb can assert all by itself, without a subject either spoken or infallibly reconstructed by the addressee'. In such cases omission of the subject could presumably produce ambiguity by Elleipsis because the omission is sanctioned by usage. Apollonius Dyscolus did in fact argue that third person verbs, unlike first and second person verbs, always need an explicit subject pronoun or noun 'to avoid being indefinite', 'ἕνεκά γε τοῦ μὴ ἀοριστοῦσθαι' (*synt.* 169.1ff.); otherwise any person or thing in the world (except the speaker and hearer) could be subject of the verb (ll. 5f.). Elsewhere he claims that pronouns, unlike nouns, are always determinate or unambiguous in their reference: *pron.* 10.4ff. Strictly, then, on Apollonius' view, only pronouns (in context, of course) will make third person verbs definite in the required way.

many ambiguities are cleared up by supplying a "missing" word or words, since discourse is naturally "gappy", and linguistic skill is in part a matter of filling out omissions correctly, by grasping unspoken assumptions or presuppositions on the basis of earlier stretches of discourse, of other bits of talk, of broader linguisitic and cultural conventions, or of shared specialised knowledge and experience. The same procedures are adopted and assumed, if to a lesser extent, by readers and composers of more formally restricted written language. Any number of expresions lifted out of context would be ambiguous; but because the filling-in process is part of what it is to use a language under constraints of time, space, attention-spans, *etc.*, not to mention rhythm or euphony, they cause no difficulty in practice, in real contexts. Elleipsis ambiguities must not be ambiguous just because they are out of context.

It was observed earlier (6.3.4, 6.3.6) that Stoic sources in particular, and ancient sources in general, offer no theoretical explication of the notions of "context" or "situation of utterance", and that this may be a reflection of what are, from a modern perspective, several important lacunae. No firm and explicit theoretical or methodological distinction was drawn between linguistic knowledge and other sorts of knowledge, or between a narrow linguistic "competence" and a broader linguistic ability, or between system and text. Sciences or disciplines to study and analyse these were in consequence lacking; and, ultimately, there was no motivation for distinguishing systematically between decontextualised utterances or sentences, and actual bits of talk or writing. Such "decontextualisation" of utterances (as one component of the process of theoretical "idealisation") is necessarily distortive if the goal is a semantics which will explain the whole of linguistic meaning, including those features of it which are essentially contextual (such as deictic reference), and especially if what is supposed to be under construction is a model of (some idealised form of) unitary user-knowledge, in the broadest sense, of a language. It is, however, often a legitimate methodological convenience, adopted to allow narrowly linguistic analysis of the phonological, grammatical, and semantic structures of utterances or system-sentences.

Resolution (or avoidance) of ambiguous utterances by users is not, standardly, thought to affect the usefulness and informativeness of "microlinguistic"[108] description of ambiguous system-sentences whose "text" counterparts may not actually constitute any sort of communicative problem in particular situations of utterance. Utterances' being ambiguous when (maximally) decontextualised is taken as criterial of their ambiguity, and the capacity of users to perform contextual or situational disambiguation may be held not to belong to narrow linguistic competence, its study being assigned to some other discipline within the broad study of language competence. The notion of context ought therefore to be made theoretically precise and comprehensive, whatever the grammarian's understanding of the preferred representation or model of the language; whether or not this is offered as a reconstruction of actual user-knowledge, the sentences it abstracts for description are still constructs, and it must be clear which properties are taken to belong to them, which have been disregarded, and how this will limit the scope of descriptions of them. And one of the most important products of decontextualisation is of course the elimination of "elleipsis" so-called, a pervasive feature of discourse, which is typically packed with so-called "sentence fragments" ostensibly derived from system-sentences by "elleipsis", whose place in descriptions of the language system has been much disputed: *e.g.* Dik 1968: 164ff.; Shopen 1973.

The Stoics did not conceive of context in this way, and alien modern preoccupations and preconceptions are not to be foisted on them. This still leaves intact and so far unmet the requirement that Elleiptic ambiguities be identified as such because of some unique defining characteristic. The Stoic

---

[108] I borrow the notions of "microlinguistics" and "maximal decontextualisation" from Lyons 1977: 591, and I am indebted to his whole discussion of "idealisation" and the methodological principles behind it (585ff.); also to Harris 1981: 32ff.

definition recorded by Diogenes may help a little here, with its specification that two or more meanings be understood 'in relation to *this* [individual] utterance'. The *de soph.* Stoics must have held, minimally, that for each Elleiptic utterance some determinate term(s) can be identified the absence of which, and of no other term(s), is sufficient for the ambiguity of the whole *lexis*. An additional condition could have been that 'this *lexis*' will be the minimal ambiguity-bearer, a particular utterance which in isolation from other particulars will be understood in two or more ways, regardless of what happens to it in association with this or that other *lexis* (or group of *lexeis*).

A possible justification in the case of the *de soph.* illustration is that in idiomatic ancient Greek two different relations of belonging, both current in contemporary culture, were signalled by use of one and the same genitive construction, and that it is the omission of appropriate qualifiers which produces the ambiguity. Sperber and Wilson 1986: 188 argue that genitives are not ambiguous but "semantically incomplete", semantic interpretation of sentences containing them requiring contextual information even if ambiguities and referential indeterminacies have been resolved. So it could be claimed on behalf of the Stoa that even at the level of the *lekton* neither signification will count as "complete". The only "incomplete", ἐλλιπῆ, *lekta* of which there is definite knowledge are, admittedly, predicates uncombined with subject cases (D.L. 7.58, 63 (33M, F3)); but it may be that ⟨ ... be of some (person)⟩ (⟨ ... εἶναι τινός⟩), say, is an incomplete predicate in the sense that it requires another case (*e.g. master's, father's*) to make it a predicate suitable for combination to form a proposition, interrogative, or other complete *lekton*. However, predicates known to require an additional, oblique, case in this way are significations of what traditional grammar came to call transitive verbs, and so are not precisely comparable either (D.L. 7.64).

Now the *lexis* will only be understood in two or more ways in some context if the addressee is a slave, or thought to be a slave, and presumably it is to be thought of as being uttered in just such circumstances. It is a presupposition (to use modern jargon) of there being an ambiguity that the person of whom the inquiry is being made, if it is a genuine request for information, is a slave or thought to be a slave. (I am assuming Sedley's emended text, and ignoring the "parasitic" possibilities that the utterance is being produced, say, in order to amuse or insult, or in a play, or said to a non-personal addressee.) That it is still counted as a case of ambiguity, and is so because of the omission of the "mediate" qualifier, illustrates the distance between the Stoic conception of ambiguity, which attaches to concrete particulars, and that of the modern linguists and semanticists who construct decontextualised and abstract objects of analysis. What obviously – obviously today – cries out for elucidation is the relation between ambiguous utterances and what are today called their presuppositions; and in general the Stoics were apparently blind to the need for a precise and comprehensive statement of the conditions under which Elleiptic ambiguity is the result of insufficient relevant information from a context, and when it is due to an utterance's inherent deficiency.

A passage from Boethius, already referred to in 4.5, is of interest here as well (*P.L.* 64, *div.* 888Dff.). A distinction is drawn between ambiguities and expressions which, while signifying only one thing, do so in many ways; Boethius calls the latter 'secundum modum', 'according to the mode [of signifying]'. What makes the semantic difference is the annexed *determinatio*: for instance, what is *infinitum* may be "determined" as limitless in measure, number, or species. In such cases there is simply too little information in an utterance for a listener to understand even one definite thing. Saying *homo*, for example, will just confuse and mislead; you must say *homo quisque ambulat* (*Some man is walking*) or *omnis homo ambulat* (*Every man is walking*) (889AB); similarly, *det mihi, let him give me*, gives no information about what is to be given, *ad me veni, come to me*, none about the place or time of meeting. Ambiguities are different because with them people are individually quite certain what they have understood, even if they come to different conclusions: and 'reasonably so', 'rationabiliter', as far as the words of the utterance are concerned. In contrast, there can be no 'reasonable', 'aliqua ratione', interpretation of *Let him give me* or *Come to me*, and the audience can only make conjectures. The interest of this passage – which, incidentally, has no obvious Stoic links – lies particularly in the rôle it assigns to hearer understanding, and in particular that of the "reasonable man". It will be remembered that the Stoics behind the D.L. definition made it a condition of ambiguity that 'two or more meanings are understood with reference to' any candidate utterance (4.9). Perhaps the *de soph.* Stoics too relied on audience reactions to utterances to decide whether what was said was determinate enough to qualify as ambiguous by Elleipsis. Such a procedure would, of course, be open to the objections that audiences might well disagree about particular utterances (as was noted in 4.9), and that in some cases agreement might be impossible in principle – even were the judgement of the appropriate expert and "reasonable man" *par excellence*, the Stoic sage, accepted as reliable whenever settlement of the matter was possible.

There are other objections to be raised. The first and most pressing is that there are in general many ways in which a person can belong to or "be of" another, and that it has not been shown even with reference to ancient Greek cultural and social conventions that there are only two such relations between which a choice must be made if it is to be clear just what is being asked of the addressee. It might also be objected (along lines suggested by Richman 1959: 89ff.) that, even if the relation of belonging between two persons, in a given cultural environment, can be exhaustively subdivided into belonging-by-blood-kinship, and belonging-by-ownership-possession, that does not make the utterance here ambiguous. Rather, it is general, and its defectiveness lies in failing to make clear in which subgroup the relation alluded to belongs, not in not indicating what kind of relation is in question. The difficulty, which has come up before (4.4), is determining when there is one, subdividable, group of things going under one name, and when there are two unrelated ones. The Stoics, as far as is known, may simply have appealed to general principles about the components and structures of the world and of people's knowledge of it to defend the principle that conceptual categories can always be made clear-cut.

Other cases are problematic because it is uncertain whether they would belong in Elleipsis or some other species, or indeed in both at once. The English sentence *Can you play?* might be assigned either to Homonymy in Compounds, because of the contextual homonymy of *play*, or to Elleipsis, on the grounds that the speaker has failed to specify the object of play (the saxophone, poker). Again, it is common practice in English and to a lesser extent in more highly-inflected Greek and Latin to clarify the reference of a pronoun by repeating its noun: would this be resolving an instance of Elleipsis?[109]

That classifiers of ambiguity really did disagree over the right way to deal with what look to be Elleipsis ambiguities will be established, I hope, by the passages from rhetoricians which I shall cite later (8.2).[110] Finally, it is worth noting another text which confirms that for the Stoics some omissions produce neither ambiguity nor obscurity. Plutarch reports:

Then again they say that the doctor orders his pupil to cut and cauterise with omission [παράλειψις] of 'at the proper time and in due measure' and the music teacher [tells him] to play and sing with omission of 'in tune and in time', so that they scold pupils who have performed unskilfully and amiss. (*St. rep.* 11.1037E)

The context of the teacher's instructions seems to be enough in itself to convey the correct conditions of fulfilment of his orders. It would be unreasonable to characterise the sentence *cut and cauterise!* as signifying two or more determinate things, unlike the *de soph.* example, but quite plausible to regard it as indeterminate in scope (the response being: *cut and cauterise whom? when? (etc.)*).

---

[109] Both of the *prog.* Significant Part examples (see 6.5.3) could be diagnosed as turning on a pronoun's ambiguity of reference, yet are classed by the Stoics as grouping ambiguities: my point is that there seems room enough for disputing that analysis.

[110] Another possibility is that Stoic Elleipsis would embrace some cases of Aristotelian Amphiboly: 6.7.4, n. 155.

6.4.5 Pleonasm (de soph. 13.10–12G, 22E)

To judge by its title the fifth species in the *de soph*. list is the contrary of Elleipsis: an expression in this group will have two or more senses because it will have some term(s) "too many". In the illustration, the "superfluous" word is μή, *not*, which must have been labelled "pleonastic" on the grounds that it is strictly unnecessary for the construction of sentences with verbs such as *forbid*, ἀπαγορεύειν, although such verbs do take what is traditionally called the "pleonastic" or the "sympathetic" negative (an example at Thucydides 1.29.3: ʽἀπεροῦντα μὴ πλεῖν ἐπὶ σφᾶςʼ). So once again a characteristic of idiomatic Greek – the use of intensifying negatives with certain verbs – is associated with the factor identified as responsible for an ambiguity.[111] The "pleonasm" tag implies that one of the two possible meanings, "he forbade him not to sail", is non-standard, as indeed it is: the (*not*) of the example is pleonastic only with reference to the standard construction with verbs of forbidding.

In the *de soph*. list Elleipsis and Pleonasm are located between an obviously word-based ambiguity species and what are obviously grouping ambiguities. Perhaps, then, they may be intended to classify complexes whose constituents are all univocal and whose constructions are constant. I have already argued that the Elleipsis example cannot be classed as syntactically ambiguous because of the authors' tacit restriction of syntax to ordering. But this argument appears not to apply to Pleonasm. The Stoics could surely have assigned at least this example of Pleonasm to the species Significant Part, which classifies expressions whose constituent words can be variously "ranged" or ordered. For it looks as though what is unclear in this sentence is whether *not* is "grouped" or "ranged" with the finite verb or with the infinitive. Only com-

---

[111] The species has nothing in common with the notion of "redundancy" current in contemporary information theory, and perhaps extendable, with caution (Hockett 1987: 36), to natural languages.

binative syntax appears in doubt, and suitable terminology is available, from Galen's account of Significant Part, to describe this sort of grouping.

A first response to this puzzle might be that for the *de soph.* Stoics μή is non-significant. But all Stoic parts of speech seem to have been significant, in some sense, and all words parts of speech (see 6.3.5.2);[112] and "non-significant parts" in this classification are not non-significant words, but mere bits and pieces of words, the letters and syllables that are parts of *lexis*.

More plausibly, the authors may have held that the sort of "ranging" left unclear by Significant Part expressions is inapplicable to this utterance. Some Stoics seem to have recognised the implicit negativeness in verbs of forbidding. This report, from Plutarch, is presented as a genuine piece of Stoic doctrine, albeit one Plutarch typically turns against the school:[113]

The Stoics say that people who make prohibitions say one thing, prohibit another, order another: for a man who says *do not steal* says [λέγει] just this, *do not steal*, ⟨forbids stealing, and orders⟩ not stealing. (*st. rep.* 11.1037D–E = S.V.F. 2.171)

One element of the analysis is that *forbid* has implicit ((συμ) παρεμφαινόμενον?) in it the negative made explicit in *do not steal*.[114] On one reading of the *de soph.* example, then, *not* will be convention's way of making that negative explicit: strictly, it belongs "inside" *forbade*. The other reading will treat *not* as

---

[112] μή is commonly listed by the grammarians as an adverb: *e.g.* D.T. *ars gr.* 79.1; Herodian (*G.G.* 3) 489.8f; A.D. *synt.* 347.12–348.4. The Stoics did not count adverbs as separate parts of speech: D.T. Sch. 520.11–17; Priscian *inst.* 2, 54.10–12.

[113] I read '... ἀπαγορεύει δὲ ⟨κλέπτειν, προστάσσει δὲ⟩ μὴ κλέπτειν' at S.V.F. 2.171, p. 49, l. 4; Mezinac's addition is plainly justified by the preceding sentence, *contra* Pachet 1978: 364f., who wants the text to reflect the ambiguity of the Pleonasm example in the *de soph.* list: this is to overlook the fact that Plutarch's report must concern the *lekta* signified by, or the *pragmata* performed by the utterance of, the *logos Do not steal*.

[114] The Stoa did have the idea of a negative's governing a proposition (Sextus *M.* 8.90 (34G5)), but did not extend it to the relation between the other constituents of a *lekton*. This governing negative is "pleonastic", *M.* 8.89 (34G2–4), but not, of course, in the way *not* is in the example. For (συν) παρέμφασις as a Stoic term: *e.g.* Chrysippus *Logical Questions* col. 10, l. 25, col. 12, l. 13 (= S.V.F. 2.298a, p. 107, l. 9, p. 108, l. 22); Alexander *an. pr.* 402.26; and see 3.5, 6.4.3.

integral to the phrase which signifies whatever is being forbidden, and it belongs with *to sail*. In consequence, only one sense of the sentence hangs on a "grouping" comparable with the combinations of Significant Part ambiguities; the first way of reading makes *not* a constituent, a "part", of the expression only by courtesy of linguistic usage.

My second proposal is more general, and looks to an aspect of the classification already familiar from discussion of the Homonymy in Simples/in Compounds distinction (6.3.6). Pleonastic ambiguities are indeed open to more than one construction: they are none the less classed separately because at least one of the parts which perform a syntactic shift is not grammatically necessary for conveying one of the possible senses. Presumably the presence of the superfluous item must be sanctioned by idiom, as is true of *not* here, just as Elleipsis ambiguities must be idiomatically, not arbitrarily, deficient. The excision of some "part" of a Significant Part ambiguity would, in contrast, alter or destroy all its possible meanings, not eliminate one of them alone. The *de soph.* Stoics may have contended that the reason Pleonastic ambiguities occur is not that they are syntactically ambiguous (although they are) but that some "extra" term is included in them. Hence a distinct species was provided to accommodate them (*cf.* Edlow 1975: 434).

This position is not unassailable. "Pleonastic" ambiguities, it might be objected, merely constitute a species of Significant Part, and should be recognised as such.[115] Still, there may be cases where there seems little to choose between a syntactic and a Pleonastic label. The rhetoricians Quintilian and Fortunatianus report some instances of just this type; and the approaches to deficient and pleonastic ambiguities taken by them and by other non-Stoic rhetoricians and grammarians will be discussed in 8.2.

---

[115] I doubt, however, whether this consideration helped prompt Galen's criticism at 14.13f.G, 23E (translation in 5.5) that the Stoic system jumbles together generic and specific groupings: his attack is rather on the Significant/Non-significant Part division: 14.14f.G, 23f.E.

6.4.6 Theon on Elleipsis and Pleonasm

Here Elleipsis has been placed after the species which classify grouping ambiguities. Perhaps Theon's dialecticians concentrated on ambiguities in which the speaker's intended grouping of the expression's constituents is in doubt, although additional items will clarify. Hence, Elleipsis' new location may be a genuinely Stoic feature of the system, even if it remains a puzzle how these Stoics would have dealt with the *de soph.* Elleipsis illustration; perhaps they argued that it is not "strictly" ambiguous.

It may still seem tempting to see Theon's hand in Pleonasm's absence from his list; there is, after all, a Pleonasm mode in his second classification of causes of obscurity: 130.23–8 (see 8.2). But his application of Pleonasm there is so wide and idiosyncratic that he is extremely unlikely to have simply relocated it there from the dialecticians' list.[116] Another possible explanation is that the *prog.* Stoics analysed all expressions which their *de soph.* colleagues would call Pleonastic as syntactically ambiguous, and removed them *en masse* to Significant Part. This case too may even have been reckoned not strictly ambiguous, on the grounds that a competent Greek speaker would not usually use it to mean "he forbade him not to sail".

Theon's account of (what is called) "obscurity on account of several words", ἀσάφεια διὰ πλείονα ⟨ὀνόματα⟩ (76.24–6), however, points to a still more radical explanation.[117] The account occurs (76.22–32) in a discussion of the exercise known as "Myth" (72.27–78.13). Obscurity is said to occur 'when what is said can be understood in several ways, nothing being either added or taken away' – which looks decidedly like a description of a sort of ambiguity, not of obscurity. The inconsistency disappears if Theon is tacitly, and illicitly, combining two sorts of material: the dialecticians' account of

---

[116] On Theon's version of Pleonasm, see 8.2.
[117] The importance of Elleipsis and the missing Pleonasm species for understanding the contents and structure of the first list of causes of obscurity has already been made, in a slightly different form, by Atherton 1988: 417.

ambiguity, and the list(s) of obscure single terms – homonyms and unusual words – drawn on again at p. 80, whose background is Aristotelian, not Stoic (as noted in 5.2.1). The most economical explanation for the anomalous definition of "obscurity" in word-complexes is that he is working from the same sources in both places. If so, the supposed definition of "obscurity in word-complexes" must be a version of the dialecticians' definition of ambiguity, for it is ambiguity they are called on to classify later, whatever Theon says about their definition. If this interpretation is correct, the *prog*. Stoics will have explicitly excluded cases of Elleipsis and of Pleonasm from their classification of ambiguities. They may have argued that saying too much, unlike saying too little, cannot produce ambiguity, although it can obscure one's point, alienate the audience's attention, and so forth. Chrysippus is reported to have held that an orator's ἐλλείψεις should be tolerated even if they offend against the canons of correct style; whether such omissions are cases of ambiguity is not recorded (Plutarch *st. rep.* 28.1047B).

Galen's criticisms of the Stoic list suggest how this understanding of Elleipsis and Pleonasm would work in practice. He mentions neither species by name in the course of his attack on the classification, and his silence is best explained by the fact that he regards both as incidental linguistic defects, not as ambiguity modes at all: they will simply be "terseness", ἔνδεια, and "long-windedness", μακρολογία, or "repetitiveness", περιττολογία, under different names (see ch. 2, 7.5G, 12E, where these three are listed as instances of non-essential stylistic defects). Further, the two are counted as separate stylistic defects in many rhetorical and grammatical accounts of style (see 8.2, 8.3). Although Pleonasm could be thought of as an offence against the peculiarly Stoic excellence of "conciseness", συντομία (D.L. 7.59), and would be undesirable whether or not it gives rise to inclarities, I suspect that here both it and Elleipsis would have been handled as sources of obscurity – which, of course, is Theon's topic, and his occasion for introducing the dialecticians' classification.

348

Where, then, can Elleipsis in the classification of the causes of linguistic obscurity in Narrative have its origin? Surely, in the same account of the causes, not of ambiguity, but of linguistic obscurity, to which the ambiguity classification originally made a contribution, and with which it has become confused. What suggests this line of reasoning is the presence of the two new species before Elleipsis, Hyperbaton and Interpolation, neither of which can plausibly be interpreted as a species of ambiguity. My hypothesis is that while using a Stoic handbook on style Theon, or his immediate source, found a section on clarity and obscurity which looked promising, and which included a classification of types of ambiguity, which was then inserted (with modifications to suit its new context) into the account of obscurity. Having got some way through the list, and having failed to notice or having temporarily forgotten that ambiguity is but one source of obscurity in the dialecticians' system, Theon or his source (and either or both may have been relying on memory) started to insert into it extraneous material from the general account of obscurity. The error or lapse of memory was noticed almost at once, and the ambiguity classification proper gets under way once more, but without explanation or apology, and with Hyperbaton and Interpolation, and possibly Elleipsis as well, having been wrongly included. In brief, Theon will have overlooked the original Stoic distinction between ambiguity and obscurity on two separate occasions: in the discussion of Myth, and in the discussion of Narrative.

The original Stoic theory will have contained Pleonasm, but as an independent cause of obscurity; and Elleipsis may have come under that heading too. The brevity of Theon's treatment of Elleipsis could be explained by his anxiety to get back to the ambiguity classification proper once he had realised his error. It is alien to that classification on two other counts. Theon does not say explicitly of Elleipsis that it produces ambiguity, merely that 'omitting certain words is contrary to clarity', 82.25f.; in contrast, all the examples of Common, Part, Significant Part, and Reference are either expressly described as, or unmistakably implied to be, ambiguous. Further, Hyperbaton, Interpolation, and Elleipsis are the only *prog.* species not illustrated.

From Theon's point of view, intruding two, or even three, species of obscurity into an ambiguity classification would be a careless lapse. Evidence already marshalled, however, suggests that he wanders from his Stoic source elsewhere; and this is not, in any case, a scholarly report of Stoic doctrine. Pleonasm and Elleipsis both appear in his classification of causes of obscurity under the heading "Law", but that version of them is at once so unorthodox, and so much in keeping with the rest of that list – which looks decidedly non-Stoic – that a Stoic model for those two species is highly unlikely.[118]

Assessment from the Stoic standpoint is still more difficult, for independent material by which to judge their position is not available, as it is in Theon's case. It might perhaps seem reasonable to expect Pleonasm and Elleipsis to form a pair, but their association is only usual, not invariable; the contrast required by context may be that between completeness and deficiency, or between harmony and excess. Many topics within Stoic dialectic were developed using these concepts:

i *logical validity*: an argument may be inconclusive or inconcludent, κατὰ παρολκήν/κατ' ἔλλειψιν: Sextus *M*. 8.431, 434 (36C3, 5), *P.H.* 2.147 ἔλλειψις, 150 παράλειψις;[119]
ii *etymology*;[120]

---

[118] In no other rhetorician have I met so broad and imaginative a treatment of Pleonasm and Elleipsis, and the rest of the classification is similarly idiosyncratic: see 8.2.

[119] I assume, *pace* Ebert 1991, that ἀπέραντος, 'inconclusive', ἀσύνακτος, 'inconcludent', are Stoic terms: see further 7.5 (esp. n. 27), 7.6.

[120] The word-formation principles of Varro's etymology (*e.g. ling. lat.* 5.6), possibly Stoic in origin, comprise the excision, addition, transposition, and transmutation of letters and syllables. Some of the etymologies attributed to Chrysippus strongly suggest he at least applied this *quadripertita ratio* (on which see n. 101): *e.g.* λύπη, pain, from λύειν, dissolve (pleonasm; Cicero *Tusc. disp.* 3.61); λαός, people, from λαλός, talk (elleipsis; Herodian *pros. cath.* (*G.G.* 3.1), 108.9ff.; ἀταλός, tender, from ἀπαλός, soft (transmutation; *Etymologicum Gudianum* cod. d², *s.v.* ἀταλός, ed. De Stefani, p. 224); καρδία, heart, from κρατία, power (transposition and transmutation; Galen *P.H.P.* 3.5.28, p. 206, ll. 15ff.); αἰών, eternity, from ἀεὶ ὄν, ever being (elleipsis and transmutation; Varro *ling. lat.* 6.11). Augustine's *de dialectica* account (ch. 6, 8.26ff.C 90ff.P) unfortunately stops short of a detailed report of the Stoic approach to word-formation.

iii *psychology and ethics*: "pleonasm" has an important rôle in the definitions of πάθος, emotion: *e.g.* Galen *P.H.P.* 4.2.8ff., p. 240, ll. 11ff. (part, 65J); and of ἁμάρτημα, error or wrong action: Stobaeus 2.93.14ff. (= *S.V.F.* 3.500 (59K));

iv *semantics*: *lekta* are either deficient or complete, αὐτοτελῆ, D.L. 7.63 (33F3), τελεῖον, Ammonius *int.* 44.20 (33q, LS 1987: 2: 203, 1. 3); and certain types of non-propositional but truth-valued *lekta* differ from propositions by containing a "redundant" part or other feature: D.L. 7.68; Ammonius *int.* 3.1–3 (and see 6.5.2).

6.4.7 *Aristotle on Elleipsis and Pleonasm*

There are no Elleipsis or Pleonasm modes in the *s. el.*, and Aristotle's rejection of a solution of such fallacies as the "Dog-father" by appeal to an ambiguity has already been mentioned (6.4.3), Elleiptic-type expressions not being necessarily πολλαχῶς λεγόμενα (24.180a19f.). Aristotle does not, however, explore the criteria under which they would be so. At *rh.* 2.24.1401b34-1402a3, Elleipsis is a mode of non-linguistic apparent enthymeme, closely related to *Secundum quid* (1402a3–28), which does figure in the *s. el.* (6.168b11–16). Later (*rh.* 3.5.1407b4f.), Aristotle remarks that soothsayers are careful to fail to specify dates, since then they have a greater chance of being correct, but it is unclear whether this sort of trick produces ambiguity (the subject of 1406b32–8) or is more like the convenient generalities discussed from 1407b1. At all events, such ambiguity, if that is what it is, is not part of any systematic classification. So there is a real puzzle as to where, if anywhere, Pleonastic and Elleiptic expressions would fit in the *s. el.* (or in any other Aristotelian account of ambiguity). Galen may have got around the problem by implying in advance of his report of the Stoic list that they are not "really" ambiguities (as observed in 6.4.6), a tactic that still allows the claim that the Stoic system contains no new, non-Aristotelian ambiguity modes (14.7f.G, 23E).

The relation of the Stoic species to the *s. el.* list (an advance? a retrograde step? or just a sideways shuffle?) hangs on whether they are genuine ambiguity species; and the only way now to settle this question is to determine whether the *de soph.*

examples are real cases of Elleipsis or Pleonasm. I have already tried to present various grounds for supposing that they cannot be located elsewhere, and that by the Stoics' own lights criteria can be supplied for their inclusion under these species, albeit not ones free from objections.

6.4.8 Elleipsis and Pleonasm: conclusions

Dissatisfaction with the Stoic analysis of these expressions must entail criticisms, which have been tentatively sketched here, of the system's classificatory principles and of its semantic and grammatical framework. The former have already come under attack for the distinction between the two Homonymies, the latter in the case of Common, and both will do so again in connection with the Part species. It may even have been these criticisms, or similar ones, which inspired the *prog.* Stoics' response.

6.5 The species of ambiguity 4: Significant Part, Non-significant Part, Part

6.5.1 The Part species: texts and translations

de soph. 13.13–14.1G, 22–3E

ἕκτην φασὶν εἶναι τὴν μὴ διασαφοῦσαν τί μετὰ τίνος ἄσημον   13
μόριον τέτακται, ὡς ἐν τῷ καινυκενηπαρελασσεν. τὸ   14
γὰρ ⟨η⟩ στοιχεῖον ⟨ἢ πρῶτον ἢ τελευταῖον⟩ ἂν γένοιτο   15
⟨ἢ⟩ διαζευκτικόν. ἑβδόμη δέ ἐστιν ἡ μὴ διασαφοῦσα τί μετὰ   16
τίνος τέτακται σημαντικὸν μόριον, ὡς ἐν τῷ   17
(p. 14 Gabler)
πεντήκοντ' ἀνδρῶν ἑκατὸν λίπε δῖος Ἀχιλλεύς.   I

(6) The sixth they say is [the species] which fails to make clear   13
which non-significant
part is ranged with which [non-significant] part, as in   14
καινυκενηπαρελασσεν;
for the element ⟨η⟩ might be ⟨the first letter [*sc.* of the word ἧπαρ,   15
liver] or the last letter [*sc.* of the word κενή, *empty*]
or⟩ the disjunction [*i.e.* 'or' in 'καί νυ κεν ἢ παρέλασσεν …', 'and   16
now he would have driven past, or …' (*Il.* 23.382)]. (7) The seventh
[species] is that which fails to make clear with
which [significant part] which significant part is ranged, as in: 17

352

(p. 14 Gabler)

Noble Achilles left 50 [out] of 100 men [or: ... 100 [out] of 50 men or: 1
... 150 [of] men].

prog. 82.3–19

ἔτι δὲ καὶ   3
ὅταν τι μόριον ἄδηλον ᾖ, μετὰ τίνος συντέτακται, οἷον   4
ουκενταυροις ὁ Ἡρακλῆς μάχεται· σημαίνει γὰρ   5
δύο, οὐχὶ κενταύροις ὁ Ἡρακλῆς μάχεται, καὶ οὐχὶ ἐν   6
ταύροις ὁ Ἡρακλῆς μάχεται. ὁμοίως δὲ ἀσαφὴς γίνεται   7
φράσις καὶ ὅταν τι σημαῖνον μόριον ἄδηλον ᾖ, μετὰ τί-   8
-νος συντέτακται, οἷον   9
οἱ δὲ καὶ ἀχνύμενοί περ ἐπ' αὐτῷ ἡδὺ γέλασσαν.   10
ἀμφίβολον γὰρ πότερον ἐπὶ τῷ Θερσίτῃ ἀχνύμενοι, ὅπερ   11
ἐστὶ ψεῦδος, ἢ ἐπὶ τῇ καθολκῇ τῶν νεῶν· καὶ πάλιν,   12
δῆμον Ἐρεχθῆος μεγαλήτορος, ὅν ποτ' Ἀθήνη   13
θρέψε Διὸς θυγάτηρ, τέκε δὲ ζείδωρος ἄρουρα.   14
πότερον τὸν δῆμον ἢ τὸν Ἐρεχθέα φησὶν ὑπὸ τῆς Ἀθη-   15
νᾶς τραφῆναι καὶ τικεῖν τὴν γῆν. παρὰ ταύτην δὲ τὴν   16
ἀμφιβολίαν τὰ Ἡρακλείτου τοῦ φιλοσόφου βιβλία σκο-   17
τεινὰ γέγονε κατακόρως αὐτῇ χρησαμένου ἤτοι ἐξεπίτη-   18
δες, ἢ καὶ δι' ἄγνοιαν.   19

And again, [there is obscurity/ambiguity]   3
whenever some part is unclear, with which [part] it is arranged, *e.g.*   4
Heracles fights ουκενταυροις: for it signifies   5
two things, "not with centaurs (οὐ κενταύροις) Heracles fights", and   6
"not amongst
bulls [*or*: in Tauri] (οὐκ ἐν ταύροις) Heracles fights". (3) Likewise,   7
there is obscure
language too whenever some significant part is unclear, with   8
which [significant] part it is arranged, *e.g.*:   9

'They [*sc.* the Greeks] despite their anger at him laughed   10
gaily' (*Il.* 2. 270):

for it is ambiguous whether they are angry at Thersites (which   11
is false) or at the drawing down of the ships; and again,   12

'The people of great-hearted Erechtheus whom Athena, Zeus'   13
daughter,
once nourished and the fruitful earth brought forth' (*Il.* 2.547–8):   14

[it is ambiguous] whether it says that it was the people or   15
Erechtheus who were nourished by Ath-
ena and whom the earth brought forth. It is because of this   16
ambiguity that the books of Heraclitus the philosopher are obscure   17
to such a degree, whether he employed it intention-   18
ally, or else out of ignorance.   19

6.5.2   Significant Part

The illustration given by Galen has already appeared in the *de soph.* as an example of the Aristotelian mode(s) Combination/Division (2.8G, 4E), and probably as a result it is not explained here in ch. 4 (14.1G, 23E). Galen borrowed it directly from the *s. el.* (4.166a37f.), but its appearance here cannot by itself prove that the author of the Stoic list had one eye on his Aristotle. One of its possible meanings is apparently not eliminated by its inherent absurdity (as noted in 6.3.6):

πεντήκοντ' ἀνδρῶν ἑκατόν λίπε ⟨δῖος Ἀχιλλεύς⟩

can be grouped as:

πεντήκοντ' (ἀνδρῶν ἑκατόν) λίπε ⟨δῖος Ἀχιλλεύς⟩
= Noble Achilles left 50 [out] of 100 men;

or as:

(πεντήκοντ' ἀνδρῶν) ἑκατόν λίπε ⟨δῖος Ἀχιλλεύς⟩
= Noble Achilles left 100 [out] of 50 men;

and also perhaps as:

(πεντήκοντ') ἀνδρῶν (ἑκατόν) λίπε ⟨δῖος Ἀχιλλεύς⟩
= Noble Achilles left 150 [of] men'.

Earlier Galen claimed that 'the difference [*sc.* in meaning] lies in *man* either being divided from *fifty* or combined with it' (2.8f.G, 4f.E). In the *s. el.*, however, the sentence appears as an application of the rule that 'the same *logos*, divided and combined, might not seem always to mean the same thing': 4.166a35f., *cf.* 20.177a34f.; this description follows Aristotle's account of Division at 166a33–5, but obviously applies equally to Combination. Possible syntactic groupings of the words in a complex can thus be neutrally characterised as combined or divided: but this is not their usual purpose in the *s. el.*, where Combination and Division are fallacy modes (see 6.2.4). Galen's explanation of the ambiguity is admirably clear, and its neutral use of the notions of combining and dividing straightforward. The problem is that he fails to observe the way his account actually distorts the system he champions. In contrast, the *de soph.* classification, and the *prog.* list in its original form, were classifications of ambiguity types, and their versions of Significant Part are neutral with regard to the actual or possible positions adopted by speakers to an expression's meanings. Whatever comparisons are made between the Stoic and Aristotelian classifications, one must always remember that, strictly, the *s. el.* is not their predecessor at all, for it classifies a quite different sort of thing.

Another peculiarity of the *s. el.* list (also already remarked on: 5.4) is that, while Combination and Division are modes of linguistic fallacy, Aristotle is not at all sure they are modes of fallacy due to ambiguity, almost certainly because he did not have a firm idea of what a *logos* is. By locating syntax primarily at the level of the *lekton*, and only secondarily at the level of relations between parts of speech, the Stoics avoided problems of this sort. (That they did indeed approach syntax in this way has been cogently argued by Frede 1977: 71f., 1978: 54ff.) A *logos* is a significant string of words, which has meaning in virtue of signifying at least one (usually complete) *lekton* whose inherent and inalienable structure it "borrows". An ambiguous *logos* is construed in different ways according to the meaning (the complex, structured *lekton*) assigned to it.[121]

In handling syntax as a relation between *lekta*, the authors of both Stoic classifications have naturally to take on board whatever weaknesses the associated semantic theory may have (see already 6.2.3). Another important consequence is that, as *logoi* may turn out to have two or more structures imposed on the same constituents, and as, in some cases of ambiguity, constituents may undergo category shifts, *i.e.* from one word-class (part of speech) to another according to how the *logos* as a whole is interpreted, the constant constituents of the *logos* whose syntactic relations change cannot, in these cases at least, be identified as such-and-such elements or parts of speech, but only as such-and-such words or such-and-such *lexeis*. It might be objected too that, as a matter of fact,

---

[121] This understanding of syntax, as a relation between νοητά, "intelligibles", akin to *lekta*, was adapted by Apollonius Dyscolos: see 8.4.

grouping ambiguities of this sort do not occur, being resolved by prosodic features – pitch and/or emphasis – of actual utterances, and by punctuation marks in writing: the *logos* which the Stoic theory envisages as having two or more meanings turns out not even to exist. The problem was of great interest to the Western schoolmen grappling with Aristotle's fallacy modes Combination and Division. One medieval scholar seems to have gone as far as trying to pronounce the sentence *Quicquid vivit semper est* (*Whatever lives always is*) in as many ways as possible, to see if it could be said with a pause (which is how the boundary appears to have been perceived): Ebbesen 1981b, esp. 332, 340.[122] Modern linguists may interpret such features as superimposed by speakers on already complete strings of words: *e.g.* Lyons 1981: 219. Besides being indicators of syntax, emphasis, contrast, and the speakers' attitudes to their own utterances (Kooij 1971: 38ff., Hockett 1987: 29ff.), they are taken as capable of altering speech-act function systematically: for example, of making a formally declarative sentence function as a question, or an interrogative sentence function as a command.[123] How might Stoic dialecticians have handled such phenomena?

If *logoi* expressing such *lekta* have to be labelled ambiguous, at least when written (pragmatically ambiguous, moderns would say), a classification of possible (systematically contextualised) secondary significations of such *logoi* would need to be compiled. Complete *lekta* appear to have been distinguished at least primarily on functional grounds; the descriptions of them at D.L. 7.66–8 suggest as much. But could a *logos* borrowing the structure of a proposition take on the meaning and/or function of (say) an interrogative utterance? Passages from Diogenes and Ammonius seem to show that form and function could be separated, if we assume,

---

[122] Kirwan 1979: 43f. argues that Aristotle assumes that 'the speaker's pauses are bound to reveal' the construction of a Combination/Division ambiguity, and that he 'is surely wrong to imply that all ambiguities' of this type 'are thus resolved in the spoken language'. But surely all that Aristotle implies is that such disambiguation is possible, as it is not with Amphibolies.

[123] *Cf. e.g.* Kooij 1971: 38ff.; Lyons 1977: 30, 59f., 374, 398ff.; Hockett 1987: 29ff.

reasonably, that sentences have the form(s) of the *lekta* they signify. Thus the "quasi-proposition", ὅμοιον ἀξιώματι (D.L. 7.67, Ammonius *int.* 2.32ff.), has a propositional content but does not count as an ἀξίωμα proper 'because of the redundancy or emotional tone of some part [of it]', 'παρά τινος μορίου πλεονασμὸν ἢ πάθος' (D.L. *ibid.*); one of Ammonius' examples 'exceeds the affirmation [*sc.* the Aristotelian declarative sentence] by the addition of the intensive adverb *how*', 'πλεονάσαντος τῆς ἀποφάνσεως ... τῇ τοῦ ὡς ἐπιτατικοῦ ἐπιρρήματος προσθηκῇ' (*int.* 3.1–3). In the three illustrations the redundant or emotionally charged "parts" are *γέ* and *ὡς* (*bis*). Again, the example of the "at-a-loss" *pragma,* ἐπαπορητικὸν πρᾶγμα (D.L. 7.68), ⟨Can it be that pain and life are somehow akin?⟩, has the form of a question (*cf.* 66) but is not classed as such, and is actually described as 'different from a proposition', 'διενηνοχὸς ἀξιώματος', as if that were the relevant comparison. Ammonius argues that both the oath, ὁμοτικὸν πρᾶγμα (*e.g.* ⟨Let Earth now know this⟩), which 'exceeds the affirmation by the calling to witness of the divine', 'τῇ μαρτυρίᾳ τοῦ θείου πλεονάσαντος τῆς ἀποφάνσεως' (3.1f.), and the quasi-proposition, being alike receptive of truth and falsity, can be assimilated to the affirmation (2.35–3.1). Two other types of truth-valued, non-propositional *pragmata,* are listed, the "ekthetic" (*e.g.* ⟨Let this be a straight line⟩) and the "hypothetical" (*e.g.* ⟨Let it be supposed that the earth is the centre of the sun's orbit⟩). In all cases, what seems to make the difference is that the attitude – emotional or cognitive – of the speaker to the propositional content is included in the *pragma* itself, effected in a variety of ways (*e.g.* an extra particle, or an interrogative or subjunctive construction).[124] But the

---

[124] In the light of this variation between the indicative and the subjunctive moods, a distinction made by Apollonius Dyscolus takes on great interest for us: that between the mood of a verb as a form, an ἔγκλισις or inflection, and the mood of a verb as an abstract or semantic distinction of the verb, a διάθεσις, more precisely the ψυχικὴ διάθεσις: see Hahn 1951, esp. 37ff. Hahn 1951: 44ff. also argues, very plausibly, that Apollonius' subtle and technical notion of the ψυχικὴ διάθεσις was grossly misunderstood by his epigones as referring to the psychological attitude of the utterer of a verb-form; there is a comparable psychological classification of types of *logoi* at Ammonius, *int.* 5.1ff. In principle, the distinction would permit a further refinement relevant here: an interrogative sentence with its main verb

distinction we are seeking goes the other way: we want cases where the form of the *logos* stays constant, while its function changes.

Another problem concerns the rôle given to contrastive or to emphatic intonation in clarifying the meaning of the particular *lexeis* which the Stoic definition makes the bearers of ambiguity. If the Stoics progressed to such subtleties, nothing whatever is known of their work. The examples of Significant Part, and of Common, might perhaps have been presented as written, not spoken, *lexeis*; this is almost certainly the case with the Non-significant Part illustration (see 6.5.3). The explanation may go deeper still. That ancient Greek could have been less marked by sentential prosodic contours of the sort under consideration surely cannot by itself account for their almost total neglect by theoreticians in antiquity. (I am leaving to one side the quite separate phenomenon of the rhetorician's practical interest in the technicalities of delivery.) Tone languages need not, of course, be deficient in sentential intonations. Some interrogative words in ancient Greek had the rising pitch within the sentence, suggesting they had a degree of autonomy (Allen 1973: 252f.), although scholars disagree as to why the final acute was retained before pauses. Allen 1973: 248 feels this may be 'a feature of sentence prosody rather than of accent alone', but, even were there a general requirement that the final word in a sentence bear a high pitch, it would still be unclear whether types of utterance were systematically differentiated by intonation, and, if so, how. Particles and interrogatives are very common in written Greek, of course, but such literary texts need not reflect the properties of all the varieties of spoken discourse. An ancient theoretical distinc-

---

in the indicative (=ἔγλκισις), for example, may have an imperative meaning (=ψυχικὴ διάθεσις). Neither Apollonius nor the Stoics, however, seem to have taken this step. Stoics are known to have used ἔγλκισις of the "inflection" of a proposition, as we saw in 6.3.3, but not, so far as is known, of variations in mood. Although it is remotely possible that the Stoics are 'the ancients' who called both formal and abstract moods διαθέσεις (Choeroboscus (*G.G.* 4.2) 5.47ff.; reference from Hahn 1951: 31), there is no evidence that they anticipated Apollonius in arriving at the idea of "illocutionary force", even if this is the correct way to understand his ψυχικὴ διάθεσις (as claimed by Householder 1981: 4, 10).

tion was developed approaching that between the syntactic/ semantic and the phonological (and graphic) unity of the sentence or *logos* (see 8.1); but there is no indication that these concepts were used to analyse intonations as separable patternings, whether or not systematically imposable on different types of sentential structure. Until the end of antiquity, prosodic and diacritical signs were rare, but they did exist (see already 6.2.3): in contrast, standardised written symbols or techniques to signal intonation or stress within the sentence (or the word) were never invented (*cf.* Lyons 1981: 219), and are not found now outside specialised linguistic literature.

Now this might be taken to reflect a wide-spread intuition that only some prosodic features are intrinsic to utterances or sentences. It remains true that, even leaving on one side scribal or typographical conventions, such as italicisation, for purposes of emphasis and contrast, scientific transcriptional systems have been and are being devised to try to meet a felt need for more and more precise descriptions of utterances. The ancient lack of interest in accurate transcription may have been one result of the attitude of orthodox grammarians and philosophers (and hence of their heterodox, especially Skeptic, "parasitic" opponents) to the proper way to study ordinary language. They – the Stoics amongst them – do not seem to have developed, or needed to develop, theoretically precise concepts of context, of the relation between utterances of the same type, on the one side, and different contexts or situations of utterance, on the other, or of the implications of context and contextualisation for theories of language use and language comprehension. Unlike their modern counterparts, they had no theoretical or methodological need for distinctions between text- and system-sentences; grammatical form and discourse function; sense and force; what is in the language system and what is non-linguistic; whether as part of a theory of linguistic description, of language comprehension, or of meaning and language use in general (*e.g.* Lyons 1977: 30). Sentential intonations were not the 'treacherous no-man's land between the clearly linguistic and the clearly paralinguistic' (Hockett 1987: 140): they were *terra incognita*.

359

All the linguistic items in the *de soph.* example can be described as "parts", μέρη, of speech, *logos*. Evidence has already been assembled (6.3.5.2) to suggest that all Stoic parts of speech are somehow significant; so the Parts may not be "parts of *logos*" after all, but parts of *lexis*, sequences of articulate sounds or their written symbols, which, in the case of Significant Part ambiguities, also happen to be significant.[125] In the *de soph.* illustration, these "Parts" are nominals and a verb. Yet, for the Stoa, nouns and verbs signify quite different sorts of thing; and the question must arise, whether all the other Stoic parts of speech will also qualify as Significant Parts of *lexis*. The same holds for the *prog.* account of the version of this species, which is properly to be called "Signifying Part", σημαῖνον μόριον; whether σημαῖνον and σημαντικόν have different senses cannot, I think, be settled on the tiny amount of evidence available. All moveable elements in the example are significant, which suggests that the description means "which ⟨significant⟩ part is ranged with which ⟨significant⟩ part". This will make the interpretation of Non-significant Part a little more straightforward.

The verb 'τέτακται' in Galen's account of the species is translated 'ranged', as being vague enough to leave open the question whether the ranging or grouping in question is or is not syntactic. A striking feature of the description is its failure to appeal, explicitly or implicitly, to any classification of types of syntactic grouping, or of syntactic unit. A Part is "ranged" with another, it seems, so long as it somehow "goes" with it. Thus *fifty* can be characterised as ranged with (*of*) men or with *hundred*, despite the fact that this change in grouping involves a change both in grammatical case (not reflected in morphology) and in syntactic function. "Ranging" of this sort

---

[125] The Stoic distinction between Significant and Non-significant Parts of *lexis* is of course not the same as the Peripatetic distinction between parts of *logos* (= nouns and verbs) and parts of *lexis* (= all other word classes): see 6.3.5.2. In 4.6, n. 14, a distinction was observed between signifying λεκτικῶς, "linguistically", and signifying συμβολικῶς, "symbolically", used by Simplicius (*cats.* 64.18ff.) to contrast conjunctions such as *however*, *moreover* with textual signs. For the Stoa, such words would have crucial logical importance: whether or not they signify individual *lekta*, they must be considered parts of *logos*.

appears to capture no more sophisticated or precise a conception of linguistic structure than that implied by bracketing a pair of written words together, or by uttering them consecutively without a pause, or by otherwise indicating a link between them. This oddly naive approach to syntax, apparently neglecting rection (government) and even agreement (concord), as well as morphology (which anyway could plausibly find a home only at the linguistic level, as in the distinction of nominal cases), first showed itself in connection with Elleipsis and Pleonasm, and it will have its consequences for assessing Non-significant Part and Reference as well.

It seems to have been shared by the *prog.* Stoics, as will emerge later; and it is perhaps hinted at too in Chrysippus' name for the parts of speech, *element* or στοιχεῖον (*e.g.* Galen *P.H.P.* 8.3.13, p. 498, ll. 7f.), which was also applied to the letters of the alphabet (D.L. 7 56) The principal relations between letters – which were treated as exact correlates to vocal elements (6.2.3) – are those of permissible and impermissible ordering and grouping. This conception of the relation between words and syntactic wholes is standard in antiquity,[126] and, while it did not altogether prevent the development of more complex and appropriate conceptions of syntax and the varieties of syntactic relation, it continued to influence, and arguably to distort and stunt, this portion of grammar. It is unsatisfactory here not because it fails to make distinctions grammarians, with their different preoccupations, would make: for example, one between simple grouping and grouping-plus-categorisation types of Significant Part ambiguities, which today might be called phrase-structure ambiguities (Lyons 1977: 400f.) or immediate constituent ambiguities (Hockett 1987: 22). It is unsatisfactory rather because it fails

---

[126] A typical expression of the analogy between physical elements, letters, and words is to be found at D.T. Sch. 356.1ff.: the philosophers call the grammarians' parts of speech "elements", because, just as the elements produce syllables, and the cosmic elements bodies, so these come together to produce *logoi*: cf. *e.g.* 36.8ff., and esp. A.D. *synt.* 2.3–15.5, where σύνταξις is used both of the combination of syllables to form words, and of the structure of the *logos*, at the linguistic and the semantic/noetic level alike (esp. 2.3–3.2). Blank 1982: 8ff. argues that orthography formed a model for the new science of syntax.

to capture some syntactic, but non-grouping, ambiguities altogether: notably those Aristotle classed under Amphiboly, where what is unclear is which word is performing which grammatical/syntactic rôle in a given *logos*, as well as so-called "deep-structure" ambiguities in which two or more "deep" constructions are in play (like *illa vulgata*, *Flying planes can be dangerous*). Such a severely restricted concept of syntax is at least as worrying as the apparent limitation of important syntactic relations to those between subject and predicate within propositions, and, within predicates, between verbal predicates and cases; such relations are themselves characterised using the same narrow vocabulary (D.L. 7.64 (33G), 'συντακτόν', 'συντασσόμενα').

For all its famed precision and formalism, the Stoa could be surprisingly lax terminologically in a way that to an uncharitable observer might suggest profound conceptual confusions: or rather, a failure to recognise important distinctions at all. The use of (συν)τάττειν/(συν)τάττεσθαι for syntactic and non-syntactic association is one such case; another, possibly, the use of συνεστός ἐκ for the relations both of the various types of simple proposition to their constituents (cases and predicates) and of a reduplicative complex proposition to its (*viz.* simple propositions) (D.L. 7.68, 70 (34K2–7)) – relations whose fundamental logical distinction might reasonably be marked at the metalinguistic level. A report of the Stoic analysis of negative sentences with definite singular subjects (Alex. *an. pr.* 402.8ff.; see already 3.5) shows that the jargon for "affixing" the negation sign either to the predicate, or to the whole proposition, is the same, προστιθέναι: cf. 'προστεθειμένου', ll. 9f., l. 11. Although it is problematic how much can be deduced from such terminological coincidences, it is clear that such ambiguities could not have been diagnosed as due to Significant Part – the negation sign can hardly be described as "arranged with" either the verb or the whole sentence – and, however they were actually classified, they slip through the net of both the *de soph.* and the *prog.* lists. Here we are, unusually, able to criticise Stoic material using Stoic material.

Theon provides two illustrations (82.10, 13–15) to Galen's

one, and both of them appear genuine. Both come from Homer (*Il.* 2.270, 547f.), not an author whom Theon, so far as is known, made especially his own – according to the Suda, he wrote commentaries (now lost) on Xenophon, Isocrates, and Demosthenes – but of course *the* author of pagan antiquity; and Homer seems to have inspired one of the *de soph.* illustrations too (that of Non-significant Part). That Theon, like Galen, uses much the same form of words in the general description of both his Part species indicates that his report of the Stoic list is reliable in this respect at least. Theon's explanation of the first example is manifestly incorrect and incomplete, but this may be put down to his own laxity.

Each illustration contains a pronoun whose reference is unclear. The *prog.* Stoics, however, apparently treated the ambiguity as one of grouping. In the first, the "some part", τι μόριον, which can be variously "arranged" is the anaphoric pronoun 'αὐτῷ'. Theon's curious explanation is that the bearer is 'ambiguous whether they [*sc.* the Greeks] are angry with Thersites, which is false, or at the drawing down of the ships' (82.11f.). The Homeric context reveals no such 'drawing down', the two possible referents being Thersites and Odysseus, in their famous confrontation. Further, another double grouping is identifiable within the one line of the example, and this may be the real ambiguity in question: the participle 'being angered' or the verb 'they laughed' may be grouped with the preposition 'at', 'ἐπί'. The Achaeans could quite reasonably be said to be 'angered at' Thersites, or else 'laughing at' him in his humiliation; or 'laughing at' Odysseus to express their approval of his treatment of Thersites. None of the authentically Stoic *prog.* illustrations is either contextually or selectionally disambiguated.

In the second illustration, the "some part" is the relative pronoun 'ὅν', which could be grouped either with ''Ερεχθῆος' or with 'δῆμον' in the same line; the surrounding text shows that the people or community mentioned is the Athenian, so there is no contextual disambiguation. Theon's account of the ambiguity seems correct, although the analysis which survives need not be Stoic.

Both examples, then, provide unimpeachable evidence that some Stoics at least regarded pronouns (their "definite articles") as in some way significant, σημαίνοντα. This supplements the general testimony to that effect in, for instance, Apollonius and the Dionysian scholiasts (see 6.3.5.2.)

The "Parts" here too are very probably "parts of *lexis*". It is unclear what exact difference of meaning, if any, attaches to the *prog.* 'συντέτακται'; but *arrange*, no more than the *de soph. range*, seems not to have been used with anything like technical precision. Yet both sorts of relation are comfortably caught in that broad net, *arranged with*; and the Part species, as will emerge shortly, lets in relations which cannot even broadly be called syntactic.

Unlike the *de soph.* illustration, each *prog.* example contains a "fulcrum", so to say, the τι μόριον which has always to be grouped with one other variable Part, and which therefore determines the sense and syntax of the whole. More precisely, the second has one fulcrum ('ὄν'), the first two fulcra ('αὐτῷ,' 'ἐπί'), and it may on that account have to be entered under Significant Part twice over. An obvious objection to the wording of the description is that there may be cases in which no such fulcrum is identifiable, that is, where there is no one Part which is always paired with one other. This may be true, for instance, of the *de soph.* illustration.[127]

Theon approves of a philosophical training for orators (*prog.* 59.1ff.), although, as it is not obvious he had one himself (see 5.2.1), he may well have picked up his reference to Heraclitus at 82.16–19 in one or other of three places: the dialecticians' list; Aristotle *rh.* 3.5.1407b11–18; or some other rhetorical text dependent on the latter. The first option is perhaps the most likely; yet professional rhetoricians and theorists of style do express interest in Heraclitus' notorious obscurity. Aristotle started the tradition with his criticisms of

---

[127] This depends on what the group of variable syntactic units comprises. If it comprises *left, fifty, hundred*, and (*of*) *men*, then there will be no "some part" which is variously ranged; but if *left* is dropped the fulcrum will be (*of*) *men*, which is ranged with either *fifty* or *hundred*.

the difficulties to which punctuating Heraclitus' sentences tends to give rise, the example given (1407b16f.) being classifiable as a case of Significant Part, or of Combination/ Division, and it is just possible that Theon knew the *Rhetoric* directly (see 5.2.1). It seems highly implausible, all the same, that he should by his own wits have recognised the connection between Aristotle's account of Heraclitus' stylistic defects – which mentions neither ambiguity nor Combination/ Division explicitly – and Stoic Significant Part. Theon's own version of Combination/Division in his final list of the causes of linguistic obscurity bears little relation to anything in the *Rhetoric*, *Poetics*, or *s. el.*; and he confuses it with Common: see 6.2.4. Demetrius *eloc.* 192 (*cf.* D.H. *Thuc.* 46), in his discussion of the plain style, criticises Heraclitus for his looseness of expression, which makes it hard to identify the beginning of each section or "colon", and thus creates obscurity; but he does not mention anything like grouping ambiguity.

Stoic interest in and respect for Heraclitus are well documented from the earliest years of the school (*cf. e.g.* Long 1975/6; Schofield 1991: 74ff.) Cleanthes and Sphaerus both wrote commentaries on him, for example: D.L. 7.174, 178. His presence here confirms that no limit was set on the types of discourse to which Stoic stylistics applied, which available evidence suggests was indeed standard policy in the school (see 3.4). Theon too gives no sign the Stoic list was thus restricted. This *obiter dictum*, that Heraclitean obscurity – obscurity *non pareil* – is precisely and concisely explicable as the product of one, easily identifiable, form of ambiguity, here plainly set forth by Stoic dialecticians, looks like a deliberate attempt to impress, as well as to inform; and the criticism thereby conveyed suggests a deliberate distancing from the unhappy limitations of Heraclitus' style (as opposed to his thought). The Stoics themselves might, of course, have connected Significant Part with Aristotle's analysis of Heraclitean obscurity. This passage would then contain the only known Stoic allusion to the *Rhetoric*: far more reasonable to conclude that they reached their own analysis independently.

6.5.3   Non-significant Part, Part

The MS version of the *de soph.* illustration at 13.14G, 22E is:

καὶ νῦν καὶ μὴ παρέλασε

which Arnim cleverly emended after *Iliad* 23.382:

καινυκενηπαρελασ⟨σ⟩ε⟨ν⟩

while Gabler produced a new version of the text of Galen's explanation of the example:

τὸ γὰρ ⟨η⟩ στοιχεῖον ⟨ἢ πρῶτον ἢ τελευταῖον⟩ ἂν γένοιτο ⟨ἢ⟩ διαζευκτικόν

both of which are adopted by Long/Sedley 1987: 2: 231, ll. 13–15 (37Q7). Unfortunately, neither the original nor the emended versions are without their difficulties. Gabler was no doubt correct to identify the στοιχεῖον mentioned by Galen as the "element" – *i.e.* element of *lexis* – or letter η. The preserved MS text does actually contain the sequence 'μη', which could be read in context either as 'μή' ('not') or – unusually – 'μ' ἤ' ('... me, or ...'). This second reading would make excellent sense of Galen's explanation in its present form, with a single addition: '... for the element ⟨η⟩ might become the disjunction [*sc.* and not part of 'μή', on the more orthodox reading]'. The insurmountable objection is that this ambiguity is, without question, a case of Common.

The illustration, as emended by von Arnim, can be read in three ways:

1. καὶ νύ κεν ἢ παρέλασσεν
2. καί νυ κενὴ παρέλασσεν
3. καὶ νύ κεν ἧπαρ ἔλασσεν

of which the first is required by the Homeric context ('and now ⟨Diomedes⟩ would either have got past ⟨Eumalus⟩ or made the race a dead heat'). If Arnim's emendation is accepted, it must be accepted too that the *de soph.* Stoics allowed ambiguities which are possible in writing only (in the absence of prosodic and/or diacritical signs). Ignoring for the moment the sequence νυ κεν, which might not form part of the core ambiguity, readings 1 and 2 will be automatically distinguished from 3 by pitch and breathing. They may be distinguished from each other too by pitch and/or junctural features (according to the view taken of such properties, which were discussed in 6.2.3). Reading 2 is the least likely candidate, given that 1 and 2 together represent another Common ambiguity ('κεν ἢ'/'κενή'),[128] whereas 1 is the reading required by context. I take the possible readings, then, to be 1 and 3 only, and the original explanation of the example to have run something like:

τὸ γὰρ ⟨η⟩ στοιχεῖον ἂν γένοιτο ⟨ἢ πρῶτον ἢ⟩ διαζευκτικόν,

and the Non-significant Parts whose ranging is unclear will be:

η, παρ, ελασσεν.

If this interpretation is correct, the Stoics can still be defended against Galen's criticism (15.8ff.G, 24f.E), already discussed in 6.2.3, that they have no Accent ambiguity species, and on the very reasonable grounds that they took accent to be integral to a word, or to any piece of *lexis*, where spoken. They can still have argued that non-contextual prosodic changes (those not determined solely by a word's relation to other words in a sequence) produce a whole new spoken word, not one and the same word with different meanings. Spoken Non-significant Part ambiguities will still be possible if prosodic changes do not accompany each different reading. This approach to accent is so far superior to any other (as will emerge later) that it would anyway be uncharitable to deny it to the *de soph.* Stoics.

At the same time, if a written utterance can be so far from a faithful representation of its spoken counterparts, it is strange, to say the least, that the Stoic doctrine of the elements of *lexis* was not revised and expanded. The ancients never developed technical forms of transcription which would allow them to represent utterances which were distinct morphologically but not (or not so clearly) phonologically; even systems

---

[128] Of course, the two species might overlap: a given utterance might belong in two or even more species at once. But it must do so by different criteria in each case; I therefore feel justified in ignoring reading 2.

of punctuation were long in developing, and rarely applied before the end of antiquity. Still more seriously, written utterances like the present example might be rejected as proper bearers of ambiguity, on the grounds that their apparent ambiguity is merely the result of purely fortuitous orthographic conventions, and that analysis of ambiguities, as of all bearers of meaning, should begin after morphological analysis, even if this is in itself problematic. These objections will be familiar from the discussion of Common in 6.2.3.

Even without a secure text of the illustration, the scope of the species can be sketched, since Galen's accounts of its general description and (in part) of the example do survive. The reliability of his general account is confirmed, I think, by the similarity between it and his characterisation of Significant Part: presumably he is following his source's precise wording very closely at this point (just as Theon seems to be – but his account of the example does not have the same authority, and must be handled with more caution). The immediate problem is to identify the ἄσημα μόρια. At least three such Parts must be in play, variously rangeable with each other, just as the Significant Parts are too.[129] Galen's explanation refers to an "element", which, as it 'might become the disjunction', has to be the letter η. Now "elements" of this sort are elements of *lexis*, and as such are not necessarily significant, even if η becomes significant as the disjunction ἤ. So the Non-significant Parts would be letters, syllables, and groups of these, mere bits and pieces of the genuine words (=parts of speech) which are the Significant Parts of *lexis*.

If this is the right way to look at the Non-significant Parts, the *de soph.* Stoics cannot have been thinking of syntactic groupings when they spoke of such parts being "ranged" with one another. For these Parts to be "ranged" is just for them

---

[129] If the grouping is of Non-significant with Significant Parts, the *de soph.* Stoics will be guilty either of inconsistency (in changing the scope of the phrase 'with which part' between the two definitions) or of negligence (in not observing that permitted groupings include those between significant and non-significant parts). *Both* species could not classify such groupings, since then one or the other would be simply redundant.

to be strung together to produce one or other of several syntactically invariable word-sequences: and this is not itself a syntactic ordering. The bland and neutral verb 'τέτακται' in the description of the species must embrace what are surely two radically different sorts of grouping. But the Stoic authors did not draw, or did not draw precisely, the distinction between syntactic construal and conglomeration (the contrary process to morphological analysis of the ambiguous *lexis*) which seems obvious to the modern reader.

The text of the example of Part in the *prog.* and of its explanation is unproblematic. The obvious difference between this species and Non-significant Part is that the semantic status of these parts is unspecified. On the assumption that Theon is faithfully recording his Stoic source, the implication is that these Stoics intended groupings of Non-significant with Significant Parts, and perhaps of Non-significant Parts with one another, to fall within the compass of this species. Again, it is unlikely that Non-significant Parts *of speech* are in play.

The clue to interpreting the illustration is in the description of the species: it is unclear 'with which ⟨part⟩ some part is arranged'. That "some Part" must be the element κ. The example

ουκενταυροις (82.5)

can be read in two ways:

1. οὐ κενταύροις = not with centaurs
2. οὐκ ἐν ταύροις = not amongst bulls [*or*: not in Tauri (?)]

The difference in arrangement, and meaning, turns on how κ is paired, that is, on whether it is arranged with the sequence ου or with the sequence ενταυροις. The second of the two Parts looks to be non-significant, a mere string of sounds. The first, however, surely is a genuine word, a part of speech, and may therefore be significant, however the ambiguous expression is read, if all Stoic parts of speech are significant (see 6.3.5.2).[130]

---

[130] Unfortunately the definition of a negative proposition has been lost from D.L. 7.69, and οὐ (like μή) is not mentioned in any extant account of the Stoic doctrine of the parts of speech. At Sextus *M.* 8.89f. (34G), the οὐ(χ) in a negative

The presence and absence of κ are governed purely by phonological rules, and have no effect on the negative's semantic status. In the *prog.* illustration the "some Part" might alternatively be the sequence εν (which is either a word in its own right, or a piece of κενταύροις); or else the sequence ταυροις (to which the same considerations apply). "Arranging" would then have to extend to strictly syntactic grouping.[131]

This alternative approach has the advantage of explaining why the semantic status of the "some Part" itself is not specified; but it has the perhaps more powerful disadvantage of making the distinction between Part and Common a fine one indeed. Let αὐλητρις (the now-familiar example of Common) be analysed as two Parts, two sound/letter sequences, αὐλη and τρις. Of each could it be said that it is 'not clear with which Part it is arranged', in the sense that it is not clear whether each is "arranged with" its fellow (both being Non-significant Parts) or with the participle πεσοῦσα (both it and the partici-

proposition is referred to as an ἀπόφασις; at Alexander *an. pr.* 402.10, as an ἀποφατικὸν μόριον. Apollonius *coni.* 222.1ff. cites (and rejects) an argument that ἤ must be a conjunction because it can be replaced by οὐ, which, some say, is a conjunction, an argument with a definite Stoic "feel": compare the definitely Stoic argument that definite articles and pronouns belong in the same part of speech because the former can substitute for the latter: A.D. *pron.* 5.13ff.; D.T. Sch. 518.34ff.

[131] Similar examples, involving what the grammarians called ν ἐφελκυστικόν, "suffixed n", such as ἐστιναξιος (= 1 ἔστι Νάξιος, *He is a Naxian*; 2 ἔστιν ἄξιος, *He is worthy*) and ἠλθενηπιος (= 1 ἦλθε νήπιος, *A young person came*; 2 ἦλθεν ἤπιος, *A gentle person came*), are frequently cited as prime cases for the application of diacritical signs: *e.g.* D.T. Sch. 17.12, 114.2ff., 566.11ff. The example οὐκετι at 455.10 is treated as a case of indecision between two words (οὐκ ἔτι, *no longer*) and three (οὔ κέ τι, (roughly) *not at all*), the former being ruled out by context. In the first two examples, the *prog.* Stoics could identify the letter ν as the key moveable Part, itself Non-significant, arrangeable either with the Significant Part ἐστι, or with αξιος, which will be a Significant or a Non-significant Part according to its grouping. Alternatively, αξιος will be the "some Part", arrangeable either with the letter ν, a Non-significant Part, or with the Significant Part ἔστιν. On cases of "ν ἐφελκυστικόν", see Allen 1973: 225, 1987: 102. Blass 1890: 130 and n. 3 lists cases of syllable division in inscriptions which may suggest – if orthography is here a guide to pronunciation – that the sequence οὐ κενταύροις could anyway have been uttered and understood as οὐκ ἐν ταύροις: *e.g. C.I.A.* 2.1, 379. 3f. ʽκ]αὶ [αὐτός οὐ/κ ὀλίγα', 'and himself not a few' (integration p. 180; shortly after 229 B.C.E.); 467. 81f., ʽκαὶ ο [ὑ/κ ἐάσας', 'and not having allowed' (integration p. 250; late 2nd/early 1st cent. B.C.E.). Apollonius *pron.* 4.11ff. classifies οὐκερω as 'ἀμφίβολον', 'ambiguous', Αἴας as 'ὁμώνυμον', 'homonymous'; the former is a clear case of (Non-significant) Part, with the element κ as fulcrum (the two possible readings are οὐκ ἐρῶ, *I shall not speak* and οὐ κερῶ, *I will not cut*).

ple being Significant Parts). Of course, αὐλή and τρίς each stand in a different syntactic relation to the participle, and Common ambiguities must often involve such a syntactic shift in the whole utterance of which the Common expression is one component, even if they are definitely distinguishable from Significant Part, the list's ostensibly "syntactic" species. Further, the sound/letter sequences αὐλη and τρις enter into a relation with each other quite different (being a mere grouping) from the (strictly syntactic) relations αὐλή and τρίς enter into with the participle. The *prog.* Stoics, however, seem to have lacked the resources to characterise any of these relations more precisely than as "arrangements". Perhaps this is to press interpretation too far, since αὐλητρις, unlike the Part illustration, is of course significant as a single term. Yet there seems no objection in principle to treating Common as a variant on the basic Part species, and it is the Stoics' vague and unsatisfactory conception of syntax which threatens to undermine this portion of their taxonomy.

The allusion to "some Part" again suggests – as with Significant Part – that such ambiguities contain a Part which on any reading must combine with one or other of several moveable Parts. This difference in the description of the species, and the lack of agreement as to whether the rangeable Parts are all Non-significant, are worth noting, for they constitute evidence of a genuine Stoic debate, and serve as a reminder (like the apparently distinct approaches to Elleipsis and Pleonasm) that there was no single, authoritative Stoic classification.

Finally, Theon's example, with its κ ἐφελκυστικόν, cannot but recall *PPar.* 2, the περὶ ἀποφατικῶν once assigned to Chrysippus, and included as *S.V.F.* 2.180 by von Arnim despite his rejection of this attribution (*S.V.F.* 1: viiff.). For, as Cavini 1985: 108–13 has shown, this curious text arrives at a series of obviously false and unacceptable conclusions – that various quotations, all negations of one sort or another, from a number of canonical authors, are not genuine propositions – by (tacitly) assuming that the sole possible negation of any affirmative proposition *p* is οὐ *p*. Cavini himself uses the *prog.*

illustration to explain why and how ambiguity – rather, its non-existence – is appealed to in order to eliminate some of the examples (nos. 16, 24 in Cavini's text (1985:115f.), 15, 23 in von Arnim's). Where a quoted expression has the form οὔκ p, it might be urged that this is ambiguous between οὔκ p – the grammatically unacceptable alternative exploited to eliminate many of the other quotations – and the grammatically orthodox but logically unacceptable οὔκ p – logically unacceptable, that is, given the assumed rule of negation. The author of the text, however, also assumes (he does not, I believe, conclude, *pace* Cavini 1985: 120), that there are no ambiguous expressions: 'οὐ [*sic*] εἰσὶν ἀμφίβολοι διάλεκτοι' (*S.V.F.* 2, p. 56, l. 8, p. 58, l. 3, substituting Cavini's – obviously correct – punctuation). He thus leaves no option but to deny that the samples are real negations.

Whether there is any closer link between Theon's example and the papyrus text is unclear, in large part because both the authorship and and the interpretation of the latter remain doubtful. The blanket rejection of ambiguity looks Diodorean (see 4.6, and *cf.* Cavini *ibid.*), and the whole is undoubtedly polemical, a *reductio ad absurdum*; but the rule of negation the author assumes in order to demolish it is not associated with any known school or logician. (The Stoics, for example, clearly included οὐχί as one sort of ἀπόφασις: D.L. 7.69 (34K2); Sextus *M*. 8.89 (34G2).) Perhaps the target was extreme formalism in general, the rule being only an Aunt Sally. Cavini 1985: 120f. claims that the author's opponents wished, by instituting the p/οὐ p rule for negation, to eliminate ambiguities of the Non-significant Part type (which Cavini, oddly, given his reference to Theon, calls ambiguities κατὰ διάστασιν, p. 116; see further, 8.1). Yet so intuitively perverse a response to normal, intelligible linguistic variation could have had few attractions, except to the professional troublemaker – a Diodorus or an Arcesilaus. Speculatively, then, I would interpret the text as one half of a double-pronged attack on any formalised rule of negation. On the one hand, any simple rule for forming negations, such as the p/οὐ p rule, is bound to fly in the face of ordinary and literary usage; on the other (and this would be the second, now lost, part of the attack), merely listing (*i.e.* ostensively defining) acceptable negation signs would not only be dangerous (for the possibility of an omission always remains), but would leave some ostensible affirmative propositions grammatically incomplete or otherwise unacceptable, so that for these more complex reformulation rules would be needed: just the sort of response to criticism, especially from the Dialecticians and Skeptics, that the Stoics, for their part, learned to make.

6.5.4   The Part species: Galen's criticisms

These can roughly be grouped as general criticisms of the whole Stoic system and as particular criticisms of individual species (see 5.5 for a translation of the relevant text). Galen's special complaint against the Part species is that they represent an offence against method, that is, the addition of specific to generic divisions (14.13–15G, 23f.E). Galen seems to mean that there should be just one all-embracing "Part" type of ambiguity comparable with the other Stoic types; the Stoics would otherwise be under an obligation to include all its specific divisions (14.16G, 24E). This complaint shows, I think, that Galen has simply not grasped the distinction between Significant and Non-significant Part. Certainly his own examples of specific divisions are not comparable with it: they are by origin (in the case of Homonymy in Simples; *e.g.* Simplicius *cats.* 31.22ff., 65.12ff.) and by cause (in the case of Homonymy in Compounds; only one survives, by 'juxtaposition of like cases', 15.4f.G 24E; *cf. e.g.* Quintilian 7.9.6). What he should have said is that the way the species are characterised masks the fundamental difference between the two sorts of "ranging" involved. That aside, Galen's criticism is unjustified, for neither species is redundant, and no further comparable divisions would be possible in a hypothetical unitary Part species.

At the general level, two of the features of the classification which come under attack, besides its alleged 'lack of method and system' (14.8f.G, 23E), have a particular bearing on the Part species. One is that the Stoic species cannot be proved

373

mutually exclusive. In 6.1 it was noted that there is no good reason to believe mutual exclusivity was in fact a virtue claimed for the Stoic classification(s), and, in any case, the two *de soph.* Part kinds can be interpreted as distinct, there being no overlap between the sorts of Part by reference to which each species is defined (rather, they are *too* distinct). More problematic is the distinction between Significant Part and Reference, which will be discussed in 6.7.2. Difficulties have already cropped up for the *de soph.* Stoics' policy of treating Pleonasm and Elleipsis on the one hand, and the Part species on the other, as distinct ambiguity types. As for Common and Non-significant Part, the latter is plainly not open to the sort of speculative re-description I earlier applied to Part in the *prog.*; and the most that can be said is that the two species have a point of similarity not shared by any other Stoic forms of ambiguity, in all of which the constituents remain fixed.

Galen's other general criticism, that there are no new Stoic ambiguity modes (14.6–8G, 23E), has already been partly re-butted as far as the Part species are concerned. If the Aristotelian modes are treated as a single species of ambiguity, the Stoic system proves superior to the extent that it operates with a more coherent notion of syntax. Nor is the division between Significant Part and Common illusory, as Galen implies when he tries to classify Common ambiguities under Combination/Division (see 6.2.4). Finally, Galen fails to see that Non-significant Part is innovatory, whatever the legitimacy of its claim to be a genuine ambiguity species. Non-significant Part indeed provides further confirmation that the choice of *lexis* as ambiguity bearer in the surviving Stoic definition of ambiguity was well motivated (see 4.3). What is ambiguous is the *lexis* whose Parts together constitute a single string of letters (and in some instances, perhaps, of speech sounds), variously divisible, and which signifies (indirectly) all the complex *lekta* signified by the various *logoi* formed by the parts in their various arrangements. Being neither word nor word-complex, this string can have no place in Galen's semantic system, or, more importantly, in Aristotle's. The Stoic classifiers thus show themselves to be more alive to the implications of contemporary scribal conventions; what is unclear is whether what they have identified are genuine cases of ambiguity, rather than of the confusion of different utterances. Compare the English inscription

GODISNOWHERE

(borrowed from Hockett 1987: 55), a clear example of written Non-significant Part: is it an example of ambiguity?

6.5.5 The Part species: conclusions

Despite difficulties thrown up by the details of interpretation, the basic distinction between Significant Part and Non-significant Part/Part seems straightforward enough. The former covers ambiguities of syntactic grouping between words, whereas ambiguities in the other two species occur when two or more word-sequences can be formed from one *lexis*, itself a set of lexical building blocks. Each type of ambiguous expression signifies more than one *lekton*, but, while a Significant Part ambiguity consists of words which can be variously construed, the syntax of a Non-significant Part/Part ambiguity is determined by the selection of a syntactically invariable word-complex from all the possible groupings of the parts of a *lexis*.

The *de soph.* illustrations of these species are the first in that list with obviously literary associations, while the *prog.* examples are both Homeric. I suggested in 6.4.6 that Theon's source may have been a Stoic ambiguity classification forming part of a broader stylistic theory, and, if this is so, then most or all of his authentic Stoic examples might well be literary. Here two of them definitely are, and the Non-significant Part illustration, although perhaps not a quotation, at least has mythological, not eristic, connections. On the other hand, two of the *de soph.* examples also have a literary flavour. The best evidence which the species provide for taking the dialecticians' list as a contribution to a theory of style is that their two Significant Part examples are not contextually disambiguated, whereas the *de soph.* Non-significant Part illustration (if correctly restored) would be; for this suggests attention in the former cases, but not in the latter, to the exigencies of relevance and acceptability in real (literary) contexts. Even more suggestive is the presence in the *prog.* classification of the next two species, Hyperbaton and Interpolation.

6.6 The species of ambiguity 5: Hyperbaton and Interpolation

6.6.1 Hyperbaton and Interpolation: texts and translations

prog. 82.19–25

παρατηρητέον δὲ καὶ τὸ μὴ ὑπερ-	19
βατοῖς χρῆσθαι, οἷά ἐστι τὰ πολλὰ τῶν Θουκυδίδου· οὐ	20
γὰρ καθόλου τὸ τῶν ὑπερβατῶν γένος ἀποδοκιμάζομεν·	21
ποικίλη γὰρ διὰ τούτου καὶ οὐκ ἰδιωτικὴ γίνεται ἡ φρά-	22
σις· μηδὲ μεταξυλογίαις, καὶ ταύταις διὰ μακροῦ· τὰ	23
γὰρ ἐγγὺς λαμβάνοντα τὴν ἀπόδοσιν οὐ λυπεῖ τοὺς	24
ἀκροατάς.	25

(4) One must also take care not to employ hyper-	19
bata [*sc.* transpositions], such as are very frequent in Thucydides; for it is not that	20
we entirely disapprove of the genus of hyperbaton;	21
for by means of it language becomes varied and unusual.	22
(5) [One must take care] not [to employ] interpolations either, that is, lengthy ones;	23
for early resumption of one's account does not trouble	24
one's audience.	25

6.6.2 The place of Hyperbaton and Interpolation in the prog. classification

Since neither Hyperbaton nor Interpolation appears in the *de soph.* list, their Stoic credentials must be suspect. I have already argued[132] that both are Stoic, but that both are in the wrong place: they rightly belong in a Stoic classification of species of linguistic obscurity, and have been inserted in error by Theon into the list of types of ambiguity. Here I shall briefly rehearse the evidence supporting this interpretation.

As noted in 6.4.6, Hyperbaton and Interpolation are the

---

[132] *Cf.* Atherton 1988: 415ff.

only *prog.* species besides Elleipsis which are not illustrated, and none of the three is explicitly said to produce ambiguity; in that respect they form a sub-group within the classification. Neither Hyperbaton nor Interpolation is described as giving rise even to obscurity, but this is clearly implied by 82.25: 'moreover [καὶ μέντοι καὶ] omission of certain words is contrary to clarity'.

Hyperbaton and Interpolation are the first species on which Theon offers what are indubitably his own comments. The first person plural 'we disapprove' ('ἀποδοκιμάζομεν', 82.21) indicates that Theon is speaking *in propria persona* here (he uses such verbs freely elsewhere), and, interestingly, both his remarks are qualifications, clumsy and belated, of general injunctions (82.20–3, 23–5; contrast 80.27–81.1, where he carefully expresses an entirely orthodox disapproval only of lengthy "digressions", παρεκβάσεις, in narrative, and has no need for disclaimers). As a professional rhetorician, Theon would have had excellent grounds for adding these disclaimers, as I shall show a little later.

Theon's other comment (82.20) is an allusion to Thucydides' fondness for Hyperbata. To judge from the rest of the *prog.*, Theon was deeply familiar with Thucydides – for example, he is one of the authors listed at 65ff. as models for memorisation and imitation by the young charges of Theon's readers (see esp. 66.22–31, 84.26ff.) – but the observation has many parallels (*e.g.* Ps.-Longinus *subl.* 22.3; Dionysius of Halicarnassus *Thuc.* 31; Marcellinus *vita Thuc.* 56)[133] and Thucydides supplies numerous rhetoricians with examples of Hyperbaton (*e.g.* 2, 438.15ff.; 3, 38.13f., 17ff., 136.19f. Sp.). The uniqueness of the *prog.* treatment lies in the stylistic advice which follows the description of Hyperbaton.

A reader of the dialecticians' list will be surprised to find that Hyperbaton – *transposition* is the usual English translation, the transposition being of a word or phrase from its own

---

[133] The comments of Russell 1964: 137ff. and of Pritchett 1975: 115–16 on Ps.-Longinus *subl.* ch. 22 and Dionysius of Halicarnassus *Thuc.* 31 respectively are also useful as general accounts of Hyperbaton and of obscurity in Greek; on the latter see also Roberts 1910: 335–41.

"natural" position in a sentence[134] – is classed by rhetoricians and grammarians exclusively as a trope or figure of speech.[135] A wide variety of subdivisions was developed, and for clarity's sake I shall start with Quintilian's discussion of style (8.6.62–7), in which Hyperbaton is treated as a figure, and which is, typically, lucid and concise. Quintilian was unusual amongst rhetorical writers for the importance he attached to clarity and to grammatical correctness, typically dismissed as mere preliminaries to rhetorical training. (His views are set out at 8.2.22.) His treatment of the causes of obscurity is accordingly full and detailed.

Quintilian distinguishes two species, ἀναστροφή or *reversio* and Hyperbaton proper, the former (8.6.65) being the reversal of the normal order of a pair of words, the latter occurring 'when a word is transferred to a greater distance [*i.e.* from its "natural" position] for ornamental effect', 'cum decoris gratia traiicitur longius verbum'. In his introduction (62–4) he explains that Hyperbaton is employed for sonority and rhythm, and a little later (66–7) it is classed as a trope, not a figure, when meaning as well as word-order is affected. Only excessive Hyperbaton and Interpolation create obscurity (8.2.14):[136]

---

[134] The term ὑπερβατός is first used of transposed words by Plato *Prot.* 343e3. The notion of a "natural" word-order, another basic tenet of ancient stylistics, was still able to influence Denniston's account of Hyperbaton, 1952: 47ff., 58f. It was not restricted to "critical" grammar or rhetoric: Apollonius Dyscolus, who is much concerned with describing and explaining departures from "normal" word-order (for which his term may be τὸ ἑξῆς: *synt.* 109.8, 17f.), makes frequent appeals to Hyperbaton: *e.g. synt.* 109.12 (ἀναστροφή), 19, 174.1ff., 447.1ff., 453.5ff. (ὑπερβιβασμός); and *cf.* 101.4ff., 202.3–5, where rival explanations appealing to Hyperbata, of a pronominal construction, a Homeric problem line, and the origin of the adverb εἴσό respectively, are rejected. At *synt.* 345.20ff. Apollonius explains *Il.* 5.118, 'δὸς δέ τ' ἔμ' ἄνδρα ἑλεῖν', as a case of Hyperbaton: 'ἄνδρα' should come after the infinitive, since the agent of an action should precede the patient (345.10ff.). Ambiguities of this sort are labelled Amphibolies by Aristotle; the Stoic pigeon-hole may be Reference or Significant Part: see further, 6.7.3.

[135] The only heterodox approach I have encountered (apart from the *prog.* list itself) is that of the rhetorician Hermogenes, who makes Hyperbaton 'an instrument of clarity' ('ὄργανον σαφηνείας', 3, 438.1ff. Sp.): an author can use interpolations as a handy way of inserting explanations of what is being said. This recalls the analysis used by Olympiodorus, *meteor.* 41.23ff., 204.18ff., 24ff., of Aristotelian "parentheses" containing an explanation and an example respectively.

[136] I take 'traiectione vel ultra modum hyperbato' at 8.2.14 (Spalding's emendation of the MS 'transiectio intra modum') to mean "by deferral, *i.e.* excessive Hyper-

properly used, they are indispensable stylistic devices,[137] and this is the rôle they would usually have had for Theon.

A Stoic dialectician's attitude would have been very different. His school's reputation for using and recommending a relatively plain, unadorned, and concise style of discourse is well known, and it set little store by rhythm (*e.g.* Cicero *orat.* 3.65f.; *Brutus* 119; *fin.* 4.7). A blanket ban on Hyperbaton (and on Interpolation) would be wholly consistent with this heterodoxy. Tropes and figures would be regarded only as disturbances or interruptions in the speaker's chain of argument or exposition, dragging the audience or reader away from the familiar patterns of everyday speech; they would be considered not merely useless, but actively pernicious: vice, not ornament. Hyperbaton and Interpolation could thus have figured in a Stoic account of stylistic defects which originally included ambiguity, just as Quintilian's does.[138] Theon's only mistake – whether the result of faulty memory, or of insufficient attention to his source – would be to insert them into the ambiguity system, instead of treating them as separate offences against clarity; and he would then quite naturally try to soften Stoic prohibitions with rhetorical orthodoxy. I find this explanation far more plausible than that Hyperbaton and Interpolation should be authentic Stoic ambiguity species: to treat them as such would be both poor logic and poor polemics. Reversing

---

baton". Since one species of Hyperbaton is simply the reversal of the normal order of a pair of words, this phrase must refer to its other species, Hyperbaton proper, where a word is deferred *e.g.* to the end of a sentence.

[137] On Hyperbaton's stylistic usefulness, see *e.g. ad Her.* 4.44: 'transposition of this sort, which does not make the matter obscure, will be very useful for periods, which were discussed before, and in which the words ought to be arranged to resemble a poetic rhythm, so as to be as perfectly and smoothly turned as possible'. Would our Stoics have allowed any poetic licence in the use of Hyperbaton and Interpolation? A ποίημα, after all, is 'metrical or rhythmical utterance artificially avoiding prose form', 'λέξις ἔμμετρος ἢ εὔρυθμος μετὰ σκευῆς τὸ λογοειδὲς ἐκβεβηκυῖα' (D.L. 7.60), this definition coming after those of the virtues and vices of *lexis* (59). Poetic style cannot have been excluded completely from consideration, since two at least of their illustrations were Homeric. Perhaps the dialecticians produced different accounts of good and bad prose and poetic style, Hyperbaton and Interpolation being banned only from prose composition.

[138] The similarities between Quintilian's and Theon's lists suggest Quintilian too may have had access to a Stoic classification of causes of obscurity, perhaps through Theon himself: see 8.2.

or otherwise altering normal word-order need not automatically give rise to ambiguity.

Unhappily it is poor stylistics, too, even for a Stoic whose concern is to adapt language to the demands of a strict and unpopular ethical code. Variations in word-order, if they help keep an audience's attention focussed on subject-matter which is itself morally acceptable, can only be welcome, and stylistic variation would be appropriate too when the Stoic orator used "emotive" language for certain approved topics (Ps.-Longinus praises the effect of emotional tension which Hyperbaton can create in an audience by delaying the completion of the expected syntactic construction: *subl.* 22.3f.; and at least one Stoic orator, and the most illustrious at that, Cato the Younger, did employ rhetorically charged language where his matter – the virtues, one's homeland, the gods, death – required it: Cicero *paradoxa Stoicorum* 3). Perhaps the *prog.* is permitting a glimpse of another internal conflict in the Stoa, a broader one than disagreement over taxonomy: the problem of how language is to be adapted to the duties imposed by ethics.

As for Interpolation, the use of parenthesis (*paremptosis, interpositio, interclusio*) was a recognised figure, and Quintilian praises it for its strong emotional effect (9.3.29). Warnings against lengthy and confusing insertions or parentheses are common in the handbooks of style,[139] but μεταξυλογία itself is a rare word, and I have come across it in just two other rhetoricians. One applies it, curiously, to the reversal of word-order, which is ἀναστροφή or *reversio* elsewhere; the other, to the insertion of a word between the halves of a compound (3, 170.14ff., 188.4ff. Sp.). Indeed, Quintilian is unusual in distinguishing between Hyperbaton and *interiectio*; the vast majority of rhetoricians and grammarians regard the insertion of a group of words into a clause or sentence as simply a form of

---

[139] First in Aristotle *rhet.* 3.5.1407a20ff.: the first item in a list of rules for achieving good Greek (Hellenism) is clever management of connectives in lucid, well-organised sentences without too many interruptions (without 'πολὺ τὸ μεταξὺ', ll. 29f.). See also Quintilian 8.2.15, 9.3.23, 27, 29; and Dionysius of Halicarnassus *ep. ii. ad Amm.* 15, who criticises 'insertions [αἱ μεταξὺ παρεμπτώσεις] which are numerous and reach a conclusion with difficulty, on account of which the language becomes hard to follow'.

Hyperbaton.[140] Theon's departure from the norm in these two points – in the Hyperbaton/Interpolation distinction, and in the use of the term μεταξυλογία – is best accounted for by their both being Stoic innovations which never became common rhetorical currency, and whose Stoic origin would not even be suspected without the evidence of this classification.

6.6.3 Hyperbaton and Interpolation: conclusions

Hyperbaton and Interpolation give the clearest indication that the *prog.* dialecticians regarded their list as part of a theory of style, although, ironically, if the interpretation put forward here is correct, what reveals their classification's original context is merely an error on Theon's part. What is strange is that Theon should have got to know their work, technically difficult and unorthodox as it was, and it is now pretty well clear that Theon must have had direct access to the Stoic list: an intermediary would have been far less likely to preserve even half-way intact a theory so uncongenial to the orthodox rhetorician. Quintilian may well have known a similar Stoic theory, but, if he did, he did not even attempt to reproduce his source's quirky originality.

6.7 The species of ambiguity 6: Reference

6.7.1 Reference: texts and translations

de soph. 14.2–5G, 23E

ὀγδόη ⟨... δ' ἡ⟩ μὴ δηλοῦσα τί ἐπὶ τί ἀναφέρεται,	2
ὡς ἐν τῷ Δίων ⟨ἐστὶ καὶ⟩ Θέων ⟨εὕροις ἂν⟩· ἄδηλον γάρ ἐστιν, εἴτε	3
ἐπὶ τὴν ἀμφοτέρων ὕπαρξιν ἀναφέρεται εἴτε ἐπὶ τοιοῦτον	4
οἷον Δίων Θέων ἐστὶ ἢ πάλιν.	5

---

[140] This unusual feature of Quintilian's account also seems to point to familiarity with a Stoic classification: further, 8.2 As for the other rhetoricians, see *e.g.* 2, 438.1ff., 3, 38.16ff., 74.19–22, 136.21ff. Sp. A broad distinction is drawn between single-word Hyperbaton (division of a compound term; deferral of a word) and word-complex Hyperbaton (all other types of word-order disturbance): *e.g.* 3, 48.5ff., 197.20ff. Sp. It is unclear where Stoic Hyperbaton leaves off and Interpolation begins; but it is very unusual to list them separately. In the rhetorical writers there is only a tendency to make ἀναστροφή and Hyperbaton distinct tropes: *e.g.* 3, 48.5ff., 18–20, 197.10–18, 20–8 Sp.

(8) The eighth [species] ⟨...is that⟩ failing to make clear what is   2
being referred to what,
⟨as you might find in⟩ *Dion* ⟨*is also*⟩ *Theon*; for it is unclear   3
whether it is being referred to the existence of both [*sc.* of both
Dion and
Theon], or to something   4
like "Dion is Theon" or *vice versa* [*sc.* "Theon is Dion"].   5

prog. 82.26–83.1

παραφυλακτέον δὲ καὶ τὸ   26
παραλλήλους τιθέναι τὰς πτώσεις ἐπὶ διαφόρων προ-   27
σώπων· ἀμφίβολον γὰρ γίνεται τὸ ἐπὶ τίνα φέρεσθαι,   28
οἷον ἐπὶ μὲν τῆς αἰτιατικῆς, ἐφ᾽ ἧσπερ καὶ μόνης τῶν   29
πτώσεων πολλοὶ γίνεσθαι τὴν ἀμφιβολίαν νομίζουσιν,   30
ὡς παρὰ Δημοσθένει κατὰ Μειδίου, ἴσασιν Εὐαίωνα   31
πολλοὶ τὸν Λεωδάμαντος ἀδελφὸν ἀποκτεί-   32
(p. 83 Spengel)
ναντα Βοιωτὸν ἐν δείπνῳ· ἄδηλον γὰρ πότερον   1
Εὐαίων ἀπέκτεινε Βοιωτὸν ἢ Βοιωτὸς Εὐαίωνα, ὅπερ ἐστὶ   2
ψεῦδος· ἀλλὰ καὶ ὁ Λεωδάμαντος ἀδελφὸς πότερον Εὐαί-   3
ων ἐστὶν ἢ Βοιωτός; ἐπὶ δὲ τῆς εὐθείας, ὡς παρ᾽ Ἡρο-   4
δότῳ ἐν τῇ πρώτῃ, εἰσὶ δὲ καὶ Αἰγύπτιοι Κολχοί·   5
ἄδηλον γὰρ πότερον οἱ Αἰγύπτιοι Κολχοί εἰσιν ἢ τού-   6
ναντίον οἱ Κολχοὶ Αἰγύπτιοι. τὸ δ᾽ αὐτὸ καὶ ἐπὶ τῆς γε-   7
νικῆς καὶ δοτικῆς, Κολχῶν δὲ ὄντων Αἰγυπτίων· καί,   8
Κολχοῖς δὲ οὖσιν Αἰγυπτίοις· ἐπὶ μὲν οὖν τῆς αἰτιατι-   9
κῆς ἀναμφισβήτητόν ἐστιν, ἐπὶ δὲ τῶν ἄλλων πτώσεων   10
φανερόν, ὅτι προσθέσει ἄρθρων οὐκέτι ἀμφίβολος γίνεται   11
ἡ λέξις· εἰσὶ δὲ Αἰγύπτιοι οἱ Κολχοί· δῆλον γὰρ γέγονεν,   12
ὅτι περὶ Κολχῶν λέγει, ὡς εἰσὶν Αἰγύπτιοι.   13

(7) One must also guard against   26
applying parallel cases to different per-   27
sons; for it becomes ambiguous to whom [*or*: which things?] [each   28
of the cases] is being referred;
e.g. in the accusative, in which alone of the   29
cases many people think this [sort of] ambiguity occurs,   30
as in Demosthenes' *Against Meidias* [§71, p. 44.10–11 ed. Goodwin]:   31
'Many people know that Euaion [or Boiotos], (Leodamas' brother),   32
kill-
(p. 83 Spengel)
ed Boiotos [or Euaion] (Leodamas' brother) at a dinner-party'; for   1
it is unclear whether
Euaion killed Boiotos, or Boiotos Euaion, which is   2
false; but also, is Leodamas' brother Euai-   3

382

on, or Boiotos ? But [this sort of ambiguity also occurs] in the	4
nominative [case], as in Hero-	
dotus Book I [*sic*; but = 2.104.1], 'Egyptians too are Colchians':	5
for it is unclear whether the Egyptians are Colchians or the opp-	6
osite, that Colchians are Egyptians; and in the ge-	7
nitive and the dative too, *of Colchians being Egyptians/of Egyptians*	8
being Colchians, and	
to Colchians being Egyptians/to Egyptians being Colchians; with the	9
accusa-	
tive [case] it is undisputed, and with the other cases	10
obvious, that by the addition of [definite] articles the expression is	11
no longer ambiguous:	
The Colchians are Egyptians; for it is now clear,	12
that it says about Colchians, that they are Egyptians.	13

6.7.2 Reference: Galen's version

In the MS the example is as follows:

Δίων Θέων εὕρω

Both Gabler and Ebbesen adopt Limanus' implicit emendation in his Latin translation:[141]

Δίων Θέων ἐστίν 14.3G, 23E

Galen's explanation of the illustration (14.3–5G, 23E) does
not support this alteration. The example as emended might
mean (a) either "Dion is Theon" or "Theon is Dion", but it
cannot mean (b) "Dion is and Theon is", as Galen implies
it does in the words 'to the existence of both'. Further, were
the Limanus emendation correct, Galen's characterisation of
"Dion is Theon/Theon is Dion" as 'something like', 'τοιοῦτο',
what the expression is "referred to" would be odd, since it (or
they) would rather be *precisely* one (or two) of its possible
meanings.

It is not even obvious that "Dion is and Theon is" is

---

[141] Edlow 1977: 64 also accepts this emendation. He also assumes, however, that
Reference is one of the Stoic examples labelled by Galen as 'homonymy in
a word-complex' (15.3–4G, 24E). This is clearly wrong, for no homonymy is
involved in Reference, which is not comparable, either, as Galen believes, to
Aristotelian Amphiboly: see further, main text.

straightforwardly one of the things the example could mean. According to Galen, the example could be being "referred" either to "Dion is Theon/Theon is Dion", which look(s) to be a proposition (or propositions), and which Stoics would therefore regard as the expression's direct signification(s); or to 'the existence of both', which looks nothing like a proposition. Either the Stoics' own explanation of the example was extremely imprecise, to say the least, or the authenticity of the analysis Galen gives is in grave doubt.

Adding to these difficulties is Galen's introduction to the species (14.2G, 23E) (which here means, any of its members)[142] as that 'which fails to make clear what is referred to what'. Or rather, this is what Galen says if the emendation in the Charterian edition, adopted by Long and Sedley without comment, 1987: 2: 231, ll. 17f., is correct:

μὴ δηλοῦσα τί ἐπὶ τί ἀναφέρεται

and can replace the MS reading:

μὴ δηλονότι ἐπὶ τί ἀναφέρεται.

Yet Galen's explanation, as just noted, puts the inclarity in what the whole ambiguous utterance is itself being "referred to". At the start of Galen's report there is a lacuna in the MS of more than 13 (Gabler) or 20–3 (Ebbesen) letters, a gap which could once have held the description proper. The word 'δηλονότι' in the manuscript may be original, and merely clarificatory of what once preceded it ('... that is to say ...'). Reading what follows as 'to what it [sc. the species, or each of its members] is being referred' will bring the text closer to Galen's explanation as it survives: but that is itself pretty well unintelligible. All that is certain is that the word ἀναφέρεται must have figured in the genuine Stoic account, and its use here has to be explained. I shall propose two different and incompatible interpretations of the text.

---

[142] Galen has already spoken of the Significant and Non-significant Part species, rather than of ambiguities falling under them, as failing to make clear how constituents are grouped: 13.13, 16–17G, 22, 23E. I take it he uses the same locution here.

I begin with the familiar technical grammatical term ἀναφορά, which was used of the mode of signifying of certain pronouns, as referring (back) to a term (= a noun) already used, and thus taking on its signification according to context.[143]

If the (near-)meaning is (b) "Dion is and Theon is", *Dion* and *Theon* may each signify different individuals, or a single individual with two names. If it is (a)(i) "Dion is Theon" and/or (a)(ii) "Theon is Dion", both names are being used to signify the same person, Dion/Theon. (I assume that successful reference of the subject-terms is guaranteed on all readings.[144]) On reading (a)(i), *Theon* is being "referred" back to *Dion*, for the names (are taken to) signify the same object; on reading (a)(ii), if it is indeed a separate reading, it is *Dion* which is "referred" in this way. On reading (b), however, this is not necessarily so: as far as can be made out from the structure of the signification itself, *Dion* and *Theon* might be being used to signify different individuals, and their syntactic rôles are independent. This interpretation of the example does appeal to a non-standard type of ἀναφορά, in which nouns, not pronouns, are "referred back" internally or intralinguistically; but I do not think it can be disregarded on this basis alone, for much of Stoic semantics was unorthodox. On the other hand, Dion and Theon might not be the same person: is this grounds for an objection? The most that can be said is that the *de soph.* Stoics did not feel constrained to deal exclusively with ambiguities which are not contextually or selectionally disambiguated, and, in any case, nothing is reported about the circumstances in which the utterance is made.

This approach is also attractive, at the very least, because it seems to identify Reference as a form of ambiguity new to the *de soph.* classification. The proper names are presumably not

---

[143] On Stoic anaphoric pronouns, see 6.3.5.2. The notion of anaphora is to be compared with Quine's "cross-reference", as opposed to reference proper, which is a word/thing relation: 1960: 137, 1965: 26f.

[144] For the Stoic analysis of singular definite terms: Alexander *an. pr.* 402.4ff.; and see 3.3, 3.5, and main text, below.

homonyms,[145] and there are no pronouns whose reference (as a modern reader would say) or grouping (as the *prog.* and perhaps the *de soph.* Stoics would say) is ambiguous. The syntax of the significations is different in (a) and (b), and they could be described as grouping ambiguities of a sort, as long as it is supposed that the *de soph.* Stoics analysed propositions constructed with the copula as the Stoa in general is known to have analysed propositions formed with verbal predicates, that is, as comprising a subject case and a predicate: *e.g.* D.L. 7.64 (33G), 69f. (34K). Gellius provides indirect evidence that the Stoics did deal with propositions formed with the copula – such as ⟨Hannibal Pocnus fuit⟩, ⟨Hannibal was a Carthaginian⟩, ⟨Neque bonum est voluptas neque malum⟩, ⟨Pleasure is neither good nor evil⟩ – even in elementary handbooks: *noct. att.* 16.8.7. There is no positive evidence for any Stoic analysis of propositions of this type; the most that can be said is that there is no evidence either that the subject/predicate structure had a restricted scope. On this interpretation, *Dion* and *Theon* would each be "ranged" separately as its subject-case with the copula *is* on reading (b) of the example, while on reading (a), either *Dion* or *Theon* or both would be "ranged" with the copula to form the predicate of a proposition whose subject-case will be the other noun.[146] ⟨Dion is Theon⟩ and ⟨Theon is Dion⟩ could thus be two distinct significations of the illustration, a curious refinement of Stoic semantics which has no support in the precise wording of Galen's report.[147]

---

[145] It is not unusual for proper names to be cited as cases of homonymy by grammatical and rhetorical writers: *e.g.* D.T. 36.2f.; Sch. 389.8; Quintilian 7.9.2; A.D. *pron.* 10.11ff.; Iulius Victor 383.13f. Halm. Note also Ammonius *int.* 73.11ff., Boethius *int.* 2, p. 106, 1.26–p. 107, 1.5 Meiser (both on Aristotle *int.* 5.17a16f.). The Stoic position is unknown (see 6.3.5.2), but it is surely impossible for homonymies to form yet another species in this classification.

[146] It would be incorrect to argue, however, that the example cannot qualify as a Significant Part ambiguity on the grounds that, when analysed as such, its constituents' various groupings have to be explicitly characterised in different ways, *e.g.* as signifying a predicate, and that this sort of syntactic description is not expressly allowed for by the *de soph.* (or *prog.*) definition of Significant Part: this weakness in the system may well have been overlooked by its authors.

[147] Galen lists the possible (near-) significations thus: 'εἴτε ... εἴτε ... ἤ', 14.3–5G, 23E, which tends to suggest that ⟨Dion is Theon⟩ and ⟨Theon is Dion⟩ are not two separate significations: at least, I have been unable to locate an author

But what the Stoics may have argued is that what is really unclear here is whether the structure of the signified propositions entails that the proper names are being internally assigned the same referent or not. The individual words in a Significant Part expression may change any type of syntactic allegiance: in a Reference ambiguity, by contrast, the only syntactic relation of importance is that of intra-linguistic "referring", which holds only between nominals, and whether or not it is exercised by a nominal determines, and is determined by, whether that nominal exercises a dependent or an independent syntactic function, as part of a predicate (or complement), or as an autonomous subject-case.

I therefore tentatively propose this emendation at 14.2G, 23E:

... μὴ δῆλον ⟨εἶτ'⟩ ἐπί τι ἀναφέρεται.

... not clear ⟨whether⟩ it [*sc.* a nominal] is being referred to something

where the "referring" relation holds between one nominal and another. What has been lost is a description of the species in which, I would guess, mention was made of the "referring" relation between nominals (ὀνόματα? πτώσεις?). Galen would then have gone on to say that of each (ὄνομα? πτῶσις?) it is 'not clear ⟨whether⟩ it is being referred to something ⟨or not⟩', which is the only part of his account to have survived. This description will thus be very close in form to what Galen says about the example, but his account of it would be badly distorted, since "reference" here will be, as noted, a special relation holding between one nominal and another within a

---

who uses this sequence in parallel construction (Xenophon *ana.* 6.6.20 and Plutarch *non posse suav. viv.* 1089D are not exceptions). Such ambiguities may, incidentally, have interesting consequences for the Stoic doctrine of the infallibility of the sage (see already Atherton 1988: 247ff. on this problem, with reference to Chrysippus' *Logical Questions*, cols. 4–5). If the reference intended by a speaker is irreducibly private, there is no way even the wise could say for sure that what he had meant was ⟨Dion is Theon⟩ or ⟨Theon is Dion⟩. Of course, the same might apply in other cases of ambiguity too, but here the truth conditions of both readings must be identical, and the wise man would need to consult the context or situation of utterance very closely even to be sure whether it is more plausible for the proposition to be about Dion or about Theon; he might not succeed even in this restricted aim.

sentence or *lekton*. Yet this is perhaps to accuse Galen unfairly of fumbling an explanation which was actually already off course when it came into his hands, and I am accordingly reluctant to endorse this interpretation and accompanying emendation wholeheartedly.

My alternative explanation of the species is a little less unorthodox, but again it does not, unfortunately, make the account which Galen reports or misreports wholly intelligible. It will take "reference" to be a relation between names and bearers, not between names. According to Diogenes Laertius proper names are said to "indicate", δηλοῦν, their significations (7.58 (33M)), but Stoic semantic jargon seems to have been neither fixed nor precise: see 4.5, 6.2.3, 6.3.5.2, 6.5.2, 6.5.3. In Apollonius the phrase ἐπί τι φέρεσθαι can be applied to a word which is itself being "applied to" or "used of something": *e.g. pron.* 61.5, *synt.* 32.9. Perhaps, then, the ambiguity of "reference" resides in the proper names, which must be constituents of the example, whatever it may be exactly.

On this interpretation, the illustration will be ambiguous because it will be unclear to which object(s) in the world Theon and Dion are being referred; the *prog.* description of his version of the species can indeed be understood in this way. What would be unclear is whether a given speaker is using the names to refer to a single individual, Dion/Theon, in which case the meaning is (a), or to two different individuals, Dion and Theon, in which case the meaning is (b). The term "reference" may be used because what is in question is how a speaker uses names to signify objects, not how those names actually signify, for which the technical label δηλοῦν may have been reserved. The text will have to be emended at 14.2G, 23E as suggested by the Charterian editor: the species will 'fail to make clear what is being referred to what', *i.e.* what name to what object. Syntax is different in the two (or three) signified propositions, but it is reference, in this technical sense, which determines syntax – that is, whether each nominal is a subject-case in an existential proposition, or a subject-case or part of a predicate in an ordinary predicate + subject proposition – so that there can be no question that such utterances might constitute a different species of ambiguity from Significant Part. (Edlow 1975: 428f., 431 presents a similar interpretation.)

This reading of the text can be given a little support from Alexander's report of the Stoic way of dealing with sentences with singular definite subjects (*an. pr.* 402.8ff.). (I assume again that sentences formed with the copula can be analysed as predicate + subject constructs.) The illustration could be taken, first, as meaning either ⟨There is a certain Dion, and he/this man is Theon⟩ or ⟨There is a certain Theon, and he/this man is Dion⟩. Here the pronouns in the two signified propositions are "being referred to" the same person. But the nominals may instead refer to different individuals, and in fact the sentence will turn out to signify a compound proposition (something like ⟨Both: There is a certain Dion; and: There is a certain Theon⟩). The problem with this interpretation (besides its failure to explain Galen's explanation) is that it too assumes reference to two individuals – which of course is not necessarily the case. That *both* of two plausible explanations make this same assumption may be another sign of indifference to contextual and/or situational factors on the part of the Stoic authors.[148]

The precise wording of the illustration has still to be established, and here a successful reconstruction is still possible, for its two (or three) significations are more or less clear. Most simply, it could be read:

ὡς ἐν τῷ Ἀίων Θέων' εὕροις ἄν

'as you might find in "Dion Theon"', easily intelligible only if a very specific context is assumed (*e.g.* if I am being asked 'which of our friends is down in the market-place?'), and might be classed as simply elliptical. It is thus less attractive than Sedley's

ὡς ἐν τῷ Ἀίων ⟨ἔστι καὶ⟩ Θέων εὕροις ἄν

'as you might find in the case of "Dion is also Theon (is)"', which accounts for the peculiar MS reading 'εὕρω', and

---

[148] I am grateful to Jonathan Barnes for comments on this text.

goes some way to explaining why signification (a) ("Dion is Theon/Theon is Dion") is only 'something like' what the illustration signifies, since (b) does not indicate the presence in the text of 'καὶ', 'also/and'.

A last word of warning. It would be all to easy to fall into the mistake of interpreting Reference too narrowly on the evidence of one case. Galen's account of this species is by far the least intelligible in his whole report; and there is no way of knowing whether this is his fault or the Stoics' own.

6.7.3   Reference: Theon's version

Theon's characterisation of the species and his choice of examples are different from Galen's, and his account of ways to disambiguate Reference expressions (83.9–13) has no counterpart in the *de soph.* As always with the *prog.*, the chief task is to pick out genuine Stoic material; and here this is especially demanding.

Theon's general description is framed as an admonition (*cf.* 'παραφυλακτέον', 82.26), which is reminiscent of the characterisation of Hyperbaton and Interpolation (*cf.* 'παρατηρητέον', 82.19); but, whereas in the case of those two species, the admonitory formula is more probably Stoic than not (since they may be drawn from a Stoic list of sources of obscurity), the balance of probabilities is against its being so here. A didactic tone would not be out of place in a Stoic stylistic manual – if that was Theon's source – but it would be oddly inconsistent of the "dialecticians" to break the pattern of neutral characterisation observed for all the other ambiguity species, which surely do not include Hyperbaton and Interpolation. In contrast, not only would it be quite natural for Theon to strike the didactic note himself, but that note has already been sounded in connection with Hyperbaton and Interpolation; his readers are not to know that these species have "crept into the text". Perhaps the original Stoic ambiguity classification was accompanied by a comprehensive prohibition, as such lists often are in surviving rhetorical and grammatical surveys.

Yet the substance of Theon's advice, that Reference ambiguities are caused by the use of like grammatical cases (82.26–8), could still be Stoic: he may simply have re-framed what was once a neutral Stoic description as a warning, appropriate to his readership and to the purpose of his book. Certainly, without some such prior information, Theon's next remark, which constitutes the explanation of why parallel cases are undesirable, and which is strikingly reminiscent of the *de soph.*, would be unintelligible: 'ἀμφίβολον γὰρ γίνεται τὸ ἐπὶ τίνα φέρεσθαι' (82.28).[149] In context, this must translate as 'it becomes ambiguous to whom ⟨each of the cases is⟩ being referred', or, perhaps, '... to which things ...'. Were persons only meant, 'ἐπὶ τίνας' would give a smoother reading; but this, while appropriate to Theon's examples, would be an intolerable restriction on the scope of the species.[150] Although the thought is highly compressed, together *explanandum* and *explanans* are just about comprehensible; and the similarity between the latter and Galen's account surely guarantees at least *its* authenticity.

The real problem is posed by the *explanandum*. The text of the *de soph.*, which might perhaps have contained just this sort of information about the items being referred, is incomplete, as already seen, and there is thus no way of checking directly the reliability of Theon's report of the scope of the species,

---

[149] I very much doubt that Ebbesen's suggested emendation 'ἀναφέρεσθαι' in the *prog.* text is necessary, 1981a: 1: 37. The simple verb is perfectly intelligible, and the different descriptions of Significant Part in the two lists (6.5.2) are unimpeachable evidence that their authors did not always use identical terminology. As well as using the locution φέρεσθαι ἐπί τι to mean "be applied to a thing" (already noted in 6.7.2 (p. 388)), Apollonius also employs it to mean something like "be construed with": *e.g. synt.* 84.3ff., 'εἴπερ τὰ ἄρθρα ἐπὶ τὰ ὑπακουόμενα φέρεται', 'if indeed the articles are construed with the ⟨words⟩ which are being taken as understood' (possibly a paraphrase of Habro, but clearly to be understood as synonymous with Apollonius' own description at 83.15f., 'ἥν δὲ ἡ σύνταξις ...', 'the grammatical construction is ...'; *cf.* 344.3–4), 343.2, 15f., 344.2 (verbs being "construed with" nouns in the various oblique cases), 490.8f., *adv.* 127.14. But I doubt this can be its meaning in the context of the Stoic classification, for Reference would then be barely distinguishable from Significant Part. On Apollonius' treatment of double-accusative ambiguities, see 6.6.2, n. 134.

[150] Some such restriction on the scope of the *prog.* species, whether original, or imposed by Theon, is suggested by the term 'persons', 'προσώπων', 82.27f. It is very hard to see why the ambiguous application of parallel cases should be so limited, and the word perhaps carries here a grammatical meaning, being equivalent to *case*, πτῶσις.

which is what the *explanandum* amounts to. Further, even the examples are suspect, there being good grounds for believing them his own, and the first of them at least is not at all easy to analyse as a Reference ambiguity in either of the two ways I suggested for the *de soph.* case. Of course, the *prog.* version of the kind may have been different, and both of Theon's illustrations, even if not Stoic, might be appropriate; but I shall argue that the *explanandum* cannot be Stoic as it stands, and that Theon has almost certainly failed to grasp and accurately record Reference's true boundaries.

Both Theon's examples are literary, one from Demosthenes (*Against Meidias* §71, p. 44.10–11 Goodwin), the other from Herodotus (2.104.1).[151] An illustration from Demosthenes, on whom Theon wrote a commentary, and who would no doubt already have been familiar to trainee orators, is, frankly, suspicious. As for Herodotus, Theon was obviously familiar with his work; both he and Demosthenes, like Thucydides, are among the numerous authors mentioned as models of excellence at *prog.* 66–9 (Herodotus: 66.23, 25; 67.12–16; Demosthenes: 66.28–31).

In the Demosthenes example (82.31–83.1) there are two sources of ambiguity: (i) either Euaion or Boiotos might be the killer; (ii) either of them may be Leodamas' brother (see 83.1–4). It is unclear, however, which of the grammatical cases is to be thought of as open to ambiguity of reference. I shall try to adapt the second of the two interpretations of the *de soph.* illustration, since that is closer to Theon's general account of the species, although the relevant questions can easily be rephrased, if desired, to apply to the alternative interpretation of Galen's example: (i) Is it that either *Euaion* or *Boiotos* might be being referred to the killer, or the participle *killed* (ἀποκτείναντα) to either Euaion or Boiotos? (ii) Is it that *Euaion* or *Boiotos* might be being referred to Leodamas' brother, or the phrase *Leodamas' brother* to Euaion or to Boiotos? As so little is known of the Stoic use of φέρεσθαι, or

---

[151] Curiously, Theon's reference, 'ἐν τῇ πρώτῃ', 'in the first book', 83.5, is wrong: which is as consistent with the illustration's being Stoic as not.

about which objects and linguistic items could be related by the act of "referring", it would be impossible to decide between these alternatives, on current information, even were the illustration proved authentic. What is more, there is surely something to the claim that the expression belongs under Significant Part, since syntax depends on whether *Euaion* or *Boiotos* is "arranged with" (i) *killed*, and (ii) *Leodamas' brother*. I shall come back to this point shortly.

The second example (83.5), εἰσὶ δὲ καὶ Αἰγύπτιοι Κολχοί, is not an identity statement in its original context. It is ambiguous because Herodotus might be saying that, of Egyptians, some are Colchians (his intended meaning, as the context shows); or that, of Colchians, some are Egyptians. The second *de soph.* analysis is again easy to apply: either *Colchians* is being used to refer to (some) Egyptians, or *Egyptians* is being used to refer to (some) Colchians. The example is still not precisely parallel to the *de soph.* illustration. It cannot mean "there are Colchians and there are Egyptians". Moreover, as it is not a straightforward expression of identity, the example's two significations have different truth-conditions, and accordingly do not resemble the proposition(s) ⟨Theon is Dion⟩/ ⟨Dion is Theon⟩.

Having given a nominative-case illustration, Theon reworks it in the dative and genitive (83.7–9). In so doing he is very much aware of teaching a novelty (82.29–30): 'for instance, in the accusative case, in which alone of the cases many people think this ambiguity occurs'. In every other rhetorical and grammatical ambiguity classification which I have consulted and which contains a version of this ambiguity type, examples are invariably framed with the accusative case. The implication is that Theon's eyes have been opened by his dialectical source, even if the examples he presents are not Stoic. Only in the *prog.*, and the *de soph.*, is a nominative-case illustration given.

Theon must already have known of an ambiguity species which reminded him of Reference when he came across the Stoic list, but which was associated exclusively with the imposition of like accusative cases. He may well be right to claim

393

that Reference does occur in association with every grammatical case. But it would be improper to infer from an illustration that may well not be Stoic that Stoic dialecticians assigned to Reference at least some of the ambiguities Aristotle would have classed as Amphibolies. I raise this issue here because one common Amphiboly ambiguity is an expression containing two accusative cases.

A description of Amphiboly may be helpful. Aristotle's own account, unfortunately, is brief and obscure, and much has to be deduced from his examples (most straightforwardly at *s. el.* 4.166a6–14), which, although all syntactic ambiguities, do not fall under Combination/Division. This is because what is unclear is the precise syntactic rôle played by terms in some given word-complex, not whether they are syntactically associated in some way or other. The only general description Aristotle offers is just that in an Amphibolous expression no constituent is ambiguous, whereas the whole is (4.166a17–18). In all but one of the illustrations in *s. el.* 4 (a representative sample) there is a term that – to use the traditional grammatical categories – could be either subject or object of the verb (*e.g.* 166a7f., τοῦτο γινώσκει (*this one knows*), 18f., ἐπίσταται γράμματα (*knowing letters*)).[152] In the remaining example, either of two terms could be object or subject (agent) (6f.). It is this expression which in the modern reader's eyes Theon's Demosthenes illustration most closely resembles, since both *Euaion* and *Boiotos* could be subject or object of the participle.

In the first chapter of the *de soph.*, and again in the fourth (1.12–2.1G, 2f.E; 15.5f.G, 24E), Galen uses examples very like Aristotle's two-case one; and when he describes the second as 'due to the juxtaposition of like cases' (15.5G, 24E), there can

[152] Aristotle's own explanation of one of his illustrations of Amphiboly, 4.166a12, assumes that one of its components ('σιγῶντα') is itself ambiguous (between the masculine singular accusative participle, and the neuter plural nominative participle, of the verb meaning *be silent* – an instance of syncretism for today's linguists, of συνέμπτωσις, "formal coincidence", for Apollonius Dyscolus (see 8.4)); but this must be an oversight. In another example, 4.166a9f., what is unclear is whether 'τοῦτο' is (to borrow traditional grammatical jargon) subject or complement of the verb. So here, too, it is the pronoun's precise syntactic relation with the verb that is in doubt. It should be noted that it is not the anaphoric reference of *this* which is unclear, but its syntactic function.

be no doubt that he has in mind the Reference example, or that he regards Reference as one-half of the Stoic counterpart to Amphiboly. In 6.3.4 his attempt to interpret Homonymy in Compounds as the other half was roundly rejected. Could his interpretation of Reference be correct none the less?

It is safe to say that neither of the main subdivisions of Aristotelian Amphiboly can fall within the compass of Reference. Expressions having two like grammatical cases are of most immediate relevance. Take Galen's 'εἴη Μελήτον Σωκράτην νικῆσαι', 'May Meletus defeat Socrates/Socrates defeat Meletus' (15.5f.G, 24E). The references of both proper names are clear and fixed, and the only appropriate classificatory pigeon hole seems to be Significant Part. Yet classifying the expression in this way is not justified by the general description of Significant Part. It would have to be possible to characterise what is unclear as, for instance, whether *Meletus* and *prevail over*, or *Socrates* and *prevail over*, are grouped as signifying a predicate; saying that they are "ranged" together would not do, since each of these pairs of terms might also and alternatively be "ranged" together as subject and verb. A similar difficulty attaches to locating Theon's quotation from Demosthenes under Reference, as far as the syntactic grouping of ἀποκτείναντα is concerned; it must be described as, for example, having *Euaion* (or *Boiotos*) as its subject-case (or part of the predicate).

In any event, Amphibolies of this type cannot be Reference ambiguities, for there is no possibility that two syntactically different propositions are involved. In consequence, Theon's association of Reference with the simple imposition of parallel grammatical cases must be unwarranted, and presumably is not Stoic. Like cases will produce such ambiguities only where the reference of each case is unclear. Thus, for instance, that famous line of Ennius, 'aio te Aeacida Romanos vincere posse', 'I say that you, son of Aeacus, the Romans can conquer', will not fall under Reference. The parallel cases in the Demosthenes passage must have misled Theon into presenting it as an example of Reference, and his familiarity with versions of this form of Aristotelian Amphiboly – which are common

395

enough in rhetorical and grammatical manuals[153] – into identifying it with the Stoic species.[154]

Amphiboly's other chief form, in which a single term's syntactic rôle or function is unclear, presents an equally serious difficulty for both Stoic systems. (I am not supposing the Stoics were familiar with the *s. el.*, only observing that they were apparently unaware of ambiguities assignable to the Aristotelian mode.) Sentences such as τοῦτο ὁρᾷ (*s. el.* 4.166a10) and ἐπίσταται γράμματα (166a18f.) seem not to fall under any of the Stoic species. What the Stoic approach to these expressions would have been remains obscure.[155] Galen, then, failed to see the one clear instance in which the Stoic classification is less comprehensive than Aristotle's.[156]

Both examples are contextually disambiguated, but, not being certainly Stoic, they cannot be used as evidence that the *prog.* Stoics accepted as ambiguous bearers disambiguated by their actual linguistic environments. Further, as Butts 1986: 379–80 observes, the position of the names in the first illustration would in any event normally be assumed to indicate their

[153] Esp. Quintilian 7.9.7, 8.2.16; Charisius (*G.L.* 1) 27.28; Diomedes (*G.L.* 1) 450.3. Both the latter authors, and Quintilian 7.9.7 (and also Cicero *div.* 2.56), have the same example: Ennius *Annales* 6.132, just quoted in the main text. Note also *Anec. Helv.* 1 (*ed.* Hagen, Teubner 1870), p. XLVI. 24, 25–8; Diomedes 450.4; Trypho 3, 204.2 Sp.; Cocondrius 3, 243.13, 15 Sp.

[154] Although Theon has explicitly associated ἀμφιβολία with the dialecticians (80.30f.), the remark that 'many people think τὴν ἀμφιβολίαν occurs only in the accusative case' at 82.29f. appears to suggest that he is misidentifying Stoic Reference with Aristotelian ἀμφιβολία. Yet in the classification of obscurities at pp. 129–30, Theon gives as one instance of what he calls 'ἀσάφεια περὶ τὴν σύνταξιν', 'inclarity in the syntax' (130.5ff.), an expression which is plainly a case of Aristotelian Amphiboly (130.5f.). Further, Amphiboly as a distinct fallacy/ ambiguity mode appears only in the *s. el.*, with which Theon was almost certainly not acquainted. Whether he met it elsewhere – say, in another rhetorical text – is unknown.

[155] One possibility is that expressions in the second group were classed under Elleipsis. A prominent characteristic of ancient Greek is that third-person verbs can have their subjects either explicit or understood from context; hence, where it is unclear whether a substantive is or is not the verb's subject-case, such expressions can be classed as giving rise to Elleipsis ambiguities, according to the rules sketched for the species in 6.4.4.

[156] Of course the *s. el.* also lists Form of Expression ambiguities: see Appendix, and 6.3.4, n. 55. But the Stoics cannot be criticised for failing to recognise a form of ambiguity which is explicitly associated with the Aristotelian categories (*s. el.* 22.178a4ff.), and which it is hard to accept as a class of ambiguities at all, rather than as, say, a class of anomalies.

syntactic rôles; and this is precisely the position adopted by Apollonius with regard to what are classifiable as cases of Aristotelian Amphiboly (*synt*. 345.10ff.; *cf*. Priscian *inst*. 18, 234.19ff.).

Theon's last point (83.9–13) is that prefixing the definite article to the grammatical subject of a Reference expression cancels its ambiguity, whatever the nominals' case. Galen actually employs this device in describing the second of his illustration's possible significations (14.5G, 23E); and the same policy is advised by the author of the *Rhetorica ad Alexandrum* (25). Theon does not realise that the addition of one definite article has failed to clear up the ambiguity as to the identity of Leodamas' brother in his first illustration – which may far more plausibly be said to have been resolved, instead, by the relative position of the nouns – but the device would serve to indicate the subject of the participle. His observation may be drawn from the dialecticians; on balance, however, it is far more likely his own. The didactic tone of the *prog*. will be familiar by this stage, and there is no sign that the other Stoic species were accompanied by comments on appropriate disambiguation procedures, just as there is no hint that the summary of such procedures which rounds off Quintilian's ambiguity classification is one of his list's specifically Stoic features (see 8.2).

6.7.4   Reference: conclusions

It is especially frustrating that this last species should be one of the hardest to interpret. It must remain obscure how the elaborate *de soph*. division was wound up, and the meagre amount of information from the *de soph*. cannot be securely supplemented by a comparison with its *prog*. counterpart. Reference's position in the *de soph*. list points to its being some sort of syntactic mode: locating the point of difference between it and Significant Part is not easy, however, given the state of the text, and the obscurity and possible unreliability of Galen's report. Theon's account is fuller, and the text unproblematic, but it diverges at a number of important points from Galen's,

397

and most of what is fresh in it has turned out to be of very doubtful authenticity. On the other hand, comparison of Theon's first example with one sub-group of Aristotelian Amphiboly has brought Reference's scope, as far as it can be reconstructed, into sharper focus.

An unexpected outcome of this investigation has been a further glimpse of that now familiar deficiency in the Stoic system, the lack of a precise and comprehensive syntactic terminology. In this respect the Stoa seems to have made little progress over Aristotle: or at least they did not apply advances in that field to the taxonomy of ambiguity. To be precise, what is required is some description of the important, indeed logically fundamental, syntactic distinction between the referential and the predicative positions occupied by terms (cases). What little is known of Stoic work on the theory of reference reveals nothing in this area.[157]

6.8   General conclusions

The two Stoic classifications are the earliest known contributions to the explicit and systematic taxonomy of ambiguity. The only truly comparable earlier material, from Aristotle, is importantly different. His various lists, for all their outstanding merits – and they do, in some respects, surpass the Stoic ones – either have been subordinated to some specialist interest, such as the classification of fallacies or apparent enthymemes, or literary critical problem-solving, or are sketchy, and lacking a secure foundation on a precise conception of linguistic ambiguity; or both. The *de sophismatis* classification, in contrast, is constrained in its application only by the bound-

---

[157] The most important contributions to the reconstruction of the Stoic theory of reference are Frede 1974a: 53ff., Lloyd 1978, Egli 1978. Lloyd points out, 288f., that the Stoic theory is by modern standards incomplete, since it has nothing to say, so far as we know, about opaque contexts, and that token-reflexives are outside its scope, since its objects are disambiguated propositions. However, such token-reflexives as *this* produce not ambiguity, but generality or multiple applicability: see 4.5, with Denyer 1988. Egli 1978 offers an alternative to standard quantificational theory, based on Stoic texts relating to anaphoric pronouns.

aries of the whole of Stoic dialectic, while the *progymnasmata* list, even if a servant of stylistics, seems not to have suffered for its narrower loyalties, and may even have gained somewhat, by its attention to the exigencies of actual contexts.

At the same time, both Stoic classifications are marred by faults which *prima facie* are not to be expected in a creation of Stoic dialecticians famed for their precision and exhaustiveness in logic, as well as for their pioneering work in grammar. Their conception of syntax as mere linear association or grouping, comparable with the ordering of letters or syllables, is inadequate and simplistic. It leaves the systems apparently quite unable to cope with the ambiguities Aristotle listed under Amphiboly. This deficiency is especially surprising given that such ambiguities typically turn on uncertainty of grammatical function, where what is unclear is which word in a complex is subject and which object (to use the traditional descriptions): for the fundamental distinction of Stoic syntax is that of subject and predicate, and the Stoic classification of predicates included "transitive" constructions. It is possible that such distinctions played some part in the identification of Reference ambiguities (Galen himself associates these with Amphibolies), or that Amphibolies were reclassified; but the evidence is too shaky in the one case, and too meagre in the other, to accept either explanation without qualms.

Further, a more detailed defence would be required before Common, Part, and Non-significant Part could be accepted as ambiguity species at all; and the apparent failure to provide identity criteria between written and spoken *lexeis*, given that these species allow for homographic ambiguities, is grave. The fundamental problems are that the Stoics have identified *lexeis* as ambiguity-bearers without taking into consideration the serious short-comings of traditional orthography, and without giving grounds for accepting *lexeis*, spoken or written, as bearers of meaning, when as such they could not form part of the *logoi* which are the authentic semantic productions of speakers of a language (D.L. 7.55ff.). The question is whether the Stoics have not spread the notion of ambiguity too wide, to include cases where what is unclear is not, primarily, meaning, but which utterance or inscription is in play. Given that there is no universal consensus on the scope of ambiguity in this difficult area, and that almost all the supporting framework of the lists has been lost, the Stoic position cannot be dismissed as hopeless. But there is certainly a difficulty with identifying *logos* as "significant articulate vocal sound issuing from the mind" of a speaker, and at the same time making room for some *lexis* which is significant, but is not a *logos* or part of one. All that distinguishes the *logos* from significant *lexis* is that some intelligent being has uttered it (and not, say, a prattling babe or a parrot). Phonologically, morphologically, grammatically, and semantically, they are – or should be – identical.

Further, the Stoics' principles of division, especially regarding the two Homonymies, and Elleipsis and Pleonasm, as well as Common and the Part species, are unsatisfactory, and it is hard to believe that these defects are all illusions induced by Galen's hostility and negligence. It is not just that the Stoics seem never to have provided a precise account of context: it is also that contextualisation of utterances is more than redundancy, it is a grave theoretical error, if its effects are taxonomically restricted to single terms. Both the association of the Part species in both lists, and the dissociation of Common and Part in the *prog.* classification, were seen to be open to very serious objections.

The Stoic principles of classification can now be reviewed.

The first is by *bearer*. Leaving Common and (Non-significant) Part on one side for the moment (the move is, of course, revealing), two types of bearer, single term and multiple term, can be differentiated. Into the first falls Homonymy in Simples; into the second, all the remaining species. This latter group can be divided by reference to the utterance's constituents: is the ambiguity one of grouping of these, or not? Grouping ambiguities will comprise Significant Part, and perhaps Reference too, whose status and identity remain puzzling. Non-grouping species comprise Elleipsis, Pleonasm, and Homonymy in Simples. How are these to be subdivided?

A second principle is now applied, *defect*. Elleipsis and Pleonasm must belong together, given their designations, utterances assigned to them being perceived as defective in one or other of two ways; but it is hard to see why only two sorts of defect, superfluity and deficiency, should be chosen, or how, exactly, these are themelves to be securely identified. The textual grounds for believing that the *prog.* Stoics may have rejected this principle of classification altogether have already been sketched.

Homonymy in Compounds utterances, uniquely, owe their ambiguity to *the presence of a term otherwise classifiable, i.e.* under Homonymy in Simples – hence the species' close association. But, as noted, hiving these off from cases in which word-complexes of indeterminate length are made ambiguous by the presence of some member of one or other of the other ambiguity species, is arbitrary and unacceptable (a problem which prompted the alternative, speculative, explanation of Homonymy in Compounds as the class of "dual focus" homonymies). The problem remains even if the two Homonymies are initially grouped together on the grounds that their ambiguity is due to the same primary bearer, *i.e.* some homonymous term, either in isolation, or contextualised.

As for Common and (Non-significant) Part, the fact that their members are undifferentiated *lexeis* strongly suggests they should be placed together, as classing *similar bearers*, the *differentia* being whether or not the *lexis* can or cannot form a single part of speech. But the regrettable association of syntactic and graphic/phonetic linear grouping has split up what should, surely, have formed a single species.

The fact that neither classification has come down in its original context, and in the case of Theon's list almost certainly not in its original form either, prevents complete and exhaustive analysis. In particular, the associated definitions do not (definitely) survive; and it is not even clear that the classifications were intended to be exhaustive, as far as possible (although this is a reasonable assumption, given the aspirations of Stoic dialectic to provide the authoritative theoretical account of all rational discourse). Unclear too is whether each species is supposed to classify non-arbitrarily – that is, whether for any given species there will be at least one utterance(-type) which will fall under this one species and no other, even if other utterances fall under several species (either because they are multiply ambiguous, or because none of the possible classificatory pigeon-holes is preferable to all the others).

That theoretically complex questions like these cannot be answered on the basis of such a tiny store of information is not surprising. We should be as grateful that Theon had the wit to appreciate Stoic practical utility, as that Galen at least took the trouble to report the system he misunderstood. Comparison of the two classifications allows precious insights into their interior workings which no other exegetical tactic – investigation of Galen's criticisms, or of Aristotle's list, or of the rhetorical and grammatical treatments – could provide. It is rare for scholars of Stoicism to have the luxury of two independent sources; to have even one who regards his Stoic material as worth recording in some detail, in something like its original form, is a boon indeed.

Finally, I shall also review the place which these and similar classifications of ambiguities may have had in dialectical education and practice. They will not, I take it, alert anyone for the first time to the existence of some instances of ambiguity, for, Stoic and general ancient presumptions of authoritativeness in linguistic matters notwithstanding, such untrained awareness is presumably part of normal linguistic knowledge. But the Stoa could still make a broad and persuasive response to Skeptic criticism of the uselessness of dialectic for coping with ambiguities, by proposing a three-part programme of combined theoretical and practical education. It will prove the dangerous potential of ambiguity, by identifying it as a cause of superficial and deceptive plausibility (as noted in 3.1, and to be explored in detail in Chapter Seven). It will offer important illustrations of this danger in the case of technical philosophical terms (like those listed in 3.3). And it will sharpen the intuitive ability to recognise and distinguish ambiguities, by making it conscious and active in the broader striving for rational and moral consistency, and by providing classificatory frameworks, like those examined in this chapter. However this learning process would have been described, a prospective philosopher or sage will be made actively aware, not only that there are utterances meeting the proper criteria of ambiguity, but also, as argued in 3.4, that ambiguities must be shunned in one's own discourse, and detected and neutralised in that of others. Only dialectic – Stoic dialectic – can help, because it alone offers the appropriate combination of spheres of competence: a justification I shall explore in 7.6.

Yet, even if it proves practically (which means, primarily, morally) relevant to familiarise oneself with ambiguity as part of a course in technical philosophy, what possible function can the classification of ambiguities serve? Why should one need to know, as a matter of theory, that there are different types of ambiguity, or that ambiguity can occur in different species of linguistic bearer? The answer I shall offer to this criticism is speculative, for no evidence directly relevant to it has survived; it is not even known whether Stoics actually had to meet it.

Classification presupposes some sort of account, the clearer and more coherent the better, of what ambiguity is, or is assumed to be; and the Stoa did draw up at least one detailed and precise definition. Although there may have been internal disputes about the scope and varieties of ambiguity (and discrepancies between the two surviving classifications strongly suggest that there were), no doubt seems to have been felt that what was being defined and classified is actually out there to be defined and classified, an objective linguistic phenomenon. Just as there simply are such things as impressions, parts of speech, and *lekta*, so there simply are such things as ambiguities. All that need be done is to identify it and to classify its types by appropriate application of the apparatus of Stoic dialectic. Other theoreticians may disagree with the Stoa, but their accounts are not true competitors: inasmuch as they fail to apply the linguistic, semantic, and logical categories and concepts identified and deployed by the Stoic expert, they are simply wrong, and their work has no value.

The Stoa is thus laying claim to an authoritative account (or as near authoritative as possible) of what ambiguity is. Its confidence in this matter is an application of the all-encompassing, philosophically indispensable assurance that there is an objectively existing, objectively knowable reality. Of course, Stoics are not unique in this belief. What distinguishes their conception of the cosmos is its pervasive, radical rationality: the reason that the world is knowable to any degree by the human mind is precisely that it too is by nature rational. True wisdom consists in bringing one's individual reason into tune with the reason that governs and organises the whole, by understanding god's causal rôle, the logical laws of reasoning, and one's own rationality. It is this capacity to appreciate the workings of the divine reason, and to grasp the principles of reasoning, which distinguishes humans from brutes, and gives them their special rôle in the cosmos.[158]

From this perspective, classifying ambiguities no longer looks like stamp-collecting. It is a contribution to meeting the obligations humans have as 'students of god and his works', as Epictetus puts it.[159] Further, the mere possibility of orderly and comprehensive taxonomy is a fresh assurance of the rationality of the world. Ambiguity is not in itself a desirable phenomenon, although perhaps even it could be justified, had we only Chrysippus' ingenuity. (Plutarch mockingly reports his teleological explanations of "blessings in disguise", such as bedbugs and mice: *st. rep.* 21.1044D (540); *cf.* Porphyry *de abstinentia* 3.20.1ff. (part, 54P).[160]) A probable Stoic explanation of ambiguity's presence in language as it exists today is that it is the result of the corruption of language over time, as the basic correspondence between linguistic terms and struc-

---

[158] *E.g.* Seneca *ep.* 124.13f. (60H), 76.9f. (63D); and esp. Epictetus *diss.* 1.6.12ff. (63E).

[159] *Diss.* 1.6.21 (63E5).

[160] Schofield 1991: 82f. observes how such explanations purport to demonstrate the anthropocentric focus of the Stoic cosmos. Explanations of this type have a long history, however. Aristotle gives as an example of the rhetorical fallacy of "Accident" the praise heaped on the mice who gnawed through Assyrian bowstrings: *rhet.* 2.24.1401b14ff. (with Herodotus 2.141). Ammonius argues that the gods deliberately use ambiguous oracles in order to benefit us, treating us, as they always do, as autonomous individuals who must make their own decisions: *int.* 137.12ff.; contrast Plutarch's claim that people have become less tolerant of ambiguity and obscurity in oracles: *orac. Delph.* 26.406F–407A.

tures, on the one hand, and the constituents of the world, with all their activities, passivities, and interrelations, on the other, began to break down, and language became, not a faithful guide to the world, but an intermittently unreliable and deceiving one. Yet even here the intelligible orderliness of things is not lost. Ambiguity does not simply happen, in any fashion, in any chance linguistic grouping: it may be a paradigm of degeneration, and is certainly a stumbling-block for the unwary, but it is categorisable and analysable by the enlightened intellect. In their systematic intelligibility its manifestations are as much a demonstration of the fundamental rationality of the world and the perfectible rationality of humans as are the "pathologies" elaborated by Stoic moral psychology (*e.g.* D.L. 7.111–15). Classifications will be serviceable only in so far as they are accurate and theoretically rigorous, since what is needed, strictly, is not some rough-and-ready rule of thumb for sorting out linguistic impressions, but a faithful reconstruction of objective divisions and distinctions. Any less demanding project would mean allowing our perfectible apprehension of the world, to remain imperfect and so would vitiate, however small and apparently negligible the flaw, the whole enterprise of achieving the perfection of human reason.[161]

It would be naive to assume that Stoic dialecticians always kept in mind as they worked such an elaborate justification of their interest in ambiguity. Ambiguities represented then a tough and fascinating theoretical and diagnostic challenge, just as they do today. The development of characteristically Stoic taxonomic principles which meet independently-agreed expectations of what would count as successful and appropriate classification in this field could not only provide convincing backing for Stoic claims of superiority in one more disputed territory: it could also attract and stimulate those who simply felt intellectual curiosity about language and logic.

---

[161] A survival of Stoic interest in the detection of regularities in degenerative states, or pathology, may be the doctrine of linguistic πάθη in later rationalist grammar: see p. 492 and n.

Later Stoics warned against the seductive charms of the higher reaches of logic,[162] and slotting hitherto uncategorised ambiguities into their proper pigeon-holes, or challenging some other analyst's findings, might have held similar attractions.

Nor should the more narrowly practical usefulness of classifications be forgotten.[163] The dialectician can operate in the secure knowledge that he has grasped exactly how many possible ways there are for an utterance to be ambiguous, and can compare any given suspect utterance against a comprehensive range of examples. But classifications will be useful too to aspiring philosophers: as "how-(not)-to" guides for those eager to apply their Stoic stylistic principles; as handy *aides-memoire*; and, most obviously, as convenient vehicles for dealing with such complex and difficult logico-linguistic topics as context, autonymy, syntax, and reference, and with any number of relevant fallacies (the Wagon, the Dog-father), with all of which we have grappled, as best we might, in the course of this investigation.

---

[162] *E.g.* Epictetus *diss.* 2.23.44–6 (31T); Seneca *ep.* 89.18: 'Haec [*sc. logica*] … quo minus legas non deterreo, dummodo quicquid legeris, ad mores statim referas'.

[163] A modern parallel for classification of ambiguity as a paedogogic aid is Black 1952: 183–200, which perhaps suggests how a Stoic classification might originally have been fleshed out with examples, explanations, and argument. The Stoic classifications use grammatical categories, however, in a way that Black, who focusses on single term or "conceptual" ambiguities, does not. On the other hand, the Stoic lists can be contrasted with the typologies of ambiguity formulated by *e.g.* Robinson 1941, esp. 145: the reason there is such a lot of ambiguity is that 'since we shall never have done clearing up confusions, our words will always be concealing differences'.

7

AMBIGUITY AND THE FALLACY

7.1 Stoic interest in fallacies

It is recognised today that interest in sophisms, puzzle arguments, and paradoxes was neither a casual diversion nor an accident of the Stoa's origins, but a formative influence on the school. Zeno's own intellectual origins lie partly in the minor "Socratic" schools (*e.g.* D.L. 7.16, 25 (31M); Stobaeus 2.22.12ff. (= *S.V.F.* 1.49 (31K)); frr. 105, 106D), whose fascination with sophisms and puzzles was, or became, their chief claim to notoriety, and he himself is reported to have recommended the study of dialectic to his students precisely because it would teach them to solve fallacies: Plutarch *st. rep.* 8.1034E (31L5). Later, Chrysippus was to express contempt for "Megarian questions", whose authors 'had acquired a great reputation for their wisdom, but now their mode of argument [λόγος] is turned into a reproach against them, on the grounds that some parts of it are rather clumsy and others manifestly sophistical' (Plutarch *st. rep.* 10.1036F, *cf.* E (31P3)). Yet he himself wrote many treatises on the "sophistical" arguments which are most closely associated in the sources precisely with the Megarians, the Dialecticians, and other "Socratic" schools: D.L. 7.196–8 (= *S.V.F.* 2.15–16, pp. 7, l. 34–8, l. 20 (37B3–6)).

Stoic dialectic grew far beyond the narrow ambit sketched for it by Zeno into a science able to distinguish truth from falsehood across the board: *e.g.* D.L. 7.47 (31B7). The felt need to recognise, solve, and classify logically and philosophically important puzzle arguments was none the less a major impetus to its creation and development as an intrinsic part of the Stoic philosophical system. Puzzles could also be memorable, striking, and concise vehicles for important teachings,

407

especially within logic itself, and means of attack or counter-attack on the school's critics and rivals. Opponents of the Stoa used the same method. One of the best known incidents in the war between the Stoa and Skepticism is the New Academy's deployment of the Liar and the Sorites (the "Heaping" argument), as challenges to the certainty and scope of Stoic logic and epistemology, while Diodorus Cronus' Master Argument forced careful re-examination and formulation of Stoic modal concepts.[1]

It is therefore surprising that no extensive classification of fallacies which is firmly known to be Stoic has survived: certainly nothing comparable with Aristotle's vastly influential classification in the *Sophistical Refutations*. What made that classification possible, and helped its longevity, was, ironically, its theoretical indeterminacy, or, less charitably, its theoretical inadequacy (see 5.1). The work cannot boast a conception of validity fully independent of the negative constraints – the ways an argument fails to go through – which are imposed by the illegitimate "dialectical" manoeuvres Aristotle is classifying (note esp. 5.167a23ff., 26.181a1ff.). A sophistical refutation is conceived of as something deliberately employed to mislead, to score debating points; the neutral notion of an argument which simply goes wrong, regardless of use or context, is still weak and unformed. Thus, at 11.171b21f., a syllogism which only appears to be appropriate to a given

---

[1] A puzzle argument which could well have been a contribution to exposition of doctrine is the Wagon, D.L. 7.187 (37R): see 6.3.4; almost certainly a weapon against other schools was the puzzle of Dion and one-footed Theon, Philo *aet. mundi* 48 (= *S.V.F.* 2.397 (28P)), with Sedley 1982b: 267ff.; more briefly at LS 1987: 1: 175f. On the Liar: D.L. 7.44 (37C), 196f. (= *S.V.F.* 2.15, p. 7, l. 34–p. 8, l. 6 (37B3)), the list of Chrysippus' works on the topic; Cicero *acad.* 2.95f. (37H5–6); Plutarch *comm. not.* 2.1059DE (37I); *cf.* Rüstow 1910; Ebbesen 1981a: 1: 42–5. On the Sorites: Chrysippus *Logical Questions* col. 9, ll. 7–12 (= *S.V.F.* 2.298a, p. 106, ll. 7–10 (37G)); D.L. 7.197 (= *S.V.F.* 2.15, p. 8, ll. 9f. (37B4)), 7.44, 82 (37C, D); Galen *med. exp.* 16.1ff. Walzer (37E); Sextus *M.* 7.416 (37F); Cicero *acad.* 2.92–4 (37H); and *cf.* esp. Ebbesen 1981a: 1: 45f.; Barnes 1982; Burnyeat 1982; and further, 7.4. On the Master Argument: LS 38A–F; and see Sedley 1977: 96–102; Giannantoni 1981; Denyer 1981; Prior 1955/8. On Zeno's intellectual debt to paradox as a form of argument: Schofield 1983: 49ff. On the whole topic of sophisms: Ebbesen 1981a: 1: 49; LS 1987: 1: 229f.

subject-matter (*i.e.* to operate with the principles of a given science) is thereby as much eristic or sophistic, and hence as 'deceptive and unfair', as the "syllogism" which only appears to be a syllogism; and the distinction between eristic and sophistic (22ff.) does not help. On the other hand, Aristotle is clear that the intention to deceive is the sophist's, the appearance of genuineness his argument's.

Aristotle's conception of ambiguity is also unsatisfactory, in part because his identity criteria for linguistic items appear to be confused and fluctuating, and the result is a discrepancy between the number of fallacy types and the number of modes of ambiguity (see 5.4). Yet his classification of sophisms "dependent on language" (παρὰ τὴν λέξιν) is immensely impressive none the less, with applications far outside the limited scope of the *s. el.* Finally, although the systems of the *s. el.* and the *Rhetoric* cannot be translated into the formal language of the *Analytics*, which has no proper place for ambiguity, generations of commentators have tried their hand at doing so.[2]

The Stoic logician's world, in its maturity, was very different. Arguments are carefully distinguished from their linguistic expressions. At least one definition, elegant, complex, and precise, of ambiguity, had been constructed. Systems for classifying invalid arguments, a variety of accounts of invalidity, and a sophisticated and expanding metalogic are all available. Exploration of the nature and forms of plausibility was motivated by peculiarly Stoic ethical concerns, for the attractiveness of at least some fallacious reasoning will be

[2] The structure of formal syllogisms and proofs tends to limit Aristotle's interest anyway to homonymies, and his comments on these tend to occur where he is discussing discovery of premisses, definitions, and explanations, and connected problems: *an. po.* 1.11.77a9, 24.85b10f., 2.13.97b29ff., 17.99a7. Elsewhere, linguistic factors are irrelevant: the assumption is that homonymous terms (always the middles: 1.12.77b28) are absent. Barnes 1975: 145 identifes the 'παραλογισμός' of 1.12.77b27 as including or comprising the fallacy of equivocation, and thus as different from that of 77b20: but this earlier paralogism could be a fallacious argument from appropriate scientific premisses, as distinct from both a syllogism from the opposite premisses (*i.e.* opposed to the true ones) (19f.) and a syllogism using premisses from another science (21f.).

deeply worrying to a philosopher who is committed both to the ultimate reliability of human cognitive capacities and to the moral gravity of correct assent. Already in the early Stoa lists were being compiled of the variants of fixed-format sophisms, such as the Horned, the Veiled Man, the No-Man, and the Mowing (or Reaping), as well as the Heaping and the Liar already mentioned, whose traditional titles reflect the content of the archetype's premisses and conclusion, and in some cases hint as well at the difficulty posed by any argument of that pattern.[3] Allusions to Stoic classifications of sophisms – their principles now obscure – are also preserved. There are fallacies παρὰ τὴν φωνὴν καὶ τὰ πράγματα, "due to vocal sounds and the meanings(?)", D.L. 7.43 (31A7), and a trichotomy, 'deficient and insoluble and conclusive', is mentioned, whose members presumably share something other than conventional formatting (7.44 (37C)). Treatment of fallacies is given special mention in accounts of mature Stoic dialectic (7.43f. (31A7), 82 (37D); Cicero *acad.* 2.45f., 92ff. (37H)), and the number and range of Chrysippus' works on fallacies are especially impressive: D.L. 7.196–8 (=*S.V.F.* 2, p. 7, l. 34–8, l. p. 19 (part, 37B)).[4]

---

[3] Fallacies of this sort include the Sorites or Heaping Argument (references in n. 1) and the Horned, D.L. 7.44, 82 (37C, D), 187. On the No-man, which played an important rôle in anti-Platonic polemic: Simplicius *cats.* 105.8ff. (30E), quoted in 6.3.4; and *cf.* Ebbesen 1981a: 1: 46–9; Sedley 1985: 88. On the Mowing or Reaping Argument, a problem in modal logic devised by the Dialectical school: D.L. 7.25 (31M), Ammonius *int.* 131.24ff. (38I). The Veiled was known to Aristotle, who analysed it as due to the (non-linguistic) fallacy mode Accident, *s. el.* 24.179a26ff.; see *e.g.* Barnes 1979; Matthews 1982; Mignucci 1985. Epicurus' response to this fallacy is explained by Sedley 1973: 72f.; see also 3.5. The Horned is said to have been invented by Eubulides: D.L. 2.108, 7.187; by Diodorus Cronus: 2.111; and by Chrysippus: 7.187. Ebert 1991: 191ff. argues, but without direct, reliable evidence, that the peculiar "out" version of the Horned quoted by Sextus *P.H.* 2.241 is Diodorean; see also 7.6, n. 33. The Growing Argument was central to the development of Stoic metaphysics: Plutarch *comm. not.* 44.1083A and ff., (28A), anon. *in Tht.* 70.5ff. (28B), with Sedley 1982b.

[4] Many of the patterns of argument now generally claimed as fallacious, *e.g.* those *ad* something-or-other (*ad hominem, ad verecundiam, etc.*), and the so-called "inductive fallacies", do not fall comfortably within the framework of the criteria for validity and soundness of a deductive logic, and perhaps, as an extreme view, tend to show that what are classed by lay standards as "good" or "bad" arguments – or indeed simply as arguments – cannot be formalised within such systems. On these issues, see Hamblin 1970. They can be safely ignored here because they are irrelevant to the reconstruction of the Stoic theories of argument and of the linguistic

7.2 The principles of classification of fallacies

Even in very broad outline Stoic taxonomic principles for the fallacy cannot now be reconstructed with any certainty from reliable sources. But *a priori* two approaches seem appropriate, and should, minimally, be consistent and complementary, in any theoretical account of fallacies (*cf.* Kirwan 1979: 37). First, a classification of logical defects might be compiled; any argument classed as "fallacious" or "sophistic" will, presumably, exhibit one or more of these. This is a task for the logician. Second, those features of a fallacious argument might be identified which, despite its unsoundness, tend to induce assent to its conclusion; its similarity to some sound argument or arguments may well be prominent in this part of the account.

This dual approach was already known in antiquity. Almost at the beginning of the tradition Aristotle wrote: 'That there are syllogisms on the one hand, and on the other what are not syllogisms but seem to be, is clear. For just as in other cases too this comes about through some similarity, so also it holds in the case of arguments' (*s. el.* 1.164a23–6).[5] Galen, whose *de sophismatis* is a defence of Aristotle's classification of ambiguities in the *s. el.* (see 5.1, 5.4), must have read at least its first four chapters, and so must have known this passage; and he clearly shared the view it expresses: the inexperienced can be deceived by similarities between true and false arguments even where a conclusion is manifestly false; giving the solution of a fallacy is identifying its similarity to some true argument (*an. pecc.*

fallacy, which clearly did not take any (systematic) account of them. Brunschwig 1980: 141–3 argues forcefully against taking a – probably Stoic – distinction, reported by Sextus *M.* 8.308f., *P.H.* 2.141f. (36B8–10)), between arguments which reach their conclusions ἐφοδευτικῶς, "progressively", and those which do so both ἐφοδευτικῶς and ἐκκαλυπτικῶς, "progressively and in a revelatory manner", as something like that between arguments from reason and arguments from authority. On the other hand, the dialecticians, who may be Stoics, behind the classification of fallacies recorded by Sextus, seem to have raised the issue of the relativeness of plausibility, of appearing true: see 7.6.

5 *Cf.* Hamblin 1970: 13f.: Aristotle's scheme makes the modes of the appearance of soundness coincide with the modes of unsoundness, for the latter at once lack and mimic those features of arguments which guarantee their validity.

dign. 2.3, pp. 55.4ff., esp. 56.3f., 57.8ff. Marquardt (*script. min.* 1) (= (part) *S.V.F.* 2.272)).[6]

This second task would fall within the broad sweep of Stoic dialectic, which could call on its resources of formal logic, epistemology, semantics, grammar – indeed on any aspect of the study of human reasoning and language use – in order to explain unforced errors in the cognitive and ratiocinative processes, as well as to offer that explanation as a safeguard against misuse and abuse of the power of assent. At the highest level this will be a vital contribution to the moral welfare of agents, the distinctively Stoic motivation for doing logic and dialectic. The virtue of dialectic embraces the virtues of "freedom from precipitancy", ἀπροπτωσία, which is the knowledge of when to assent and when not; and "uncarelessness", ἀνεικαιότης, a firm rational principle directed against the (merely) "likely", εἰκός: D.L. 7.46 (31B2, 3). Precipitate assent is not some minor intellectual failing, but a danger to the orderliness and control necessary for a happy and fulfilled life: 7.48 (41B8); *cf. PHerc.* 1020, cols. 1, 4 (41D). As a virtue, dialectic is the prerogative of the wise, but it can assist ordinary people too 'when, surrounded, even deceived, by fallacious and captious questions, and unable to solve them, they may abandon the truth' (Cicero *acad.* 2.46).[7]

---

[6] The scheme was inherited from Aristotle by the scholastic philosophers, in east and west alike – see Ebbesen 1987: 115ff. for the western distinction between the *causa non existentiae/causa defectus* and the *causa apparentiae/principium motivum* – but this did not prevent a *s. el.* commentator from criticising Aristotle himself for not giving both 'the principle by which it appears [*sc.* to be valid] and by which it is defective', 'principium quo apparet et quo deficit' (Ebbesen 1981a: 1: 7; text at 1981a: 2: 430, ll. 38–45).

[7] Of course, it can be disputed how far any of the infamous "named" fallacies in particular (see nn. 1, 3), with their notoriously absurd conclusions, could have any effect on an ordinary person's cognitive state. The point, I take it, is that some applications of these fallacy-types require expert attention because they are *not* obviously false, and that these cases tend to be directed against philosophical technicalities (Arcesilaus' and Carneades' versions of the Sorites, for instance (*cf.* n. 19)); and also that some sophisms, while having manifest absurdities for their conclusions, may yet lead to doubt and confusion, because their flaws will be clear only to the trained dialectician. It is the beginning philosopher, then, who is most at risk, with just enough knowledge to see problems and not enough to solve them: hence Chrysippus' careful instructions as to how they are to be introduced to Skeptical argumentation: Plutarch *st. rep.* 10.1035Fff. (part, 31P).

The Stoics, unlike Aristotle, could not dismiss an argument as sophistic on the grounds that it contains an ambiguity, for the simple reason that in Stoic logical theory arguments are not linguistic items, but systems of *lekta*: *e.g.* D.L. 7.63 (33F1); Sextus *P.H.* 2.107.[8] Language and what it signifies are not entirely isomorphic or complementary. Flaws and distortions exist today in what was once a (near-)perfect mirror of the cosmos, its structure and inhabitants. Arguments, in particular, may be badly framed, or wrongly interpreted, simply because of their linguistic form, which as a result will come high on the list of factors inducing unfounded assent. Ambiguity will be perhaps most often responsible for the mismatch between what is being argued and how it is expressed in words.

On this view, a Stoic classification might or might not include a "fallacy due to ambiguity", or more broadly a "linguistic sophism", according as it was intended to capture modes of defective argument, or species of deceptively plausible rational impressions. Any adequate classification of sophisms should, however, describe both sides of the counterfeit coin. An argument cannot be classed as fallacious because it contains an ambiguity, any more than it can be sonorous, or triangular; but it may be counted as such on the grounds that its success as a means of getting someone to accept a proposition – as an argument in that sense – is solely the product of the language in which it is expressed. There will then be two separate questions: first, what is wrong with the argument (*qua*

---

[8] It might be objected that, as propositions contain cases, πτώσεις, and as these are words (see 6.3.4), propositions, as well as sentences, could be ambiguous; there is no evidence for this, however (but see 4.5, n. 7). And it is obscure how the Stoic semantic scheme can use *lekta* to explain the ambiguity of a *lexis* ambiguous because of the presence of an homonymous nominal (an appellative or (?) a proper name). It cannot signify a single proposition in which the case corresponding to the nominal is ambiguous (or homonymous), for then one proposition will have to bear opposite truth-values simultaneously (and here there will be no *linguistic* ambiguity anyway). If it signifies two tokens of the same type proposition, one true and the other false, differentiated only by the signification of the case – so there will be two πράγματα in *that* sense – the Stoics will still have to explain how such ostensible ambiguities differ from sentences of multiple application, *e.g.* those containing indexicals, even if it is precisely one of the differences between names and cases that the references of occurrences of cases in *lekta* are single and fixed. See already 4.6 on these problems.

concatenation of premisses and conclusion), which belongs to the subsection of dialectic which deals with formal logic; and second, what is so attractive about its linguistic appearance, which belongs to the rest of dialectic. The odd thing is that it has to be determined first what the defective argument actually is.

Arguments are true if and only if their premisses are true and they are valid ('δι' ἀληθῶν συνάγοντες': D.L .7.79 (36A8). Thus *true*, used of an argument in a Stoic context, will, strictly, be the equivalent in modern logical jargon of *sound*.[9] Consider a very simple case. Suppose that a homonym figures in both of the sentences used to signify the premisses of an argument, and the contents of the remainders of each sentence ensure that each of the signified propositions will be true if and only if the homonym has a different sense in each, that appropriate to its context. (I shall ignore other factors bearing on the premisses' truth value.) The signified argument can be declared false either on the grounds that at least one premiss of this argument is false, although the argument is concludent, or else on the grounds that the premisses of this argument are both true, but, thanks to their linguistic expression, (only) appear to have something in common. In the jargon of Stoic logic, this argument is invalid because it is incoherent: the premisses have nothing to do with one another (see further, 7.3). But in each case it is a different argument which is being assessed.

7.3 The dialectical context

Which of the alternative analyses of the ambiguity fallacy I have sketched – by falsity, or by incoherence – found favour with the Stoa, and why?

I shall argue here that the second was preferred, and that this was primarily for dialectical reasons, to do with the secur-

---

[9] To be distinguished from the use of the technical term ὑγιές of "sound" conditionals, as at *e.g.* Sextus *P.H.* 2.104 (35C3), *M.* 8.245, 417, 427; ὑγιές itself is apparently often used in such contexts as a synonym of ἀληθές, true: *e.g. M.* 8.416, 418, D.L. 7.73 (35A6), and *cf.* Mates 1961: 136; Barnes 1980: 169, n. 11.

ing of assent to premises in the course of a public exchange. Which course was followed where such considerations were irrelevant, where merely false or unsound arguments were in question, regardless of their attractiveness, is unclear. In one important sense, ambiguity is simply not interesting to a formal logician: its effects at the level of the *lekton* are reducible without remainder to independently specifiable properties of arguments (falsity, incoherence). There is an obvious parallel between modern formal logics, in which ambiguity is not carried over into the logical calculus from natural language, and Stoic formal logic, which analyses certain properties of *lekta*, of which ambiguity cannot be one. To a Stoic dialectician, in contrast, who is also concerned with the ways in which arguments are or can be framed or deployed in actual exchanges, the interest, and the seriousness, of ambiguity cannot be doubted.

Ambiguity's deceptive properties may have been what prompted the description of some sophisms as "παρὰ τὴν φωνήν" (D.L. 7.43 (31A7)): they are "dependent on vocal sound" in so far as they can only be successfully deceptive by courtesy of their linguistic dress.[10] Take the following system of sentences, almost certainly an authentically Stoic creation:

The tunic is ἀνδρεῖος (brave/men's wear);
whatever is ἀνδρεῖος (brave) is εὔψυχος (stout-hearted);
so: the tunic is εὔψυχος (stout-hearted).

Whatever vanishingly small plausibility attaches to the conclusion plainly does so thanks to the occurrence of the word ἀνδρεῖος in the linguistic expression of the premises; it could not have exercised even this minimal level of persuasive power had ancient Greek lacked a word meaning both "brave" and "*pour homme*". From the rest of the report of this argument it is fairly certain that ἀνδρεῖος is to be interpreted appropriately to its context at each occurrence, and the resulting argument will presumably be incoherent. For sophisms like this

---

[10] So already Ebbesen 1981a: 1: 33. I agree with much of Ebbesen's invaluable discussion of the Stoic analysis of defective arguments and of ambiguity (25ff.), and his comments and explanations are consistently useful and stimulating.

one to appear sound, the ambiguity of, say, ἀνδρεῖος must be capable of generating both true but unrelated premisses (in one argument), and related but false premisses (in another). The two arguments are identical at the linguistic level, and language can (or could, in a subtler case) induce the mistaken belief that there is just one, sound, argument, or at least encourage doubt as to whether "the argument" is or is not sound. The two possible Stoic positions thus seem together to meet the minimal criteria laid down in 7.2 for a theoretical account of the fallacy. A form of words seems to express a single, sound argument, and does so precisely because it is *this* form of words; in actual fact, it represents two (or more) unsound arguments, unsound because they turn out to contain premisses which are either false or unconnected and whose apparent *simultaneous* truth and coherence with each other is a product of mere linguistic legerdemain.

Before examining the evidence available for actual Stoic views and the reasoning behind them, a pair of objections to the reconstruction offered here must be met.

Sextus *M.* 8.429ff. (part, 36c) (*cf. PH* 2.146ff.) ascribes to the Stoics a four-fold classification of "inconclusive", ἀπεραίνοντες, or "inconcludent", ἀσύνακτοι, arguments:[11] by "incoherence", διάρτησις, "deficiency", ἔλλειψις, "redundancy", παρολκή, and "defective [*i.e.* asyllogistic] form", μοχθηρὸν σχῆμα. The first is illustrated as follows:

If it is day, it is light;
but wheat is being sold in the market;
so: it is light (*M.* 8.430 (36c2)) (*or*: so: Dion is walking, *P.H.* 2.146),

which might be rendered:

If p, q; but r; so q [*or*: so s].

The premisses lack κοινωνία and συνάρτησις (*M.* 8.430 (36c2)) or ἀκολουθία (*P.H.* 2.146) towards each other and the conclusion. *M.*'s general description, with the requirement that lack of coherence characterises the relation between the premisses and the conclusion, as well as that between the premisses,

---

[11] On this terminology, and the authorship of these classifications, see n. 27.

suggests that its illustration may be incorrect. Now, would it not be true to say, in the case of most ambiguity fallacies, that *only* the premisses can be unconnected, or *only* one premiss and the conclusion? Whether it is Sextus' illustration or his general account of διάρτησις in *M.* which embodies the authentic Stoic doctrine, it is hard, all the same, to see what other Stoic analysis is available of the argument's defectiveness.

The second difficulty is that incoherence is surely supposed to characterise arguments regardless of the truth-value of their premisses, whereas the analysis of linguistic fallacies as incoherent appears to rest on the assumption that their premisses are true. But of course they may be false: only their being false cannot be the result of an incongruity or impossibility caused by their linguistic expression's being given a meaning inappropriate to its context. This second objection actually strengthens the original conviction that an adequate theoretical account of ambiguity fallacies in the Stoa must take account of both analyses. Two arguments are in play, the one contributing true premisses, the other, formal validity, to the linguistically generated appearance of a single argument.

Given that both analyses are required to explain at once the plausible appearance and the implausible actuality, why would the Stoa plump for truth over validity? What motive could the school have had for taking the truth of the premisses for granted?

In the *ἀνδρεῖος* example the glaring falsity of the conclusion might seem enough to warrant rejection of the whole argument, even were one uncertain where the trick lay. Or else one might immediately distinguish the meaning on the basis of which one is giving assent, as soon as an ambiguous term or expression is used, thereby forestalling any advance to a false conclusion, obvious or not. Both these policies – and both were advocated in antiquity – assume a context of discourse for such arguments: being sophisms, they must not only be unsound, they must appear or be capable of appearing *to someone* to be sound (as Aristotle saw: *s. el.* 8.170a12ff.). The context that they operate in, or at least recall, is that

417

of the lively public dialectical exchanges which seem to have exercised so powerful an influence on the Stoa and its contemporary rivals. The working assumption is that an argument is being posed by one individual to another, in order to win assent, first to premisses, and thereby to some conclusion.

In a dialectical context, as ancient and medieval authorities describe it,[12] progress towards a conclusion can be made only if the respondent does not disagree. The rules always specify that if the party questioned will not or cannot assent to a proposition, it can play no (legitimate) rôle in the construction of the argument. The parties need not be attacking or defending a thesis to which they are otherwise committed or opposed, but premisses conceded must form an internally consistent set. Platitudinously, premisses which are obviously true will win assent more easily than those which are obviously false or whose truth-value is unclear. Of course, obviousness and clarity are relative to some state-of-affairs and to some observer, even if a fair degree of general agreement obtains about what is or is not obviously true or false within (and between) exchanges.

Thus, in the ἀνδρεῖος illustration, assent could easily be secured to the obviously true *The tunic is "pour homme"* (assuming the tunic in question really is male attire, as is the case in the situation which our source for the argument describes). Anyone participating in a dialectical exchange will assume, *ceteris paribus*, that that is the premiss to which assent is being asked: no competent disputant would expect *The tunic is brave* to pass muster. The same will hold where the context is sophistic, with deliberately illicit manoeuvres being

---

[12] One of Aristotle's criteria for sophistic reasoning is that it is *only ad hominem*, whereas true dialectical reasoning is also an argument ἁπλῶς, *simpliciter*, or without qualification: *s. el.* 8.170a12–19, 20.177b31–4, 22.178b16–23, with *top.* 8.1.155b9–10, *de caelo* 2.13.294b7–13; and *cf. top.* 6.4.141b15ff., for a parallel distinction, which of course connects with central themes of Aristotelian epistemology, between genuine definition – definition ἁπλῶς – and definition for the comparatively ignorant; also *meta.* 10.5.1061b34ff., for the famous discussion of the Principle of Non-Contradiction. On the ancient dialectical contest in general: Hamblin 1970: 50ff.; in the Academy and Aristotle: Owen 1986d; Ryle 1968; Moraux 1968; Evans 1977. On dialectical strategies in ancient philosophical debate: Burnyeat 1976, 1979; Sedley 1977. On the medieval "obligation game": Hamblin 1970: 126ff.; De Rijk 1974.

carried out over much the same territory as, and under the guise of, legitimate dialectical exchanges. No self-respecting sophist will expect to win an argument with such questions as *This tunic is brave, isn't it?*

Hence, any Stoic analysis of ambiguity in argument which focusses on fallacies as intended to deceive, or at least perplex, would be bound to lean to the "incoherence" option, since progress to a conclusion requires assent, and assent is likelier, and so more likely to be sought by sensible and experienced persons, to (obvious) truths. There may be cases where internal consistency on the respondent's part demands assent to a falsehood; and others where both interpretations of an ambiguous sentence are acceptable. But if one is most interested in deliberately deceptive moves in the argument game, including the unscrupulous exploitation of ambiguities intended to induce assent to absurdities, or create the shamefaced semblance of it, then the sort of argument illustrated by the ἀνδρεῖος fallacy will be the chief object of concern.

Evidence for a general Stoic commitment to disambiguation by context has already been marshalled, in the shape of the distinction between the two Stoic types of ambiguity due to homonymy, discussed in 6.3. Augustine's testimony on the point will be briefly recapitulated in 7.8. Two other pieces of evidence, from Simplicius and Sextus Empiricus, strongly suggest that the analysis by incoherence was favoured by at least some Stoic dialecticians. That both this and the alternative/ complementary analysis by falsity were known and put to work in antiquity will be demonstrated with the help of a passage in Galen.

7.4   Incoherence I: Simplicius *cats.* 24.13–20 (37S)

Simplicius reports as follows:[13]

And that is why, in syllogisms due to homonymy, the dialecticians recommend keeping quiet [ἡσυχάζειν], so long as the questioner transfers the

---

[13] Simplicius cites the dialecticians' advice as support for his response to a criticism (*cats.* 24.6–9) that, if the subject-matter of the *Categories* is significant *lexeis*, which is Simplicius' own view, and if there are only homonyms (things which share a name but not a definition) because there are homonymies (words with more than

word to another signification;[14] for example, if someone asks if the tunic is ἀνδρεῖος, we will assent, if it happens to be ἀνδρεῖος; and if he asks if the ἀνδρεῖος is courageous [εὔψυχος] we will assent to this too, for it is true; but if he concludes that the tunic is therefore courageous, here ⟨they recommend⟩ distinguishing the homonymy of ἀνδρεῖος and pointing out that this is said in one way of the tunic, in another of what possesses bravery.[15]

one signification), Aristotle should really have talked about the latter. Simplicius' reply is curious, for he starts, apparently, by agreeing (24.10) that 'homonyms become clear from things' (*i.e.* it becomes clear which things are homonyms from the (concepts of) things associated with homonymies); yet he needs rather to establish that 'strictly things, not words, make homonymies' (24.20f.; *cf.* Porphyry *cats*. 61.13ff.). But whatever interpretation Simplicius wants to force on the dialecticians' advice – presumably, that people do in fact associate a number of different concepts (and thus things) with homonymies – the dialecticians originally must have had something quite different in mind.

[14] LS translate, 1: 228, 'until the questioner transfers the word to another sense'; *cf.* Ebbesen 1981a: 1: 31, Baldassari 1987 (vol. 5B): 117. But, *contra* Ebbesen *ibid.*, the "transfer" to another meaning must occur when the second premiss is posed, *not* at the conclusion, whereas we 'keep quiet' (see the main text) until then, that is, so long as the questioner continues to change his meaning. This is not possible reading 'μεταγάγη' at 24.14 (*i.e.*, with an aorist subjunctive). I thus read 'μετάγη' with two of the MSS (*L*, which never has *iota mutum*, and *A*, which has it only very rarely: see Wallies's introduction in *C.A.G.* viii, pp. ix, xii).

[15] Thus the only extant example of what is almost certainly a Stoic analysis of a linguistic sophism is of a categorical syllogism, whose premisses, if assumed true, will be of the form:

Every φ is ψ; a is ω; so, a is ψ,

where the terms φ and ω share the same linguistic expression; the premisses are clearly unconnected, but they could not, as they stand, form a characteristically Stoic syllogism (in one of the indemonstrables, or a form reducible to one: D.L. 7.78 (36A5)). Perhaps the original Stoic formulation was:

If ((whatever is φ is ψ) and (a is φ)), then (a is ψ); but ((whatever is φ is ψ) and (a is ω)); so, (a is ψ)

which could be reformulated with propositional variables as:

If (p and q), then r; but (p and s); so, r

and this comes close to the illustration at *M*. 8.430 (quoted in 7.2). (The lack of connection between the premisses is clearer still if the argument is conditionalised:

If p then (if q, r); but p; so, (if q, r); but s; so, r.

The Stoics seem not to have known the rule of conditionalisation, however: Corcoran 1974a: 179.) Barnes 1980: 171, n. 15 suggests that Sextus used a source for *M*. which was either unreliable or actually corrupt. He also points out, 169–73, the link between modern "logics of relevance" and the συνάρτησις criterion of the truth of a conditional, which is Stoic and probably Chrysippean: Cicero *fat*. 12 (38E1), with Frede 1974: 80ff., LS 1: 211, 236, 264.

The dialecticians' advice makes sense only if the ambiguous term ἀνδρεῖος is disambiguated on each occasion of utterance, and is intended by the sophist in the sense appropriate to its context. There is equivocation, a change of sense between the two sentences, but this is perfectly acceptable: indeed, it is a linguistic commonplace.[16]

Simplicius' source here is very probably Stoic. His use of the label διαλεκτικός (and of the term διαλεκτική) is usually no more than consistent with taking these dialecticians as Stoics, although, whoever they are, they are plainly not engaged in Aristotelian dialectic.[17] But at *cats.* 25.13f., where Simplicius is meeting an objection that Aristotle talks only of homonymous nouns, ὀνόματα, when verbs, participles, and conjunctions are also ambiguous, he reports that 'the dialecticians have handed down many distinctions [διαφοράς] of *or* and *or else*'. Stoic logicians of course had a vested interest in identifying varieties of *or*.[18] As for Simplicius' sample syllogism,

---

[16] Kirwan 1979: 35 has a useful distinction between ambiguity, a kind of inclarity, and equivocation, meaning two or more things (a) successively or (b) simultaneously by the same expression; the latter need not be, and often is not, a fault. He does not, however, make explicit the vital point that equivocation presupposes linguistic ambiguity. If the definition of ambiguity reported by D.L. has been correctly understood, then at least the Stoics behind it cannot have had such a distinction, for their ambiguity is defined without reference to speaker's intentions, and is explicitly *simultaneous* semantic multiplicity (4.9). Further, if the difference between the two Homonymy species was also correctly interpreted (in 6.3), then for the *de soph.* Stoics, only (single-term) instances of (b) will count as cases of ambiguity. This sort of *appropriate* meaning shift makes void Hamblin's suggested "presumption of meaning constancy" in dialectical exchanges (1970: 294–5).

[17] Simplicius' commonest use of the terms is in the sense familiar from the *Topics*: e.g. *cats.* 70.18, *phys.* 16.27, 42.25, 71.31–72.2, 476.26, *an.* 15.20, 21.19, *cael.* 28.20 (a νόμος διαλεκτικός regulating the correct form of the negation of modal propositions).

[18] ἤτοι and ἤ are used to frame disjunctions both in the fourth and fifth indemonstrables, D.L. 7.81 (36A14f.), and in isolation, 7.72 (35A4); the former 'announces that one of the propositions is false'. (The precise meaning of *announce*, ἐπαγγέλλειν, in these contexts is unclear.) Plutarch *quaest. Plat.* 10.4.1011AB argues that just because 'the dialecticians [that is, the Stoics, whose account of the parts of speech he is criticising here: cf. 6.3.5.2] above all need conjunctions' for forming complex propositions, that does not make conjunctions parts of speech. Leaving "preposed conjunctions" (*i.e.* prepositions) to one side, there seem to have been at least seven main types of Stoic σύνδεσμοι: conjunctive ((*both* ...)*and*), disjunctive (*or, or else*), conditional (*if*), para-conditional (*since*), causal (*because*), syllogistic (*e.g.*: *but, however, therefore*; *i.e.*, those used to introduce minor premises and conclusions in arguments), and expletive (see 6.3.5.2, n. 76 there).

Galen gives ἀνδρεῖος as an example of the Stoic ambiguity mode Homonymy in Simples, with the comment 'for it is either a tunic or a man' (*de soph.* 13.4f.G, 22E (37Q3); *cf.* 6.3.4); and it is a fairly safe bet that all Galen's illustrations are authentically Stoic.

One other point confirms this piece of doctrine's Stoic origin, as well as its dialectical background. Simplicius' describes the dialecticians' procedure as ἡσυχάζειν, a term familiar above all in philosophical contexts from the response recommended by Chrysippus to the Sorites, or, more precisely, from one part of that response, which has to do with handling such arguments in a dialectical situation. The tactic allows a debater not to commit himself in debate to propositions whose truth-value is obscure (whether temporarily or naturally and for all time) for he is cautioned to "fall silent" *before* the questions become obscure: Cicero *acad.* 2.93 (37H3; less coherently at Sextus *M.* 7.416 (37F)).[19] According to Simplicius, respondents are explicitly told to assent to the premisses *The tunic is male attire* and *The brave is courageous.* What he failed to note is that they will not make their assent public, and that they will make no contribution to the proceedings, either openly agreeing or openly objecting, until the fraudulent attempt to draw a conclusion. "Keeping quiet" covers, and must cover, silent assent even in the case of the Soritic arguments, since it would be absurd and wrong to withhold assent from the obvious truths leading up to the unclear premisses. As with Soritic arguments, a further assumption is at work: that questioning by the interlocutor will continue until an explicit response, positive or negative, is won. It is hardly surprising that Simplicius should have missed the crucial point that the respondent does not signal assent, for

---

[19] On Skeptical use of the Sorites and Chrysippus' response to it, see Barnes 1982; Burnyeat 1982; LS I: 229f. (briefly). Barnes 1982: 50ff. argues that Chrysippus' falling silent masks a genuine suspension of assent at some point. But, as Burnyeat 1982: 334 points out, that is to neglect the dialectical context; and what is gained is escape from having to state openly where the unclear cases (*i.e.* those whose truth-value is unclear) begin, as well as where the cut-off point between true and false premisses lies. Sextus' interpretation of "falling silent" as Skeptical ἐποχή, *P.H.* 2.253, is malicious and polemical.

he need not even have been aware of Chrysippus' response to the Sorites.[20]

"Keeping quiet" confers two advantages. On the one hand, there will be no need for blushing disclaimers that assent to the first premiss was given with ἀνδρεῖος meaning one thing, and to the second with it meaning another, since no assent has been publicly given: even the embarrassing appearance of assent to absurdity is avoided. On the other hand, the objection is framed as an objective statement of the senses of ἀνδρεῖος, not as an account of subjective understanding of it. The sophist's desired conclusion can be rejected with a combined display of our linguistic expertise and justified contempt for his ignorance.

The procedure recommended here may not, however, have been the only Stoic, even the only Chrysippean, line. Chrysippus wrote a treatise in two books *Against those who do not distinguish*, πρὸς τοὺς μὴ διαιρουμένους, which opens the list of his works on ambiguity, D.L. 7.193 (= *S.V.F.* 2.14, p. 6, l. 23 (37B2)). Schmidt saw in this work Chrysippus' proof that his teaching about ambiguity, contained in his many books on the topic, was necessary (1839/1979: 52/73, n. 75 (1979: 141)), while Cavini 1985: 119 suggests it may have concerned 'ambiguità di composizione e divisione' – that is, Common ambiguities, those 'κατὰ διάστασιν' (116; and see already 6.5.4). But in the *s. el.*, Aristotle offers the following piece of practical criticism and advice:

But of course, since it is unclear whether someone who did not determine [ὁ μὴ διορισάμενος] the ambiguity has been refuted or not, although it is permissible to distinguish [διελεῖν] in arguments, it is obviously a mistake to assent without determining the question, but in an unqualified way; so that, even if not the man himself, at least his argument closely resembles one that has been refuted. Now it frequently happens that those who are aware of the ambiguity hesitate to distinguish it [διαιρεῖσθαι], because of the crush of people who put forward such premisses, so that they will not seem to be making difficulties about everything; then, although they would not have thought that it was on this point that the argument depended, a paradox

---

[20] Simplicius clearly knows the Sorites – at *phys.* 1177.2ff. he distinguishes it from another fallacy, that of false proportion – but he does not mention any solutions to it.

often confronts them. So, since it is permissible to distinguish, one must not hesitate to do so, as was said before.   (17.175b28–38)

Aristotle's counsel is based on what he introduces as a contemporary dialectical rule: to distinguish the ambiguity in the question to which assent is being sought, in order to make clear which premiss one is agreeing to. Assent can be openly given without risking the appearance of being refuted, or of admitting a paradox. Avoiding the appearance of refutation is Aristotle's subject throughout ch. 17 (175a31ff.); his concern is explained by the facts that sophistic syllogisms are not really syllogisms at all (175a33–6), and that, if a question is ambiguous, its associated syllogism cannot be a real refutation (36–8): the distinction of senses thus serves, not to avoid a genuine refutation, but to avoid appearing to be refuted (40f.). A similar point is made at *top.* 8.1.156b36ff.; and Alexander *top.* 532.1ff. comments that such people will resort, *inter alia*, to the distinction of ambiguities to get out of their self-imposed difficulties.

Aristotle speaks of division or distinction as a recognised dialectical procedure. (Such "distinction" of meanings seems to be a special application of the now familiar method of *distinguo*, as applied, for example, in a proposed solution of what Aristotle calls fallacies due to Accident, which he himself rejects: 24.179b7ff.)[21] It may have found its way from the Academy into the Stoa, and once more become subject for debate, some theorists maintaining that it was better to distinguish senses of ambiguous items as an argument proceeds, others that the wisest course is τὸ ἡσυχάζειν. I shall come back to these procedural points in 7.6.

7.5   Incoherence 2: Sextus Empiricus *P.H.* 2.236–8

At *P.H.* 2.256–9 Sextus argues that dialectic is unnecessary and inappropriate for the resolution of ambiguities wherever

---

[21] There may be an even earlier reference to the method, in very general terms, at *Euthydemus* 295d1f.: Socrates fears the sophist is angry with him 'διαστέλλοντι τὰ λεγόμενα', 'distinguishing what is said', and this seems to be a reference back to 295b4, when he wants to reply that he knows 'with his soul' not just 'with something'.

such resolution is useful, whether in ordinary language, or in technical jargon. In 257 he refers back to an earlier example, at 237, of the sort of ambiguity which only those trained in the different expertises can distinguish.[22] At 236–40 Sextus had examined two fallacious arguments, both drawn from the field of medicine, which, it is claimed, only the doctor can solve, while the dialectician stands helpless and tongue-tied on the sidelines.[23] The dialectician's purportedly general knowledge, which should distinguish true arguments from false (229 (37A1)) apparently regardless of subject-matter, is proved useless in comparison with the range of varied expertises practised by those 'who in each expertise possess practical understanding' (236). There "the dialectician" stands in solitary opposition to "the doctor", who represents the class of experts. (Sextus' choice is presumably determined by his own interests.[24]) Likewise, 256–7 present "the dialectician" in lonely,

---

[22] Sextus' own technical term, διαστολή, neatly suggests a non-dogmatic procedure for distinguishing meanings (rather than things), for the word was used by Empiricists in preference to διορισμός, with its essentialist connotations: see e.g. Galen subfig. emp. 59.2ff., meth. med. 10.138.1K. Similarly, Sextus' experts have ἐμπειρία and training, not ἐπιστήμη, P.H. 2.256; cf. 'τὴν ἐπὶ τῶν πραγμάτων παρακολούθησιν ἐσχηκότες', 236.

[23] Sextus' description of the dialectician's reaction to the second fallacy, 'ἡσυχάσει', 239, might be taken as a reference to the "keeping quiet" tactic just described in 7.4. The parallel passage at 237, however – 'the dialectician would have nothing to say to help in solving the sophism' – shows that the dialectician actually falls silent in bewilderment, in contrast to the doctor's confident assertion ('λέξει', 238) of the argument's incoherence; and Sextus' conclusion to this whole stretch of argument (241) confirms this interpretation. There is another non-Stoic use at M. 1.311.

[24] The second of the two sophisms which Sextus quotes looks like a puzzle a Methodic doctor might set: only he would claim to know that it is the underlying πάθος, the contraction or expansion, which must be treated: cf. Galen sect. ingred. 1.79ff.K, esp. p. 86. Sextus, who argues that the Methodic school is the closest to Pyrrhonism (P.H. 1.236f.), may thus also be setting cats amongst medical pigeons. There are medical examples too in the classification of sophisms at 2.230f. (37A3): 'no-one gives absinthe to drink'; 'the doctor qua doctor kills' (37A4); 'you look frenzied' (37A6) (cf. the description of phrenitis victims at [Hipp.] morb. 3.9, 'καὶ ἀτενὲς βλέπουσι'); 'you look at an inflamed spot' (37A6) (cf. morb. 3.1, 7 on phlegmasia). Like Ebbesen 1981a: 1: 23, I hesitate to suggest they are Sextus' own, but they are almost too well adapted to Sextus' polemic. (Contrast the presumably genuine quotations from philosophers and poets used to illustrate the grammarians' ignorance, one passage from Euripides requiring medical treatment: M. 1.300ff., esp. 308.) All could have been constructed on the basis of genuine dogmatic examples which did not make such pertinent references to materia medica (on absinthe, see e.g. Dioscorides mat. med. 3.23, with Riddle 1985: 38; Arnold 1989), medical ethics (e.g. Edelstein 1967: 9–20; Carrick 1985; more briefly Phillips 1973: 114–21), and the theory of humours (e.g. Carrick 1985: 15ff.). The story of

fumbling opposition to 'those trained in each expertise', and
even to linguistically competent slaves, who need no dialectic
to distinguish ambiguities.

Sextus' first illustration runs as follows:

In diseases, during abatements [ἐν ταῖς παρακμαῖς], a varied diet and wine are
to be approved;
but in every form of disease an abatement occurs before ⟨the end of⟩ the
first three-day period;
therefore, it is necessary to take a varied diet and wine, for the most part,
before ⟨the end of⟩ the first three-day period.

Only the doctor 'will solve the sophism, knowing that abatement [παρακμή] is said in two ways, one of the whole disease
and one of the tendency of each local strain to improve after
the crisis' (238), and that the prescription of a varied diet and
wine only applies to the general abatement of the disease;[25]
'in consequence, he will say that the premisses of the argument are also incoherent [διηρτῆσθαι], one sort of abatement
being assumed in the first premiss, that is, that of the whole
condition, another in the second, that is, that of the local
condition.' In other words, the doctor knows that the conclusion is false, and knows that *abatement* has two uses or
senses.[26]

The doctor's rejection of the first argument thus starts from
his technical knowledge, but ends with the diagnosis that the
argument's premisses are "incoherent" because of the differ-

Diodorus Cronus' appeal to the doctor Herophilus at 245, on the other hand,
while too good to be true, need not be Sextus' own invention. On the nature and
authorship of this classification, see 7.6.

[25] On "abatement": *e.g.* Galen *subfig. emp.* 57.1.1–9, in the context of the empiricists'
account of disease; more generally *de totius morbi temp.* (*ed.* I. Wille, Diss. Kiel
1960) 81.3, 112.3, *meth. med.* 10.228.1, 689.7, 690.7, 932.3K, with reference to
dietary requirements.

[26] It is irrelevant here that Sextus moves at 238 from talk of the word *abatement* as
ambiguous ('abatement is said in two ways') to talk of types of abatement ('one
abatement being assumed in the first premiss ... another in the second'), for there
is no need to assume that Sextus, or his token expert, will bother with such niceties.
The crucial points are the use of the Stoic jargon *διηρτῆσθαι, be incoherent,* and
that Sextus refers back to the fallacy, at 257, as a case of ambiguity. Note that the
incoherence characterises only the relation between the premisses, which may bear
out the earlier suggestion (7.2) that such restricted incoherence suffices to make an
argument invalid.

ence in meaning of *abatement* between them. This terminology
will be remembered from *P.H.* 2.146, from the classification
of "inconcludent", ἀσύνακτος, arguments. A comparison with
the parallel passage in *M.* 8.429ff. (36C) confirms that for
Sextus the doctrine of incoherence is Stoic.[27] The dialecticians
mentioned at *P.H.* 2.235 plainly include the Stoics, whose
indemonstrable arguments were given the usual Skeptic treatment at 156ff. So, going simply by Sextus' use of the term here,
"the dialecticians" referred to both in the previous sentence,
and in the introductory paragraph (229 (37A1)), may be Stoics.
They need not be, of course, for Sextus says explicitly that the
classification is the work of 'some dialecticians; for others have

---

[27] Ebert 1991: 130ff. argues, partly on terminological grounds, that the *P.H.* classification (2.146–150) of invalid arguments is a product of the Dialectical school,
improved on by the Stoics in their own list, that at *M.* 8.429–34. (He would thus
still allow that an analysis of ambiguity as giving rise to διάρτησις, *incoherence* (as
described in 7.3) could be Stoic.) A detailed reply to all of Ebert's contentions
on this point would be impossible here (and his book came into my hands too late
to include replies to his numerous other claims about the relationship between
Dialectical and Stoic logic – although see also n. 28, 7.6, nn. 33, 38, and generally
7.6). But a comparison of the *M.* and *P.H.* lists suggests that *Sextus himself* was
not aware of any difference in origin between them. Thus, having shown at *M.*
8.396ff. that proof is non-apprehensible according to Stoic τεχνολογία, "technical
treatment" of the subject, Sextus turns to attacking its logical foundations, 'κατὰ
τὴν διαλεκτικὴν θεωρίαν', 'by way of their logical theory', 411. He starts on a
demonstration that the valid argument of the Stoics is 'undiscoverable', chiefly by
showing that all ostensibly valid arguments fail by one or other of the Stoics' own
prescriptions for inconcludency: 426–8, 428–46 (part, 36C). Admittedly, the sort
of argument under discussion at *M.* 8.428ff. is called "inconclusive", ἀπέραντος,
while that at *P.H.* 2.146ff. is "inconcludent", ἀσύνακτος, but Sextus is surely using
the terms synonymously: for, after arguing at *M.* 8.424–8 that the Stoics' "concludent", συνακτικός, argument is undiscoverable, he proposes at 428f. to deal with
the specific Stoic teaching about (not the ἀσύνακτος, but) the ἀπέραντος argument.
This does not mean that the two terms were synonymous for their users, or
that they belonged to the same school or to the same stage of development within a
school. (There is a possible sign of terminological fluidity in this area in D.L., who
uses the jargon περαντικός, *conclusive*, yet distinguishes amongst the conclusives a
subgroup of 'οἱ συνάγοντες μὴ συλλογιστικῶς', 'those drawing a conclusion not
by way of a syllogism', 7.78 (36A6), and defines true arguments as 'οἱ δι' ἀληθῶν
συνάγοντες', 79 (36A8).) All that matters is that *for Sextus* there was no difference
in meaning.
   Again, although the definitions of incoherence in *P.H.* and *M.* differ (see already
7.3), Sextus gives no sign at all that for him two doctrines are in play, and the only
indisputable attribution of the incoherence analysis of invalidity is to the Stoa.
Any differences between the lists as reported by Sextus can be easily and plausibly
accounted for by different stages of development, or by different factions, within
the Stoa.

other things to say'.[28] But it can be safely inferred that at 237f. Sextus is trying to turn the tables on Stoic opponents, by putting doctrinaire logical jargon into the mouths of the only people who (Sextus contends) can apply it in practice. At the same time, his precise line of attack strongly suggests that the doctrine of incoherence was used by Stoics to explain sophisms due to ambiguity; and incoherence is the link between fallacy and ambiguity which Sextus, for his own reasons, suppresses later, when he turns to the dogmatic distinction of ambiguities.

There is another clue to the identity of Sextus' opponents in the attack on dialectical treatment of ambiguities at 256ff.: the definition of ambiguity presented at 256, 'ἡ ἀμφιβολία λέξις ἐστὶ δύο καὶ πλείω σημαίνουσα'.[29] In case of doubt, another glance at D.L. 7.62 (text in 4.2) should confirm its Stoic origin.

[28] If Sextus is actually reporting a Dialectical classification here, as argued at length by Ebert 1991: 176ff., and tentatively assumed by LS 1: 229; 2: 222, then the most charitable interpretation must be that he does not know it, since an unannounced move from what is known to be a specific piece of work by certain "Dialecticians", *i.e.* members of the Dialectical school, to what is presented as a quite general attack on "dialecticians", *i.e.* logicians, who clearly include Stoics (the mention of indemonstrables in 235 confirms this), would be intolerable. Now, if Sextus does not know that the authors of the classification belong to the Dialectical school – is even perhaps unaware of that school's existence – then his mentioning οἱ διαλεκτικοί can never, on its own, be a reliable guide to the precise identity of the thinkers so designated. If, on the other hand, he does know of the school, but is so careless of keeping the generic and the specific references of *διαλεκτικοί* apart, then, once again, independent evidence must be forthcoming that a Dialectician is the author of whatever doctrine is in question. *P.H.* 2.166 is another passage in which the "dialecticians" are undoubtedly logicians of the Stoic (156ff.) and Peripatetic (163ff.) schools. The 'perhaps', 'ἴσως', at 235 indicates merely that it may not already be obvious from the earlier, broad criticisms of such dogmatic notions as truth, proof, *etc.*, that the special treatment of fallacies is useless and redundant, which is why Sextus will go on to argue the point explicitly and in detail at 247–55. Certainly the introduction to (247) and the conclusion of (255) that stretch of argument betray no lack of confidence in the force or the applicability of the criticisms voiced; the only doubt expressed, at 235, is as to whether the connection between the undermining of the broad logical theory and the collapse of the narrow account of fallacies is 'already', 'ἤδη', clear. I believe that neither the content of the classification, nor Sextus' manner of introducing it, require us to award it to the Dialectical school; unfortunately, as already explained in n. 27, I am unable to reply here to Ebert's arguments in the detail they demand.

[29] 'Ambiguity is an utterance signifying two and [*or:* or] more things.' 'Two or even [ἤ καὶ] more' would be closer to the Stoic definition. But presumably the 'καὶ' here is corrective ('two or more'), and the difference is a slight one. Hülser 1982: 3: 399f. comments that Sextus 'schwächt ... ab' the Stoic definition, 'bzw. er greift den für sein Argument relevanten Teil heraus'.

Sextus' next assumption might seem to undermine this confident attribution: 'and *lexeis* signify by imposition [θέσει]'. This cannot be Stoic doctrine; it is Aristotle's, or a misleading version of Epicurus', or even, perhaps, Diodorus Cronus', although he denied the possibility of ambiguity.[30] What is Sextus about here?

Sextus states explicitly that he is going to explore dogmatic distinctions of ambiguities elsewhere, and that 'if some dogmatist or other tries to argue against any of these points, he will strengthen the Skeptic argument, by himself adding support to the suspension of judgement about matters under inquiry, as a result of argumentation from both sides and undecidable disagreement', 259. Such further treatment (which does not survive) would have been justified by covering in greater detail what is dealt with here compendiously. Sextus' short, swift attack on the dogmatists unites doctrines from a number of schools into a skilful composite which none could accept, which can give no assistance in resisting Sextus' immediate criticisms, and which helps intensify the διαφωνία supposed to induce Skeptical ἐποχή. A Stoic definition of ambiguity unacceptable to Aristotelians, Dialecticians, Epicureans, *et al.* is followed by a rejection of Stoic orthodoxy about the nature of language and then a selection of cases of ambiguity, two out of three of which are signally incompatible with linguistic naturalism – technical jargon and proper names.[31] Yet a semantic conventionalist could take no comfort from this last manoeuvre: if names really are a mere matter of

---

[30] Aristotle: *int.* 16a26ff.; Epicurus: see 3.5; Diodorus: see 4.6. Ebert 1991: 179f. suggests that a subgroup of the Dialectical school may have rejected Diodorus' denial of the possibility of ambiguity, but there is no reliable evidence for internal dissension on this score; Chrysippus' *Reply to Panthoides* '*On ambiguities*', D.L. 7.193 (=*S.V.F.* 2.14, p. 6, l. 27 (37B2)), could simply be an indirect attack on Diodorus.

[31] It was argued that proper names are suitable to their possessors, and thus "natural" in that sense (*e.g.* Stephanus *int.* 9.29ff.), and even that *cognomina* are 'quasi naturalia' because 'they are as it were born with us, for they are given to us as soon as we are born': Pompeius (*G.L.* 5) 141.21f. As far as Sextus is concerned, however, questioning the ambiguity of one or other of his examples would be just another case of pointless dogmatic disagreement. As already noted in 4.5 and elsewhere, it was a common ancient assumption, and one which there is no reason to believe the Stoics rejected, that proper names can be homonymous or ambiguous.

arbitrary imposition, then those responsible for it are still those best able to judge usage correctly, and dialecticians will be out of a job just the same. Of course, an argument could be made that imposition is not necessarily arbitrary; but that in itself would do little to confirm the usefulness of dialectic in the practical, everyday business of distinguishing the senses of bits of jargon and the references of proper names – and, in any case, would be yet more grist to the Skeptic mill.

In 3.5 it was noted that Sextus restricts the area of dispute to single terms, and I take this to be a deliberate attempt to disqualify any claim from the dialecticians to a recognised sort of linguistic expertise, that ostensibly exercised by grammarians. Correct use and interpretation of single terms also require linguistic knowledge of some kind, knowledge which might be thought, and was thought in antiquity, to require at least training and expertise. It does so less obviously, however, than correct use and interpretation of syntactic complexes, and least conspicuously where the references of proper names and the meanings of technical jargon are in question. Sextus' third example, in which the slave who asks his master to specify 'which wine' he wants to drink, would not even count as a case of linguistic ambiguity (but rather of referential indefiniteness) for modern linguists and semanticists. Its being presented as one here might hint at a far broader conception of ambiguity, but Sextus may just as well be making hay out of yet another doctrinaire problem: in 4.5 the absence was noted from the Stoic definition of ambiguity of any explicit distinction between ambiguous and general or non-specific multiple signifying.

As for Sextus' assumption of linguistic conventionalism, this is plainly no more than polemical. The Stoa is his principal naturalist enemy, as *P.H.* 2.214 confirms, where he turns on Chrysippean dialectic with the support of entirely unoriginal conventionalist arguments (one of which looks Diodorean).[32] Its usefulness in illustrating the internecine

---

[32] *P.H.* 2.214 retails an argument that there can be no science of dialectic, since sciences must be firm and unchangeable, while language, being 'by imposition', is,

strife amongst the dogmatic dialecticians, both within and between schools, is clear too. The Stoics resurface at 258, where the jargon *non-apprehensible* ('ἀκαταλήπτοις') is used. But Sextus' invitation to join in the debate is perfectly general.

So Sextus provides fairly clear evidence that the Stoics did analyse fallacies due to ambiguity by incoherence. His criticisms of the ways ambiguities and fallacies were handled by the doctrinaire philosophers have not yet exhausted their interest, however, and it will be worth digging deeper into what he reports on the topic and into his complaints.

7.6 Sextus, the Stoa, and sophisms

It is fairly clear that the dialectician (256, 258) and the dogmatist (259) whose activities Sextus mocks may be Stoic, but need not be, whereas the dialectician who fails to deal with the first of the medical fallacies almost certainly is. The continuity in the form and direction of Sextus' attack, explicitly announced at 256 ('And we have similar things to say in the case of the discrimination of ambiguities . . .'), would anyway suggest that the dialecticians and dogmatists criticised for useless technicalities about ambiguities are the same as the dialectician(s) and dogmatists criticised for indulging in idle speculation about fallacies. Moreover, the Stoa is definitely one of Sextus' targets, perhaps his principal one (and Sextus knows it), when the general doctrinaire treatment of sophisms within the context of formal logic and logical theory comes under fire.[33]

---

like all such things, malleable: the meanings of terms can be altered by *fiat*. The argument assumes a dialectic which is "the science of signifiers and signified", and this definition, not attributed here to any particular dogmatist(s), closely resembles the account of the subject-matter of dialectic reported by D.L. 7.62 as Chrysippus': see 3.1.

[33] Sextus has two main lines of attack besides the contention that dialecticians cannot solve genuinely dangerous sophisms. First, the doctrinaire treatment of unsound argument makes a specific account of sophisms unnecessary (247ff.) (not strictly true, of course, as the special pleading at 251–3 reveals). Second, the well-known Hellenistic debate about the propriety of responses to Skepticism (see esp. Cicero *acad.* 2.17f. (part, 68U), 45f.) is exploited; it is outlined generally and explicitly, in quasi-Epicurean terms, at 244ff., but Aristotle too seems to have been brought into this debate: compare *P.H.* 2.250 with *s. el.* 1.165a6–17, 24.179b17–26. Disputes

That leaves unclear who, exactly, drew up the classification of fallacies reported at 229–31 (37A2–6). Given the analysis of the Stoic ambiguity fallacy reconstructed in 7.4 and 7.5, one easy explanation presents itself of how the classification of fallacies could be Stoic, and yet not contain a species of sophism due to ambiguity: it is explicitly a list of types of arguments, *logoi*, and Stoic *logoi* are by definition systems of *lekta*.[34] So, is it really Stoic?

Its logical and semantic sophistication do point *prima facie* to some group of Stoics. The Stoa is known to have worked on "changing", μεταπίπτοντες, propositions and arguments, those which change truth-value according to context,[35] like

within and between dogmatist schools about the need for dialectic to combat absurdities and about what counts as a fallacious argument anyway are deliberately highlighted. Thus Sextus lists four sophisms from doctrinaire sources at 241–4: one each from Diodorus (who is thus firmly in the camp of the dogmatists whose sophisms, or "sophisms", are to be solved by the (equally doctrinaire) dialectician), Gorgias (?), and Anaxagoras, and another whose author is unknown (although see 7.1, n. 3, for one conjecture); these the dialectician is supposed to solve, 244. Sextus' skeptical strategy turns out to be complex and many-layered, but it remains true that the Stoics are one of his targets; that the definition of dialectic at 247 is Posidonius' (D.L. 7.62); that the difference between the definitions of validity at 137 and 249 is unimportant, since the example of a concludent argument at 137 is framed in precisely the same way as the later definition; and that it is impossible to believe that Sextus, given his explicit references at 235 and 254f. to earlier criticisms of logical theory, and given the similarities between 137ff. and 248–50, somehow failed to notice that he was shifting to a new account of validity in the second passage.

34 It is no objection to interpreting it as Stoic that the classification includes 'solecising arguments', 231 (37A10). Solecism can characterise linguistic groupings, as in the definition of it at D.L. 7.59; but, like all syntactic properties, it presumably belongs primarily to improperly constructed complex *lekta*: see already 6.5.2, and also n. 36, below; and *cf.* Frede 1977: 6off., 1978: 56ff.

35 Propositions which change from true to false are mentioned at D.L. 7.76; they seem to have been dealt with at greater length by his source. The treatises dealing with "changing arguments" listed in the Chrysippean bibliography are marked as spurious, D.L. 7.195 (= S.V.F. 2.15, p. 7, ll. 22f.), but there is plenty of other, firm, evidence for Stoic interest: *e.g.* Alexander *ap.* Simpl. *phys.* 1299.36ff. (37K); Epictetus *diss.* 1.7.1, 10–21 (37J). See further Nuchelmans 1973: 8of.; Frede 1974: 44–8; Denyer 1988: 385f. The logico-semantic and more broadly philosophical issues underlying the classification are sketched by Ebbesen 1981a: 1: 24, who sees it as a list of challenges to be met by the (Stoic) philosopher. Ebbesen 1981a: 1: 23 also sees the influence of the *s. el.* in the classification, but (i) it uses no explicitly linguistic/non-linguistic dichotomy; (ii) it is clearly not restricted to the *s. el.* context of one-on-one sophistic combat (*e.g.*, there is nothing about the dialectician's and the sophist's primary goal, achieving (the appearance of) self-contradiction by the interlocutor); (iii) paradoxical does not mean "resembling the false", as Ebbesen claims; (iv) the ἄδηλον category is altogether new; (v) the goal of reducing your opponent to "babbling" (meaningless repetition) is missing.

the major in the example of the third type of fallacy, and on solecisms (*e.g.* D.L. 7.59), which are exploited in at least some members of the fourth group.[36] The school was also interested in the sort of distinction of levels of discourse that includes the use/mention distinction (or however one describes it) which is flouted in the illustration of the first fallacy species, and invoked to explain the illustrations of the second and third types. If the classification is to be counted as a product of the Dialectical school, as has been argued recently, then at the very least strong independent evidence for activity in these areas by members of that school must be presented; Sextus' attributing it to οἱ διαλεκτικοί tells us almost nothing,[37] and internal evidence is slight.[38]

The case for the list's being Stoic would be a little strengthened if it could be shown to be (minimally) consistent with what is known already of Stoic principles for classifying fallacies. Unfortunately, as noted in 7.1 and 7.2, this is not very much; and, as the Sextus list is obviously not intended to codify (just) the famous fixed-format sophisms, information about Stoic solutions to these cannot be taken as paradigmatic. I shall consider two small pieces of evidence.

First, Diogenes Laertius 7.44 (37C) describes certain

---

[36] Interestingly, given the description of this last group of "solecistic" arguments as 'otherwise unacceptable', 231 (37A6), Apollonius *synt.* 300.8ff. argues that where formally distinct nominal cases are changed, they will either constitute an acceptable figure of speech, or will be regarded as 'unacceptable', 'ἀπαραδέκτους', because of their lack of conformity to the rules of correct syntax, 'κατὰ τὸν τοῦ ἀκαταλλήλου λόγον'. See also n. 44, and 8.3, n. 22.

[37] See nn. 27, 28.

[38] Even the allusion in the example of the second kind of sophism to the Diodorean criterion of a true conditional, in which 'it neither was nor is impossible for the antecedent to be true and the consequent false', *P.H.* 2.110 (35B3), *M.* 8.115, need not point to the classification's origin in the Dialectical school. Already in antiquity Diodorean implication was regarded as paradoxical, since it makes any proposition at all imply a proposition always true, even its own contradictory: *P.H.* 2.111 (35B3). Of course, Philonian (=(roughly) material) implication has its own paradoxes: *M.* 8.113, with Kneales 1964: 128–33; Mates 1961: 42–51; Frede 1974a: 80–93; but some Stoics continued to use it: D.L. 7.81; Cicero *fat.* 12–15 (38E), and the school as a whole had good reason to try to discredit Diodorean implication. In the illustration, 'the doctor *qua* doctor kills' turns out not to be ἄτοπον only in the sense that it is or signifies a well-formed proposition: see n. 44 on this technical usage of the term. Similarly, some Diodorean implications would turn out not ἄτοπα only because they, too, would be (conditional) propositions. In brief, the illustration may be a Stoic witticism at Diodorus' expense, and, like Hierophilus' (245), one with serious intent.

sophisms, curiously, as περαίνοντες, "conclusive". One possible explanation is as an allusion to arguments which are "conclusive in being posed", that is, those one or more of whose constituent propositions change(s) truth-value as the argument is being posed,[39] such as the example of the group of fallacies with ἄδηλα, "unclear", conclusions. Or the whole list, 'defective and insoluble and conclusive', may have been grouped as those 'similar to', 'τοὺς ὁμοίους τούτοις', the fixed-format sophisms just enumerated (implicit in, for example, the LS translation, 1987: 1: 222). But the label might be explained by appeal to the second species of fallacy, *P.H.* 2.230 (37A4), arguments whose conclusions 'resemble the false' and which actually turn out sound, 233 (37A8), despite appearances to the contrary as far as the (logically) uneducated are concerned. They count as sophisms, presumably, because they are 'cunningly fashioned to have their conclusions accepted', 229 (37A2) on the basis of their premises, even though the conclusions may seem in themselves unacceptable.[40]

Second, the sophisms dealt with by Stoic dialectic are described by D.L. 7.43 (31A7) as those 'due to language [strictly, 'to vocal sound, φωνή'] and the *pragmata*'. This is generally assumed to represent a simple dichotomy;[41] but in that case Diogenes would more plausibly to refer to 'sophisms due to vocal sound *or* to the *pragmata*'. The φωνή/πράγματα pairing of course strongly suggests that *pragmata* here are significations of linguistic expressions, and *pragmata* at least include *lekta* (see 6.2.3). So perhaps these two, linguistic form and signified content, are being paired to provide a compendious explanation of how there can be deceptively unsound (or sound) arguments. In a fallacy, as a rule, there will be something wrong with the *pragmata*, that is, either some one or other of the *lekta* will be false or ill formed, or the *lekta* will

[39] Arguments of this type are mentioned by Epictetus *diss.* 1.7.1, 10ff. (37J1, 4, esp. LS 2: 228, ll. 24–8).

[40] Galen at one point (*subfig. emp.* 82.10ff.) describes sophisms as 'arguments appearing to prove something opposed to what is self-evident'. This is actually a very good description of the illustration of the "apparently false" sophism – but not in the way Galen meant it.

[41] *E.g.* Ebbesen 1981a: 1: 25ff.

be invalidly connected. Neither defect would by itself be sufficient to yield a sophism (a bad argument which looks sound), for there must also be something to create the appearance of a valid argument; and both defect and *causa apparentiae* (to borrow the medieval jargon) must be components in any adequate explanation of the existence of sophisms (see 7.2). Conjecturally, this additional factor will be linguistic expression. In a logically perfect language, in which the components, internal structures, and relations of *lekta* are reproduced with total precision, reasoners could not be led astray by any misrepresentation of these properties into believing they had met or devised a valid argument when they had not. In particular, they could not be confused by any verbal similarity between the invalid argument and whatever valid argument acts as its "cover". (This is not to say that the Stoa had such a perfect language as a goal; it seems to have been content with *ad hoc*, piecemeal improvements (3.5).)

A fallacy due to ambiguity will be one obvious case in which there is an inconcinnity between linguistic and "logical" form (which can here be given a precise meaning: the structure(s) and relations of all components of propositions and their complexes). But could *all* fallacies be accounted for in this way? The Stoic conception of ambiguity articulated in the D.L. definition is narrow and rigid. Apparent instances of ambiguity might turn out, by its standards, to be instances of something else: for example, Chrysippus' reformulation of sentences (or propositions) of the form

if *p*, then *q*

as

not both (*p* and not-*q*)

(Cicero *fat.* 12ff. (38E)) might not be a concession that the conjunction *if* is ambiguous, signifying both strong Chrysippean and weak Philonian implication. It might indicate instead that what *if* signifies, strictly, is the coherence of a sound Chrysippean conditional; or that the two significations of *if* belong to two different ἔθη, a possibility allowed for by the

435

D.L. definition (4.7); or that *if*, albeit lacking full linguistic signification in the way that nouns and verbs have it, is none the less associated with one sort of logical function at the level of the *lekton*, and *not* (*both . . . and not . . .*) with another. If one or other of these interpretations is correct,[42] no ambiguity would be involved (even if a non-Stoic might easily believe that there was); yet it is undoubtedly still the language which is responsible for masking the logical distinctions involved.

It remains questionable, even with such an appropriately broad understanding of the possible effects of language, whether linguistic form can account for *all* plausibility. Surely, for example, a Sorites may be plausible simply because of the similarity between its constituent premisses, which no amount of re-formulation could affect. So suppose instead that linguistic expression is not to be the sole cause of the plausible appearance of sophisms, although still, perhaps, the single most important component in this portion of the Stoic account, so that the group of fallacies "due to language and the *pragmata*" will be a large one. Errant *lekta* may also be to blame, where their falsity is unclear. Clarity, being relative, must itself be analysed further: premisses are "obviously" true or false, and "persuasive" or not persuasive, or both or neither, only to observers and in certain relations.

The Stoics said that the impressions people receive of the ἄποροι λόγοι, literally "impassable arguments", or those which are "hard to manage", which are or form a subgroup of all sophisms,[43] are both plausible and implausible, sometimes one, sometimes the other (Sextus *M*. 7.243 (39G4)), according as, I suppose, the conclusions are considered in isolation, and

---

[42] I offer several because the semantic status of connectives is unknown: see 6.3.5.2. Chrysippus' *On mode ambiguities* and *On conditional mode ambiguities*, D.L. 7.193 (= *S.V.F.* 2.14, p. 6, ll. 25f. (37B2)), might have dealt with this issue.

[43] The list 'deficient and ἄποροι and conclusive' at D.L. 7.44 (37C) is hard to square with the introduction of the Veiled, Elusive, Sorites, Horned, and No-man arguments as all ἄποροι, D.L. 7.82 (37D); it is also hard to believe that Stoics would admit that some arguments – even the Liar – are ἄποροι in that they are insoluble or intractable, as accepted, uneasily and with qualifications, by Ebbesen 1981a: 1: 42ff.; *cf.* Barnes 1982: 41, n. 64. At D.L. 7.82 the word seems to mean no more than "puzzle" or "problematic". A different, and more precise, meaning would be likely at 7.44, but what it was remains puzzling itself.

436

in relation to the independently plausible (and very possibly true or even apprehensive) impressions of the premises which appear to imply them. Since their conclusions are implausible in the ordinary run of things, but plausible in the light of the independently plausible and apparently supportive premisses, the arguments as whole systems both call for assent and urge us to withhold it. Later Stoics actually added a qualification to the definition of the apprehensive impression as criterion of truth, that it have no obstacle; that is, an impression cannot be criterial if rendered unbelievable, ἄπιστος, by circumstances: Sextus *M*. 7.253ff. (40K). A sense-impression cannot be grasped unless the sense-organ, the object perceived, the location, the manner of perception, and the mind of the perceiver are all in normal condition: *M*. 7.424 (40L). Perhaps impressions produced in the course of argument and discourse are subject to similar qualifications, with abnormal conditions for judging a propositional impression extending to its association with impressions urging its acceptance and rejection at the same time, as with the conclusion of a fallacy.

That impressions of puzzle arguments are both plausible and implausible may perhaps also mean that to different observers the same arguments may seem plausible and implausible. A Stoic distinction was drawn between "expert" and "non-expert" impressions, D.L. 7.51 (39A7), and, although the expertise there is one of the visual arts, and although the emphasis is also on visual impressions in Lucullus' account of how familiarity and training can enable observers to distinguish closely similar objects (*acad*. 2.56ff. (part, 40I)), the point must have general application. Lucullus in fact draws an explicit distinction between *usus* and *ars*, that is, the art of dialectic (57), which the wise man applies to his perceptions. The dialecticians behind the classification of fallacies had certainly marked out and begun to explore this difficult terrain. They had made explicit allowances for arguments which appear unsound, that is, are unpersuasive, to some, yet not to others; this is the case with the argument which concludes that 'the doctor *qua* doctor kills is not

437

absurd', which turns on an abstruse, technical sense of *absurd*, probably to mean something like "well-formed", of a proposition.[44] Further, they isolated a species of sophism in which the conclusion is ἄδηλον, "unclear, obscure", a parody of proof where the "revealed" conclusion is beyond human apprehension (καθάπαξ ἄδηλον, "completely obscure), is not "revealed" by the premisses, and, in Stoic terms, although 'neither plausible nor implausible' in itself (Sextus *M*. 7.243 (39G5)), is made 'both plausible and implausible' (*ibid*. (39G4)) by its place in this seemingly valid argument. Stoics would also be able to explain why a classification of fallacies can reasonably contain sound arguments which appear false only to the logically ignorant. The wise man, as the consummate dialectician, would have a firm grasp on the technical vocabulary and concepts of dialectical theory; and of course he does not withhold firm assent from truths clearly perceived as such,[45] any more than he grants it to known or possible falsehoods, where knowledge is humanly attainable (as it is not, for example, in the case of the number of the stars).

The examples also display great sensitivity to the persuasive value of language. In the linguistic expression of the second premiss of the first illustration at *P.H.* 2.230 (37A3)),

No-one offers a predicate to drink;
but drinking absinthe is a predicate;
so, no-one offers absinthe to drink,

---

[44] This use, not attested elsewhere, is elucidated by *P.H.* 2.235 (37A10): 'The final arguments, they say in this case [reading 'ἔνθα'; or, reading 'ἔνιοι', 'some of them say'], the solecistic ones, draw conclusions [reading 'ἐπάγειν' with the MSS and Bekker for the Latin translation's 'ἐπάγεσθαι] ἀτόπως, contrary to linguistic usage'. The unacceptability of the conclusions of these arguments as descriptions of states-of-affairs will scarcely count as an explanation of the defects they display comparable with the explanations of all the other examples. Rather, this "absurdity" must lie in the ill-formedness of the conclusions, which turn out not even to be propositions: unlike, for example, 'the doctor, *qua* doctor, kills', which is absurd as regards its content, but not badly formed *qua* proposition, 'there is at an inflamed spot' is ill-formed.

[45] It is a characteristic of ordinary people that, although they do have apprehensions, they do not assent firmly to cognitive impressions: this seems to be why δόξα, "opinion, belief", is defined as 'weak and false assent', Sextus *M*. 7.151 (41C3), as covering both false assent, to falsehoods, and weak and changeable assent, to apprehensive truths.

the second premiss, 'κατηγόρημα δέ ἐστι τὸ ἀψίνθιον πιεῖν', is so expressed that the neuter singular article, 'τό', 'the', left untranslated here, might belong with 'ἀψίνθιον' or with the phrase designating the whole predicate. The latter, being a case (a πτῶσις in standard Stoic jargon: 6.3.4), also properly takes an article. The fallacy would still be plausible were the article excised, but it lends the premiss greater authority. The real fault is that language does not capture the structure of the premiss. Precisely the opposite holds in the case of the second illustration (*ibid.* (37A4)).

That which neither was nor is possible is not absurd (ἄτοπον);
but 'the doctor *qua* doctor kills' neither was nor is impossible;
so, 'the doctor *qua* doctor kills' is not absurd.

Its second premiss employs the same neuter singular article, but here to indicate, correctly, that a proposition is merely being referred to, just as in the previous example a predicate is merely being mentioned. Language can still play tricks on the uninitiated, as they may yet be misled by the novel use of ἄτοπον, which is, I suppose, disambiguated by its context: an important assumption for us, perhaps, if the classification is Stoic. The disguised shift in the temporal reference of the token-reflexive *first*, πρῶτον, between the first and the second premisses of the next sample fallacy at 231 (37A5) may also have been accounted a linguistic trick, the difference in time-reference being hidden by the use of an ordinary adverb.[46]

It is not the case both that I have asked you a question first, and
that it is not the case the stars are even in number, ⟨is it?⟩;
but I have asked you a question first;
so, it is the case that the stars are even in number.

The plausibility of the solecistic arguments at 231 (37A6) of course rests entirely on the exploitation of the lack of perfect correspondence between the properties of the constituents of linguistic signifiers and those of propositions. The first runs:

[46] See Nuchelmans 1973: 8off. on the bearing this question may have on the understanding of the Stoic proposition (Nuchelmans takes the sophism classification to be Stoic).

What you look at, exists;
but you look at your wits' end;
so, your wits' end exists

(I borrow Long and Sedley's excellent translation, slightly modified). Here the second premiss, 'βλέπεις φρενιτικόν', is properly understood as 'you have a frenzied look'. In the other example.

What you turn your eyes on, exists;
but you turn your eyes on an inflamed spot;
so, on an inflamed spot exists.

the second premiss, 'ὁρᾷς φλεγμαίνοντα τόπον', comprises a verb governing an accusative-case noun with accompanying adjective, also in the accusative case; these accusative forms are then illicitly carried forward to the conclusion, 'ἔστιν ἄρα φλεγμαίνοντα τόπον'.

This examination of the classification assumes that the sophisms it lists must be, not systems of *lekta* alone, but those systems together with their linguistic expression; language plays a principal part in the "cunning fashioning" (*cf.* 'δεδολιευμένον', 229 (37A2)) of the fallacy. It may seem curious that ambiguity, surely the linguistic defect *par excellence*, is nowhere mentioned. Its absence is explained by the fact that identifying an ambiguity in the sentences expressing an argument comes before the argument can itself be identified (and so, *a fortiori*, before it can be rejected as false or incoherent). Ambiguity is important enough in this context to have been given separate treatment, including an account of its appropriate logical analysis, which we recovered earlier, from the rest of Sextus' report. But sophisms which exploit ambiguities could not form a distinct group within a classification, like this one, which takes as its chief principles of division the truth-value and the epistemic status of conclusions, for these principles simply presuppose some sort of autonomous account of validity and invalidity,[47] whereas ambiguity fallacies

---

[47] The first illustration and its solution, 230, 232 (37A3, 7), indicate this point most clearly: the conclusion established is said not to follow from the premisses (although a true, validly drawn conclusion is possible), but there is no attempt to

are united by the analysis appropriate to their logical status, as incoherent or false arguments.[48] Sextus represses the connection because it does not serve his purpose, a compendious polemic whose barrage of general criticism would be interrupted by such technical *minutiae*. It is enough for him to sketch the full-scale attack promised at 259: in particular, to point out the uselessness of the Stoic analysis (by incoherence) in the hands of people who cannot even recognise ambiguities when they see them.

Sextus' intention to cover the whole field, albeit at a brisk trot, also explains why he does not think it worth while to reveal exactly who the classification's authors were. The classification is useful to him because it gives him a firm base from which to argue, as noted, that the dialecticians' own logical theory makes it redundant, where fallacies have clearly true or clearly false conclusions, and then to suggest that any tactic but Skeptical ἐποχή, "suspension of judgement", in the face of all arguments is sheer folly, since all arguments, by Skeptic standards, are more or less ἄδηλα, "obscure", Sextus sets up an opposition, not between Skepticism and some one doctrinaire school, but between Skepticism and all dogmatic speculation about fallacies. His strategy is obviously a sensible one: if dogmatists cannot establish firm criteria for distinguishing fallacies from sound arguments, all claims to knowledge through ratiocination are in danger of collapse, and dialectic, 'the distinguisher of true and false', has no 'help for life when it totters' (229 (37A1)).

It is above all remarkable that the classification is of conclusions, of the range of propositions a sophist tries to get one to accept in argument, not of (defective) argument-patterns. If

relate the analysis of the argument's defectiveness to a complete syllogistic (precisely, to some set of rules for instantiation and detachment). Similarly, the solution of the "changing argument" invokes, without justification, a metalogical rule for the simultaneity of premisses and conclusion – an obvious requirement for governing a tensed logic such as the Stoic or Diodorean, and one captiously ignored in Sextus' criticisms of the Stoic proposition (*P.H.* 2.109, *M.* 8.83f., 136).

48 Thus the "Wagon" argument, discussed in 6.3.4, which is false if the conclusion is taken to refer to actual wagons with wheels, but true if premiss and conclusion refer to the word *wagon*, might fall into two classes, or just one, the "resembling the false". This is presumably always the case where the conclusion is ambiguous.

the list is not to function only as a vehicle for a series of
lessons in logic and semantics – and clearly it could carry out
such a task satisfactorily, although Sextus never suggests it
was designed or used for that purpose – but is also to help
people cope with fallacious arguments in actual discourse,
then there seem to be two ways it could be put to practical use.
First, it would alert agents to the fact that not all sophisms
have false conclusions, contrary to received wisdom (*e.g.*
Galen *an. pecc. dign.* 2.3, 56.18ff. Marquardt). Second, if all
sophisms have conclusions of one or other of these four types,
and no other, then a fallacy could be recognised as such on the
basis of its conclusion alone. But then, of course, interlocutors
must wait until an argument, any argument, is over before
they can safely pass judgement on it; and they might think
Sextus was right, after all, that the Skeptic's "wait-and-see"
strategy is the best one (*P.H.* 2.253). The classification need
not force them to withhold assent in all cases, however. Like
Simplicius' dialecticians they can "keep quiet", assenting privately if they choose, while maintaining the tactical advantage
of silence, at least in situations in which they suspect funny
business may be afoot (gauging such dangers will require general dialectical experience, of course).

Sextus' denial of usefulness to dialectic rests in part on a
fresh objection, that logic is useful only in the hands of scientists and other experts. His doctor is sure on independent
grounds that the conclusion of the "abatement" sophism is
false, and he knows, also on independent grounds, both that
an ambiguous term occurs in each of its premiss-sentences,
and that the second premiss is true only if παρακμή is understood to apply there to the relaxation in the local strain. But
his next step, which is to observe that the ambiguity destroys
the coherence between the premises, shows that Sextus' criticisms contain the seeds of their own undoing. Sextus claims
the mere recognition that an argument has a false conclusion
is enough (250). Here he is trying to establish the redundancy of the dogmatists' τεχνολογούμενα, "technicalities",
about sophisms by showing that knowledge of their broader
logical account of truth and falsity is enough for identifica-

tion of an argument as false.[49] In other words, the dialecticians' τέχνη, "expertise", about fallacies is to be proved, not merely useless in practice (unlike, for example, medicine) and so no τέχνη at all,[50] but also a quite superfluous addition to the τέχνη of dialectic (247), which itself turns out to be of no practical use (254f.). If an argument has a false (obviously false) conclusion, people will know at once that it is false.

A Stoic dialectician's opening countermove would surely be to urge that it is manifestly not enough merely to assume that ambiguity can be a defect of argument. People's thinking it a fault cannot, or should not, be arbitrary; they must have some reason for thinking it so; and to determine just why it is a fault requires independent criteria for validity and soundness, a good few steps beyond pretheoretical, intuitive understanding of what counts as a "good" or a "bad" argument. The same necessity, and the same heuristic and explanatory procedure, will hold in other cases of defective argument. For the Stoa, the capacity to infer, to grasp the relation of ἀκολουθία – literally "following (from)", that is, logical consequence – is a natural human gift: Sextus *M* 8.275f. (53T), Galen *med. off.* 18B.649K (= *S.V.F.* 2.135); but it must be trained, D.L. 7.48 (31B7–8), because the components of the ultimately reliable human cognitive apparatus may conflict or break down: Cicero *acad.* 2.46. It may be possible to tell in this or that case that an argument is "good" or "bad", but systematic, reliable assessment demands and rests on explicit, coherent, comprehensive logical theory. Of course, Sextus will want to complain that such non-arbitrary distinctions are by the dogmatists'

---

[49] Sextus actually says '... is not true or concludent' (reading 'ἤ' with Mau for the MSS 'οὐδέ'); but arguments with false conclusions, which must be either inconclusive, with true premisses, or conclusive, with false premisses (248f.), are all "false" as that term is (implicitly) defined at 248, where *true* is equivalent to *sound*. The same usage is evident at 250: 'that the not-concludent or not-true argument is, according to them [*sc.* the dialecticians], not probative either'. But I see no reason to detect anything more than a harmless equivocation on Sextus' part.

[50] Stoic definitions of τέχνη, expertise, which became standard, emphasise its practical usefulness as well as its theoretical content: *S.V.F.* 1.73 (part, 42A), 2.93–7; Sextus *M.* 2.10. Philosophy for the Stoa is also the practice of an expertise – the expertise of what is useful, Aetius 1 *pr.* 2 (= *S.V.F.* 2.35 (26A)) – but its being of practical use as ordinarily understood is a debatable philosophical tenet.

standards a feeble mirage, and useless to boot, and will disown his deployment of the doctor's logical diagnosis as merely polemical; hence, any possible settlement of the dispute between the dialectician and the doctor about the usefulness of their activities hangs on far wider issues than the analysis of the rôle of ambiguity in the formation of fallacious reasoning, as Sextus' own strategy in the remainder of *P.H.* 2 confirms. My purpose here is simply to construct a Stoic defence against the usurpation of logic by non-logicians.

That Stoics actually did have to face this challenge is shown by this passage from Cicero:

What is there that can be perceived by reason? You say that dialectic was discovered as the, so to say, discriminator and judge of true and false. Of which true and false, and in what subject? Will the dialectician judge what is true or false in geometry, or in literature, or in music? But he has no knowledge of those things. In philosophy, then? What has the question of the size of the sun to do with him? What gives him the ability to judge what the supreme good is? What, then, will he judge? What a true conjunction is, what a true disjunction, what is said ambiguously, what follows from each thing, what conflicts with it? If it [*sc.* dialectic] judges these and similar matters, it is its own judge; but it made a larger promise, for it is not enough for the many and important matters in philosophy to judge just these. But, since you do attach such significance to that art, watch out that it is not of its nature entirely against you ... (*acad.* 2.91)

The later, Posidonian, Stoa, at least, seems to have presented philosophy as providing the special sciences with their general principles; and it may have also advocated this approach to logic, as the discipline privileged to produce models for all scientific reasoning.[51] It may therefore be significant that Sextus attributes to his dialecticians both a Posidonian defini-

---

[51] Posidonius' Platonising hierarchy of philosophy and the sciences is probably that described by Seneca, *ep.* 88.25–8 (=(part) fr. 90EK (26F)). It should certainly not be understood as assigning philosophy the rôle of *ancilla scientiarum*. A major difference between Stoic and Aristotelian theorising about the fallacy is that the early Stoa at least did not deal with the extra complication of arguments of the type Aristotle called ψευδογραφήματα, that is, ones merely purporting to conform to the principles of a particular science or expertise: *e.g. s. el.* 11.171b11ff., *top.* 8.12.162b7f., *an. po.* 1.12.77b16ff.; or, more generally, with the question, central for Aristotle, of what does and does not fall within the ambit of the special sciences: *e.g. phys.* 1.2.185a14ff.

tion of dialectic, and a reason for doing dialectic – enabling them to judge not only which arguments are valid, but also which are probative, 247 – which brings to mind Posidonius' reported fascination with the nature and criteria of proof.[52] If Posidonian dialectic is to the fore at this point, then Sextus must be seen as continuing to attack the (later) Stoa despite the shift in his line of approach, that is, even though his target has now become the redundancy of all special teaching about fallacies.

Sextus would certainly be unpersuaded by the practical usefulness of what is claimed as dialectical "knowledge" – does it really matter if the wise man is bamboozled by such trivia (cf. 'ὕθλους', 244)? – and would complain (at least as a polemical tactic) that the expert, such as the doctor and his fellows, seems to have been quite unwarrantably deprived of his claims to specialised knowledge, of ambiguities in particular. But Stoic logicians will not pretend that their expertise is a substitute for medical or other scientific knowledge. They cannot claim to pronounce on the truth or falsity of the whole empirical content of sciences. Rather, their case is that it is dialectic which constructs the rules for correct reasoning in all the sciences, and reflects on its qualifications for, and success in, setting up and testing that model. This relation between logic and the sciences is characteristically Stoic, according to Ammonius: logic is a part of philosophy, but is merely used by scientists, such as doctors:

If someone says that other expertises too use logic, as medicine uses syllogisms, and all the other expertises use syllogisms, we [Stoics] will say that they too use it, but they lack scientific knowledge of the methods [οὐκ εἰσὶν τῶν μεθόδων ἐπιστήμονες], and are not primarily concerned with this; e.g., the doctor is not primarily concerned with the syllogistic method, nor would you say that it is a part or division of medicine, but he takes over as an instrument from the dialectician just so much [of it] as is useful for him for the demonstration of medical theorems; but the philosopher has above all scientific knowledge of this sort of method. (an. pr. 8.20ff. (=(part) S.V.F. 2.49; (part) 26E))

---

[52] Posidonius' geometrical training is praised by Galen P.H.P. 4.4.38, p. 258, ll. 19ff. (=T83EK); see further, Kidd 1978: 12.

Chrysippus appears to have assumed that philosophers and doctors should use (roughly) the same methods for establishing the truth – sense-perception and inference from signs, τεκμηρία – when they are available (*cf.* Galen *P.H.P.* 3.1.10–15, p. 170, ll. 9–27; on this passage, see already 3.5). The rules formulated for argument and proof are, in Stoic eyes, universal; Sextus may attack their foundations, but his own illustration makes the point admirably.

A further Stoic step would be to claim that the precise fault committed by every fallacious argument must be identified, for a codification to be drawn up of all possible defects, even, and especially, in arguments whose fallaciousness is not immediately apparent. Not all such arguments will fall within the province of this or that science or expertise, and in the last analysis none is trivial, not because some fallacy or other may escape universal notice, but because, despite their fallaciousness, they may encourage unwarranted doubt, or because they enshrine logical defects which may be hard to detect in more serious fallacies. Their solution will thus usefully point the way to correct doctrine, both within and without the strict confines of logic.[53] The classification of fallacies which Sextus records underscores this last reason for interest in "trivial" fallacies by its inclusion of a "sophism" whose soundness will actually be obvious to someone in possession of the relevant logical knowledge. The dialecticians themselves have thus also raised the notion of the relativeness of what is "(un)clear" or "(im)-plausible", which is central to Sextus' critique: his case rests on the fallacious medical arguments being obviously false, and so implausible, to doctors, opaque to dialecticians; the dialecticians', on the illustration of the "resembling-the-true" sophism being obviously true, and so plausible, to the logically initiated, apparently false, and so implausible, to the logically ignorant (233 (37A8)). Sextus nowhere openly tackles this problem.

Nor need Stoics feel discomfited by the reminder that doc-

---

[53] The "Wagon" argument is just such a frivolous (*cf.* LS 1: 230) illustration of a serious dialectical issue, the distinction between use of a word to signify itself, and its use to signify an external object: see 6.3.4, 6.3.5.

tors may be said, catachrestically, to "know" things sages
do not, since the wise are not literally omniscient, merely
infallible in their assents.[54] Presumably the wise man would be
little more inclined to assent to the conclusions of the medical
fallacies, given the obscurity to him of the arguments, than
to the ἄδηλον, "obscure", conclusion of the μεταπίπτων,
"(truth-value) changing", sophism (231, 234 (37A5, 9)), impressions of which will be universally 'neither plausible nor
implausible' (M. 7.243 (39G5)). At most, he might assent to
the proposition that 'it is plausible [πιθανόν]' or 'reasonable
[εὔλογον] that such-and-such diet is to be adminstered'.[55]

Sextus' own recommendation, P.H. 2.253, is to wait until
an argument is complete, suspending judgement about each
premiss in turn, in cases where the argument concludes something "absurd" or "unacceptable". He seems to be looking
back to the characterisation of the conclusions of the fourth
and last species of fallacy in the classification, the "solecistic
arguments" of 235 (37A6, 10), although he may have intended
to include in this group those which conclude something "unclear" as well (perhaps the καθάπαξ ἄδηλα, "completely
obscure", but their scope is uncertain).[56] But, in any case,

---

[54] On the nature and limits of the wise man's knowledge: esp. Kerferd 1978: 129–131.
[55] The plausibility/reasonableness qualification: Cicero *acad.* 2.100f. (part, 421), D.L.
7.177, Athenaeus 8, 354e, p. 276, ll. 23ff. (both = 40F)). He could never assent to
the plausibility of the stars' being odd (or being even) in number, since this is
καθάπαξ ἄδηλον, "completely obscure" (to humans), and so neither plausible nor
implausible: Sextus *M.* 7.243 (39G5).
[56] On καθάπαξ and other varieties of ἄδηλα: Barnes 1980: 177–181. Any argument
purporting to "reveal" what it does not, as well as what cannot be revealed by any
human effort, would perhaps fall into this class; the point is that the inclarity of
the conclusion is not dispelled by these premisses, even if it could be by other
means. On the revelatory nature of proof: Brunschwig 1980: 146–7, and ff.; a
different view in Barnes 1980: 176–181; LS I: 266. On "changing arguments":
n. 35. The explanation of this illustration is defective. At 231 (37A5), the argument
is to be analysed:

$-(p \ \& \ -q)$; but p; so, q.

The only hidden step is, trivially, $-(-q)$ to q. At 234 (37A9) however, the analysis
runs: $-(p \ \& \ -q)$ is true at first, because of the presence of p, which is false, but
then becomes false after the asking of the question because 'what was false in the
negated conjunction has become true', *viz.* p, 'I have asked you a question first';
so, now that $(p \ \& \ -q)$ is true, $-q$ must be true too. But the argument as given at
231 rests on the assumption that the negated conjunction $-(p \ \& \ -q)$ *stays* true,

447

his advice is itself absurd. If it is not until the conclusion is drawn that it becomes clear whether or not it is "acceptable", must not the same procedure hold for all arguments, without exception? Further, his earlier counsel (250), to reject any argument with a false conclusion, even if the source of its fallaciousness is unclear, is vitiated by its unexamined assumption that the truth-value of all propositions will be equally clear. Here he seems to be advising suspension of belief about all premisses, something he has not shown to be appropriate, and which is *prima facie* unwarranted.[57]

The solution to this apparent inconsistency is that towards the end of his diatribe against the dogmatists Sextus moves closer to his own philosophical position. At 254f. he explicitly contrasts Skeptic and dogmatic approaches to fallacies. If the dogmatists were the serious, rational creatures they claim to be, they would always suspend judgement about premisses, just in case something unacceptable turns up as conclusion; and Skepticism tentatively suggests that, given the state of people's knowledge of the world and of logic, this is the only sensible policy if we are to avoid 'falling into absurdity' (253; *cf.* Plato *Parm.* 130d7). The Stoic's policy is different because of a confidence that the truth of most premisses and most arguments can be determined, in practice or in principle. If there is an objection to be raised, it is rather that agents may not be able to be certain of other persons' intentions; and this has to be raised and met precisely because of what is known of the Stoic analysis of ambiguity fallacies. I have argued that, in a dialectical or sophistic context, a working assumption will

---

so that *q*, not −*q*, will be true. What Sextus should have said, presumably, is that the conjunction becomes ἄδηλον (as noted by LS 1987: 2: 222, *ad* l. 40), since the truth value of only one of its conjuncts is and can be known. I am reluctant to say whether the fault is his or his source's. The 'question' referred to, of course, is just the asking of this first premiss – a forceful reminder of the importance to our classifiers of the live context of dialectical exchange. Hamblin 1970: 92f. sees this point, but still regards the classification as one of 'involuntary lapses of reasoning rather than tricks of a sophist'.

[57] Galen's description of and advice for those who lack experience of the ways in which false arguments may resemble true ones is an excellent example of the practical usefulness of the logical training he consistently recommended: *de an. pecc. dign.* 2.3, pp. 55.4ff., Marquardt (*script. min.* 1), 5.72K (=(part) *S.V.F.* 2.272); and see already 7.2.

hold to the effect that assent is being sought to the premisses proposed, and thus that absurd interpretations of linguistic expressions will be avoided. Yet I am far from certain that such an approach is advisable, whether in the context of debate, or in discourse generally.

Consider again the exchange described in 7.3, but this time as (part of) a dialogue between genuine, if not especially astute, inquirers after truth:

The tunic is ἀνδρεῖος (brave/men's wear);
whatever is ἀνδρεῖος (brave), is εὔψυχος (stout-hearted);
so, the tunic is εὔψυχος (stout-hearted).

The "incoherent" argument,

Whatever is brave is stout-hearted;
the tunic is men's wear;
so, the tunic is brave,

need not be that intended by one of the interlocutors. It may not have been realised by one or both parties, in all innocence, that the homonym must change its meaning to preserve truth. It may not even have been noticed that it has two meanings: each party may have so poor a grasp on the language that what ordinary usage recognises as two distinct senses might simply have not been distinguished at all. Hence, one of the premisses offered for approval may have been false, but false without the knowledge of the speaker; and the argument as a whole will then be, not formally defective (always provided there is no other, independent, logical flaw), but materially false.

The analysis by incoherence is only applicable where an item ambiguous in isolation is consistently assigned the meaning appropriate to its context. But there is no guarantee that that is the meaning assigned to each occurrence of the item by any given speaker or hearer. Whether it is appropriate to invoke incoherence, or some other defect, depends on which argument is in play, and that in turn will be determined by which factors (context, speaker's/hearer's meaning, *etc.*) are deemed to disambiguate, and when, and more broadly by what the rules and conventions governing rational human

449

intercourse are assumed to be.[58] And it is not in dialectical exchanges alone that the precise meaning of utterances must be agreed if discourse is to be possible.

Where the focus of interest is deception, the truth-values of premises offered for assent will be highly relevant. It seems correct to take for granted that the item has the sense appropriate to its context wherever the alternative(s) would make the sentence signify something obviously false, and perhaps obviously absurd. The presumption, apparently reasonable, is that no-one would knowingly, sincerely, and without further explanation offer for assent something so obviously bizarre. Yet mistakes about both fact and usage are made; and when it comes to reconstructing an argument's premises, what the speaker intended must surely take priority over the meaning demanded by context, where one or more of the premises being put up for approval is false, or (more radically) where there turns out to be no combination of premises and conclusion which is both permitted by the rules of recognised usage and which corresponds to "the" argument which has deluded the speaker. The interesting linguistic and methodological questions are: how to go about determining what a speaker's intentions are, and whether the criteria selected are justifiable. These questions will come up for further investigation in 7.7 and 7.9.

7.7 Incoherence 3: Galen *P.H.P.* 2.5.1–97, p. 128, l. 15–p. 148, l. 6 (2.5.9–13 = 53U)

A doubt has been raised about the universal appropriateness of a Stoic analysis of ambiguity fallacies by διάρτησις, "incoherence". It seemed especially out of place where the intentions of the propounder of an argument are irrecoverable. Galen's critical examination of a set of related Stoic arguments

---

[58] Compare Socrates' clash with Euthydemus, *Euth.* 295b6ff.: the sophist assumes that it is enough if Socrates understands something by the question; Socrates wants the same thing understood by both interlocutors. The sophism being foisted on him is not due to ambiguity, but the point has universal application for dialectical exchanges.

to do with the seat of the "ruling part", the ἡγεμονικόν, of the soul, which is the mind, διάνοια, shows how even a double analysis, by incoherence and by falsity, can be inadequate.

Galen's discussion is complex and repetitive. He examines not only Zeno's original, negative version of the argument, 2.5.8, p. 130, ll. 2–5, establishing that the mind is not in the brain, but also Chrysippus' and Diogenes of Babylon's positive reformulations, 2.5.15–20, p. 130, l. 24–p. 132, l. 2; 2.5.9–13, p. 130, ll. 7–19 (53U), which aim to show that the mind's real *locus* is the regions around the heart, and offers damning criticisms before presenting his own version, which he claims to be correct or perfect: 2.5.74–93, p. 142, l. 11–p. 146, l. 27. His basic objections remain the same, and the differences between the versions are largely of interest for reasons unconnected with the treatment of ambiguity,[59] so I shall simply reproduce what Galen presents as the Zenonian original, as reported by Diogenes at the start of his *On the ruling part of the soul* (2.5.7, p. 128, ll. 33ff.), and supplement it as necessary:

1 Vocal sound comes ⟨out⟩ *via* the windpipe (φωνὴ διὰ φάρυγγος χωρεῖ);
2 if it were coming from the brain, it would not come ⟨out⟩ *via* the windpipe (εἰ δ᾿ ἦν ἀπὸ τοῦ ἐγκεφάλου χωροῦσα, οὐκ ἂν διὰ φάρυγγος ἐχώρει);
3 where rational discoures comes from, vocal sound comes from too (ὅθεν δὲ ὁ λόγος καὶ φωνὴ ἐκεῖθεν χωρεῖ);
4 rational discourse comes from the mind (λόγος δὲ ἀπὸ διανοίας χωρεῖ); so (ὥστε) 5 the mind is not ⟨located⟩ in the brain (οὐκ ἐν τῷ ἐγκεφάλῳ ἐστὶν ἡ διάνοια).

Of Galen's two chief criticisms the second is the more relevant, but the first must be sketched in too. First, Zeno's argument omits 'premisses needed for being perfectly posed' (2.5.74, p. 142, l. 11), principally the "axiom" 'everything emitted through something is emitted from the contiguous parts', 'πᾶν τὸ διά τινος ἐκπεμπόμενον ἀπὸ τῶν συνεχῶν αὐτῷ μορίων ἐκπέμπεται' (2.5.76, p. 142, ll. 18–24, esp. ll. 22–3). The

---

[59] Students of Galen's logic will find interesting his conviction of the need for universal premisses (and for including them in the explicit formulation of demonstrations), which grew into the theory familiar from the *Institutio logica*, that all proofs work through axioms. The theory was a late one, Galen himself recording that it made no appearance in his (lost) *magnum opus On Proof* (*inst. log.* 17.1), except in the case of relational syllogisms (17.2).

omission of this vital (*cf.* 'κυριώτατα', 2.5.90, p. 146, l. 10; 'ἀναγκαιότατον', 2.5.82, p. 144, ll. 9–10) universal premiss is either sophistical, or the result of ignorance of the probative method (2.5.86, p. 144, ll. 25–31). Second, the preposition ἀπό in what Galen takes to be the two most important premisses – *viz.* 4 in Zeno's argument, and the omitted axiom – has to be understood in two different ways if the premisses are to come out true: as *by the agency of* in 4, as *out of* in the axiom. That is, ὑπό can be substituted *salva veritate* for ἀπό in one, ἐκ in the other (2.5.30, p. 134, ll. 2–7), but a consistent use of one or the other will make one premiss true, one false (2.5.83, p. 144, ll. 14–17). If, on the other hand, the appropriate substitution or interpretation is made in each case, the argument as a whole will be ἀπέραντος, "inconclusive" (2.5.84, p. 144, l. 19; 2.5.92, p. 146, l. 22), although the premisses will be true (p. 146, l. 21). The chief premisses will then be unconnected ('οὐ γὰρ ἔτι συναφθήσονται πρὸς ἀλλήλας', ll. 22f.), yet they must share the same preposition 'in order for some conclusion common to them to be drawn' (2.5.93, p. 146, ll. 26–7).

It is easy to see that Galen's account of this defect may well be a survival of a Stoic analysis. This holds even though Galen hovers between treating ἀπό as a substitute for one or other of the two prepositions ὑπό and ἐκ (*e.g.* 2.5.30, p. 134, ll. 2–7, 'ἀντὶ', 'instead of'; *cf.* 2.5.28, p. 132, ll. 30–1, 2.5.83, p. 144, ll. 14–17, 20–1), and taking ἀπό as ambiguous (implied, 2.5.26, p. 132, l. 27; 2.5.48, p. 136, l. 35; explicit at 2.5.84, p. 144, l. 17); the locutions 'κατὰ τὴν ἐξ/ὑπὸ πρόθεσιν', 'with (*or*: by way of) the prepositions *out of, by the agency of*' (*e.g.* 2.5.85, p. 144, ll. 22f.; 2.5.88, p. 146, ll. 1–2) could be interpreted either way. But it is hard to know just what firmer conclusion to draw from this passage. Galen does not employ the technical term διάρτησις, and his other criticisms do not suggest he is applying the four-fold Stoic scheme of unsoundness (described in 7.3) in its original form. Zeno's version is described as 'lacking', 'ἐλλείπειν' (2.5.14, p. 130, l. 21; *cf.* 2.5.79, p. 142, l. 31) premisses 'for being perfectly framed', 'πρὸς τὸ τελέως ἠρωτῆσθαι', 2.5.74, p. 142, l. 11), Diogenes' as being 'redundant', 'πλεονάζειν' (2.5.14, p. 130, l. 22; cf. 2.5.79, p. 142, ll. 31–2), and his own version as having 'the premisses changed into a clearer form' (2.5.75, p. 142, l. 12) and as making it 'easier to see' that the argument really rests on the use of ἀπό and on the partially obscured premiss about the position of the heart (2.5.82, p. 144, l. 12, 2.5.90, p. 146, ll. 10–11). So the Stoic versions are not actually rejected as invalid on the grounds that they are deficient or redundant, but merely reformulated, made clearer, in a way that primarily reflects or anticipates Galen's conviction of the probative power of axioms.

Galen certainly points out the inconclusiveness of Zeno's argument, but its real defect, in his eyes, is its dependency on sophistic premisses rather than on the 'primitive and demonstrative premisses' which characterise proof (2.5.44, p. 136, ll. 17f., 2.5.74, p. 142, ll. 8–9) – the result of the Stoa's tendency to ill-formed, slap-dash argumentation (2.3.8, p. 110, ll. 15ff.). The Stoics simply fail to observe the vital distinction in probative power between different types of premiss, scientific, dialectical, plausible or rhetorical, and sophistic, which means, in the main, ambiguous (2.3.9–22, p. 110, l. 22–p. 114, l. 21; cf. 2.8.2, p. 156, l. 28–p. 158, l. 2; 3.1.3, p. 168, ll. 12–21). On the other hand, although the Aristotelian logical tradition could have alerted Galen to the fact that premisses 'will not be connected with each other' (2.5.92, p. 146, ll. 22–3) because of ambiguity,[60] his reference to deficiency and redundancy as defects of argument does suggest that his ultimate source is Stoic. But that does not mean the combined analysis, by incoherence and by the falsity of premisses, was taken from a Stoic authority; and I feel sure that, had he been aware of its Stoic origin, he would have exploited his knowledge at so convenient a juncture.

It is still worth exploring why Galen considers what

---

[60] Cf. esp. Philoponus *an. pr.* 158.16ff: a paralogism is not really a syllogism, having instead 'δύο προτάσεις διεσπασμέναι ἀπ' ἀλλήλων', 'two premisses separated' from each other'', because of the presence of a homonymous middle.

happens to Zeno's argument both if its premisses are true but unconnected, and if they are false. He is clear that Zeno's second premiss belongs to his lowest, fourth class of premisses, those which are sophistic, 'if it has indeed put on some sophistic linguistic form that has been deceptively framed to produce ambiguity, in the hope of escaping refutation thereby', 'εἴ γε δὴ σχῆμά τι λέξεως ὑποδύεται πεπανουργημένον τε καὶ σεσοφισμένον πρὸς ἀμφιβολίαν, ἐκ ταύτης τὸν ἔλεγχον ἐλπίζον ἀποδράσεσθαι' (2.5.26, p. 132, ll. 26–8). Zeno could have used one or other 'clear' preposition (2.5.28, p. 132, l. 31), so that the premiss would have been 'precisely and clearly and distinctively framed', and thus have belonged to the second, dialectical class (2.5.48, p. 136, ll. 32–4); but he did not, and as a result the premiss as it stands 'as regards its linguistic form has acquired a cunningly deceptive ambiguity' (ll. 34–5). Galen does not accuse Zeno himself of being a sophist: that charge would stick only were the ambiguity intentional, and it may simply be that Zeno's logical education is at fault (2.5.49, p. 136, l. 36–p. 138, l. 2; cf. 2.5.54, p. 138, l. 14); but he does find the Stoics guilty of deceiving whoever is unable to see which of the premisses is true, that framed with *out of* or that with *by the agency of* (2.5.88f., p. 144, l. 31–p. 146, l. 6).

So the question whether the argument is sophistic is never quite settled, despite a distinction between sophistic premisses and sophistic intentions; and that is itself an interesting indecision on Galen's part, for he bases his four-fold classification of types of premiss on the Aristotelian corpus, including the *s. el.*, which is said to deal with sophistical premisses. In the *s. el.*, of course, Aristotle does not deal with innocent errors of reasoning due to unnoticed ambiguities, but with fraudulent equivocation intended to deceive and embarrass one's opponents (see 5.4). Aristotle does not need the distinction, but Galen does, and so do the Stoics, as a general strategy for analysing and coping with the effects of ambiguity on ratiocination.

The reason Galen does not commit himself to identifying the defect as either incoherence or falsity of a premiss is precisely that it is unclear what Zeno meant.[61] And that must be the case because the argument holds together, and looks like a proof, only if the ambiguity goes undetected. If Zeno genuinely found his attempted proof so plausible (which I think must be taken for granted), then for some reason he cannot have been aware of the shift in meaning required to preserve the truth of the premisses. Galen, understandably, claims that this is because he failed to formulate the universal premiss which would have made it obvious that *out of* is required in one premiss, but *by the agency of* in another (2.5.88f, p. 146, ll. 2–6). Whichever argument is reconstructed, false or invalid, neither can be the argument Zeno thought he was constructing. His formulation of his argument is crucially ambiguous, and yet his philosophical commitment to the truth of his argument very strongly suggests that he was deceived as much as anyone. Either his logic was so poor that he saw the change in meaning but thought it irrelevant – which is unlikely, even for so amateur a logician – or his use of ἀπό reflected some deeper conceptual confusion of, or failure to distinguish, different types of source.[62] Relevant beliefs (including philosophical convictions), based on conceptual structurings of the world, can thus make inapplicable the simple procedure recommended by Simplicius' Stoics (7.4) for determining which signification of ambiguous expressions is intended by speakers.

Galen's critique of the Stoic arguments, impressive as it is, is very restricted as a study of ambiguity. Like Simplicius'

---

[61] Ebbesen 1981a: 1: 84, who has a useful and concise account of Zeno's argument and Galen's improved version, comments that, according to Galen's analysis, arguments exploiting an ambiguity cannot be called materially or formally defective until after disambiguation. He does not, however, observe the evidence in Galen (or in Sextus) for the Stoic incoherence analysis.

[62] That Chrysippus treats his own version of the argument as merely 'εὔλογον', "reasonable", 2.5.15, p. 130, l. 24, and 'πιθανόν', 'plausible', 2.5.20, p. 130, l. 34, does not show that he came close to detecting his master's confusion, for he falls into the same error himself (see 7.9), and the cautious wording rather reflects, I would guess, a more sophisticated epistemology: in fact Galen says not that Chrysippus himself, but rather 'most of the Stoics', accepted the argument as demonstrative: 2.5.74, p. 142, ll. 8f.; and see already 3.5.

dialecticians, he is interested in ambiguity as a flaw in argument. It is for this reason that he thinks it important to observe ambiguities, such as the one he himself describes, the homonymy of the word *heart*, καρδία, between "the heart in the chest" and "the mouth of the stomach", 'an homonymy which escapes no-one conversant with the writings of the ancients' (2.8.7, p. 158, ll. 18f.). All he has suggested is an expansion of the range of factors appropriate to the selection of utterers' meanings in the context of argument, where arguments are intended as authentic contributions to a philosophical system; for obvious reasons, he does not dwell on the difficult, and for us central, issues of linguistic and speaker's meanings and their relation. The important distinction for him is between deceiving intentionally and unintentionally. He speaks as though Zeno could have employed one or other of the 'clear' prepositions (2.5.28, p. 132, ll. 31f.), although, if Zeno really were unclear about the significations or uses of ἀπό, he could hardly have chosen between them in this way. And, of course, the virtues of Galen's account, like its flaws, may be Galen's only, as far as can be judged today.

7.8   Incoherence 4: Augustine *de dialectica* chs. 8, 9, *de magistro* ch. 8.22ff.

In 6.3.5.1 I argued that Augustine adopted and adapted, probably in tandem, Stoic doctrines of contextual disambiguation and of autonymy. In the *de dialectica* he retails what may be Stoic argumentation defending the Chrysippean thesis 'every word is ambiguous by nature', in which an assumption is made of the possibility of disambiguation of single terms by context. In the *de magistro* a "rule of discourse" is stated to the effect that, *ceteris paribus*, extra-linguistic significations or uses will have priority. This rule, although illustrated and supported by sophisms of the "Wagon" sort, has general application, and likewise the *de dialectica*'s assumption of contextual disambiguation is general in scope. As the precise extent and weight of the Stoic element in Augustine's reasoning are unknown, it is impossible to be sure what limits the Stoics had set to the power of context to disambiguate, and whether the Stoics had in fact developed a systematic account of its workings.

7.9 Incoherence: Conclusions

The Stoics, it seems, did accept contextual disambiguation, but no actual arguments survive for this or that particular contextual factor as disambiguating. They may have reflected on the contextual factors imposed by eristic questioning, and on the relations of linguistic to speaker's or hearer's meaning, but the precise considerations they brought into play, and what their conclusions were, can only be the objects of speculation, so that a very large lacuna remains open in our understanding of the Stoic theory of ambiguity. That the *de sophismatis* Stoics failed to extend their Homonymy in Simples/Homonymy in Compounds distinction to other species of ambiguity tends to suggest that they did limit the power of context, and the only motivation for the restriction for which even indirect evidence is available is the greater usefulness of homonyms to the sophist, given their brevity and the traditional terseness of sophistic argumentation: but neither explicitly nor implicitly does the Homonymy in Compounds example limit the scope of the distinction between the two kinds to that of the sophistic exchange. It thus remains unclear whether the assumption that context or situation of utterance disambiguates was generated exclusively by the demands of the dialectical arena, or whether the Stoics' recommended response to sophistic exploitation of ambiguities, as reported by Simplicius, is but one special application of a doctrine having independent, general force.

This lack of testimony to further discussions about other forms of discourse may be the result of historical accident. In fact one piece of relevant evidence amongst those already examined points to the existence of Stoics who studied ambiguity outside the limits of sophistic argument, in the broad fields of rhetoric and stylistics, and the illustrations suggest a lively awareness of contextual factors in actual texts. This is the classification of ambiguity types recorded by Theon. So it cannot be taken as read that all Stoics came to grips with disambiguation only on the field of sophistic combat.

What was new and important about the Stoic understanding of the relation between the fallacy and ambiguity? As 3.5 has already shown, although the Stoics were not the only or the earliest Greek philosophers to associate ambiguity with fallacious reasoning (an association which was to become commonplace: *e.g.* Clement *strom.* 6.1.11.5ff.), there is little strong evidence for direct connections with or reactions to their predecessors' or contemporaries' work in the field. Certainly nothing has suggested they knew of Aristotle's pioneering study in the *s. el.*, any more than that they were aware of his imaginative and powerful applications of the concepts of πολλαχῶς λέγεσθαι, "semantic multiplicity", and focal meaning. The first systematic association of ambiguity with sophisms is probably Aristotle's, but the system he constructed was very different from the Stoa's. Where he associated each (linguistic) fallacy type with a single species of ambiguity making the argument at once actually unsound and apparently sound, the Stoics seem to have slotted fallacies due to ambiguity into an independent logical scheme for analysing and classifying all unsound arguments, while at the same time conceding, with Aristotle, that in such cases ambiguity can make such an argument attractively plausible. Again, while both Aristotelian and Stoic formal logic have no place for ambiguity, the reason in each case is importantly different: the Stoics consciously locate all arguments, their constituents, and their relations at the level of the *lekton*, while still having to rely heavily on their much-criticised formalism to ensure clarity and precision in the "metalanguage" and absolute consistency in the logic itself; Aristotle sees himself as working with words and their complexes (*e.g. an. pr.* 1.39.49b3ff.), but seems to have assumed total elimination of ambiguities at the level of the logical "object-language".[63]

---

[63] His commentators, in contrast, working on the basis of *int.* 1.16a3–8, tended to regard the "real" terms, propositions and syllogisms as mental objects, so that ambiguous sentences signify several non-ambiguous mental propositions:

Another important distinction is that the Stoics never had to make the linguistic fallacy comprehensible within an intellectual scheme shaped by a dialectic which explicitly and by definition operates with and on "reputable opinions", ἔνδοξα, as Aristotle's did. Aristotle himself may not have seen the problems inherent in this situation, but his commentators had to grapple with them. Alexander, for example, stipulates on the basis of *top.* 1.1.100b23–5 that a materially defective syllogism has at least one false *endoxon* for a premiss, such as 'Everything ἀνδρεῖος has ἀνδρεία' (*top.* 21.5ff.), and also that apparent *endoxa* are very easy to detect, and, unlike the real thing, easy to prove false (20.5–21.4), as 'What you have not lost, you have' (14) and 'What you say comes out of your mouth' (*e.g. wagon*, 12f.). The jargon of "material" and "formal" defectiveness is not Aristotle's, of course, and the distinction may be ultimately Stoic: see Ebbesen 1981a: 1: 33ff., 127ff., 1987: 114. Certainly Alexander's examples suggest he has been reading a Stoic textbook on fallacies.

Alexander seems not to have completely realised, however, the force of the facts that false and apparent *endoxa* are not the same thing (since an opinion may be a real *endoxon*, in good standing with everyone or the many or the wise, and yet still be false, as Alexander himself observes: 21.23ff.), and that, if apparent *endoxa* are obvious for what they are, presumably by going to make obviously false arguments, they can hardly help explain the attraction of the fallacies they are used to construct: surely false but real *endoxa* are far more dangerous (as 20.19ff. seem to suggest).[64] A full description and

---

Alexander *an. pr.* 379.23; Porphyry *cats.* 64.28ff., 101.26ff.; Ammonius *int.* 22.9ff., 23.12ff., and *cf.* 73.8ff. (as many premisses as there are meanings of the terms); Boethius *int.* 2 I c. 1, p. 36, ll. 10ff., p. 39, ll. 25ff., II c. 5, p. 106, l. 26–p. 107, l. 5. Meiser (on Porphyry) (and *cf.* Magee 1989: 118 for Boethius' sources); Dexippus *cats.* 7.1ff., 10.3ff. (also Porphyrian). On this whole issue: Ebbesen 1981a: 1: 127ff., 159ff.

[64] Ebbesen 1987: 114f. observes that in the medieval West 'the class of defective syllogisms was not considered coextensive with the class of paralogisms committing one of the thirteen [*s. el.*] fallacies, since a fallacy in this sense is only committed when the paralogism is such as to be (in principle) capable of deceiving somebody', and 'the scholastics showed they had grasped the fact that by listing the thirteen fallacies Aristotle does not pretend to list the ways in which an argument may fail to be sound, but the ways in which it is possible to produce a sound-looking bad argument' (117).

classification of fallacies, including those due to ambiguity, needs an account both of their unsoundness – what makes them false arguments – and of their plausibility – what makes them appear sound (see 7.2). Thus, Aristotle's classification later in the *Topics* (8.12.162b3ff.) of false arguments (not fallacies) into four types, of which the first and last are those which only appear to draw a conclusion (the "eristic") and those which have false premises, would need to be supplemented with a classification of the ways in which such false arguments can look true, if it is itself to be used to substitute for or supplement the classification of eristic syllogisms (not false arguments) at the start of the first book, the one which Alexander tries to rework in Hellenistic terms. For that classification, besides asking whether a syllogism really is a syllogism or not, whatever its premises, also asks whether it is formed from real or from apparent *endoxa*. It still needs to be stated why some invalid syllogisms look valid; but it is not enough to be told, if what is wanted is an explanation *of fallacies*, why some apparent *endoxa* are only apparent – because some real *endoxa* may be false, and really perilous.

Stoic dialectic never had to sort out problems of this type. At least in the context of analysing and classifying fallacies, the school seems not to have drawn a line between merely superficial, easily refuted false beliefs, and more deeply misleading falsehoods whose disproof demands greater philosophical expertise; and I take it that this was, on the one hand, because the threats posed by even apparently trivial fallacies had had such an important influence, separately and collectively, on the formation and development of its doctrines, and, on the other, because *every* falsehood was counted a potential disturbance of the psychological tranquillity and "easy flow of life" which is happiness. For of course the Stoics were principally concerned with seeing why fallacies are plausible, and how the danger they pose to us can be averted, not with testing *endoxa*. It is important for Aristotelians that some *endoxa* are easy even for beginners at dialectic to identify as merely apparent, because they can then be safely eliminated relatively early on in the discussion, whether as gambits in dialectical argument, or as possible contributions to the construction of philosophical doctrines. It is important for Stoics that the ways in which any bad argument can look good can be identified by dialecticians (although some arguments are more dangerous or harder to disarm than others). This, of course, is one major difference between Aristotelian and Hellenistic dialectic.

Equally striking when the *s. el.* and Stoic work on fallacy are compared is the care Aristotle lavishes on locating eristic in relation to other, more reputable, intellectual disciplines (didactic, peirastic, dialectic proper, the special sciences) and their respective argument-types, including crucial distinctions between syllogisms which are irrelevant to a given subject-matter and syllogisms which are not but are flawed in some other way (*e.g.* 10–11.171a1–172b8), and "syllogisms" which are only apparent, not genuine, syllogisms (1.164a23ff.). His ancient commentators, and the medieval schoolmen, were to tie themselves in knots trying to decide which "syllogisms" are the real thing.[65] Stoic dialecticians seem not to have inherited a comparable interest in the genres of argument, or at least they did not exploit it in a comparable way, just as Aristotle's versions of dialectical method have few parallels in the Stoa, despite their common origin (see 3.5). The sources never hint that Stoics felt the same anxiety about, and the same need for justification of, the study of sophisms which inspired that commonplace of the Aristotelian commentators, the *sophistica docens/utens* ("teaching/making use of sophistry") distinction (see Ebbesen 1981a: 1: 88ff.); and this was presumably just because the Stoa never contemplated the existence of such a dangerous and disreputable mock-discipline as eristic, the black sheep of the intellectual family. Moreover, since Stoic logical theory consistently defined argument, λόγος, structurally or formally – as a construct of assumption, λῆμμα, additional assumption, πρόσληψις, and conclusion, ἐπιφορά (D.L. 7.76 (36A1)) – and the syllogism by a formal relation of reduction to one or more of the five indemonstrables (78, 79ff.

[65] See Ebbesen 1981a: 1: 95ff., 1987: 114f.

461

(36A5, 11–16)), without reference to content or validity, all talk of "appearance" must have been confined to "apparent validity" or "apparent soundness". In fact, inconclusive arguments with syllogistic form were explicitly called "asyllogistic" (ἀσυλλόγιστοι) and conclusive arguments lacking syllogistic form "specifically conclusive" (περαντικοὶ εἰδικῶς) (78; cf. Alex. an. pr. 373.28ff.).

A theoretical or general association of ambiguity with sophisms goes back even earlier, of course, at least to Plato, as we saw in 3.5, where the Stoa's possible debt to the *Euthydemus* was tentatively sketched; and we saw there too that at some stage in his career Epicurus may, just possibly, have associated all error with the conventional usage of language, but does not seem ever to have made a close or specific link between ambiguity and the creation of sophisms. As for the other obvious fallacy hunters (or fallacy-mongers) who might in some way have influenced the Stoa, the members of the various minor Socratic schools, there is, perhaps oddly, no sign of interest in sophisms or types of sophism which were explicitly linked with ambiguities. The disagreement between Chrysippus and the Dialectician Diodorus, which I have already tried to reconstruct (4.6), concerned a broader issue, the autonomy of language, and not, or not only, linguistic fallacies. The Megarian Stilpo, perhaps, is behind the illustration of Elleipsis (6.4.3), unless the influence of the *Euthydemus* is at work again instead. Another doxographical anecdote (D.L. 2.135 (=fr. 84D)) has Alexinus[66] criticising the Eretrian Menedemus for not solving the 'ἀμφιβολίαν' of the hoary *Have you stopped beating your father?* puzzle. But this "ambiguity" is probably a different sort of "doubleness" from the semantic variety: the word may point to the dilemma which the fallacy presents, a classic case of "being attacked on both sides" (or "no way

---

[66] Alexinus is reported to have been a pupil of Eubulides who earned the nickname *Elenxinus* for his love of refutation, D.L. 2.109, and the other brief doxographical references tend to give him a reputation for sophistry and quibbling, frr. 76–80, 81–7 D; but Schofield 1983: 34ff. has restored at least his dialectical honour, for his witty and potentially devastating παραβολαί, "parallels", of Zeno's syllogisms (on which see already 3.2).

out") which is the word's standard pretheoretical meaning.[67] This interpretation ties in neatly with Menedemus' reply ('It would be absurd to follow your laws, when I can meet you at the gates'). Less plausibly, given that it is Alexinus who uses the word, it may indicate that the sophism is a case of what Aristotle would call the fallacy-mode "Many Questions", the trickery lying in the illicit presupposition that the victim has agreed that he has in the past beaten his father, and is being quizzed only about his present activity: the single question conceals two premises.[68]

If the reconstruction of Stoic doctrine offered in this chapter is correct, then the Stoics could certainly give a precise account of how ambiguity produces both unsoundness and the appearance of soundness without collapsing one into the other (as Aristotle does in the *s. el.*) or making arguments mental entities (as the Neoplatonists did).[69] But their analysis commits them to a particular ontology, one including *lekta*, as Aristotle's does not; and, what is more, Galen's critique of Zeno's argument suggested possible limitations inherent in an assumption that one or other linguistic sense of an ambiguity *must* be that intended by the propounder of an argument (perhaps by any party to rational discourse). Of course, the triviality of the dialecticians' example reported by Simplicius should not cozen us into thinking that their concern was solely with the sort of hostile argument which is primarily what

---

[67] *E.g.* Thucydides 4.32.3 (and *cf.* 4.36.3), where the Athenians are said to have occupied the island of Pylos in a certain way 'in order to give their enemies the greatest amount of trouble, in that they would be encircled on all sides, and not have one direction in which to draw up the line of battle, but for the most part be attacked on both sides', '... ἀλλ᾽ ἀμφίβολοι γίγνονται τῷ πλήθει'. *Cf.* also Herodotus 5.74, with ch. 1, n. 7.

[68] For Alexinus' demand that Menedemus reply with a simple *Yes* or *No*, *cf. s. el.* 17.175b7ff., where what is at issue is the correct reponse to an ambiguous question; but the alleged dialectical "rule" has general application: Aulus Gellius *noct. att.* 16.2. Hintikka 1959: 4ff. = 1973: 15ff. cites two cases where Aristotle uses the phrase διχῶς λέγεσθαι to describe what are clearly not cases of ambiguity; in the first, a sentence turns out to be a disjunction of two propositions (not a conjunction as here, *i.e.* (*p* and *q*) or (*p* and -*q*), where *p* = *You have beaten your father* and *q* = *You are beating your father*).

[69] See n. 63, and esp. Ebbesen 1981a: 1: 165–9.

Aristotle wanted to analyse and classify in the *s. el*. Armed with the complex Stoic conceptual apparatus, a dialectician could face down even serious philosophical challenges by appeals to ambiguity of key terms – the very investment of ingenuity denounced as useless speculation by Sextus (*P.H.* 2.259). What is still lacking is an explanation in Stoic terms of how ambiguities can cause error and confusion outside the dialectical/eristic situation; and I am not sure that the resources of Stoic epistemology, psychology, and semantics can meet this need.

Modern logicians have devised formal languages in part specifically to eliminate (and assist in identifying) ambiguities: *e.g.* Kirwan 1979: 41; Scheffler 1979: 4ff.; for a famous illustration, Geach 1972: 12f. Similarly, ambiguities are not possible at the level of the *lekton*. In general, because of the isomorphism between language and *lekton*, moving from what is said to what is meant will be straightforward and easy, but the dialectician's competence does extend to identifying and explaining difficult cases – for example, those involving ambiguities. It is even possible that the felt need to eliminate ambiguity and other such irritations was one of the factors that prompted the removal of logical items and relations from the linguistic arena altogether. The failure of the Stoics to construct logical calculi, however, made this manoeuvre no more practically effective than a stipulation that word-complexes designating logical items (*lekta*) signify only one thing.[70]

The problem is that it is hard to see how, say, the confusion about types of source or origin which characterises not only Zeno's, but also Chrysippus' and Diogenes' versions of the

---

[70] The analogy between modern and ancient approaches can be pushed too far (see already 6.2.3). The Stoics did not think of the system of *lekta* as constituting an interpreted formal language, and they lacked formal, disambiguated, ways of talking about logical relations between *lekta*: hence *e.g.* Chrysippus' reformulation in a natural language of Philonian conditionals (see 7.6). Hamblin complains, 1970: 218ff., that a formal theory of linguistic fallacies using a translation model (*viz.* between an object-language and a privileged logical language) is unacceptable because it allows *all* fallacies to be explained in this way; but the model itself is surely inappropriate for Stoic and perhaps all pre-modern logics.

argument described in 7.7 can be interpreted in terms of *lekta* and the rational impressions which they articulate. *Lekta* are supposed to be objectively real, albeit not existent, items which can be shared by numerically different impressions and *logoi* in such a way that thoughts can be shared and communicated. At the level of linguistic expression it is clear that all three versions of the argument are infected by some systematic error or confusion. Thus, Zeno argues that speech does not come from, ἀπό, the brain but that rational discourse comes from, ἀπό, the mind (*P.H.P.* 2.5.8, p. 130, ll. 3, 4), where the first claim concerns local and the second causal origin. Chrysippus' version has it that rational discourse and the mind have the same "source", πηγή, as do speech and rational discourse, and thus that the source of speech and the *locus* of the ruling part are the same (2.5.16, p. 130.25–8). Diogenes contended that both speech and discourse come from, ἐκ, the same region, around the heart, that discourse is sent from, ἐκ, the mind, and that *logos* is in fact often defined as 'significant speech sent out from [ἀπό] the mind', being loaded with semantic content by, ὑπό, the mind's resident conceptions (2.5.9–13, esp. p. 130, ll. 9, 11, 13, 14, 15; and see already 6.2.3 on this passage). Thus the simple ambiguity of ἀπό detected by Galen seems to form part of an interlocking set of errors, extending to other words and phrases, especially ἐκ, ὅθεν, πηγή, about the kinds of source there are.

That last phrase inevitably raises an awkward question. The Zenonian argument, with its variants, is a prime example of a difficulty first raised, in a general form, in Chapter 4: is it possible, even in principle, to determine whether what is in play is a case of ambiguity – an expression's having two quite different meanings – or of generality – where some expression applies to one, broad type or class of object, divisible into two or more sub-types or -classes? Are the "sources", πηγαί, to which Chrysippus refers, for example, in fact members of different species of a single genus? Intuitively, they may "feel" related, yet this does not show that πηγή is *not* ambiguous; and "relatedness" may itself be simply too diffuse, or too

465

subjective, or too much in need of theoretical explication, to be a useful or even coherent concept. Did Zeno even perhaps intend to break new conceptual ground, by drastically revising what is or can be meant by *source*? These problems have a particular relevance for Galen's chosen analysis of the arguments, but they must be confronted by all codifiers of ambiguity. I glance at them here as a further reminder that any application of the Stoic definition of ambiguity, whether or not to fallacious reasoning, involves making assumptions the original justifications for which are unknown, and which may even be unjustifiable.

One other striking feature of the definition was that a *lexis* would count as ambiguous if it has several meanings (linguistic, strict, and so on) and if it is actually understood in more than one way by some, unspecified, audience. Intentions of speakers are ignored as irrelevant, by way not so much of a simple rebuff to Diodorus Cronus, I take it, as of an application of the thesis that ambiguity must be a joint product of linguistic rules and discourse situations. But a problem does arise in the case of the arguers' own understanding of the ambiguous *logoi* (let us assume that they are ambiguous) in Zeno's argument and its variants (let us also overlook the curious fact that by the Stoic definition it appears they could not even have been candidates for ambiguity before Galen cast his critical eye over them: see 4.9). He and the others seem guilty of a gross conceptual error or a gross error in reasoning: either they have failed to keep distinct the two sorts of source in play, or in a fit of absence of mind they have failed to observe a switch between the two.

The difficulty with the first of these explanations is fairly obvious. If Zeno, for example, can use ἀπό, or Chrysippus πηγή, or Diogenes ἐκ, to express exhaustively and accurately a genuine belief about what is taken to be one signal property of the ruling part of the soul, it is only because they have associated with it a linguistically incorrect, fused concept covering both local origin and productive agency. The expressibility of their thought, in Stoic eyes – indeed its being a rational thought at all – should consist in its correspondence to some *lekton* or a determinate set of *lekta*.[71] But analysis into *lekta*, required for formulating the various versions of the argument, cannot yield a set of propositions which the reasoners themselves believe and which they are trying to put into words: for the linguistic meaning(s) of ἀπό, πηγή, or ἐκ, and the meaning which the reasoners attach to them, will not be the same. Linguistic meaning and speaker's meaning, which ought both to be explicable in terms of (the same) *lekta* (roughly, speaker's meaning ought to coincide with or constitute a subset of linguistic meaning(s)), turn out not to be. Yet if direct articulation in meaningful discourse of such conceptual fusions requires that there exist corresponding composite or fused *lekta*, the existence of such *lekta* in turn threatens the general usefulness of *lekta* as providing a mode of linguistic communication. Far from preserving the rational and objectively valid order and structure which language has already partly lost, they would instead begin to reproduce particular individuals' arbitrary, personal, and unpredictable errors.

The alternative explanation is that, while there is indeed some linguistically legitimate set of discrete *lekta* associated with Zeno's, or Chrysippus', or Diogenes' thoughts, as there is with their thoughts' linguistic expression, the thinkers themselves were unaware of the lack of internal connection between them. I take it that none of them reasoned innocently as if *only* local origin or *only* causal origin were involved; and deliberate fraud is out of the question. Further, as their error was plainly not one of selecting, whether out of ignorance, carelessness, or justifiable bias, some one or other of all the possible propositions which together constitute all or most of the content of a given impression (as one may neglect ⟨This is white⟩ in favour of ⟨This is a man⟩ because one is not interested in the object's colour, although the impression contains that information as well), this additional complication can be safely ignored. But if we do suppose that certain linguistic expressions played *some* rôle in leading these Stoics

---

[71] I ignore the non-propositional content, if any, of Zeno's belief, for only the propositions to which he subcribes are relevant here: *cf.* 3.1, n. 12.

into thinking that a single type of source was in play (and the assumption is a plausible one), then only two explanations of their error can be found. Either their impressions were carelessly analysed, and articulated into what seemed the most appropriate words. Or the impressions were articulated carelessly, thus producing the unfortunate and misleading linguistic connection. Yet now our supposed alternative explanation collapses back into our first: surely reasoners of the calibre of Zeno, Chrysippus, and Diogenes could have used their chosen linguistic expressions as they did only so long as they detected no difference in meaning between them.

It might be urged instead that so ignorant were they of the contents of their own thoughts, and of the way they were structuring the world through their concepts (perhaps in part because of a prior conviction of the truth of the desired conclusion), they failed to see the meaning shift in this one instance, even if they would not have missed it in others. If a set of linguistically possible *lekta* supervenes automatically on an impression, misinterpretation should be explicable as misselection from that permitted range. (Striker 1977: 134 speaks of 'a kind of automatic translation' of sense impressions into propositions: talk of translation is a little misleading, but the process thereby described is precisely that in question here.) The problem is to see how this will work in practice where ambiguities are in play. *Lekta* should be precisely those discrete semantic contents on which the Stoic theory of linguistic communication ultimately rests. How, then, can *lekta* themselves be confusable? A far more attractive option is to suppose that error occurs at the linguistic level, that is, at the level of *logoi* which turn out to be defective in one or other of a variety of ways – such as being ambiguous – with the result that semantic differences between the *logoi* or their constituents get overlooked. But the most credible explanation of the failure to see those differences is that the reasoners had a fused concept of origin or source after all.

It would of course be reasonable to expect some sort of explanation from the Stoics of how sentences can be interpreted as if the ambiguities in them did not exist where people do not know of one or other possible meaning, or where they are so stupid and careless that they do not notice some shift in meaning. But it would also be reasonable to look for an explanation of cases where they have fused two or more of the linguistic meanings into one. What is proving difficult is to construct an explanation of this phenomenon using the most important and distinctive feature of Stoic semantics, *lekta*, if *lekta* automatically supervene on impressions. And it seems more plausible anyway that in the case of the argument about the seat of the mind Zeno, Chrysippus, and Diogenes just had arrived at a genuinely unitary, non-standard, concept of source, and that they had different, genuinely unitary impressions associated with it. The Stoics have very little to say which is precise and informative about concept formation,[72] but, like the Epicureans, they appear to have assumed that the basic concepts – those acquired naturally, which are criteria of truth – are the same for all; there are no Lockean ambiguities in a Stoic universe.[73] Nor do they do seem to have felt anxiety about terms which might signify a conceptual range or continuum, or about dangerous unperceived shifts from whole to part or part to part of some broad, complex concept. They acknowledge that people can and do misinterpret impressions, just as Orestes thought that he was seeing a Fury when he was actually seeing Electra; his impression was thus both true and false, Sextus *M.* 7.244f. (39G9). If the failure is particularly embarrassing here, it is because Zeno and Chrysippus must have misinterpreted impressions one of which – that of discourse, λόγος – should be true and definitional (*P.H.P.* 2.5.11, p. 130, ll. 13f., 17, p. 130, ll. 28f. (53U6); *cf.* D.L. 7.56f. (33A, H)),[74] the other – that of

---

[72] Cicero *acad.* 2.19–22 (part, 39C, 40M) contains a very sketchy account of concept formation, closely allied with the learning of language, which is probably mostly Stoic (albeit with Peripatetic elements); *cf.* Barnes 1989: 83, who comments that it is 'thin and feeble'.

[73] On Locke: *e.g.* Robinson 1941: 142.

[74] A passage in Varro, *ling. lat.* 6.56 (= *S.V.F.* 2.143) might suggest that a far stronger requirement for a *lexis* to qualify as a *logos* was imposed than that it be linguistically significant and issue from the mind (D.L. 7.49 (33D), 57 (33A)): that it issue from some *actual speaker's* mind. According to Varro, Chrysippus denied that parrots, or children just learning to talk, can be properly said to "speak" at all:

speech, φωνή – true, sensory, and very possibly cognitive, as if both were articulating the same relation to the same sort of source. People also do tend to acquire concepts which are wrong, and/or wrongly ordered, and which thus structure the world incorrectly; for example, they may have a concept of the good which correctly takes it to be what is beneficial (Sextus *M*. 11.22 (60GI)), yet incorrectly associates the beneficial with, say, what is pleasurable. The heart of the issue is not this one bad argument, however, nor the frailty of the human cognitive apparatus, but the weakness implied in Stoic semantics, epistemology, and psychology. Even if Zeno, Cleanthes, and Chrysippus could show themselves justified in this one instance, by making out that they had arrived at a hitherto unrecognised *but correct* meaning of *origin* (the justification, I presume, being by way of arguments borrowed from Stoic aetiology and metaphysics), there must be other cases where ostensible conceptual "innovations" turn out to be no more than simple errors. The difficulty in finding a satisfactory explanation of this sort of error which can be couched in Stoic terms points to a general restriction on the range of explanations which the school's own relevant doctrines can supply. This must, I fear, rank as the single most serious flaw to show itself in the Stoic theory of ambiguity.

just as a likeness of a man is not a man, so the words they utter are not really words at all, but mere imitations of words, because they can be said only to 'sort-of speak', 'ut loqui'. The parrot or prattling babe produces more or less articulate *lexeis* which are also, at least sometimes, linguistically significant; adult human language users understand something by them, and what they understand are not meanings arbitrarily attached to the utterances by their speakers, but ones sanctioned by the rules of the linguistic community whose genuine discourse is being imitated. So if the parrot's cry *pieces of eight* does not count as a piece of *logos*, this must be because the utterer of the words does not itself understand what it is saying, and has no communicative intentions. It has no internal *logos* (= reason) attaching meaning to its cries. So it looks as though for Chrysippus at least any *logos* must actually issue from a rational speaker. But it is entirely consistent for him to insist that *logos* is what *could have* so issued, while denying that parrots utter *logoi*: the question is whether the *logos conventionally associated with* the *lexis* uttered by the parrot is a real *logos*, intended (and understood) as a piece of significant discourse according to the rules of the language – which of course it is not.

THE INFLUENCE OF STOIC TEACHING

8.1 Introduction

In this chapter I shall try to discover what influence Stoic teaching about ambiguity had outside the school itself, primarily on rhetorical and grammatical writers who had to deal with the subject in the course of their own work and from their own peculiar perspectives. Comparison of the two classifications in Chapter Six strongly suggested that the *prog.* system was originally part of a more comprehensive stylistic theory. Outside philosophical circles, Theon seems to be unique amongst writers on ambiguity in recording a Stoic classification more or less as a whole; but there are others who called on Stoic work piecemeal when they compiled their own definitions of ambiguity and lists of its species.

Treatment of ambiguity in the grammarians and rhetoricians is usually restricted to a terse definition and one or two examples of a small range of types or species. Stoic influence can be felt in the second of these areas, with Stoic survivals in the shape of one or more characteristically Stoic kinds, under a variety of names; but there are no grammatical or rhetorical lists to compare for precision and completeness with the *de soph.* or *prog.* systems, and none explicitly acknowledges a debt to Stoic innovation or systematisation. The Homonymy in Simples/in Compounds distinction is not found; neither is (Non-significant) Part, although Common is frequent, if displaced, since many lists use a dichotomy between single terms and word complexes[1], which is alien to both surviving Stoic

---

[1] For example, Charisius (*G.L.* 1) 271.26–30 distinguishes between *dictiones* and *sententiae*, Trypho 3, 203.25 Sp. between *lexeis* (words) and *logoi*. A *lexis* is defined as 'minimum part of a syntactic complex' by D.T. 22.4; *cf.* Sch. 56.24ff., 211.24ff., 212.2ff., 353.8ff., where this definition is criticised, and 'articulate vocal sound completing a thought' is substituted – which in turn comes to grief over non-

systems (*e.g.* Quintilian 7.9.4; Hermogenes 2, 141.21, 26ff. Sp.;[2] Capella 5.229.21ff.; Fortunatianus 99.26ff. Halm). Grouping ambiguities, such as *vidi statuam auream hastam tenentem*, *I saw a golden spear carrying statue* can be classed as "divisional", 'per distinctionem' (*e.g.* Diomedes (*G.L.* 1) 450.13; Iulius Victor 383.10–13 Halm), a label with an Aristotelian (κατὰ διαίρεσιν?) rather than a Stoic feel. The scholiast on Hermogenes' work on *staseis* (see 8.2) lists such ambiguities as 'due to transposition of words', 'κατ' ὑπέρθεσιν λέξεων', also not a known Stoic grouping: *R.G.* 7.1, 229.4ff. Some categories do not look Stoic at all.[3] Some authors, on the other hand, most notably Quintilian, Theon, and Fortunatianus, seem to have had more or less direct contact with a Stoic classification, as we shall see in 8.2, although it is probably not safe to infer

significant parts of speech (212.24ff.). Another alternative is 'minimum indivisible vocal sound which is independently utterable and conceivable, expressed (either written or spoken) as a unit as regards accent and breathing': 352.35ff., *cf.* 513.1ff. One scholiast draws a clumsy, but striking, distinction between the phonological divisibility of a *lexis* and its semantic unity: 514.11ff. For Apollonius, *lexeis* are 'parts of a syntactically complete *logos*' (*synt.* 2.8f.), but he also draws a distinction between parts of *lexis* and parts of *logos*, the latter being 'conceived of on the basis of juxtaposition [ἐκ παραθέσεως]', *i.e.* as words in a sentence, the former merely 'on the basis of combination [ἐκ συνθέσεως]', *i.e.* being combinable to form words proper) (*synt.* 446.11ff.). Herodian implicitly identifies parts of speech and *lexeis*, *orth.* (*G.G.* 3.1.2.1) 407.20f., 'ἐν ἑνὶ μέρει λόγου ἤγουν ἐν μίᾳ λέξει'; *cf.* Priscian *inst.* 2 (*G.L.* 2), 53.8–10, 'dictio est pars minima orationis constructae, id est in ordine compositae: pars autem, quantum ad totum intellegendum, id est ad totius sensus intellectum'. Dionysius Thrax's definition of the *logos* as a 'complex of prose *lexeis* indicating a complete thought' is rejected as excluding poetic discourse, Sch. 214.3ff., 355.16ff., in favour of 'well-formed [κατάλληλος] complex of words completing a thought' and the like; *cf.* Priscian *inst.* 2, 53.28f.: 'oratio est ordinatio dictionum congrua, sententiam perfectam demonstrans'.

2 This is a version of Common under the heading 'περὶ διάστασιν συλλαβῶν', 'concerning syllable division', with an example also retailed by Quintilian, 7.9.6. The other mode of ambiguity he lists, ll. 21–6 (*cf.* 173.13ff.), that 'ἐκ προσῳδίας', is given the illustration used for the species "Pronunciation" in Theon's second classification of sources of obscurity, *prog.* 129.17ff. (see 8.2); it also recalls the example of Common in Theon's dialectical classification, 81.32–82.1. Rendered into Latin, and used by Cicero *inv.* 2.118, it turns not on accent, however, but on grouping syntax. The anonymous scholiast on Hermogenes, who adds ambiguities of pitch, breathing, syntactic grouping, and homonymy to Hermogenes' original two, observes explicitly that one of his examples (ἐν δέκα ἔτεσι/ἕνδεκα ἔτεσι, *i.e.* in [=for] ten years/[for] eleven years) can be analysed equally as due to prosody, breathing, or division of syllables: *R.G.* 7.1, 227.12ff., esp. 228.19ff.

3 For instance, ambiguities *per communia verba*, *i.e.* in verbs which can be either deponent or passive, *e.g. criminor*, "I accuse"/"I am accused": Diomedes (*G.L.* 1) 450.10–12; or classifiable as Aristotelian Amphibolies, as at Diomedes 450.1–7, *Anec. Helv.* p. XLVI. 23–8 ('per casum accusativum' only).

that such authors' immediate source was specifically a Stoic text on rhetoric, as Reichel 1909: 26, n. 3 supposes was the case with the αὐλητρίς example adopted or adapted by Fortunatianus and Iulius Victor.

Stoic influence might also be expected in the matter of definitions. Although his account of ambiguity as a trope is independent of all known Stoic models, Trypho's definition of ἀμφιβολία, for example, closely resembles the first part of the Stoic definition (D.L. 7.62): λέξις ἢ λόγος δύο ἢ καὶ πλείονα πράγματα δηλοῦσα' (3, 203.25f. Sp.). A *lexis* for Trypho, however, is a single term, a word, as it is for most grammarians. In other authors' definitions, there is little or no clear evidence of Stoic influence.[4] In many cases definitions are so vague it is impossible to say whether they look back to a Stoic model or not; but numerous writers do use the characteristic Stoic term ἀμφιβολία/*amphibolia* (*amfibolia*) (see 6 1)

8.2 Rhetoric

Rhetoricians tend to treat ambiguity exclusively in one or other of two rôles: as a source of legal dispute, and as a cause of the stylistic defect, obscurity. The latter I shall deal with in 8.3, since many features of the grammatical and rhetorical treatments of this portion of stylistic theory are shared.

The rhetoricians had their own special place for ambiguity, in *stasis* theory, as a source of legal dispute. *Stasis* does not now appear on any education syllabus, but in its day it formed

---

[4] *Cf.* Charisius' definition, 271.26f.: 'dictio sententiave dubiae significationis', 'a word or sentence of doubtful meaning'; [Gregory's], 3, 223.15f. Sp. = West 1965: 245: 'φράσις δύο ἢ πλείονας ἐννοίας σημαίνουσα', 'language signifying two or more thoughts'; Cocondrius', 3, 243.8f. Sp.: 'φράσις δύο ἢ καὶ πλείονα σημαίνουσα δι' αὐτῆς', 'language signifying two or even more things in and of itself'; Iulius Victor's, 383.7f. Halm: 'quotiens varia pronuntiatione vel varia significatione quaestio nascitur', 'whenever a ⟨legal⟩ problem is created by a difference in pronunciation or in meaning'. *Cf.* also Cicero *inv.* 2.116: 'cum quid senserit scriptor obscurum est, quod scriptum duas pluresve res significat', 'when what the writer intended is unclear, because what is written signifies two or more things' and Cassiodorus 497.8f. Halm: 'cum id quod scriptum est duas aut plures res significare videtur', 'when what is written appears to signify two or more things'. Both these last two writers understandably restrict ambiguity to writing, their main topic being *stasis* theory. Their definitions are so vague, however, that it is impossible to say whether they conform to any model, Stoic or not.

473

the backbone of what was probably the largest division of ancient secondary education. The theory of *stasis*, *status*, or *controversia* identifies for each legal dispute a single issue or point of contention – the *stasis* - which, if decided, decides the whole case. There was, typically, disagreement about almost everything, starting with its name (*e.g.* Quintilian 3.6.2ff.). Quintilian devotes most of one book (Bk. 3) merely to outlining the enormous variety of rival divisions and subdivisions, and another (Bk. 7) to describing his own favoured version of the theory. An outline of one chief variant will suffice here. *Staseis* are often divided into those which are "rational", that is, having to do with what is alleged to have been done, or the nature or quality of what was done by the accused; and those which are "legal", which turn on points of law, and are usually classified as due to five causes: letter and intention of the law; contradictory laws; syllogism; ambiguity; and competence of the court (*e.g.* Quintilian 3.6.66ff.; and *cf.* Seneca *contr.* 1.2.15, 1.4.6).

Thus, the *stasis* of ambiguity is that which turns on deciding which interpretation of an ambiguous statute, decree, will, contract, or other legal document is to be accepted by the court. It is mentioned, at the very least, by just about every general rhetorical handbook after the first century B.C.E., but was certainly invented earlier than this; indeed, an ancestor of it can be found in Aristotle, although not, of course, in the context of any version of *stasis* theory: *rhet.* 1.15.1375b11–13. Treatment of ambiguity *staseis* can be very cursory, being more than likely limited to a definition and a small stock of wearily familiar examples; but the best writers are happily not content with superficial orthodoxy. Indeed it seems to be chiefly their attitude to the investigation and codification of ambiguities by dialecticians – who are generally Stoics, or Stoic-influenced – which has shaped their own exposition: an exposition which can be favourably discursive (as in Cicero), or scornfully polemical, as in the *ad Herennium* (2.16ff.), or both discursive and dismissive, as in Quintilian (7.9.1ff., esp. 14f.).

It may have been Posidonius' contribution to the field which was the means of transmission of Stoic teaching to the rhetorical tradition, for he is the only major Stoic known to have interested himself in *stasis* theory (Quintilian 3.6.37 = F189, p. 173EK; vol. 2(ii), pp. 686–9). Posidonius is said to have divided *status* into two categories, *vox* and *res*, and defined the former by prescribing four questions: 'an, quid, quam multa, quo modo significet?', 'whether, what, how many things, how it signifies?' An ambiguity classification would not have been out of place in connection with the third of these.[5] An alternative explanation is that Hermagoras, who made *ambiguitas* one of his four *quaestiones legales* (Quintilian 3.3.61), and is traditionally the father of *stasis* theory,[6] had earlier gone directly to Stoic dialectical teaching. But another Stoic, Nestor, is reported to have argued against the inclusion of ambiguity in the list of *status*: see further, 8.5.

---

[5] Ebbesen 1981a: 1: 34 detects a correspondence between each of Posidonius' categories of *vox* and *res status*, and each of the Stoic "categories"; but, as the names of only two of the *res* questions are known, and are mysterious themselves, this correspondence can only be speculative. Kidd 1988: 687f. claims a definite link with the Stoic distinction between φωνή and *pragmata*, which is more likely, but equally uninformative. Curiously, in the course of speculating on the details of the connection, Kidd associates the 'quam multa?' group with ambiguity, yet seems to identify them with cases of polynymy. Stough 1978: 215 suggests ways in which an alleged agent might try to show, in a Stoic context, that a given act was 'not *his doing* [and so not his responsibility], perhaps because someone else did it or ... because what he actually did does not fall under the description of the action attributed to him or even, let us say, because what occurred was not really a doing at all but a kind of mishap' (Stough's emphasis). Extending this speculative reconstruction to Posidonius' rhetorical scheme, we can see that such a negative system could easily form the foundation of a positive classification of actions, one which would recall a typical list of (rational) *staseis*, including Posidonius' own: *coniectio*, "conjecture" (did the alleged agent do what he is said to have done?); *(de)finitio*, "definition" (what, exactly, did he do?); *qualitas*, "quality" (what sort of thing did he do? in particular, was it right, or good, and so justifiable, regardless of the law?) (*e.g.* Cicero *inv.* 1.10, *orator* 45; Quintilian 3.6.66). Posidonius' third *res* class, *ad aliquid*, normally covers the *stasis translatio*, that is, appeals to have the case transferred to another court or dismissed altogether as not suitable to the court before which it is being tried, as technically legal (or illegal) but moral or socially unacceptable (or acceptable), *etc.*: *e.g.* Quintilian 3.6.84. This might not have been Posidonius' own understanding of it, however.

[6] Hermagoras' work is now extant only in fragments preserved by the many later writers who adopted and adapted his system; on his work see esp. Matthes 1959. On *stasis* theory: *e.g.* Volkmann 1885: 38ff.; Bonner 1977: 296ff.; Russell 1983, ch. 3. Posidonius may have attacked a follower of Hermagoras for allowing rhetoricians to fish in philosophical and scientific waters: Plutarch *vit. Pomp.* 42.5 (=F43, T39EK), with Cicero *inv.* 1.8, *de or.* 2.65ff.

There is no explicit evidence about the route(s) by which Stoic teaching found its way into non-Stoic rhetorical textbooks; yet Stoic classifications must have quite swiftly become fixtures in such handbooks and lectures, for already by c. 85–c. 75 the author of the *ad Herennium* – perhaps under Epicurean influence[7] – is ridiculing "the dialecticians'" efforts: 'sunt qui arbitrentur ad hanc causam tractandam vehementer pertinere cognitionem amphiboliarum eam quae ab dialecticis proferatur. nos vero arbitramur non modo nullo adiumento esse, sed potius maximo inpedimento' ('Some people are of the opinion that the knowledge of ambiguities which is on offer from the dialecticians is of especial relevance to the handling of this [legal] cause. We, however, are of the opinion that not only is it of no assistance, it is rather a very great hindrance', 2.16).[8] The immediate context is *stasis* theory, but from the way they are described it is obvious that these dialecticians – almost certainly Stoics – did not study ambiguity in any one type of discourse, and that in this particular field their work was being used, and use of it advocated, by rhetoricians, not by the dialecticians themselves. But there may still have been Stoics (like Posidonius?) who constructed their own versions of the ambiguity *status*. The conventionality of what is known of Stoic rhetorical teaching (stylistics aside) is entirely consistent with there being Stoic rhetoricians who took over accounts of ambiguity worked out in dialectic and used them to adapt or expand versions of *stasis* theory taken over from the professionals.[9]

---

[7] The authorship of the *ad Herennium* is discussed by Kennedy 1972: 110–13, 120ff., who argues that the writer 'is by no means a doctrinaire Epicurean, who would have had little use for rhetoric', although Epicurean influence has been detected at 2.34, the fear of death as a motive to crime, and at 4.24, a possible allusion to one of Epicurus' maxims; and certainly the broadside against dialectic smacks of Epicureanism.

[8] On ambiguities with absurd meanings: 6.3.6; on the dialecticians' fear of speaking their own names: 6.3.4; and see further, 8.5.

[9] The conventionality of Stoic rhetorical teaching emerges from the brief report at D.L. 7.42f. (31A6), which mentions the traditional three types of rhetorical speech; four of the traditional areas of rhetorical expertise, invention, expression, arrangement, memory (delivery may have been deliberately excluded as irrelevant); and the five-way division of the (forensic) speech (assuming, reasonably, that the division "proof" has simply dropped out of the text).

In stark contrast to the scornful hostility of the *ad Herennium* is Cicero's fulsome praise of the philosopher–orator. Indeed, one of the numerous benefits to orators from a dialectical training is the ability to distinguish ambiguities: *orator* 16, 115 (*cf.* Capella 5.230.6–7), *Brutus* 152f., *de or.* 2.110f. (where Antonius complains that the rhetoricians do not understand the subject as well as the dialecticians). Presumably the ambiguity *status* will be one area in which this ability can be usefully exercised, although dialectic is not mentioned in the relevant section of the *de inventione*. Theon took Cicero's side of the debate over the usefulness of philosophy, especially dialectic, to the orator: 'The orators of old, especially those of good repute, thought one should not take up rhetoric at all before engaging to some extent in philosophy, and getting one's fill of magnanimity from that source' (*prog.* 59.1–4). Theon may well not have studied dialectic, and actually cites it, alongside geometry, as an 'obscure' subject unsuitable for ordinary narrative (80.12), yet he considered at least one of its products, the Stoic ambiguity classification, valuable and beneficial, even for the education of budding orators. He does not recommend the study of dialectic specifically in his opening pages, but the combination of his warm praise for philosophy and his use of the dialectical classification is strikingly Ciceronian.[10]

Quintilian is less favourable toward complicated ambiguity classifications; but his reservations are probably limited to the context of *stasis* theory, where what matters is to show, if possible, that the favoured interpretation of a document is that intended by its author, 'nec refert, quo modo sit facta amphibolia, aut quo resolvatur' ('and it does not matter how an ambiguity is made or how it is corrected', 7.9.14). Iulius Victor lists the recommended considerations for comparing rival interpretations of an ambiguously-framed law as 'utrum honestius, utrum iustius, utrum legibus congruentius, utrum

---

[10] On Theon's (lack of) acquaintance with dialectic: 5.2.1, 5.3. His mention of 'orators of old' brings to mind Pericles and Demosthenes, and the Roman Servius Sulpicius, as described by Cicero *orator* 14ff., *Brutus* 152f., and praised for their dialectical skill, in, amongst other things, the distinction of ambiguities.

disciplinae aptius: in quo quid credibile sit voluisse latorem cernitur' ('whether it is more honourable, more just, more consonant with the laws, more productive of good order: in which the object of attention is what it can be believed the lawmaker intended', 394.31f. Halm; and see already 6.3.6). Techniques of diagnosis and resolution, like those Quintilian himself lists, 7.9.9–12, will assist literary composition and criticism – indeed, in Book 8, where ambiguity is classed as one cause of obscurity in Quintilian's own theory of style, he refers the reader back to the Book 7 classification – but in the forensic arena they could easily seem superfluous and merely confusing. Cicero's *de inventione* lacks a classification altogether, concentrating instead on resolution procedures for dealing with (ostensible) ambiguities; some of these[11] form Quintilian's other target at 7.9.14f.

It is perhaps curious, then, that Quintilian includes an ambiguity classification at all, especially one so elaborate and impressive, in Book 7; he may simply have bowed to rhetorical convention. Elsewhere, he indicates only grudging approval of the very minor rôle played by dialectic's fallacy- and ambiguity-solving powers (*cf.* 1.10.5), although there is nothing like the sort of bitter and wide-ranging offensive launched in the *ad Herennium*. His source-materials may have included classifications of ambiguity considered as a stylistic defect, as three of his illustrations are literary (7.9.6 (Ennius), 7 (Virgil), 10 (Virgil?)), while the list of disambiguation procedures would not interest a *stasis* theorist but could be a valuable diagnostic or corrective tool in stylistics. So did Quintilian know a Stoic system something like the one Theon records?

What the classification in Book 7 does is to insert a very small number of recognisably Stoic elements into a basically

---

[11] A similar list of such procedures is found at *ad Her.* 2.16, immediately before the anti-dialectical polemic. Ebbesen 1981a: 1: 32 suggests that the disambiguation procedures outlined at Quintilian 7.9.10ff. are 'Stoic rather than anything else', if they do indeed belong to any philosophical school. But there is nothing to suggest that they were culled from any philosophical source, and they fit both known Stoic classifications only very loosely: see main text, further, below.

non-Stoic framework. Quintilian's broad division of ambiguity bearers is into *singula* and *coniuncta*, and the former ranges what are obviously Common expressions alongside homonyms.[12] (Non-significant) Part, which also spans the word/word-complex divide, has disappeared altogether. There are four sub-groups, by cause, of *coniuncta* ambiguities, the last three of which together apparently correspond to Significant Part (the illustration of ambiguity *per flexum*, "through inflection (of the voice)", is actually the *de soph.* example of Significant Part), while the first closely resembles Theon's version of Reference (although only 'accusativi geminatio', with two accusative cases, is mentioned); Reference itself is absent. The *singula/coniuncta* dichotomy, and the tetrachotomy of *coniuncta*, have no (known) Stoic parallels, and neither does Quintilian's version of Accent (7.9.13).

The only other hint at a possible Stoic past is the absence of his versions of Pleonasm and Elleipsis from the first part of the classification, that not concerned with disambiguation, although both appear, separately, in his list of sources of obscurity in Book 8, a list which also includes excessive Hyperbaton and lengthy Interpolation (see 6.6.2). These versions of Pleonasm and Elleipsis (here dubbed *adiectio* and *detractio*) may originally have belonged to a different classification, one which treated disambiguation procedures as divisional principles: at least, Quintilian's attempt to associate each species of ambiguity in word-compounds with just one disambiguation technique is unsuccessful.[13] So Quintilian may perhaps be

---

[12] Quintilian's dichotomy of Common ambiguities has already been mentioned: 6.2.5.

[13] For example, the following testatory clause is given as an illustration of ambiguity which occurs when it is unclear 'utri duorum antecedentium sermo subiunctus sit', 'to which of two antecedents an expression is to be connected': 'heres meus uxori meae dare damnas esto argenti, quod elegerit, pondo centum', 'let my heir be bound to pay to my wife one hundred pounds of silver which he/she has chosen' (7.9.9). Later this is diagnosed as due to *detractio* ('ipse', 'he', or 'ipsa', 'she' can be added to 'elegerit', 'has chosen'); yet it could be resolved just as well by the removal, *translatio*, of 'quod elegerit' to a position after 'heres' or 'uxori', or – a course not even mentioned by Quintilian – the relative clause might be changed to a participle. There is a comparable list of techniques, applying the *quadripertita ratio* (on this see 6.4.3, n. 101, and also next note) to word-complex ambiguities, at Boethius *div.* 890BC, already discussed in 6.3.6; this lacks an explicit restriction

using, and like Theon adapting, a Stoic treatment of style similar to the one Theon records; but to all appearances he took very little from any of the Stoic classification(s) he may have known, and it would be rash to assume on the basis of this one text that the resolution procedures he describes are Stoic, since no other author reports that they were adopted or developed in connection with ambiguity classifications by the Stoa.[14]

Theon is known to have had access to Stoic material: as a result, his second list of causes of ἀσάφεια, "inclarity" (pp. 129f.), under the heading of the *progymnasma* "law",[15] might be expected to show signs of Stoic influence, even if it marks the transition to *stasis* theory. The classification itself is, however, highly unorthodox; only the Scholiast on Hermogenes' *On staseis* seems to approach Theon's flexibility in interpreting traditional groupings. It comprises:

1. *Pronunciation or prosody*, 'περὶ τὴν προφοράν, ἥν τινες περὶ τὴν προσῳδίαν καλοῦσιν', 129.11f., 17–22; *cf. e.g.* Hermogenes 2, 141.21–26 Sp., Quintilian 7.9.13.[16]
2. *Name* (129.22–7), where 'what is written is new or quite old or foreign' (23f.). These are separate classes in the earlier clas-

to any type(s) of discourse, although other passages make it probable that Boethius is thinking primarily or exclusively of two standard Aristotelian activities, the dialectical exchange and scientific or philosophical inquiry: note especially the distinction between *contentio* and *veritas* at 890A.

[14] The tetradic system *adiectio/detractio–diminutio/divisio/transmutatio* has been attributed to the Stoa, but available evidence suggests rather that it was common Hellenistic property: see already 6.4.3, n. 101. In any case, there is no reason to suppose that these classifications of ambiguity types and of resolution procedures came from the same source, for the match between them is decidedly imperfect.

[15] "Law" does not survive intact in the Greek manuscript tradition, the text breaking off after only one source of controversy – obscurity – has been described and classified. The Armenian version contains four of five further chapters entirely lost from the Greek, a loss which Butts 1986: 20 plausibly attributes to Theon's work having been trimmed and re-arranged (probably by the early 5th cent. C.E.: Butts 1986: 22.) in order to bring it closer in form and content to Hermogenes', Aphthonius', and Nicolaus' students' handbooks of *progymnasmata*.

[16] The Stoics had a special term, προφορά, for the "pronunciation" of linguistic items, as opposed to the "enunciation", ἐκφορά, of *lekta*: see 6.3.4. There is thus a remote possibility that the "dialecticians" may have had a Pronunciation, προφορά, mode, which for some reason Theon omitted from his earlier list, but mentions here. As already observed in n. 2, the rhetorician Hermogenes lists only two species of ambiguity, of which one ("Division of syllables") is clearly Common, the other the "missing" Accent, προσῳδία, kind: 2, 141.19ff. Sp.

sification of causes of obscurity at 81.8ff, which lists invented, coined, metaphorical, old-fashioned, foreign, and homonymous terms.

3. *Homonymy* (129.28–130.1). Theon's for once orthodox treatment contrasts with that of Hermogenes' commentator, who lists the following as cases of Homonymy: Demosthenes *On False Embassy* 298, where the 'guardians' mentioned in an oracle may be generals or orators (*R.G.* 7.1, 226.24ff., 229.10ff.); Apollo's famous oracle recommending recourse to the 'wooden wall' of Athens (229.15ff.); two slaves, both called Leon, quarrelling over who is meant by a clause in their late master's that 'Leon should be freed' (230.11ff.); a convicted murderer on the run pleading he is being tried twice for the same crime when he is found guilty a second time after the god refuses to grant him an oracle (again!), the dispute being whether δίκη means "trial" or "penalty" (230.20ff.).

4. *Polynymy or Synonymy*, where one thing has many names (130.1–5); these are of course the Peripatetic and Stoic names for the same phenomenon· *e g.* Simplicius *cats.* 36.8ff. (− *S.V.F.* 2.150).

5. *Syntax* (130.5–13), which seems to be a combination of Aristotelian Amphiboly with Aristotelian Combination/Division or Stoic Significant Part.

6. *Combination and Division* (130.13–22), which seems to be Theon's own invention, and corresponds neither to the Aristotelian modes nor to Stoic Common, despite the claim that 'some call this περὶ τὴν κοινὴν τοῦ διῃρημένου καὶ τοῦ διαιρέτου', 'concerning the ⟨ambiguity?⟩ which is common to the divided and the undivided (*or*: the indivisible) (14f.). The examples are: (a) a law that a brother's children can inherit: does this mean that the brother takes precedence, and they inherit only if he is dead (= "Division"), or that they all inherit equally (= "Combination")?; and (b) a law that 'ὁ ψευδομαρτυρῶν ἁλοὺς τρὶς χιλίας διδότω': does this mean that a three-times perjurer pays a thousand, or a one-timer three thousand? (b) clearly belongs under "syntax"; (a) does not, and their being grouped together is curious indeed.

7. *Pleonasm* (130.23–8), 'ὅταν δυνατὸν ᾖ πλέον τι τοῦ γεγραμμένου συλλογίζεσθαι, ὡς καὶ αὐτὸ δυνάμει δηλούμενον', 'whenever it is possible to infer something more than what is written, as also being indicated potentially' (130.23–8). Theon's example is as follows: a law allows maternal relatives to inherit; a mother contends that she herself should therefore have priority. The type thus resembles, and presumably replaces, the orthodox *stasis* type συλλογισμός, and it is a long way from the Stoic *de soph.* kind Pleonasm, as I have already observed (6.4.6), and widely different

too from anything else I have found in rhetorical or grammatical classifications. It is easy to object that it is far too wide and vague to be informative, a class of narrowly linguistic pleonastic expressions being more useful.

8. *Elleipsis* (130.28–36, the end of the text in the Greek manuscript tradition, from which the obscurity type 'περὶ μάχην', "concerning conflict" (129.16), possibly concerned with conflicting laws (Reichel 1909: 111), is lost): not defined, but at least two examples were provided: (i) a man who strikes his father is to lose his hand; what of the man who strikes his father unwittingly? (a Greek but apparently not a Roman law: Bonner 1949: 96f.); (ii) a traitor's children are to be disinherited; does this apply equally to natural and to adopted children? Theon adds that 'elleipsis of the person' is 'multiform', embracing failure to specify nature, age, kinship, or fortune (*e.g.* should a traitor's adopted children, or his girl-children, die with him?). Again, the class is generous to the point of uselessness.

Perhaps surprisingly, then, the only remnants of the Stoic classification are Common (misinterpreted), Syntax (in part) or Combination and Division (again in part; all recall Significant Part), Pleonasm, and Elleipsis (the scope of which Theon greatly changes and expands).

The closest approach, besides Theon's and Quintilian's, to the known Stoic classifications is made by the rhetorician Fortunatianus. His system (79.18ff. Halm) comprises five modes: *per discretum et indiscretum* (corresponding to Significant Part, not Common);[17] *per distinctionem* (corresponding to Common); homonymy; and *per abundantiam* and *per deficientiam*. These last two kinds, if present at all, are commonly listed as species of linguistic defect separate from ambiguity (as in Quintilian 8.2.17ff.), but this need not imply unawareness of, or lack of interest in, Stoic work on ambiguity, since the *prog.* Stoics at least may have dealt with Pleonasm and Elleipsis as types of obscurity, not of ambiguity (see 6.4.6, and 8.3, below).

---

[17] Like Theon, Fortunatianus or his source must, I think, have confused Common with some version of Combination/Division, as does Reichel 1909: 110 and n. 5, who describes it, revealingly, as concerned 'de syllabis et verbis separandis', 'concerning the division of syllables and words'.

8.3   Stylistics

As a fault of style ambiguity appears frequently in both rhetoricians' and grammarians' accounts, and occasionally, too, as a trope. The framework of virtues and vices of style – standardly purity, clarity, appropriateness, and embellishment – is one of the commonest theoretical and didactic constructs in ancient stylistic writing. It seems to have its origins in Aristotle, was apparently first formulated by Theophrastus with material culled from the *Rhetoric* and *Poetics*, adapted with characteristic eccentricity by the Stoa, and then used in one form or another by most later writers on style and composition. In place of Aristotle's original understanding of ambiguity in the *Rhetoric*, 3.5.1407a32ff., as an offence against "Hellenism", or "good Greek" in a wide sense, it became one source of a distinct stylistic fault, obscurity, Hellenism itself being restricted to correctness or purity; the Romans later introduced their own counterpart to it, *Latinitas*. In late Roman grammars, ambiguity is usually treated under the heading of the virtues and vices, as one of the "other vices" of style, after solecism and barbarism; but there is no good evidence that the standard tripartite division of these treatises (phonology and orthography; parts of speech; virtues and vices of style) is a Stoic survival, as Barwick 1922 argued. The routes Stoic stylistic doctrines may have taken to Diomedes, Charisius, and their fellows remain mysterious.[18]

Ambiguity's relegation to the stylistic vices was not seriously challenged until this century. Its identification as a

---

[18] For the weaknesses in Barwick's famous thesis, see Baratin and Desbordes 1987: 42. Yet their own case – that the Romans extended the stylistic portion of the *ars grammatica* to cover some parts at least of another of the standard excellences, *ornatus*, κατασκευή, besides *Latinitas* – is also unconvincing, based as it is on a rigorous theoretical distinction, that between 'langue' (to be endowed with Hellenism/Latinity) and 'discours' (amenable to the other stylistic excellences) (1987: 53), which may not have been observed in practice. Grammar's quarrel with rhetoric about their respective duties and areas of competence must be taken to reflect changing social pressures and demands and professional ambitions as much as, or even more than, the theoretical or methodological conflicts which interest historians of the language sciences.

fault assumes a conception of language, all language, as a transmitter of some single and straightforwardly separable message or meaning. The approach is still taken by modern pedagogical writers. In Taha 1983, for example, types of syntactic ambiguity are described using a simplified technical jargon (admittedly, and unsurprisingly, one more complex and precise than that used in most ancient textbooks), illustrated with instances from ordinary, non-literary, language (another significant difference), and matched with appropriate disambiguation techniques, where differences between the resources of spoken and written discourse are stressed. Ambiguity is explicitly described as 'a defect that learners of English should avoid in their writing' (1983: 252, *cf.* 265). Stageburg 1975 is a similar treatment aimed explicitly at American college students, for whom 'ambiguity is an ever-present peril to clearness of expression' (303). In antiquity, however, what was appropriate for schoolchildren and their teachers seems often to have shaped advanced literary criticism and elementary προγυμνάσματα alike, in so far as the dominant model was that of rhetorical composition, a model which makes language the adaptable medium of a single, preselected content, and which both judges and teaches stylistic technique on that basis (*cf.* Russell 1981: 4ff.).

The unworkability of this scheme shows up nowhere so well as in that notorious rhetorical and grammatical double-act, figures of thought and figures of speech. Ancient authors will almost, but not quite, admit that the distinction is incoherent and impossibly rigid. Ambiguity was sometimes, however, included amongst these stylistic adornments, perhaps as a result of of its long-standing contribution to the philological techniques by which plausible resolutions of problematic verses in Homer and the classics generally could be devised. (This was not, to all appearances, a distinctively Stoic approach to ambiguity.[19]) From here it could have been but a short step to classifying ambiguities as deliberate stylistic flourishes, when the intended double or triple meaning was seen as witty

[19] See 3.5, and nn. 65, 66 there, on this use of ambiguity.

and entertaining, a flattering challenge to the audience's intelligence, rather than an obstacle to their understanding (*cf. e.g. ad Her.* 4.67 on this distinction). Tropes and figures are, after all, sometimes reckoned as intentional, artistic barbarisms and solecisms; and the same features of style – Pleonasm, Elleipsis, Hyperbaton, and so on – tend to crop up also as stylistic advantages, provided they are well-handled and deliberate.[20] Quintilian lists homonymies and rare words as items in literary texts for the grammarian to explain, 1.8.15, but for the orator to avoid, as being causes of obscurity, 8.2.12ff. (*cf.* Baratin and Desbordes 1987: 60). Apollonius Dyscolus criticises grammarians who merely collect tropes 'as some did who merely pointed out the solecisms, but did not teach their cause – something which, if one does not understand the cause, will make the collection of the tropes pointless' (*synt.* 271.5ff.). Ambiguity's appearance in this rôle is, though, relatively rare: *e g ad Her.* 4.67, where ambiguity is one form of the figure Emphasis; [Gregory] *trop.* 3, 223.14ff. Sp.;[21] Cocondrius 3, 243.7ff. Sp.[22]

The Stoics, who have been credited with inventing the traditional figures and tropes, may also sometimes have conceived of ambiguity in this way; but the unconventional treatment of Hyperbaton and Interpolation (6.6.2) is evidence against.[23]

---

[20] Solecisms as "bad" figures: *e.g.* Servius *Comm. in. Don.* 447.5ff.; D.T. Sch. 456.23. Diomedes 440.4ff. divides up the four literary dialects according to their characteristic defects, which are stylistic ornaments (tropes, figures, *metaplasmos*) in the hands of the 'docti'; κοινή 'communis est, in qua omnes idem sentimus', 'is common, in which we all express ourselves in the same way'. Contrast Quintilian 8.2.14 with 8.6.62ff., *ad Her.* 4.18, for "bad" and "good" Hyperbaton; and *cf.* Quintilian 1.8.14ff.: the "vices" of barbarism, solecism, and *catachresis* acquire new names when they occur as stylistic ornaments in poetry. For further, extensive documentation, see Baratin and Desbordes 1987: 46ff.

[21] West 1965: 230–2 argues that this *On tropes* is perhaps a version of Trypho's book on the topic, and is certainly not by Gregory.

[22] Apollonius *synt.* 300.11ff. claims that where the cases of a nominal are formally distinct, any changes in them are either figures or solecistic: 7.6, n. 36.

[23] The traditional tropes and figures can be found in *e.g. ad Her.* 4.19ff.; Cicero *de or.* 3.148–70; Quintilian Bks. 8–9; Ps.-Longinus *sublim.* 16–29; [Gregory] *trop.* (see n. 21); Tiberius *fig.* (*ed.* Ballaira 1968); and many other sources. Barwick 1957: 88ff. argues that the traditional doctrine of tropes is Stoic in origin, and that their division is parallel to the divisions constructed by Stoic etymology of the ways in which words were originally formed (as described by Augustine in his *de dialectica*, ch. 6). His similar argument for figures is less persuasive, however; and, as Baratin and Desbordes observe, 1981: 28ff., the orthodox *lexis/logos* opposition

The Roman grammarians' seemingly bizarre double treatment of departures from "ordinary" usage as both "good" (*metaplasmos*, figures and tropes, in the poets) and "bad" (catachresis, barbarisms and solecisms, in everyone else) may be simply a sign of a deeper theoretical incoherence, the simultaneous rejection of poetic discourse as "abnormal" and its elevation to the status of an ideal. (For a different explanation, see Baratin and Desbordes 1987: 46ff.). A wilder guess would be that it reflects an authentic Stoic survival. Hyperbaton and Interpolation at least were probably treated by the *prog*. Stoics as causes of obscurity, not as figures or tropes (6.6.2). These Stoics may also have listed Ambiguity, Elleipsis and Pleonasm as separate offences against clarity, which is standard in the Latin *artes* (see 6.4.6). So the guess would be that some Stoic lists of offences against (a) correct speech and (b) clarity found their way into Roman manuals, but had to be adapted to a more generous literary canon.

8.4 Technical grammar

Ambiguity's next appearance is, I think, the one that best gives both a handle on the dominant conception of ambiguity in antiquity, and a measure of its distance both from the Stoa and from the modern world.

This is not the place to review the recent scholarly shift in perspective on ancient grammar, especially ancient technical grammar (which tends to take the form of a rather belated application of Kuhnian historiography of science, followed, with dazzling inconsistency, by the substitution of some hybrid of modern generative grammar as the new "normal science"). I shall try only to identify the homes found for ambiguity in all varieties of professional, self-styled "grammar", as a prelude to identifying Stoic survivals. This very

---

underpinning that between tropes and figures is in any case a word/word-complex dichotomy alien to the Stoic tradition. The unusual treatment by Theon's Stoics of Interpolation and Hyperbaton was discussed in 6.6.2; their presence alone – especially if it was in a list of causes of obscurity – does not prove these Stoics had or even had access to an extensive system of figures.

limited project itself demands some background information; I shall confine myself to the barest essentials.

Perhaps the most famous division of the field of grammar, that of Dionysius Thrax, provides a serviceable starting-point, when taken together with the one most useful for present purposes, that of Sextus Empiricus. Six parts are described by Dionysius (5.2ff.): accurate recital; interpretation, with respect to the poetic tropes (or methods); ready explanation of unusual words and of narratives (themselves subdivided, Sextus *M*. 1.252f.); discovery of etymologies; the working out of regularities (= analogy); and finally literary (*i.e.* poetic) criticism, 'the noblest part of the art'. As this account comes at the very beginning of the *Ars*, it has a good chance of being authentic and early, even if the rest of the work is not.[24] The treatise itself shows scant respect for the division it retails, being primarily concerned with the elements and parts of speech and their properties. Sextus *M*. 1.91ff. offers a comparable, but three-way, division into "historical" grammar (explaining references to persons, places, *etc.* (92)); "special" or "interpretive" grammar (explaining unclear and unsound passages in authors, and establishing which works are spurious, which genuine (93)); and "technical" grammar, which is concerned with orthography and Hellenism (92, 97ff.). A primary or "first" grammar, sometimes called γραμματιστική, concerned with teaching basic reading, writing, and comprehension skills, was also distinguished (*e.g.* 44, 49; Quintilian 1.9.2). (The long-running dispute with rhetoricians as to who should teach what – *e.g.* Quintilian 1.9.6, 2.1.4ff.; Suetonius *gr.* 4 – can be ignored here.) These schematic descriptions should be allowed neither to obscure the complexity, changeability, and internecine strife which characterised linguistic and grammatical studies, those "awkward" qualities which can now be

---

[24] Di Benedetto 1958/9, 1973 has argued against the authenticity of the Dionysian *Ars*, which he dates to the third or fourth century C.E., with the exception of chs. 1–5 (including the division of grammar); his case has been found wanting by Erbse 1980. Wouters 1979: 36, who gives a useful summary of reactions to Di Benedetto's thesis, assumes its basic genuineness, while allowing for modifications over the centuries. Taylor 1987a: 8ff. surveys the evidence in the broad context of the development of grammar as an independent discipline.

admired in some of the papyrus remains of grammatical manuals and technical treatises alike (*cf.* Wouters 1979: 38ff., 214); nor to give an impression of uniformity between Greek and Roman grammars, or of development in either toward preordained goals (*cf.* Taylor 1987a). But they do allow a working basis for marking out areas in which use may have been made of Stoic work on ambiguity, and ones which show little or no sign of Stoic influence.

The grammarians discussed in 8.3 were generally concerned directly with the interpretation and assessment of literature, and with teaching composition. Technical grammar, whose field of operations is of interest here, is, in its advanced form, comparable to some extent with the modern disciplines of phonetics and phonology, morphology, and syntax, as well as semantics and historical linguistics; and modern linguists would recognise in the more theoretically and methodologically sophisticated sort of technical grammar a remote (and, typically, a sadly misguided) forerunner to their own work, even if technical grammar was ostensibly a contribution to what was accepted as the highest form of grammatical activity, literary criticism.[25] An outstanding example – perhaps un-

---

[25] So *e.g.* A.D. *synt.* 2.1f. It may be relevant that Suetonius *gr.* makes textual-cum-literary criticism the oldest, and by implication the most prestigious, type of grammar – in fact it is dominant in his little work; the earliest native grammarians are poets themselves (§1), and those taught by Crates of Mallos edited and commented on poetry, while the only two exceptions, those who 'instruxerunt auxeruntque ab omni parte grammaticam', 'taught and extended the whole of grammar', are mentioned by name (§2). Blank 1982: 52, however, points out that Apollonius neither restricts the study of syntactic regularity to its applications in literary criticism (*cf.* esp. *synt.* 51.7–9, 10–12), nor consistently advocates alteration of poetic usage on the grounds that it is irregular. Apollonius, who expends an enormous amount of ingenuity defending the "regularity", καταλληλότης, of literary "problem" lines, will sometimes reject as ungrammatical constructions which we would find acceptable: thus at *synt.* 453.11f., taking κατά as a preposition is disallowed, even though this would be normal Homeric usage; at 37.6f., the removal of an article is said to make a sentence 'unintelligible', 'ἀσύνετον', yet would be perfectly acceptable in poetry. (Householder 1981: 33, 234 alerted me to both these passages; the use made of them here is mine, however.) The question – central to understanding ancient language studies – to what extent technical grammarians genuinely took the reading and appreciation of literary texts to be the supreme goals of grammar as a whole, and thus regarded poetic usage as at the same time deviant and ideal, is too large to be pursued here.

orthodox, but admirably clear in plan – was Varro's great treatise on Latin, now largely lost. Its author's own words show that it originally followed a trichotomy of language, *oratio*, into (i) *impositio* or origin ('quemadmodum vocabula rebus essent imposita', 'how names were imposed on things'); (ii) *declinatio*, that is, both inflection (*declinatio naturalis*) and derivation (*declinatio voluntaria*) ('quo pacto de his declinata in discrimina ierint', 'how ⟨words⟩ were differently derived from these ⟨imposed words⟩'), the study of which seeks to explain 'cur et quo et quemadmodum in loquendo declinata sunt verba' ('why and to what end and how words are derived in speech'); and lastly (iii) syntax ('ut ea inter se ratione coniuncta sententiam efferant', 'how ⟨words⟩ when coherently conjoined produce a sentence' (or '... express a thought')) (*ling. lat.* 7.110, 8.1–2).

The influence of Stoic logic and semantics on one of the greatest contributers to technical grammar, the second-century C.E. Alexandrian Apollonius Dyscolus, was wide and heavy, although in some ways he departs from known Stoic models – notably in his conception of the sentence or *logos*[26] – and he can be explicitly critical of Stoic ideas, about

---

[26] Apollonius' conception of grammar as a development of Stoic ideas about the rationality and regularity of language has been explored by Blank 1982, who argues convincingly that in Apollonius' case at least the traditional divide between technical and philosophical grammar is non-existent. A distinction has still to be drawn between Apollonius' programme and his success in executing it, including and especially the provision of a firm and coherent theoretical basis. For example, syntax is made as much a relation between (forms of) words (φωναί, λέξεις, σχήματα: for the distinction between these and ὀνόματα, see *e.g. synt.* 62.10f.; for this type of syntax, see *e.g. synt.* 275.6f.) as one between thoughts or meanings (ἔννοιαι, νοητά) or between the parts or elements of speech that meanings differentiate (*pron.* 67.6f.). Apollonius' weakness is that he seems not to have fixed precisely the connection between the two types of syntax; this flaw is particularly noticeable in the key passage *synt.* 2.3–3.2, which exploits a dual conception of the *logos* as both a combination of forms and a combination of νοητά; but both *lexeis* and their associated "intelligibles" are merely said to be 'in a way' elements of the *logos*.

Another important departure from the Stoa (*cf.* Blank 1982:32ff.) is the treatment of certain formal properties of words, such as case, gender, or number, elsewhere typically called παρεπόμενα (*e.g.* D.T. 46.5ff.), as παρυφιστάμενα, "subsistent on" them, which the more radically materialist Stoics are unlikely to have initiated; note that the relation between *lekta* and impressions is that of "subsistence", D.L. 7.63.

pronouns and articles, for example.[27] Apollonius treats ambiguity primarily as a limitation on thorough-going linguistic regularity, καταλληλότης, τὸ κατάλληλον. Ancient Greek shows many instances of what Apollonius calls συνέμπτωσις or σύνοδος or simply ὁμοφωνία, when (to use a modern jargon) different lexemes share a form or forms, or else the same lexeme has different morphosyntactic words sharing or realising the same form ("syncretism").[28] For example, the word-form 'ἐμοῦ', 'mine', is the genitive case of two words or lexemes, ἐγώ, *I* and ἐμός, *mine*, (*synt.* 216.8ff., *cf.* 314.3ff., 'ἐμοί', 'to/for me'); some nouns have a formally identical nominative and vocative case, or a nominative and accusative (41.18, 293.1ff., 318.5ff., 371.5ff.); and the ordinary and the possessive genitive forms may be identical (145.5ff.). In fact, Apollonius criticised the Stoics for overlooking the ὁμοφωνία of articles and pronouns when they argued that these belong to one part of speech (*pron.* 7.20; *cf.* D.T. Sch. 519.12ff.).

To eliminate such ambiguities, certain additional features of language come regularly into play: for example, if the verb with which a noun is used is imperative, the noun must be vocative and not nominative (*synt.* 371.5ff.); an adverb may show that a verb is imperative and not indicative (*adv.* 123.10ff.); the addition of the article can distinguish between a preposition and a prefix, as in παρὰ τοῦ νόμου, *against the law*, and παρανόμου, the adjective meaning "unlawful", in the genitive case (*synt.* 445.10ff.); or the construction as a whole must be examined, as in the cases of 'ἐμοῦ' (216.8ff.), 'αὐτοῦ' (= 'there', 'his/her/its', *adv.* 176.8ff.), and 'ἤ', which may be a disjunction (= 'or') or have a clarificatory meaning or function (= '*i.e.*') according to context (*coni.* 223.4ff.). It does not seem to have been felt as a difficulty for the theory of linguistic regularity that, were it not for such safety nets, the prin-

---

[27] *Pron.* 5.13ff.; and also possibly D.T. Sch. 214.29ff., 357.18ff., 522.5ff., if these passages are indeed excerpts from Apollonius and not from Trypho, as Schneider G.G. 2.3, pp. 30f. argues. *Coni.* 213.1–214.3 is a good summary of Apollonius' (overt) attitude to Stoic grammatical theory. Wouters 1979: 68 (commentary at 77ff.) gives the text of one papyrus manual in which something like the Stoic thesis that pronouns and articles are the same part of speech is endorsed.

[28] For Apollonius' concept of formal coincidence, see esp. *synt.* 45.3ff., 292.17ff.

ciple of regularity would inevitably, in some cases, lead to ambiguity.

Ambiguity cannot be invoked to explain such phenomena *ad lib.* Apollonius argues all too persuasively for the arbitrariness of Trypho's derivation of the exclamation ὦταν, *Sir!*, from ὦ, *Oh!*, together with the syllable τα (on the lines of δῆτα, *certainly*), the letter ν having been added to distinguish it from ὦτα, *ears* (*adv.* 159.15ff.). Again, the notion that articles were introduced in order to distinguish cases of nominals which do not reveal gender is rejected not merely on the grounds that it is a false generalisation (*e.g.* it cannot apply to genitive plurals, when the whole context, if anything, will disambiguate), but also because it offends against the principle that each part of speech has its own independent force or meaning, and cannot be explained as an adjunct to something else (*synt.* 35.5ff.).[29] On the other hand, apparently incongruous constructions can be made genuinely acceptable simply by recognising the ambiguity of the sentence in question; and *vice versa*, ambiguities can easily be resolved by adhering to the principle of καταλληλότης or regularity: *e.g. synt.* 293.1ff., 305.7ff., *pron.* 71.2ff. Sometimes ambiguity is indeed resolvable by the addition of articles: at *synt.* 56.3ff. it is argued that the homonymy of proper names is removed in epistolary contexts by attaching epithets and definite articles to them (*cf.* 446.5ff., and see 6.2.3). Ambiguity too is what explains the absence of a vocative form of ἐμός, *mine*, which would be formally identical with the accusative 'ἐμέ', 'me' (*synt.* 312.15ff.).

Apollonius' confident assumption is thus that, although it may force language to abandon strict regularity, in order to avoid too much formal coincidence, ambiguity merely conceals the original perfect congruity of words, meanings, and

---

[29] This general principle must be distinguished from Theon's specific claim that the addition of articles can clear up Reference ambiguities: *prog.* 83.9ff. There is an example of the sort of explanation for the existence of the various parts of speech which Apollonius is rejecting in Pompeius (*G.L.* 5) 199.21–3, who argues that pronouns were introduced to avoid excessive repetition of nouns. Apollonius himself can argue, *synt.* 20.4ff., that pronouns 'were invented', 'ἐπενοήθησαν', in order to combine with verbs.

structures, whose pristine correctness is recoverable by application of the appropriate methods. This explanation of apparently aberrant word-forms or constructions as, in some cases, a prophylactic against potential ambiguities, is part of an overarching scheme to discover all the rules for the orderliness of the whole of Greek. To supplement the more general rules of καταλληλότης, subsidiary, more specific rules can be found which constitute a παθολογία, a system to explain and organise all deviations or πάθη (literally, "experiences"; here, "deviant properties"; cf. Blank 1982: 41ff.). The only indication of Stoic influence in this area is that its originator, Philoxenus, is associated with the Stoic-influenced grammarian Trypho.[30]

Apollonius' linguistic pathology points to what is perhaps the most basic difference between ancient and modern grammars. It offers a prime illustration of what is now criticised as the fundamental weakness of his discipline: its normativeness. Apollonius' purpose was to provide and apply criteria of correctness at various levels of description – phonological, orthographic, formal, syntactic, etymological – and that aim was constant and uniform throughout ancient grammar whether the grammarian is rationalist, like Apollonius himself, seeing analogy or regularity as a genuine governing principle of language and thus a vital heuristic technique for the grammarian, or empirical, taking usage as the standard and relying on observation of it alone. Sextus Empiricus castigates all technical grammar as useless speculation, and rejects its big brother, κριτική, "critical grammar" just as forcefully; but the challenge is to the grammarians' claims to knowledge, and to the objectivity, coherence, and usefulness of their concepts and categories, not to their common aim, which is to describe,

---

[30] See Theodoridis 1976: 315, fr. 491; on Philoxenus, see Reitzenstein 1901: 86ff.; Theodoridis 1976, esp. 191ff., frr. 224ff.; Blank 1982: 42, nn. 1, 83. The tendency to construct more, and more particular, rules to account for ostensible exceptions is also mentioned by Wouters 1979: 213. There may be a hint of it in Augustine's argument, *civ. dei* 13.11, that *mortuus, dead,* belongs by its form amongst the nominals (*e.g. fatuus, arduus*), not the participles of analogous verbs (*e.g. oritur, ortus;* but *moritur, mortuus*) – a classification which the logic of *mori, to die,* reveals as perfectly appropriate.

not Greek, but good Greek (*cf.* D.T. Sch. 446.6: 'the goal
of grammar is Hellenism').[31]

It is probable that Apollonius borrowed from the Stoa the
model of a language as conveying autonomous, precise, detachable meanings, into which words and linguistic structures
can import confusion, imprecision, and, *imprimis*, ambiguity,
the (implicit) ideal being of a language free from such features
– although he, like they, did not embrace a programme of
actual language reform. So it is only fair, after this brief allusion to one of the crucial differences between Apollonian

[31] The normativeness or prescriptiveness of ancient grammar (often, rather, of its
elementary portion) has been repeatedly criticised – as by Robins 1951: 45 – and
abusively labelled: thus Lyons 1968: 9 has identified the "classical fallacy" that
language is always deteriorating, Harris 1980: 7, n. 3, the "orthological dogma"
that some usages are "right", others "wrong". A preliminary defence (the complexity of historical evidence and of the theoretical issues alike permit no more
here) would be to argue that such criticisms perhaps tend to confuse the pedagogic
principle of prescriptiveness – which, if to some extent predictable in school
textbooks of grammar and composition, is definitely open to abuse – with the
theoretical and methodological principle of normative regularity, implicit even in
descriptive grammar as that is envisaged by some modern theorists (*e.g.* Itkonen
1978). A failure to separate high-level technical grammar from school manuals
(*e.g.* Harris 1980: 96f., 105ff.) is a connected fault. The dialectical contexts of the
debates over the proper criteria for correctness, and their complexity and quality
(Sextus *M.* 1.176ff., Quintilian 1.6.1ff.), may be ignored. Of course, *usus* or
συνήθεια as criterial of linguistic purity was commonly (although not always) the
usage of acknowledged masters of spoken or written language; at the same time,
practical constraints and needs could be given due weight: *e.g.* Quintilian 1.6.3;
Varro *ling. lat.* 9.4, where it is observed that 'it is one thing to say that there is
analogy in words, another to say that one ought to use analogies'. It was recognised too that constant change occurs in ordinary language, and does so *for
better or worse*: *e.g.* Varro 9.17; and *cf.* Uhlfelder 1963/4.
     A much graver defect seems to be the ethnocentricity of ancient grammar, as
well as of other disciplines concerned with language: *e.g.* Allen 1949: 560: 'To sum
up, comparative philology in ancient times can scarcely be said to deserve the
name'; Robins 1979: 11, 23; Pedersen 1931: 2 (who, unsurprisingly, has no doubts
on the matter.) Grammatical concepts and categories appropriate to Greek may
have unduly influenced some Latin grammarians: *e.g.* Robins 1979: 52, on Varro:
but note Quintilian's – perhaps exaggerated – criticisms of such practices, 1.5.58ff.
A good knowledge of Greek is usually taken for granted, as is the propriety of
comparative analysis: *e.g.* Priscian *inst.* 18, 278.7ff., a sequence of comparisons of
constructions in the two languages. Roman grammarians tend to compare their
own tongue exclusively with Greek (Uhlfelder 1966: 586f., 593), even though other
foreign words were known and their treatment in Latinised form debated: *e.g.*
Quintilian 1.5.57ff.
     Another serious weakness has been found in what seems to be comparative lack
of interest in syntax (see esp. Donnet 1967): but this may be in part a result of
misinterpreting ancient grammatical methodology: see esp. Blank 1982: 6ff. (on
Apollonius).

grammar and modern linguistics, to offer a modern parallel he would surely have found both intelligible and congenial. One of the most promising forms of explanation of Greenbergian linguistic universals (that is, of empirically-based generalisations about the properties of all languages, or the relations between their properties: see esp. Greenberg *et al.* 1966, Greenberg 1978) is the "functional" one: accounting for the presence of a feature or its regular association with or dissociation from another feature by appeal to the contribution thereby made to the semantic efficiency of the language. Avoidance of ambiguity could be one such conspicuous contribution, and it has been appealed to to explain the use of different cases to mark agent and object in transitive constructions (*cf.* Anderson 1976, Comrie 1978, 1981).[32] Payne 1990: 304, to whom I owe this example, describes the functionality of universals as increasing 'the ease with which the semantic content of an utterance can be recovered from its syntactic structure'. Both the content/form division, and the use to which it is put, would be quite at home in Apollonius. He himself, as noted, claims that the order of accusative case nominals in *oratio obliqua* indicates the structure, and thus the meaning, intended, with the subject of the infinitive verb preceding it, the object following; and this implies that the formal differentiation of cases in *oratio recta* has a semantic function, which is taken over entirely by position in *oratio obliqua*. On the other hand, Apollonius would have attributed the distribution of cases to mark different syntactic rôles to the workings of rationality in language, perhaps even to the foresight of the inventors of language. On one occasion he compliments the στοιχειωταί for inventing a dual accentuation for prepositions, so that the position of the accent (oxytone or paroxytone) will indicate with which nominal a preposition in a

---

[32] Other examples of the explanation of particular linguistic phenomena as ways of avoiding ambiguity can be found in Mallinson/Blake 1981: 322ff.: where there is extraposition of relative clauses, a 'judicious use of variable relation markers', if available, as they are in English, will help remove ambiguities and misbracketings; 341ff.: strategies for avoiding ambiguities caused in some languages by the absence of case-markers are noted; 366f.: it is observed that 'languages employ remedial strategies' where grammatical 'relations [between sentence constituents] are particularly opaque'.

sentence or phrase is to be construed, even when it is, unusually, postposed (*synt.* 442.8ff.; *cf.* 20.4ff., 35.10ff., for similar cases of "invention"). These "elementalists" must be the originators of speech, and Apollonius thus appears to accept a conception of the origin of language, presumably borrowed from the Stoa, in rational, benevolent design, which is quite alien to modern linguistics, even when it appeals to diachronic or psycholinguistic factors.

8.5   Conclusions

Both the rhetorical and grammatical traditions were too complex and too independent, and their interests too restricted, to accept Stoic work on ambiguity as authoritative or transmit it in an unadulterated form. Only Theon, probably Cicero and Quintilian, and perhaps Fortunatianus, seem to have had direct contact with Stoic material, whether classifications or more general treatments of the topic. But there was no slavish copying, at least in extant manuals and technical treatises; and the general tendency in textbooks to simplify and schematise can itself go some way toward explaining why the Stoic contribution, which, with all its taxonomic defects, is subtle, innovative, and profound, was quarried piece-meal, rather than preserved intact, and why some of its most important features – contextual disambiguation, autonymy, and the species Common, Non-significant Part, and Reference – were radically reworked, or sank without trace. (Wouters 1979: 214f. has pointed out that the market for both pedagogical and scholarly epitomes and commentaries on grammar as a whole tended to lead to the disappearance of the originals.) We might compare the tendency to piecemeal survival of Stoic grammatical doctrine in later writers, although much of this, too, is lost, and what exists often too fragmentary for certainty. (For two possible examples of Stoic influence in the grammatical papyri, see Wouters 1979: 68 (text) and 77ff. (commentary) (articles and pronouns); 176 (text) and 177ff. (commentary) (proper names and common nouns)).

Even allowing for simplification and condensation, two issues in particular should permit application of the standard "compare and contrast" method between Stoic and non-Stoic material. How far its context and situation of an utterance should be, and can be, discounted as irrelevant to identifying and explicating its ambiguity is one of the problems regularly faced in modern studies. Ancient discussion, in contrast, is rare, and then almost always cursory. But the Stoics were clearly to some extent aware of the problem as a general one in the definition and classification of ambiguity, even if the shape their discussions took can only be guessed at. The *de soph.* Stoics seem to have believed that the presence of a homonym does not always result in an ambiguous sentence, and that what would today be called its context can also be a factor; while the Stoic definition of ambiguity suggests that the effects of context must be taken into consideration when judging whether a given utterance is ambiguous, not just in the case of homonyms, but across the board.

I have found no discussion of the problem of context for correctly defining and classifying ambiguity in the grammarians, while the rhetoricians, for their part, when they do appreciate that there might be a problem, or at least acknowledge that someone had raised it, see it squarely in the context of their own preoccupations. Quintilian, for example, dismisses it as trivial, as seen already in 6.3.6; one notable Stoic absentee from his classification is Homonymy in Compounds; and it is just possible that it was the Homonymy in Simples/in Compounds distinction which provoked him to this robust observation:

For it is clear that two things are signified, and, as far as what is written or said is concerned, the balance on each side is equal. Hence, 'try to swing the expression itself over to our side of the case' is a useless precept in this sort of issue. For, if that can be done, there is no ambiguity.

(duas enim res significari manifestum est, et, quod ad scriptum vocemve pertinet, in utramque par est partem. ideoque frustra praecipitur, ut in hoc statu vocem ipsam ad nostram partem conemur vertere. nam, si id fieri potest, amphibolia non est.) (7.9.14)

One of the weaknesses in the Stoic system preserved by Galen was that the distinction between the two Homonymies seemed to allow a bearer to be (or appear) ambiguous in one context, unambiguous in a second, richer, one embracing the first (see 6.3.6). Stoic taxonomic difficulties aside, this seems fairly uncontroversial, and it is surprising Quintilian makes such heavy weather out of it: hence the suspicion that Quintilian's attack may have been prompted at least partly by dissatisfaction with this portion of the Stoic ambiguity classification. On the other hand, an apparent Stoic parallel for this position does exist. The Stoic Nestor, who wanted ambiguity removed from the list of *status*, argued his case on two grounds: that investigation of the properties of vocal sound is the province of the grammarian; and that this supposed *status* 'will lack internal coherence, for no limit or solution can be found for it, for it makes utterances equal' ('ἀσύστατα ἂν εἴη, οὐ γὰρ δυνατὸν πέρας ἢ λύσιν αὐτῆς εὑρεθῆναί τινα, ἰσάζει γὰρ τὰ λεγόμενα') (anon. *scholia in Herm. stas.*, *R.G.* 7.1, 226.15ff) The first point seems irrelevant as it stands – the rhetorician is surely not debarred from making use of the grammarian's findings – and perhaps Nestor's intention was rather to rule out impractical obsession with phonological niceties. The second can be interpreted as the result of a failure to acknowledge the effects of context, as well as of situation of utterance more broadly construed; the scholiast himself points to 'the different qualities of persons' (226.23) (the speaker or writers, presumably) as decisive. The Stoic classifications also left unclear what weight to attach to considerations of reasonableness, or its opposite, in accepting multiple interpretations of utterances. Unsurprisingly, Quintilian, with practical concerns uppermost, explicitly warns against using expressions which, while grammatically open to more than one construction, could be reasonably intended and understood in only one sense (*e.g. visum a se hominem librum scribentem, he himself saw a book reading ⟨a⟩ man*), and does so without exploring the question of whether they are genuine ambiguities, 8.2.16. A similar position seems to have been adopted by the grammarian Charisius, who lists ambiguity as a defect of language, and whose account is unfortunately incomplete: 'ut si quis se dicat hominem occidisse, cum appareat eum qui loquitur occisum non esse', 'as one who should say he has killed a man [*or*: a man has killed him], when it is obvious the speaker has not been killed' ((*G.L.* 1) 27.26–32, esp. 30–32).

Cicero's first batch of recommended procedures for dealing with "ambiguous" documents, in contrast, sees no conflict between the fact that the *stasis* he is describing is that of ambiguity, and the recommendation that it be demonstrated, if possible, that there is no ambiguity in the problem document and thus that the author's intention can safely be recovered:

> First, if it can be done, it must be proved that what is written is not ambiguous, because in everyday discourse everyone habitually uses this single word, or ⟨these⟩ several words, in the sense in which the pleader will prove that it should be understood. Next, it must be shown that the question is cleared up by the text which precedes and follows. For, were words looked at in themselves, in isolation, all or most would seem ambiguous; but words which become clear when the whole of what is written is looked at should not be thought ambiguous.

> (primum, si fieri poterit, demonstrandum est non ambigue scriptum, propterea quod omnes in consuetudine sermonis sic uti solent eo verbo uno pluribusve in eam sententiam in quam is qui dicet accipiendum esse demonstrabit. deinde ex superiore et ex inferiore scriptura docendum id quod quaeratur fieri perspicuum. quae si ipsa separatim ex se verba considerentur, omnia aut pleraque ambigua visum iri; quae autem ex omni considerata scriptura perspicua fiunt, haec ambigua non oportere existimare.) (*inv.* 2.116f.)

Cicero then goes on to recommend that the advocate should look not merely to the immediate or even the wider written context, but to the "situation of utterance" or "inscription" (as it would be described today) in the broadest possible sense: the writer's other writings, doings, sayings, his whole character and way of life, must be examined to find anything that is consistent with the favoured interpretation, and inconsistent with the opponent's. Cicero's treatment is thus entirely practical, geared to the needs of the courtroom. His reader is looking, not for the only or the optimal interpretation of an ambiguity, but for the interpretation he himself needs to support, and his reading of this and other documents (and of everything else too) will be governed by the requirement to find evidence to fit the chosen "facts".

Cicero's distance from the philosophical perspective on ambiguity can be measured by the nature of his allusion in the passage just quoted to Chrysippus' thesis that 'every word is by nature ambiguous', which is the second Stoic achievement in the classification of ambiguity to disappear almost without trace outside a tiny philosophical circle. Quintilian seems to have been familiar with the simple outline of the thesis, but neither he nor Cicero (at least in his youth) had any idea of the real reasoning behind it. Cicero's formulation is qualified in a way Augustine's is not (note 'all *or most* words will *seem* ambiguous'), but the argument behind it is similar in both authors: it is words' being isolated that makes them, or makes them appear, ambiguous. Wherever Cicero had come across Chrysippean ambiguity,[33] he had obviously not (yet) encountered autonymy; and neither, I think, had Quintilian, who makes the following untypically vapid and irrational comment:

The species of ambiguity are countless – to the extent that some philosophers think there is no word which does not signify many things.

(amphiboliae species innumerabiles sunt, adeo ut philosophorum quibusdam nullum videatur esse verbum quod non plura significet.) (7.9.1)

I can find no other allusions even as vague as this to the thesis, in its true form, anywhere in the rhetorical, or grammatical, traditions: only the husk of Chrysippus' idea was preserved outside philosophical circles. The reason is not far to seek. Autonymy would be of little or no interest or importance to the practical experts who compiled classifications of ambiguities for students of *stasis* theory and style. It is the product of a concern with the mechanisms of language in themselves, the work of a linguist or a philosopher of

---

[33] Kennedy 1972: 137 concludes that the only Stoic known to Cicero personally at the time of writing the *de inventione* (c. 91–c. 88) was Aelius Stilo. His dialectical studies with Diodorus did not begin until the late 80s, and the meeting with Posidonius took place only in 78. Accordingly, it would be perfectly understandable for Cicero to have heard of universal ambiguity, but not (yet) to have fully grasped its theoretical basis, and thus for him to have misidentified it – just as Augustine was to do much later – as universal lexical ambiguity of isolated terms which are or can be disambiguated by their contexts.

language, who will try to clarify its autonymous function to further that project. It is no coincidence that modern books on semantics always contain, and frequently start off with, a description of the ways in which language can be used to talk about itself (*e.g.* Lyons 1977: 5ff.). Even if Stoics regarded ambiguity as, on the whole, a symptom of language's decayed condition, they may also have acknowledged the need to make formal, precise, and unambiguous the linguistic means they themselves made use of, and had to use, in order to try to be dialecticians – which in part meant to be experts in formal, precise, and unambiguous talk about talk about the world.

The moral of all this is not the bland and unsurprising fact that it is no use hoping for systematic, theoretical explications in authors whose interests are entirely practical, and that expectations must be shaped by the purposes and methods of the disciplines being examined. When the Stoa defined and classified ambiguity, it did so, in the last analysis, because of its concern for the moral welfare of human beings who could benefit, however indirectly, from its work. Its motivation looks austere alongside the professional practicality of *stasis* and stylistics, and immensely odd beside the professionalised philosophy and linguistics which cover some of the same topics and problems today. But in one important respect Stoics and non-Stoics in antiquity could meet. For reasons which are admittedly sharply different, they agreed, even if implicitly, that ambiguity is a problem. It is an obstacle in the way of the realisation of whatever ideal of language governs and structures the theory in which ambiguity has been placed. Of course, the use of ambiguities may occasionally count as a stylistic accomplishment, and the undesirability of ambiguity has been formalised and to some extent neutralised in *stasis* theory, which, after all, is a classification of problems. But the underlying conception of language – whether as rational discourse, the instrument of persuasion and delight, or the medium for the communication of legal dispositions – is consistently as a conduit for or conveyor of a detachable message or meaning; and this cannot but make ambiguity, primarily, both undesirable and straightforwardly eliminable. There is little room for ambiguity as a manifestation of the creativity of language and its users, even in literary or sub-literary discourse.

9

A SURVEY OF CONCLUSIONS

This final chapter will be brief: each individual chapter has included a summary of results, and particular discoveries will by now, I trust, be familiar enough not to require repetition. I intend only to draw together the threads that connect them, and to place the Stoic work we have examined in its ancient and modern contexts.

Stoic dialectic in its highest form was a single body of knowledge, and even as a set of imperfect teachings it has an impressively organic unity. But its treatment of ambiguity can be seen in two different ways. One way is to focus on its more purely formal-logical content: here lies the analysis of the relation between ambiguity and unsoundness in argument, itself resting on an independent account of logical validity. The other is to highlight the broader interrelated logico-linguistic doctrines which support and explain that account, and which are themselves given purpose and meaning by the deep ethical motivation of Stoic philosophical activity. Ambiguity thus reveals itself as a threat to secure happiness, but one disarmed by a dialectic which imparts correctness in the use of language, and in the interpretation of impressions, as well as in reasoning.

Perhaps the most surprising outcome of this investigation is the insight that the Stoics' logical analysis of ambiguity's rôle in creating fallacious arguments is far better adapted to explaining deliberate exploitation of ambiguity – fraudulent equivocation – in a dialectical context than it is to accounting for innocent errors in reasoning induced by unconscious conceptual confusions. Thus, although the Stoic wise man is an expert in the whole of rational discourse (D.L. 7.48 (31B7–8)), the dialectical tradition that shaped so much Hellenistic philosophy can be seen at work here too, and perhaps, it has to be said, to the detriment of the Stoic theory. It certainly brings that theory far closer to the treatment of linguistic fallacies in Aristotle's *Sophistical Refutations* than might be expected, given the enormous differences between the logical and linguistic schemes which he and they devised, and between the Stoic and Aristotelian conceptions of the nature and purpose of dialectical method. It also sets Stoic work apart from that of Epicurus and his followers, who had little interest in either form of dialectic, and puts it firmly in the long tradition, going back at least to Plato, of associating ambiguity with fallacy and of conceiving of it as a defect of reasoning – but this is reasoning of a certain sort, public, semi-formal, almost institutionalised. And it sets it apart too from the work of those philosophers who have tried to explore ambiguities in so far as they shape, illumine, or distort our conceptual schemes, or (like Aristotle) as they cast light on the structure and contents of the world.

The usefulness of the definition and classification of ambiguity for imparting a mass of abstruse and complicated material, on a wide variety of dialectical topics, in a vivid and memorable form, emerged clearly enough from the attempts to understand the few texts still available: they would be wholly unintelligible without a solid background in Stoic grammar, semantics, and philosophical logic. Modern contributions from linguistics and the philosophy of language to the study of ambiguity, especially ones regarding autonomy, autonymy, the bearers of meaning, and context, proved their worth repeatedly as tools of interpretation and criticism, precisely because the Stoics had themselves seen the importance and relevance of such issues, even if the detailed background to their doctrines has, sadly, been lost.

It did not turn out, of course, that what we had on our hands were comprehensive classifications of the ambiguous lexical and syntactic structures of ancient Greek, or definitions of ambiguity binding it to a specific model for a specific natural language – but such things are not to be found in ancient grammarians either. Grammarians, and rhetoricians too, quarried Stoic teachings on language in general, and am-

503

biguity in particular, for material to add to their own professional constructs. They had no use for Stoic stylistics, or for such technical details as autonymy or the theory of reference, but Stoic treatment of ambiguity species could be useful both pedagogically and exegetically. More fundamentally, they shared with the Stoa, with (almost) the whole of the ancient world, and with many moderns too, the assumption that ambiguity is (almost) always a defect, a failure of communication, without which language – all language, literary, rhetorical, philosophical, or whatever – can only be better and more efficient. The Stoics did not so designate it in their one surviving definition, and the assumption did not, apparently, affect their detailed work in taxonomy: in fact, definition and classification alike could have served as useful teaching vehicles. But, if the modern world parts company from them anywhere, it will be over this failure to accord ambiguity any greater positive value than it borrows from its merely subordinate pedagogic rôle. Aristotle came to see systematic ambiguity as an invaluable analytical and constructive philosophical tool; moderns can see both ambiguity's literary richness and its creativity in the mouths of ordinary language users; the Stoics, for all their originality and insight, saw only its dangers.

APPENDIX

THE CLASSIFICATION OF LINGUISTIC FALLACIES IN ARISTOTLE'S *SOPHISTICAL REFUTATIONS*

One feature of the *s. el.* that must be borne in mind is that it contains a classification of modes of fallacy, not of ambiguity species, so that direct comparison with the Stoic systems is strictly speaking improper. Further, Aristotle's exposition relies primarily on examples, not definitions. As a result, any summary account of his theory will inevitably introduce some degree of distortion.

1. Homonymy, ὁμωνυμία. There is no definition, but homonymy is one of the fallacy modes παρὰ τὸ διττόν "by doubleness (*sc.* of meaning)", at 6.168a24f. Enough examples are provided (esp. 4 165b30–166a6) for it to be plain that fallacies due to homonymy exploit polysemy of a single term: *e.g.* μανθάνειν, *learn* or *understand*. The sophist gets his conclusion by assuming that the word has the sense not given it by his interlocutor/victim: 4.165b30–166a6.
2. Amphiboly, ἀμφιβολία. Again, there is no real definition. To judge from Aristotle's illustrations (esp. 4.166a6–14), Amphiboly produces fallacies when a syntactically variable group of words is given one construal by the sophist, another by his victim: *e.g.* τοῦτο γινώσκει, *this one knows, i.e. this knows ⟨something⟩* or *⟨someone⟩ knows this* (166a7f.). Aristotle says merely that amphibolous complexes have more than one meaning, though none of their components is homonymous (4.166a17f.); the difference in meaning is produced by at least one word's being able to play two or more grammatical/syntactic rôles in relation to (one of) the others. In the example quoted, *this* could be subject or object of the verb (to use traditional grammatical jargon; how Aristotle would characterise it is unclear).

Curiously, he takes one of his own examples – ἆρ' ἔστι σιγῶντα λέγειν;, *Is speaking of the silent possible?* – to contain a single-word ambiguity, 'σιγῶντα', an instance of what would today be called syncretism: it can be the accusative singular participle or the neuter plural participle, nominative or accusative, of the verb σιγᾶν, *be silent*, 166a12, 13f.; compare the newspaper headline *Police found drunk in shop window.* The formal identity of the nominative and accusative cases is sufficient to produce an ambiguity, σιγῶντα being either subject or object (again borrowing the traditional jargon) of the infinitive. I take this to be an oversight induced by the authority of the probable source for this puzzle, *Euthydemus* 300b1ff., where σιγῶντα does undergo this shift: compare 'σιγῶντα λέγειν', 300b1f., with 'λέγοντα σιγᾶν', 300b3, and 'σιγῶντα λέγεις', 300b4.

3. Combination and Division, σύνθεσις, διαίρεσις. Considered as a single ambiguity type, Combination/Division will produce cases where a set of words can be differently combined or divided into one or other of a selection of syntactic groupings (4.166b23–38): *e.g.* ἐγώ σ᾽ ἔθηκα δοῦλον ὄντ᾽ ἐλεύθερον, *I made you, free, a slave/I made you, a slave, free*, (166a36f.). As fallacy modes, each exploits this syntactic fluidity contrariwise, Combination occurring when the sophist combines a group of words his victim had assumed were syntactically divided, Division when the sophist divides words the victim had assumed were syntactically combined. Aristotle signals the distinction between Combination and Division in these two different rôles, as fallacy modes and as ambiguity (?) types, at 166a35f.

Combination, Division and Amphiboly are all syntactic fallacy modes, but in the case of Amphiboly it is unclear which syntactic relation certain words have to one another, not whether they are or are not closely associated syntactically. It is important to note too that Aristotle does not consistently treat Combination and Division (or Accent) as modes of linguistic fallacy due to ambiguity: see 5.4.

4. Accent, προσῳδία. The main problem of interpretation has just been mentioned: it is unclear whether Aristotle regards Accent sophisms, introduced at 4.166b1–9, as due to the exploitation of ambiguity, for he oscillates between treating words formed from identical letters, but differently pronounced, as ambiguous, and treating them as two distinct words. Aristotle is not even sure there are really any Accent fallacies at all: 21.177b35–7, *cf.* 4.166b1f.; only a single, feeble, example is offered, 177b37–178a3. See further, 6.2.3.

5. Form of Expression, σχῆμα τῆς λέξεως. Grammatical form belies ontology: the outward "form" of an expression suggests that what it signifies belongs in another category than the true one, 4.166b10–19; as for example the verb ὑγιαίνειν formally resembles words signifying activities (*e.g.* τέμνειν, *cut*), but itself applies to something which is 'qualified and disposed in a certain way', *viz.* "flourishing" (166b16–19). Aristotle's inclusion of this mode shows he is working within the metaphysical framework of the categories: *cf.* 22.178a4–6 and ff.[1]

---

[1] Evans 1975 discusses the principles of division for the *s. el.* system. Also helpful are Hamblin 1970, esp. chs. 1–3; Edlow 1977, ch. 3; and Ebbesen 1981a: 1: 6–10.

BIBLIOGRAPHY

All references are to works cited or quoted in the text or footnotes.

Bibliographical abbreviations:
A.G.P.   *Archiv für die Geschichte der Philosophie*
C.E.   *Cronache Ercolanesi*
C.Q.   *Classical Quarterly*
J.H.P.   *Journal of the History of Philosophy*
P.A.S.   *Proceedings of the Aristotelian Society*
P.B.A.   *Proceedings of the British Academy*
P.C.P.S.   *Proceedings of the Cambridge Philological Society*
P.Q.   *Philosophical Quarterly*
P.R.   *Philosophical Review*
P.T.R.S.   *Philosophical Transactions of the Royal Society of London*
T.A.P.S.   *Transactions of the Americal Philological Society*
T.P.S.   *Transactions of the Philological Society*

Allen, J. P. B. and van Buren, P. (1971) *Chomsky, Selected Readings* (Oxford).
Allen, W. S. (1947) 'Ancient ideas on the origins and development of language', *T.P.S.* 35–60.
  (1949) *Linguistic problems and their treatment in antiquity* (Diss., Cambridge).
  (1966a) 'Prosody and prosodies in Greek', *T.P.S.* 107–48.
  (1966b) 'A problem in Greek accentuation', in C. E. Bazell *et al.* ed. *In Memory of J.R. Firth* (London), at 8–14.
  (1973) *Accent and Rhythm. Prosodic features of Latin and Greek: a study in theory and reconstruction* (Cambridge).
  (1981) 'The Greek contribution to the history of phonetics', in: *Towards a History of Phonetics, edd.* R. E. Asher and E. J. A. Henderson (Edinburgh), at 115–22.
  (1987) *Vox Graeca* (3rd edn.; 1st edn., 1968) (Cambridge).
Allen, W. S. and Brink, C. O. (1980) 'The old order and the new: a case history', *Lingua* 50, 61–100.
Alston, W. (1971) 'How to tell whether a word has one, several, or many senses?', in Steinberg and Jacobovits, at 35–47.

Amsler M. (1989) *Etymology and Grammatical Discourse in Late Antiquity and the Early Middle Ages* (Amsterdam Studies in the Theory and History of Linguistic Science; Series III, Studies in the History of the Language Sciences, vol. 44) (Amsterdam/Philadelphia).

Anderson, S. R. (1976) 'On the notion of subject in ergative language', in *Subject and Topic, ed.* C.N. Li (N.Y.), at 3–23.

Annas, J. and Barnes, J. (1985) *The Modes of Skepticism. Ancient texts and modern interpretations* (Cambridge).

Anton, J. (1968) 'The Aristotelian doctrine of homonyma in the Categories and its Platonic antecedents', *J.H.P* 6, 315–26.

(1969) 'Ancient interpretations of Aristotle's doctrine of homonyma', *J.H.P.* 7, 1–18.

Appiah, A. (1986) *For Truth in Semantics* (Oxford).

Arnim, I. von ed. (1903–5) *Stoicorum Veterum Fragmenta* (Leipzig, 3 vols.; vol. 4, indices, M. Adler, Leipzig, 1924).

Arnold, W. N. (1989) 'Absinthe', *Scientific American* 260/6, 86–91.

Arthur, E. P. (1983) 'The Stoic analysis of the mind's reactions to impressions', *Hermes* 111, 69–78.

Asmis, E. (1984) *Epicurus' Scientific Method* (Ithaca/London).

Atherton, C. (1986) 'The Stoics on ambiguity' (Diss., Cambridge).

(1988) 'Hand over Fist: the failure of Stoic rhetoric', *C.Q.* 38, 392–427.

Aubenque, P. ed. (1980) *Concepts et catégories dans la pensée antique* (Paris).

Ax, W. (1987) '*Quadripertita Ratio*: Bemerkungen zur Geschichte eines aktuellen Kategoriensystems (*Adiectio–Detractio–Transmutatio–Immutatio*)', in Taylor 1987b, at 17–40.

Bach, K. and Harnish, R. M. (1979) *Linguistic Communication and Speech Acts* (Cambridge, Mass./London).

Baker, G. P. and Hacker, P. M. S. (1984) *Language, Sense, and Nonsense* (Oxford).

Baldassarri, M. (1984–) *La Logica Stoica: testimonianze e frammenti. Testi originali con introduzione e traduzione commentata* (Como, 9 vols.; vol. 1, *Introduzione* (1984); vol. 2, *Crisippo. Il catalogo degli scritti e i frammenti dai papiri* (1985); vol. 3, *Diogene Laerzio. Dalle 'Vite dei Filosofi' VII* (1986); vol. 4, *Sesto Empirico* (1986); vol. 5A, *Alessandro di Afrodisia* (1986); vol. 5B, *Plotino, I commentatori aristotelici tardi, Boezio* (1987); vol. 6, *Cicerone* (1985); vol. 7A, *Galeno* (1986); vol. 7B, *Le testimonianze minori del sec. II d.c. Epitteto, Plutarco, Gellio, Apuleio* (1987); vol. 8, *Testimonianze sparse ordinate sistematicamente* (1987); vol. 9 (Indices, Bibliography, Conclusions; forthcoming)).

Ballaira, W. (1968) *Tiberii de figuris Demosthenicis libellus cum deperditorum operum fragmentis* (Rome).

Baratin, M. (1982) 'L'identité de la pensée et de la parole dans l'Ancien Stoïcisme', *Langages* 65, 9–22.

Baratin, M. and Desbordes, F. (1981) *L'Analyse linguistique dans l'antiquité classique 1: les théories* (Paris).

(1982) 'Sémiologie et métalinguistique chez saint Augustin', *Langages* 65, 75–90.

(1987) 'La "troisieme partie" de l'*Ars Grammatica*', in Taylor 1987b, at 41–66.

Barnes, J. (1971) 'Homonymy in Aristotle and Speusippus', *C.Q.* n.s. 21, 65–80.

(1975) *Aristotle's 'Posterior Analytics'* (Oxford).

(1980) 'Proof destroyed', in Schofield *et al.* 1980, at 161–181.

(1982) 'Medicine, experience, and logic', in Barnes *et al.* 1982, at 24–68.

(1984/5) 'The *Logical Investigations* of Chrysippus', *Berliner Wissenschaftskolleg, Jahrbuch*, 19–29.

(1985a) 'πιθανὰ συνημμένα', *Elenchus* 6, 453–67.

(1985b) 'Theophrastus and hypothetical syllogisms', in Fortenbaugh 1985, at 125–41.

(1986) 'Nietzsche and Diogenes Laertius', *Nietzsche Studien* 15, 16–40.

(1989) 'Antiochus of Ascalon', in Griffin and Barnes 1989, at 50–98.

(1991) 'Galen on logic and therapy', in *Galen's Method of Healing*, edd. F. Kudlien and R. J. Durling (Studies in Ancient Medicine, vol. 1) (Leiden/N.Y./Cologne/Copenhagen), at 50–102.

Barnes, J., Brunschwig, J., Burnyeat, M. F. and Schofield, M., edd. (1982) *Science and Speculation. Studies in Hellenistic theory and practice* (Cambridge/Paris).

Barnes, K. T. (1979) 'Aristotle on identity and its problems', *Phronesis* 22, 48–62.

Barwick, K. (1922) *Remmius Palaemon und die römische ars grammatica* (*Philologus* suppl. 15) (Leipzig).

(1957) 'Probleme der stoischen Sprachlehre und Rhetorik', *Abhandlungen der sächsischen Akademie der Wissenschaften zu Leipzig*; phil.-hist. Kl. 49, Heft 3.

Bäuerle, R., Egli, U. and von Stechow, A. edd. (1979) *Semantics from Different Points of View* (Springer Series in Language and Communication, vol. 6) (Berlin/Heidelberg/N.Y.).

Bernhardy, G. (1853) *Suidae Lexicon* (*post* Th. Gaisford, Oxford, 1834) (Halle/Brunswick; 2 vols. in 4).

Bierwisch, M. (1970) 'Semantics', in *New Horizons in Linguistics*, ed. J. Lyons (Harmondsworth), at 166–84.

Black, M. (1949) 'Vagueness: an exercise in logical analysis', in *Language and Philosophy: studies in method* (Ithaca, N.Y.), at 23–58; repr. from *Philosophy of Science* 4 (1937), 427–55.

(1952) *Critical Thinking* (N.Y.).

(1970) 'Reasoning with loose concepts', in *Margins of Precision* (Ithaca, N.Y.), at 1–13.

Blank, D. (1982) *Ancient Philosophy and Grammar. The Syntax of Apollonius Dyscolus* (A.P.A. American Classical Studies, no. 10) (Chico, California) .

Blass, F. (1890) *Pronunciation of Ancient Greek* (tr. of *Über die Aussprache des Altgrieschischen* (3rd edn., Berlin, 1888) by W.J. Purton) (Cambridge).

Bloomfield, L. (1926) 'A set of postulates for the science of language', *Language* 2, 153–64.

(1935) *Language* (London, rev. edn.; American edn., N.Y., 1933).

Bochenski, I. M. J. (1951) *Ancient Formal Logic* (Studies in Logic and the Foundations of Mathematics) (Amsterdam).

(1970) *A History of Formal Logic* (2nd edn., N.Y.; tr. of *Formale Logik* (Munich, 1962) by I. Thomas).

Bonhöffer, A. (1890) *Epictet und die Stoa* (Stuttgart).

Bonner, S. (1949) *Roman Declamation in the Late Republic and Early Empire* (Berkeley/Los Angeles).

(1977) *Education in Ancient Rome* (Berkeley/Los Angeles).

Bostock, D. (1988) *Plato's 'Theaetetus'* (Oxford).

Bréhier, E. (1951) *Chrysippe et l'ancien stoïcisme* (rev. 2nd edn.; 1st edn. 1910) (Paris/London/N.Y.).

Brotman, H. (1956) 'Could space be four dimensional?', in *Essays in Conceptual Analysis*, ed. A. Flew (London, 1956), at 253–65.

Brunschwig, J., ed. (1978a) *Les Stoïciens et leur logique* (Paris).

Brunschwig, J. (1978b) 'Le modèle conjonctif', in Brunschwig 1978a, at 59–86.

(1980) 'Proof Defined', in Schofield *et al.* 1980, at 125–60.

Burnyeat, M. F. (1976) 'Protagoras and self-refutation in later Greek philosophy', *P.R.* 85, 44–69.

(1979) 'The upside-down back-to-front sceptic of Lucretius IV.472', *Philologus* 122, 197–206.

(1980) 'Can the skeptic live his skepticism?', in Schofield *et al.* 1980, at 20–53; repr. in Burnyeat 1983, at 117–148.

(1982) 'Gods and heaps', in Schofield and Nussbaum 1982, at 315–38.

ed. (1983) *The Skeptical Tradition* (Berkeley/Los Angeles/London).

(1984) 'The skeptic in his place and time', in Rorty *et al.*, at 225–54.

(1987) 'Wittgenstein and Augustine *de magistro*', *P.A.S.* Suppl. 61, 1–24.

Butts, R. E. (1986) *The 'Progymnasmata' of Theon. A new text with translation and commentary* (Diss., Claremont).

Cargile, J. (1979) *Paradoxes: A study in form and predication* (Cambridge).

Carnap, R. (1937) *The Logical Syntax of Language* (London).

Carrick, P. (1985) *Medical Ethics in Antiquity. Philosophical perspectives on abortion and euthanasia* (Philosophy and Medicine Series, vol. 18) (Dordrecht/Boston/Lancaster).

Cavini, W. (1985) 'La negazione di frase nella logica greca', in *Studi su Papiri Greci di Logica e Medicina*, W. Cavini, M. C. Donnini Macciò, M. S. Funghi and D. Manetti (Florence) (Studi e Testi per il Corpus dei Papiri Filosofici Greci e Latini, 1), at 7–126.

Celluprica, V. (1980) 'La logica stoica in alcune recenti interpretazioni', *Elenchos* 1, 123–150.

Chao, Y. R. (1959/60), 'Ambiguity in Chinese', in *Studia serica Bernhard Karlgren dedicata: Sinological Studies dedicated to B. Karlgren on his 70th birthday*, edd. S. Egard and E. Glahn (Copenhagen), at 1–13.

Cherniss, H. (1944) *Aristotle's Criticism of Plato and the Academy* (Baltimore).

Chomsky, N. (1959) Review of *Verbal Behaviour* by B. F. Skinner, *Language* 35, 26–57.

(1965) *Aspects of the Theory of Syntax* (Cambridge, Mass.)

(1967) 'The formal nature of language', in *The Biological Foundations of Language*, ed. E. H. Lenneberg (N.Y.), at 397–442.

(1971) 'Topics in the theory of generative grammar', in *The Philosophy of Language*, ed. J. R. Searle (Oxford), at 71–100.

(1980) *Rules and Representations* (Oxford).

(1981) 'Knowledge of language: its elements and origins', *P.T.R.S.* 295, 223–34.

(1985) 'Methodological preliminaries', in Katz 1985a, at 80–125.

(1986) *Knowledge of Language: its nature, origin, and use* (N.Y.).

Christensen, J. (1962) 'An essay on the unity of Stoic philosophy' (Diss., Copenhagen).

Christensen, N. E. (1962) 'The alleged distinction between use and mention', *P.R.* 76, 358–67.

Clark, D. L. (1957) *Rhetoric in Greco-Roman Education* (N.Y.).

Colish, M. (1983) 'The Stoic theory of verbal signification and the problem of lies and false statement from antiquity to St. Anselm', in *Archéologie du Signe*, edd. L. Brind'Amour and E. Vance (Toronto), at 17–43.

Collinge, N. E., ed. (1990) *An Encyclopaedia of Language* (London/N.Y.).

Comrie, B. (1978) 'Ergativity', in *Syntactic Typology: Studies in the phenomenology of language*, ed. W. P. Lehmann (Austin, Texas), at 329–94.

BIBLIOGRAPHY

(1981) *Language Universals and Linguistic Typology* (Oxford).

Corcoran, J. (1974a) 'Remarks on Stoic deduction', in Corcoran 1974b, at 169–81.

Corcoran, J., ed. (1974b) *Ancient Logic and its Modern Interpretations* (Dordrecht/Boston).

Cortassa, G. (1978) 'Pensiero e linguaggio nella teoria stoica del λεκτόν', *Rivista di Filologia e di Istruzione Classica* 106, 385–94.

Courcelle, P. (1969) *Late Latin Writers and their Greek sources* (tr. of 2nd French edn., Paris, 1948, by H. E. Wedeck) (Cambridge, Mass.).

Crönert, W. (1901) 'Die Λογικὰ Ζητήματα des Chrysippos und die übrigen Papyri logischen Inhalts aus der herculanensischen Bibliothek', *Hermes* 36 (1901), 548–79; Italian tr. by E. Livrea, in W. Crönert, *Studi Ercolanesi, Collana di Filologia Classica*, dir. da M. Gigante (Naples, 1975), at 63–101.

Dahlmann. H. (1932/64) *Varro und die hellenistische Sprachtheorie* (Berlin 1932/Zürich 1964).

DeFrancis, J. (1989) *Visible Speech. The diverse oneness of writing systems* (Honolulu).

Delamarre, A. J.-L. (1980) 'La notion de ΠΤΩΣΙΣ chez Aristote et les Stoïciens', in Aubenque 1980, at 321–45.

Denniston, J. D. (1952) *Greek Prose Style* (Oxford).

Denyer, N. (1981) 'Time and modality in Diodorus Cronus', *Theoria* 47, 31–53.

(1985) 'The case against divination: an examination of Cicero's *de divinatione*', *P.C.P.S.* 211 (n.s.31), 1–10.

(1988) 'Stoicism and token reflexivity', in *Matter and Metaphysics*, edd. J. Barnes and M. Mignucci (Naples), at 375–96.

De Rijk, L. M. (1974) 'Some 13th century tracts on the game of Obligation', *Vivarium* 12, 94–123.

Di Benedetto, V. (1958/9) 'Dionisio Trace e la Techne a lui attribuita', *Annali della Scuola normale superiore di Pisa*, Serie 2, 27, 169–210; 28, 87–118.

(1973) 'La Techne spuria', *Annali della Scuola normale superiore di Pisa*, Serie 3.3, 797–814.

Dik, S. C. (1968) *Co-ordination: its implications for the theory of General Linguistics* (Amsterdam).

Donnellan, K. S. (1966) 'Reference and definite descriptions', *P.R.* 75, 281–304.

(1979) 'Speaker reference, descriptions, and anaphora', in French *et al.* 1979, at 28–44.

Donnet, D. (1967) 'La place de la syntaxe dans les traités de grammaire grecque, des origines au XIIᵉ siècle', *L'Antiquité Classique* 36, 22–48.

BIBLIOGRAPHY

Döring, K. (1972) *Die Megariker. Kommentierte Sammlung der Testimonien* (Amsterdam).
Dougherty, R. C. (1967) 'Coordinate conjunction', *P.E.G.S.* paper 10, Nov. 14, 1967; reference from Kooij 1973: 65.
Dummett, M. (1975) 'Wang's paradox', *Synthèse* 39, 301–24.
Düring, I. (1966) *Aristoteles* (Heidelberg).
Ebbesen, S. (1977) 'Can equivocation be eliminated?' *Studia Mediewistyczne* 18, 103–24.
(1981a) *Commentators and Commentaries on Aristotle's 'Sophistici Elenchi'* (Leiden; 3 vols.).
(1981b) 'Suprasegmental phonemes in ancient and medieval logic', in *English Logic and Semantics from the End of the Twelfth Century to the Time of Ockham and Burleigh*, edd. H. A. G. Braakhuis, C. H. Kneepkens and L. M. de Rijk (*Aristarium* Suppl. 1) (Nijmegen), at 331–59.
(1987) 'The way fallacies were treated in scholastic logic', *Cahiers de l'Institut du Moyen-Age Grec et Latin*, Université de Copenhagen, 55, 107–134.
Ebert, T. (1991) *Dialektiker und frühe Stoiker bei Sextus Empiricus. Untersuchungen zur Entstehung der Aussagenlogik. Hypomnemata* vol. 95). (Göttingen).
Edelstein, L. (1967) *Ancient Medicine. Selected papers of Ludwig Edelstein*, edd. O. and C. L. Temkin (Baltimore).
Edelstein, L. and Kidd, I. G. *edd.* (1972) *Posidonius. Volume One: The Fragments* (Cambridge).
Edlow, R. B. (1975) 'The Stoics on ambiguity', *J.H.P.* 13, 423–35.
(1977) *Galen on Language and Ambiguity* (Leiden).
Egli, U. (1967) 'Zur stoischen Dialektik' (Diss., Basel).
(1979) 'The Stoic concept of anaphora', in Bäuerle *et al.*, at 266–83.
(1981) *Das Diokles-Fragment bei Diogenes Laertios*, Arbeitspapiere Sonderforschungsbereich 99 Linguistik, Universität Konstanz 55 (Konstanz).
(1987) 'Stoic syntax and semantics', in Taylor 1987b, at 107–32 (rev. version of article in Brunschwig 1978a, at 135–54).
Eikmayer, H. J. and Rieser, H. (1983) 'A nominalistic approach to ambiguity and vagueness, considered from a mildly Platonistic point of view', in *Approaching Vagueness*, edd. T. T. Ballman and M. Pinkal (Amsterdam/N.Y./Oxford), at 393–422.
Empson, W. (1953) *Seven Types of Ambiguity* (3rd edn., London; repr. Harmondsworth, 1961; 1st edn., 1930).
Epp, R. H. (1985a) 'Stoicism bibliography', in Epp 1985b, at 125–71.
ed. (1985b) *Recovering the Stoics. Spindel Conference 1984* (*Southern Journal of Philosophy*, suppl.).

513

BIBLIOGRAPHY

Erbse, H. (1980) 'Zur normativen Grammatik der Alexandriner', *Glotta* 58, 236–58.

Evans, J. D. G. (1974) 'The Old Stoa on the truth-value of oaths', *P.C.P.S.* 200 (n.s. 20), 44–7.

(1975) 'The codification of false refutations in Aristotle's *De sophisticis elenchis*', *P.C.P.S.* 201 (n.s. 21), 42–52.

(1977) *Aristotle's Concept of Dialectic* (Cambridge).

Fehling, D. (1950) 'Varro und die grammatische Lehre von der Analogie und der Flexion', *Glotta* 35, 214–70; cf. 36 (1951), 48–100.

(1965) 'Zwei Untersuchungen zur griechischen Sprachphilosophie. 1: Protagoras und ὀρθοέπεια. 2: φύσις und θέσις', *Rheinisches Museum für Philologie* n.s. 108, 212–17, 218–29.

Flashar, H. (1975) *Aristoteles: Problemata Physica, übersetzt von H. Flashar* (Berlin; Aristoteles Werke in deutscher Übersetzung, Band 19).

Flew, A. *ed.* (1953) *Logic and Language* (second series) (Oxford).

Fodor, J. A. (1983) *The Modularity of Mind* (Cambridge, Mass./London).

Fortenbaugh, W. W. (1985) (with P. M. Huby and A. A. Long) *Theophrastus of Eresus. On his life and work* (Rutgers University Studies in Classical Humanities, vol. 2) (New Brunswick/Oxford).

Frazier, L. (1988) 'Grammar and language processing', in Newmayer 1988, at 15–34.

Frazier, L. and Rayner, D. (1982) 'Making and correcting errors during sentence comprehension: eye movements in the analysis of structurally ambiguous sentences', *Cognitive Psychology* 14, 178–210.

Frede, M. (1974a) *Die stoische Logik* (Göttingen).

(1974b) 'Stoic vs. Aristotelian syllogistic', *A.G.P.* 56, 1–32.

(1977) 'The origins of traditional grammar', in *Historical and Philosophical Dimensions of Logic, Methodology, and Philosophy of Science.* Part Four of the Proceedings of the Fifth International Congress of Logic, Methodology, and Philosophy of Science, London, Ontario, Canada, 1975 (The University of Western Ontario Series in Philosophy of Science, vol. 2), *edd.* R. Butts and J. K. K. Hintikka (Dordrecht), at 51–79.

(1978) 'The principles of Stoic grammar', in Rist, at 27–75.

(1979) 'Des Skeptikers Meinungen', *Neue Hefte für Philosophie* 15/16, 102–29.

(1980) 'The original notion of cause', in Schofield *et al.*, at 217–49.

(1983) 'Stoics and Skeptics on clear and distinct impressions', in Burnyeat, at 65–93.

(1984) 'The skeptic's two kinds of assent and the question of the possibility of knowledge', in Rorty *et al.*, at 255–78.

(1986) 'The Stoic doctrine of the affections of the soul', in Schofield and Striker, at 93–110.

French, P. A., Uehling, T. E. and Wettstein, H. K., *edd.* (1979) *Contemporary Perspectives in the Philosophy of Language* (Minneapolis).

Fries, C. C. (1952) *The Structure of English* (N.Y.).

Fudge, E. (1990) 'Language as organised sound', in Collinge 1990, at 30–67.

Gabler, C. G. (1903) 'Galeni libellus de captionibus quae per dictionem fiunt' (Diss., Rostock).

Geach, P. T. (1962) *Reference and Generality* (Ithaca, N.Y.).

(1969) *God and the Soul* (London).

(1972) *Logic Matters* (Oxford).

Giannantoni, G. (1981) 'Il κυριεύων λόγος di Diodoro Crono', *Elenchus* 2, 239–72.

Gleason, H. A. Jr (1965) *Linguistics and English Grammar* (N.Y.).

Glidden, D. (1983) 'Skeptic semiotics', *Phronesis* 28, 313–55.

(1985) 'Epicurean *prolêpsis*', in *Oxford Studies in Ancient Philosophy* 3, ed. J. Annas, at 175–217.

Goldschmidt, V. (1972) 'Υπάρχειν et ὑφιστάναι dans la philosophie stoïcienne', *Revue des Etudes Greques* 85, 331–44.

(1978) 'Rémarques sur l'origine Epicurienne de la "prénotion"', in Brunschwig, at 155–69.

Görler, W. (1984) 'Zum Virtus-Fragment des Lucilius (1326–38 Marx) und zur Geschichte der stoischen Güterlehre', *Hermes* 112, 445–68.

Graeser, A. (1973) *Die logischen Fragmente des Theophrast* (Kleine Texte für Vorlesungen und Übungen 191) (Berlin/N.Y.).

(1978) 'The Stoic categories', in Brunschwig, at 199–221.

Greenberg, J. H. ed. (1978) *Universals of Human Language* (Stanford, 4 vols.)

Greenberg, J. H., Osgood, C. and Jenkins, J. (1966) 'Memorandum concerning language universals', introduction to *Universals of Language: Report of a conference held at Dobbs Ferry, N.Y., April 13–15, 1961*, ed. J. H. Greenberg 2nd edn.; 1st edn., 1963) (Cambridge, Mass.).

Griffin, M. (1986) 'Philosophy, Cato, and Roman suicide', *Greece and Rome* 33, 64–77, 192–202.

(1989) 'Philosophy, politics, and politicians at Rome', in Griffin and Barnes, at 1–37.

Griffin, M. and Barnes, J., *edd.* (1989) *Philosophia Togata. Essays on Roman philosophy and society* (Oxford).

Gudeman, A. (1934) *Aristoteles*, περὶ ποιητικῆς, *mit Einleitung, Text und Adnotatio Critica, exegetischem Kommentar, kritischem Anhang, und Indices Nominum, Rerum, Locorum* (Berlin/Leipzig).

Haack, S. (1978) *Philosophy of Logics* (Cambridge).

Hadot, P. (1966) 'La notion de "cas" dans la logique stoïcienne', in *Le Langage. Actes du XIIIᵉ Congrès des Sociétés de Philosophie de langue française. Genève, 2–6 Août 1966, par la Société Romande de Philosophie* (Neuchâtel), at 109–112.

(1980) 'Sur divers sense du mot PRAGMA dans la tradition philosophique grècque', in Aubenque, at 309–19.

Hahn, E. A. (1951) 'Apollonius Dyscolus on mood', *T.A.P.A.* 82, 29–48.

Hall, R. A. Jr (1987) *Linguistics and Pseudo-Linguistics. Selected essays 1965–85* (Amsterdam Studies in the Theory and History of Linguistic Science; Series IV, Current Issues in Linguistic Theory, vol. 55) (Amsterdam/Philadelphia).

Hamblin, C. L. (1970) *Fallacies* (London).

Hambruch, E. (1904) *Logische Regeln der platonischen Schule in der aristotelischen Topik* (Berlin).

Harris, R. (1980) *The Language Makers* (London).

(1981) *The Language Myth* (London).

(1986) *The Origin of Writing* (London).

Harrison, B. (1972) *Meaning and Structure* (N.Y.).

(1979) *An Introduction to the Philosophy of Language* (London).

Heitsch, E. (1972) *Die Entdeckung der Homonymie* (Akademie der Wissenschaften und der Literatur. Abhandlungen der Geistes- und Sozialwissenschaftlichen Klasse, Jahrgang 1972, n. 11) (Wiesbaden).

Hiersche, R., Ising, E. and Ginschel, G. (1955) *Entstehung und Entwicklung des Terminus* πτῶσις. *Aus der Arbeit an einem historischen Wörterbuch der sprachwissenschaftlichen Terminologie* (Berlin).

Hintikka, J. (1959) 'Aristotle and the ambiguity of ambiguity', *Inquiry* 2, 137–51; revised version in *Time and Necessity. Studies in Aristotle's theory of modality* (Oxford, 1973), at 1–26.

(1971) 'Different kinds of equivocation in Aristotle', *J.H.P.* 9, 368–72.

Hirst, G. (1987) *Semantic Interpretation and the Resolution of Ambiguity* (Cambridge).

Hockett, C. F. (1954) 'Two models of grammatical description', *Word* 10, 210–34 (repr. in *Readings in Linguistics*, ed. M. Joos (Washington, 1957)).

Hockett, C. F. (1958) *A Course in Modern Linguistics* (N.Y.).

(1968) *The State of the Art* (Janua Linguarum, Series Minor, no. 73) (The Hague).

(1987) *Refurbishing our Foundations: Elementary linguistics from an advanced point of view* (Amsterdam Studies in the Theory and History of Linguistic Science; Series IV, Current Issues in Linguistic Theory, vol. 56) (Amsterdam/Philadelphia).

Hockett, C. F. and Altmann, S. (1968), 'A note on design features', in *Animal Communication*, ed. T. A. Sebeok (Bloomington, Indiana), at 61–72.

Hoenisgswald, H. M. (1951) Review of Robins 1951. *Language* 29, 180–2.

Horrocks, G. (1987) *Generative Grammar* (London).

Householder, F. W. (1981) *The Syntax of Apollonius Dyscolus. Translated, and with commentary* (Amsterdam Studies in the Theory and History of Linguistic Science; Series III, Studies in the History of Linguistics, vol. 23) (Amsterdam).

Hülser, K. (1979a) 'Expression and content in Stoic linguistic theory', in Bäuerle *et al.*, at 284–303.

(1979b): see Schmidt 1839/1979.

(1982) *Die Fragmente zur Dialektik der Stoiker: zusammengestellt, ins Deutsche übersetzt und teilweise kommentiert*, Sonderforschungsbereich 99 Linguistik (University of Konstanz; 8 vols.).

Imbert, C. (1975) 'Sur la méthode en histoire de la logique', in *Proceedings of the International Summer Institute and Logic Colloqium, Logic Conference, Kiel 1974*, edd. G. H. Müller, A. Oberschelp and K. Potthoff (Lecture notes in Mathematics 499) (Berlin/Heidelberg/N.Y.).

Innes, D. C. (1985) 'Theophrastus and the theory of style', in Fortenbaugh, at 251–68.

Inwood, B. (1985a) *Ethics and Human Action in Early Stoicism* (Oxford).

(1985b) 'The Stoics on the grammar of action', in Epp 1985b, at 75–86.

Inwood, B. and Gerson, L. P. (1988) *Hellenistic Philosophy: Introductory readings* (Indianapolis/Cambridge, Mass.).

Itkonen, Esa (1978) *Grammatical Theory and Metascience. A critical investigation into the methodological and philosophical foundations of 'autonomous' linguistics* (Amsterdam Studies in the Theory and History of Linguistic Science, Series IV: Current Issues in Linguistic Theory, vol. 5) (Amsterdam).

Jackson, B. D. (1969) 'The theory of signs in St Augustine's *de doctrina Christiana*', *Revue des Études Augustiniennes* 15, 9–49.

(1975) See Pinborg 1975a.

Janáček, K. (1972) *Sextus Empiricus' Skeptical Methods* (Prague).

Jesperson, O. (1964) *Language: its nature, development, and origin* (12th edn.; first edn., 1922) (London).

Joos, M. (1968) *The English Verb. Form and meanings* (2nd edn.; 1st edn. 1964) (Madison/Milwaukee/London).

Kaplan, A. (1950) 'An experimental study of ambiguity and context', in *Selected Publications of the Rand Corporation*, vol. 1 (Santa Monica, California; quoted by Kooij 1971).

Kaplan, D. (1979) 'DTHAT', in French *et al.*, at 383–400.

Katz, J. J. (1981) *Language and Other Abstract Objects* (Oxford).

ed. (1985a) *The Philosophy of Linguistics* (Oxford); Introduction, pp. 1–16.

(1985b) 'An outline of a Platonist grammar', in Katz 1985a, at 172–203.

Katz, J. J. and Fodor, J. A. (1963) 'The structure of a semantic theory', *Language* 39, 170–210; repr. in *The Structure of Language: Readings in the Philosophy of Language*, edd. J. A. Fodor and J. J. Katz, (Eaglewoood Cliffs, N.J., 1964), at 479–518.

Kennedy, G. A. (1963) *The Art of Persuasion in Greece* (Princeton/London).

(1972) *The Art of Rhetoric in the Roman World, 300B.C.–A.D. 300* (Princeton).

Kerferd, G. B. (1978) 'What does the wise man know?', in Rist, at 125–36.

(1982) 'Two problems concerning impulses', in *On Stoic and Peripatetic Ethics. The work of Arius Didymus*, ed. W. W. Fortenbaugh (Rutgers University Studies in Classical Humanities 1), at 87–98.

Kess, J. F. and Hoppe, R. A. (1981) *Ambiguity in Psycholinguistics* (Amsterdam).

Kidd, I. G. (1978) 'Philosophy and science in Posidonius', *Antike und Abendland* 24, 7–15.

ed. (1988) *Posidonius. Volume Two: Commentary* (Cambridge; 2 vols.).

Kirwan, C. (1979) 'Aristotle and the so-called fallacy of equivocation', *P.Q.* 29, 35–46.

Kittay, E. F. (1987) *Metaphor: its cognitive force and linguistic structure* (Oxford).

Kneale, M. (1935) 'Implication in the 4th century', *Mind* 44, 484–95.

Kneale, W. and M., (1964) *The Development of Logic* (corrected edn.; 1st edn., 1962) (Oxford).

Kooij, J. G. (1971) *Ambiguity in Natural Language. An investigation of certain problems in its linguistic description* (North-Holland Linguistics Series 3) (Amsterdam/London).

Kress, J. and Odell, S. J. (1982) 'A paraphrastic criterion for difference of sense', *Theoretical Linguistics* 9, 181–201.

Kretzmann, N. (1971) 'Plato on the correctness of names', *American Philosophical Quarterly* 8, 126–38.

(1974) 'Aristotle on spoken sound significant by convention', in Corcoran 1974b, at 3–21.

Kripke, S. (1979) 'Speaker's reference and semantic reference', in French *et al.*, at 6–27.

(1980) *Naming and Necessity* (Oxford; 1st edn. Dordrecht/Boston, 1972).

Lakoff, G. (1970) 'A note on vagueness and ambiguity', *Linguistic Inquiry* 1, 357–9.

(1971) 'On generative semantics', in Steinberg and Jacobovits, at 232–96.

Lammert, F. (1920) 'Eine neue Quelle für die Philosophie der mittleren Stoa', *Wiener Studien* 42, 34–46; *cf.* 41 (1919), 113–121.

Lana, I. (1951) *Quintiliano, Il 'Sublime', e gli 'Esercizi Preparatori' di Elio Teone* (Turin).

(1959) *I 'Progimnasmi' di Elio Teone. Volume Primo: La storia del testo* (Turin).

Langendoen, D. T. (1966) 'A note on the linguistic theory of M. Terentius Varro', *Foundations of Language* 2, 33–6.

Laum, B. (1928) *Das alexandrinische Akzentuations-system* (Paderborn).

Lear, J. (1980) *Aristotle and Logical Theory* (Cambridge).

Lloyd, A. C. (1970) 'Activity and description in Aristotle and the Stoa', *P.B.A.* 56, 227–40.

(1971) 'Grammar and metaphysics in the Stoa', in Long 1971b, at 58–74.

(1978) 'Definite propositions and the concept of reference', in Brunschwig, at 285–95.

Long, A. A. (1971a) 'Language and thought in Stoicism', in Long 1971b, at 75–113.

ed. (1971b) *Problems in Stoicism* (London).

(1975/6) 'Heraclitus and Stoicism', ΦΙΛΟΣΟΦΙΑ 5/6, 133–56.

(1978) 'Dialectic and the Stoic sage', in Rist, at 101–24.

(1986) Hellenistic Philosophy (2nd edn.; 1st edn., 1974) (London).

Long, A. A. and Sedley, D. N. *edd.* (1987) *The Hellenistic Philosophers* (Cambridge; 2 vols.).

Lyons, J. (1963) *Structural Semantics. An analysis of part of the vocabulary of Plato* (Publications of the Philological Society, 20) (Oxford).

(1968) *Introduction to Theoretical Linguistics* (Cambridge).

(1972) 'Human language', in *Non-Verbal Communication, ed.* R. A. Hinde (Cambridge), at 49–95.

(1977) *Semantics* (Cambridge; 2 vols., numbered consecutively).

(1981) 'Language and speech', *P.T.R.S.* 295, 215–221.

519

McCawley, J. D. (1968) 'The role of semantics in a grammar', in *Universals in Linguistic Theory*, edd. E. Bach and R. T. Harms (N.Y.), at 124–69.

(1980) *Everything that Linguists Have Always Wanted to Know about Logic* (Chicago).

Madec, G. (1975) 'Analyse du *De magistro*', *Revue des Etudes Augustiniennes* 21, 63–71.

Magee, J. (1989) *Boethius on Signification and Mind* (*Philosophia Antiqua* vol. 52) (Leiden/N.Y./Copenhagen/Cologne).

Mallinson, G. and Blake, B. J. (1981) *Language Typology* (North-Holland Linguistic Series, no. 46) (Amsterdam).

Maloney, C. J. (1984) 'Scheffler on ambiguity' (review of Scheffler 1979), *Southern Journal of Philosophy* 22, 195–202.

Mandouze, A. (1975) 'Quelques principes de "linguistique augustinienne" dans le "de magistro"', in *Forma Futuri: Studi in onore del card. M. Pellegrino* (Turin), at 789–95.

Mansfeld, J. (1986) 'Diogenes Laertius and Stoic philosophy', *Elenchus* 7, 297–382.

(1989) 'Chrysippus and the Placita', *Phronesis* 34, 311–42.

Markus, R. A. (1957) 'Augustine on signs', *Phronesis* 2, 60–83.

Marrone, L. (1982) 'Nuove letture nel *PHerc*. 307 (*Questioni Logiche* di Crisippo)', *C.E.* 12, 13–18.

(1984a) 'Il problema dei "singolari" e dei "plurali" nel *PHerc*. 307', in *Atti del XVII Congresso Internazionale di Papirologia (Napoli, 1983)* (Naples; 2 vols.), vol. 2, at 419–27.

(1984b) 'Proposizione e predicato in Crisippo', *C.E.* 14, 135–46.

(1987) 'Testi stoici ercolanesi', *C.E.* 17, 181–4.

(1988a) 'Il mentitore nel PHerc 307', in B. G. Mandilaras *ed.*, *Proceedings of the XVIIIth International Papyrology Congress (Athens, 1986)*, (Athens), at 271–6.

(1988b) 'Testi stoici ercolanesi II', *C.E.* 18, 223–5.

Marrou, H. (1956) *A History of Education in Antiquity* (London).

Mates, B. (1961) *Stoic Logic* (1st edn., 1953) (Berkeley/Los Angeles).

Matthes, D. (1959) 'Hermagoras von Temnos 1904–1955', *Lustrum* 3, 58–214.

Matthews, G. B. (1982) 'Accidental unities', in Schofield and Nussbaum, at 223–40.

Mejer, J. (1978) *Diogenes Laertius and his Hellenistic Background* (*Hermes* Einzelschr. 40) (Wiesbaden).

Mignucci, M. (1967a) *Il significato della logica stoica* (2nd edn.) (Bologna).

tr. (1967b) '*Analitici Primi' di Aristotele* (Naples).

(1985) 'Puzzles about identity. Aristotle and his Greek commentators', in *Aristoteles Werk und Wirkung. (1) Aristoteles und seine Schule*, ed. J. Wiesner (Berlin/N.Y.), at 57–97.

Montague, R. (1974) *Formal Philosophy. Selected Papers of Richard Montague*, ed. R, Thomason (New Haven).

Moraux, P. (1968) 'La joute dialectique d'après le huitième livre des Topiques', in Owen 1968b, at 277–311.

Mühl, M. (1962) 'Der λόγος ἐνδιάθετος und προφορικός von der älteren Stoa bis zur Synode von Sirmium 351', *Archiv für Begriffgeschichte* 7, 7–56.

Müller, H. E. (1943) *Die Prinzipien der stoischen Grammatik* (Rostock).

Neubecker, A. J. (1986) *Philodemus: Über die Musik IV. Buch. Text, Übersetzung, und Kommentar* (Naples).

Newmayer, F. J., ed. (1988) *Linguistics: the Cambridge survey. Vol. III: Psychological and Biological Aspects* (Cambridge).

Nicholls, J. (n.d.) 'The Alexander Technique', leaflet for the Society of Teachers of the Alexander Technique.

Nuchelmans, G. (1973) *Theories of the Proposition. Ancient and medieval conceptions of the bearers of truth and falsity* (Amsterdam).

Nutton, V. (1978) Review of Edlow 1977, *Classical Review* 92 (n s 28), 347–8.

Odell, S. J. (1984) 'Paraphrastic criteria for synonymy and ambiguity', *Theoretical Linguistics* 11, 117–25.

Ong, W. J. (1944) 'Historical backgrounds of Elizabethan and Jacobean punctuation theory', *Publications of the Modern Language Association of America* 59, 349–60.

(1982) *Orality and Literacy: the technologising of the word* (N.Y./London).

Owen, G. E. L. ed. (1968) *Aristotle on Dialectic. The Topics* (Oxford).

Owen, G. E. L. (1986a) *Logic, Science and Dialectic. Collected papers in Greek philosophy*, ed. M. Nussbaum (London).

(1986b) 'Logic and metaphysics in some earlier works of Aristotle', in Owen 1986a, at 180–199; originally in *Aristotle and Plato in the mid-Fourth Century*, edd. I. Düring and G. E. L. Owen (Göteborg, 1960), at 163–190; also repr. in *Articles on Aristotle 3: Metaphysics*, edd. J. Barnes, M. Schofield and R. Sorabji (London, 1979), at 13–32.

(1986c) 'Aristotle on the snares of ontology', in Owen 1986, at 259–78; originally in *New Essays on Plato and Aristotle*, ed. R. Bambrough (London, 1965), at 69–95.

(1986d) 'Dialectic and eristic in the treatment of the Forms', in Owen 1986, at 221–38; originally in Owen 1968, at 103–25.

Pachet, P. (1978) 'L'impératif stoïcien', in Brunschwig 1978a, at 361–74.

Palmer, L. R. (1980) *The Greek Language* (London/Boston).

Palmer, F. R. (1981) *Semantics* (2nd edn.) (Cambridge).

Pasquino, P. (1978) 'Le status ontologique des incorporels dans l'ancien Stoïcisme', in Brunschwig 1978a, at 375–86.

Patzig, G. (1961) 'Theologie und Ontologie in der Metaphysik des Aristoteles', *Kant-Studien* 52, 185–205.

Payne, J. R. (1990) 'Language universals and language types', in Collinge, at 281–330.

Pears, D. F. (1953) 'Incompatibilities of colours' in Flew, at 112–22.

Pedersen, H. (1931) *Linguistic Science in the Nineteenth Century. Methods and results* (tr. by J. W. Spargo of first Danish edn. (Copenhagen, 1924) (Cambridge, Mass.).

Peirce, C. S. (1902) 'Vague', in *Dictionary of Philosophy and Psychology, ed.* J. M. Baldwin (London/N.Y.), at 748.

(1966) *Collected Papers, edd.* C. Hartshorne, P. Weiss and A. W. Burks (Cambridge, Mass.; 8 vols.; repr. of edn. of 1931–58).

Pembroke, S. G. (1971) '*Oikeiosis*', in Long 1971b, at 114–49.

Pépin, J. (1976) *St. Augustin et la dialectique* (1972 Lecture in the Saint Augustine Lecture Series, Augustinian Institute, Villanova University) (Villanova).

Pfeiffer, R. (1968) *History of Classical Scholarship. From the beginnings to the end of the Hellenistic Age* (Oxford).

Phillips, E. D. (1973) *Greek Medicine* (London).

Pinborg, J. (1962) 'Das Sprachdenken der Stoa und Augustins Dialektik', *Classica et Mediaevalia* 23, 148–77.

ed. (1975a) *Augustine, 'de dialectica'. Translated with an introduction and notes by B. Darrell Jackson* (Dordrecht/Boston).

(1975b) 'Classical antiquity: Greece', in *Current Trends in Linguistics 13: The Historiography of Linguistics, ed.* T. A. Sebeok (The Hague), at 69–126.

Pohlenz, M. (1939) 'Die Begründung der abendländsichen Sprachlehre durch die Stoa', *Nach. Ges. Wiss. Göttingen, phil.-hist. Kl.* N.F. 3, 6, at 151–98.

(1970–2) *Die Stoa* (4th edn.) (Göttingen).

Poste, E. (1866) *Aristotle on Fallacies, or the 'Sophistici Elenchi'* (London).

Prantl, K. (1855) *Geschichte der Logik im Abendland* (Leipzig, vol. 1; repr. Graz, 1955).

Prior, A. N. (1955/8) 'Diodorean modalities', *P.Q.* 5, 205–13; 8, 226–30.

Pritchett, W. K. (1975) *Dionysius of Halicarnassus, 'On Thucydides'. English translation, with commentary* (Berkeley/Los Angeles).

Quine, W. V. O. (1951) *Mathematical Logic* (rev. edn.; 1st edn., 1946) (Cambridge, Mass.).

(1960) *Word and Object* (N.Y./London).

(1961) *From a Logical Point of View* (rev. 2nd edn.; 1st edn., 1953) (Cambridge, Mass.).

(1965) *Elementary Logic* (rev. edn.) (Cambridge, Mass.).

(1976) *The Ways of Paradox and Other Essays* (rev. and enlarged edn.; 1st edn., 1966) (Cambridge, Mass./London).

(1981) *Theories and Things* (Cambridge, Mass./London).

Reddy, M. J. (1979) 'The conduit metaphor: a case of frame conflict in our language about language', in *Metaphor and Thought, ed.* A. Ortony (Cambridge), at 284–324.

Reesor, M. (1989) *The Nature of Man in Early Stoic Philosophy* (London).

Reichel, G. (1909) 'Quaestiones Progymnasmaticae' (Diss., Leipzig).

Reitzenstein, R. (1901) *M. Terentius Varro und Joh. Mauropus von Euchaita* (Leipzig).

Replici, L. (1977) *La Logica di Teofrasto. Studio critico e raccolta dei frammanti e delle testimonianze* (Milan).

Richman, R. J. (1959) 'Ambiguity and intuition', *Mind* 68, 87–92.

Riddle, J. M. (1985) *Dioscorides on Pharmacy and Medicine* (Austin, Texas).

Rist, J. M. (1969) *Stoic Philosophy* (London).

ed. (1978) *The Stoics* (Berkeley/Los Angeles).

Roberts, L. (1984) 'Ambiguity and generality: removal of a logical confusion', *Canadian Journal of Philosophy* 14, 295–313.

Roberts, W. R. (1910) *Dionysins of Halicarnassus on Literary Composition; being the Greek text of the 'de compositione verborum', ed. with introduction, translation, notes, glossary and appendices* (London).

Robins, R. H. (1951) *Ancient and Medieval Grammatical Theory in Europe* (London).

(1966) 'The development of the word class system of the European grammatical tradition', *Foundations of Language* 2, 3–19.

(1979) *A Short History of Linguistics* (2nd edn.; 1st. edn., 1967) (London).

(1980) *General Linguistics* (3rd edn.; 1st edn., 1964) (London).

Robinson, R. (1941) 'Ambiguity', *Mind* 50, 140–55.

Rorty, R., Schneewind, J. B. and Skinner, Q., *edd.* (1984) *Philosophy in History. Essays on the historiography of philosophy* (Cambridge).

Ruef, H. (1981) *Augustin über Semiotik und Sprache: Sprachtheoretische Analysen zu Augustins Schrift "De Dialectica"* (Bern).

Russell, B. (1923) 'Vagueness', *Australasian Journal of Philosophy* 1, 84–92.

Russell, D. A. (1964) *"Longinus", 'On the Sublime'. Edited with Introduction and Commentary* (Oxford).

(1981) *Criticism in Antiquity* (London).
(1983) *Greek Declamation* (Cambridge).
Rüstow, A. (1910) *Der Lügner. Theorie, Geschichte, und Auflösung* (Leipzig).
Ryle, G. (1968) 'Dialectic in the Academy', in Owen 1968b, 68–79
Sandbach, F. H. (1971a) '*Phantasia kataléptikê*', in Long 1971b, at 9–21.
(1971b) '*Ennoia* and *Prolêpsis*', in Long 1971b, at 22–37.
(1985) *Aristotle and the Stoics* (Cambridge Philological Society Suppl. vol. 10) (Cambridge).
Sandys, E. (1921) *A History of Classical Scholarship* vol. 1 (3rd. edn.; 1st edn., 1903) (Cambridge).
Sapir, E. (1933/85) 'The psychological reality of phonemes', in *Selected Writings of Edward Sapir in Language, Culture and Personality*, ed. D. G. Mandelbaum (Berkeley/Los Angeles/ Cambridge, 1949), at 46–60, originally published as 'La réalité psychologique des phonèmes', *Journal de Psychologie Normale et Pathologique* 30 (1933), 247–65; repr. in Katz 1985a, at 65–79.
Saussure, F. de (1916/83) *Cours de Linguistique Générale*, edd. C. Bally, A. Sechehaye and A. Riedlinger (Paris, 1916/72); tr. and annot. by R. Harris (London, 1983).
Scheffler, I. (1979) *Beyond the Letter: a philosophical inquiry into ambiguity, vagueness, and metaphor in language* (London/ Boston/Henley).
Schmidt, R. (1839/1979) *Stoicorum grammatica* (Halle 1839 (repr. Amsterdam 1967)); German tr. by K. Hülser as *Die Grammatik der Stoiker*, with introduction and annotated bibliography by U. Egli (Brunswick/Wiesbaden, 1979).
Schofield, M. (1980a) 'Preconception, argument, and god', in Schofield *et al.*, at 283–308.
(1983) 'The Syllogisms of Zeno of Citium', *Phronesis* 28, 31–58.
(1991) *The Stoic Idea of the City* (Cambridge).
Schofield, M., Burnyeat, M. F. and Barnes, J., edd. (1980) *Doubt and Dogmatism. Studies in Hellenistic epistemology* (Oxford).
Schofield, M. and Nussbaum, M., edd.(1982) *Language and Logos. Studies in ancient Greek philosophy presented to G.E.L. Owen* (Cambridge).
Schofield, M. and Striker, G., edd. (1986) *The Norms of Nature. Studies in Hellenistic Ethics* (Cambridge/Paris).
Schwyzer, E. (1938/53/59) *Griechische Grammatik I* (Munich).
Searle, J. R. (1969) *Speech Acts* (Cambridge).
(1975) 'Indirect speech acts', in *Speech Acts. Syntax and Semantics*, vol. 3, edd. P. Cole and J. Morgan, (N.Y.) at 59–82.
Sedley, D. N. (1973) 'Epicurus *On nature* Book 28', *C.E.* 3, 5–83.

BIBLIOGRAPHY

(1977) 'Diodorus Cronus and Hellenistic philosophy', *P.C.P.S.* n.s. 23, 74–120.
(1980) 'The protagonists', in Schofield *et al.*, at 1–19.
(1982a) 'On Signs', in Barnes *et al.*, at 239–72.
(1982b) 'The Stoic criterion of identity', *Phronesis* 27, 255–75.
(1983) 'The motivation of Greek Skepticism', in Burnyeat, at 9–29.
(1984) 'The Negated Conjunction in Stoicism', *Elenchos* 52, 311–16.
(1985) 'The Stoic theory of universals', in Epp 1985b, at 87–92.
(1989) 'Philosophical allegiance in the Greco-Roman world', in Griffin and Barnes, at 97–119.
(forthcoming) 'Chrysippus on psychophysical causality', forthcoming in *Passions and Perceptions*, edd. J. Brunschwig, M. Nussbaum (Cambridge).
Sharples, R. (1983) *Alexander of Aphrodisias 'On Fate'. Text, translation, and commentary* (London).
Shopen, T. (1973) 'Elleipsis as grammatical indeterminacy', *Foundations of Language* 10, 65–77.
Sittig, E. (1931) *Das Alter der Ausordnung unserer Kasus* (Stuttgart; *Tüb. Beitr. Altertumswissensch.* 13).
Smiley, T. (1982/3) 'The schematic fallacy', *P.A.S.* n.s. 83, 1–17.
Soames, S. (1985) 'Semantics and psychology', in Katz 1985a, at 204–26.
Sommerstein, A. H. (1973) *The Sound Pattern of Ancient Greek* (Oxford).
Sperber, D. and Wilson, D. (1986) *Relevance. Communication and cognition* (Oxford).
Stageburg, N. C. (1975) 'Ambiguity in college writing', in: *Introductory Readings on Language*, edd. W. L. Anderson and N. C. Stageburg (4th edn.; 1st edn., 1962) (N.Y.).
Steinberg, D. D. and Jacobovits, L. A. edd. (1971) *Semantics* (London/N.Y.).
Stitch, S. P. (1971) 'What every speaker knows', *P.R.* 80, 476–96.
(1985) 'Grammar, indeterminacy, and psychology', in Katz 1985a, at 126–45 (repr. from *Journal of Philosophy* 1972: 799–818).
Stough, C. (1978) 'Stoic determinism and moral responsibility', in Rist, at 203–31.
Striker, G. (1974) Κριτήριον τῆς ἀληθείας. *Nachrichten der Akademie der Wissenschaften in Göttingen*, phil.-hist. Kl., 1974, Nr. 2, S. 47–110 (Göttingen).
(1977) 'Epicurus on the truth of sense-impressions', *A.G.P.* 59, 125–42.
(1980) 'Skeptical strategies', in Schofield *et al.*, at 54–83.

Sturtevant, E. H. (1940) *The Pronunciation of Greek and Latin* (2nd edn., Philadelphia, repr. Groningen, 1968; 1st edn., Chicago, 1920).

Taha, A. K. (1983) 'Types of syntactic ambiguity in English', *International Review of Applied Linguistics in Language Teaching* 21, 251–66.

Tarán, L. (1978) 'Speusippus and Aristotle on homonymy and synonymy', *Hermes* 106, 73–99.

Tate, J. (1934) 'On the history of allegorism', *C.Q.* 28, 105–14.

Taylor, D. J. (1987a) 'Rethinking the history of language science in classical antiquity', in Taylor 1987b, at 1–16.

Taylor, D. J. ed. (1987b) *The History of Linguistics in the Classical Period* (Amsterdam Studies in the Theory and History of Linguistic Science; Series III, Studies in the History of the Language Sciences, vol. 46) (Amsterdam/Philadelphia).

Theodoridis, Chr. (1976) *Die Fragmente des Grammatikers Philoxenus* (Berlin).

Todorov, T. (1982) *Theories of the Symbol* (English tr. by C. Porter of *Théories du Symbole* (Paris, 1977)) (Oxford).

Tsekourakis, D. (1974) *Studies in the Terminology of Early Stoic Ethics* (Wiesbaden).

Uhlfelder, M. L. (1963/4) 'The Romans on linguistic change', *Classical Journal* 59, 23–30.

(1966) 'Nature in Roman linguistic texts', *T.A.P.A.* 97, 583–95.

Unger, P. (1979) 'I do not exist', in *Perception and Identity. Essays presented to A. J. Ayer*, ed. G. F. Macdonald (London), at 235–51.

Vallance, J. (1990) *The Lost Theory of Asclepiades of Bithynia* (Oxford).

Vendryes, J. (1929) *Traité d' Accentuation Grecque* (Paris).

Vlastos, G. (1946) 'On the pre-history in Diodorus', *American Journal of Philology* 67, 51–9.

Volkmann, R. (1885) *Die Rhetorik der Griechen und Römer* (Leipzig).

Wackernagel, J. (1893) *Beitrage sur Lehre vom griechischen Akzent* (Basel).

Waismann, F. (1951) 'Verifiability', in *Logic and Language*, ed. A. Flew (Oxford) 1951, at 117–44.

(1953) 'Language strata', in Flew, at 11–31.

Watson, G. (1966) *The Stoic Theory of Knowledge* (Belfast).

Wehrli, F. (1948) *Die Schule des Aristoteles*, vol. 1/3 (Basel/Stuttgart).

Wells, R. S. (1947) 'Immediate constituents', *Language* 23, 81–117.

West, M. (1965) 'Tryphon, "de tropis"', *C.Q.* 15, 230–48.

Whittaker, J. (1990) *Alcinoos. Enseignement des Doctrines de Platon. Introduction, Texte établi et commenté par J. Whittaker, traduit par P. Louis* (Paris, Budé).

Wiggins, D. (1971) 'On sentence-sense, word-sense, and difference of word-sense. Towards a philosophical theory of dictionaries', in Steinberg and Jakobowitz, at 14–34.

Witt, R. E. (1971) *Albinus and the History of Middle Platonism* (Amsterdam; repr. of edn. of 1937).

Wouters, A. (1979) *The Grammatical Papyri from Graeco-Roman Egypt: Contributions to the study of the 'ars grammatica' in antiquity* (Verhandelingen van de Koninklijke Academie voor Wetenschappen, Letteren en Schone Kunsten van Belgie; Klasse der Letteren XLI.92 (Brussels).

Wright, C. (1975) 'On the coherence of vague predicates', *Synthèse* 30, 325–65.

——— (1976) 'Language mastery and the Sorites paradox', in *Truth and Meaning, edd.* G. Evans and J. McDowell (Oxford).

——— (1987) *Realism, Meaning and Truth* (Oxford).

Zwicky, A. M. and Sadok, J. M. (1975) 'Ambiguity tests and how to fail them', in *Syntax and Semantics*, vol. 4, *ed.* J. P. Kimball (N.Y./San Francisco/London), at 1–36.

INDEX LOCORUM

INDEX LOCORUM

GALEN (*cont.*)
  (15.7ff.G, 24f.E), 213 n. 27; (15.8ff.G, 24f.E), 231, 367; (15.10–15G, 25E), 206;
    (15.19–16.3G, 25E), 225 n. 8
Outline of Empiricism (subfig. emp.) (ed. K. Deichgräber, *Die griechische Empiri-*
    kerschule, Berlin/Zurich 1965; cited by page and line of Greek) (57.1–9), 426
    n. 25; (59.2ff.), 425 n. 22; (82.10ff.), 434 n. 40
On the Stages of a Complete Illness (de totius morbi temp.) (ed. I. Wille, Kiel, 1960)
    (81.3), 426 n. 25; (112.3), 426 n. 25
On the Usefulness of the Parts of the Body (de usu partium) (11.8, vol. 2, p. 135, ll.
    14ff. Helmreich), 193
GELLIUS, *Aulus*
  Attic Nights (noct. Att. (ed. P. K. Marshall, O.C.T. 1968) (7.2.6ff. (62D)), 123;
    (11.12.1ff. (37N; *S.V.F.* 2.152; fr. 111 Döring)), 154, 298, 300; (16.2), 463 n. 68;
    (16.3.12f.), 118 n. 84; (16.8.1), 252
[GREGORY]
  On Tropes (vol. 3 Sp.; also in M. West, *Classical Quarterly* 15, 1965) (223.14ff.), 485
    and n. 23; (223.15f. (p. 245W)), 473 n. 4

HERMOGENES
  On staseis (vol. 2 Sp.) (141.19ff.), 480 n. 16; (141.21), 472; (141.21–26), 480;
    (141.26ff.), 472; (141.26–30), 270
[HERMOGENES]
  On the Treatment of Forcefulness (vol. 3 Sp.) (438.1ff.), 378 n. 135, 381 n. 140;
    (438.15ff.), 377
HERODIAN
  On Orthography (orth.) (ed. A. Lentz, *G.G.* 3.2. 1867) (407.20f.), 471 n. 1 (472)
  On Prosody (pros. cath.)
  (ed. A. Lentz, *G.G.* 3.1. 1867) (Book 5, 108.9ff.) 286, 350 n. 120
  (G.G. 3.3) (489.8f.) 345 n. 112
[HERODIAN]
  On Barbarism and Solecism (de barbarismo et soloecismo) (p. 304.14ff. Nauck), 203
    n. 20; (p. 309.7 Nauck), 232
HERODOTUS *(ed.* H. B. Rosen, Teubner, 1987–) (1.142), 169 n. 35; (2.104.1), 191, 392;
    (2.141), 404 n. 160; (5.74), 463 n. 67
[HIPPOCRATES]
  On Diseases (morb.) (ed. P. Potter, Loeb, 1988) (3.1), 425 n. 24; (3.7), 425 n. 24;
    (3.9), 425 n. 24
HOMER *(O.C.T.)*
  Iliad (1.129), 233; (2.270), 189, 353, 363; (2.547f.), 189, 353, 363; (13.41), 233;
    (15.241), 233; (17.720), 289; (23.382), 182, 352, 366
  Odyssey (1.52), 233

ISISDORE
  Etymologies, or the Origins of Words (orig.) (O.C.T.) (1.29.2), 158
IULIUS VICTOR
  Art of Rhetoric (ed. Halm) (383.7f.), 473 n. 4; (383.10–13), 472; (383.13f.), 386 n.
    145; (394.31f.), 478

[LONGINUS]
  On the Sublime (subl.) (ed. D. A. Russell, Oxford, 1964) (16–29), 485 n. 23; (22), 377
    and n. 133, 380
  LS *(q.v.)* (34), 45; (40), 43 n. 6; (45), 50 n. 16; (58), 55

538

INDEX LOCORUM

539

541

GENERAL INDEX

"abatement" (παρακμή), 426 and
n., 427, 442
Academy, Platonic, 424; interest in
homonymy and synonymy, 103n.
Academy, Skeptic, method of arguing,
101f. and n.
accents: see ambiguity; Greek language
acceptability, of utterances or sentences,
126, 149
Aelius Stilo, late 2nd/early 1st cent.
B.C.E. Stoic, 499n.
Alexander, of Aphrodisias, 2nd/3rd
cent. C.E. commentator on Aristotle,
37, 40n., 247n.; critique of Stoic
theories of negative sentences and of
reference. 78–80; criticism of Stoics
on *luck, chance, that which is up to us*,
122–4; use of word/complex
dichotomy, 223; on *endoxa* and
fallacies, 459f.
Ps.-Alexander, author of commentary
on Aristotle's *s. el.,* identity, 317f.; on
autonymy. 287, 324; on contextual
"ambiguation", 318, 334n.
Alexinus, "Eristic", 462; and Zeno of
Citium, 28n., 74, 462 and n., 463
and n.
Allen, J. P. B., 19
Allen, W. S., 155, 225 and n., 226n., 228
and n., 229 and n., 358, 370n., 493n.
Alston, W., 144.
Altmann, S. 14n.
ambiguity, linguistic: and analytic *vs.*
synthetic statements. 80; and
linguistic autonomy, 65, 503; and
autonymy, 37f., 65, 243, 503; bearers,
10, 16, 17, 18, 22, 23, 138, 145, 205,
206f., 223, 243–50, 309; and singular
definite terms, 37; in negative
sentences, 37, 79f.; in non-declarative
discourse, 23; changed attitudes
towards, 25–7, 88n., 174, 483f., 500f.,
504; and contexts or situations, 10,
17, 19, 65, 148f., 171, 313 and n.,
314n., 503; and co-ordination, 141n.;

its creative value, 25–6, 501, 504;
criteria for, 16, 18, 77f., 141n.; as a
defect, 24f., 173, 8.3 *passim*, 500;
(preliminary) definition of, 16f.; and
disambiguation, 125, 320, (by
prosodic features) 356; and disci-
plinary boundaries, 22–4; effect
on discourse, 14; usefulness of
distinguishing, 69, 109; "distinction"
(διαίρεσις/διαστολή/διορισμός), of,
423f., 425n.; *vs.* equivocation, 37, 172,
421 and n., 502; and fallacies, 6, 7, 24,
35, 36, 36f., 62, 108 and n., 129, 5.4
passim, ch. 7 *passim*; and linguistic
generalisations, 238f., 241n., 314n.;
vs. generality, 16n., 22, 141n., 143–5,
342, 465; *vs.* contextual indefiniteness, 337f.; and ideal language(s), 10,
26n., 238, 500; as a feature of natural
language(s), 17f., 23, 26 and n.; and
lexicography, 23, 83; and linguistic
intuitions, 12, 14–16, 17, 18–21, 77f.,
82f., 85f., 125, 133, 250; and linguistics, 5, 6, 10, 14–16, 18–21, 22,
23, 24, 25–6, 80, 125f., 133, 141, 145,
148, 157f., 238, 241n., 494 and n.,
500, 503; and levels of linguistic
description/representation, 22, 245;
and language "processing", 23; and
literary criticism, 24, 88n., 504; and
logic, 5, 7, 10, 11, 23, 25, 78, 80;
and meaning(s), 1, 10, 14, 16, 17, 20,
21, 23; and medieval logic, 68f.;
and metaphor, 22; and modern
philosophy, 5, 7, 22, 23, 24, 75 and n.,
77f., 79, 80, 145, 238, 500, 503; *vs.*
multiple applicability, 22, 141; and
paraphrases, 16n.; as a philosophical
resource, 108; and punctuation, 206,
226n., 228; and obscurity, 6, 21, 24,
88n., 201, 203; and reference, 65, 79,
141; and "referring" *vs.* "attributive"
usages, 80; and "rigid" *vs.* "non-rigid"
designation, 80; and selectional
restrictions, 145, 147f.; and semantic

GENERAL INDEX

Inwood, B., 30n., 45n. (46), 81, 118, 138, 152n.
ἰσοσθένεια, Skeptical method of "counterbalancing", 36n.
Itkonen, E., 17n., 75n., 493n.

Jackson, B. D., 292n., 293n., 294nn.
Jesperson, O., 14n.
Joos, M., 337n.

Kalbfleisch, C., 177
Kaplan, A., 75n.
Kaplan, D., 80
Katz, J. J., 17 and n., 266
Kennedy, G. A., 315n., 499n.
Kerferd, G. B, 50n., 447n.
Kidd, I. G., 127n., 306 and n., 445n., 475n.
Kirwan, C., 241n., 356n., 411, 464
Kittay, E. F., 163n.
Kneales, W. and M., 433n.
Kooij, J. G., 21, 26n., 75., 128, 168n., 244, 245, 320, 331, 356 and n.
Kress, J., 16n.
Kretzmann, N., 147n. (148), 155 and n.
Kripke, S., 75n., 77n., 80

Lakoff, G., 20, 150n.
Lana, I., 184 and n.
language, arbitrariness vs. iconicity of, 153f. and n.; autonomy of, 11, 65, 153, 154f., 157n, 243f.; autonymy in, 11, 37f., 65, 155n., 274, 326f.; "conduit" metaphor for, 24f., 259; and contexts, 10, 17, 65; (non-)declarative/descriptive functions of, 22, 25; "deep" structure of, 19, 266; definition(s) of, 17; formal vs. natural, 9, 10, 12, 22, 23, 260; "hierarchical" structure of (Hockett), 20, 21; ideal, 10, 26n.; knowledge of, 12, 13, 15f., 17, 18, 20, 86n.; kn. of not an ancient problematic, 146f., 338; and non-linguistic knowledge, 13, 86n., 146, 338; "language-myth" (Harris), 25n., 259; modularity of l., 26n., 338f.; "natural" (φύσει) vs. "conventional" (θέσει) origin of, 67 and n., 146, 155, 157 and n., 243f., 429 and n.; "object" vs. "meta" l., 294n.; "processing" of, by users, 23; "purity" (Hellenism, Latinitas) of, 83f.; and rationality, 147f.; and rules and conventions, 25, 153, 244; "self-reference", 295; spoken vs.

544

written, 5, 137; (trans)formation rules, 264; "use" vs. "mention", 288, 294n., 295; l. vs. "the world", 163f., 185
Latin, language, 216, 227 and n., 245, 343
Laum, B., 225
λεκτά: see Stoics, philosophy
letters, γράμματα, 69f.
lexeme, 235, 237
lexicography, 23, 83
linguistics, 2, 4, 5, 12, 13, 22, 24, 83; use of abstractions, 237 and n., 314n.; attitude to ancient grammar, 488, 493n.; branches, 24; contexts and "(maximal) decontextualisation" (Lyons), 312, 313n., 317, 320, 338, 339 and n.; on "deep" structure, 266; descriptiveness of, 21, 493n.; on disambiguation, 320; by prosodic features, 356; need for generalisations, 237, 238; goals of, 6, 14–16, 18–21, 148, 238, 261, 338f.; "idealisation" in, 338, 339 and n.; and theories of meaning, 259f.; "microlinguistics", 339 and n.; and pragmatics, 22; on proper names, 157f.; on strict, literal, metaphorical usages, 163, 165 and n.; subject-matter of, 14–16, 17–19, 261; need for precise transcriptions, 359; "universals", Chomskyan, 261, Greenbergian, 494; on utterances, 243, 244f., 246; on types of word, 305; on word-identity, 232n.
linguistic description, levels of, 22
linguistic philosophy, 116f.
literalness, 10
literary criticism and theory, modern, 22, 24, 25f.
literary criticism and theory, ancient, 8, 24, 25, 8.3 passim; on ambiguity vs. metaphor, 166; on contexts and disambiguation, 322
Lloyd, A. C., 45n., 47, 76n., 97n., 263, 264, 309n., 398n.
"Lockean" ambiguities, 61f.
logic, ancient, 9, 24
logic, medieval, on ambiguity, 68f., 356; on causa apparentiae vs. causae defectus, of fallacies, 295n., 412n.; on formal vs. material supposition, 288; res vs. vox, 295n. (296)
logic, modern, 2, 5, 7, 9, 13, 464n.; on ambiguity, 415, 464; on vagueness, 149f.

GENERAL INDEX

Stoic philosophy (cont.)
412 and n., 413, 414, 443–7, 460f.,
502, 503; relation to sciences, 444–7;
and Aristotle's dialectic, 102n., 461,
503; as "science of true and false and
neither" (Posidonius), 54 and n., 445;
pre-Chrysippean dialectic, 41n., 407;
subject-matter of d., 41, 48, 253, 302;
ideal dialectician and wise man, 21,
49–51, 52n., 53, 55, 61, 74, 90, 102,
386n. (387), 438, 445, 447 and n., 502;
and Plato's philosopher-kings, 102;
possible loss of wisdom, 55n.;
"disjunction", 118n.; "disposition"
(ἕξις), 169n.; "duty", see "appropriate
action"; "emotion" (πάθος), 351;
epistemology, 7, 9, 32n., 39, 40, 41,
50f., 56, 62, 116, 133, 260; and
uniqueness of individuals, 236n.;
"error" (ἁμάρτημα), 351; ethics and
moral philosophy, 9, 31, 39, 50–2, 87,
90, 260, 351; etymology, 68, 95–7,
154, 156, 167, 350 and n.; euphony,
33; "evidence" (τεκμήρια), 127n.
(128); "expertise" (τέχνη), 43, 45,
84n., 443 and n.; fallacies, 7, 33,
36f., 41, 56, ch. 7 passim, esp. 7.1, 7.6;
and the "plausible", "implausible"
(πιθανόν, ἀπίθανον), 436–8, 446;
Stoic (?) classification of f., 432–
41; motives for, 442, 445f.; no
Aristotelian influence on, 432n.;
differences between Arist. and Stoic
handling of false arguments, 458–62;
falsehoods, danger of, 460f.; fate, see
providence; god, 51, 52n., 70, 72n.,
113n. (114); rejection of Platonic
forms, 76f., 77n., 283 and n., 284n.;
genera and species, 144; geometry,
127n. (128); "good" (ἀγαθός),
ordinary conception of, 116, 470;
Stoic conception of, 105, 118n.;
grammar, 6, 7, 9, 39, 48, 83f., 85, 127
and n. (128), 130, 133, 217, 300f., 302,
490n., 495; and philosophy, 84n.;
"Hellenism" (linguistic purity), 84
and n., 88n., 95, 127, 328; on
Heraclitus, 364f.; on Homer, 90;
imagination, 43; imperatives, 81, 260,
345 and n.; imperfection, of persons,
55f., 65, 67; "impression" (φαντασία),
42–3, 45n., 48, 54n., 62, 75, 115n.,
165f., 236, 335, 469; "cognitive/
apprehensive (καταληπτική)" i., 43,
50, 56 and n., 65f., 255, 437, 438 and

n.; "expert", "non-expert" (τεχνική,
ἄτεχνος) i., 437; "plausible",
"implausible" (πιθανή, ἀπίθανος) i.,
56, 435–7, 438; "rational (λογική)" i.
(= "thought", νόησις), 43, 91, 93 and
n., 115, 254, 257, 259, 466–8; "true"
(ἀληθής) i., 107; relation to lekta
problematic, 468, 469; and language,
91, 92; "impulse" (ὁρμή), 54;
incorporeals, 44n., 45n.; "incoherence" (διάρτησις), 201, 416f., 419,
7.4, 7.5, 7.7, 7.8 passim; "indicate"
(δηλοῦν), 302, 303; "inflection"
(ἔγκλισις), 76n., 262n., 264f.,
281n., 357n.; "knowledge/science"
(ἐπιστήμη), 43, 45, 49f., 69n.;
language, natural origin of, 68, 155;
heuristic/philosophical value of,
95–7, 102–3, 115f., 118–22; written
vs. spoken, 137, 138; knowledge of,
42f.; and rationality, 42f., 51f., 65, 92,
147f.; λεκτά, 42n., 44–9, 54n., 91,
97n., 141, 142, 152, 237, 250, 259, 281
and n., 302, 316n., 354, 464;
complete, 351; complete truth-valued,
45 and nn., 54n., 117, 260, 351, 357;
complete non-truth-valued, 253n.,
260; incomplete, 337, 340, 351;
functions of, 126, 250, 258, 259, 263,
465, 467, 468; identity criteria for,
142f.; and causation, 284f.; and
concepts 115n.; and πράγματα, 139,
141, 143, 251, 252–4, 284; and
σημαινόμενα, 253; syntax of, 126, 141,
142, 260, 263, 266, 328 and n., 333,
355, 362, 389, 398, 399, 464; linguistic
theory, 40, 42; logic, 7, 11, 32f., 37,
39, 40, 41, 260; unity of, 133; as a
part of philosophy, 40 and n., 49, 69,
127n. (128); formal logic, 126, 133,
262f., 266, 414, 415, 458, 461f.;
as tensed, 440n. (441); formalism,
in logic, 118 and n.; "logical
consequence" (ἀκολουθία), 443;
λόγος, as rational discourse or
language, 40n., 89, 91, 3.5 passim,
147n. (148), 255, 257, 261, 399, 400,
451, 465, 469; as argument, 45n., 48,
54n., 107, 253n., 413, 432, 464;
structure of: "(major) premiss/
assumption" (λῆμμα), 461; "(minor)
premiss/additional assumption"
(πρόσληψις), 309, 461; "conclusive"
(περαίνων) l., 434; "inconclusive"
(ἀπέραντος), "inconcludent"

560